Business Communication

A Problem-Solving Approach

Kathryn Rentz
University of Cincinnati

Paula Lentz
University of Wisconsin–Eau Claire

Anupam Das
Indian Institute of Management Kozhikode

McGraw Hill Education (India) Private Limited

Published by McGraw Hill Education (India) Private Limited
Registered Office: Anjana Complex No: 5/90 A, Butt Road, St. Thomas Mount, Chennai – 600016

Special Indian Edition 2020

First reprint 2022

This edition can be exported from India only by the publishers,

Sales Territories: India, Pakistan, Nepal, Bangladesh, Sri Lanka and Bhutan

Fictious names of companies, products, people, characters and/or data that may be used herein (in case studies or in examples) are
not intended to represent any real individual, company, product or event.

Print Edition
ISBN-13: 978-93-90185-83-2
ISBN-10: 93-90185-83-1

E-Book Edition
ISBN-13: 978-93-90185-84-9
ISBN-10: 93-90185-84-X

02 03 04 05 06 RAJ 26 25 24 23 22

Managing Director: *Lalit Singh*
Director—Product: *Tanweer Ahmad*
Head of HED Portfolio: *Nikhil Wadhera*
Associate Portfolio Manager: *Chandrabhanoo Chakrabarti*
Project Manager—Production Services: *Atul Gupta*
General Manager—Production: *Rajender P Ghansela*
Manager—Production: *Reji Kumar*

Typeset at APS Compugraphics, 4G, PKT 2, Mayur Vihar Phase – III, Delhi 96 and
Printed and Bound in India at Rajkamal Electric Press, Plot No. 2, Phase – IV, Kundli, Sonepat, Haryana

Cover Image Source: Lightspring/Shutterstock
Cover Designer: APS Compugraphics
Cover Printer: Rajkamal Electric Press

Visit us at: www.mheducation.co.in
Toll free in India: 1800 103 5875
Write to us at: info.india@mheducation.com
CIN: U80302TN2010PTC111532

Dedication

Kathy dedicates this book to Kitty O. Locker, who taught the graduate seminar on teaching business and technical writing, and Robert Gieselman, who was executive director of the Association for Business Communication, when Kathy was a Ph.D. student at the University of Illinois-Urbana. They turned out to have determined the major focus of Kathy's professional work for the next 30+ years. For that, she is deeply grateful.

Paula dedicates this book to business communication instructors everywhere who work tirelessly to equip their students for the workplace and inspire these students to become their best professional selves. She is grateful for the instructors' work and for their advocacy of business communication as an essential part of a 21st-century education.

Anupam dedicates this book to his mother Mrs. Sima Das and Professor Susan C. Herring who was Anupam's doctoral advisor at Indiana University Bloomington. Anupam has acquired many important life skills from them that have helped him navigate both in his personal and professional life. As a teacher he draws inspirations from his mother's acts of kindness. His advisor has constantly provided him intellectual stimulus and extended emotional support whenever needed. Anupam's active research interests in Computer-Mediated Communication are highly influenced by Professor Herring's vast body of research works. He is forever indebted to his mother and doctoral advisor for shaping his life.

About the Authors

Dr. Kathryn Rentz

Dr. Kathryn Rentz is a Professor of English at the University of Cincinnati. She taught her first business writing class as a doctoral student at the University of Illinois at Urbana-Champaign in the early 1980s and has been teaching workplace writing ever since. She helped establish the University of Cincinnati's professional writing program and has served as its coordinator. She has also won the English Department's teaching award, directed the department's graduate program, and helped direct the composition program.

Dr. Rentz's affiliation with the Association for Business Communication goes back to her beginnings as a business writing teacher. She has performed many roles for the ABC, including serving on the board of directors and chairing the publications board. She served two terms as an Associate Editor of the *Journal of Business Communication* and was Interim Editor from 2000–2001, for which she won the Francis W. Weeks Award of Merit. In 2008 she won the ABC's Meada Gibbs Outstanding Teacher Award. In 2011 she was elected Second Vice President for the association. She served as President in 2013–2014 and Past President in 2014–2015.

Dr. Rentz has published articles on business communication pedagogy and research in such journals as *Business Communication Quarterly*, the *Journal of Business Communication*, *Technical Communication Quarterly*, and the *Journal of Business and Technical Communication*. She has participated in many professional meetings and seminars over the years and is always learning from her colleagues and her students.

Dr. Paula Lentz

Dr. Paula Lentz is an Associate Professor and Academic Program Director in the Department of Business Communication at the University of Wisconsin–Eau Claire. She teaches Business Writing, Business Writing II, Advanced Business Writing, and the MBA Communicating for Success course. She is also a developer and coordinator of the department's Business Writing Fundamentals Program, which ensures that students have basic writing skills essential for success in their first business writing course.

Dr. Lentz is particularly interested in qualitative research that explores narratives and organizational cultures, genre theory, and writing pedagogy in online environments. She has published in such journals as *Academy of Educational Leadership Journal, Wisconsin Business Education Association Journal, Equal Opportunities International, Business and Professional Communication Quarterly,* and *Qualitative Research in Organizations and Management.* She has also presented her research at several national and regional conferences, including those of the Association for Business Communication and the Academy of Management.

Prior to becoming a full-time academic, she worked as a technical writer and publications editor. She continues to do freelance editing and provides consulting and writing services. She received a BA from Coe College, an MA from UW–Eau Claire, and a PhD in Rhetoric and Scientific and Technical Communication from the University of Minnesota.

Dr. Anupam Das

Dr. Anupam Das is an Associate Professor in Humanities and Liberal Arts in Management at the Indian Institute of Management Kozhikode. He teaches courses on Organisational Communication including Communication as Impression Management and Public Speaking. His research interests include Computer-Mediated Communication, Pragmatics, Discourse Analysis, and Pedagogy of Organizational Communication. He has published in various international journals which include, *Information, Communication & Society, Language & Communication*, and *International Journal of Designs for Learning.* He earned his PhD in Linguistics with a minor in Information Science from Indiana University Bloomington, USA.

A Problem-Solving Approach

Combining the fundamentals of clear communication with visual rhetoric and critical thinking, Kathy Rentz, Paula Lentz, and Anupam Das' problem-solving approach gets directly to the heart of great business communication and helps students gain a professional advantage.

Additionally, with the help of business and management cases in the Indian contexts, the book helps the Indian students grasp the contemporary issues of business communication effectively.

A Unique Focus on Problem Solving

Business is all about solving problems, and communication is part of every solution. The students who will do well in the workplace will be those who approach communication tasks with an analytical, creative mindset. Rentz, Lentz, and Das acquaint students with goals they're likely to encounter on the job—from resolving ethical issues, solving management problems, and crafting company policies to reporting information, selling a product or idea, and managing customer relations—and provide students with the principles and practice they'll need to meet those goals.

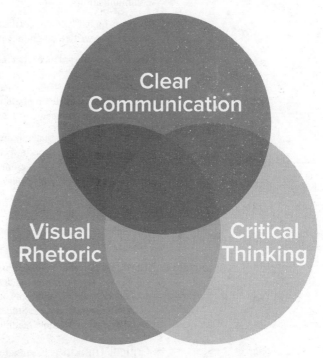

Good problem solvers don't start from scratch. They start with what they know and then find the additional resources they need to meet new challenges successfully. That's why *Business Communication: A Problem-Solving Approach* focuses on three overlapping areas: clear communication, visual rhetoric, and critical thinking.

Clear Communication Students need basic writing and speaking skills to be able to solve communication problems. Rentz, Lentz, and Das make sure students get this "basic training."

A chapter on writing effective sentences and paragraphs provides thorough but accessible advice on using an appropriate style free of grammatical problems. Each chapter ends with a "Power Charge Your Professionalism" activity that reinforces a grammatical concept relevant to the chapter. Connect also provides grammatical instruction and practice via LearnSmart Achieve and other online activities. A reference chapter on correctness supports these materials.

Another chapter focuses on the writing process, the conventions of different media, and audience analysis. It teaches students to consider specific contextual factors as they craft their letters, emails, proposals, reports, social media posts, or any form of communication.

This chapter also discusses helpful technologies for every phase of the writing process. To plan and communicate well, students must know what kinds of communication technologies are available, how their usage differs, and how to use them responsibly. "From the Tech Desk" boxes throughout the book, as well as related material in the later chapters, build on the technology discussion in this chapter.

Because of the importance of trust in workplace relationships, a whole chapter is devoted to using an appropriate tone and making ethical communication decisions. The next chapter extends this discussion by addressing the special challenges raised by cross-cultural communication.

Numerous chapters provide examples of common types of workplace communication, and "Communication Matters" boxes share additional professional tips. Equipped with this kind of knowledge, students can start their professional careers with greater skill and efficiency.

A reference chapter on citing sources explains when, why, and how to credit others in their communications.

Chapters on interpersonal skills and oral presentations show students how to apply the principles for effective written communication to oral communication.

The authors also practice what they preach by writing in a style that is efficient, engaging, and real.

Visual Rhetoric "Visual rhetoric" refers to the way the visual features of a message communicate. These features include not only photos, drawings, charts, graphs, and tables but also fonts, colors, the placement of text on a page, and even paragraph length and use of headings.

In our increasingly visual culture, good business communicators must understand how the visual presentation of their work affects the audience's ability to understand and respond positively to a message. Good business communicators must also be aware of how the visual presentation of their work impacts their professional image.

With one chapter devoted to document design and another chapter to communicating with visuals, Rentz, Lentz, and Das provide practical strategies students can use to communicate visually. Principles of visual rhetoric are also discussed within chapters as they relate to topics such as using visual appeal in sales messages.

These principles have also been incorporated into the book's design. The exhibits, photos, fonts, colors, and layout engage readers and communicate key content. Annotated examples of correspondence, reports, proposals, and résumés model the use of effective visual communication in different business genres. Students and instructors alike will find that this is a visually friendly text designed to promote reading and comprehension.

Critical Thinking Essential to the problem-solving approach is a focus on critical thinking. This is the element of effective communication that requires students to take the leap from known concepts and familiar territory to innovative, effective solutions.

Each chapter begins with a "Problem-Solving Challenge"—a real-life scenario that invites students to solve a communication problem. This beginning prepares students to approach the chapter's content thoughtfully rather than passively. Instead of preaching, the chapters challenge students to anticipate how they will apply the concepts in different situations.

Reinforcing this effort are "You Make the Call" prompts throughout the text. Each prompt asks students to think about the part of the chapter that they're currently reading. The questions thus encourage not only critical thinking but also more active reading, and they can serve as great discussion starters. They also reinforce the point that there is rarely just one right answer to a communication-related question.

Each chapter also ends with "Critical-Thinking Questions" that ask students to delve more deeply into the "why" behind the book's advice or explore exceptions to the rule. The chapters that focus on preparing various kinds of communications also end with an extensive collection of "Problem-Solving Cases" that can serve as the course's main assignments. These have been carefully designed to accommodate different levels of knowledge and skill, but they all require both analysis and resourcefulness.

Book End Appendices At the end of the book, five comprehensive appendices are included that provide a combination of the three fundamental components of business communication, namely–clear communication, visual rhetoric, and critical thinking.

These appendices help Indian students internalize the fundamental concepts of business communication and apply them in Indian contexts. Consequently, the 'glocal' approach of the book aims to enable the Indian students to go global while drawing from the behavioural and cultural traits of their own society.

Where It All Comes Together

Never before has the workplace required so many different skills and so much flexibility. Whatever the course or curriculum, *Business Communication: A Problem-Solving Approach* will equip your students for a successful professional journey while keeping them focused on the essentials.

Acknowledgments

Through the Association for Business Communication and our other professional connections, many dedicated business communication instructors and practitioners have contributed to this book. We extend our sincere thanks to them for their ideas and inspiration. We'd also like to thank our students, who never stop challenging and rewarding us.

We are particularly indebted to the reviewers and event participants who helped shape the first edition of this book.

Reviewers:

Colleen D. Armstrong, Colorado State University–Pueblo

Cynthia Eve Ash, Oklahoma State University–Tulsa

Bev Augustine, Elgin Community College

Jeanine Elise Aune, Iowa State University

Lisa Bailey, University of South Carolina

Cynthia Barnes, Lamar University

Larry Barraza, Mt. San Jacinto College

Judith Haywood Bello, Lander University

Roxanne Bengelink, Kalamazoo Valley Community College

Yvonne Block, College of Lake County

Gregory Brecht, University of South Florida–St. Petersburg

Sheryl Broedel, University of North Dakota

Edward Brown, Alabama State University

Shanti Bruce, Nova Southeastern University

Suzanne Buck, University of Houston

Brennan J. Carr, Long Beach City College

Annette Castagna, Long Beach City College

Debbie Cook, Utah State University

Mark Courtright, Elon University

Sandra G. Ehrlich-Mathiesen, University of Alaska–Anchorage

Megan Lee Endres, Eastern Michigan University

Robert Goldberg, Prince George's Community College

Constance Golden, Lakeland Community College

Heather Griffo, Portland Community College

Elizabeth R. Guerrero, Texas State University

Karen Head, The Georgia Institute of Technology

Candy Henry, Westmoreland County Community College

Kathy L. Hill, Sam Houston State University

Debra Hoffmann, Southeast Missouri State University

Cole E. Holmes, University of Utah

Matthew Houseworth, University of Central Missouri

Harold A. Hurry, Sam Houston State University

Ralph Jagodka, Mt. San Antonio College

Norma Johansen, Scottsdale Community College

William T. Jones, State University of New York at Canton

Stephanie Kelly, North Carolina A&T State University

Susan Kendall, Arapahoe Community College

Carolyn E. Kerr, University of Pittsburgh

Sonia Khatchadourian, University of Wisconsin–Milwaukee

Arthur Khaw, Kirkwood Community College

Janet M. King, Indiana University-Purdue University Indianapolis

Lisa Kleiman, Boise State University

William R. Kohler, University of Illinois at Chicago

Melinda Kramer, Prince George's Community College

Daria LaFave, Wayne State University

Nancy K. LeGrand, Southeast Missouri State University

Kathy Leslie, California State University–Northridge

Michael Levy, University of Wisconsin–Stout

Holly Littlefield, University of Minnesota

Mrs. Joyce Lopez, Missouri State University

Jo Mackiewicz, Iowa State University

Marla Mahar, Oklahoma State University

Rebecca J. Mahr, Western Illinois University

Lara Mandrell, Texas Tech University

Steve Merriam, San Diego State University

Annie Laurie I. Meyers, Northampton Community College

Susan Meyers, Seattle University

Karl Mitchell, Queens College–CUNY

Wayne Moore, Indiana University of Pennsylvania

Christina J. Moore, Texas State University

Gregory H. Morin, University of Nebraska–Omaha

Gwen H. Moultrie, Midlands Technical College

Nancy Nygaard, University of Wisconsin–Milwaukee

Lisa O'Laughlin, Delta College

David M. Owens, Valparaiso University

Ranu Paik, Santa Monica College

Audrey M. Parajon, Wilmington University

Melinda L. Phillabaum, Indiana University–Indianapolis

Greg Rapp, Portland Community College

Georgi Ann Rausch, University of Utah

Rob Rector, Delaware Technical Community College

Teeanna Rizkallah, California State University, Fullerton

Joseph A. Rosendale, Indiana University of Pennsylvania

Sharon Rouse, University of Southern Mississippi

Kristina Schaap, Oklahoma State University

Nanette Shackelford, Hastings College

Michael Shuman, University of South Florida

Lucia Stretcher Sigmar, Sam Houston State University

Rachel V. Smydra, Oakland University

Carolyn A. Spillers, Fayetteville State University

Jo Ann Starkweather, Northeastern State University

Ann Still, Finger Lakes Community College

JoAnn Syverson, University of Minnesota

Cecil V. Tarrant III, Western Illinois University

Elizabeth Tomlinson, West Virginia University

Donald Urmston, Orange County Community College

Janet Voas, Westmoreland County Community College and Community College of Allegheny County

Kathleen Voge, University of Alaska Anchorage

Jie Wang, University of Illinois at Chicago

McClain Watson, University of Texas at Dallas

Susan Hall Webb, University of West Georgia

Teresa G. Weldy, University of South Alabama

Raholanda White, Middle Tennessee State University

Elisabeth Wicker, Bossier Parish Community College

Kadi Wills, Northwest Vista College

Brandon H. Wood, College of DuPage

Event Participants:

Marilyn Chalupa, Ball State University

Jennifer D'Alessandro, Niagara County Community College

Debra Gosh, Cleveland State University

Mary Groves, University of Nevada–Reno

Jeanette Heidewald, Indiana University–Bloomington

Jo Mackiewicz, Iowa State University

Marla Mahar, Oklahoma State University–Stillwater

Becky Mahr, Western Illinois University

Lisa O'Laughlin, Delta College

Anita Satterlee, Liberty University

Erik Timmerman, University of Wisconsin–Milwaukee

Emil Towner, Saint Cloud State University

Doris Wright, Troy University

In addition, we would particularly like to thank Heather Smith for her excellent work on the auxiliary materials for this book.

We would like to recognize and thank the entire editorial and marketing teams at McGraw-Hill that have made this publication possible: Kelly Pekelder, Anke Weekes, Michael Gedatus, Mary Powers, Matt Backhaus, Deborah Nicholls, Kristine Janssens, Bhanoo Chakrabarti, Piyaray Pandita, Shweta Pant and all of the talented McGraw-Hill publisher's representatives.

On our respective home fronts, Kathy would like to thank her husband Dave for his wonderful patience and support during this project. Paula is forever grateful to her husband John for his thoughtfulness and encouragement and Anupam would like to thank his wife Tua and daughter Anusha (Evo) for their constant support and encouragement. He is grateful to his father Dr. Pares Chandra Das who has inspired him through his publications.

These acknowledgments would not be complete without our expression of thanks to Ray Lesikar and Marie Flatley, who brought Kathy on board as a co-author for the 11th edition of their textbook in 2006. While much has changed since then, their forward-thinking focus on audience adaptation, core structural patterns, stylistic clarity, and technological currency is as timely as ever and continues on in this product.

Brief
Contents

Reference Chapters

(On the Online Learning Center of the book at **www.mheducation.co.in**)

Appendices

Contents

© McGraw Hill Education/Mark Dierker, photographer

© Denis Krasavchikov/123RF

Part Two Essential Components of Business Communication

© Nonwarit Pruetisirirot/123RF

© PhotoDisc/Getty Images

Chapter 6   Building Positive Relationships through Communication 166

Part Three   Structures and Strategies for Common Business Documents

© scyther/Shutterstock

© Shutterstock / fizkes

Chapter 10   Writing Persuasive Messages and Proposals 294

© Stockbyte/Getty Images

© Mark Adams/123RF

Part Four   Strategies for Oral Communication and the Job Search

© hxdbzxy/123RF

© George Doyle/Stockbyte/Getty Images

Reference Chapters
On the Online Learning Center of the book at
www.mheducation.co.in

© Ingram Publishing RF

Appendices

Business
Communication

A Problem-Solving Approach

Communicating in
the Workplace

Chapter One

A s head of his own talent-development company and former Director of Learning for Facebook, Stuart Crabb knows what it takes to be an attractive job candidate and a successful employee. He has over 20 years' experience helping companies hire the right people and develop their talent.

What does it take to flourish in today's workplace? According to Crabb, the answers are "critical thinking," "problem solving," "creativity," and "performance." It also takes being "motivated," "individually accountable," and a "good fit" with the company culture.

These happen to be key traits of successful business communicators, too. They understand that communicating well takes analysis, judgment, and even ingenuity. It takes being attuned to people and to each communication situation. And it takes not only verbal skill but also technological and visual literacy.

Like business itself, business communication can be challenging. But the challenge can be fun, and solving communication problems can bring enormous rewards. This book will help prepare you for an exciting future as both a businessperson and a communicator.

Stuart Crabb
Courtesy of Stuart Crabb

Learning Objectives

LO1-1 Explain the importance of communication to you and to business.

LO1-2 Explain the ways in which business communication is a form of problem solving.

LO1-3 Describe the skills that are needed by today's business communicators.

LO1-4 Define professionalism and its importance to business communicators.

LO1-5 Describe the three main categories of business communication.

LO1-6 Describe the two types of communication networks in an organization.

LO1-7 Describe the main factors that affect the types and amount of communicating that an organization does.

LO1-8 Describe the contexts for each act of business communication.

LO1-9 Describe the business communication process.

Problem-Solving Challenge

Demonstrating Your Value on a High-Profile Team

You were thrilled to be hired a few months ago as a customer service representative for OrgWare, a software developer that sells management platforms to professional associations to help them run their operations and support their members' activities. This is your first "real," professional job, and you intend to make a great impression.

The company is doing well. In 12 years, it has grown from a five-person business into one that employs 120 people and has six regional U.S. sales teams, and there's even a tech-development team in Malaysia. But this growth has created a problem: The extensive face-to-face communication that helped make OrgWare a thriving business has, in many cases, become difficult or impossible. As a result, the sense of teamwork in the organization is weakening. And it is clear that phone calls, emails, and instant messaging are not sufficient to keep employees engaged and well informed.

The CEO has formed a task force to find an internal communication solution. Will it be an intranet? An electronic newsletter? A secure social networking site? Virtual meetings? A combination? Which would the employees be most likely to read and use? How should the solution be implemented, and what will it cost?

To your surprise, you were asked to help find the answers. The CEO felt that your familiarity with new media could be an asset to the team. You'll also be expected to represent the customer service area and the viewpoints of young employees like yourself.

Everyone on the team will need to research the pros and cons of different media, acquire employees' opinions, write progress reports, share ideas, and ultimately help present the team's recommendation to the top executives.

What will you need to know about communicating in business to meet this challenge? Chapter 1 will give you a good grounding for answering this question thoroughly and well.

LO1-1   Explain the importance of communication to you and to business.

The Role of Communication in Business

Your work in business will involve communication—a lot of it—because communication is critical to every area of an organization's operations. The overview that follows will help you prepare for the countless communication challenges ahead of you.

The Importance of Communication Skills

What assets will you need to bring with you into the job market? The first answer that might pop into your head is "everything I learned in my major." Not a bad answer. You're working hard to master an area of study, and that knowledge will certainly assist your entry into a profession. But check out the Communication Matters box titled "Take It from Today's Executives." The knowledge needed for many jobs is changing so fast that employers are looking for skills that transcend particular jobs, industries, time, and places. Communication ranks at or near the top of these skills.

For example, in the most recent annual survey conducted by the National Association of Colleges and Employers (NACE), employers rated leadership, ability to work on a team, written communication skills, and problem-solving skills as the top attributes they look for in applicants' résumés. Oral communication skills and a strong work ethic were rated just under these top four choices.[1] In another study, the 431 managers and executives who responded to a survey about graduates' preparedness for the workforce named "oral communications," "teamwork/collaboration," "professionalism/work ethic," "written communications," and "critical thinking/problem solving" as the top "very important skills" job applicants should have.[2]

Why is the ability to communicate effectively so highly valued? As one professional trainer explains, "You will need to request information, discuss problems, give instructions, work in

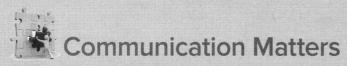
Communication Matters

Take It from Today's Executives: What You Can Do Is Even More Important Than What You Know

In its latest two surveys of executives, the Association of American Colleges and Universities found that "cross-cutting capacities" like communication skills are now more valued than a particular choice of major. More specifically,

- Nearly all those surveyed (93%) agree that "a candidate's demonstrated capacity to think critically, communicate clearly, and solve complex problems is more important than their undergraduate major"—and an even higher percentage (96%) believe that "all college students should have experiences that teach them how to solve problems with people whose views are different from their own."

- More than 9 in 10 of those surveyed say it is important that those they hire demonstrate ethical judgment and integrity, intercultural skills, and the capacity for continued new learning.

- More than 3 in 4 employers say they want colleges to place more emphasis on helping students develop critical thinking, complex problem solving, written and oral communication, and applied knowledge in real-world settings.

Sources: "It Takes More than a Major: Employer Priorities for College Learning and Student Success," AACU, April 10, 2013, accessed February 2016, https://www.aacu.org; "Falling Short? College Learning and Career Success," AACU, January 20, 2015, accessed February 2016, https://www.aacu.org.

teams, and interact with colleagues and clients" to achieve cooperation and team efficiency. To advance, you'll also need to be able to think for yourself, "take initiative," and "solve problems."[3] On the managerial level, you'll find that communication skills are even more essential. In the words of an international business consultant, "nothing puts you in the 'poor leader' category more swiftly than inadequate communication skills."[4]

Unfortunately, businesses' need for employees with strong communication skills is often unfulfilled. According to Solari Communications, "poor communication costs business millions of dollars every single day" in the form of wasted time, misunderstandings, eroded customer loyalty, and lost business.[5] SIS International Research found that poor communication is a problem for small and midsize businesses, not just for big corporations. In 2009 a business with 100 employees spent an average downtime of 17 hours a week on clarifying its communications, which translated into an annual cost of $524,569.[6] A recent study by the Project Management Institute revealed that one in five projects is unsuccessful due to ineffective communication, costing companies millions of dollars.[7]

The communication shortcomings of employees and the importance of communication in business explain why you should develop your communication skills. Whatever position you hold, your performance will be judged largely on the basis of your ability to communicate. If you perform and communicate well, you are likely to be rewarded with advancement. And the higher you advance, the more you will need your communication ability. The evidence is clear: Improving your communication skills makes you a better contributor and a more successful professional.

Business Communication as Problem Solving

Communication is involved in everything businesses do. Even in businesses based largely on manual labor, somebody has to inform the employees how to run the machinery or perform their jobs, and the employees need to be able to explain their needs and describe problems. Communication is thus a huge problem solver in business; indeed, almost no business problem could be solved without it.

But there's another way in which communication is problem solving. Every communication challenge you will face will involve factors that require at least a somewhat unique solution. For this reason, business communication itself—that is, figuring out what to say or write, and how—is a form of **problem solving**.

LO1-2 Explain the ways in which business communication is a form of problem solving.

Researchers in many fields—management, medicine, writing, psychology, and others—have studied problem solving. In general, they define *problem* as a gap between where you are now and where you want to be.[8] Some problems can be solved by following a set procedure. These are well-defined problems. When you find out how much money is left in your budget or fill in a report with routine data, you are solving a well-defined problem. But most significant business communication problems are ill-defined problems. They involve too many unmeasurable factors and allow for too many possible options to be routinely solved. With ill-defined problems, you cannot *find* the answer; you have to *develop* one by gathering information, analyzing it, and making decisions. In fact, you often have to construct a definition of the problem before you can construct the solution.

One reason why so many business communication tasks are ill defined is that communication is a transaction between people—and people are both complex and unique. But the business context itself is complex, often presenting you with multiple ways to handle a situation. For example, if a customer has complained, what will you do about it? Nothing? Apologize? Imply that the customer was at fault? Give a conciliatory discount? Refuse to adjust the bill? Even a "simple" ill-defined problem like this one requires thinking through not only how to solve the business problem (what to do with an unhappy customer) but also how to solve the communication problem (what to say and how to say it).

Fortunately, once you've studied this book, you'll have several **heuristics** in your toolbox that'll help you meet any communication challenge. Heuristics are tools to think with. They're basic guidelines, rough models, previous scenarios, and other aids that keep you from having to treat each problem as a brand new problem. Good problem solvers rely on heuristics. When facing a problem, the first thing they ask is, "Have I seen this kind of problem before?" And then, depending on the answer, they consider strategies they've already learned and used in other situations to see if some of those might apply. This is the kind of problem solving we encourage you to use. The concepts, structures, and strategies offered here are meant to save you time when planning communication solutions, but you must use your own good judgment to figure out how and when to apply them.

Of course, people will handle communication tasks differently depending on who they are, how they interpret the situation, and who they imagine their recipients to be. Does this mean that all communication solutions are equally good? Absolutely not. While there is no perfect solution, there can be many bad ones that have been developed without enough effort. Focused analysis, research, and planning will not guarantee success in the shifting, complex world of business communication, but they will make your chances of success as high as possible. Following the advice in this book, you can generate effective solutions for many common communication problems.

Communication Skills—A Breakdown

LO1-3 Describe the skills that are needed by today's business communicators.

When you approach business communication as problem solving, you draw on skills that you may not have realized are necessary for effective workplace communication.

Certainly **verbal literacy** is a core component of communication skill. The greater the range of words and sentence patterns you're familiar with, and the stronger your knowledge of grammar and mechanics, the better you can communicate appropriately with a given audience. Chapter 5, Chapter 6, and Reference Chapter A will help you craft a correct, reader-focused style.

But these days, **visual literacy** is almost as important. Extensive exposure to the Internet, with its graphics-rich content, has led readers to expect all types of written communication to look inviting and easy to read. Anything that doesn't look this way is likely to be ignored. Visuals are also critical to conveying information. Research indicates that 80 to 85% of all our perception is mediated through vision, and visually enhanced text has been proven to generate more effective learning than text alone.[9] Chapters 3 and 4 will explain about how to boost your communication's effectiveness through purposeful visual design.

While verbal and visual literacy will be your core communication skills, many other skills will come into play as you solve business communication problems. Listed below are the ones most frequently mentioned by employers and by analysts of the contemporary workplace.

Interpersonal Skill Every business, even a one-person business, is a social enterprise. Someone has to make or acquire what's being sold, someone has to sell it, and someone has to manage the whole operation—all of which involves communicating with others. Being able to work with people is thus a highly prized business skill.

Of particular interest to employers these days is employees' ability to work on a team. The respondents to the latest NACE survey ranked this trait second in terms of the skills they like to see indicated in a résumé, and it is similarly prized by many other employers.[10] There is good reason for this: As the hierarchical structure that characterized 20th-century businesses has given way to flatter, more shifting organizational shapes, the workgroup approach to business has become widespread.

Many workplace groups manage a functional area of the company, such as sales or tech support. But others are cross-functional teams set up on a temporary basis to solve particular problems or pursue particular initiatives. And you'll notice that even large companies sometimes refer to their employees as the "team." Putting together different types of people with different kinds of expertise has become essential to most organizations' success. Chapter 14 will help you become a valued contributor in this environment.

Analytical Ability When you communicate on the job, you will often be presenting your analysis of a situation or a set of information. Adapting to a quickly changing business landscape requires being able to scan the available facts, focus on the relevant ones, and interpret them reliably and usefully. As data-gathering devices are built into more objects, there will be more numerical data for us to process. Thus, the need for **computational thinking**—the ability "to interact with data, see patterns in data, make data-based decisions, and use data to design for desired outcomes"[11]—is increasing, and, with it, the need for the ability to create and read data-based graphics.[12]

But your **interpretive skills** need to go beyond interpreting numbers. Being able to understand situations and people—that is, to guess the meaning behind the facts you can see—is critical. As "smart machines" have automated many workplace tasks, employees are spending more time on tasks that require "the ability to determine the deeper meaning or significance of what is being expressed."[13] As one expert put it, "high-value work" has "an *imaginative* component."[14] This quality is required to discern the key facts, to explore "what ifs," and to choose the best solution—all central components of successful business communication. Every communication task in this book draws on such analytical skills.

Media Literacy When email arrived on the scene in the late 1980s, it created something of a revolution. Instead of being restricted to letters, memos, and printed reports and proposals, business writers could now correspond electronically. As a result, many tasks formerly conducted via print documents—memos in particular—were performed through email instead, and email replaced many phone and face-to-face conversations as well.

As you know, we now have many additional media options for our communication. In addition to instant messaging and text messaging, businesses are now using blogs, tweets, podcasts, virtual meetings, videos, animation, simulations, and even online games. Collectively referred to as **new media**, these forms of communication and the mobile devices with which people access them are causing another revolution.

The impacts of this change are many and far reaching. It is easy now to network with others, even on the other side of the world, and to tap the intelligence of those outside the boundaries of the

Exhibit 1-1	Communication-Related Skills for 21st-Century Business

- Verbal and visual literacy
- Interpersonal/collaborative skill
- Analytical ability (computational thinking, interpretive skill)
- Media literacy/social intelligence
- Cross-cultural competency
- Ethical awareness

Communication Matters

Why Companies Promote Workplace Diversity

Diversity programs are becoming widespread. Why? An article on OPENForum.com, a site offering resources and advice for businesses, lists these benefits:

1. **It builds your employer brand.** You can attract better talent from around the world. Also, a company that has a strong diversity program will have a good reputation because it will be seen as having fair employment practices.

2. **It increases creativity.** When you bring a variety of different people from various backgrounds together, you'll end up getting better solutions to business problems.

3. **It encourages personal growth.** Employees, especially younger ones, are striving to use their corporate experience to learn and to grow their careers. Workplace diversity supports this professional development because it helps employees learn new ideas and perspectives and connect intellectually and personally to different people.

4. **It makes employees think more independently.** If you have similar people at a company, it will be harder to solve complex problems. One study by Katherine Phillips, a professor at Kellogg, shows that adding even one employee from a different background can get people out of their comfort zones and thinking differently about a situation.

Source: Dan Schawbel, "Why Diversity Matters in the Workplace," *American Express OPEN Forum,* November 8, 2012, https://www.americanexpress.com/us/small-business/openforum/articles/why-diversity-matters-in-the-workplace/. All rights reserved. Used with permission.

organization. Obviously, these "new ways for groups to come together and collaborate" require that employees be "highly conversant with digital networking and virtual collaboration."[15] But new media also increase the need for employees with **social intelligence**—the ability "to quickly assess the emotions of those around them and adapt their words, tone, and gestures accordingly."[16]

With information coming in so fast and from so many sources, organizations are becoming more brainlike, with each employee acting as a kind of sensor. As a result, front-line employees now have a higher level of decision-making power than ever before.[17] Performing well in such an environment takes "novel and adaptive thinking,"[18] a willingness to "embrace change," and "fierce problem-solving skills."[19] Chapter 2 and many of the later chapters will help you choose your media wisely and strengthen your ability to use them well.

Cultural Awareness Countries and cultures continue to grow more interconnected as businesses expand around the world.

Cross-cultural competency should thus be a part of your skillset.[20] You will need to be aware that your assumptions about business and communication are not shared by everyone everywhere. As Chapter 7 explains, businesspeople from other countries may have distinctly different attitudes about punctuality and efficiency. They can also differ from you in their preference, or lack thereof, for directness and the show of emotion. And the core features of their culture—such as their preference for individualism or collectivism, their religious beliefs, their political environment, their ideas about social hierarchy, and their attitudes toward work itself—can make their view of how to do business quite different from yours.

You will encounter other kinds of diversity as well. To have adequate retirement income, the Baby Boomers—those born soon after World War II—are extending their careers. This means that organizations are likely to have employees in their twenties, in their sixties and seventies, and every age in between. The influx of women into the workplace has meant increased gender diversity. Moreover, each generation of U.S. workers has grown more ethnically diverse, with the youngest generation having the most ethnic diversity.[21] You will definitely need to have cultural agility to communicate successfully in the workplace.

Ethical Awareness One more widespread trend underway in business will likely affect your work and the goals of the organization you work for: an increased focus on ethical, socially responsible behavior.

Ethical scandals have plagued businesses throughout modern history, but several have fueled particular concern. In the 1990s, a series of articles about Nike's outsourcing its manufacturing operations to Asian countries focused the public's attention on the widespread problem of exploitation of foreign labor. In 2001, Enron and WorldCom were found to have falsified their accounting statements, which cost their shareholders and employees millions of dollars and ultimately led to these companies' bankruptcy (as well as to the conviction of one of the former "big five" U.S. accounting firms, Arthur Andersen). In 2008 came unprecedented discoveries of mismanagement, predatory lending, and fraud on the part of many of the United States' largest financial institutions—discoveries that caused the Great Recession, global economic panic, and the loss of countless homes and jobs. The explosion of a BP oil rig in the Gulf of Mexico in 2010 caused the worst oil spill in U.S. history, and Mexico is still trying to collect compensation for damage caused by the disaster. Walmart and other companies have recently been sued for wage theft and other types of mistreatment of employees. And companies are routinely taken to court for defective products and/or deceptive advertising.

On a moral level, doing business in a way that harms others is wrong. On a practical level, doing so undermines trust, which is critical to the success of business. The more an organization builds trust among its employees, its shareholders, its business partners, and its community, the better for the business and for economic prosperity overall. This helps explain why businesses place a high premium on the ethical integrity of their members and on honest, trustworthy communications.

But there's another reason. The Internet and social media have brought a new transparency to companies' business practices, with negative information traveling quickly and widely. Nongovernmental organizations (NGOs) such as CorpWatch, Consumer Federation of America, and Greenpeace can exert a powerful influence on public opinion and even on governments. Businesses now operate in an age of social accountability, and one of their responses has been the development of **corporate social responsibility (CSR)** departments and initiatives. Although the business benefits of CSR have been debated, the public demand for such programs is strong. Accountability to the various groups affected by your organization will—and should—influence how you work and communicate in business.

Professionalism 101

There's one more highly valued trait to mention, and it should come into play during every interaction you have. It's **professionalism**.

LO1-4 Define professionalism and its importance to business communicators.

Like communication, professionalism seems a simple concept until you start to unpack it. What exactly is professionalism?

Surely a part of it is **business etiquette**. This is the set of behaviors that's expected from you as an employee when you're in social situations, whether with your colleagues, your superiors, or such outsiders as partners and customers. Good table manners, polite conversation, and appropriate attire are part of business etiquette, but it goes deeper than this. As one source puts it, the ultimate goal of good manners "is to build positive relationships that enable a working environment to function in the most favorable way to all concerned."[22]

Courtesy is a part of business etiquette. In terms of communication, this means that you allow others to speak, you listen carefully, you don't interrupt, and you keep your tone of voice under control. Respect also plays a role. You demonstrate awareness of and appreciation for others' expertise and accomplishments, as well as their cultural norms.

Nongovernmental organizations (NGOs) such as CorpWatch attest to the growing importance of social responsibility in business.

Source: *CorpWatch*, February 18, 2016, accessed February 20, 2016, http://corpwatch.org/section.php?id=181.

But professionalism goes beyond etiquette because it extends beyond behavior in social situations. It means being responsible, conscientious, and cooperative in every area of your work. It means being loyal to the organization that pays you, having a strong work ethic, and adapting gracefully to change as needed. It also means having high standards for your written communications. As one blogger put it, "professionalism results in carefully prepared reports, accurate presentation of information, and constantly bearing in mind that the company exists for its customers."[23]

Research shows that employees are now changing jobs at a faster rate than ever before. According to Integral Talent Systems, recent graduates are staying at one organization only 1.8 years, and 60% of them are "résumé building" while working for their current employer.[24] As you plot your upward path, be a professional in whatever job you hold. It will lead to better learning on your part, more impressive accomplishments, and stronger letters of reference, as well as

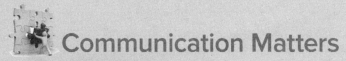

Communication Matters

How to Spot a Professional

You've seen them, and probably worked with them—they're the ones who are responsible, easy to work with, and under control without being stuffy or unfriendly. They're professionals. Here are some of their most noticeable behaviors:

- When responding to others, especially in sensitive situations, they do not blurt out the first thing that comes to mind. Instead, they listen and think and then give a considered response.
- They realize that they represent their organization. They don't say anything to an external

party that they wouldn't want their boss to overhear.

- They do not needlessly make work for other people. They answer messages appropriately and efficiently, come through with their part of a project, pay attention to instructions and feedback, and try to find the information they need before asking others for it.
- They're willing to go beyond their own job description to contribute something that will help the team. When they pick up the slack for a co-worker, they don't make a big deal out of it; they

realize that everyone is expected to give extra occasionally and that, at some point, a co-worker will return the favor.

- When in important meetings or at important presentations, they put their phones on silent and do not look at them unless they've been invited to tweet their feedback to the speaker, they're researching something for the group, or it's clear that using one's phone in such situations is okay.

What else do they do? See how many other professional behaviors you can add to this list.

rewarding relationships and a personal sense of pride. Remember that people will know you largely through your communications. Make sure your content, your wording, and the look of your written work all convey your professionalism.

The Business Communication Environment

Seeing the big picture is an important part of communication success. The Project Management Institute reports that one of the main reasons projects fail is that the team members don't understand how the project fits into the company's larger business strategy.[25] Trying to grasp a situation in its entirety before figuring out how to act is also what effective problem solvers do.[26]

But social researchers and managers have noted that, compared to the generations before them, today's graduates tend to be weak at reading the big picture.[27] Having grown up with information overload, they have developed the habit of quickly assessing messages, spending as little time as possible on each task before moving to the next one, and doing more than one thing at once (a.k.a. multitasking). In other words, they focus on the immediate and tend to work too fast on too many things to pick up on the more subtle features of a situation, some of which can be extremely important.

Efficiency is highly prized in business, but not taking the time to gather and think through all the important facts will lead to inefficiency, as well as to decisions that backfire. The discussions that follow will help you identify communication factors that may be lurking behind the more obvious ones.

Main Categories of Business Communication

All the communicating going on in your workplace can seem so overwhelming that you can be tempted to ignore all messages that do not concern you directly. But as mentioned, ignoring the big picture can lead to poor communication choices.

LO1-5 Describe the three main categories of business communication.

A way to make sense of the big communication picture is to view all communications as being one of three types: internal operational, external operational, or personal. This categorizing scheme is an oversimplification, of course. For example, a blog post or tweet can fall into all three categories if it is read by people both inside and outside the company and has a distinctive personal voice. Many business emails also include brief personal touches to help build goodwill.

Still, an understanding of these three primary categories can help you see where your communications fit in and decide what to say, how, why, and to whom.

Internal-Operational Communication All the communication that occurs in conducting work within a business is internal operational. This is the communication among the business's employees that is done to perform the work of the business and track its success.

Internal-operational communication takes many forms. It includes the ongoing discussions that senior management undertakes to determine the goals and processes of the business. It

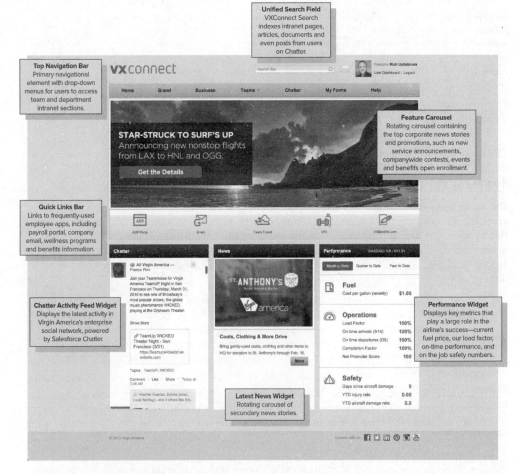

Companies often use carefully designed intranets, such as this one from Virgin America, to communicate with employees and enable them to communicate with each other.

Source: Virgin Atlantic. Reprinted with permission.

includes the orders and instructions that supervisors give employees, as well as written and oral exchanges among employees about work matters. It includes reports that employees prepare concerning sales, production, inventories, finance, maintenance, and so on. It includes the messages that they write and speak in carrying out their assignments and contributing their ideas to the business.

Most internal-operational messages should use the conversational style discussed in Chapter 6. This style is pleasant without being too chummy and professional without being stiff. Another style can be appropriate depending on what kind of communication you're engaging in—for example, a chat with a co-worker can be more casual, while a report to your boss can be more formal. But none of your internal messages should lapse into profanity, goofiness, or poor grammar.

External-Operational Communication
The work-related communicating that a business does with people and groups outside the business is **external-operational communication**. This is the business's communication with suppliers, service companies, customers, government agencies, the general public, and others.

External-operational communication includes all of the business's efforts at selling—from sales letters, emails, and phone calls to Web and television ads, trade-show displays, the company website, and customer visits. Also in this category is all that a business does to gain positive publicity, such as promoting its community-service activities, preparing appealing materials for current and prospective investors, writing press releases for the media, and contributing expert insights at professional meetings and on webinars. In fact, every act of communication with an external audience can be regarded as a public-relations message, conveying a certain image of the company. For this reason, all such acts should be undertaken with careful attention to both content and tone.

The importance of these kinds of external-operational communication hardly needs explaining. Because the success of a business depends on its ability to attract and satisfy customers, it must communicate effectively with them.

But businesses also depend on one another in the production and distribution of goods and services. Coordinating with contractors, consultants, and suppliers requires skillful communication. In addition, every business must communicate to some extent with a variety of other external parties, such as government agencies and public-interest groups. Some likely external audiences for today's businesses are illustrated in Exhibit 1-2.

Communication with such parties can be friendly, but it is typically more formal than internal communication unless you know your co-communicator well. When conversing with outsiders, you'll want to be especially aware that you are representing your organization. Be sure to do so with discretion and professionalism.

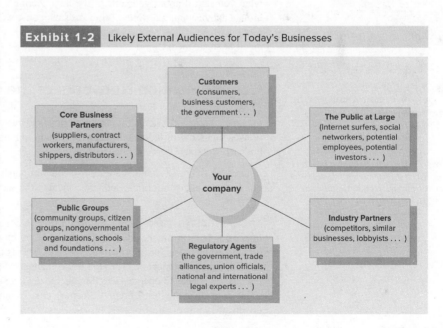

Exhibit 1-2   Likely External Audiences for Today's Businesses

Customers
(consumers, business customers, the government . . .)

Core Business Partners
(suppliers, contract workers, manufacturers, shippers, distributors . . .)

The Public at Large
(Internet surfers, social networkers, potential employees, potential investors . . .)

Your company

Public Groups
(community groups, citizen groups, nongovernmental organizations, schools and foundations . . .)

Regulatory Agents
(the government, trade alliances, union officials, national and international legal experts . . .)

Industry Partners
(competitors, similar businesses, lobbyists . . .)

Personal Communication Much of the communication that occurs in business is interpersonal dialog that has no clear connection to the business's operations. But do not underestimate its importance. **Personal communication** helps make and sustain the relationships upon which businesses depend.

The employees' attitudes toward the business, one another, and their assignments directly affect their productivity, and the nature and amount of personal talk at work affect those attitudes. Wise managers understand the importance of chitchat at doorways, around the water cooler, or in the breakroom; it encourages a team attitude and can often be the medium in which business issues get discussed. In fact, to encourage random connections and spontaneous collaboration, many businesses have switched to an open-space office design (though, as many critics point out, providing quiet spaces to concentrate is necessary, too).[28]

Using both online and face-to-face networking, you will also cultivate business-related friends. Your relationships with these contacts will not only help you do your current job; they will also be an important resource as you change jobs or even careers.

Personal communication in business is both inevitable and important.
© Creatas/Getty Images

As with operational communication, the personal communication you engage in as an employee should have boundaries. Undue familiarity with colleagues can be distracting or even offensive, and too much complaining can lead others to regard you as a negative influence. Be careful, too, what you reveal about yourself; as the next section discusses, stories have a way of getting around and becoming distorted. Blow off steam only with your most trusted work friends and in a place where you're sure you won't be overheard (as Chapter 2 points out, never do this via email or social media!).

You Make the Call
What are some examples of personal communication that would probably be inappropriate in the workplace?

LO1-6 Describe the two types of communication networks in an organization.

Communication Networks of the Organization

Looking over all of a business's communication (internal, external, and personal), we see an extremely complex system of information flow and human interaction. We see dozens, hundreds, or even thousands of individuals engaging in untold numbers of communication events throughout each workday.

In fact, as Exhibit 1-3 shows, there are two complex networks of information in any organization—one formal and one informal. Both are critical to the success of the business.

The Formal Network The information flow in a modern business is much like the network of arteries and veins in the body. Just as the body has blood vessels, the business has major, well-established channels for information exchange. This is the **formal network**—the main lines of operational communication. Through these channels flows the bulk of the communication that the business needs to operate. The flow includes the upward, lateral, and downward movement of information in the form of reports, memos, email, and other media within the organization; the downward movement of orders, instructions, advisories, and announcements; and the broad

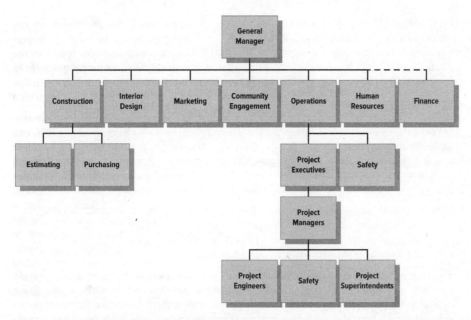

An organizational chart, like this one for a construction company, can provide clues about the company's formal communication network—for example, who reports to whom, what areas of operations are likely to communicate routinely with what other areas, and how widely different types of documents would be shared.

dissemination of company information through the organization's newsletter, bulletin boards, email, intranet, or social media platform.

As we have seen, information routinely flows outward as well. Order acknowledgments, invoices, receipts, correspondence with suppliers and consultants, and other standard external-operational communications can make external audiences part of the formal communication network.

These officially sanctioned lines of communication cause certain stable forms of communication, or **genres**, to exist within the organization (you can read more about genres in Chapter 2). For example, it may be customary in one company for project leaders to require a weekly report from team members. In another company, the executives may hold monthly staff meetings. Whatever the established form, it will bring with it certain expectations about what can and cannot be said, who may and may not say it, and how the messages should be structured and worded. You will need to understand these expectations in order to use the approved lines of communication appropriately and well.

Understanding your organization's formal network can also help you see what role your communications play in the big picture. Knowing this can help you align your comments better with the organization's goals and anticipate all possible readers of the comments you write.

Exhibit 1-3

Formal and Informal Communication Networks in a Division of a Small Business

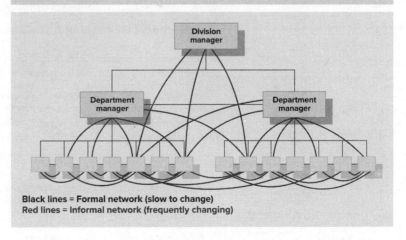

Black lines = Formal network (slow to change)
Red lines = Informal network (frequently changing)

The Informal Network Operating alongside the formal network is the **informal network**. It consists of the thousands upon thousands of personal communications that may or may not support the formal communication network of a business. Such communications follow no set pattern; they form an ever-changing and infinitely complex structure linking the members of the organization to each other and to many different external audiences.

The complexity of this informal network, especially in larger organizations, cannot be overemphasized. Typically, it is really not a single network but a complex relationship of smaller networks consisting of certain groups of people. These people may also belong to more than one group, and the members can change as employees come and go, projects begin and end, and external partners are replaced by new people. The department you belong to, the other employees with whom you come in contact in the course of your workday, and the many connections you make with those outside your organization can cause links in this network to form.

The informal network inside an organization is often referred to as the **grapevine**. This communication network is more valuable to the company's operations than you might think. Though it can spread gossip and rumors, it usually carries far more information than the formal communication system, and on many matters it is more influential in determining the course of an organization.

As an employee, you need to be careful about how you participate in the informal network. Be aware that the most influential people on the grapevine are often not those with high-ranking positions in the company. Try to identify these people, and be careful what you share with them. Such communication can either help or hurt the company, and the same holds true for communication with outsiders. Unwise remarks can get you known as a troublemaker and even get you fired, whereas representing yourself and your company well can result not only in more pleasant relations but also in professional success.

Factors That Influence an Organization's Communication

How much and what kind of communicating a business does depends on the factors listed below, as well as others you might be able to think of. Being aware of the kind of organization you work for will help you adapt your communication practices appropriately.

- **The nature of the business.** What the business does has an enormous influence on the kind of communication it needs. Insurance companies have a great need to communicate with their customers, especially through letters and other mailings, whereas housecleaning service companies have little such need. A financial services company puts almost every communication to employees in writing, whereas a construction company does not.

- **The organization's size and complexity.** Relatively simple businesses, such as auto repair services, require far less communication than complex businesses, such as automobile manufacturers.

- **The structure of the company.** Is your company highly structured, with the entry-level employees at the bottom of the organizational chart and the executives at the top, with various levels of command in between? Or is the structure relatively flat and team based? Structure strongly determines the topics you may communicate about and with whom.

- **How geographically dispersed the business is.** Obviously, internal communication in a business with multiple locations will differ from that of a one-location business. Enabling employees to work from home, requiring them to travel, or relying on outside contractors can also affect the kinds of communication a business needs and the media it uses.

- **How culturally diverse the company is.** A business whose employees are similar in background and who come from the same local area will have distinctly different communication norms from those of a multicultural organization, which must accommodate its employees' diverse perspectives and even language skills.

- **The organization's culture.** When people come together in an organization and spend many hours a day there, they form a social world with its own goals, values, behaviors, and idiosyncrasies. This

You Make the Call

Think back over the jobs you've held. Which co-workers had considerable influence on the business even though they were not high-ranking employees? What was the source of their power?

LO1-7 Describe the main factors that affect the types and amount of communicating that an organization does.

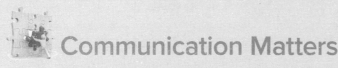

Communication Matters

What's the Dominant Metaphor in *Your* Workplace?

Management scholar Gareth Morgan asserts that companies are shaped by powerful, yet often unconscious, metaphors. Below are the eight metaphors he discusses in his book *Images of Organization*. How do you think communication practices would vary across these different types of cultures?

The organization as a machine. An organization based on this way of seeing will be hierarchical and bureaucratic—strong on control but poor at adaptation.

The organization as an organism. This type of organization understands itself as a living organism that must pay attention to its various environments as well as foster healthy development internally.

The organization as a brain. Here the emphasis is on enabling quick adaptability through "organizational intelligence," which is achieved by establishing a minimal set of rules and then allowing employees at all levels to gather, share, and act on information.

The organization as a culture. This vantage point enables us to see organizations as meaning-making systems, with rituals, myths, heroes, values, and shared frames of reference that sustain an interpretive world, much like that of a tribe.

The organization as a political system. All organizations are "intrinsically political" because the people who work there will have diverse and conflicting interests. But conflict, coalition building, and the use of power will be more pronounced in some organizations than in others.

The organization as a psychic prison. "Organization *always* has unconscious significance," Morgan asserts: People bring their egos, anxieties, repressions, and many other psychic elements to the workplace, and the organization as a whole can develop tunnel vision or neuroses. These can block positive change and even threaten organizational survival.

The organization as flux and transformation. Organizations that embrace change (and understand that change is inevitable) are more willing than others to redefine the business they're in, question the traditional boundaries between themselves and other organizations, and let their identities continually evolve.

The organization as an instrument of domination. Organizations can and often do have a dark side, with the will to compete and expand taking precedence over regard for individuals, society, and the well-being of other countries.

Morgan's list is not exhaustive; an organization could be like a sports team, for example, or a family. And several different metaphors could be operating within the same company. But looking for your organization's dominant metaphor will help you interpret your place of employment and make more successful communication choices.

Source: Gareth Morgan, *Images of Organization*, *Executive Edition* (San Francisco: Berrett-Koehler, 1998).

is its **organizational culture**.[29] You can think of a given company's culture as its customary, but often unstated, ways of perceiving and doing things. Employees at T.G.I. Friday's, for example, are expected to behave differently from those at Procter and Gamble, Google, or any bank or insurance agency, but only some of the behavioral rules are spelled out. As you know from your own experience, the ins and outs of each workplace's culture can take quite a while to learn. Making this effort is essential to successful communication in that environment.

Organizational culture is strongly influenced by the leaders at the top, but they do not have full control. While they may promote a certain culture through such communications as mission statements and mottoes, the actual culture of a company is a living medium constructed daily through infinite behaviors and communications at all levels of the company. (See the Communication Matters feature "What's the Dominant Metaphor in *Your* Workplace?" for eight common metaphors that shape companies' cultures.) All the factors listed above can help shape the kind of culture an organization has.

The Business Communication Process

So how do you solve business communication problems? Just throw yourself in there and hope your intuition steers you in the right direction? Or is there a better way?

Even though business communication problems are often not clear-cut, you can take a systematic approach to solving them. Exhibit 1-4, Exhibit 1-5, and the discussion in this section will help you do so.

Exhibit 1-4 The Business Communication Process

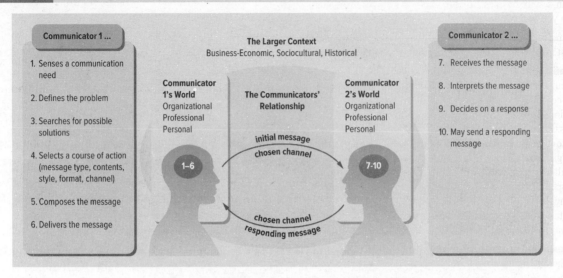

A Model of Business Communication

Exhibit 1-4 shows the basic elements of a communication event. You'll notice that the two communicators in the figure are labeled simply Communicator 1 and Communicator 2 instead of Sender and Receiver or Communicator and Audience. Certainly any communication event begins with someone deciding that communication is needed and initiating that communication, with an intended recipient on the other end. But in many situations, especially those involving real-time conversation, the two parties work together to reach a mutual understanding. Even in situations where a communicator is attempting to deliver a complete, carefully prepared message—as in a letter, report, or oral presentation—the intended recipients have already participated in the construction of the message because the writer or presenter has kept them in mind when composing and designing the message. The labels in this model are thus intended to convey the cooperative effort behind every successful act of communication.

The Contexts for Communication Certain features of the communication situation are already in place as the communicators in our model begin to communicate.

The **larger communication context** includes the general business-economic climate; the language, values, and customs in the surrounding culture; and the historical moment in which the communication is taking place.

Think about how these contexts might influence communication. For example, when the country's economy or a particular industry is flourishing, a communicator's message and the recipient's response may well be different from what they would be during an economic slump. The sociocultural context also affects how individuals communicate. Whether they are communicating in the context of U.S. urban culture, for instance, or the culture of a particular region or another country, or whether they are communicating across cultures, their communication choices will be affected. The particular historical context of their communication can also be a factor. Consider how the financial scandals in the United States or the increased focus on the environment have influenced the language of business. The skillful communicator is sensitive to these larger contexts, which always exert an influence and, to some extent, are always changing.

The **communicators' relationship** also forms an important context for communication. Certainly, communication is about moving information from point A to point B, but it is also about interaction between human beings. Your first correspondence with someone begins a

LO1-8 Describe the contexts for each act of business communication.

relationship between the two of you, whether as individuals, people in certain business roles, or both. All future messages between you will continue to build this relationship.

The communicators' *particular contexts* exert perhaps the strongest influence on their business communication.

Like this technician and manager, you will often need to adapt your communication when speaking to those whose areas of expertise are different from your own.

© Jupiterimages/Stockbyte/Getty Images

- **Organizational contexts**. As we've discussed, the type and culture of the organization you represent will shape your communication choices in many ways, and the organizational contexts of your audiences will, in turn, shape theirs. In fact, in every act of business communication, at least one of the parties involved is likely to be representing an organization. What you communicate and how you do so will be strongly shaped by the organization for whom you speak. In turn, the organization to which your audience belongs—its priorities, its current circumstances, even how fast or slow its pace of work—can strongly influence the way your message is received.

- **Professional contexts**. You know from school and experience that different professionals— whether physicians, social workers, managers, accountants, or those involved in other fields— possess different kinds of expertise, speak differently, and have different perspectives. What gets communicated and how can be heavily influenced by the communicators' professional roles. Be aware that internal audiences as well as external ones can occupy different professional roles and therefore favor different kinds of content and language. Employees in management and engineering, for example, have been demonstrated to have quite different priorities, with the former focusing on financial benefit and the latter on technological achievement.[30] Part of successful communication is being alert to your audiences' different professional contexts.

- **Personal contexts**. Who you are as a person comes from many sources: the genes you inherited, your family and upbringing, your life experiences, your schooling, the many people with whom you've come in contact, and the culture in which you were reared. Who you are as a person also depends to some extent on your current circumstances. Successes and failures, personal relationships, financial ups and downs, the state of your health, your physical environment—all can affect a particular communicative act. Since much business communication is between individuals occupying organizational roles, personal matters are usually not disclosed. But business professionals should be mindful of the effect that these can have on the communicators. If you're aware, for example, that the intended recipient of your message is under stress or having a bad day, you can adapt your communication accordingly.

The Process of Communication

No one can know exactly what occurs inside the minds of communicators when they create messages, but researchers generally agree that the process includes the following steps:

L01-9 Describe the business communication process.

1. *Sensing a communication need.* A problem has come to your attention, or you have an idea about how to achieve a certain goal. You believe that some form of communication will help you achieve the desired state.

2. *Defining the situation.* To create a successful message or plan a communication event, you need to have a well-informed sense of the situation. What exactly is the problem? Who is involved? What further information might you need to acquire? How might your or your organization's goals be hindered or helped depending on your communication choices?

3. *Considering possible communication strategies.* As your definition of the situation takes shape, you will start considering different communication options. What kind of communication event will you initiate, and what will you want to achieve with it? What image of yourself, your company, and your communication partners might you project in your message? What will be your recipient's likely expectations and preferences?

Communication Matters

Channel Choice—It Matters in Business, Too

It's considered so uncool to break up with someone by texting that this has become the classic example of poor channel choice. But choosing the wrong medium can also be decidedly uncool in business.

Check out the article listed in the source note, which tells the story of a dancer who was fired by text message. As you can see from the comments and from other such cases on the Internet, bosses who choose the wrong medium for such messages are judged insensitive and cowardly, and they run the risk of having their poor communication decision widely publicized, to their discredit.

It is naive to assume that the medium is simply a means for transmitting words. The choice of communication channel contributes significantly, along with the words, to the success of the message.

So when selecting a channel, consider such factors as the message content, the communicators' levels of competency with the channel, the recipient's access to the channel, and the assumptions associated with the channel. Appropriate choice of your communication medium will help you get the response you desire.

Source: Laruen Weber, "Text from the Boss: UR Fired," *The Wall Street Journal,* July 18, 2013, accessed February 27, 2016, http://blogs.wsj.com.

4. *Selecting a course of action.* Considering the situation as you've defined it and looking at your communication options, you will consider the potential costs and benefits of each option and select the optimum one. Your decision will include preliminary choices about the message type, contents, structure, verbal style, and visual format, and about the channel you will use to deliver the message. (Read about a poor choice of channel in the Communication Matters feature "Channel Choice—It Matters in Business, Too.")

5. *Composing the message.* Here is where you either craft your written message or plan your presentation or conversation. If you have decided to convey your message orally, you will make careful notes or perhaps even write out your whole message and also design any visuals you need. If you have decided to write your message, you will draft it and then revise it carefully so that it will get the job done and reflect well on you (see Chapter 2 for helpful writing and revising techniques).

6. *Sending the message.* When your message is prepared or carefully planned, you are ready to deliver it to your intended recipients in the channel you have chosen. You choose a good time to deliver it, realizing, for example, that Monday morning may not be the best time to make an important phone call to a busy executive. You also consider sending auxiliary messages, such as a "heads-up" phone call or email, that could increase your main message's chances of success.

While these activities tend to form a linear pattern, the communicator often needs to revisit earlier steps while moving through the different activities. In other words, solving a communication problem can be a **recursive process**. This is particularly true for situations that have many possible solutions or heavily involve the audience in the communication process. A communicator may begin a communication event with a certain view of the situation and then find, upon further analysis or the discovery of additional facts, that this view needs to be revised in order to accommodate all the involved parties and their goals.

If all goes as planned, here is what will happen on the recipient's end:

7. *Receiving the message.* Your chosen channel has delivered your message to each intended recipient, who decides to read or listen to your message.

8. *Interpreting the message.* Just as you had to interpret the situation that prompted your communication, your recipient now has to interpret the message you sent. This activity will involve not only extracting information from the message but also guessing your communication purpose, forming judgments about you and those you represent, and picking up on cues about the relationship you want to promote between yourself and the recipient.

You Make the Call

Think about a recent communication situation you handled that didn't go well. Where did your decision-making process go wrong?

9. *Deciding on a response.* Any time you send a message, you hope for a certain response from your recipient, whether it be increased goodwill, increased knowledge, a specific responding action, or a combination of these. If your message has been carefully adapted to the recipient, it has a good chance of achieving the desired response.

10. *Replying to the message.* The recipient's response to your message will often take the form of replying to your message. When this is the case, the receiver acts as a communicator, following the process that you followed to generate your message.

Exhibit 1-5 lists the main questions to consider when solving a communication problem. Taking this analytical approach will help you think consciously about each stage of the process and give you the best chance of achieving the desired results.

Exhibit 1-5   Planning Your Communication Strategy: A Problem-Solving Approach

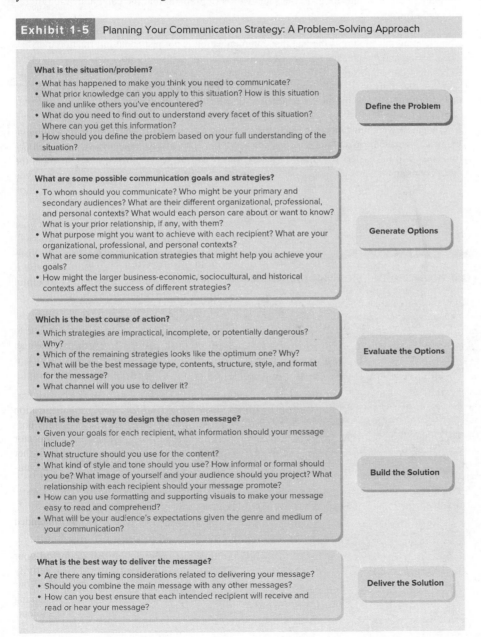

What is the situation/problem?
- What has happened to make you think you need to communicate?
- What prior knowledge can you apply to this situation? How is this situation like and unlike others you've encountered?
- What do you need to find out to understand every facet of this situation? Where can you get this information?
- How should you define the problem based on your full understanding of the situation?

Define the Problem

What are some possible communication goals and strategies?
- To whom should you communicate? Who might be your primary and secondary audiences? What are their different organizational, professional, and personal contexts? What would each person care about or want to know? What is your prior relationship, if any, with them?
- What purpose might you want to achieve with each recipient? What are your organizational, professional, and personal contexts?
- What are some communication strategies that might help you achieve your goals?
- How might the larger business-economic, sociocultural, and historical contexts affect the success of different strategies?

Generate Options

Which is the best course of action?
- Which strategies are impractical, incomplete, or potentially dangerous? Why?
- Which of the remaining strategies looks like the optimum one? Why?
- What will be the best message type, contents, structure, style, and format for the message?
- What channel will you use to deliver it?

Evaluate the Options

What is the best way to design the chosen message?
- Given your goals for each recipient, what information should your message include?
- What structure should you use for the content?
- What kind of style and tone should you use? How informal or formal should you be? What image of yourself and your audience should you project? What relationship with each recipient should your message promote?
- How can you use formatting and supporting visuals to make your message easy to read and comprehend?
- What will be your audience's expectations given the genre and medium of your communication?

Build the Solution

What is the best way to deliver the message?
- Are there any timing considerations related to delivering your message?
- Should you combine the main message with any other messages?
- How can you best ensure that each intended recipient will receive and read or hear your message?

Deliver the Solution

Business Communication: The Bottom Line

The theme of this chapter might be summed up this way: The goal of business communication is to create a shared understanding of business situations that will enable people to work successfully together.

Timely and clear transfer of information is critical to businesses, now more than ever. But figuring out what kind of information to send, whom to send it to, how to send it, and what form to use requires good decision making. Because every person has his or her own mental **filters**—preconceptions, frames of reference, and verbal worlds—wording the information so that it will be understood can be a challenge. You and your audience may even attach completely different meanings to the same words (a problem that the communication literature calls **bypassing**).

Complicating this picture is the fact that communication is not just about information transfer. The creation and maintenance of positive human relations is also essential to business and thus to business communication. Every act of communication conveys an image of you and of the way you regard those to whom you're speaking or writing. Successful business communicators pay careful attention to the human relations dimension of their messages.

Yes, business communication can be challenging. It can also be extremely rewarding because of the results you achieve and the relationships you build. The advice, examples, and exercises in this book will jump-start you toward success. But it will be your ability to analyze and solve specific communication problems that will take you the rest of the way there.

Power Charge Your Professionalism: Use the Right Word (Part I)

Select the word that completes each sentence below. The choices are pairs of words that are sometimes confused. You'll find these and other misused words listed in Reference Chapter A. To be sure you use them accurately, consult a dictionary.

1. The performance of our stock will (affect/effect) our shareholders' willingness to continue investing in our company.
2. Roy, Sydney, and Ming have all applied for the promotion. We will have a difficult time choosing (among/between) the three of them.
3. Jeanette knew she had to raise more (capital/capitol) before starting her new business.
4. We will be conducting interviews on (cite/sight/site) next Thursday.
5. Jorge and Mira work well together because their skills are (complimentary/complementary).
6. The CEO asked for everyone's (cooperation/corporation) as we moved through the software conversion.
7. Guests always receive (deferential/differential) treatment when they visit our company.
8. Good team members do not (desert/dessert) their teams just because the work isn't going well.

Choosing the right word is important because . . .

- Using the wrong word can confuse readers or even make them completely misunderstand your meaning.
- Using the wrong word can make you appear to be poorly educated and/or careless, neither of which is an impression you want to convey.

Key Terms

problem solving 5
heuristics 6
verbal literacy 6
visual literacy 6
computational thinking 7
interpretive skills 7
new media 7
social intelligence 8
cross-cultural competency 8
corporate social
   responsibility (CSR) 9

professionalism 9
business etiquette 9
internal-operational
   communication 12
external-operational
   communication 13
personal communication 14
formal network 14
genres 15
informal network 16
grapevine 16

organizational culture 17
larger communication
   context 18
communicators'
   relationship 18
organizational contexts 19
professional contexts 19
personal contexts 19
recursive process 20
filters 22
bypassing 22

Critical-Thinking Questions

1. Why do you think employers value transferable skills more highly now than in the past? What changes in business over the last 20 years or so might account for this change? LO1

2. "If there's no definitive solution, then all ways of handling a business communication problem are equally good." Using the discussion of business communication problem solving in this chapter, explain why this statement is false. LO2

3. In what ways is imagination important in business? In business communication? LO2, LO3

4. Think of a time when insufficient verbal skills on the part of someone in the workplace or in the public sphere led to a negative result. What kind of wording mistake did this person make, and what kind of damage did it cause? LO3

5. Think of or find an example of a time when someone used a visual effectively to make a point. Why does the visual work so much better than words, or words alone? LO3

6. Think back through your work history and any team projects you've been on, and identify someone who, in your opinion, was a great team player. What qualities and skills made this person skillful at working with others? LO3

7. To get a feel for the importance of media literacy on the part of business communicators, make a list of all the information technologies (devices, media platforms, and applications) that you've used over the last two years. What kind of knowledge is required to be able to use each of these technologies well? LO3

8. "People need to leave their cultures and values at the door when they come to work and just do business." Discuss the possible merits and flaws of this attitude. LO3

9. How might people's definition of "professional behavior" depend on which industry or type of company they're in? LO4

10. "Never mix business with personal matters—it just leads to damaged relationships, poor business decisions, or both." In what ways might this be a fair statement? In what ways is it unwise advice? LO5

11. Describe the formal communication network in an organization, division, or department with which you are familiar (preferably a simple one). Discuss why you think the communication network has taken this form and how successfully it seems to meet the business's needs. LO6

12. As noted in this chapter, companies develop specific forms of communication, or genres, that enable them to get their work done. In a place where you have worked or another organization you have been a member of, what were the main forms of communication with the employees or members? To what extent were these uniquely adapted to the needs of the organization? LO6

13. Review the Communication Matters box at the end of "The Business Communication Environment" to see what management scholar Gareth Morgan has to say about types of workplace cultures. Then think of an organization you know well and decide what its dominant cultural metaphor is. Is it one of Morgan's? Or is it a family? A team? A community? A prison? A mixture of several kinds? Once you settle on your metaphor, be prepared to explain how this organization's culture affects, and is affected by, its communication practices. LO7

14. Think of a recent transaction you had with a businessperson or with a staff member at your school. Describe the contexts of your communication, from the larger context (business-economic, sociocultural, and historical) down to the personal (to the extent you know them). How did these likely influence the outcome of your communication? LO8

15. Using this chapter's discussion of communication, explain how people reading or hearing the same message can disagree on its meaning. LO8, LO9

Skills-Building Exercises

1. Interview a successful professional in an area of business you're interested in to find out how he or she feels about the importance of communication skills. See how this person defines such skills and their importance. Ask for a positive and a negative example of a time when communication helped determine an important outcome. LO1

2. You purchased two pairs of expensive shoes (or substitute another product) about six months ago at a specialty store located 20 miles from where you live. One of the pairs needed to be ordered from the manufacturer because the store did not have the color you wanted. The manager told you that he would call you when that pair came in, but three months passed, and you heard nothing. So you called the store and left a message. The manager called you back to say that those shoes wouldn't be available for another three months and asked if you wanted to wait for them. You said yes—but then four more months passed, with no word from him. You called again and left a message, but, so far, no one has called you back. Use Exhibit 1-5 to help you decide how to use communication to solve this problem. Explain which communication solution you think would be best and why. LO2, LO8, LO9

3. Choose a certain national or regional culture, ethnicity, or generation—one different from your own—and find out what values the people in this demographic are generally known for. How might working or doing business with a person from this group require you to adapt your own values and communication style? LO3

4. Using the Internet, find a company that has a corporate social responsibility program and study what the company's website says about that program. What kind of image as a corporate citizen is the company trying to project, and how? How convincing is this effort, in your opinion, and why? LO3

5. What do you think would be the most professional way to handle the following situations? LO4, LO5
   a. You're the lead student employee of your school's technology help desk. Each day, you field questions from faculty, staff, and students about their email account, the Internet, and other tech topics. The volume of calls and emails is high, so you're worn pretty thin by the end of your shift each day. Today, late in the day, you get an email from a faculty member expressing interest in having her students design a tutorial to help faculty and students learn one of the school's tech tools better and asking which IT person would be best to contact about this idea. You have no idea. How do you answer?

b. You're the chair of the employee volunteerism committee at your workplace. After three years in this role, you're ready to step down. At your latest meeting, one of the committee members eagerly volunteered to be the next chair. The thing is, this person actually hasn't done much of the work, and you suspect that he wants the job just to make himself look good to the company's leaders. You didn't say anything right then, but now the HR director, in whose area this committee falls, has come to your desk to ask if the person who wants the job should be appointed to it. What do you say?

c. You recently served on a team that prepared an important proposal for your company. During the presentation of the proposal to management, one of your teammates indicated that she had done most of the work, when in fact she had done very little compared to you. Do you say or do anything in response or just let it slide?

d. You've had a long, successful relationship with the supplier of some of the materials that your company uses in its products. The company is reliable, and the quality of their products is solid. But the sales rep you usually dealt with at this company was recently replaced by someone who isn't very pleasant. She seems to regard each phone call or email from you as an annoyance and is quick to become defensive when you call any little issue to her attention. What, if anything, would you do about this situation?

6. Find two websites of companies in the same industry—for example, two manufacturers of household products or two wireless service providers. Using the evidence presented on their websites, compare their company cultures. Look at their stated mission (if any), their history (if provided), the gender and qualifications of their personnel (if given), their employee benefits, their information for job applicants, their information for investors, the company image projected by the visual elements on the site—anything that suggests who they are or who they want you to think they are. Write up your comparison in a well-organized, well-supported message to your instructor. LO7

7. After noticing that some workers were starting work late and finishing early, a department head wrote this message to subordinates:

It is apparent that many of you are not giving the company a full day's work. Thus, the following procedures are implemented immediately:
a. After you clock in, you will proceed to your workstations and will be ready to begin work promptly at the start of the work period.
b. You will not take a coffee break or consume coffee on the job at the beginning of the work period. You will wait until your designated break times.
c. You will not participate in social gatherings at any time during the workday except during designated break periods.
d. You will terminate work activities no earlier than 10 minutes prior to the end of the work period. You will use the 10 minutes to put up equipment, clean equipment, and police the work area.
e. You will not queue up at the exit prior to the end of the work period.

The message was not well received by the workers. In fact, it led to considerable anger and confusion. Using the discussion of communication planning in this chapter, explain where the department head's problem-solving process went awry. What did he or she fail to take into account? LO8, LO9

8. Find an article in the business press or general news about a recent incident involving a company—for example, a merger or acquisition, a scandal or crisis, or the launching of a new product. What kind of communication challenges might this event have posed for the company, both internally and externally? What kinds of messages probably needed to be prepared, and for whom? LO1–LO9

Writing Effectively for Your Audience, Purpose, and Medium

© Shutterstock / GaudiLab

Two

M uch of this book focuses on writing in business. Is oral communication important? Absolutely. How about visual communication? Definitely.

We focus on written communication because experienced businesspeople tend to place writing skills ahead of other communication skills when asked what they seek in job applicants. In fact, according to the National Association of Colleges and Employers 2016 *Job Outlook,*[1] written communication skills are among the top skills employers value in new employees, along with problem-solving, leadership, team, quantitative, and analytical skills. Also, as employees advance, they do more knowledge work, which often requires expertise in written forms of communication. Therefore, your written communication skills are ones you want to continuously develop as a business professional.

Developing your oral communication skills is essential as well, and you'll likely find that many of the strategies for developing written messages apply to oral messages as well.

Learning Objectives

LO2-1   Understand the importance of skillful writing in business.

LO2-2   Describe the writing process and effective writing strategies.

LO2-3   Describe the use of computer tools to facilitate planning messages.

LO2-4   Describe the use of computer tools to facilitate drafting messages.

LO2-5   Describe the use of computer tools to facilitate revising messages.

LO2-6   Describe the purpose and form of letters.

LO2-7   Describe the purpose and form of memorandums (memos).

LO2-8   Describe the purpose and form of email.

LO2-9   Understand the nature and business uses of other communication media.

LO2-10   Describe how technology will continue to impact communication in the future.

Problem-Solving Challenge

Managing Multiple Media

Introduce yourself to this chapter by shifting to the role of Julie Evans, a recent college graduate in her first job as an accounts manager at a small company that manufactures windows. You are amazed (and sometimes overwhelmed) by the types of messages you send each day. Every day you process dozens of internal email messages. Occasionally you write and receive memorandums. Then there are the more formal communications you exchange with people outside the company—both email and letters. You also write messages for social media sites and daily rely on text messaging and instant messaging for quick communication.

With so many audiences and so many ways to send messages with your co-workers, you often wonder if you're making good choices. Are you choosing the right channel for your communication? Are your messages accomplishing your business and communication goals? Are you using communication and computer technologies effectively and efficiently? Are your readers able to understand your messages and act on them?

This chapter guides you through the main types of business messages so that you are sure to meet the needs of your audience.

LO2-1 Understand the importance of skillful writing in business.

The Importance of Good Business-Writing Skills

Writing is in some ways more difficult to do well than other kinds of communication because the words alone must communicate the message. Essentially, you have no safety net; you can't rely on your facial expressions, body language, or voice to set the tone for a message. To be an effective business writer, then, you must develop the ability to capture a complex reality in words, which requires you to use ingenuity, discipline, critical thinking, and problem solving.

The first major section of this chapter will help you capture the complex nature of writing by showing you how to divide the writing process into parts. You will also learn tips for using technology to be more efficient in each part of the writing process. The remainder of the chapter will discuss the features and conventions associated with the main forms of business messages.

LO2-2 Describe the writing process and effective writing strategies.

The Writing Process

The writing process is really the process of problem solving and critical thinking. Familiarizing yourself with this process will help you become a more deliberate, effective business writer.

As Exhibit 2-1 shows, preparing any piece of business writing involves three stages: **planning**, **drafting**, and **revising**. In other words, you figure out what you want to say, you say it, and then you say it better. Each of these stages can be divided into various specific activities. However, as the arrows in the figure suggest, you should not think of the three stages as strictly chronological or separate. In practice, the stages are interrelated. Like the steps for solving business communication problems described in Chapter 1, they are **recursive**. For example, you may start writing pieces of the draft during the planning stage. Or you may find when drafting that gathering more information is necessary. Or you may decide to revise a piece of the document carefully before continuing with the drafting. In other words, you should make sure your process is flexible if you want to achieve the best results in creating your messages.

A good practice for beginning business writers is to spend roughly one-third of the writing time in each of the three stages. A common mistake that writers make is spending too much time on drafting and too little on the other two stages—planning and revising. Preparing to write and improving what you have written are as critical to success as the drafting stage, and careful attention to all three stages can actually make your writing process more efficient. Once you have become an experienced business writer, you will be able to write many messages without as much planning and revising. Even so, some planning and revising will still be essential to getting the best results with your messages.

Planning the Message

Chapter 1 presents a problem-solving approach to business communication. As Exhibit 1-5 indicates, you need to develop a definition of the problem that you are trying to solve. Once you have defined your problem, you can plan your message by answering several questions regarding your context and audience. As you plan written documents in particular, you can make the planning process more manageable by thinking about it in five smaller steps: determining goals; analyzing the audience; gathering information; analyzing and organizing the information; and choosing the form, channel, and format the document will take.

Planning a good message takes time, especially when you are writing to an audience you may not know all that well. The investment of your time pays dividends when you are able not only to achieve the goal of your message but also to enhance your professional image by writing a coherent, concise message.

Determining Goals Because business writing is largely performed in response to a certain situation, one of your main planning tasks is to figure out what you want to do about that situation. Bear in mind that in business communication, "what to do" means not only what you want your communication to achieve but also any action related to solving the larger business problem. Let's say, for example, that you manage a hotel where the air conditioning has stopped functioning. You will need to decide what to communicate to your guests about this problem. However, this decision is related to other decisions. How and when will you get the air conditioning problem solved? In the meantime, will you simply apologize? Make arrangements for each guest to have a free continental breakfast or complimentary beverages? Rent fans for meeting rooms and any guest rooms occupied by people with health problems?

As Exhibit 2-2 shows, solving the business problem is closely related to both your communication goals and business goals. You will need to bring your **business goals** (e.g., increase profits, ensure customer satisfaction) to bear on your **writing goals** (e.g., communicate your message, promote your professional image, build goodwill)—and clarifying your writing goals will help you generate business solutions.

Analyzing the Audience Once you know your purpose—what you want your message to do—you need to **analyze the audience** who will read your message. Who will be affected by what you write? What organizational, professional, and personal issues or qualities will affect the audience's response to your message? What organizational, professional, and personal issues or qualities do you have that affect how you will write your message? What is your relationship with your reader? Are you writing to your superior? Your colleagues? Your subordinates? Clients? Answers to these questions and others (see Exhibit 2-3) will influence your choices regarding your channel of communication, tone, style, content, organization, and format.

| Exhibit 2-2 | |

The Interrelated Nature of Business Goals and Communication Goals

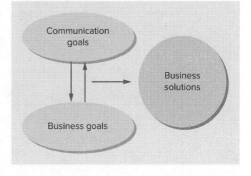

Exhibit 2-3 Audience Analysis Checklist

✔ Your relationship to your audience

What is my relationship **to** my audience?

- ☐ Colleague or someone of equal rank
- ☐ Manager or someone of superior rank
- ☐ Client of customer
- ☐ Other: _____

What is my relationship **with** my audience?

- ☐ Friendly and informal. I know my audience well. We communicate often and have a social business relationship.
- ☐ Friendly and formal. We've met and have a cordial, business-like relationship.
- ☐ Neutral or no relationship. I don't know my audience personally.
- ☐ Unfriendly or hostile.
- ☐ Other: _____

✔ Your audience's reaction

What is my audience's likely reaction to my message?

- ☐ Positive
- ☐ Negative
- ☐ Neutral

What do I want my audience to think, feel, do, know, or believe as a result of my message?

- ☐ _____
- ☐ _____
- ☐ _____

What factors in my company culture or other background information should I consider?

- ☐ _____
- ☐ _____
- ☐ _____

What factors in my audience's culture or background should I consider?

- ☐ _____
- ☐ _____
- ☐ _____

What does my audience need to know?

- ☐ _____
- ☐ _____
- ☐ _____

What does my audience already know?

- ☐ _____
- ☐ _____
- ☐ _____

✔ Your communication channel

What is the best way for your reader to receive your message?

- ☐ _____ would be the best channel for delivering the message.
- ☐ This channel is best because _____.

In the hotel manager scenario, for instance, how might your approach in an announcement to guests who are currently at the hotel differ from your approach in a response to a guest's complaint letter a week after the incident? Though you should take time to analyze your audience early in the planning process, you should continue to think of your audience as you proceed through the rest of the planning stage and through the drafting and revising stages, too. Always be thinking about what kind of information will matter most to your audience. If you fail to meet your audience's needs, you compromise your professional image and your ability to meet your business and communication goals.

Gathering Information Once you have a sense of what you want your message to achieve and what the audience needs to know, you may need to do some research. In many cases this research can be informal—finding past correspondence; consulting with other employees or with outside advisers; or reviewing sales records, warranties, and product descriptions. In other cases you will do formal research such as conducting surveys or reviewing the literature on a certain subject. In general, you will collect any information that can help you decide what to do and what to say in your message.

Gathering information by using your memory, problem-solving skills, and creativity is also important. For example, you can visualize your readers to determine their interests. Likewise, you can list pertinent facts and then **brainstorm** (generate possible solutions without censoring them) to develop creative solutions. You might also diagram your ideas to collect your thoughts.

Analyzing and Organizing the Information Once you have ideas, you can analyze them. If your data are numerical, you will do the calculations to see patterns and meaning in the numbers. You will put other kinds of data together as well to see what course of action they might indicate, weighing what the parties involved stand to gain or lose from each possible solution.

As you think about what to say in your message, you will, of course, keep your readers in mind. What kind of information will matter the most to them? In our scenario, will the hotel guests want information about what caused the air conditioning problem or about when it will be fixed and what they can do to stay comfortable? As always, your intended readers are your best guide to what information to include.

The readers are also your guide for organizing the information. Whatever order will draw the most positive reaction from your readers is the best order to use. If you have information that your readers will consider routine, neutral, or positive, then put it first. This plan, called the **direct order**, is discussed in Chapter 8. On the other hand, if you think your information could run the risk of evoking a negative response, you will employ an **indirect order**, using your message's opening to prepare the reader to receive the news as positively or neutrally as possible. As you will see in Chapter 9, such a message usually requires a more skillful use of organization and word choice than one written in the direct order. Regardless of the situation, all readers appreciate logically organized information.

Choosing a Form, Channel, and Format Students typically produce writing of two types: essays or research papers. But on the job you have a wide range of established forms of communication **(genres)** from which to choose. Which one you use has a significant impact on your planning. For instance, if you want to advertise your company's services, how will you do it? Write potential customers a letter? Email them? Send a brochure? Create a website? Post a message on your company's social media sites? Use some combination of these? Each form of communication (genre) has its own formatting, stylistic, and content conventions. As a businessperson, you want to start your writing tasks with some sense of the genre you are using. The genre itself helps you know what to say and how to say it.

Communication Matters

Do I Need to Write It?

When you have a substantial message to convey—that is, one not suitable for a quick text or instant message—is it better to write it or speak it? You'll probably want to write it if one or more of the following applies:

- You want a written record of the communication.
- You want the communication to be perceived as somewhat formal.
- You think you can explain better in writing, and you don't want the recipient to interrupt you until you're done.
- Your reader will want to be able to review what you said.
- You have to reach a lot of people at once with the same message.
- The situation isn't so sensitive or timely that it requires an oral communication channel such as a phone call.

You Make the Call

If you were the hotel manager, how would your responses to the guests differ?

You can make decisions about a document's format or visual design at any point in the writing process, but usually the planning stage involves preliminary decisions about how your document will look. How can you make the information easily readable and accessible to your audience? Will you be dividing the contents with headings? Could a bulleted or numbered list help your reader? Will you use any visual elements such as a logo, picture, or diagram? Anticipating the format can help you plan an inviting and readable message.

Formatting and visual appeal impact readers' reactions. For example, Exhibit 2-4 shows the starting text of an email from a university registrar to the faculty with the subject line "'X' and 'WX' Grades Effective for Autumn 2018 Grading." How inviting do you find the format, and how easy is it to understand the information about the two new grades?

Exhibit 2-4	Illustration of the Difference That Formatting Makes

At its October 20, 2018, meeting, the Faculty Senate, having received a favorable recommendation from the Academic Affairs Committee, voted to approve the creation and Autumn Quarter implementation of two new grades: "X" and "WX." Instructors will record an "X" on the final grade roster for students who never attended any classes and did not submit any assigned work. The "X" will appear on the transcript and will carry zero (0.00) quality points, thus computed into the GPA like the grades of "F" and "UW." Instructors will record a "WX" for those students who officially withdrew from the class (as denoted on the grade roster by either EW or W) but who never attended any classes and did not submit any assigned work. The "WX" may be entered to overwrite a "W" appearing on the grade roster. An assignment of "WX" has no impact on the student's GPA. A "W" will appear on the student's online grade report and on the transcript. The "WX" recognizes the student's official withdrawal from the class and only records the fact of nonparticipation. The need to record nonparticipation is defined in "Rationale" below. With the introduction of the "X" and "WX" grades to denote nonparticipation, by definition all other grades can only be awarded to students who had participated in the class in some way. Instructors will record a "UW" (unofficial withdrawal) only for students who cease to attend a class following some participation. Previously, instructors utilized the "UW" both for those students who had never attended classes and for those who had attended and participated initially but had ceased to attend at some point during the term. In cases of official withdrawal, instructors have three options available at the time of grading: "W," "WX," and "F." If the student has officially withdrawn from the class, a "W" (withdrawal) or "EW" (electronic withdrawal) will appear on the grade roster. If the student participated in the class and the withdrawal was in accordance with the instructor's withdrawal policy as communicated by the syllabus, the instructor may retain the student's "W" grade by making no alteration to the grade roster. . . .

Now look at the first part of the actual message that was sent out. What formatting decisions on the part of the writer made this document much more readable?

At its October 20, 2018, meeting, the Faculty Senate, having received a favorable recommendation from the Academic Affairs Committee, voted to approve the creation and Autumn Quarter implementation of two new grades: "X" and "WX."

Definition of "X" and "WX" Grades, Effective Autumn Quarter 2018

"X" Grades (no withdrawal, nonattending):

- Instructors will record an "X" on the final grade roster for students who never attended any classes and did not submit any assigned work.
- The "X" will appear on the transcript and will carry zero (0.00) grade points, thus computed into the GPA like the grades of "F" and "UW."

"WX" Grades (official withdrawal, nonattending):

- The "WX" may be entered to overwrite a "W" appearing on the grade roster. An assignment of "WX" has no impact on the student's GPA. A "W" will appear on the student's online grade report and on the transcript. The "WX" recognizes the student's official withdrawal from the class and only records the fact of nonparticipation. The need to record nonparticipation is defined in "Rationale" below.
- Instructors will record a "WX" for those students who officially withdrew from the class (as denoted on the grade roster by either "EW" or "W") but who never attended any classes and did not submit any assigned work.

Participation and Nonparticipation Grades

With the introduction of the "X" and "WX" grades to denote nonparticipation, by definition all other grades can only be awarded to students who participated in the class in some way.

Instructors will record a "UW" (unofficial withdrawal) only for students who stop attending a class following some participation. Previously, instructors used the "UW" both for those students who had never attended classes and for those who had attended and participated initially but stopped attending at some point during the term.

Official Withdrawals

In cases of official withdrawal, instructors have three options available at the time of grading: "W," "WX," and "F."

1. *If the student has officially withdrawn from the class,* a "W" (withdrawal) or "EW" (electronic withdrawal) will appear on the grade roster. If the student participated in the class and the withdrawal was in accordance with the instructor's withdrawal policy as communicated by the syllabus, the instructor may retain the student's "W" grade by making no alteration to the grade roster. . . .

Source: Dr. Douglas K. Burgess, University Registrar, University of Cincinnati.

Using Computer Tools to Plan a Writing Project

Sometimes, a writing project requires significant planning. Other times, writing a document is part of a larger project, and you need to schedule the writing among the other tasks in the project. It could also be that you are writing short documents that have specific deadlines or time lines associated with them, and you want to make sure you have allotted enough time in your schedule to write them.

Whatever the case, you may find it helpful to use **project planning tools** such as Microsoft Visio. Project planning tools are a great way to visualize the scope of a project and see how all of the pieces will come together to create a final product or achieve a business goal. A Gantt chart (Exhibit 2-5) is commonly used to identify all the tasks needed to complete a project and to determine how much time each task will take. It can also help you track your progress and determine how to reallocate your resources to complete a project on time or within budget.

LO2-3 Describe the use of computer tools to facilitate planning messages.

Finding time for writing, of course, is one of the major challenges for businesspeople. By using an annotated **electronic calendar**, you can plan time for completing your writing projects. One such desktop tool is Microsoft Outlook. Exhibit 2-6 shows an Outlook calendar, which allows you to view your calendar in multiple formats, see others' shared calendars, schedule meetings, set appointment reminders, and perform many other functions to manage your time.

Good business writers always take the time to plan, using whatever tool helps their planning process. Using the powerful features that both project management and electronic calendars provide will give you the potential to produce high-quality work in a timely fashion.

Exhibit 2-5 Illustration of a Gantt Chart Created with a Microsoft Visio Template

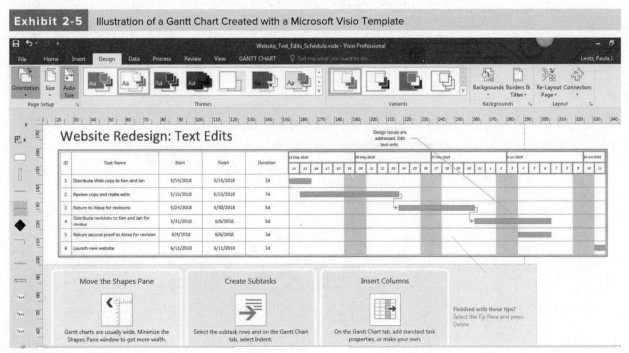

Source: Microsoft Office 2016.

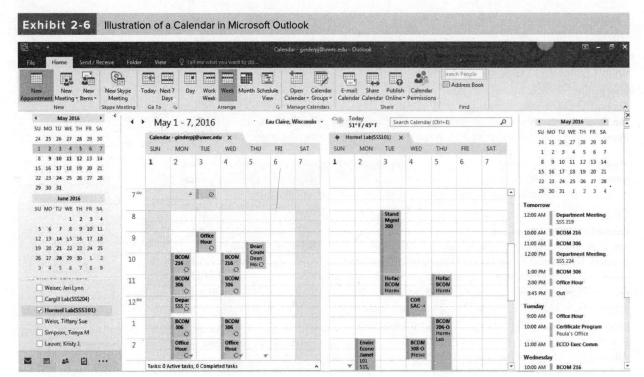

Source: Microsoft Office 2016.

Using Computer Tools to Gather and Organize Information

As we've discussed in previous chapters, before you can write, you need to know what information you require to accomplish your business and communication goals. Gathering information is one of the business writer's most important jobs.

Technology can help a writer create effective business messages.
© Paul Bradbury/Getty Images

Chapter 11 introduces you to many resources for conducting secondary research—databases, reference materials, library catalogs, company webpages, listservs, professional organizations, social networking sites (e.g., Facebook, LinkedIn, and Twitter), and other helpful websites.

While it's nice to be able to seek information using these resources, it's also convenient to have information come to you via an RSS (really simple syndication) reader. Readers such as Flipboard or Feedly pull content from around the Web based on your interests. Because you can use these readers with either a desktop or mobile device, you can always access information immediately or save it for later reading.

Whatever method you choose to gather data, you want to be aware of the latest trends, news, and research in your field and have ready information for your writing needs.

Organizing Your Information

Once you have gathered the facts, you will want to store them in some organized fashion so you can retrieve them easily. **Database tools** will help you here. For instance, if your company is interested in developing a product for a newly defined market niche, you may want to collect information about the targeted market, potential suppliers of components of your new product, sites for producing the product, projected labor costs, and so on. You could organize your information by entering your notes about target markets, names of suppliers, and other data in an individually designed form created with database tools. The information you have collected will be available whenever you need it. You can search and sort it on any of the categories (fields) you set up in your database.

Variations of the generic database are specialty tools such as EndNote, ProCite, and RefWorks. These specialty programs allow you to transfer bibliographic information automatically from a wide variety of online databases.

Microsoft Word 2016 also provides a database for managing sources (Exhibit 2-7). To use the database, click References > Citations & Bibliography tab > Insert Citation. After you have inserted your citations, you can organize them by clicking the Manage Sources icon.

Organizing Your Ideas

Organizing your ideas is essential for writing a clear message. You may find it helpful to organize ideas using an **outlining or concept-mapping program** (Exhibit 2-8). Some, such as Edraw, have both free and at-cost programs available. Once you have captured your ideas and grouped related ideas, you can rearrange them into an order that will be meaningful to your audience.

Using Computer Tools to Present Information

Once you've gathered and organized your information, you need to think about how you will present the information to your audience. Deciding how to present your data requires that you think about how you will organize your data and content to best meet your audience's needs.

Statistical programs such as SPSS and SAS are now user friendly, allowing writers to organize raw numbers into meaningful pictures of their data. In addition, spreadsheet programs such as Excel (Exhibit 2-9) will compute a broad range of data to help writers interpret the data and make it visually accessible.

Exhibit 2-7 Illustration of the References Tool in Word 2016

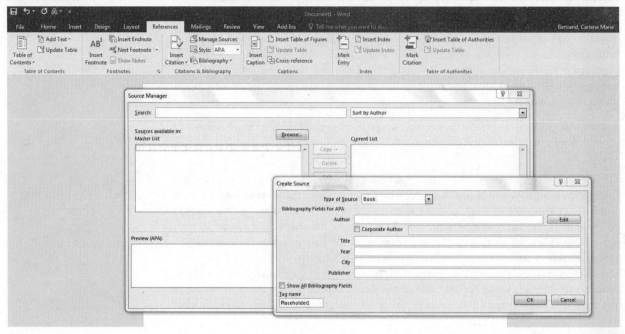

Source: Microsoft Word 2016.

In addition, as you think about presenting your information, you'll need to consider how different computer tools meet different needs. Picking the right tool makes your work as a writer easier and helps ensure that your message is communicated in ways appropriate for the genre or medium of communication.

- To develop **multimedia presentations**, consider programs such as Microsoft MovieMaker, Camtasia, PowerPoint, Articulate's Storyline, or Jing; you'll also want to consider programs such as Audacity to record and edit audio. All of these allow you to integrate video, music, still photos, screen captures, and narration into one presentation. Keep in mind, though, that with multimedia presentations you want to make them accessible to people of all abilities. For example, if you're creating a multimedia presentation that includes narration, you will want to accommodate listeners with hearing impairments by providing a transcription of your narration or include the text of the narration in the presentation. Likewise, if your presentation contains Flash elements, which are not recognized by the screen readers used by people with visual impairments, you'll want to provide a transcript as well.

- To give your documents a professionally designed look, consider desktop publishing programs such as Microsoft Publisher or Adobe InDesign. Word processing programs provide many layout and formatting options, but desktop publishing programs provide flexibility and precision for placing information on the page, formatting your text, and placing visual elements.

- To create documents for **online publication**, you can use programs such as Dreamweaver, Weebly, Kompozer, or SeaMonkey; however, programs such as Microsoft Word or Publisher let you save documents as .html files for Web publication.

Exhibit 2-8	Illustration of the Edraw Concept-Mapping Tool for Organizing

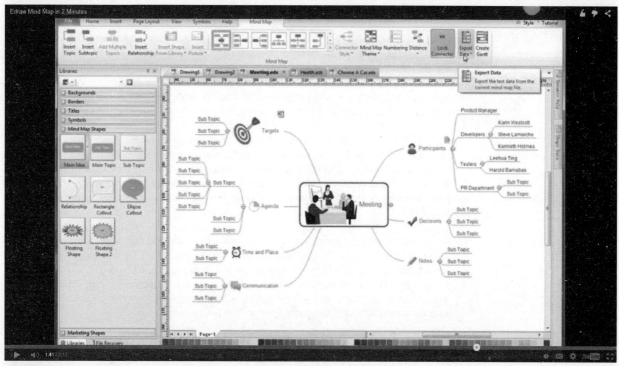

Source: EdrawSoft.

Exhibit 2-9	Illustration of Data Visualization Using Excel

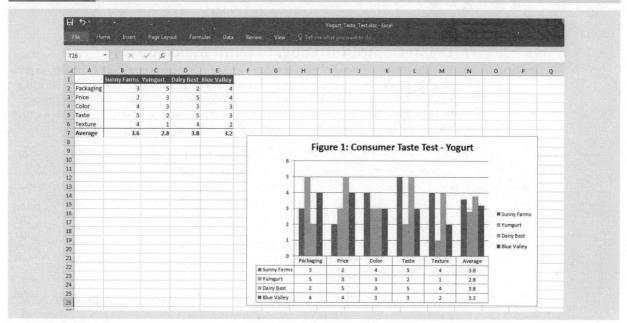

Source: Microsoft Excel 2016.

Choosing the right technology for a writing task makes at least part of your job easier. The time invested in learning the technology may save you time later by helping you make your writing process more efficient.

Drafting

Flexibility is the key to creating drafts of your business documents. Writers often hinder themselves by thinking that they have to write a finished document on the first attempt with all parts in their correct order and with perfect results. The following suggestions can help you draft your messages as painlessly and effectively as possible.

Avoid Perfectionism When Drafting
Trying to make your first draft perfect causes two problems. First, spending too much energy perfecting the early parts can make you forget important pieces and purposes of the later parts. Second, perfectionism can make drafting frustrating and slow and thus keep you from wanting to revise your message when you're done. You will be much more inclined to review your message and improve it if you have not agonized over your first draft.

Keep Going
When turning your planning into a draft, don't let minor problems with wording or grammar distract you from your main goal—to generate your first version of the document. Have an understanding with yourself that you will draft rather quickly to get the ideas down on paper or onto the screen and then go back and carefully revise. Expressing your points in a somewhat coherent, complete, and orderly fashion is hard enough. Allow yourself to save close reexamination and evaluation of what you've written for the revision stage.

Use Your Own Favorite Strategies
The idea with drafting is to keep moving forward at a reasonably steady pace with as little stalling as possible. Do anything you can think of that will make your drafting relatively easy. For example, write at your most productive time of day, write in chunks, start with a favorite part, talk aloud or write to yourself to clarify your thoughts, take breaks, let the project sit for a while, create a setting conducive to writing—even promise yourself a little reward for getting a certain amount accomplished. Your goal is to get the first orderly expression of your planned contents written just well enough so that you can go back and work with it.

Using Computer Tools to Draft Messages

You are likely familiar with Microsoft Word or another word processing program as a technology for creating your documents. In addition to the basics of using the software to open files, draft, edit, cut and paste, change a font size and style, and print a document, this software offers many more options for helping you with the drafting process. Because of its popularity, we reference Microsoft Word, but many of the tools we discuss are readily available in other word processing programs as well.

Use the Help Feature
When using your software, be sure that you control the software rather than letting it control you. That is, if you need your software to do something, look for a way to accomplish the task. "The computer wouldn't let me" is really not an issue anymore. For example, in Microsoft Word 2016, the default line spacing is 1.08 spaces, and the default paragraph spacing is 8 points. If you are not a proficient user of Word, you may think that you are stuck with this spacing. However, if you use the *"Tell me what you want to do. . ."* search feature located on the Word toolbar or think logically that the controls for line and paragraph spacing would be the *Paragraph* settings (found on the *Home* ribbon), you can make changes quickly.

Take Advantage of Built-In Styles and Themes
Word processing programs also offer a variety of styles, document themes, and templates that you may use to ensure consistency in your documents. The built-in styles in Word 2016 are particularly useful not only to ensure

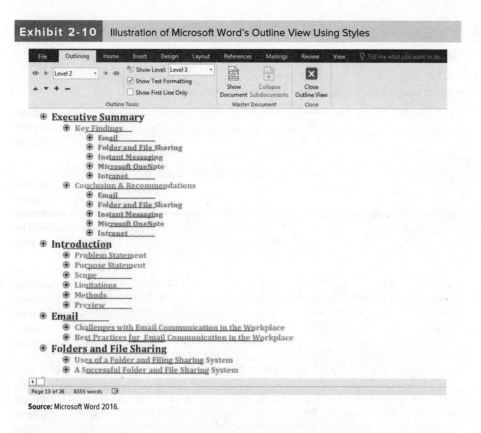

Source: Microsoft Word 2016.

consistency but also to create a table of contents. If you use the styles (or create your own using the *Styles* tool), Word can use them to automatically generate a table of contents. Styles also let you use Word's outline view (Exhibit 2-10) to move text just by clicking and dragging the heading to a new location in the outline. If you use the themes and templates, though, be aware that many of these have specially set formatting for line and paragraph spacing, bullets, and alignment. You can manipulate these settings to meet your preferences, but if you are not comfortable doing so, you may find it easier to create your own formatting. Again, the *Tell me what you want to do. . .* search feature can help you make these changes.

Explore Other Interesting Features Microsoft Word 2016 offers the following additional features. If you use other word processing software, you may have access to similar features as well.

- Equation builder: Lets you write equations.

- Quick Parts (also called Quick Words and AutoText in other software): Lets you create a collection of information that you frequently use in documents so that you do not have to retype the information every time you create a document.

- Word count: Allows you to keep track of your document's length.

- Collaboration: Enables you to merge, view, or compare multiple documents.

- Digital signature: Validates the authenticity of the writer much like the signature on a printed document.

- Smart Art, Clip Art, Charts: Lets you create appealing, informative visuals.

- Multiple *Save* options: Allows you to save your document as a Word file, a .pdf, or an .html file.

Exhibit 2-11   Illustration of the Many Tools in Microsoft Word 2016

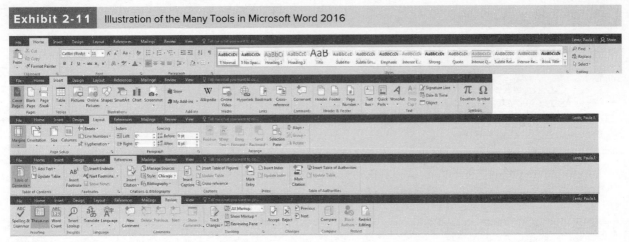

Source: Microsoft Word 2016.

Exhibit 2-11 shows the various ribbons and their tools in Word 2016. Some people may find it useful to take courses to learn how to use word processing software, but many learn successfully by exploring the software and using the *Tell me what you want to do...* feature to accomplish their tasks.

Save Your Document Correctly
If your readers are getting printed copies of your document, you can save your file in whatever software format you are using. However, if your readers will view your document electronically, you need to save it in a format that your reader's software will recognize. For instance, Word 2016 files save as .docx files. However, you may find that some of your readers are still using older versions of Word that recognize only .doc files, which means they will not be able to open your file without first downloading a special utility program. To accommodate this reader, you will need to do a File > Save As and save your document as a .doc file—though if you save your .docx file as a .doc, you may lose some of the formatting from the themes or Smart Art that are not recognized by earlier versions of Word.

If your reader's software is not compatible with your current version of Word, you can save your document as a .pdf (portable document format) file so that your reader can open it with the formatting preserved. As with the actual composing process itself, saving your documents is an audience-centered effort. You don't want your reader to be angry and frustrated at not being able to open your documents, nor do you want to spend time (and the reader's time) backtracking to save the document in another format and then resending it.

Use Speech Recognition Tools
If you have mobility issues or find it easier to talk through your thoughts as you draft, you may want to consider using a speech recognition tool. You train the software to recognize your voice and speech patterns so that it can enter text in your document as you speak. Some programs, such as Dragon Naturally Speaking, can be purchased, whereas Google Chrome's Dictation App or Microsoft's Windows Speech Recognition (All Programs >> Accessories >> Ease of Access >> Windows Speech Recognition) can be accessed from your computer without an additional purchase.

Revising
Getting your draft ready for your reader requires going back over it carefully—again and again. Do you say what you mean? Could someone misunderstand or take offense at what you have written? Is your information organized effectively? Is each word the right one for your goals? Are there better, more concise ways of structuring your sentences? Can you move the reader more smoothly from point to point? Does each element of format enhance readability and highlight the

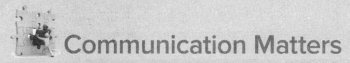

Communication Matters

Why Accurately Proofreading Your Own Work Is Difficult

You have likely had the experience of writing what you think is the perfect document only to have someone point out a misspelling or other error. You are not alone. Proofreading your own work is difficult, and there is a reason for it.

Psychologist Tom Stafford explains that when you write and edit, your brain engages in a high-level process called "generalization." That is, it generalizes the simple parts of the message such as letters and words so that it can spend its time on more complex parts of the message such as content. As a result, when you proofread your own work, your brain leads you to see words as you expect to see them, not to see what is typed on the page. When you proofread others' work, you have no expectations regarding what you will see on the page, which makes it easier for you to pay attention to details and see errors.

Stafford says that to improve your ability to proofread your own work well, you need to make it visually unfamiliar so that your brain does not draw on what it has generalized—that is, change the color or the font or print the document and edit by hand rather than edit on screen.

Source: Nick Stockton, "What's Up with That: Why It's So Hard to Catch Your Own Typos," *Wired*, August 12, 2014, accessed May 2, 2016, http://www.wired.com.

structure of the contents? When revising, you become your own critic. You challenge what you have written and look for better alternatives. Careful attention to each level will result in a polished, effective message.

Any given message has so many facets that using what professional writers call **levels of edit** may be helpful. The levels this term refers to are **revising**, **editing**, and **proofreading**.

When revising, you look at top-level concerns: whether or not you included all necessary information, whether the pattern of organization is logical and as effective as possible, whether the overall meaning of the message comes through, and whether the formatting is appropriate and helpful.

You then move to the editing level, focusing on your style. You examine your sentences to see whether they pace the information in such a way that the reader can easily follow it, whether they emphasize the right things, and whether they combine pieces of information coherently. You also look at your word choices to see whether they are right for your audience and purpose.

Finally, you proofread, looking at mechanical and grammatical elements—spelling, typography, punctuation, and any grammar problems that tend to give you trouble. Editing functions in your word processing program can help you with this task.

Getting feedback from others is also helpful during the revision stage. As you may well know, finding weaknesses or errors in your own work is difficult. Seek assistance from willing colleagues, and if they give you criticism, receive it with an open mind. Hearing this feedback from them is better than hearing it from your intended readers when costly mistakes may have already been made.

Using Computer Tools to Revise and Edit

Word processing software also offers several tools for proofing and editing your documents. If your editing consists of reading from the computer monitor or printing a document and simply reading it, you may be missing issues or errors that could be quickly fixed. Again, we use Word 2016 as our reference to illustrate helpful editing tools, but these tools are readily available in other software as well. Remember, though, that while your software may help you identify some of the things you need to revise, you still need to be able to revise for issues your software does not detect.

Successful writers often seek others' perspectives on important documents.
© Image Source/Stockbyte/Getty Images

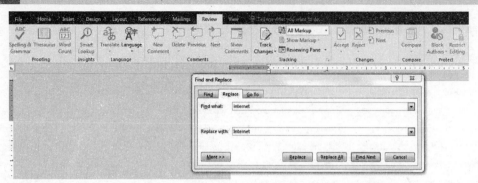

Source: Microsoft Word 2016.

The Find Feature   The Find feature (Ctrl+F, or Home > Editing > Find) can search for and highlight parts of the text you want to check. Let's say that you are writing a letter, and you know you have a problem with comma splices. You could have the software find and highlight every comma in the letter. Then, you can review the highlighted commas and fix any errors.

The Find and Replace Feature   This feature (Ctrl+H, or Home > Editing > Replace) allows you to make multiple changes simultaneously (Exhibit 2-12). You can find and replace words or text formatting. If, for example, you spelled *internet* with a lowercase *i* and want to capitalize it instead, you would tell Word to search for all instances of *internet* and replace them with *Internet*. You can also find and replace line spacing, paragraph formatting, tabs, styles, and special characters much more efficiently than selecting all individual instances of a word, sentence, or paragraph and making changes one at a time.

Comments and Track Changes Features   Though these features can be used separately, they are often used together when writers collaborate on documents, as Chapter 11 explains. However, you may also want to use them to leave comments for yourself (e.g., "Check the date of this source") or to keep a record of your changes. Because you can accept or reject the changes, you are not committed to them, and because you still have a record of your earlier work, you can simply reject a change and revert to your original version.

Auto Correct Features   As we discuss in Chapter 5, the Auto Correct feature lets you enable the software to recognize common errors you may make. For example, if you type quotation marks inside a period (e.g., ".), you can set the auto correct feature to always correct your text to read ." instead.

Spelling Checkers   Along with Quick Parts, AutoText, and QuickWords, spell checkers are tools business writers rely on daily. However, they are only effective at identifying words that are not in their dictionary. Therefore, spell checkers will not identify as errors words that are spelled correctly but used in the wrong sense. For example, a spell checker will not identify wrong-word errors such as *compliment* for *complement* or *imply* for *infer*. A spelling checker also may miss errors such as *desert* for *dessert* or misused words such as *good* for *well*. Therefore, careful proofreading is still in order after a document has been checked with a spelling checker. To access the spelling checker in Word 2016, select the Review ribbon and then ABC Spelling & Grammar or press F7.

Thesaurus Software   Microsoft Word 2016 also includes a Thesaurus that you can access by going to the Review ribbon and selecting Thesaurus. You can also find a Thesaurus online. The Merriam-Webster website (www.m-w.com) includes a free online thesaurus, as well as a dictionary and other tools.

Grammar and Style Checkers   Grammar and style checkers identify possible problems and give suggestions for revision. Your responsibility is to decide whether the possible problem

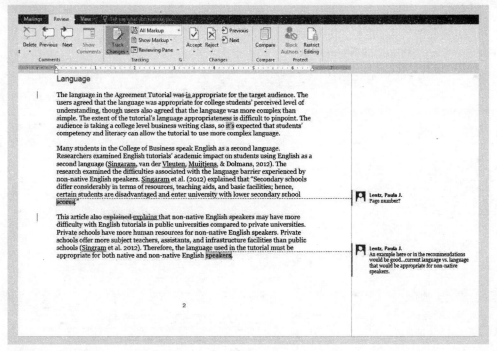

Source: Microsoft Word 2016.

is a problem and whether the suggestion is the best solution. Making this decision requires that you have a good understanding of basic grammar (see Reference Chapter A).

In addition to checking grammar, style, word usage, and punctuation, Word 2016 reports readability indexes. It also analyzes sentence structure, suggesting that you use simpler sentences, vary the sentence beginnings, use more or fewer prepositional phrases, and make various other changes. Grammar and style checkers also identify possible problems with specific words that might be slang, jargon, misspelled, misused, negative, or difficult for readers to understand. A complementary feature, Word Count, reports statistics for number of pages, words, characters, paragraphs, and lines. An example of the interactive use of one grammar checker is shown in Exhibit 2-14.

Exhibit 2-14   Illustration of a Spelling and Grammar Checker in Microsoft Word 2016

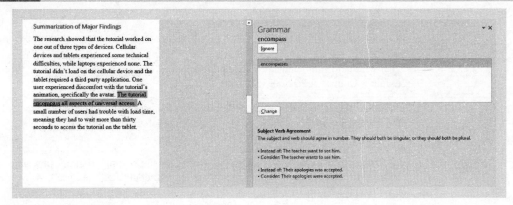

Source: Microsoft Word 2016.

Backing Up Frequently Is the Writer's Responsibility

Most writers know how difficult it is to create a document, much less recreate it, so they are willing to spend a little time to protect their investment. In the Save Options dialog box of Word (File > Word Options > Save > Save Documents), a writer can set up the program to have Word always create a backup file, to run these backups every 10 minutes, and to do it in the background. This backup helps protect you from losing your work if your computer goes down unexpectedly whether from crashes, power outages, accidents, or viruses.

To protect your documents further, you might want to vary the backup media you use so that if your computer is damaged or becomes infected with a computer virus, you still have copies of your files. This media could range from simple backups on disks or USB drives to backups at offsite locations. You might also back up your work by saving it to online services such as Dropbox or Google Drive.

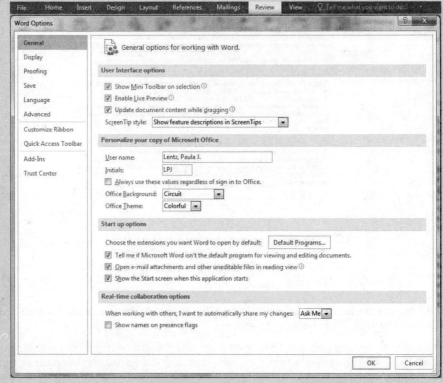

Source: Microsoft Word 2016.

Recent versions of grammar and style checkers are much more flexible than older versions. In Word 2016 you can customize your grammar and style settings to fix common errors or to adapt your writing to your company's style preferences. To customize your settings in Word 2016, go to File > Options > Proofing.

Grammar and style checkers are definitely important for the business writer. As with all tools, the more appropriately you use them, the better the job they do for you.

Information Rights Management (IRM) Many writing programs now give writers the ability to specify how their documents are shared, controlled, and used. As you can see in Exhibit 2-15, Word 2016 offers several levels of security for a document.

Exhibit 2-15 Illustration of Security Options in Microsoft Word 2016

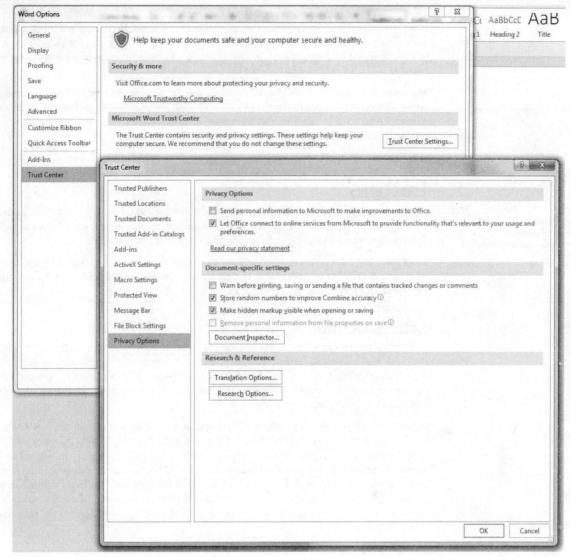

Source: Microsoft Word 2016.

Writers can determine how their documents are shared by specifying who can read, change, or have full control over them. Additionally, the writer can set an expiration date on these permissions. Not only do these features help businesses prevent sensitive information from getting into the wrong hands either accidentally or intentionally, but they also give writers control over documents once they leave their computers. If only certain people have permissions, forwarded and copied files will be protected from unauthorized use.

IRM tools have prompted many businesses to establish practices or policies on the kinds of permissions required for various types of information to protect their intellectual property. These tools also help decrease inbox clutter because they force writers to think about who really needs the document and for how long.

Technology is certainly an important tool for constructing messages. While word processing is the writer's primary tool, a wide variety of other tools can help with the planning, gathering and organizing, presenting, drafting, and revising and editing. By using the tools discussed in this section, you will find that your writing process is more efficient and your writing more polished.

The remaining sections of this chapter describe specific purposes and traits of different message types. Chapter 4 provides in-depth advice about their physical design. No matter what you're writing, taking time to make careful formatting decisions during your writing process will significantly enhance your chances of achieving your communication goals.

Letters

LO2-6 Describe the purpose and form of letters.

Letters are the oldest form of business messages. The ancient Chinese wrote letters, as did the early Egyptians, Romans, and Greeks. In fact, American businesspeople used letters as early as 1698 to correspond about sales, collections, and other business matters.[2]

From these early days letters have continued to be used in business. Although their use and purpose have evolved as other business communication genres have developed, they are still the best choice for many communication tasks.

Letters Defined

The general purpose of a letter is to represent the writer and his or her topic rather formally to the recipient. For this reason, **letters** are used primarily for corresponding with people outside your organization. When you write to internal readers, they are often familiar to you—and even if they are not, you all share the connection of being in the same company. Your messages to such audiences tend to use less formal media.

However, when you write to customers, to suppliers, to citizens and community leaders, and to other external audiences, you will often want to present a formal, polished image of your company by choosing the letter format, complete with an attractive company letterhead and the elements of courtesy built into this traditional format. Once you have established a less-formal relationship with your audience, you may find you conduct your business through emails, phone calls, instant or text messaging, and social media. However, especially when corresponding with an external party whom you do not know well, a letter is often the most appropriate form to use.

Letter Form

The format of the business letter is probably already familiar to you. Although some variations in format are generally acceptable, typically these items are included: date, inside address, salutation (e.g., Dear Ms. Smith or Dear Dr. Smith), body, and complimentary close (Sincerely). Other items sometimes needed are an attention line, subject line, return address (when letterhead is not used), and enclosure information. Exhibit 2-16 presents one option for formatting a letter. More options are presented in Chapter 4.

Letter Formality

As formal as letters can be, they are not nearly as formal as they used to be. Business messages in general have grown more conversational, and this is true of letters as well as of other forms of correspondence.

Exhibit 2-16 Illustration of a Letter in Full-Block Format

 RALSTON'S PLUMBING AND HEATING
2424 Medville Road, Urbana, OH 45702 | P: 555.555.5555 | F: 555.555.5544 | E: ralstons@rph.com

March 15, 2017

Ms. Diane Taylor
747 Gateway Avenue
Urbana, OH 45702

Dear Ms. Taylor:

Thank you for allowing one of our certified technicians to serve you recently.

Enclosed is a coupon for $25 toward your next purchase or service call from Ralston.
It's just our way of showing that we appreciate your business.

We look forward to serving you again. Please be sure to visit our website
(www.ralstonheatingandplumbing.com) or our Facebook page for our latest products, services, and
sales.

Sincerely,

Jack Ralston

Jack Ralston
Owner and President

For instance, in the past, women were always addressed as "Mrs." Today, women are addressed as "Ms." unless you know the reader prefers "Mrs." In the past, too, if writers did not know the reader's name, wrote to a mass audience, or wrote to someone whose gender could not be determined by the reader's name (e.g., Pat Smith), they might have used a salutation such as "To Whom It May Concern," "Dear Sir/Madame," or "Dear Ladies and Gentlemen." These expressions are now considered impersonal and old fashioned. More modern options include "Dear Human Resources" or "Dear Pat Smith." Alternatively, writers can omit the salutation, perhaps adding a subject line (a brief phrase stating the writer's main point) instead, much in the same way they would create a subject line in a memorandum or email. Chapter 4 provides more information on placing a subject line in a letter.

Some business writers also consider the use of the terms "Dear," "Sincerely Yours," and even "Sincerely" outdated or excessively formal. These writers will omit "Dear," replace "Sincerely yours" with "Sincerely," omit the complimentary close, or use "Best regards" or some other cordial phrase. Your audience and company culture will determine what is appropriate for you.

Regardless of its formality, the letter should always be regarded as a personal exchange between people as well as a strategic means for accomplishing business goals and building business relationships.

Businesses with multiple locations send many of their internal messages by email as well as by instant and text messages

© Chad Baker/Jason Reed/Ryan McVay/Photodisc/Getty Images

Memorandums (Memos)

Memorandums Defined

Another business genre is the **memorandum** (or **memo**). It is a hard-copy (printed on paper) document used to communicate inside a business. Though in rare cases they may be used to communicate with those outside the business, they are usually exchanged internally by employees as they conduct their work. Originally, memos were used only in hard copy, but their function of communicating within a business has been largely replaced by email. Even so, they still are a part of many companies' communications. They are especially useful for communicating with employees who do not use computers in their work.

Memos can be used for a wide range of communication tasks. For example, as Chapter 12 points out, some memos communicate factual, problem-related information and can be classified as reports. As with the letter, the purpose and use of the memo have evolved as other business communication genres have emerged, but the memo is still an important means for communicating in many organizations.

Memorandum Form

Memorandums can be distinguished from other messages primarily by their form. Some companies have stationery printed especially for memos, while many use standard or customized templates in word processors. Sometimes the word *Memorandum* appears at the top. But some companies prefer other titles, such as *Interoffice Memo* or *Interoffice Communication*. Below this main heading come the specific headings common to all memos: *Date, To, From, Subject* (though not necessarily in this order). This simple arrangement is displayed in Exhibit 2-17. As the figure indicates, hard-copy memos are initialed by the writer rather than signed, and the memo does not contain a salutation or complimentary closing.

Large organizations, especially those with a number of locations and departments, often include additional information on their memorandum stationery. *Department, Plant, Location, Territory, Store Number*, and *Copies to* are examples (Exhibit 2-18). Because in some companies memos are often addressed to more than one reader, the heading *To* may be followed by enough space to list a number of names.

You Make the Call

Even if all employees have email access, can you think of instances when you would send a memo instead?

Memorandum Formality

Because memos usually are messages sent and received by people who work with and know one another, they tend to use casual or informal language. Even so, some memos use highly formal language. As in any business communication, you will use the level of formality appropriate to your audience and writing goals.

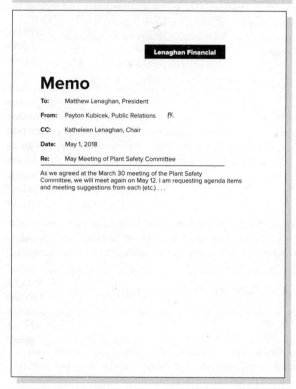

Source: Kathryn Rentz and Paula Lentz, *M: Business Communication* (New York: McGraw-Hill Education, 2014).

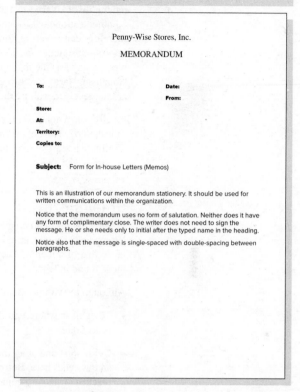

Source: Kathryn Rentz and Paula Lentz, *M: Business Communication* (New York: McGraw-Hill Education, 2014).

Email

Although businesspeople routinely communicate via social media, text messaging, and instant messaging, email remains a primary tool in the workplace. In fact, according to one study of white-collar workers, Americans spend 6 hours a day (or 30 hours a week) using email.[3]

Email Defined

It's easy to see why **email** remains popular. In contrast to letters and memos, emails can be used with either internal or external audiences and can vary widely in their types of content and levels of formality. Email addresses are readily available, and anyone can send a message to any email address (or multiple addresses simultaneously), regardless of who provides the email account. The speed at which readers receive a message can also make email more attractive than a letter or a memo. Consequently, businesses continue to use email as a low-cost, quick, and efficient means of communicating with both internal and external audiences either formally or informally. Furthermore, email provides HTML and other formatting options that text messaging, instant messaging, and social media may not, and it does not limit the writer to any number of characters

LO2-8 Describe the purpose and form of email.

or amount of text. In addition, emails can be archived and filed for easy access to a written record of correspondence.

Email, however, also presents communication challenges. Sometimes people use email to avoid having difficult face-to-face or phone conversations, which is not a good way to accomplish communication goals or cultivate the audience's goodwill. Emails are also easily forwarded and therefore can never be considered confidential. Additionally, many businesspeople deal with **spam**—unsolicited messages or mass emails that are not relevant to their work. Moreover, some writers may assume that an informal email message is not held to the same standards of professionalism, clarity, or correctness as a more formal message might be; as a result, their messages are not received well by their audiences.

Finally, when not used properly, email can be costly. According to one Fortune 100 company, the time employees spent on "irrelevant email" was costing the company $909,000 per day and $236 million per year.[4] It is important, then, that business writers ensure their emails communicate a clear message, cultivate goodwill, and promote a professional image.

Email Form

When you look at an email, you likely notice that its form contains elements of both memos and letters. For example, emails generally contain a *Date, To, From, Subject* heading structure similar to that of a memo. They may also contain salutations and complimentary closes similar to those found in letters.

Although the various email systems differ somewhat, email format includes the following:

- **To:** This is where you include the email address of the recipients. Be sure the address is accurate.

- **Cc:** If someone other than the primary recipient is to receive a *courtesy copy,* his or her address goes here. Before people used computers, *cc:* was called a *carbon copy* to reflect the practice of making copies of letters or memos with carbon paper.

- **Bcc:** This line stands for *blind courtesy copy.* This line is also for email addresses of recipients. However, each recipient's address will not show in the sent message; that is, recipients will not know who else is receiving a copy of the message.

- **Subject:** This line describes the topic of the message. The reader should get from it a clear idea of what the message is about. Always include a subject line to get your reader's attention and indicate the topic of the message. In the absence of a subject line, a reader may think your message is junk mail or unimportant and delete it.

- **Attachments:** In this area you can enter a file that you want to send with the message. Attach only files the reader needs so that you do not take up unneeded space in his or her inbox.

- **The message:** The information you are sending goes here. Typically, email messages begin with the recipient's name. The salutations commonly used in letters (Dear Mr. Dayle, Dear Jane) are sometimes used, but something less formal ("Hi, Ron") or no salutation at all is also common. If you know the recipient well, you can use the reader's first name. If you would normally address the reader by using a title (Ms., Dr., Mr.), address him or her this way in an initial email. You can change the salutation in subsequent messages if the person indicates that you are on a first-name basis. A friendly generic greeting such as "Greetings" is appropriate for a group of people with whom you communicate. As we discussed in the section on letters, you'll want to avoid outdated expressions such as "To Whom It May Concern."

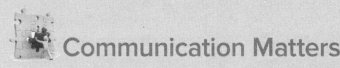

Communication Matters

Email: Your Ticket to a Successful Marketing Campaign

While it is true that businesspeople use email to conduct business within and outside organizations, many businesses use email as part of their marketing strategy.

MarketingCharts (MC) cites a report from BlueHornet in which over 1,800 people ages 18–64 were surveyed about their email use. Many respondents reported not only that they check their emails frequently throughout the day but also that they do not maintain separate email accounts for marketing or advertising messages. And even those who maintain separate accounts for marketing emails check those accounts frequently.

MC cites additional research indicating that "opt-in emails drive purchases among more Millennials than all paid advertising save for TV ads" and that given a variety of communication channels email marketing is "second only to word-of-mouth in purchase influence" among women.

The BlueHornet study indicated the factors that influence the audience's responses to an email marketing campaign include the subject line and the frequency with which messages are sent. Regardless, the study found that for nearly 75% of the 1,800 respondents email influenced their purchases at least once per month.

Source: "B2C Email Marketing Very Much 'Alive and Kicking,'" *MarketingCharts*, August 11, 2015, accessed March 11, 2016, http://www.marketingcharts.com.

Like a letter, an email message often ends with a complimentary close followed by a signature block containing the writer's name, job title, company, and contact information. Some writers also use the signature block as an opportunity to promote a sale, product, or service. Exhibit 2-19 shows a standard email format.

| **Exhibit 2-19** | Illustration of Email Form Using Microsoft Outlook |

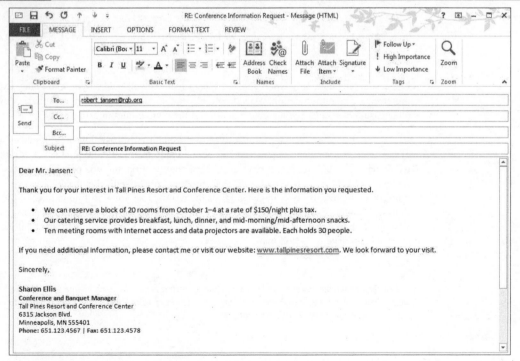

Source: Microsoft Word 2016.

Email Formality

A discussion of email formality is complicated by the fact that email messages are extremely diverse. They run the range from highly informal to formal. The informal messages often resemble face-to-face oral communication; some even sound like chitchat that occurs between acquaintances and friends. Others, as we have noted, have the increased formality of reports.

A helpful approach is to view email language in terms of three general classifications: **casual**, **informal**, and **formal**.[5] Your audience should determine which type of language you choose, regardless of your personai style or preference.

Casual By casual language we mean the highly informal language we use in talking with close friends in everyday situations. It includes slang, colloquialisms (informal expressions), contractions, and personal pronouns. Its sentences are short—sometimes incomplete—and it may use mechanical emphasis devices and initialisms (e.g., LOL, BTW) freely. Casual language is best limited to your communications with close friends. Following is an example of casual language:

Are you on the way?

I'll be there in 20 minutes.

The meeting has been Changed to 9:45 am. Can you make it?

Many businesspeople use their phones to send and receive emails and text messages. With such a small display screen, conciseness and clarity are especially important.
© Wavebreak Media LTD/123RF.

Hey, Cindy,

Props for me! Just back from reps meeting. We totally nailed it . . . plan due ASAP. Meet, my office, 10 AM, Wed?

Brandon

Use casual language only when you know your readers well—when you know they expect and prefer casual communication. You should also avoid slang, initialisms, emphasis devices, or other casual elements if you are not certain that they will communicate clearly.

Informal Informal language retains some of the qualities of casual writing. It makes some use of personal pronouns and contractions. It occasionally may use colloquialisms but more selectively than in casual writing. It has the effect of conversation, but it is polished conversation. Its sentences are short, but they are well structured and organized. They have varied patterns that produce an interesting style. In general, it is the writing that you will find in most of the illustrations in Chapters 8–10. You should use it in most of your business email messages, especially when writing to people you know only on a business basis. An example of an email message in informal language is the following:

Cindy:

The management team has approved our marketing plan. They were very complimentary. As you predicted, they want a special plan for the large accounts. They want it as soon as possible, so let's get together to work on it. Can we meet Wednesday, 10 AM., in my office?

Brandon

Formal A formal style of writing maintains a greater distance between writer and reader than an informal style. It avoids personal references and contractions, and its sentences are well structured and organized. Formal style is well illustrated in the examples of the more formal reports in Chapters 11 and 12. It is appropriate to use in email messages resembling formal reports, in messages to people of higher status, and to people you do not know.

As with any business message, formal or informal, your emails should achieve your communication goal, promote goodwill, and present a professional image. To do this, follow the advice in Chapter 5 for writing clear, courteous messages. You will also want to follow the guides in Reference Chapter A to ensure your messages are expressed correctly.

Additional Media in Business Writing

Sometimes writers in today's fast-paced, global business world need to communicate more immediately and quickly than a letter, a memo, or an email will allow. Technology provides business writers with many more channels for immediate, quick communication including text messaging, instant messaging, and social networking. Exhibit 2-20 illustrates Old Navy's many uses of social media.

LO2-9 Understand the nature and business uses of other communication media.

However, as with more traditional business writing media such as letters, memos, and emails, the use of these more immediate channels should be driven by audience needs and expectations as well as the writer's goals and purposes.

Exhibit 2-20	Illustration of Old Navy's Many Uses of Social Media

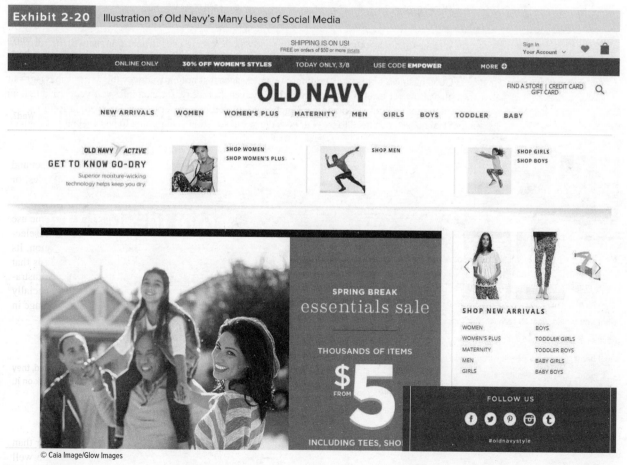

© Caia Image/Glow Images

Source: oldnavy.com.

Text Messaging

Text messaging, also called short message service (SMS), is, as its name suggests, used for sending short messages, generally from a mobile device. Because the purpose of a text message is to convey a quick message, text messages are much shorter than messages conveyed by more traditional forms. Also, mobile service providers may limit the number of characters in a text message.

The need for brevity has led to the use of many abbreviations. In fact, a dictionary of over 1,400 text-messaging abbreviations has been compiled at Webopedia, an online computer technology encyclopedia (www.webopedia.com/quick_ref/textmessageabbreviations.asp). Some examples include the following:

b4 (before)	NP (no problem)
gr8 (great)	FBM (fine by me)
CU (see you)	TC (take care)
u (you)	HRY (how are you)
BTW (by the way)	TYT (take your time)

In addition to abbreviations, writers use typed symbols to convey emotions (emoticons), which can also be found at Webopedia:

:-) standard smiley	:-! foot in mouth
;) winking smile	:-(sad or frown
:-0 yell	(((H))) hugs

Whether and when these abbreviations and emoticons are used depends on the writer's relationship with the audience.

Good business writers will compose text messages that not only convey the writer's message but also allow for brief responses from the receiver. Let's say, for example, you've learned that an important visiting customer is a vegetarian and you have reservations for lunch at Ruth's Chris Steakhouse. You need to let your boss know this location is not going to work—before the lunch

From the Tech Desk

Using Good Email Etiquette Helps Writers Achieve Their Goals

Using proper email etiquette is as easy as applying a bit of empathy to your messages: Send only what you would want to receive. The following additional etiquette questions will help you consider more specific issues when using email.

• Is your message really needed by the recipient(s)?

• Is your message for routine rather than sensitive messages?

• Are you sure your message is not spam?

• Have you carefully checked that your message is going where you want it to go?

• Has your wording avoided defamatory or libelous language?

• Have you complied with copyright laws and cited sources accurately?

• Have you avoided humor and sarcasm that your reader may not understand as intended?

• Have you proofread your message carefully?

• Is this a message you would not mind having distributed widely?

• Does your signature avoid offensive quotes or illustrations, especially those that are religious, political, or sexual?

• Is your recipient willing or able to accept attached files?

• Are attached files a size that your recipient's system can handle?

• Are the files you are attaching virus free?

meeting. However, the boss is leading an important meeting in which a phone call would be disruptive and inappropriate, so you decide to send a text message.

Marina Smith is a vegetarian. Where should we take her for lunch today?

Although your message does convey the major fact and is only 77 characters counting spaces, it forces the recipient to enter a long response—the name of another place. It might also result in more message exchanges about availability and time.

A better version might be this:

Marina Smith is a vegetarian. Shall we go to 1) Fish House, 2) Souplantation, 3) Mandarin House? All are available at noon.

This version conveys the major fact in 130 characters and allows the recipient to respond simply with 1, 2, or 3. As the writer, you took the initiative to anticipate your reader's needs, identify appropriate alternatives, and then gather information—steps that are as important with text messaging as they are with other messages. If your text messages are clear, complete, and concise and have a professional and pleasant tone, you will find them a valuable tool for business use.

Instant Messaging

Instant messaging, commonly referred to as IM-ing or online chatting, is much like telephone conversation in that parties communicate in real time (instantly). It differs primarily in that it is text-based (typed) rather than voice-based communication, though voice-based instant messaging is possible. Many writers will use the same abbreviations and emoticons when instant messaging as they would in text messaging. Here again, the use of these devices depends on your audience and purpose. Exhibit 2-21 shows the Skype for Business instant messaging tool.

Because **instant messages** are similar to phone conversations, you should write them much as you would talk in conversation with another person. Whether the person is a friend or your business associate, your language should reflect this relationship. In business situations you should consciously direct the flow toward your objective and keep your language and content professional.

Social Media

You are probably familiar with such **social media** sites as Facebook, Twitter, Pinterest, Instagram, or LinkedIn. Perhaps you have a blog where you keep an online diary or journal that you share publicly. Although you may use these sites to connect with friends, family, or classmates, many business writers also use them to connect with clients, customers, colleagues, and supervisors, as they answer questions, promote products, network with other professionals, or interact briefly with co-workers. Business professionals, then, are using social networking sites for purposes that are likely very different from your purpose in using them (see the corporate blog in Exhibit 2-22).

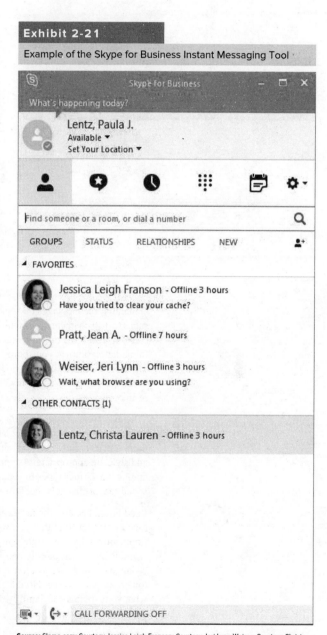

Exhibit 2-21

Example of the Skype for Business Instant Messaging Tool

Source: Skype.com; Courtesy Jessica Leigh Franson; Courtesy Jeri Lynn Weiser; Courtesy Christa Lauren Lentz.

Exhibit 2-22   Illustration of a Corporate Blog

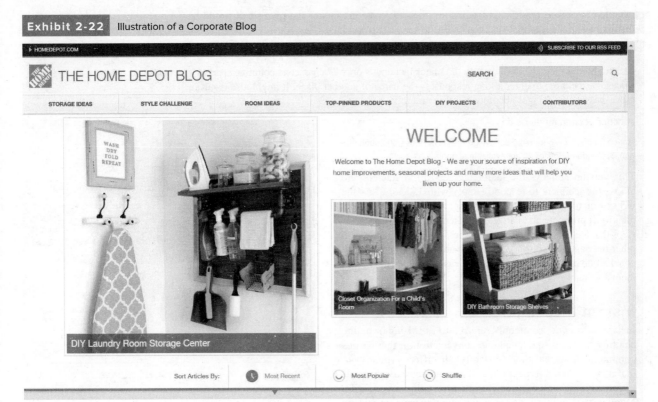

Source: homedepot.com.

Generally, the messages on social networking sites are brief; Twitter, for example, restricts messages to 140 characters. As with text messaging, messages must not only be brief but concise and clear. If you have only so much space for your message, you need to make sure your reader immediately knows your point and has enough detail to act on your message. Therefore, messages on social media sites should begin with your main point (what you need your reader to do, think, feel, or believe as a result of reading your message) and then follow with details in order of importance.

Whatever form of social media you use, you want to be sure you analyze your audience, purpose, and context before you write. You wouldn't, of course, want to spend much time posting to Instagram if your audiences primarily use Twitter and Pinterest. And you want to be sure your tone and style are appropriate. As you can see in Exhibit 2-23, the audience demographics vary widely among the various types of social media channels. Knowing your audiences will help you use the social media channels that best reach them.

In addition, because the messages on these sites are public, you never want to use language or a tone or writing style that you would be embarrassed to have your boss see, that may have legal implications, or that might get you fired. In fact, if you currently have a page on a social networking site where family and friends are your audience, you will want to remove any pictures or language that you wouldn't want a prospective employer, current employer, co-worker, customer, or client to see. No matter how private you believe your page to be, you can never know what your friends and family are sharing with other people.

In fact, cleaning up your social media accounts may actually help you during the job search. In one study, most employers said they check social media sites during the hiring process. While it was true that employers said they would not consider a candidate whose social media sites

showed inappropriate photos, drug or alcohol use, poor communication skills, negative comments about an employer, or discriminatory language, they also said they looked favorably on candidates whose sites demonstrated evidence of job qualifications, creativity, professionalism, good communication skills, and the potential to fit into the company's corporate culture.[6]

Regardless of the type of business messages you send, remember that on the job, companies often monitor employees' computer activity. They can detect excessive use, inappropriate or unethical behavior, disclosure of proprietary information, use of sexually explicit language, and attachments with viruses. Companies' monitoring systems also have features that protect the company from legal liabilities. As a business professional, you must know your company's computer use policy and avoid writing anything that would reflect poorly on you or your company or put you or your company at risk.

A Look to the Future

Given the recent explosion of communication-related technologies, you can anticipate further rapid advancements in how businesses use technology to support or enhance communication.

For example, innovative social media sites such as Pinterest, Snapchat, and Instagram are continually being developed as businesses seek new and creative communication channels to help them achieve their business goals. And mobile applications such as those that let people

You Make the Call
Should companies allow employees to use social media at work for personal reasons?

LO2-10 Describe how technology will continue to impact communication in the future.

Communication Matters

Do U Txt?

Odds are you've sent text messages using standard texting abbreviations. If you do this frequently, do you wonder whether your common use of text messaging has compromised your understanding of standard English conventions and usage? A study in *New Media and Society* indicates that tweens' use of texting language may affect their use of standard English. Though this is only one study, its implications are interesting in that it underscores the importance of not becoming so comfortable with one style of writing or one technology that we neglect to tailor our messages to our audiences and communication goals.

Texting is used in business every day—and rightly so given its speed and efficiency. Standard English usage and spelling, though, are still expected. If you don't know your audience or context well enough to know whether you can use a smiley face or text-message speak, you'll want to use a more standard writing style. Otherwise, the response you get might be "C U L8r."

Source: Drew P. Cingel and Shyam S. Sundar, "Texting, Tech-speak, and Tweens: The Relationship between Text Messaging and English Grammar Skills," *New Media & Society* 14 (2012): 1304–1320.

photograph checks and then use the photograph to deposit the funds into their bank accounts are changing how people access and use companies' products and services.

In addition, **cloud computing** continues to change the way business communicators access and store their software and their work. For instance, because software and information are stored on websites—in the **cloud**—rather than on the computer, nearly everyone has access to the software programs (e.g., Microsoft Word) used most frequently to communicate in business. Because cloud applications have no system requirements and require no software on the user's computer, a current challenge for businesspeople is remembering to back up data just as they would if they were working locally from their own computers.

Chapter 12 discusses more thoroughly how technology has increasingly facilitated collaborative writing in the workplace through means such as Dropbox and Google Drive/Google Docs.

Smaller, smarter technology lets people be mobile in their work.
© Mike Kemp/Blend Images LLC

Whatever technologies develop, human minds will still need to control communication using good judgment and skill. As Chapter 1 points out, the need for effective problem solving through skillful use of technology is dramatically increasing. Businesspeople who use technologies in ways that promote clear, professional communication will be assets to their companies and increase their odds of success in their careers.

Power Charge Your Professionalism: Use the Right Word (Part II)

Select the word that completes each sentence below. The choices represent words that are sometimes confused, but as a savvy businessperson, you will want to know how to use them to project your best professional image. You'll find these words listed in Reference Chapter A, but to find the definitions, you will want to use a dictionary.

1. Ling is conducting the training sessions to (ensure/insure) all employees know how to use the new intranet portal.
2. Once you (except/accept) the terms of the license agreement, you can download your new software.
3. Even though the instructions did not (implicitly/explicitly) provide a deadline, everyone assumed the forms were due at the end of the month.
4. Did Rick's email (imply/infer) that we would all be getting a raise this year?
5. Last Thursday Kerstin (lead/led) the hospital's board of directors on a tour of the remodeled emergency room.
6. Business letters are usually sent on company letterhead, but personal letters are usually sent on (plane/plain) paper.
7. Paying extra on a loan (principal/principle) each month can help you pay off the loan more quickly.
8. Even though we send most of our messages electronically, we still use (stationary/stationery) for our printed messages.

Choosing the right word is important because . . .

- Using the right word is essential if you want your sentences to be clear.
- Using the right word lets you portray yourself as an educated, competent businessperson.

Key Terms

Critical-Thinking Questions

1. Explain why writing can be more difficult than other forms of communication. LO1

2. Describe ways in which the writing process might be recursive. LO2

3. Explain how technology can help the writer with both creative and tedious writing tasks. LO2–LO5

4. Identify specific software tools that assist with constructing written messages. Explain what each does. LO3

5. Word processing programs are the writer's primary tool. Identify five basic features and two advanced features useful to business writers. LO3–LO5

6. Discuss the advantages and disadvantages of spelling checkers and grammar and style checkers. LO5

7. Brainstorm some practices or policies that businesses might develop for using the information rights management (IRM) tool effectively. LO5

8. How have text messaging or other technologies affected your writing? LO2, LO9

9. How will technology continue to affect business writing? LO10

Skills-Building Exercises

1. Investigate your school and/or local libraries to determine what current (or future) computer sources will help you find information about businesses. Report your findings to the class.

2. Compile an annotated list of at least 10 websites with good links to sources of business information (e.g., labor statistics, stock market trends). Three of these links should be for local business information.

3. Select a multimedia technology, and as your instructor directs, write a memo discussing considerations for accommodating audiences with special needs (e.g., those with visual, hearing, or mobility impairments).

4. Choose a feature from your word processor (such as index, table of contents, templates, or citation manager) that you have not used much. Learn how to use it and create an example of its use in a business document. Write a brief description of its application and then teach your classmates to use the feature.

5. From a current business magazine, find an article that relates to communication in business. As your instructor directs, write a one-paragraph reaction to it and post it to a blog, post it to the "Comments" section of an online article, or submit your reaction in memo format.

6. Find a recent news article about a company's unsuccessful use of social media. As your instructor directs, write a memo or email in which you describe the situation, analyze what led to the failure of the message, and offer suggestions for what the company should have done differently.

Designing Documents
with Visual Appeal

Chapter Three

The appearance of a letter, memo, email, report, or any other business document plays a significant role in communicating a message. Attractively presented messages reflect favorably on you and your company. They give an impression of competence and care, and they build your credibility. The principles covered in Chapter 3 will help you make your documents visually appealing. This chapter on document design, along with Chapter 4 on visual communication, helps you see the importance of visual rhetoric in the problem-solving approach to business communication. **Visual rhetoric** refers to the way the visual features of a message communicate. These features include not only photos, drawings, charts, graphs, and tables but also fonts, colors, the placement of text on a page, and even paragraph length and the use of headings. Once you have studied this chapter, you can use what you know as you work through Chapter 4, which shows you how to create visuals and integrate them into your business documents.

Learning Objectives

LO3-1   Describe the four principles of document design: contrast, repetition, alignment, and proximity.

LO3-2   Lay out documents effectively to enhance readability and visual appeal.

LO3-3   Choose fonts that enhance readability and visual appeal.

LO3-4   Understand the impact of color on business documents.

LO3-5   Design documents for print and online reading.

LO3-6   Format business letters according to commonly accepted practices.

LO3-7   Format memorandums (memos) according to commonly accepted practices.

LO3-8   Format letter and memorandum (memo) reports.

LO3-9   Format formal business reports.

LO3-10   Design a brochure.

Problem-Solving Challenge

Promoting a Professional Look

Assume that you are a mid-level manager at Masterson Insurance Agency, an agency with several offices in the Midwest region of the United States. At a recent meeting of managers and agents, Reid Knuth, one of your best agents, raised a question about the correspondence between the company and its clients and among employees within the agency.

Reid noted that whenever he receives interoffice messages from other branches, the messages are not consistently formatted. In fact, he said that if he were not familiar with the employees' names, he might think the messages had been sent from another company. Plus, he says,

the writing itself does not look good—long paragraphs, inconsistent formatting, multiple fonts—which does not entice employees or customers to look at the messages they receive. He also noted that customer-facing messages such as Masterson's webpage, Facebook page, and letterhead/letters do not have a consistent look.

You agree. You just read an article on the importance of visual communication to a company's brand and have noticed, too, that your company's documents do not have a consistent or appealing look. Furthermore, you feel your company's internal documentation should reflect the company's standards for professionalism.

Because you and Reid spoke up, you are assigned the job of establishing standards for internal and external correspondence and a uniform look for Masterson's social media platforms and website. While you do not have to do the design work yourself, you do have to communicate with a graphic designer regarding your company's desired look and brand. Plus, you and Reid have been assigned to lead a company-wide webinar with employees about writing professional-looking documents, so you need to know what design features make a document. The information in this chapter will help you make good decisions as you work through these tasks.

Basic Principles of Document Design

LO3-1 Describe the four principles of document design: contrast, repetition, alignment, and proximity.

You do not have to be a graphic designer to create attractive business documents. All you need is an understanding of a few basic principles that will guide the decisions you make when you write or present information to an audience. Of course, your audience, communication goals, and business goals will drive your choices, but these principles will help you make informed decisions about presenting your documents in a way that best meets your audience's needs.

Graphic designers frequently communicate about design using four principles: contrast, repetition, alignment, and proximity. These principles also apply to the design and presentation of business documents.

Exhibit 3-1 Illustration of Good Contrast in a PowerPoint Slide

Online and In-Store Sales: 2017

Contrast

Contrast means that you use conventions of typography, layout, color, or other visual elements to ensure that your most important content is readily accessible to the reader. Contrast could mean that you use dark text on a light background in a PowerPoint presentation so that the text stands out to the reader. Contrast could also mean that you use bold, italics, or color to make your main points stand out, or it could mean that you use a different font or capital letters to make headings more obvious in a document such as a long report.

Keep in mind that the secret to effective formatting is simplicity. For example, if you bold or italicize too many items, your page becomes visually messy, and nothing stands out to the reader. Exhibit 3-1 illustrates a good contrast. Notice how the dark bars contrast with the light background and how the red line, blue bars, and green bars are distinct from one another.

Repetition

Repetition includes the repeated use of elements such as color, placement, fonts, or visuals to help the reader easily recognize where he or she is in a document. For example, if you consistently use the same formatting for the major headings of a report and a consistent but different formatting for subheadings, your reader will easily recognize where major and minor sections of your document begin and end. Or you may create repetition, for instance, by using one icon to indicate a warning and another to indicate a tip or shortcut. Exhibit 3-2 illustrates the use of repetition in font, layout, and color to create a clear, readable document. You can see that the article titles look the same, that each article is accompanied by a photograph to the right of the article title, and that each article title is followed by a brief statement and "read more." The repetition of these elements provides consistency and uniformity that let you immediately navigate the page.

Alignment

Alignment refers to the positioning or placement of text and other elements on a page so that every element looks intentionally placed. You do not want page elements to look as though you randomly placed them on the page.

You are most likely familiar with text alignment, which is also called text justification (Exhibit 3-3). Left-, right-, or center-justified text is appropriate for headings. Generally, left-justified text and full-justified text are appropriate for paragraphs. When using full-justified text, you will want to keep in mind that this alignment requires extra spaces within lines of text so that the text aligns at the left and right margins. The result is that these extra spaces may be distracting. For this reason, many writers prefer left-justified text for paragraphs. Full-justified text, though, may create a more formal or traditional look for a report or book.

Aligning nontext elements to the left, right, or center is also a consideration for business writers. These visual elements should be aligned so that it is obvious they are connected to the text that surrounds them.

Proximity

Proximity is the idea that similar elements appear together, while text or other visual elements that are not similar are separated from each other by space or other means. Exhibit 3-4 shows the effect that the proximity principle can have on making a document more readable.

Exhibit 3-2 Illustration of Repetition in a Business Document

Source: The Washington Post. Photos (top to bottom) © joeppoulssen/123RF; © Lenny Ignelzi/AP Images; CXC/MIT/S. Rappaport et al./NASA/STScI; © Shutterstock/Minerva Studio RF; © mike davies/Alamy RF; © Getty Images/iStockphoto

Exhibit 3-3 Illustration of Types of Text Alignment

Savvy businesspeople tailor their communication to the audience's needs. Whether writing or speaking, a message's success rests on its ability to reach the reader.

However, businesspeople should keep in mind that written and oral messages should reflect positively on a person's professional image. Messages should also reflect a company's professional image.

Left Justification

Savvy businesspeople tailor their communication to the audience's needs. Whether writing or speaking, a message 's success rests on its ability to reach the reader.

However, businesspeople should keep in mind that written and oral messages should reflect positively on a person's professional image. Messages should also reflect a company's professional image.

Full Justification

Savvy businesspeople tailor their communication to the audience's needs. Whether writing or speaking, a message's success rests on its ability to reach the reader.

However, businesspeople should keep in mind that written and oral messages should reflect positively on a person's professional image. Messages should also reflect a company's professional image.

Centered Justification

Savvy businesspeople tailor their communication to the audience's needs. Whether writing or speaking, a message's success rests on its ability to reach the reader.

However, businesspeople should keep in mind that written and oral messages should reflect positively on a person's professional image. Messages should also reflect a company's professional image.

Right Justification

Source: Microsoft Word.

Exhibit 3-4 Illustration of the Proximity Principle

Our advisory board meeting is in six months, so we need to meet to discuss the following details:

- Sending invitations
- Sending a follow-up message and thank you
- Planning for refreshments
- Moderating the discussion
- Reserving projectors and technology
- Creating the meeting agenda
- Assigning staff roles for the meeting
- Reserving a meeting room
- Incorporating guests and student speakers
- Distributing the minutes

Before applying the principle of proximity

Our advisory board meeting is in six months, so we need to meet to discuss the following details:

Before the Meeting

- Sending invitations
- Planning for refreshments
- Reserving a meeting room
- Reserving projectors and technology
- Creating the meeting agenda

During the Meeting

- Assigning staff roles for the meeting
- Moderating the discussion
- Incorporating guests and student speakers

After the Meeting

- Sending a follow-up message and thank you
- Distributing the minutes

After applying the principle of proximity

Taken together the principles of contrast, repetition, alignment, and proximity can help you create more professional and more effective documents or presentations. The following sections of this chapter will show you how to achieve these principles by making informed choices regarding your text and visual elements.

Layout

LO3-2 Lay out documents effectively to enhance readability and visual appeal.

One way to achieve contrast, repetition, alignment, or proximity in a document is through a good layout of the text. A good layout will help your audience easily move through your document to find your main points and understand your message.

Gutenberg Diagram and Z-Pattern

Two common ways of laying out text on a page require you to follow the **Gutenberg diagram** or **Z-pattern**. These patterns are similar in that they both account for how people read and process text. The Gutenberg diagram, however, uses a grid to explain this process and assumes that the eye automatically moves diagonally from the document's start to its finish. The Z-pattern explains the process using the letter Z to show how a reader's eye moves across the page, eventually stopping at the end of a document.

Essentially, the most visually critical areas of your documents are the beginning and ending points. Readers will start at the top left, move across or through the page, and then end in the bottom right corner. It's not that readers ignore information in the middle of a document; they simply attend to the beginning and ending more unless you've given some type of emphasis to the information in the middle.

Exhibits 3-5 and 3-6 illustrate how both the Gutenberg diagram and Z-pattern can be applied to a routine message. In Chapter 8, you will learn more about routine messages, but in general, a routine message begins with the main point, provides relevant details, and ends with any

Exhibit 3-5 Illustration of the Gutenberg Diagram Applied to a Business Message

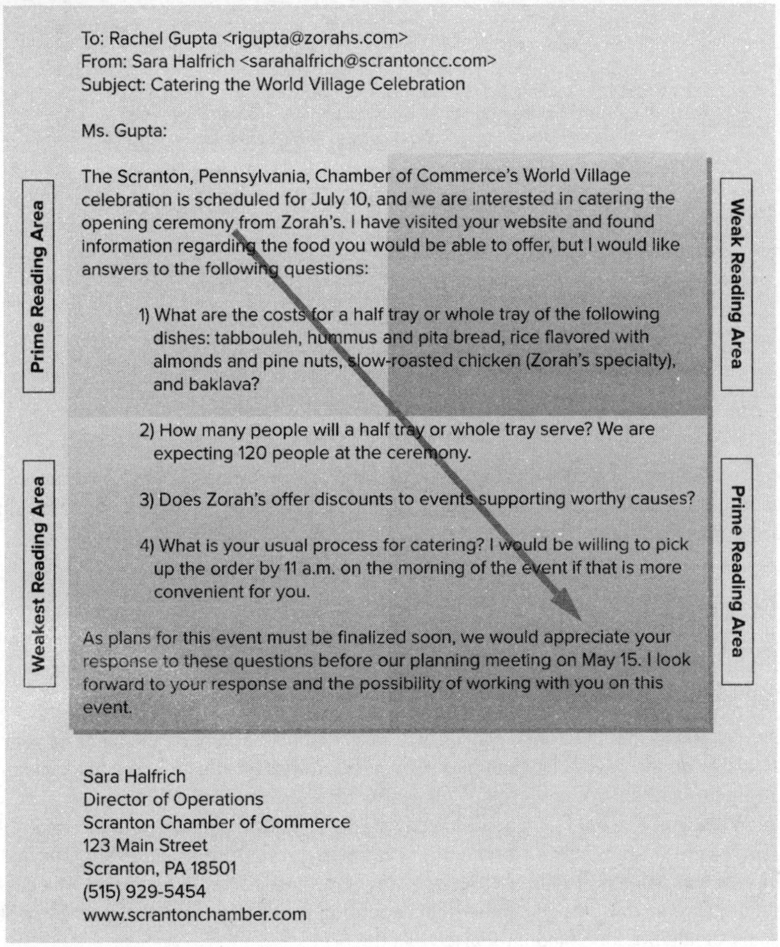

To: Rachel Gupta <rigupta@zorahs.com>
From: Sara Halfrich <sarahalfrich@scrantoncc.com>
Subject: Catering the World Village Celebration

Ms. Gupta:

Prime Reading Area / **Weak Reading Area**

The Scranton, Pennsylvania, Chamber of Commerce's World Village celebration is scheduled for July 10, and we are interested in catering the opening ceremony from Zorah's. I have visited your website and found information regarding the food you would be able to offer, but I would like answers to the following questions:

1) What are the costs for a half tray or whole tray of the following dishes: tabbouleh, hummus and pita bread, rice flavored with almonds and pine nuts, slow-roasted chicken (Zorah's specialty), and baklava?

2) How many people will a half tray or whole tray serve? We are expecting 120 people at the ceremony.

3) Does Zorah's offer discounts to events supporting worthy causes?

4) What is your usual process for catering? I would be willing to pick up the order by 11 a.m. on the morning of the event if that is more convenient for you.

Weakest Reading Area / **Prime Reading Area**

As plans for this event must be finalized soon, we would appreciate your response to these questions before our planning meeting on May 15. I look forward to your response and the possibility of working with you on this event.

Sara Halfrich
Director of Operations
Scranton Chamber of Commerce
123 Main Street
Scranton, PA 18501
(515) 929-5454
www.scrantonchamber.com

To: Rachel Gupta <rigupta@zorahs.com>
From: Sara Halfrich <sarahalfrich@scrantoncc.com>
Subject: Catering the World Village Celebration

Ms. Gupta:

The Scranton, Pennsylvania, Chamber of Commerce's World Village celebration is scheduled for July 10, and we are interested in catering the opening ceremony from Zorah's. I have visited your website and found information regarding the food you would be able to offer, but I would like answers to the following questions:

1) What are the costs for a half tray or whole tray of the following dishes: tabbouleh, hummus and pita bread, rice flavored with almonds and pine nuts, slow-roasted chicken (Zorah's specialty), and baklava?

2) How many people will a half tray or whole tray serve? We are expecting 120 people at the ceremony.

3) Does Zorah's offer discounts to events supporting worthy causes?

4) What is your usual process for catering? I would be willing to pick up the order by 11 a.m. on the morning of the event if that is more convenient for you.

As plans for this event must be finalized soon, we would appreciate your response to these questions before our planning meeting on May 15. I look forward to your response and the possibility of working with you on this event.

Sara Halfrich
Director of Operations
Scranton Chamber of Commerce
123 Main Street
Scranton, PA 18501
(570) 348-5454
www.scrantonchamber.com

deadlines or actions the reader must know. You can see in Exhibits 3-5 and 3-6 that laying out text according to the Gutenberg diagram or Z-pattern helps the reader see two critical pieces of information: the request for help and the deadline for response.

Grids

Sometimes you will work with documents that require both text and visuals. When creating these documents, using a grid can be helpful in making sure that your visuals and text comply with the design principles of contrast, repetition, alignment, and proximity.

Grids are the nonprinted horizontal and vertical lines that help you place elements of your document precisely on the page. The examples shown in Exhibit 3-7 illustrate the placement of text on two-, three-, and six-column grids. You can readily see how important it is to plan for this element. When you place information on a page, you'll want to consider whether multiple columns (such as in a newsletter or brochure) will better present information to your audience. Programs such as Microsoft Publisher let you view gridlines as you work so that you can easily map and align your text. Just remember that according to the principle of alignment, your text and visuals should not look randomly placed on the page.

From the Tech Desk

Using Microsoft Word 2016's Insert, Position, and Text Wrap Features to Place Visuals on a Page

The principle of alignment requires that visuals do not look randomly placed on a page. Fortunately, Microsoft Word can help you position your visuals for the best effect:

1. From the Insert ribbon, select Pictures.
2. Select the picture you want, and click Insert to put the visual in your document.
3. Click the visual.
4. Click the tab for the Format ribbon.
5. Click the Position dropdown arrow to select where you want your visual to appear on the page.
6. Click either the Wrap Text icon next to your picture or select Wrap Text from the Format ribbon to locate your visual relative to the text around it.

Source: Microsoft Word 2016; © Fuse/Getty Images.

Exhibit 3-7 Layouts Using Different Grids

Two-column grid

Three-column grid

Six-column grid

Spacing

To make your document look its best, you must consider both external and internal spacing. **External spacing** is the white space on a page. Just as the amount of text denotes importance in writing, so, too, does white space. Surrounding text or a graphic with white spaces sets it apart, emphasizing it to the reader. Used effectively, white space also has been shown to increase the readability of your documents. Thus, white space should be a careful part of the design of your document.

Internal spacing refers to both vertical and horizontal spacing. The spacing between letters on a line is called **kerning**. With word processing programs, you can adjust how close the letters are to each other. You can also adjust how close the lines are to one another vertically, which is called **leading**. Currently, many still refer to spacing in business documents as single or double spacing. However, this is a carryover from the typewriter era when a vertical line space was always ⅙ inch or when six lines equaled an inch. Today's software allows you to control this aspect of your document much more exactly. The best spacing for your document depends on the typeface.

Margins

Another aspect of layout is the setting of your margins. Ideally, you want your document to look like a framed picture. One-inch margins are standard, though you can always adjust your margins to any width that creates the look you want.

From the Tech Desk

Fine-Tuning the Line Spacing in Microsoft Word 2016

You can adjust the line spacing (leading) in your documents by accessing Microsoft Word's paragraph tools:

1. Click the Home ribbon.
2. From the Paragraph tools, click the arrow to open the Paragraph dialog box.
3. Under Spacing, select the amount of space you want before or after a paragraph of text and deselect the check box for "Don't add space. . . ."
4. Under Line Spacing, select the type of space you want between lines of text. If you select At Least, Exactly, or Multiple, use the At: box to indicate how much space you want between lines.

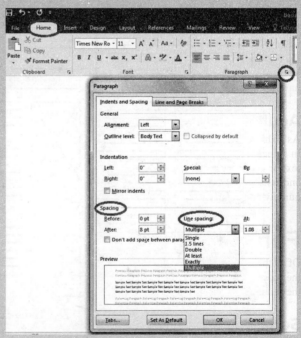

Source: Microsoft Word 2016.

Kerning in Microsoft Word 2016

Occasionally, when you type text—especially in headings—you'll notice that some letters in a word appear closer to each other than other letters in the word. When this happens, your reader may initially misread your text. For example, an "o" followed by an "l" may look like a "d." To make sure your text is clear, you can use Microsoft Word's kerning feature to create space between letters:

1. Select the letters in your document you want to kern.
2. Click the Home ribbon.
3. From the Font tools, click the arrow to open the Font dialog box.
4. Click either Spacing > Normal, Expanded, or Condensed *or* Kerning for fonts.
5. Use the By: dialog box to enter the amount of spacing you want between letters.
6. Check the Preview box to see what the spacing will look like in your document.

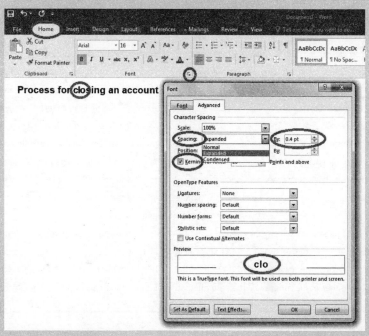

Source: Microsoft Word 2016.

You can also balance the white space above and below the text on a page by centering the document vertically. In Microsoft Word 2016, you can do this by going to the Layout ribbon, clicking the Page Setup dialog box launcher, selecting the Layout tab, and selecting "center" from the Vertical Alignment options. Although all margins will not be exactly equal, the page will still have horizontal and vertical balance.

Additional Layout Considerations

As Exhibits 3-5 and 3-6 illustrate, using a list is a good way to achieve contrast or proximity in a document. In addition, many designers will use boxes or rules (lines) to call attention to text or visual elements in a document. As we discuss later in this chapter, using boxes, rules, and lists in documents such as a brochure ensures that your reader sees your main points quickly and clearly.

Fonts

Of all the issues a writer considers when writing an effective business message, the font is among the most important. Choosing the right font can make your documents look as professional as they sound.

LO3-3 Choose fonts that enhance readability and visual appeal.

Serif and Sans Serif Fonts

Generally, business writers prefer **serif fonts** (e.g., Times New Roman, Cambria) or **sans serif fonts** (e.g., Arial, Calibri). Script fonts such as Monotype Corsiva are used less

Communication Matters

One Space or Two after a Period?

Few issues have created more debate recently than the spacing after the period. Should a period be followed by one space or two? In truth, it's not an issue of whether one or two spaces is right or wrong but an issue of whether the second space is necessary.

When businesspeople had only the typewriter to write their documents, they had few fonts available and these fonts, such as Courier, were monospaced fonts. Each letter in a monospaced font occupies the same amount of space on the page. For example, the wide "w" and the narrow "I" or the small period take the same amount of space, even though the "w" is wider than either of the other two. The result is that

the white space within and between words and sentences is fairly uniform. The second space was added as a visual element to make the white space between sentences clearer and, as a result, improve readability.

Today, businesspeople use computers with proportional fonts, which means that each letter takes up exactly as much room as it requires. The result with proportional fonts is that white space within and between words is sufficient for clarity and readability.

Because the second space after a period is no longer needed for clarity and readability, some business writers believe its use is unnecessary. Furthermore, typesetters and graphic designers

have always had monospaced fonts and have traditionally used only one space after the period. Thus, writers feel as though using only one space creates the look of a more professionally designed document.

Others feel the use of the second space is a defining element of business genres that provides a traditional and professional look.

When you start a job, you will want to know your company's preferences. If you have to change your practice, just know that Microsoft Word's Auto Correct features or Find and Replace features (see Chapter 2) can help you easily change the spacing after the period.

---

frequently. As Exhibit 3-8 shows, letters in serif fonts such as Times New Roman have "tails" or "feet" (serifs). Letters in sans serif fonts such as Arial do not. The presence or absence of serifs is an important design consideration for business writers. Serifs connect letters, which makes the space between words more distinguishable and the text therefore more readable—at least in printed documents. As we discuss later in this chapter, in electronic documents, the serifs may actually hinder readability depending on the font size and monitor resolution. Sans serif fonts, however, allow for more white space, which makes letters and words clearer in electronic documents.

Number of Fonts per Document

Another consideration when choosing fonts for your documents is the number of fonts to use. Generally, limit yourself to no more than two fonts. It's fine to use only one font, either serif or sans serif. However, if you use more than two, you will have a document that looks cluttered and visually confusing. Because serifs help connect letters and thus emphasize white space between words, some writers will use a sans serif font for headings and a serif font for body (paragraph) text.

If you decide to use two fonts in a document, make sure that one is a sans serif font and one is a serif font. Choosing one of each font category means that the fonts will complement each other. If you choose two serif fonts or two sans serif fonts, the fonts will compete with each other.

Font Sizes

Yet another consideration in choosing a font is the font size for headings and body text. The font size you choose depends on the font. The point size of a font is

Serif Font   Sans Serif Font

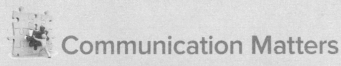

Communication Matters

What Is Your Font Really Communicating?

With so many font choices, you can easily become overwhelmed when selecting a font for your document. Logos are just one example of the importance of taking time to make the right choice.

Timothy J. Pritchard, senior SEO and digital marketing and e-commerce analyst for Seller-Deck, says that the font you use in a logo is likely to influence your audience's first impression of your company. In fact, if you look at his renderings of several logos for Expresso Delights, you can see that they all create a different impression of the same business.

Pritchard says fonts such as Comic Sans are likely never appropriate, but many other fonts may be. The font you choose is determined by the desired look. Do you want to be seen as traditional? Contemporary? Serious? Humorous? Family friendly? Elegant? Rustic? Upscale?

Timothy J. Pritchard, "What Your Font Choices Say about Your Business," *LinkedIn,* August 17, 2015, accessed March 25, 2016, https://www.linkedin.com. Copyright © 2015 by Timothy J. Pritchard. All rights reserved. Used with permission.

The possibilities are many, but your choice must be targeted and precise if you are to achieve your business goals. While Pritchard discusses logos, it is easy to see how the font you choose for any document could impact a reader's perception of you and your company.

Source: Timothy J. Pritchard, "What Your Font Choices Say about Your Business," *LinkedIn,* August 17, 2015, accessed March 25, 2016, https://www.iinkedin.com.

determined by **x-height**—the size of the letter "x" in that font. This is why a sans serif font such as Arial appears bigger at 10 points than a serif font such as Times New Roman. To start, you can choose a font at 9 to 12 points for the body of your document. Then you can choose a font that is 2 points larger than your body text. Whatever size you choose, be sure the text is readable and looks professional. Fonts that are too small are hard to read. Fonts that are too big look amateurish and visually shout at the reader.

Font Choices

The font or fonts you choose will depend on what kind of document you're writing and to whom. Which would be more appropriate in a print ad for party supplies? In an annual report to investors? In an invitation to a formal event? Fonts such as Arial and Times New Roman are traditional fonts used in business documents. Fonts such as Futura, Cambria, or Calibri may communicate a more contemporary look. Choose your font carefully to match your audience and context.

You Make the Call

What is your favorite font? Would you use it in a business document? Why?

Color

Color is an important tool, especially for achieving contrast and repetition in business documents. Many times the colors you choose will be determined by colors found in your company's logo or by specifications in your company's style guide. Many times, however, you will have to select the colors you use. In these cases, it is important for you to know a little bit about color theory so that the colors you choose help you present a professional, readable, and visually appealing business document.

LO3-4 Understand the impact of color on business documents.

Color Theory

Before combining colors, you should know some basic terminology. **Primary colors** (red, blue, and yellow) are the colors from which all other colors originate. **Secondary colors** are created when you combine two primary colors (e.g., mixing blue and yellow creates green). **Tertiary colors** are created when you mix a primary color with a secondary color. From these three types of colors, you can create a variety of shades or tones of any color.

One of the easiest ways to see the variety of color possibilities is to look at the color wheel (Exhibit 3-9). Colors that are next to each other on the wheel are called **analogous colors**; those across the wheel from each other are called **complementary colors**. If you struggle to choose colors for your document, you can always start by choosing analogous or complementary colors, as these colors generally form good color combinations. Of course, Microsoft Word, Publisher, and Excel all provide a color palette that you can use, and many Web resources such as Session College's Color Wheel Color Calculator (https://www.sessions.edu/color-calculator/.) can help you choose a palette as well.

Color and Meaning

Although color theory and the color wheel can help you pick a color palette, you should be aware that color can have emotional, social, or cultural meanings as well. For example, in some cultures, the color black can signify death, while in others the color white has this same meaning. And even within cultures, the same color can have different meanings. For example, in the United States, the color green can signify wealth, money, nature, or environmentally safe practices; yet we often describe someone who is ill as "looking a little green."

You Make the Call

What colors do you react positively to? Negatively? Why?

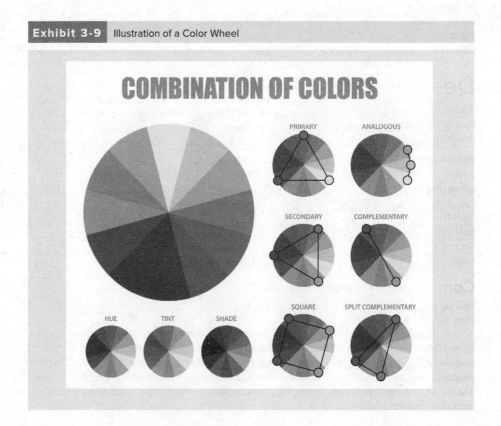

Exhibit 3-9   Illustration of a Color Wheel

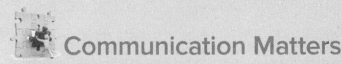

Communication Matters

What Does the Color of Your Logo Say about Your Business?

Marketo notes that many brands are recognized primarily by the colors they use (e.g., the McDonald's golden arches). But have you ever thought about how color affects purchasing choices? According to Marketo,

- A product's color affects 60 to 80% of a customer's purchasing decisions.
- Customers are aware when a logo color does not connect with a company brand.
- Color is the first thing audiences will notice about a logo.

- A study of the world's top 100 brands revealed that the most popular choice for a logo color is blue (33%), which communicates trustworthiness, dependability, security, and responsibility. The least popular color is yellow (13%), which communicates positivity, light, warmth, motivation, and creativity.
- Nearly all companies (95%) use only one color in their logos.

Marketo notes (as we do earlier in this chapter) that the use of color in a logo is industry

dependent. That is, a color such as yellow may be the least popular choice for a logo overall, but it is generally a good choice for company logos in the energy, household, or food industries.

Choosing colors is one of the most important decisions you will make whether you are creating a logo or writing a report. Be sure your color choice is consistent with your brand and company image.

Source: Marketo, "True Colors: What Your Brand Colors Say About Your Business [Infographic]," accessed March 25, 2016, https://www.marketo.com/infographics/true-colors-what-your-brand-colors-say-about-your-business-infographic/.

Keep in mind that nearly 8% of men and 0.5% of women are color blind,[1] meaning that to varying degrees, they cannot see colors. If you are using color to indicate meaning, for example in a chart or graph, you will want to take special care to ensure you use color the readers can see or select alternative formatting such as different degrees of shading to create contrast.

Design Considerations for Online Text

As we have discussed, business professionals use a variety of print and electronic genres for business writing. The basic principles of business writing apply to both print and electronic text; that is, your text must be reader centered, accessible, complete, concise, and accurate.

LO3-5 Design documents for print and online reading.

But no matter how great your blog or website looks, if your message is unclear or incomplete, your blog or website serves no purpose. Business writers also have to realize that many audiences may be viewing a company's website on a mobile device with a small viewing area. In fact, Janice Redish, an expert on writing for the Web, says, "Understanding your site visitors and their needs is critical to deciding what to write, how much to write, the vocabulary to use, and how to organize the content on your website."[2] While this advice also applies when writing print documents, writing for online delivery presents special considerations. The following are the main ones to keep in mind.

Comparing Print and Online Text

One of the keys to successful writing for online readers is understanding how online readers view and process text.

Linear versus Nonlinear Text Jakob Nielsen, noted usability expert, has found that online readers read an average of 20% of the words on a page.[3] He says that print text can be distinguished from online text in that print text tends to be linear, whereas online text is nonlinear. That is, when people read print documents, they often start at the beginning and continue reading until they reach the end using the Z-pattern described earlier in this chapter. By contrast, online

Exhibit 3-10 Illustration of the F-Pattern of Online Reading

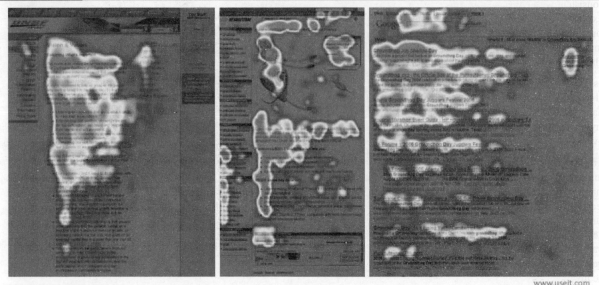

www.useit.com

Jacob Nielsen, "F-Shaped Pattern for Reading Web Content," April 17, 2006, accessed March 24, 2016, https://www.nngroup.com/articles/f-shaped-pattern-reading-web-content/. Used with permission.

readers scan for relevant information and may be diverted by links or other features of the display in their search.

F-Pattern of Reading

Nielsen's eye-tracking research used heat maps to identify this online reading style as following an **F-pattern**. Using an F-pattern, online readers generally skim the text across the top of a webpage twice and then read vertically down the left side of the page. Exhibit 3-10 shows these patterns in Nielsen's heat maps, with the reds and yellows indicated as the strongest areas of reader focus.

Task-Focused Reading

In addition, Nielsen says that when people look for information in electronic documents, particularly on the Web, they do so not necessarily to read what an author has to say about an issue but to accomplish a specific task (e.g., locate a statistic, fill out a form). Therefore, online text needs to facilitate the reader's ability to find and use information.

Furthermore, Nielsen notes that online text can produce comprehensive data more concisely than a print document, making online text in many ways more efficient for helping readers accomplish a task. Because technology allows writers to embed links to relevant or related information rather than include that information in a paragraph or on a page, electronic documents can incorporate a lot of information in a relatively small space. Print documents, though, could become quite long and unwieldy if an author were to include every fact, statistic, or resource related to the topic at hand.

Writing Style

Lastly, print documents generally require that thoughts be expressed in complete sentences, with occasional bulleted lists added for clarity and visual appeal. In electronic documents, writers tend to rely much more on bulleted lists and other terse forms of text. Depending on the medium, online text may use fragments and frequent abbreviations.

Organizing Content

Consistent with Nielsen and with research on the F-pattern for reading online text, Redish notes that most people visit webpages because they need to *do* something. Consequently, they do not read so much as they scan for information, and they want what they need quickly, which means that writers should "think 'information,' not 'document.'"[4]

As with print documents, online information must be organized well. Redish advocates organizing webpages in the **inverted pyramid style**, where the main point is presented first, followed by supporting information and then by any historical or background information (Exhibit 3-11). As you can see, this inverted pyramid style will enable efficient F-pattern reading for key content.

If readers are merely scanning for information, they may not scroll for information, which means that the main point must stand out. Therefore, you must analyze your audience and goals to know which information should be embedded in links and which information should appear on the page the reader is currently reading. In addition, similar to information in printed business documents, information in electronic documents should be chunked in short paragraphs and contain headings and lists that emphasize a logical structure and presentation of the information. Exhibit 3-12 provides an example of writing in the inverted pyramid style.

Exhibit 3-11

Illustration of the Inverted Pyramid

Primary information: Content essential to understanding or acting on the message

Secondary information: Supporting details and other helpful content

Tertiary information: Content that is interesting but not necessary for understanding or action

Presenting the Content

Your choice of design elements (font, color, graphics) depends on your audience. Redish notes that one of the important differences between print and electronic documents is that the

Exhibit 3-12   Illustration of an Article Written in the Inverted Pyramid Format

MADISON MEDICAL ANNOUNCES EXTENDED URGENT CARE SUMMER HOURS

From June 1–September 1, Madison Medical Clinic's urgent care center will be open Monday–Friday from 9 am–9 pm, and Saturday and Sunday from 9 am–6 pm. No appointment is necessary.

You will find our clinic at 9823 Madison Street, just off the interstate at Exit 51. If you have questions, be sure to call us at 715-920-1902 or visit our website at http://www.madisonmedicalurgentcare.org.

We know the beautiful summer weather means many of us are spending time outdoors, and that means more opportunity for those little accidents that require medical attention. So whether it's a sprain,

© Blend/Image Source

a rash, a little too much sun, or another routine medical need, you can be sure our medical staff are here to serve you. Of course, in an emergency you want to call 911 or head to your nearest emergency room. We accept most forms of insurance and can arrange payment plans for our services.

resolution (sharpness of the letters and images) is lower on a screen than in print. Thus, while you can use a variety of serif and sans serif fonts in a variety of sizes in print documents, you will want to choose sans serif fonts in at least a 12-point size for most online documents so that the serifs do not obscure the text.

You should also keep in mind that while readers usually see printed documents on 8.5 × 11 paper, readers may see electronic documents in screens or monitors of varying sizes. For this reason, Redish recommends a line length of 50 to 70 characters, or 8 to 10 words. Short lines are also more quickly and easily read, though you do not want lines so short that your text does not capture the main point.

Likewise, text-formatting conventions differ in print and electronic environments. In both environments, writers can use emphasis devices such as bullets, headings, bold text, or italics. However, because underlining also represents links in electronic environments, writers should favor italics or bold text in that context.

As with printed text, writers should use colors that are visually appealing and appropriate for the message and audience. For most readers, this will be a dark text on a light background.

Creating Searchable Content

Search engine optimization (SEO) refers to strategies writers use to ensure their sites appear in the top results of a reader's online search. An important point to note about search engine optimization is that some of the writer's work is done behind the scenes in a webpage's **HTML code** (the coding language used to create webpages that the reader does not see) (Exhibit 3-13). Therefore, if you write for the Web, you must consider audiences both in terms of information the readers will see in the final published webpages and information that functions in the background but that your readers still need in order to access your content when they search for it online (e.g., keywords embedded in the HTML code).

According to Emil Towner and Heidi Everett, experts in Web and e-communication, you can increase the chances that your site will appear in a reader's search by doing the following:[5]

- Researching and understanding key words that consumers use to search for the product/service being offered

- Incorporating those key words into meta-descriptions (key words that appear in the website's HTML code but not on the webpage that the reader sees), first- and second-level headings (formatted using H1 and H2 HTML coding options), page titles, and even URLs when possible (e.g., www.XYZcompany.com/LawnMowers) to help improve a website's ranking in searches and get users to the correct page in the website with fewer clicks

- Using those keywords as links on other pages in the website

Making Your Web Writing Accessible

Many businesses have seen the wisdom of ensuring that their websites are accessible to people with disabilities; in fact, accessibility is generally required by law. Many features of the Web that we take for granted may present difficulties for those with disabilities. For instance, how do people with hearing impairments access audio content on a website? How do people with visual disabilities access text? How does a person with a motor impairment use a mouse?

Incorporating text along with audio files gives people who have hearing impairments access to a site, while people with motor disabilities can be helped with voice-activated features or key commands rather than mouse-controlled navigation.

Visually impaired people use screen readers to access Web content; therefore, any text or images you use must be adapted for interpretation by these screen readers. Towner and Everett offer

Exhibit 3-13 | Illustration of HTML code

HTML ⊗

```
1    <!DOCTYPE html>
2    <html xmlns="http://www.w3.org/1999/xhtml" designation="" enumeration
     ="" data-uuid="     ">
3        <head>
4            <meta charset="utf-8" />
5            <link type="text/css" rel="stylesheet" title="default" href="
     ../../assets/css/core.css" />
6            <link type="text/css" rel="stylesheet" title="default" href="
     ../../assets/css/main.css" />
7            <link type="text/css" rel="stylesheet" title="default" href="
     ../../assets/css/color.css" />
8            <link type="text/css" rel="stylesheet" title="default" href="
     ../../assets/css/custom.css" />
9            <link type="text/css" rel="stylesheet" title="default" media
     ="print" href="../../assets/css/print.css" />
10           <title>Designing Documents with Visual Appeal</title>
11       </head>
12       <body>
13           <header class="chapter-intro3 border-top color1" data-uuid="    

14           <div class="title-info" data-uuid="     ">
15               <div class="chapter-number" data-uuid="     ">
16                   chapter three
17               </div>
18               <h1 data-uuid="     ">Designing Documents with Visual
     Appeal</h1>
19           </div>
20           <aside class="sidenote-7 color2" data-uuid="     ">
21               <h4 data-uuid="     ">Learning Objectives</h4>
22               <p data-uuid="     "><span class="step-title">LO 3-1 
```

Source: McGraw-Hill Education.

these best practices for creating text that screen readers can easily interpret. Many of these tips will also be helpful for all readers of your website.[6]

- Add alt-tags to images. "Alt" refers to alternative text that describes what the image is. The screen reader can then read this description for a visually impaired Web reader.

- Add descriptive captions to all images that connect the meaning of the image to the text on the page. Even readers who are not visually impaired will appreciate the explanation.

- Use the HTML tags for headings (e.g., H1 for Heading 1, H2 for Heading 2) rather than format headings manually with bold text or a change in font size. Using the HTML code ensures the screen reader will help visually impaired readers skim a website's content. As we discussed, the HTML-formatted headings also improve search engine optimization.

- Use descriptive headings for links rather than just "click here." For example, a link to a company's "contact us" page should read: "<u>Contact us</u> for help with your order" instead of "<u>Click here</u> to contact us." If a descriptive phrase isn't used, the screen reader will state: "Link: Click here." When a descriptive phrase is used, however, the screen reader will state: "Link: Contact us."

- Use periods at the ends of items in a list so that the screen reader knows that the line has ended.

As a businessperson, you may never be called on to design a website, but you are likely to write the content that appears on a website or to work with the designers who put your content online. If you would like to learn more about customizing your Web writing for access by all readers, you can find information at the Web Accessibility Initiative (WIA).

Devices such as screen readers help people with disabilities access Web content.
© zlikovec

Format for Business Letters

LO3-6   Format business letters according to commonly accepted practices.

The layout of a letter will often be the first impression a reader has of you as a businessperson. Therefore, showing that you know standard business letter formats will speak to your professional credibility.

Exhibit 3-14 illustrates four common letter formats. In all formats, single spacing in paragraphs and double spacing between paragraphs is the general rule.

Regardless of the style you choose, most letters have the following components, though you may expect some variation depending on your company practices or preferences, and some elements may not be relevant to your document. For example, you do not need to include "Enclosure" if you do not enclose anything in the envelope with the letter.

Letterhead

The **letterhead** is a visual rendering of your company's address and general contact information. It may contain a company's logo, phone number, email address, website address, or social media addresses. The information is usually at the top of a letter.

Return Address

The **return address** is the writer's address. Your letters should always contain a return address. In business letters, the return address appears in your company letterhead. In personal letters, the return address goes at the top of the page. It does not contain your name, just your street address, city, state, and zip code.

Date Line

You should use the **conventional date form**, with month, day, and year spelled out for the reader (September 7, 2019). The conventional date form is preferred because abbreviated date forms such as 9-7-19 or Sept. 7, '19 are informal. Further, 9-7-19 in the United States is September 7; in other countries where the month commonly appears before the date, people will read the date as July 9. Spelling out the date is the surest way to be clear. Most word processors allow you to set up your preference and will use that preference when you use the date feature.

Exhibit 3-14 Illustration of Letter Formats

Full Block

June 10, 2019

Mr. Cuyler Semingson
1298 Elm Street
Eau Claire, WI 54701

Dear Mr. Semingson:

On behalf of ECCO Board of Directors, thank you for your generous donation to Eau Claire Chamber Orchestra. Your support is vital to the viability of this organization, and we very much appreciate your partnership with us in bringing chamber music to the Chippewa Valley. Your tax statement is enclosed.

Your support not only enables us to deliver beautiful music but also to provide an annual free family concert to the community. Ticket revenue only accounts for approximately a 40% of the production cost for each concert. The balance must be covered by grants, corporate sponsorships, and individual donation.

We hope to see you this season! Visit eauclairechamberorchestra.org or befriend us on Facebook for more details.

Best regards,

Elizabeth Hart
General Manager

Enclosure

Modified Block, Blocked Paragraphs

June 10, 2019

Mr. Cuyler Semingson
1298 Elm Street
Eau Claire, WI 54701

Dear Mr. Semingson:

On behalf of ECCO Board of Directors, thank you for your generous donation to Eau Claire Chamber Orchestra. Your support is vital to the viability of this organization, and we very much appreciate your partnership with us in bringing chamber music to the Chippewa Valley. Your tax statement is enclosed.

Your support not only enables us to deliver beautiful music but also to provide an annual free family concert to the community. Ticket revenue only accounts for approximately a 40% of the production cost for each concert. The balance must be covered by grants, corporate sponsorships, and individual donation.

We hope to see you this season! Visit eauclairechamberorchestra.org or befriend us on Facebook for more details.

Best regards,

Elizabeth Hart
General Manager

Enclosure

Modified Block, Indented Paragraphs

June 10, 2019

Mr. Cuyler Semingson
1298 Elm Street
Eau Claire, WI 54701

Dear Mr. Semingson:

On behalf of ECCO Board of Directors, thank you for your generous donation to Eau Claire Chamber Orchestra. Your support is vital to the viability of this organization, and we very much appreciate your partnership with us in bringing chamber music to the Chippewa Valley. Your tax statement is enclosed.

Your support not only enables us to deliver beautiful music but also to provide an annual free family concert to the community. Ticket revenue only accounts for approximately a 40% of the production cost for each concert. The balance must be covered by grants, corporate sponsorships, and individual donation.

We hope to see you this season! Visit eauclairechamberorchestra.org or befriend us on Facebook for more details.

Best regards,

Elizabeth Hart
General Manager

Enclosure

Simplified

June 10, 2019

Mr. Cuyler Semingson
1298 Elm Street
Eau Claire, WI 54701

YOUR GENEROUS DONATION TO ECCO

On behalf of ECCO Board of Directors, thank you for your generous donation to Eau Claire Chamber Orchestra. Your support is vital to the viability of this organization, and we very much appreciate your partnership with us in bringing chamber music to the Chippewa Valley. Your tax statement is enclosed.

Your support not only enables us to deliver beautiful music but also to provide an annual free family concert to the community. Ticket revenue only accounts for approximately a 40% of the production cost for each concert. The balance must be covered by grants, corporate sponsorships, and individual donation.

We hope to see you this season! Visit eauclairechamberorchestra.org or befriend us on Facebook for more details.

ELIZABETH HART, General Manager

Enclosure

Because business letters are read by audiences external to a company, they must convey a professional image for you and your company.

© Dragon Images/Shutterstock

Inside Address

The **inside address** is your reader's mailing address, complete with **courtesy title** (i.e., Mr., Ms., or Dr.). In business correspondence women are addressed as "Dr." or "Ms." Courtesy titles such as "Miss" or "Mrs." are not used unless you know that your reader prefers this title. The reason for using "Ms." is a practical one: It is the the most neutral. You may not know whether your audience is married, but if you use "Miss" or "Mrs." you assign a marital status. Even if you know a woman is married, she may not wish to use a courtesy title that ties her business or personal identity to her marital status, especially when her male counterparts have no courtesy title that is the masculine equivalent of "Miss" or "Mrs."

Attention Line

Some businesspeople prefer to use the company name rather than an individual name in the inside address. Thus, they address the letter to the company in the inside address and then use an **attention line** that directs the letter to a specific office or department. The attention line is placed two lines below the inside address and two lines above the salutation. The typical form of the attention line is

Attention: Mr. Donovan Price, Vice President

Salutation

The **salutation** is your opening greeting to your reader. It is the equivalent of "Hello" and is followed by a colon. The salutation should reflect your familiarity with the reader and the formality of the situation. If you know your reader well, you can address the reader by first name (e.g., *Dear Joan*). If not, you use the reader's courtesy title and last name (e.g., *Dear Mr. Baskin*). As with the inside address, you should use "Mr." or "Ms." or "Dr." as a courtesy title before the reader's name.

If you do not know and cannot find out the name of the person to whom you are sending the letter, use a position title. By directing your letter to *Director of Human Resources* or *Public Relations Manager,* you are helping your letter reach the appropriate person. Avoid greetings such as "To Whom It May Concern" or "Dear Sir," as these are considered outdated and not audience centered. If you don't know the person or position title, you can omit the salutation and use a subject line.

Mixed or Open Punctuation

The punctuation following the salutation and the closing is either mixed or open. **Mixed punctuation** employs a colon after the salutation and a comma after the complimentary close. **Open punctuation**, on the other hand, uses no punctuation after the salutation and none after the complimentary close. These two forms are used in domestic communication. In international communication, you may see letters with **closed punctuation**—that is, punctuation distinguished by commas after the lines in the return and inside addresses and a period at the end of the complimentary close.

Subject Line

So that both the sender and the receiver may quickly identify the subject of the correspondence, many writers use the **subject line** in their letters. The subject line tells what the letter is about.

In addition, it contains any specific identifying material that may be helpful such as the date of previous correspondence, invoice number, or order number. It is usually placed two lines below the salutation.

Subject lines are generally written as fragments. They may be capitalized as book titles (every important word capitalized), or they may be capitalized as sentences (the first word and proper nouns capitalized). Remember that using all capital letters in a subject line may create the impression that you are shouting at your reader.

The subject line is usually formatted in one of two ways:

Subject: Your July 2 inquiry about an estimate

RE: Please Refer to Invoice H-320.

Second-Page Heading

When the length of a letter exceeds one page, you should set up the following page or pages for quick identification. Always print pages 2 and onward on plain paper (no letterhead). These two forms are the most common:

Ms. Helen E. Mann   p. 2   May 7, 2019

Ms. Helen E. Mann
May 7, 2019
Page 2

Be sure there is no number on the first page. In Microsoft Word 2016, you can omit the number on the first page by clicking in the header area of your document and then from the Design ribbon, checking the "Different First Page" box.

Complimentary Close

By far the most commonly used **complimentary close** is *Sincerely. Sincerely yours* is also used, but in recent years the *yours* has been used less frequently, as some see it as too personal. *Truly* (with and without the *yours*) is also used, but it also has lost popularity for the same reason. Such closes as *Cordially, Regards, Best regards,* and *Respectfully* are appropriate when their meanings fit the writer–reader relationship. A long-standing friendship, for example, would justify *Cordially;* the writer's respect for the position, prestige, or accomplishments of the reader would justify *Respectfully.*

Signature Block

The writer's signature appears in the space between the closing and the printed signature. The **signature block** usually appears under the writer's signature. It contains the writer's name and title usually on the same line, though if either the name or title is long, the title appears on the following line, blocked under the name. It may also contain the company name when the letter continues on a second page without the company letterhead, as well as contact information not found in the letterhead.

Information Notations

Below the signature block and aligned to the left are **information notations** for the reader regarding the document. *Enclosure, Enc., Enc.—3,* and so on indicate materials enclosed with the letter. If the writer and the typist are not the same person, the initials of the writer and the typist may be noted (e.g., *WEH:ga* indicates that "WEH" wrote the letter, and "ga" typed it). Indications of copies prepared for other readers also may be included: *cc:* (or *bcc:*) *Sharon Garbett, copy to:* (or *blind copy:*) *Sharon Garbett.*

Postscripts

Postscripts, commonly referred to as the PS, are placed after any notations. While rarely used in most business letters because they look like afterthoughts, they can be effective for adding promotions in sales letters.

Paper

Today, paper is still a common choice of medium. In the United States, standard business paper size is 8.5 by 11 inches; international business A4 paper is sized slightly narrower than 8.5 inches and slightly longer than 11 inches. Occasionally, half-size (5.5 × 8.5) or executive size (7.25 × 10.5) is used for short messages. Other than these standards, you have a variety of choices to make regarding color, weight, and texture.

The most conservative color choice is white. The color you choose should also be the color you use for the second and continuing pages.

The weight and texture of your paper also communicate. While "cheap" paper may denote control of expenses to some readers, other readers may associate a high-quality paper with a high-quality product or service. Usually businesses use paper with a weight of 16 to 20 pounds.

The Fold

The carelessly folded letter creates a bad first impression with the reader. Neat folding will complete the planned effect by (1) making the letter fit snugly in its cover, (2) making the letter easy for the reader to remove, and (3) making the letter appear neat when opened.

The two-fold pattern is the easiest. It fits the standard sheet for the long (No. 10) envelope as well as some other envelope sizes. As shown in Exhibit 3-15, the first fold of the two-fold pattern is from the bottom up, taking a little less than a third of the sheet. The second fold goes from the

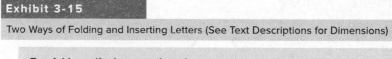

Exhibit 3-15

Two Ways of Folding and Inserting Letters (See Text Descriptions for Dimensions)

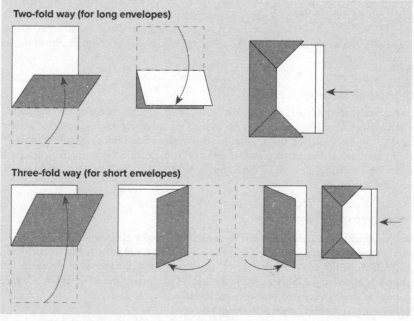

Two-fold way (for long envelopes)

Three-fold way (for short envelopes)

top down, making exactly the same panel as the bottom segment. (This measurement will leave the recipient a 0.25-inch thumbhold for easy unfolding of the letter.) Thus folded, the letter should be slipped into its envelope with the second crease toward the bottom and the center panel at the front of the envelope.

The three-fold pattern is necessary to fit the standard sheet into the commonly used small (No. 6¾) envelope. Its first fold is from the bottom up, with the bottom edge of the sheet riding about 0.25 inch under the top edge to allow the thumbhold. (If the edges are exactly even, they are harder to separate.) The second fold is from the right side of the sheet toward the left, taking a little less than a third of the width. The third fold matches the second: from the left side toward the right, with a panel of exactly the same width. (This fold will leave a 0.25-inch thumbhold at the right, for the user's convenience.)

So that the letter will appear neat when unfolded, the creases should be neatly parallel with the top and sides, not at angles that produce irregular shapes. In the three-fold form, the side panels produced by the second and third folds must be exactly the same width; otherwise, the vertical creases are off-center and tend to throw the whole carefully planned layout off-center.

The three-fold letter is inserted into its cover with the third crease toward the bottom of the envelope and the loose edges toward the stamp end of the envelope. From habit, most recipients of business letters slit envelopes at the top and turn them facedown to extract the letter. The three-fold letter inserted as described thus gives its reader an easy thumbhold at the top of the envelope to pull it out by and a second one at the top of the sheet for easy unfolding of the whole.

Envelope Address

So that optical character recognition (OCR) equipment may be used in sorting mail, the U.S. Postal Service requests that all envelopes be typed as follows (Exhibit 3-16).

- Place the address in the scannable area as shown in the white box in Exhibit 3-16. It is best to use a sans serif font in 10 to 12 point.

- Use a block address format.

- Use single space.

Exhibit 3-16 Form for Addressing Envelopes Recommended by the U.S. Postal Service, Publication 28

Return Address Area
TATUM SAYERS
7165 HERMES LANE
NEW BERLIN IL 62670-3762

Postage Area

(OPTIONAL) Non-Address Data → CRPS 03672
(OPTIONAL) Information/Attention → MS ANNA CHAN
Name of Recipient → MCGRAW-HILL/IRWIN INC
Delivery Address → 1333 BURR RIDGE PARKWAY
Post Office, State, ZIP → BURR RIDGE IL 60521-0101

← 1/2" →   2 3/4"   ← 1/2" →

5/8

Bar Code Clear Area 4 1/2"

- Uppercase or lowercase letters are acceptable.

- Do not use punctuation, except for the hyphen in the nine-digit zip code.

- Use the two-letter abbreviations for the U.S. states and territories and the Canadian provinces. Use other address abbreviations as shown in the most recent edition of the *Post Office Directory* (see www.usps.com for the most updated version). When sending mail to a foreign country, include only the country name in uppercase on the bottom line.

States and Possessions of the United States

Alabama	AL	Kentucky	KY	Ohio	OH
Alaska	AK	Louisiana	LA	Oklahoma	OK
American Samoa	AS	Maine	ME	Oregon	OR
Arizona	AZ	Marshall Islands	MH	Palau	PW
Arkansas	AR	Maryland	MD	Pennsylvania	PA
California	CA	Massachusetts	MA	Puerto Rico	PR
Colorado	CO	Michigan	MI	Rhode Island	RI
Connecticut	CT	Minnesota	MN	South Carolina	SC
Delaware	DE	Mississippi	MS	South Dakota	SD
District of Columbia	DC	Missouri	MO	Tennessee	TN
Federated States of Micronesia	FM	Montana	MT	Texas	TX
Florida	FL	Nebraska	NE	Utah	UT
Georgia	GA	Nevada	NV	Vermont	VT
Guam	GU	New Hampshire	NH	Virginia	VA
Hawaii	HI	New Jersey	NJ	Virgin Islands	VI
Idaho	ID	New Mexico	NM	Washington	WA
Illinois	IL	New York	NY	West Virginia	WV
Indiana	IN	North Carolina	NC	Wisconsin	WI
Iowa	IA	North Dakota	ND	Wyoming	WY
Kansas	KS	Northern Mariana Islands	MP		

Canadian Provinces and Territories

Alberta	AB	Newfoundland	NF	Prince Edward Island	PE
British Columbia	BC	Northwest Territories	NT	Quebec	PQ
Manitoba	MB	Nova Scotia	NS	Saskatchewan	SK
New Brunswick	NB	Ontario	ON	Yukon Territory	YT

- Type the return address in the left corner, beginning on the second line from the top of the envelope and three spaces from the left edge of the envelope.

- Print any on-arrival instructions (Confidential, Personal) four lines below the return address.

- Place all notations for the post office (Special Delivery) below the stamp and at least three lines above the mailing address.

Format for Memorandums (Memos)

LO3-7 Format memorandums (memos) according to commonly accepted practices.

Memorandums (memos) have basic components, but their form varies widely across organizations. Because memos are sent internally, they do not contain a return address or inside address. The basic components are the heading and body.

Memo Headings

The heading has four elements: *To, From, Date,* and *Subject*. These elements can be arranged in various orders, but they should all be present. Optional headings include the *cc:* or *bcc:* notation if others are copied on the memo. The information after each heading should align with the information that appears after the other headings (Exhibit 3-17). You sign your initials after your names in the *From* heading.

Memo Body

Unlike a letter, a memo does not contain a salutation. A memo moves directly from the *To, From, Date,* and *Subject* to the body, which is single spaced with double spacing between paragraphs. Usually, all text is aligned at the left margin. Headings in the body of the memo are frequently used in long memos.

A complimentary closing and signature block are not included in a memo. A memo concludes once the body is finished unless you need any notations, such as for the typist. In addition, enclosures are included just as they are in letters, but they are noted as *Attachment* or *Att.* rather than *Enclosure.* The reason for this notation is that items sent with a letter are enclosed in the envelope with the letter; items sent with a memo are attached to (e.g., stapled, paper clipped) to the memo. Exhibits 2-18 and 2-19 in Chapter 2 show correct memo format.

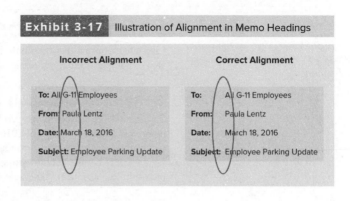

Exhibit 3-17 Illustration of Alignment in Memo Headings

Incorrect Alignment

To: All G-11 Employees
From: Paula Lentz
Date: March 18, 2016
Subject: Employee Parking Update

Correct Alignment

To: All G-11 Employees
From: Paula Lentz
Date: March 18, 2016
Subject: Employee Parking Update

Format for Letter and Memorandum (Memo) Reports

Informal business reports may be written in letter or memo format, depending upon the audience. The letter report contains the return address or company letterhead, date, inside address, and salutation; it may also contain a subject line. The memo report contains the standard *To, From, Date,* and *Subject* lines.

LO3-8 Format letter and memorandum (memo) reports.

Beginning with the second page, letter and memo reports must have a header that contains the reader's name, the date, and a page number. In Word 2016 you can find the heading feature by going to Insert > Header. From here type the text of your header and insert a page number. Because you do not want this information on the first page of your report, also check "Different First Page."

Both letter and memorandum reports may use headings to create visual appeal and guide the reader through the report. The headings are usually displayed in the margins, on separate lines, and in a different style (Exhibit 3-18). Memorandum and letter reports may also differ from ordinary letters and memos by having illustrations (charts, tables), an appendix, and/or a bibliography. Chapters 11 and 12 address reports in more detail.

Exhibit 3-18 Illustration of Heading Levels in a Report

First-Level Heading

Second-Level Heading

-
-
-

Third-Level Heading

Format for Formal Reports

LO3-9   Format formal business reports.

Like letters, formal reports should be visually appealing. Well-arranged reports give an impression of competence and professionalism.

General Information on Report Presentation

Fortunately, Microsoft Word provides you with many template options for creating formal reports, as shown in the Word 2016 template in Exhibit 3-19. However, even if you do not have to format your own reports, you should know the basics about report presentation to be sure your work is completed correctly. Your understanding of contrast, repetition, alignment, and proximity can also help you create a visually appealing format.

Conventional Page Layout   For the typical text page in a report, a conventional layout appears to fit the page as a picture fits a frame (Exhibit 3-20). This eye-pleasing layout, however, is arranged to fit the page space not covered by the binding of the report. Thus, you must allow an extra 0.5 inch or so on the left margins of the pages of a single-sided left-bound report and at the top of the pages of a top-bound report.

Special Page Layouts   Certain text pages may have individual layouts (e.g., first pages of chapters, tables of contents, executive summaries). Exhibit 3-21 illustrates that some special pages can be created with templates.

Exhibit 3-19   Illustration of a Report Template in Microsoft Word 2016

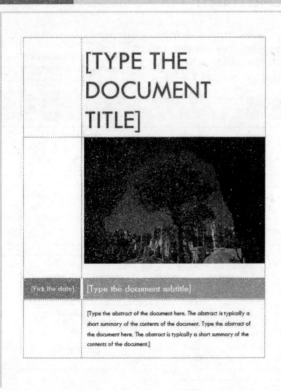

Source: Microsoft Word 2016; Image © Design Pics/Don Hammond RF

Exhibit 3-20   Examples of Page Layouts

Double-Spaced Page

Single-Spaced Page

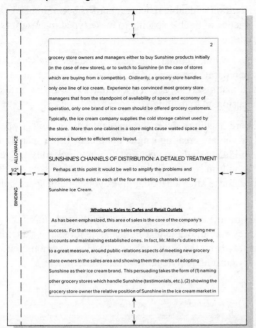

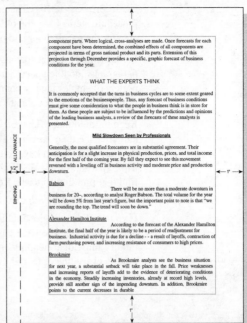

[Company]
[Street Address, City, ST ZIP Code]
Tel [Telephone]
Fax [Fax]
[Website]

ANNUAL REPORT

FY [Year]

[You can add an abstract or other key statement here. An abstract is typically a short summary of the document content.]

TABLE OF CONTENTS

Contents

Letters or memos of transmittal and authorization may also have individual layouts. They are arranged in any conventional letter or memo form.

Choice of Spacing

The convention of double spacing reports is becoming less popular. This procedure stems from the old practice of double spacing to make typed manuscripts more readable for the proofreader and printer.

In recent years, single spacing has become popular. The general practice is to single space within paragraphs, double space between paragraphs, and triple space above all centered heads. Supporters of single spacing contend that it saves space and facilitates reading because it is like the printing that most people are accustomed to reading.

Keep in mind that Microsoft Word headings styles and text styles have built-in spacing before and after the text. As a result, if you are creating single, double, or triple spacing by pressing your Enter or Return key, you will likely find that your text does not look truly single, double, or triple spaced. Microsoft Word's built-in spacing is fine to use for business reports, so you may find that pressing Enter or Return once after a heading gives you enough space before or after your headings or text.

If you need true single, double, or triple spacing, you can modify the style to set the spacing you need. Modifying the style ensures that all of the text in that style looks the same. If you try to modify individual headings or text from the Font tools on the Home ribbon, you will have to modify every line of text or every heading individually, which is inefficient.

From the Tech Desk

Modifying Styles in Microsoft Word 2016

There may be a time when you want to change Microsoft Word's preset styles for your headings or paragraphs. While it is true you can manually change each paragraph or each heading by using the Font tools on the Home ribbon, this practice is time consuming. You also risk forgetting to change a heading or paragraph text. Microsoft Word will let you simultaneously change all text formatted one style simply by modifying the style itself.

1. From the Home ribbon, locate the Styles tools.

2. Right click the style you want to modify and select Modify. Beneath the preview window, you can see all of the formatting currently applied to text with that style.

3. From the dialog box, select the new font, colors, etc. that you want to apply to the style.

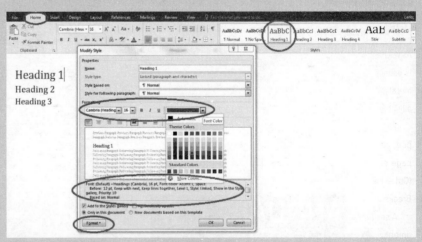

Source: Microsoft Word 2016

4. If you want to change the line spacing, apply a border, etc., click the dropdown arrow next to the Format button.

5. Click OK.

If you want to change paragraphs of text, you can tell which style is applied by clicking in the paragraph and looking for the style that is highlighted in the Styles tool. It is likely the Normal style, and you can modify that style as you would any other style.

Patterns of Indentation You should indent the paragraph beginnings of double-spaced typing. You should not indent the first line of a paragraph of single-spaced material because its paragraph headings are clearly marked by the blank lines between paragraphs.

No generally accepted distance of indentation exists. Some sources suggest 0.5 inch; others, 1 inch and more. Any decision as to the best distance to use is up to you, though you should follow the practice established in the office, group, or school for which you write the report. Whatever your selection, you should be consistent.

Page Numbers Two systems of numbers are used in numbering the pages of the written report. Small Roman numerals are standard for the front matter of the report (i.e., the transmittal document, table of contents, and executive summary) beginning with p. ii. The title page, though it is considered the first page, is not numbered. Arabic numerals are conventional for the main part of the report, normally beginning with the first page of the introduction and continuing through the appendix.

Placement of the numbers on the page varies with the binding used for the report. In reports bound at the top of the page, you should center all page numbers at the bottom of the page, two or three lines below the body and usually in a footer.

For left-sided binding, you should place the numbers in the upper-right corner, two or three lines above the top line, usually in the header, and right justified.

From the Tech Desk

Using Microsoft Word to Number Report Pages

As we have discussed, the front matter of a report is usually numbered with lowercase Roman numerals, while the main body of the report is usually numbered with Arabic numerals.

To create the two types of numbering in a report, you have to know the difference between a page break and a section break. A page break (Ctrl + Enter or Insert > Page Break, or Layout > Breaks > Page) starts a new page.

A section break starts a new section of a document, which gives you the power to apply changes to one section that do not have to be applied to other sections. To apply a section break, go to Layout > Breaks > Next Page.

To insert page numbers in the front matter:

1. Insert page breaks at the end of the title page, transmittal document, table of contents, and any other pages in your front matter *except* the last page of your front matter.

2. Insert a section break at the end of the last page of your front matter.

3. From the Insert ribbon, select the Page Number dropdown list and choose where you want your page number to go.

4. In the front matter section, choose any page number format.

5. Select the page number.

6. From the Design ribbon, check the Different First Page box so that the page number does not appear on the title page.

7. With the page number selected, either right click and choose "Format Page Numbers" or from the Design ribbon, select Page Number > Format Page Numbers.

8. Choose the page format for lowercase Roman numerals.

9. Click OK.

To apply page numbers to the main body of the report:

1. Select a page number in the body of the report.

2. Make sure that in the Design ribbon > Navigation tools, the Link to Previous option is not selected.

3. With the page number selected, either right click and choose "Format Page Numbers" or from the Design ribbon, select Page Number > Format Page Numbers.

4. From the dialog box, select the format for Arabic numerals.

5. From the dialog box, select Start At and set the number to 1.

In documents printed back-to-back, page numbers are usually placed at the top of the page even with the outside margin.

Heading Formats Headings are titles of the parts of the report. Designed to lead readers through the report, headings must show at a glance the type of information they cover.

Using Microsoft Word's Styles feature is the easiest way to create and use headings in your text. In addition to ensuring consistency in the format of your heading levels, these styles also let you automatically generate a table of contents for your report.

You can use any combination of form and placement that clearly shows the headings for major sections and subheadings for sections within the major sections (Exhibit 3-18 demonstrates one way). When you use headings, you should observe these four principles:

1. All headings of the same level must have the same placement on the page and the same formatting. That is, all Level-1 headings must have the same format and placement, all Level-2 headings must have the same format and placement, and so on.

2. Headings of the same level must be grammatically parallel within their sections of the report. In other words, all Level-1 headings must be parallel. All Level-2 headings within a Level-1 section must be parallel with one another; and all Level-3 headings within a Level-2 section must be parallel with one another.

3. If you use one of any heading level, you must have a second one within that section of the report. If, for example, you create a Level-1 heading, you must use at least one more. If you create a Level-2 heading within a Level-1 section, you must use at least one more.

4. You should place text between all headings. Don't move from one heading to the next without adding text. If you do, this is called "stacking" your headings, and it does not allow your reader to transition easily from one piece of content to the next.

Mechanics and Format of the Report Parts

The preceding notes on physical appearance apply generally to all parts of the report. However, a report may contain several sections, each with its own conventions for content and presentation. Whether a report contains these sections depends on the type and nature of the report. Chapter 12 provides a more thorough discussion of when you use each of these sections.

Title Fly The **title fly** contains only the report title. The title should be formatted in a font and style that are distinct from the report headings. The font used is usually larger than the font for any heading in the report.

Title Page The **title page** normally contains four main areas of identification.

1. The report title. The title is formatted the same as it would on a title fly.

2. The name or names of the individual (or group) for whom the report has been prepared. Introduce the name or names with "Prepared for" or "Submitted to." Include recipient's title or role, company, and address, particularly if you and the recipient are from different companies.

3. Your name. Introduce your name with "Prepared by," "Written by," or similar wording describing your role in the report. Include your job title or role, company, and address.

4. The date of the presentation or publication of the report. As with dates in letters and memos, be sure you spell out the date (e.g., March 23, 2019, not 2/23/19).

Placement of the four areas of identification on the page should be visually appealing. Many templates can help you create an attractive title page.

Letters or Memos of Transmittal

As their names imply, the **letters or memos of transmittal** are letters or memos that transfer the report from the writer to the reader. They are written in standard letter or memo format. Chapter 12 provides information on how to write these documents.

Acknowledgments

When others have helped you write a report, you usually thank them in an **acknowledgments** section somewhere in the report. If you have only a few people to acknowledge, you may do so in the introduction of the report or in the letter of transmittal. If you need to make numerous acknowledgments, you may create a special section for them. This section, titled "Acknowledgments," has the same layout as any other text page on which a title is displayed.

A well-formatted report will help readers understand your content and help you look like a prepared and knowledgeable source.
© Dmitriy Shironosov/123RF

Table of Contents

The **table of contents** is the report outline in its polished, finished form. It lists the major report headings with the page numbers on which those headings appear. Short reports will not likely require a table of contents, but long reports usually contain the table of contents to help the reader navigate your document.

The table of contents is titled "Contents" or "Table of Contents." The layout of the table of contents should be consistent with the look of the report. Below the title are two columns. One contains the report headings, generally beginning with the first report part following the table of contents; the other contains the page numbers.

In the table of contents, as in the body of the report, you should format your heading levels so that each is distinguishable. Fortunately, you do not have to do this formatting yourself. If you use Microsoft Word's styles to format your headings in the body of the report you can automatically insert a table of contents using the References ribbon.

Table of Illustrations

The **table (list) of illustrations** may be either a continuation of the table of contents or a separate table. It lists the visuals presented in the report in much the same way as the table of contents lists the report parts. The table is usually titled "Table of Charts and Illustrations," "List of Tables and Figures," "Table of Figures," or "List of Tables."

The table consists of two columns, the first for the table and figure titles and the second for the pages on which the tables and figures appear. The look of the table should match the format and layout of the table of contents. The figure or table number should precede each table or figure title.

As we have mentioned, you can automate this process by using Microsoft Word's "Insert Caption" feature for all of the visuals in your report and then inserting the list in your report.

From the Tech Desk

Generating a Table of Contents and List of Tables and Figures Using Microsoft Word 2016

As with most tasks in formatting the parts of the report, the table of contents and list of tables and figures is an automated process. To ensure you can use the automated process, however, you must do two things when creating your report:

- Use Microsoft Word's Styles tool to format your headings.
- Use Microsoft Word's References > Insert Caption feature to create titles for your tables, figures, and other visuals.

Assuming you've done these two things, you can create your table of contents and list of tables and figures by doing the following:

1. Go to the page in your report where you want to insert this content.

2. From the References ribbon, select the Table of Contents dropdown list and choose one of the options.

3. After the table of contents, type the title for your list of tables or figures.

4. From the References ribbon, select Insert Table of Figures.

5. From the dialog box that opens, select either the Figures or Tables option. Word will pull the visuals with that label to generate the list.

6. If you have both figures and tables in your list, repeat Step 6, and select the other label.

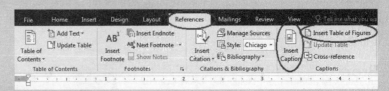

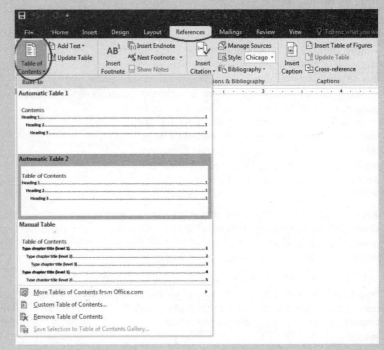

Source: Microsoft Word 2016.

References (or Bibliography) Anytime you use another's idea, you need to give credit to the source. Sometimes business writers interweave this credit into the narrative of their text, and often they use footnotes to convey their source information. But often these sources are listed in a **references or bibliography section** at the end of the report. Typically, these sections are organized alphabetically, but they also can be organized by date, subject, or type of source.

As Reference Chapter B illustrates, the format and content of citations vary depending on which citation method you use. Among the widely used formats are Chicago, Modern Language Association (MLA), and American Psychological Association (APA). Word 2016's Reference ribbon includes a reference management tool that will help you generate a bibliography in these standard formats.

Format for Brochures

It's true that many businesses today advertise their products and services on their websites and through many social media channels. However, brochures are still a viable marketing tool. According to Lance Hiley of The Marketing Centre, when people take your brochure, they can be considered "engaged" with your product or service—a critical step in getting the customer to commit. Further, he says customers are likely to want brochures when purchasing "high-value or high-risk items, especially where the time taken between making the decision to purchase and actually experiencing the product can be lengthy," such as the purchase of a cruise.[7]

LO3-10   Design a brochure.

Brochure Content

Determining the content for your brochure is much like determining the content for any other document. As you learned in Chapters 1 and 2, determining content requires you to analyze your audience and your purpose.

- What are your business goals?
- Who is your target audience for the brochure?
- What do you want the reader to think, feel, do, or believe as a result of reading your brochure?
- What does the reader need to know to act on your message?
- What visual elements will help communicate your message?

Once you have answered these questions, you can then determine your main point and the content you need in your brochure to communicate that point. One error many businesspeople make is putting too much content in a brochure. As a result, the brochure looks cluttered, random, and inconsistent, and the writer's main point is lost. If you keep your business goal in mind, you can develop your content around that one main point to ensure a clean, straightforward message.

After you determine your content, you should write your message before placing it in your brochure. Doing so will help you see your entire message apart from the visual elements and, as a result, more easily edit the content for completeness, conciseness, coherence, and accuracy. You can, however, gather visuals that you want to use when you design your brochure, such as photos of the product or your company logo.

As you write your content, you also want to think beyond the facts about your message to the persuasive elements that readers will find compelling. This content might include customer testimonials, data about your product's functionality, product reviews, or visuals showing happy, satisfied people using your product or service.

Brochure Design

The most common format for a brochure is the trifold brochure. Exhibit 3-22 presents templates illustrating common features of trifold brochures created by professional designers, but you do not need to be a graphic designer to create a nice-looking brochure. Fortunately, Microsoft Word and Microsoft Publisher offer several trifold brochure templates that include preset fonts, color palettes, and design elements you can customize for your needs.

Mapping Information One thing your template won't do for you is tell you where to put your content. Fortunately, if you think about the principles of contrast, repetition, alignment, and proximity, your task is much easier. When you map your content in your brochure, you want to apply the Z-pattern, Gutenberg diagram, and grids discussed earlier in this chapter to think about how your readers will see content both within a single panel (as they would when the brochure is folded) and across panels (as they would when the brochure is open).

As you've likely guessed, this means that your main point should be the first thing the reader sees on your front panel. For example, let's say you work for a health care

Exhibit 3-22 Illustration of Stock Agency Templates

(left-right and top to bottom respectively): © Timea Cseke/123RF; © Erika Voloncs/123RF; © Timea Cseke/123RF; © Inokentii Rybtsov/123RF.

organization that wants to encourage people to join its wellness program. The front panel should indicate that your brochure is about the wellness program and contain visual elements such as your company logo that immediately tie the wellness program to your company. You also have to think about what should go on the other panels the readers see when they look at the folded brochure.

Once you open the brochure, you are presented with yet another opportunity to apply the Z-program and Gutenberg diagram. What should your reader see first? What should your reader see last? Using the wellness program example, it would be logical to lead with your main selling point for the program and end with information that makes it easy for your reader to join. Of course, you want to be sure to group similar content according to the proximity principle. In between, you would include your facts about wellness, testimonials, and perhaps some pictures of happy participants or before-and-after pictures of successful participants.

A tip: Before you move from writing your content to putting it in a template, fold a sheet of paper as you would a trifold brochure so that you can easily see the location of the title panel, back panel, and so on. Exhibit 3-23 shows how the fold of the brochure affects the layout.

Incorporating Design Elements

You can apply what you have learned previously in this chapter about fonts and colors to brochures. Many brochures use just one font, and you do not want to use more than two. The colors and fonts you use should be consistent with the professional image you want to portray as well as with your company's image. Again, if you think about the design principles of contrast, repetition, alignment, and proximity, your task is easier.

Because people will likely scan a brochure before they read it, you want to make sure your design can be easily skimmed. This means ensuring white space, using lists rather than paragraphs of text, and using short paragraphs of text when lists are not logical.

Exhibit 3-23 Illustration of the Panels in a Tri-Fold Brochure

Inside Left Panel	Inside Middle Panel	Inside Right Panel	Inside Left Panel	Inside Middle Panel	Inside Right Panel

Visuals in your brochure should be of high quality. Chapter 4 discusses how to create visuals, but generally, you want to work with photos rather than clip art. You also want to place the visuals close to the content that they reflect and ensure that the content of the visuals accurately represents your message. Exhibit 3-24 presents a brochure that generally follows many of the principles of design discussed in this chapter for both text and visuals.

Whether your business career is in advertising, marketing, accounting, health care, operations management, information systems, or any other field, you can be sure your audiences will respond positively to a document that is not only written well but also looks good. The next time you write, incorporate the principles of design and think critically about your layout, fonts, and color. You will be impressed with your results, and your audience will, too.

You Make the Call
Critique the ways the brochure in Exhibit 3-24 follows (or does not follow) the principles of good design.

Exhibit 3-24 Illustration of a Brochure

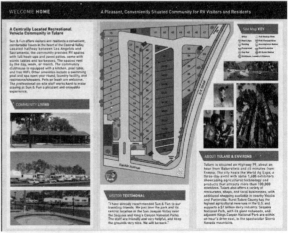

Courtesy Western Management Property Consultants

© gorillaimages/Shutterstock; © gpointstudio/Shutterstock; © Mykola Mazuryk/Shutterstock

Courtesy Western Management Property Consultants

Right panel, clockwise from top: © emeldrum/Getty Images RF; © CO Leong/Shutterstock RF; © Creatista/Shutterstock RF; © Aleksei Potov/Shutterstock

Power Charge Your Professionalism: Use Standard Capitalization

Indicate which capitalization guide you used from Reference Chapter A to determine your capitalization choices for each sentence. If the sentence is correct, leave it as it is.

1. You will find advice about writing a business plan in Chapter 3, page 46.
2. In january charlie hughes, vice president, announced he would retire this fall.
3. I wanted to major in accounting, but I enjoyed the principles of buyer behavior course so much that I decided to major in marketing instead.
4. To be reimbursed for your travel expenses, please submit your receipts to our accounting department.
5. Many companies ask job applicants to send their materials to the human resources department.
6. Our company is looking for a sales manager for the midwest region of the united states.
7. To reach our headquarters, turn left on colorado avenue and travel east for one mile.
8. Our company requires all new employees to read the book *communication and collaboration in the workplace*.

Capitalization is important because . . .

- Using capitalization is a must if you are writing more formal or moderately formal messages. It's true that many text and instant messages are sent without any capitalization. These messages are highly casual and usually appropriate among writers who have a close relationship.
- Using standard capitalization is a way to communicate your general and specific meanings in a way that your reader will readily understand. Generally, the more specific a noun, the more likely you are to capitalize it.

For further instruction on using the right word, see "Capitalization" in the "Punctuation and Mechanics" module of LearnSmart Achieve.

Key Terms

Critical-Thinking Questions

1. What are the four basic principles of document design? Why is it important that you observe these principles when writing business documents? **LO1**

2. What strategies can you use to incorporate the principles of document design in business documents? **LO1–LO4**

3. Why are the Gutenberg diagram and Z-pattern helpful for laying out information? LO2

4. How can writers use leading and kerning to improve readability? LO2

5. What are some considerations for choosing a font(s) for a business document? LO3

6. How can the use of analogous or complementary colors help you choose a color palate for your business document? LO4

7. In what ways can social, emotional, or cultural connotations impact color choices? LO4

8. How does writing text for an electronic medium differ from writing text for a print medium? LO5

9. What is SEO? How can a businessperson write online text to achieve SEO? LO5

10. What are three ways that the format for a business letter differs from the format for a business memo? LO6, LO7

11. What information goes in the header for page 2 and subsequent pages in memos and letter reports? LO8

12. What are three ways that Microsoft Word's Styles feature makes report writing more efficient? LO9

13. Why are brochures important business documents? LO10

Skills-Building Exercises

1. Lisa Richards, owner of Lisa's Childcare Center, has submitted an ad for Sunny Day Travel Agency's quarterly *Travel Adventures* magazine. You have reviewed the ad and know that it needs a lot of work if it is to attract potential customers. Plus, you have standards for the look of the material that appears in your publication, so you rewrite and redesign the advertisement to reflect the basic principles of document design. In a letter to Lisa, explain your design choices regarding the layout, font(s), and colors you used to achieve these principles. Be sure to indicate to Lisa that you have enclosed the revised advertisement for her review. Chapter 8 can help you plan and organize your content.

TEL: 555 555 5555

Lisa's Childcare Center is a family-friendly center catering to the schedule of today's busy workforce. We understand that people don't work from 8–5, so we don't either. Our center is staffed all day every day—even on Saturday and Sunday—with experienced daycare (and overnight care) providers. Whether you work the second shift or overnight or just want to get some work done over the weekend, we are here for you. If you work during the day, we are here for you also. Children love us! If you want to know more about us or talk about how we might me your needs and your child's needs, please give us a call to schedule an appointment and a tour.

Lisa's Childcare Center
Childcare Everyday, All Day

2. You are a new intern at your company. (You can pick the type of company and type of internship.) Your company is redesigning its logo and letterhead, and your boss asks your opinion about fonts and color schemes. Thinking about the field you are in and your company, pick three possible fonts and color schemes. In a memo to your boss, explain why you think the fonts and colors would be appropriate for your business. Chapter 8 can help you organize the content for your memo.

3. You work for Mayfield Medical Center (MMC) in its human resources department. MMC's policy is that whenever someone leaves a position in any department, a department supervisor must submit a proposal to human resources to request to fill the position. Human resources must then approve the request before the position can be filled. The approval process allows MMC to evaluate which positions are truly necessary and to allocate its open positions to the most needy departments.

Because your office has used the same instructions for the proposal for many years, people have continually added to the instructions without much thought to their look, organization, and readability. As a result, the instructions are a mess, and you decide to revise them so that the layout, font, colors, and other visual elements result in a form that is clear, readable, and visually appealing. The instructions you need to revise are as follows:

Mayfield Medical Center Request to Fill a Position:

To request a position in your department, submit a one-page proposal in which you describe the position qualifications, why it was originally staffed, why you need it to continue to be staffed, the cost, the consequences of not staffing the position, why the duties of the position are unique to your department, and other options you have considered. Be sure to organize the document with headings and subheadings. The more complete your document is, the more quickly we can fill the position. Remember that the more persuasive you are, the more likely you are to get the position filled. Our goal this year is to reduce our operating costs by 7%.

Include one position per proposal. Good headings are useful. If you know of any employees who are currently interested in the position and are qualified for the position, you can include that person's name. We will be sure to watch for that person's application. Make sure you describe the job duties, the time spent on each duty, whether the position is full or part time, and how many hours a week the person works. Justify why the hours are necessary and why the position cannot be done in fewer hours. In describing the history of the position, describe how the person in this position helps you achieve your department goals. Use data to explain the consequences of not replacing the position. Data include volume trends in your department, productivity measures, efficiency measures, and other department-specific measures that support your need for the position. If it's a part-time position, explain why you need to hire for the position rather than distribute the part-time hours among your current part-time employees. Provide a budget for this position that includes benefits (cost = salary × 40 percent). Describe consequences of not filling the position, keeping in mind that a lot of departments want to fill positions and that we allocate positions where they are most needed. If you include a potential applicant's name, give a brief summary of that person's qualifications. In making your case, stick with data and logic, not emotional appeals, your opinion, or claims you cannot back up with data.

4. Using a student group, company, nonprofit organization, or other organization, design a brochure for an event, product, or service. Then, write the text so that it would be appropriate for content on the organization's website. As your instructor directs, explain your design choices to your client or student group for the Web and print documents. When you write the Web document, be sure to think critically about which information appears on the page the reader sees and which information you will link to other pages.

5. You have recently assumed responsibility for assembling your company's team for a city-wide summer softball league. You inherited last year's form, and you don't want to use it in its current format. Redesign the form so that the layout, fonts, and visual elements conform to the principles of document design.

Cypress Electric Sypply

2019 Summer Softball League
Registration Form

It's time to sign up for the summer softball league. The teams are co-ed and open to all employees. Practices start on May 1, and we play on Tuesdays from June 4–August 6. No experience? No problem. We play for fun. It's a great way to relax, enjoy the summer, and get to know your colleagues. We are in a league with nine teams throughout the city.

Name: _____ Phone: _____

Address: _____ Email: _____

Emergency Contact: _____ Phone: _____

Fees: $20.00 per person   T-Shirt: $20.00 each

Grants are available to cover fees— Please note your confidential grant request and justify the need on your registration form or contact Rebecca directly.

Shirt Size (all are men's sizes): ___Sm ___Med ___L ___XL ___XXL ___XXXL

Volunteers needed.   Please consider helping us out! ALL TEAMS ARE REQUIRED TO HAVE AT LEAST ONE COACH AND ONE ASSISTANT COACH! The success of the team reflects the support given by our employees!!!!

****If we do not have coaches, we will not be able to play!!****

If you want to coach, check one: ___Coach   ___Assistant Coach

If you can't coach or play but want to sponsor a player, please donate: $_____

Please return Registration Form by Monday, April 15 to Rebecca Wilkins in the Accounting Department!

For more information, contact Rebecca Wilkins at Rebecca.wilkins@cypress.com or 715.123.4567.

Please note that when you turn in the form you will be required to sign a form releasing Cypress Electric from any liability associated with your participation.

---

6. Find a business website, letter, memo, report, brochure, or other document. As your instructor directs, write a letter report, memo report, or formal report to the company evaluating the document according to the principles of document design. Include a copy of or link to the original document. See Chapters 11 and 12 for more information on report writing.

Communicating with
Visuals

Chapter Four

Visuals are pervasive in today's media-rich society in both our work and leisure activities. We read and write documents and reports that include images; we hear and give presentations where the audience expects graphs and other visuals. Each day millions of people post or view images and videos on websites such as Instagram, Flickr, and YouTube. Additionally, other sites, such as LinkedIn SlideShare, are popular places for businesspeople to post professional slide shows that others can access and learn from. Visuals are even being used as search expressions with smartphone apps or Google.

This growing use of images for conveying information confirms that being visually literate is important not only to communicate effectively but also to communicate efficiently. One study at MIT found that people can process and retain the concepts in an image that they view for as little as 13 milliseconds;[1] people cannot process text at that same speed and will, in fact, comprehend less as their reading speed increases.[2] As you work through Chapter 4, you can also refer to the design principles covered in Chapter 3 to create visuals for your business documents. Chapter 4, along with Chapter 3, helps you see the importance of visual rhetoric in the problem-solving approach to business communication.

Visual rhetoric refers to the way the visual features of a message communicate. These features include not only photos, drawings, charts, graphs, and tables but also fonts, colors, the placement of text on a page, and even paragraph length and use of headings. It may seem like you're simply putting numbers in a table, demonstrating a trend in a chart, or getting an audience's attention, but every visual you choose tells your story and leaves the audience with an impression of you, your data, and your ideas. In other words, visuals are never neutral. Rather, they are as essential to communicating meaning and presenting a professional image as the words written in a document or spoken in a presentation.

In addition, as a consumer of visual information, you want to look critically at the visuals you encounter to ask what message is being conveyed and whether it is being conveyed clearly, accurately, and ethically.

Learning Objectives

LO4-1 Plan which parts of your document or presentation should be communicated or supported by visuals.

LO4-2 Explain the factors that are important in the effective presentation of visuals.

LO4-3 Select and use textual visuals such as tables, pull quotes, flowcharts, and organizational charts.

LO4-4 Select and use visuals such as bar charts, pie charts, line charts, scatter diagrams, pictographs, and maps.

LO4-5 Avoid common errors and ethical problems when constructing and using visuals.

LO4-6 Place and interpret visuals effectively.

Problem-Solving Challenge

Choosing the Right Visuals for Your Data and Your Audience

In your job as the sales manager for Green Living Industries, you are frequently called upon to gather data regarding your clients and their needs. You share these data with your employees as well as with your colleagues and corporate headquarters to support decisions that help achieve business goals.

In fact, you have just finished gathering data for a major report you will give orally and in writing to Green Living's upper management. These data include information on the makeup of your target markets, sales performance by division and geographic area, industry trends, and survey results on customer perceptions of your products. Although your primary audience is Green Living's upper management, you also know that these data will be used to inform decisions by managers at various district offices, sales staff, accountants, and others who develop budgets and plan the company's direction.

Essentially, you have a lot of information and several audiences who will use it. You need to think critically regarding how you will present this information so that your audiences quickly, clearly, and correctly understand what you are communicating. Because you have a lot of data, you know you will use several charts and graphs as well as text to communicate your information.

This chapter will present you with a variety of options for presenting data visually and help you make informed choices about the visuals you decide to use.

Planning the Visuals

LO4-1 Plan which parts of your document or presentation should be communicated or supported by visuals.

Your planning for visuals should be guided largely by your business and communication goals, and it should begin as soon as you have gathered your information. To determine whether you should use a visual, review your information to identify complex information, difficult information, and facts. You can also ask yourself how a visual will inform or persuade an audience and provide interest.

As you plan the visuals, remember that some can stand alone, but others will supplement the writing or speaking—not take its place. Visuals in documents or oral presentations should support your words by clarifying difficult concepts, emphasizing the important points, adding coherence, or summarizing data.

Constructing and Presenting Visuals

LO4-2 Explain the factors that are important in the effective presentation of visuals.

When constructing and presenting visuals, you can ensure clear communication and readability by following commonly accepted business conventions. The most common conventions are summarized in this section. Because many of these conventions are consistent with the principles for good design discussed in Chapter 3, you may want to review the information there as you work through this chapter.

Size

One of the first conventions to consider is size, which is determined by a visual's contents and importance. If a visual is simple (with only two or three quantities), a quarter page or less might be enough. If a visual must display complex or detailed information, a full page might be justified.

With extremely complex, involved information, you may need to use more than a full page. When you do, make certain that this large page is inserted and folded so that the readers can open it easily. You may also consider including large or complex visuals in an appendix or attachment.

Orientation

The size and contents also determine the **orientation** of a visual. Sometimes a tall orientation (**portrait**) is the answer; sometimes the answer is a wide orientation (**landscape**). For example, if you have a table with several columns or a bar chart that encompasses several years of data, you might find that the landscape orientation better accommodates the width of the visual. On the other hand if you have a table with several rows but few columns, you may find that the portrait orientation works better. To change the orientation in Microsoft Word 2016, go to Layout > Orientation.

Type

The type used in visuals throughout a report should generally be consistent in terms of **style and font**. Style refers to the look of the type such as bold or italics; font refers to the look of the letters (e.g., serif or sans serif). The size of your font should look appropriate in the context of the other elements in the visual and in your document or presentation and be easily readable.

Rules and Borders

Many businesspeople use **rules (lines) and borders** to improve the readability of the visual. Rules help distinguish one section or visual from another, while borders help separate visuals from the text. Keep in mind that rules can add clutter, so be sure to use them only when they will enhance the audience's understanding of your visual. When using borders, be sure to place them around visuals that occupy less than a full page so that your visual does not appear to be "floating" on the page. You also can place borders around full-page visuals, but these borders are usually more decorative than functional. Except in cases where visuals will not fit into the normal page layout, you should not extend the borders of visuals beyond the normal page margins.

Color and Cross-Hatching

Color and cross-hatching, appropriately used, help readers see comparisons and distinctions (Exhibit 4-1). Research has found that color in visuals improves the comprehension, retention, and extraction of information. Xerox cites research that says the use of color in business documents can increase comprehension by 78% and learning and retention by 73%.[3] Furthermore, color and cross-hatching can make your documents and presentations more attractive to your audience, which, of course, enhances your professional image.

Background

Background colors, photos, and art for your visuals should be chosen carefully. The color of your slides or paper should provide **high contrast** with your text and data and not distract from the main message. As with any photos or art, backgrounds should create a positive, professional impression. Additionally, when visuals are used cross culturally, you will want to be sure the message your background sends is the one you intended by testing or reviewing it with your audience.

Numbering

Pull quotes, clip art, and other decorative visuals do not need to be numbered. Neither does a lone table or figure in a document. All other visuals should be numbered. You can choose from a variety of numbering schemes, depending on the types of visuals you have.

If you have many visuals that fall into two or three categories, you may number each of the categories consecutively. For example, if your document is illustrated by six tables, five charts, and six maps, you may number these visuals Table 1, Table 2, . . . Table 6; Chart 1, Chart 2, . . . Chart 5; and Map 1, Map 2, . . . Map 6.

However, if your visuals comprise a wide mixture of types, you may number them in two groups: tables and figures. Figures include all visuals other than tables. To illustrate, consider a report containing three tables, two maps, three charts, one diagram, and one photograph. You would number these visuals Table 1, Table 2, and Table 3; and Figure 1, Figure 2, . . . Figure 7.

Whatever your numbering scheme, remember that each type of visual is labeled separately from other visuals. Thus, if you have tables, figures, and maps, the numbering for each type begins at 1.

Exhibit 4-1 Color versus Cross-Hatched Pie

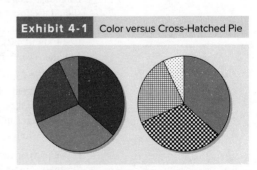

Source: Kathryn Rentz and Paula Lentz, *M: Business Communication* (New York: McGraw-Hill, 2014).

Construction of Titles and Captions

The **title** is the name you give your visual; a **caption** is a brief description of the visual. All visuals generally have titles; captions may be used if the reader will need them to interpret or better understand the visual.

Like the headings used in other parts of the report, the title or caption of the visual should concisely cover the visual's contents. As a check of content coverage, you might use the **five Ws**: *who, what, where, when,* and *why.* Sometimes you also might use *how.* Because conciseness is also important, you do not need to include all the Ws in the title. For example, the title of a chart comparing the annual sales volume of the Texas and California territories of the Dell Company for the years 2016–2020 might be constructed as follows:

Who:	Dell Company
What:	Annual sales
Where:	Texas and California branches
When:	2016–2020
Why:	For comparison

The title might read, "Comparative Annual Sales of Dell Company's Texas and California Territories, 2016–2020." For even more conciseness, you could use a major title and subtitle. The major title might read, "A Texas and California Sales Comparison"; the subtitle might read, "Dell Company 2016–2020." Similarly, the caption might read "A Texas and California Sales Comparison: Dell Company 2016–2020."

As you recall from Chapter 3, you want to use Microsoft Word's Insert Captions feature to number and title your visuals. Doing so lets you automatically generate a list of visuals for your table of contents, and Word will automatically renumber your visuals if you add or remove any. The section of Chapter 3 regarding parts of the report shows you how to use Microsoft Word to create titles for your visuals. You will notice that the defaults for visual titles are Tables, Figures, and Equations. You can use the New Label option if you are creating specific label types for a map, chart, or other visual.

Placement of Titles and Captions

You should place titles above tables. You can place titles either above or below other visuals, though it is most common to place titles above the visual. Captions, on the other hand, are generally placed below tables and other visuals to indicate descriptions, sources, or footnotes. When typing titles and captions, use **title case** (the kind of capitalization used for book titles). For long captions, you may opt to use **sentence case** (capitalization of the first word and any proper nouns).

Footnotes and Acknowledgments

Parts of a visual sometimes require special explanation or elaboration. When this happens, you should use **footnotes**. These footnotes are concise explanations placed below the illustration by means of a superscript (raised) number or symbol (asterisk, dagger, double dagger, and so on) (see Exhibit 4-2). Footnotes are placed immediately below a visual with no caption. If a visual contains a caption, the footnote is placed below the caption.

Usually, a **source acknowledgment** is the bottom-most component of a visual. A source acknowledgement refers to the person, group, or organization that deserves the credit for gathering the data used in the illustration. The entry consists of the word *Source* followed by a colon and the source information (in some cases, simply the source name will suffice). See Exhibit 4-2 for an illustration of source acknowledgment.

If you or your staff collected the data, you may either omit the source note or give the source as "Primary," in which case the note would read like this under your visual:

Source: Primary

Communication Matters

Telling Your Story with an Infographic

An **infographic** is essentially a visual that uses a mashup of text and several types of graphics to capture large amounts of data that tell one single story.

Researchers from Colorado State University say that effective infographics accomplish the following:

1. They tell a story that is relevant to the reader, actionable, and answers the five Ws.
2. They cite evidence-based research or other research-based data.
3. They group information logically and use visuals to present it in a way that appeals to the reader.
4. They are easily available to and accessible by their target audiences.

Infographic World refers to infographics as "visual shorthand" and cites research suggesting they are effective, in part, because they streamline and simplify the barrage of content people see every day. Further, their compact yet encompassing nature allows readers to easily share infographics online, causing many of them to go viral—a definite marketing advantage. Plus, the content of infographics can generally be linked to a company's site in order to improve a company's SEO (see Search Engine Optimization in Chapter 3).

Anna Mazereeuw says that infographics also present information in a way that is compatible with how we process visual information and promote better retention. If you visit the URL in the source information for "The Power of Push" infographic by Raconteur shown here, you'll see that you can interact with the infographic by hovering over specific content for an enlarged view.

You can search the Internet to locate many tools for creating infographics. You'll also see you can create beautiful data visualizations on widely varying topics—everything from survey results to résumés. Like any type of visual, an infographic is only useful if it looks professional and tells a story clearly and effectively. As in any business communication, you must analyze your audience, communication goals, and context to know if an infographic is appropriate.

Sources: Kelly Niebaum, Leslie Cunningham-Sabo, Jan Carroll, and Laura Bellows, "Infographics: An Innovative Tool to Capture Consumers' Attention," *Journal of Extension* 53 (2015): 2, accessed April 20, 2016, https://joe.org/joe/2015december/tt8.php; IGW, "How to Leverage Infographics for Your Business," *Infographic World,* September 25, 2015, accessed April 20, 2016, http://infographicworld.com/blogs/how-to-leverage-infographics/; Anna Mazereeuw, "Why Infographics Work," *LifeLearn,* May 12, 2015, accessed April 20, 2016, http://www.lifelearn.com/2015/05/12/why-infographics-work/; "The Power of Push Notifications," Raconteur Media, Ltd., 2015, accessed April 20, 2016, http://raconteur.net/infographics/the-power-of-push-notifications.

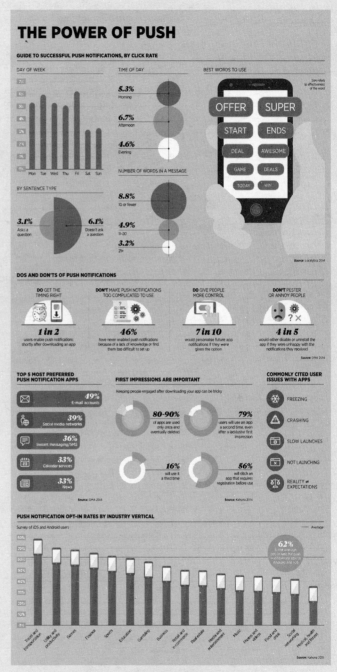

"The Power of Push Notifications," Raconteur, 2015. http://raconteur.net. All rights reserved. Used with permission.

Selecting and Using Textual Visuals

LO4-3 Select and use textual visuals such as tables, pull quotes, flowcharts, and organizational charts.

Visuals for communicating information fall into two general categories: those that communicate primarily through textual content (words and numerals) and those that communicate primarily through visual elements (charts and graphs). Included in the textual group are tables, pull quotes, and a variety of process charts such as flow charts and organizational charts.

Tables

A **table** is an orderly arrangement of information in rows and columns. Aside from the title, footnotes, and source, a table contains heads, columns, and rows of data, as shown in Exhibit 4-2. Row heads are the titles of the rows of data, and column heads are the titles of the columns.

Exhibit 4-2 Illustration of the Parts of a Table

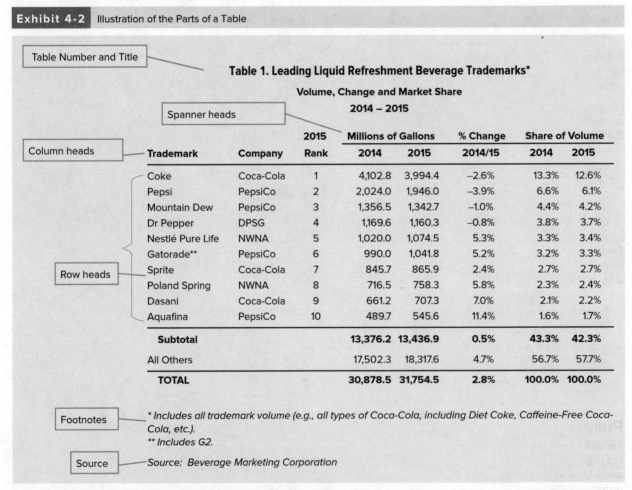

Table Number and Title

Table 1. Leading Liquid Refreshment Beverage Trademarks*

Volume, Change and Market Share
2014 – 2015

Spanner heads

Column heads / Row heads

Trademark	Company	2015 Rank	Millions of Gallons		% Change	Share of Volume	
			2014	2015	2014/15	2014	2015
Coke	Coca-Cola	1	4,102.8	3,994.4	–2.6%	13.3%	12.6%
Pepsi	PepsiCo	2	2,024.0	1,946.0	–3.9%	6.6%	6.1%
Mountain Dew	PepsiCo	3	1,356.5	1,342.7	–1.0%	4.4%	4.2%
Dr Pepper	DPSG	4	1,169.6	1,160.3	–0.8%	3.8%	3.7%
Nestlé Pure Life	NWNA	5	1,020.0	1,074.5	5.3%	3.3%	3.4%
Gatorade**	PepsiCo	6	990.0	1,041.8	5.2%	3.2%	3.3%
Sprite	Coca-Cola	7	845.7	865.9	2.4%	2.7%	2.7%
Poland Spring	NWNA	8	716.5	758.3	5.8%	2.3%	2.4%
Dasani	Coca-Cola	9	661.2	707.3	7.0%	2.1%	2.2%
Aquafina	PepsiCo	10	489.7	545.6	11.4%	1.6%	1.7%
Subtotal			**13,376.2**	**13,436.9**	**0.5%**	**43.3%**	**42.3%**
All Others			17,502.3	18,317.6	4.7%	56.7%	57.7%
TOTAL			**30,878.5**	**31,754.5**	**2.8%**	**100.0%**	**100.0%**

Footnotes

Includes all trademark volume (e.g., all types of Coca-Cola, including Diet Coke, Caffeine-Free Coca-Cola, etc.).
***Includes G2.**

Source

Source: Beverage Marketing Corporation

"Press Release: The U.S. Liquid Refreshment Beverage Marketing Enlarged in 2014, Reports Beverage Marketing Corporation," *Latest News,* March 25, 2015, accessed March 26, 2016, http://www.beveragemarketing.com/news-detail.asp?id=335

The construction of text tables is largely influenced by their purpose. Nevertheless, a few rules generally apply:

- If rows are long, the row heads may be repeated at the right side of the table.

- The em dash (—) or the abbreviation *n.a.* (or *N.A.* or *NA*), but not the zero, is used to indicate data not available.

- Because footnote numbers might be confusing in a table already full of numbers, footnote references to numbers in the table should be keyed with asterisks (*), daggers (†), double daggers (‡), section marks (§), and so on. Small letters of the alphabet can be used when many references are made.

- Totals and subtotals should appear whenever they help readers interpret the table. The totals may be for each column and sometimes for each row. Row totals are usually placed at the right, but when they need emphasis, they may be placed at the left. Likewise, column totals are generally placed at the bottom of the column, but they may be placed at the top when the writer wants to emphasize them. A ruled line (usually a double one) separates the totals from their components.

- The units used to represent the data must be clear. Unit descriptions (e.g., bushels, acres, pounds, dollars, or percentages) appear above the columns as part of the headings or subheadings. If the data are in dollars, however, placing the dollar mark ($) before the first entry in each column is usually sufficient.

Tabular information need not always be presented in formal tables. In fact, short tables of data may be presented more effectively as parts of the text. In these situations, rows and columns are organized with leaders or text tabulations.

Leaderwork is the presentation of tabular material in the text without titles or rules. **Leaders** are the repeated dots with intervening spaces. Typically, a colon precedes the tabulation, as in this illustration:

August sales of the representatives in the Western Region were as follows:

Micha Brown	$33,517
Courtney Capp	39,703
Chua Vue	38,198

Text tabulations are simple tables, usually with column heads and sometimes with rules and borders, but they are not numbered and they have no titles. They are made to read with the text, as in this example:

As these figures show, the August sales of the representatives in the Western Region increased sharply from those for the preceding month:

Representative	July Sales	August Sales	Increase
Micha Brown	$32,819	$33,517	$ 698
Courtney Capp	37,225	39,703	2,478
Chua Vue	36,838	38,198	1,360

Pull Quotes

The **pull quote** is a textual visual that is often overlooked yet extremely useful for emphasizing key points. It is also useful when the text or content of the report does not lend itself naturally or easily to other visuals. By selecting a key sentence, copying it to a text box, enlarging it, and perhaps even enhancing it with a new font, style, or color, you can break up the visual uniformity of a full page or screen of text. You can easily wrap text around shapes as well as along curves

From the Tech Desk

Using Pivot Tables and Charts in Microsoft Excel

Many times in business you will have a complex set of data that is not easily explained or organized in a traditional table or chart. Fortunately, Microsoft Excel offers you the option of pivot tables and charts to help you with this type of data.

To create a pivot table, you first arrange your data by category in columns and rows. Then go to the Insert ribbon and select Recommended Pivot Table. With this option Excel will generate a pivot table for you. From there, you can create a pivot chart by clicking in the table, selecting the Insert ribbon, and choosing a table from the Pivot Chart options.

These examples present monthly sales data for four sales territories over two years. In the data table, you can see most of the data for 2018. The table continues through 2019, resulting in a total of nearly 100 rows—that's a lot of data for a viewer to comprehend! A pivot table can let the viewer see all of this data in a variety of formats. In the pivot table and chart example, you can see how neatly the data are arranged in table, bar graph, and line chart formats.

Because the table and charts still contain a lot of data, you may want to limit how much data readers see by selecting various filters or by using the dropdown lists to show the data by month, year, sales, territory, or a combination thereof. In the table, you can expand or collapse lists by selecting the plus or minus sign. You can use the Design ribbon to format your table and your chart.

	A	B	C	D
1	Month	Year	Territory	Sales
2	January	2018	Northern	$ 154,895
3	January	2018	Southern	$ 365,415
4	January	2018	Eastern	$ 264,897
5	January	2018	Western	$ 225,489
6	February	2018	Northern	$ 264,958
7	February	2018	Southern	$ 348,957
8	February	2018	Eastern	$ 265,483
9	February	2018	Western	$ 156,485
10	March	2018	Northern	$ 295,648
11	March	2018	Southern	$ 213,455
12	March	2018	Eastern	$ 341,234
13	March	2018	Western	$ 178,956
14	April	2018	Northern	$ 246,132
15	April	2018	Southern	$ 215,634
16	April	2018	Eastern	$ 265,532
17	April	2018	Western	$ 111,454
18	May	2018	Northern	$ 444,121
19	May	2018	Southern	$ 225,643
20	May	2018	Eastern	$ 135,642
21	May	2018	Western	$ 225,645
22	June	2018	Northern	$ 235,641
23	June	2018	Southern	$ 332,216
24	June	2018	Eastern	$ 115,648
25	June	2018	Western	$ 223,654
26	July	2018	Northern	$ 215,643
27	July	2018	Southern	$ 221,564
28	July	2018	Eastern	$ 215,642
29	July	2018	Western	$ 663,125
30	August	2018	Northern	$ 456,123
31	August	2018	Southern	$ 486,521
32	August	2018	Eastern	$ 442,653
33	August	2018	Western	$ 332,156
34	September	2018	Northern	$ 221,564
35	September	2018	Southern	$ 556,432
36	September	2018	Eastern	$ 112,356
37	September	2018	Western	$ 225,645
38	October	2018	Northern	$ 228,745
39	October	2018	Southern	$ 421,435
40	October	2018	Eastern	$ 326,256
41	October	2018	Western	$ 235,645
42	November	2018	Northern	$ 223,546
43	November	2018	Southern	$ 226,548
44	November	2018	Eastern	$ 456,532
45	November	2018	Western	$ 221,556
46	December	2018	Northern	$ 584,659
47	December	2018	Southern	$ 221,564
48	December	2018	Eastern	$ 364,512
49	December	2018	Western	$ 232,156

Table of Data before Converting It to a Pivot Table and Chart

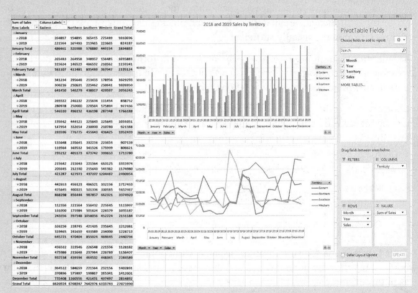

Table of Data Presented as a Pivot Table and Pivot Chart

Exhibit 4-3   Illustration of a Pull Quote

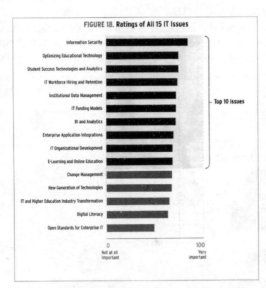

Top 10 IT Issues, 2016

FIGURE 18. Ratings of All 15 IT Issues

Information Security
Optimizing Educational Technology
Student Success Technologies and Analytics
IT Workforce Hiring and Retention
Institutional Data Management
IT Funding Models
BI and Analytics
Enterprise Application Integrations
IT Organizational Development
E-Learning and Online Education

Top 10 issues

Change Management
New Generation of Technologies
IT and Higher Education Industry Transformation
Digital Literacy
Open Standards for Enterprise IT

0
Not at all
important

100
Very
important

Managing, securing, and using data was common to 5 of this year's Top 10 IT issues:

1. Information Security
3. Student Success Technologies
5. Institutional Data Management
7. BI and Analytics
8. Enterprise Application Integrations

Data issues are pertinent to divestment, reinvestment, and differentiation. The data challenge of divestment is how to move away from local control in order to adopt institution-level data governance, standardization, and integration. Because data is critical to the ways in which institutions are hoping to achieve strategic differentiation—including student success, e-learning, and analytics—IT organizations need to reinvest in information security to secure this data, which is increasingly

important and increasingly at risk.

Securing, managing, and integrating data is foundational to achieving higher education's most strategic technology needs. The role of data will become only more important and differentiated over time. Analytics is being applied to numeric, text, image, and even video

data. However, data is only the fuel for the models and algorithms that will drive alerts, customizations, triggers, and other tools for personalized learning, student success services, and additional applications of analytics (e.g., to optimize resources, contain costs, improve service quality, increase productivity). Data is necessary and critical, but not sufficient, to produce analytics useful enough to inform decision making. Ultimately the models derived from data will prove to have more value than the data itself. In future years, the data concerns of higher education will likely extend to governing, securing, and optimizing analytic algorithms.

Leadership as the Multiplier

Again and again, the EDUCAUSE IT Issues Panel members emphasized the importance of leadership. If information technology is to have a meaningful impact, institutional leaders must be enduringly, enthusiastically, and publicly committed to investing in information technology and to accommodating institutional practices to IT solutions. IT leaders are masters of the workaround: they know how to adapt, pivot, and make do in the face of roadblocks and setbacks. But there are no workarounds for tepid or reluctant leadership.

Information technology is now embedded in every institutional activity and mission. IT organizations can accomplish little on their own.

> "IT professionals should adopt the perspective, culture, values, and language of a business professional and frame their work within this context. Once viewed as a business professional in their own right, managing change within the broader community of end users becomes much, much easier."
>
> —Timothy M. Chester, Vice President for Information Technology, University of Georgia

58 EDUCAUSEreview JANUARY/FEBRUARY 2016

and irregular lines. Exhibit 4-3 shows an example that is simple yet effective in both drawing the reader's attention to a key point and adding visual interest to a page.

Bulleted or Numbered Lists

Bulleted lists are listings of points arranged with bullets (•) to set them off. **Numbered lists** are also listings of points, but their numbered order means that the order of the items is important (e.g., a series of steps that must be done sequentially). These lists can have a title that covers all

You Make the Call

Can a document contain too many lists? Is it possible for lists to be distracting?

the points, or they can appear without titles. When you use these arrangements, make the points grammatically parallel. If the points have subparts, use **sub-bullets or numbers** for them. Make the sub-bullets or numbers distinct (e.g., different by color, size, shape, or weight or using "a, b, c" instead of numbers).

Flowcharts and Process Charts

Business professionals use a variety of specialized charts in their work. Often these charts are a part of the information presented in reports. Perhaps the most common of these is the **organizational chart** (Exhibit 4-4). This type of chart shows the hierarchy of levels and positions in an

| Exhibit 4-4 | Illustration of an Organizational Chart |

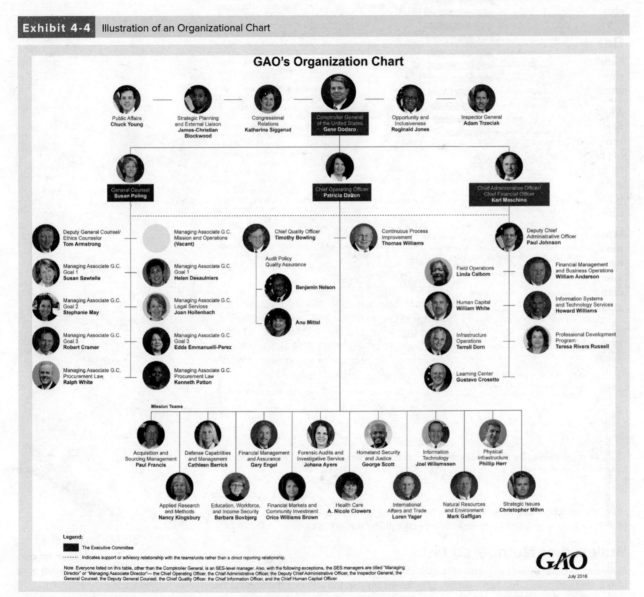

Source: U.S. Government Accountability Office, "The Government Accountability Office Organization Chart," accessed November 25, 2016, http://www.gao.gov/about/workforce/orgchart.html.

organization. A **flowchart** (Exhibit 4-5), as the word implies, shows the sequence of activities in a process. Flowcharts use specific designs and symbols to show possible process paths. A variation of the organization and flowchart is the **decision tree**, which helps people follow a path to an appropriate decision. See Chapter 2 for suggestions on constructing these charts.

Selecting and Using Charts, Graphs, and Other Visuals

Visuals built with raw data include bar, pie, and line charts and all their variations and combinations. Illustrations include maps, diagrams, drawings, pictographs, and photos.

Bar and Column Charts

Simple bar and **column charts** compare differences in quantities using differences in the lengths of the bars to represent those quantities. You should use them primarily to show comparisons of qualities or quantities side by side.

As shown in Exhibit 4-6, the main parts of the bar chart are the bars and the grid (the field on which the bars are placed). The bars, which may be arranged horizontally or vertically (then called a column chart), should be of equal width. You should identify each bar or column, usually with a caption at the left or bottom. The grid (field) on which the bars are placed is usually needed to show the magnitudes of the bars, and the units (e.g., dollars, pounds, miles) are identified by the scale caption below. It is often a good idea to include the numerical value represented by each bar for easy and precise comprehension.

When you need to compare quantities of two or three different values in one chart, you can use a **clustered (or multiple) bar chart**. Cross-hatching, colors, or other formatting on the bars distinguish the different kinds of information (Exhibit 4-7). Somewhere within the chart, a **legend** explains what the different bars mean. Because clustered bar charts can become cluttered, you should usually limit comparisons to not more than three kinds of information in one of them.

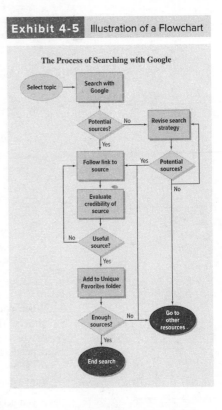

Exhibit 4-5 Illustration of a Flowchart

The Process of Searching with Google

LO4-4 Select and use visuals such as bar charts, pie charts, line charts, scatter diagrams, pictographs, and maps.

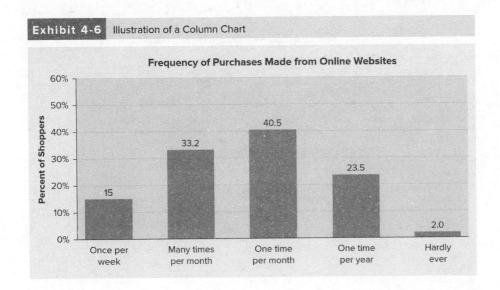

Exhibit 4-6 Illustration of a Column Chart

Frequency of Purchases Made from Online Websites

Percent of Shoppers

- Once per week: 15
- Many times per month: 33.2
- One time per month: 40.5
- One time per year: 23.5
- Hardly ever: 2.0

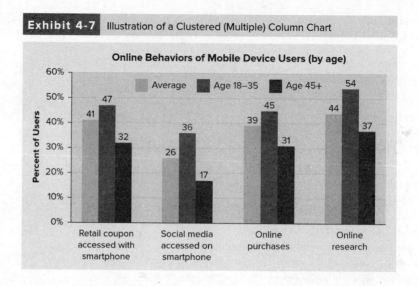

Exhibit 4-7 Illustration of a Clustered (Multiple) Column Chart

When you need to show plus and minus differences, you can use **bilateral bar or column charts**. The bars of these charts begin at a central point of reference and may go either up or down, as illustrated in Exhibit 4-8. Bar titles appear either within, above, or below the bars, depending on which placement works best. Bilateral bar or column charts are especially good for showing percentage changes, but you may use them for any series that includes plus and minus quantities.

If you need to compare subdivisions of bars, you can use a **stacked (subdivided) bar or column chart**. As shown in Exhibit 4-9, such a chart divides each column into its parts. It distinguishes these parts with color, cross-hatching, or other formatting; and it explains these differences in a legend. Subdivided bars may be difficult for your reader to interpret since both the beginning and ending points need to be found. Then the reader has to subtract to find the size of the bar component. Clustered bar charts or pie charts avoid this possibility for error.

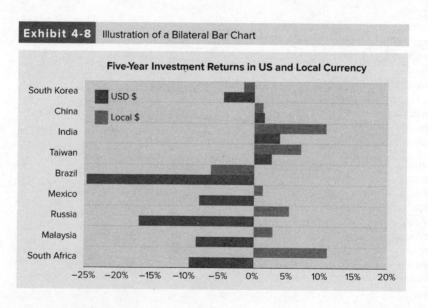

Exhibit 4-8 Illustration of a Bilateral Bar Chart

Exhibit 4-9 Illustration of a Stacked Column Chart

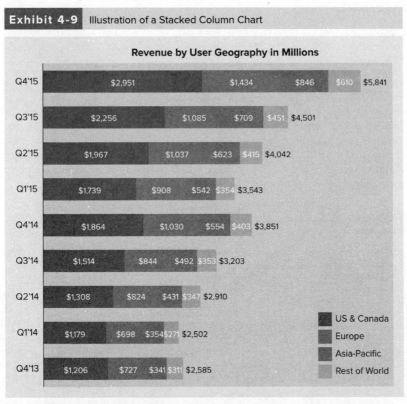

Exhibit 4-9 Illustration of a Stacked Column Chart

Revenue by User Geography in Millions

	US & Canada	Europe	Asia-Pacific	Rest of World	Total
Q4'15	$2,951	$1,434	$846	$610	$5,841
Q3'15	$2,256	$1,085	$709	$451	$4,501
Q2'15	$1,967	$1,037	$623	$415	$4,042
Q1'15	$1,739	$908	$542	$354	$3,543
Q4'14	$1,864	$1,030	$554	$403	$3,851
Q3'14	$1,514	$844	$492	$353	$3,203
Q2'14	$1,308	$824	$431	$347	$2,910
Q1'14	$1,179	$698	$354	$271	$2,502
Q4'13	$1,206	$727	$341	$311	$2,585

Source: Jillian D'Onfro, "Facebook Explodes on Q4 Earnings Beat," *Business Insider,* January 26, 2016, accessed March 10, 2016, http://www.businessinsider.com/facebook-2015-q4-earnings-2016-1.

Another feature that can lead to reader error in interpreting bar or column chart data is the use of three dimensions when only two variables are being compared. Therefore, unless more than two variables are used, choosing the two-dimensional presentation over the three-dimensional form is usually better. (Later in this section, Exhibit 4-19 illustrates the appropriate use of a three-dimensional visual to compare three dimensions.)

A special form of stacked (subdivided) bar or column chart is used to compare the subdivisions of percentages. In this form, all the bars are equal in length because each represents 100%. Only the subdivisions within the bars vary. The objective of this form is to compare differences in how wholes are divided. The component parts may be labeled, as in Exhibit 4-10, or explained in a legend.

Exhibit 4-10 Illustration of a 100% Stacked Bar Chart

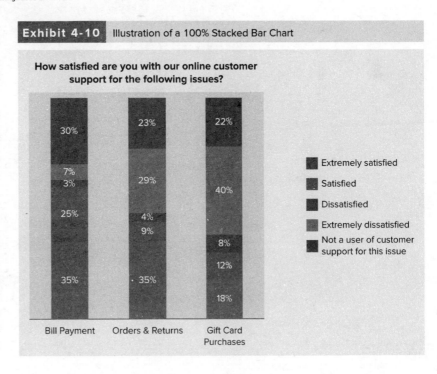

How satisfied are you with our online customer support for the following issues?

Legend:
- Extremely satisfied
- Satisfied
- Dissatisfied
- Extremely dissatisfied
- Not a user of customer support for this issue

	Bill Payment	Orders & Returns	Gift Card Purchases
	30%	23%	22%
	7%	29%	40%
	3%		
	25%	4%	8%
		9%	12%
	35%	35%	18%

Pictographs

A **pictograph** is a bar or column chart that uses bars made of pictures. The pictures are typically icons of the items being compared. For example, in Exhibit 4-11 each picture represents approximately 10 women.

In constructing a pictograph, you should follow the procedures you used in constructing bar and column charts. In addition, you must make all the picture units equal in size. The human eye cannot accurately compare geometric designs that vary in more than one dimension, so show differences by varying the number, not the size, of the picture units. Also, be sure you select pictures or symbols that fit the information you are illustrating. In comparing the cruise lines of the world, for example, you might use ships. In comparing computers used in the world's major countries, you might use computers. The meaning of the picture or symbol you use must be immediately clear to the readers.

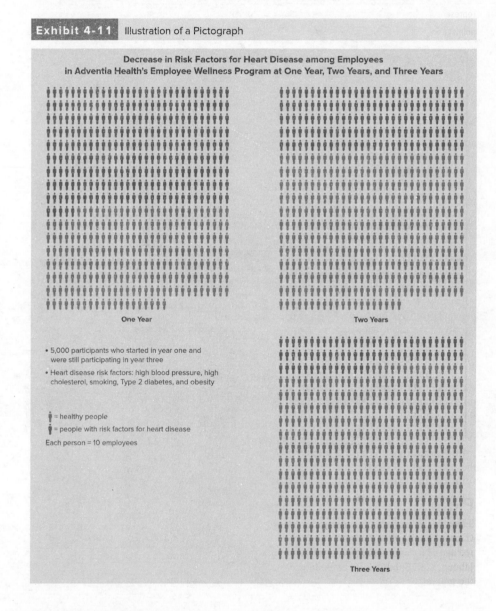

Exhibit 4-11 Illustration of a Pictograph

Decrease in Risk Factors for Heart Disease among Employees in Adventia Health's Employee Wellness Program at One Year, Two Years, and Three Years

One Year

Two Years

Three Years

- 5,000 participants who started in year one and were still participating in year three
- Heart disease risk factors: high blood pressure, high cholesterol, smoking, Type 2 diabetes, and obesity

= healthy people
= people with risk factors for heart disease
Each person = 10 employees

Using Pictures to Chart Data in Excel

Pictographs (see Exhibit 4-11) represent data by assigning a number or data point to each picture or icon in the visual. Similarly, Excel allows you to use pictures as data points in the visuals you create. However, unlike the pictures in a pictograph, the pictures in an Excel chart may not necessarily represent a discrete number or represent a data point; they may be only decorative like the scales of justice in the example here. Nevertheless, as long as your data are clear, using pictures to chart data can make your visuals interesting and meaningful to your audience.

To create visuals in Excel such as the chart depicting law school enrollment,

1. Create a table of data.
2. Select the table.
3. From the Insert ribbon > Charts menu, select the Bar Charts option to create a 2-D bar chart.
4. Double click one of the bars in your chart.
5. From the Format Data Series box, select Fill (the paint bucket).
6. Select Picture or Texture Fill.
7. Insert a picture.
8. Select Stack.

Readability Statistics

Counts

Words	1625
Characters	7716
Paragraphs	30
Sentences	85

Averages

Sentences per Paragraph	3.8
Words per Sentence	18.5
Characters per Word	4.5

Source: Microsoft Excel 2016.

Pie Charts

The most frequently used chart in comparing the subdivisions of a whole is the **pie chart** (Exhibit 4-12). As the name implies, pie charts show the whole of the information being studied as a pie and the parts of this whole as slices of the pie. The slices may be distinguished by labeling and color or cross-hatching. A single slice can be emphasized by pulling it out from the pie or enlarging it. Because the exact values of the slices may not be readily evident, it is

Exhibit 4-12 Illustration of a Pie Chart

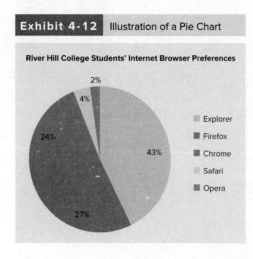

River Hill College Students' Internet Browser Preferences

- Explorer
- Firefox
- Chrome
- Safari
- Opera

good to include the percentage values within or near each slice. Some businesspeople will also put labels next to each piece rather than in a legend when doing so makes the data clearer. A good rule to follow for ordering the pieces of the pie is to begin by slicing the largest piece at the 12 o'clock position and then ordering the pieces largest to smallest; however, you should order the pieces in the way that will make the most visual sense to your audience.

Line Charts

Line charts are useful for showing trends or changes in information over time such as changes in prices, sales totals, employment, or production over a period of years.

In constructing a line chart, you represent data in a continuous line on a grid that is scaled to show time changes from left to right (the X-axis) and quantity changes from bottom to top (the Y-axis). You should clearly mark the scale values and the time periods in equal increments.

You also may compare two or more series on the same line chart (see Exhibit 4-13). In such a comparison, you should clearly distinguish the lines by color or form (e.g., dots or dashes). You should also label them on the chart or with a legend somewhere in the chart. The number of series that you can effectively compare on one line chart is limited. As a practical guide, the maximum number is three to five.

Line charts that show a range of data for particular times are called *variance* or *hi-lo* charts. Some variance charts show high and low points as well as the mean, median, or mode. When used to chart daily stock prices, they typically include closing price in addition to the high and low.

It is also possible to show parts of a series using an **area** chart. Such a chart, though, can show only one series. You should construct this type of chart, as shown in Exhibit 4-14, with a top line representing the total of the series. Then, starting from the base, you should stack the

Exhibit 4-13 Illustration of a Line Chart

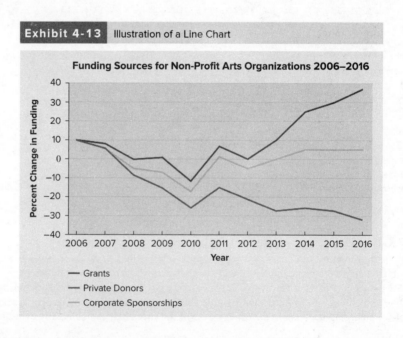

Funding Sources for Non-Profit Arts Organizations 2006–2016

- Grants
- Private Donors
- Corporate Sponsorships

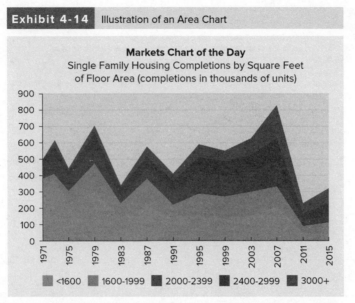

Exhibit 4-14 Illustration of an Area Chart

Markets Chart of the Day
Single Family Housing Completions by Square Feet
of Floor Area (completions in thousands of units)

Legend: <1600, 1600-1999, 2000-2399, 2400-2999, 3000+

Source: Miles Udland, "America Isn't Building Enough Homes for First-Time Buyers," *Business Insider*, May 22, 2016, accessed November 25, 2016, http://www.businessinsider.com/single-family-housing-completions-by-square-foot-2016-3.

parts, beginning with the largest and ending with the smallest or beginning with the smallest and ending with the largest. You may use cross-hatching or coloring to distinguish the parts.

Scatter Diagrams

Scatter diagrams are often considered a variation of the line chart. Although they do use X- and Y-axes to plot paired values, the points stand alone without a line drawn through them. For example, you might use a scatter diagram in a report on digital cameras to plot values for price and resolution of several cameras. While clustering the points allows users to validate hunches about cause and effect, they can only be interpreted for correlation—the direction and strength relationships as positive, negative, or nonexistent. Additionally, by examining the tightness of the points, the user can see the strength of the relationship. The closer the points are to a straight line, the stronger the relationship. In Exhibit 4-15, the paired values are insurance premium cost increases and number of accidents.

Maps

You also may use maps to communicate quantitative as well as physical or geographic information. **Statistical maps** are useful primarily when quantitative information is to be compared by geographic areas. On such maps, the geographic areas are clearly outlined, and formatting techniques are used to show the differences between areas (Exhibit 4-16). Statistical maps are particularly useful in illustrating and analyzing complex data.

Of the numerous formatting techniques available to you for statistical maps, these are the most common:

- Showing different areas with color, shading, or cross-hatching. Maps using this technique must have a legend to explain the quantitative meanings of the various colors or cross-hatchings.

- Placing visuals, symbols, or clip art within each geographic area to depict the quantity for that area or geographic location.

- Placing the quantities in numerical form within each geographic area.

Exhibit 4-15 Illustration of a Scatter Diagram

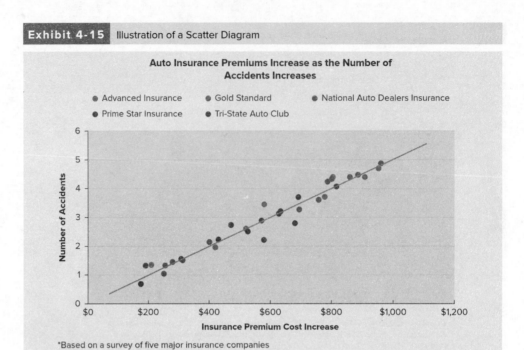

Auto Insurance Premiums Increase as the Number of Accidents Increases

- Advanced Insurance
- Gold Standard
- National Auto Dealers Insurance
- Prime Star Insurance
- Tri-State Auto Club

*Based on a survey of five major insurance companies
*Assumes the company's insured driver is at fault

Exhibit 4-16 Illustration of a Map (Quantitative)

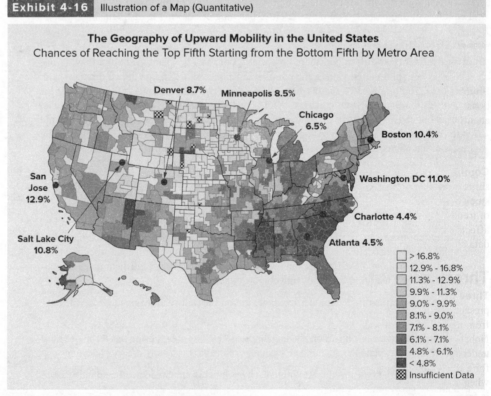

The Geography of Upward Mobility in the United States
Chances of Reaching the Top Fifth Starting from the Bottom Fifth by Metro Area

Denver 8.7% Minneapolis 8.5%
Chicago 6.5%
Boston 10.4%
San Jose 12.9%
Washington DC 11.0%
Salt Lake City 10.8%
Charlotte 4.4%
Atlanta 4.5%

- > 16.8%
- 12.9% - 16.8%
- 11.3% - 12.9%
- 9.9% - 11.3%
- 9.0% - 9.9%
- 8.1% - 9.0%
- 7.1% - 8.1%
- 6.1% - 7.1%
- 4.8% - 6.1%
- < 4.8%
- Insufficient Data

Source: Raj Chetty, Nathaniel Hendren, Patrick Kline, and Emmanuel Saez, "Where Is the Land of Opportunity? The Geography of Intergenerational Mobility in the United States," *Quarterly Journal of Economics* 29 no. 4 (2014): 1553–1623. Map on page 36 of the Appendix. Reprinted with permission of the author.

Exhibit 4-17   Illustration of a Map (Physical)

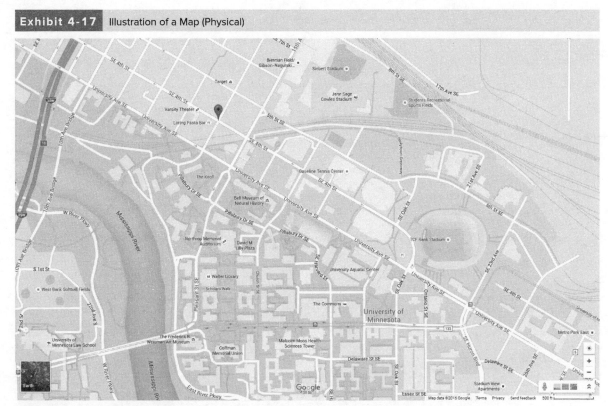

Google and the Google logo are registered trademarks of Google Inc., used with permission.

Physical or geographic maps (Exhibit 4-17) can show distributions as well as specific locations. Colors, icons, and labels for streets or landmarks are frequently used to call the reader's attention to specific locations on the map.

Combination Charts

Combination charts often serve readers extremely well by allowing them to see relationships of different kinds of data. The example in Exhibit 4-18 shows the reader the price of stock over time (the trend), the volume of sales (comparisons), and the MACD (an indicator of trends in stock performance). It allows the reader to detect whether the change in volume affects the price of the stock. This kind of information would be difficult to get from raw data alone.

Three-Dimensional Visuals

Three-dimensional graphs can be useful when you have three or more variables. Many times, presenting these variables in three dimensions is an option for helping your readers see the data from multiple perspectives and gain additional information. In fact, Francis Crick, who won a Nobel prize for discovering the structure of DNA, once revealed that he and his collaborators understood the configuration of DNA only when they took a sheet of paper, cut it, and twisted it for a three-dimensional view. Keep in mind that three-dimensional visuals are most effective when you have at least three variables; using three-dimensional visuals with only two variables is frequently unnecessary in helping the reader see the data from multiple perspectives and in some cases may be visually confusing.

Exhibit 4-18   Illustration of a Combination Chart

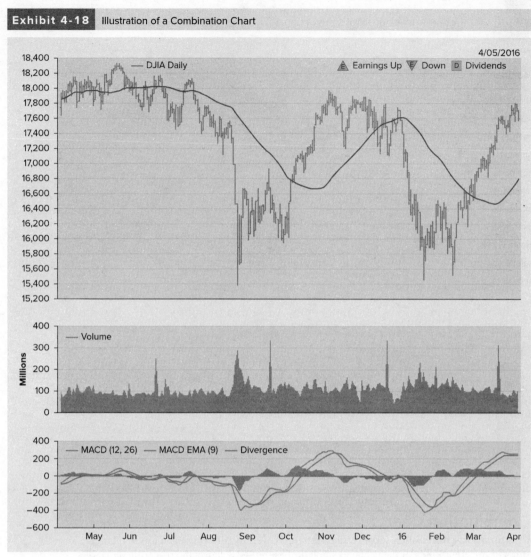

4/05/2016

Source: Market Watch, "Dow Jones Industrial Average," April 7, 2016, accessed April 8, 2016, http://www.marketwatch.com/investing/index/djia/charts.

Exhibit 4-19 shows a three-dimensional visual plot of factors identified as the major ones consumers use when deciding which laptop computer to purchase. Five products are plotted on three variables: cost, battery life, and weight. This visual could help a company identify its major competitors and help consumers identify those products that are best suited to their needs. The more products or data that are plotted, the more valuable the graph is at helping the reader extract meaning. If these data had been displayed on a two-dimensional graph, the lines would have overlapped too much to be distinguishable, thus requiring you to accompany this visual with a table, enable the reader to rotate the visual, or both in order to make the data clear.

In deciding whether to use a three- or a two-dimensional representation, you need to consider your audience, the context, and the goal of your communication. Overall, multidimensional presentation on paper is difficult; multiple representations can be made from separate two-dimensional views but not always effectively. Moreover, if the three-dimensional visual is being presented online or digitally where the reader can rotate it to see perspectives, it is likely to be much more effective.

From the Tech Desk

Making the Most of Excel

Microsoft Excel presents exciting options for data visualization—and the best part is that you don't have to know a lot about Excel to use them. Among other things, Excel 2016 suggests visuals appropriate for your data, provides numerous templates to ensure your data look sharp, and offers a Quick Analysis feature, which, as its name indicates, lets you quickly calculate data and create visuals. A sample of a template and color palette options, and the Quick Analysis feature, appears here.

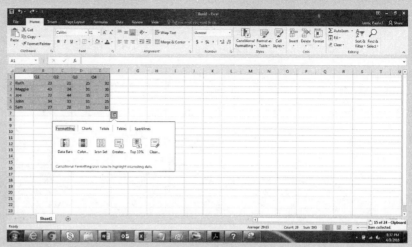

Source: Microsoft Excel 2016.

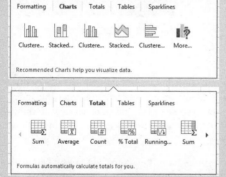

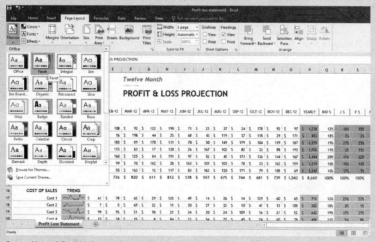

Source: Microsoft Excel 2016.

Exhibit 4-19

Illustration of a Three-Dimensional Visual

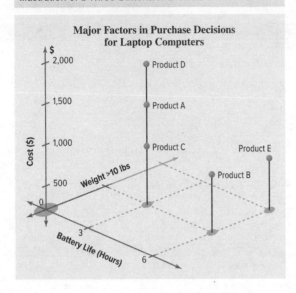

Exhibit 4-20 Illustration of a Photo

© Shutterstock/belkos

Photographs

Cameras are everywhere today, enabling anyone to capture images. Royalty-free photos intended for commercial use are readily available on the Internet, too. Many businesspeople use photos to document events as well as to show products, processes, or services. Exhibit 4-20 illustrates how a photo creates a message. What does the context created by the split image (half fall/half summer) suggest to you?

Photos can be found easily, but you must follow copyright laws when using them. If a photo is not specifically released into the public domain, you should seek permission to use the photo in addition to citing the source of the photo.

Clip Art

Today you can get attractive clip art easily—so easily, in fact, that some writers often overuse it. Although clip art can add interest and bring the reader into a visual effectively, it also can overpower and distract the reader. The general rule is to keep in mind the purpose your clip art should serve: to help the reader understand the content. It should be appropriate in both its nature and size; and it should be appropriate in its representation of gender, race, age, and any other demographic considerations. Clip art, like photos, may have copyrights attached, so be sure to seek permission before using it in your business documents.

Other Visuals

The types of visuals discussed thus far are the ones most commonly used in business. Other types also may be helpful. **Diagrams** (Exhibit 4-21) and drawings may help simplify a complicated explanation or description. **Icons** are visuals that capture a command, action, or concept. Computer programs frequently use them, for example, to indicate Save or Print. You can create new icons, or you can select one from an existing body of icons with easily recognized meanings, such as Ø. Even carefully selected **cartoons** can be used effectively. **Video clips** and

You Make the Call

Can you provide an example of when it would be appropriate to use clip art in a business document?

LO4-5 Avoid common errors and ethical problems when constructing and using visuals.

animation are now used in many electronic documents. For all practical purposes, any visual is acceptable as long as it helps communicate the intended story.

Visual Integrity

In writing a business document, you are ethically bound to present data and visuals in ways that enable readers to interpret them easily and accurately. By being aware of some of the common errors made in presenting visuals, you learn how to avoid them and how to spot them in other documents. Keep in mind that any errors—deliberate or not—compromise your credibility, casting doubt on the document as well as on other work you have completed. Therefore, you need to ensure that visuals accurately and honestly represent the data they contain.

Exhibit 4-21 Illustration of a Diagram

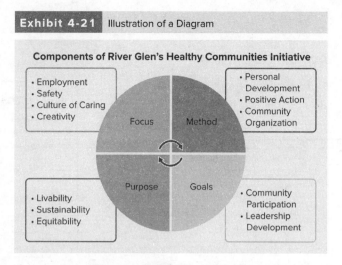

Components of River Glen's Healthy Communities Initiative

- Employment
- Safety
- Culture of Caring
- Creativity

Focus   Method

- Personal Development
- Positive Action
- Community Organization

Purpose   Goals

- Livability
- Sustainability
- Equitability

- Community Participation
- Leadership Development

Avoiding Errors in Graphing Data   Common graphing errors are errors of scale and errors of format. Another category of error is inaccurate or misleading presentation of context.

Errors of scale occur whenever the dimensions from left to right (X-axis) or bottom to top (Y-axis) are unequal. Three sources of scale errors include no uniform scale size, scale distortion, and beginning at a point other than zero.

No uniform scale size occurs when intervals in data points on the X- or Y-axis are not consistent. Determining the distances that present the most accurate picture is a matter of judgment, but note in these graphs how the unequal intervals on the Y-axis in the second graph create a different presentation of the data:

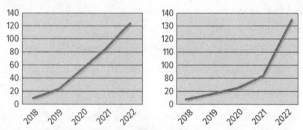

Source: Kathryn Rentz and Paula Lentz, *M: Business Communication* (New York: McGraw-Hill, 2014).

Scale distortion occurs when a visual is stretched excessively horizontally or vertically to change the meaning it conveys to the reader. Notice the different looks of these visuals when they are stretched vertically and horizontally:

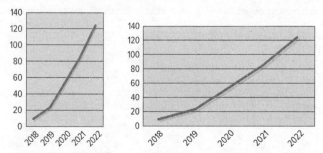

Source: Kathryn Rentz and Paula Lentz, *M: Business Communication* (New York: McGraw-Hill, 2014).

Avoiding Chartjunk

Edward Tufte, a pioneer and leading expert in data visualization, invented the term *chartjunk* to refer to any elements in a visual that are either unnecessary or irrelevant to the reader's understanding of the data or that impede or distract from a reader's ability to understand the data.

Technology enables business communicators to incorporate many features (e.g., colors, lines, images) into their visuals—some that will enhance a visual's message and some that will not. Charley Kyd from the ExcelUsers blog explains that the distinction between visual elements that enhance a visual versus those that are chartjunk is the extent to which visual elements make the reader work to understand the information.

To illustrate, Kyd presents variations on the same visual about Juicy sales. The one on the left contains chartjunk; the one on the right is Kyd's rendering of the visual minus the chartjunk.

Kyd acknowledges that neither visual makes the data impossible to understand; what makes

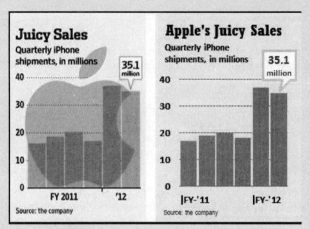

Reprinted with permission of Charley Kyd, ExcelUser.com.

the elements chartjunk in the visual on the left is that the visual elements "act as noise where your readers need silence." That is, the shape of the bite in the apple appears to alter the shape of the bars in the chart, making the reader look twice to see that the bars, indeed, retain their shape. Is this a lot of work for the reader? No, but why make your reader work at

all? When you create visuals, just as when you create text, all elements should be immediately clear.

Sources: Charley Kyd, "Oh, No! Chart Junk from *The Wall Street Journal*," *ExcelUser Blog: Insight for Business Users of Microsoft Excel*, May 12, 2012, accessed April 20, 2016, http://www.exceluser.com/blog/1152/oh-no-chart-junk-from-the-wall-street-journal.html; Jessica E. Vascellaro and Ian Sherr, "Apple Rides iPhone Frenzy: Quarterly Profit Nearly Doubles as Tech Giant Taps China, New Markets," *The Wall Street Journal*, April 24, 2012.

Finally, another type of scale error is the **missing zero beginning** of the series. For accuracy you should begin the scale at zero. But when all the information shown in the chart has high or low values, it is awkward to show the entire scale from zero to the highest value. For example, if the quantities compared range from 1,320 to 1,350 and the chart shows the entire area from zero to 1,350, the line showing these quantities would be almost straight and very high on the chart. Your solution in this case is not to begin the scale at a high number (say 1,300), which would distort the information, but to begin at zero and show a scale break. Realize, however, that while this makes the differences easier to see, it does exaggerate them. You can see this effect here:

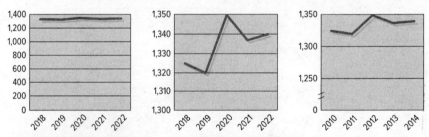

Source: Kathryn Rentz and Paula Lentz, *M: Business Communication* (New York: McGraw-Hill, 2014).

Computer applications enable writers to easily create a wide variety of visuals from small to huge data sets.

© Sebnem Ragiboglu/123RF

Occasionally, though, a writer needs to use good judgment when the guides for starting at the zero point are not practical. For example, Exhibit 4-22 compares race times of three runners, all of whom have times that cluster in the 14- to 17-second range. Beginning the time scale at zero would hinder the reader's interpretation of the information. In this context, presenting the data at a scale that begins at 14 efficiently presents the data while maintaining integrity.

Exhibit 4-22   Illustration of a Line Graph That Considers Context

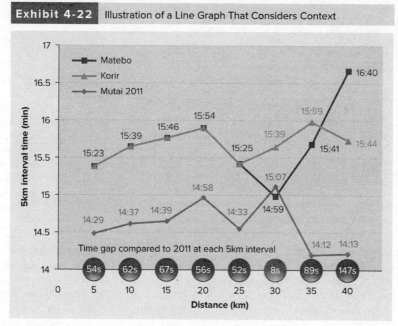

Communication Matters

The Periodic Table of Visualization Methods

This chapter presents many of the most common options for using visuals to present your text and data. The Periodic Table of Visualization Methods provides an array of many other possibilities to help you choose the best visual as well. To see your options, just visit the website www.visual-literacy.org/periodic_table/periodic_table.html, move your mouse over any of the visual types, and view the example that appears. As you view the many creative options, you may be tempted to choose a visual format based on its novelty rather than its functionality. Remember, though, that the main purpose of any visual is to communicate. Choose wisely. You want your visuals to look good, but more importantly you want them to be appropriate for your message.

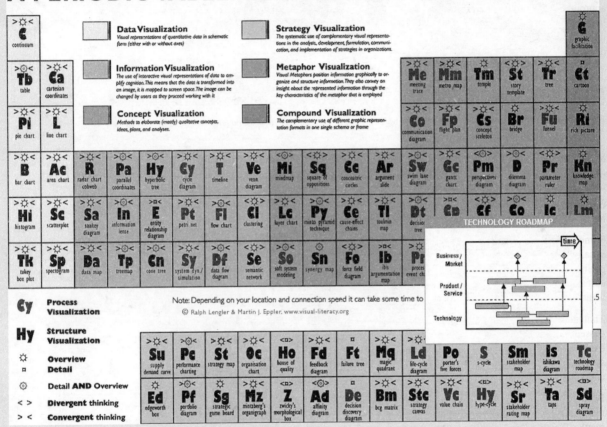

Source: Ralph Lengler and Martin J. Eppler, "Periodic Table of Visual Elements," *Visual-Literacy.org*, accessed October 28, 2016, http://www.visual-literacy.org/periodic_table/periodic_table.html.

Errors of format come in a wide variety. Some of the more common ones are choice of wrong chart type, distracting use of grids and shading, misuse of typeface, and problems with labels. For example, if a company used pie charts to compare expenses from one year to the next, readers might be tempted to draw conclusions that would be inappropriate because, although the pies would both represent 100% of the expenses, the size of the business and the expenses may have grown or shrunk drastically in a year's time. If one piece of the pie is colored or shaded in such a way as to make it stand out from the others, it could mislead readers. And, of course, small type or unlabeled, inconsistently labeled, or inappropriately labeled visuals confuse readers.

Avoiding Other Ethical Problems Another ethical challenge is accounting for the context. For example, as we have discussed, the number and size of visuals should be proportionate to the importance of the topic and appropriate for the emphasis a topic deserves.

Using visuals presents other ethical issues to consider. One issue in particular is the appropriate selection of the content. Are people or things over- or underrepresented? Are the numbers of men and women appropriate for the context? Are their ages appropriate? Is ethnicity represented appropriately? Have colors been used appropriately and not to evoke or manipulate emotions? To avoid these ethical issues, you will need to select and design visuals carefully to maintain integrity.

Placing and Interpreting the Visuals

For the best effect, you should place each visual near the place where you discuss it. Exactly where on the page you should place it, however, should be determined by its size. If the visual is small, you should place it within the text that discusses it. If it is a full page, you should place it on the page following the first reference to the information it covers.

Some writers like to place all visuals at the end of a document, usually in the appendix. This arrangement may save time in preparing the document, but it makes the readers' task more difficult because they have to flip through pages every time they want to see a visual. Therefore, be sure to place visuals where they are most helpful to readers.

That said, sometimes you may have a visual that is necessary for completeness but is not discussed in the document (e.g., screen captures of an online survey on which your report data are based). Or you may have summary charts or tables that apply to the entire document but to no specific place in it. When such visuals are appropriate, you should place them in an appendix, and you should refer to the appendix at an appropriate point in the document.

Because visuals communicate most effectively when the readers view them at the right point in their reading, you should tell the readers when to look at a visual and what to look for. Of the many wordings used for this purpose, these are the most common:

As Figure 4 shows, ...

. . . , indicated in Figure 4, ...

. . . , as a glance at Figure 4 reveals, ...

. . . (see Figure 4) . . . .

If your visual is carrying the primary message, as in a detailed table, you can just refer the reader to the information in the visual: "As Table 1 illustrates, our increased sales over the last three years. . . ." No further explanation or discussion may be necessary.

Communication Matters

Practicing Visual Ethics

As you have learned in this chapter, visuals can serve several useful purposes for the business writer. However, the writer needs to be accountable in using visuals to present images that in the eye and mind of the reader communicate accurately and completely. To do this, the careful writer pays attention to both the design and content of the visual. These are particularly important, for readers often skim text but read the visuals. Research shows that people remember images much better and longer than text.

Donna Kienzler offers the following guides to help you evaluate the visuals you use:

- Does the visual's design create accurate expectations?
- Does the story told match the data?
- Is the implied message congruent with the actual message?
- Will the impact of the visual on your audience be appropriate?
- Does the visual convey all critical information free of distortion?
- Are the data depicted accurately?

We would also add that ethical use of visuals requires you to cite the source of any data that you did not produce. In addition, you must get permission to use visuals that you do not create or own—including those found through Web searches.

Adapted from Donna Kienzler, "Visual Ethics," *Journal of Business Communication* 34 (1997): 171–187.

You Make the Call
Your boss has asked you to present data in a way that you think is not honest. How would you handle the situation?

LO4-6 Place and interpret visuals effectively.

However, sometimes the visual is part of a more detailed discussion or presentation of your data. In these cases, you will start with a summary statement that reveals the big picture. For example, you might say, "As Figure 17 shows, areas of the country where sales are highest are the High, Central, and Southern Plains states." After presenting the figure, you would call your readers' attention to more specific points in the visual, such as patterns or general trends. Then you would give the exception to the trend, if there is one. For example, you might say, "The data show that sales in the Southern Plains states, especially, are high compared not only to the region but also to other territories across the country."

Visual communication and visual rhetoric are important components of business communication. Your readers will appreciate well-chosen, well-designed, and well-explained visuals, and you will achieve powerful communication results if you pay attention to both your data and how you present it.

Power Charge Your Professionalism: Use Numbers Correctly

Numbers, like capitalization, probably have the most variation in standards for their use. Reference Chapter A presents standards that are common to business. Keep in mind that if you work in the sciences or the humanities, these standards may be different, but for this exercise, be sure you use Reference Chapter A as your guide as you work through this exercise.

1. According to our market research, _____% of our customers pay their bills online.

   a. 25   b. twenty-five   c. either a or b

2. Our shareholders are meeting on March _____.

   a. twenty-first   b. 21st c. 21

3. The graduation rate for students who are involved in campus organizations is _____% greater than it is for those who are not.

   a. 2.5   b. 2 and one-half   c. two and one half

4. You can receive _____ off on your next order if you take our online survey.

   a. 10 dollars   b. $10   c. ten dollars   d. either a or b   e. either b or c

5. Your checked bag should not weigh more than _____ pounds.

   a. fifty   b. 50   c. either a or b

6. The deadline for submitting applications is the _____ of June.

   a. 1st   b. first   c. 1

7. The closet in my office is _____ feet long and _____ feet wide.

   a. 10, two   b. 10, 2   c. ten, two

8. Our division's staff consists of _____ manager, _____ supervisors, _____ administrative assistants, _____ senior accountants, and _____ junior accountants.

   a. one, three, four, 11, 13   b. one, three, four, eleven, twenty-three   c. 1, 3, 4, 11, 23

Number use is important because . . .

- Using numbers correctly will ensure that your reader does not misinterpret or misunderstand your meaning.
- Representing numbers in a way that is consistent with standards in business or the field in which you work shows that you are a professional in that community.

For further instruction on using the right word, see "Numbers" in the "Punctuation and Mechanics" section of LearnSmart Achieve.

Key Terms

visual rhetoric 103
orientation 104
portrait 104
landscape 104
style and font 105
rules (lines) and borders 105
color and cross-hatching 105
high contrast 105
title 106
caption 106
five Ws 106
title case 106
sentence case 106
footnotes 106
source acknowledgment 106
infographic 107
table 108
leaderwork 109
leaders 109

text tabulations 109
pull quote 109
bulleted lists 111
numbered lists 111
sub-bullets or numbers 112
organizational chart 112
flowchart 113
decision tree 113
simple bar 113
column charts 113
clustered (or multiple)
  bar chart 113
legend 113
bilateral bar or column
  charts 114
stacked (subdivided) bar or
  column chart 114
pictograph 116
pie chart 117

line charts 118
area 118
scatter diagrams 119
statistical maps 119
physical or geographic
  maps 121
combination charts 121
three-dimensional
  graphs 121
diagrams 124
icons 124
cartoons 124
video clips 124
animation 125
errors of scale 125
no uniform scale size 125
scale distortion 125
missing zero beginning 126
errors of format 128

Critical-Thinking Questions

1. For the past 20 years, Professor Clark Kupenheimer has required that his students include five visuals in the long, formal report he assigns. Evaluate this requirement. LO1

2. Because it was easier to do, a report writer prepared each of the visuals on a full page. Some of these visuals were extremely complex; some were very simple. Comment on this practice. LO1, LO6

3. A report has five maps, four tables, one chart, one diagram, and one photograph. How would you number these visuals? LO2

4. How would you number these visuals in a report: seven tables, six charts, and nine maps? LO2

5. Discuss the techniques that may be used to show quantitative differences between areas on a statistical map. LO4

6. Give examples of data that are suited for presentation in three dimensions. LO4

7. Discuss the advantages and disadvantages of using pictographs. LO4

8. Find a graph that uses scale breaks. Discuss the possible effects of its use on the reader. LO5

9. Find a visual with errors in format. Tell how you would correct the errors to present the chart's data more clearly to the reader. LO5

10. "I have placed every visual near the place I write about it. The reader can see the visual without any additional help from me. It just doesn't make sense to direct the reader's attention to the visuals with words." Evaluate this comment. LO6

Skills-Building Exercises

1. Construct a complete, concise title for a line chart representing employment placement rates for graduates in your major at your school from 2014 to the present. LO2

2. The chart prepared in Exercise 1 requires an explanation for the years 2015 and 2016. In each of those years, data were collected in January (mid-academic year) rather than June (end of the academic year). Provide the necessary explanation. LO6

3. For each of the types of information described, which form of visual would you use? Explain your decision. LO1–LO4
   a. Record of annual sales for Kenyon Company for the past 20 years
   b. Comparison of Kenyon Company sales, by product, for this year and last year
   c. Monthly production of the automobile industry in units
   d. Breakdown of how the average middle-income family in your state (or province) disposes of their income dollar
   e. How middle-income families spend their income dollar as compared with how low-income families spend their income dollar
   f. Comparison of sales for the past two years for each of B&B Company's 14 sales districts. The districts cover all 50 states, Canada, and Puerto Rico
   g. National production of trucks from 1950 to present, broken down by manufacturer
   h. Relationship between list price and gas mileage of alternative and gasoline-fueled cars
   i. Home purchases by home value, geographic region, and income

4. For each of the following sets of facts, (a) determine the visual(s) that would be best, (b) defend your choice, and (c) construct the visual. LO1–LO5
   a. Average (mean) amount of life insurance owned by Mutual Life Insurance Company policy-holders; classification is by annual income

Income	Average Life Insurance
Under $30,000	$ 40,000
$30,000–34,999	97,500
$35,000–39,999	112,500
$40,000–44,999	129,000
$45,000–49,999	142,500
$50,000 and over	225,000

   b. Profits and losses for Organic Whole Foods Stores, by store, 2014–2018, in dollars

	Store			
Year	Able City	Baker	Charleston	Total
2014	234,210	132,410	97,660	464,280
2015	229,110	−11,730	218,470	435,850
2016	238,430	−22,410	216,060	432,080
2017	226,730	68,650	235,510	530,890
2018	230,080	91,450	254,820	576,350

   c. Share of real estate tax payments by ward for Bigg City, 2014 and 2018, in thousands of dollars

	2014	2018
Ward 1	17.1	21.3
Ward 2	10.2	31.8
Ward 3	19.5	21.1
Ward 4	7.8	18.2
City total	54.6	92.4

d. Percentage change in sales by employee, 2018–2019, District IV, Abbott, Inc.

Employee	Percentage Change
Joan Abraham	+7.3
Helen Calmes	+2.1
Edward Sanchez	−7.5
Clifton Nevers	+41.6
Wilson Platt	+7.4
Clara Ruiz	+11.5
David Schlimmer	−4.8
Pa Yang	3.6

5. Determine what percentage of each type of registered vehicle is owned in the United States, including hybrid vehicles as appropriate. Choose an appropriate visual type and create it to convey the data. Consult the U.S. Department of Transportation for statistics. LO1–LO5

6. Through research, find the approximate milligrams of caffeine in the following items and create an appropriate visual for Affiliated Food Products, Inc., to illustrate your findings. LO2–LO5
   a. 5-oz. cup of coffee (drip brewed)
   b. 7-oz. glass of iced tea
   c. 6-oz. glass of soda with caffeine
   d. 1-oz. dark chocolate, semisweet

7. Choose five or six types of exercise. In a visual, identify the activity as a type of (1) cardiovascular training, (2) strength training, or (3) muscle stretching and toning. You can assume that some forms of exercise will incorporate all three types. You work for the Parks and Recreation Department of a city of your choosing. Provide an interpretation of your visual. LO1–LO6

Crafting Effective Sentences
and Paragraphs

© PhotoDisc/Getty Images

Chapter **Five**

nce you have analyzed your commu-nication task, decided what kind of message to write, and planned your verbal and visual content, you're ready to get down to the challenge of writing—putting one word, sentence, and paragraph after another to communicate what you want to say.

While each document you write will need to respond to the unique features of the situation, keeping in mind certain guidelines can help you make good writing choices. This chapter offers advice on selecting appropriate words, writing clear sentences and paragraphs, and achieving the desired effect with your readers. The goal is documents that communicate clearly, completely, efficiently, and engagingly.

Learning Objectives

LO5-1 Simplify your writing by selecting familiar and short words.

LO5-2 Use slang and popular clichés with caution.

LO5-3 Use technical words and acronyms appropriately.

LO5-4 Use concrete, specific words with the right shades of meaning.

LO5-5 Avoid misusing similar words and two-word expressions.

LO5-6 Prefer action verbs.

LO5-7 Write short, clear sentences by limiting sentence content and economizing on words.

LO5-8 Manage emphasis with sentence structure.

LO5-9 Keep sentences unified by omitting irrelevant points and unnecessary detail.

LO5-10 Word sentences logically.

LO5-11 Keep paragraphs concise.

LO5-12 Make sure each paragraph has one main idea.

LO5-13 Make paragraphs coherent.

LO5-14 Give each paragraph a strategic job to do.

Problem-Solving Challenge

Learning from an Unclear Message

This summer you're making some college money by working as a groundskeeper at a local hotel. Recently, you and the other hotel staff—including the rest of the maintenance crew and the house-keepers—received this written message from the new assistant manager:

> It has come to my attention that certain standards of quality are not being met by personnel in service positions. For successful operations, it is imperative that we adhere to the service guidelines for staff in each functional area, as set forth by corporate in the training materials that were reviewed during your orientation and onboarding. Be advised that there will be two mandatory training sessions on May 1, one at 4:00 p.m. for daytime employees and the other at 3:00 for the late shift, to reinforce your understanding of performance standards. Just as a machine cannot work properly if the pistons are all firing at different times, we cannot achieve our goals if individuals are setting their own criteria for how to serve our guests. I assume that I will see each and every one of you at a training session so that we may move forward with better comprehension of our roles and responsibilities.

You're no management pro, but you're sure this is a faulty message. In addition to being bossy and impersonal, it is wordy and difficult to understand. And the key point—that everyone will need to attend a training session—is buried in the middle of the message.

You get to thinking . . . how would you rewrite this message for a better effect? If only you had a few stylistic pointers to go on. . . .

Adapting Your Style to Your Readers

This chapter provides many tips for writing effectively. But the most important advice is this: Write in a style that is appropriate for the reader. As Chapter 1 explains, readers occupy particular organizational, professional, and personal contexts. They do not all have the same vocabulary, knowledge, or values, and you do not have the same relationship with all of them. Plus, as Chapter 7 explains, some of your readers may be from cultures very different from yours.

To communicate clearly and with the appropriate tone, you should learn everything possible about those with whom you want to communicate and consider any prior correspondence with them. Then you should word and organize your message so that it is easy for them to understand it and respond favorably.

Here's how Lynn Marmer, the first female corporate officer for the Kroger Company, describes her communication strategy:

Courtesy of Lynn Marmer

Lynn Marmer
Executive Director, Child Poverty
Collaborative, Cincinnati, OH
Former Group Vice President for Corporate
Affairs, The Kroger Company

> Whatever the medium (traditional, social, speeches, or television interviews) or audiences (employees, external, investors, policymakers), I always strive to follow my own four cardinal rules:
>
> - Tailor the medium and the message to the interests/needs of the audience.
>
> - Make the writing clear, unambiguous, and easy to understand.
>
> - Be honest, transparent, and authentic.
>
> - Strive to connect with the audience in a way that supports and reinforces the company's brand promise.

Tailoring your message to your readers is not only strategically necessary; it is also a sign of consideration for their time and energy. Everyone benefits when your writing is reader focused.

Selecting Appropriate Words

Choosing the best wording requires thinking about what you want to achieve and with whom. Do you and your readers know each other, or are you writing to strangers? How well educated are your readers, and what kinds of knowledge can they be presumed to have? How do you want your readers to feel about you, your company, and what you're writing about? The following sections will help you think through your choices.

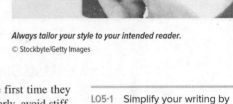

Always tailor your style to your intended reader.
© Stockbyte/Getty Images

Use Familiar Words

To communicate clearly, you must use words that your readers will understand. Because words that are familiar to some people may be unfamiliar to others, you will need to choose the appropriate wording for each reader.

In general, using familiar words means using the language that most of us use in everyday conversation. The U.S. government calls this kind of wording **plain language** and defines it as "communication your audience can understand the first time they read or hear it."[1] (Read more about plain language in Exhibit 5-1.) To write clearly, avoid stiff, difficult words that do not communicate precisely or quickly. For example, instead of using the less common word *endeavor*, use *try*. Prefer *begin* to *initiate, find out* to *ascertain, share* to *disseminate,* and *show* to *demonstrate*.

LO5-1 Simplify your writing by selecting familiar and short words.

The following examples illustrate the communication advantage of familiar words.

Unfamiliar Words	Familiar Words
This machine has a tendency to develop excessive and unpleasant audio symptoms when operating at elevated temperatures.	This machine tends to get noisy when it runs hot.
Purchase of a new fleet is not actionable at this juncture.	Buying new trucks is not practical now.
We must leverage our core competencies to maximize our competitiveness.	Relying on what we do best will make us the most competitive.
Company operations for the preceding accounting period terminated with a deficit.	The company lost money last year.

Prefer Short Words

According to studies of readability, short words generally communicate better than long words. One reason is that short words tend to be familiar words. But another reason is that heavy use of long words—even long words that can be understood—creates an impression of difficulty that hinders communication.

This point is illustrated by the following examples. Notice how much easier the short-word versions are to understand.

Long Words	Short Words
The *proposed enhancement is under consideration*.	We are *considering your suggestion*.
They *acceded* to the *proposition to undertake a collaborative venture*.	They *agreed* to *work with* us.
Prior to *accelerating productive operation*, the supervisor inspected the machinery.	Before *speeding up* production, the supervisor inspected the machinery.
This *antiquated merchandising strategy* is *ineffectual in contemporary* business *operations*.	This *old sales* strategy *will not work* with *today's* customers.

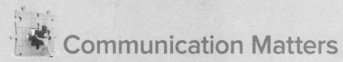
Communication Matters

The Most Annoying Clichés in Marketing

Each year, *Marketing Magazine* publishes the 10 most annoying marketing clichés as determined by Michael Sugden, CEO of a prominent marketing agency in London. Here were his picks from 2015:

1. Growth hacking.
2. Fail forward.
3. Let's socialize this.
4. Shift the dial.
5. Let's workshop this.
6. Level the playing field.
7. Let's not boil the ocean.
8. Content is king.
9. I may have a window for you.
10. Think outside the box.

Take a look at the rest of his post, as well as the comments, and you'll see many other nominees—e.g., "Let's circle back on this," "Run it up the flagpole," "Bandwidth crunch," and "Low-hanging fruit." What do all these expressions mean? Why do you think they became popular?

Source: "The 10 Most Annoying Phrases in Marketing," *Marketing Magazine*, December 11, 2015, accessed March 4, 2016, http://www.marketingmagazine.co.uk.

Use Slang and Popular Clichés with Caution

LO5-2 Use slang and popular clichés with caution.

At any given time in any society, certain slang expressions and clichés are in vogue. In the United States, for example, you're likely to hear young people say "I know, right?" (as in "I totally agree!"), "no worries," "that was the *worst*," and "on fleek" (as in "on point"), while other such expressions—"get out," "LOL," and "chill"—have become somewhat passé.

Business clichés come and go as well. "State of the art," "cutting edge," and "world class" gave way to such phrases as "moving forward," "thought leaders," and "best practices," and now these expressions are growing stale. More such examples are listed in the Communication Matters box "The Most Annoying Clichés in Marketing."

Admittedly, business clichés can sometimes increase your credibility with other businesspeople. These expressions can also add color to your language and quickly convey an idea. But they can also work against you. As Harvard professor Marjorie Garber puts it, "Jargon marks the place where thinking has been."[2] Clichés catch on because they represent popular concepts, but with overuse, they begin to sound like a replacement for thinking. Plus, they run the risk of sounding out of date, and they can create problems in cross-cultural communication.

Google "annoying clichés" and you will see that popular expressions can soon become unpopular. Use them sparingly and only in communication with people who will understand and appreciate them.

Use Technical Words and Acronyms Appropriately

LO5-3 Use technical words and acronyms appropriately.

Every profession—from accounting, information systems, and marketing to law, nursing, and teaching—has its technical language. As you work in your chosen field, you will learn its terms and acronyms and use them often when communicating with others in your field, as well you should. Frequently, one such word will communicate a concept that might otherwise take dozens of words to describe. Moreover, specialized language can signal to other specialists that you are qualified to communicate on their level.

However, communication can fail when you use technical terms with people outside your field. Remember that not everyone will have your specialized vocabulary. For example, does everyone know what an *annuity* is? How about *supply chain management*? Or *opportunity cost*? When possible, use your reader's language, and if you must use a technical term, explain it.

Initials (including acronyms) should be used with caution, too. While some initials, such as IBM, are widely recognized, others, such as SEO (search-engine optimization) and CRM (customer relationship management), are not. Exhibit 5-2 lists common business acronyms that may be unfamiliar to your readers. If you have any doubt that your reader will understand the initials, the best practice is to spell out the words the first time you use them and follow them with the initials. You may also need to go one step further and define them.

Use Precise Language

Good business communicators use words that convey sharp, clear meanings as well as the right emotional tone. Choosing such words means being concrete, specific, and sensitive to shades of meaning.

Concrete is the opposite of **abstract**. Whereas abstract words are vague, concrete words stand for things the reader can see, feel, taste, smell, or count.

The most concrete words are those that stand for things that exist in the real world, such as *chair, desk, computer, Bill Gates*, and the *Empire State Building*. Abstract nouns, on the other hand, cover broad, general meanings, as in these examples: *administration, compatibility, conservation, distinction,* and *integration*. It is difficult to visualize what these words stand for.

Notice how much clearer the concrete words are in the following examples:

Abstract	Concrete
A significant loss	A 53 percent loss
A more efficient process	Saved 23.2 hours of operating time
The majority	62 percent
In the near future	By noon Thursday
Effective leader (from a résumé)	Led a 5-person team that produced a 204-page website

Closely related to being concrete is being **specific**. Even if you are talking about something intangible, you can still make your wording as precise as possible. These examples show what we mean:

Vague	Specific
We have a great company.	We've been voted one of the *Business Courier*'s "Best Places to Work" for the last five years.
Our batteries are better.	Our batteries cost less and last longer.
Please respond soon.	Will you let me know by June 1?

But being specific isn't your only concern. Good writers possess a sensitivity to words' shades of meaning. Some words are forceful and some timid; some are positive and some negative; some are formal and some informal. Any given word can occupy a place on many different scales of tone and meaning. To achieve your communication goals, you need to choose the words that will achieve the desired response from your intended readers.

Consider the different associations of the words in each of these groups:

sell, market, advertise, promote

money, funds, cash, finances

improve, enhance, fix, correct

concern, issue, problem, incident

secretary, administrative assistant, support staff, coordinator

Exhibit 5-2 Alphabet Soup

Do you know what the following business abbreviations stand for?

B2B	CMS	EPS	FIFO	KPI	SWOT
GAAP	ROI	SAAS	TQM	CTR	ERP

Find out by Googling each acronym followed by "stands for"—and be sure your readers also know what it means before you use it.

LO5-4   Use concrete, specific words with the right shades of meaning.

Like different clothing styles, connotations project different moods and meanings.

(left): © ONOKY - Eric Herchaft/Getty Images, (middle): © Sam Diephuis/Getty Images, (right): © ONOKY - Eric Audras/Getty Images

Though the words in each list share the same **denotation** (basic meaning), they vary widely in their **connotations** (their social and emotional associations). Being attentive to what different words imply will make you a more skillful and effective writer.

Select Words for Appropriate Usage

LO5-5 Avoid misusing similar words and two-word expressions.

Certain pairs of words in English can cause trouble for writers. For example, do you know the difference between *fewer* and *less*? *Fewer* is used with items that can be counted (e.g., customers), while *less* is used to refer to an overall quantity of something that can't be counted (e.g., traffic). *Affect* and *effect* are often used interchangeably. But *affect* is most often used as a verb meaning "to influence," whereas *effect* is most often used as a noun that means "a result" of something (in its verb form, *effect* means "to bring about"). Similarly, careful writers use *continual* to mean "repeated regularly and frequently" and *continuous* to mean "repeated without interruption." They write *farther* to express geographic distance and *further* to indicate "more."

You'll find more examples of often-misused words in the Communication Matters feature "Don't be Hoodwinked by Homophones" and in the "Wrong Word" section of Reference Chapter A. Watch out for them.

In your effort to be a skillful writer, you should also use **two-word expressions** (sometimes called **idioms**) correctly. Many of these expressions seem arbitrary, but to avoid unclear or distracting writing, you need to use the word combinations that people expect. For example, the correct expression is "attitude toward," not "attitude about." You "agree to" a proposal but "agree with" a person. You are "careful about" a sensitive situation, but you are "careful with" your money. Here are some additional illustrations:

Faulty Wording	Correct Wording
authority about	authority on
comply to	comply with
different than	different from
equally as bad	equally bad
seldom or ever	seldom if ever
based off of	based on

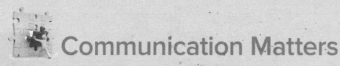

Communication Matters

Don't Be Hoodwinked by Homophones

Words that sound alike (or nearly alike) but are spelled and used differently are called *homophones*. Some English homophones, like "beat" and "beet" or "allowed" and "aloud," are easy for native speakers to keep straight—but many can be tricky. Be sure you know when to use each word here:

Accept	To take in
Except	Other than
Affect	To influence
Effect	A result (or to bring about)
Aid	To help
Aide	An assistant
Cite	To quote or refer to
Site	A specific location

Compliment	Words of praise (or to give words of praise)
Complement	Something that completes (or to complete)
Discreet	Tactful
Discrete	Distinct
Elicit	To evoke
Illicit	Illegal
It's	A contraction meaning "it is"
Its	A possessive pronoun (e.g., "its handle")
Its'	[no such word]
Led	Guided
Lead	A type of metal (or to guide)

Passed	Moved ahead
Past	The time before the present (or beyond, as in "we went past the school")
Personal	Private or pertaining to a particular person
Personnel	Employees or staff
Principle	A rule or standard
Principal	The highest ranking person; main or primary
Their	A possessive pronoun (e.g., "their employees")
There	Beginning of a clause or sentence (e.g., "There are . . . ")
They're	A contraction meaning "they are"
Your	A possessive pronoun (e.g., "your application")
You're	A contraction meaning "you are"

As you can see, some word choices are unwise, some are awkward, and some are just plain wrong. If you are unsure which word you need or would have the best effect, consult a dictionary.

Prefer Action Verbs

Of all parts of speech, verbs do the most to make your writing interesting and lively, and for good reason: They contain the action of the sentence.

LO5-6 Prefer action verbs.

But not all verbs add vigor to your writing. Overuse of the verb "to be" and passive voice can sap the energy from your sentences. To see the difference between writing that relies heavily on forms of "to be" and writing that uses action verbs, compare the following two passages (the forms of "to be" and their replacements are italicized):

Version A (weak verbs)

There *are* over 300 customers served by our help desk each day. The help desk personnel's main tasks *are* to answer questions, solve problems, and educate the callers about the software. Without their expert work, our customer satisfaction ratings *would be* much lower than they *are*.

Version B (action verbs)

Our help desk personnel *serve* over 300 customers each day. They *answer* questions, *solve* problems, and *educate* the users about the software. Without their expert work, our customer satisfaction ratings *would* drop significantly.

As these examples show, using action verbs adds impact to your writing, and it usually saves words as well.

One way to minimize the use of "to be" verbs is to avoid the **dummy subject**. Sentences that start with "there is," "it is," and variations on these expressions are said to use dummy subjects because the words that are the real subjects of these sentences come after the verb. For example, the real subject in the sentence "There were over 40 people in attendance" is

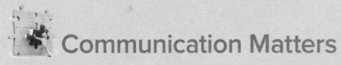

Communication Matters

Everything You Wanted to Know about Active and Passive Voice

Students are often confused by the terms *active voice* and *passive voice*. Here's the lowdown.

Broadly speaking, there are two main categories of verbs in English: those that can take direct objects and those that can't. To illustrate, the verb *repair* can take a direct object (that is, you can repair something), while the verb *happen* cannot (you can't happen anything).

Sentences with verbs that can take direct objects are the ones that can be written in either active or passive voice. When you write in active voice, the sentence is in "who + does/did what + to what/whom" order, as in this example:

An authorized technician repaired the new laser printer.

    [who]   [did what]   [to what]

When you write the same idea in passive voice, the direct object moves to the start of the sentence and bumps the real subject to a phrase at the end of it (or out of it altogether). With this move, you now have . . .

The new laser printer was repaired by an authorized technician.

    [what]   [had something done to it]   [by whom]

. . . or even just . . .

The new laser printer was repaired. [real subject removed]

As you can see, inverting the word order this way makes the sentence less energetic, more roundabout, and sometimes less informative.

You can find instances of passive voice in your own writing by looking for two- and three-word verbs that consist of

- a form of the verb *to be* (for example, *is, was, has been, will be*); and
- a verb in past-tense form (for example, *installed, reduced, chosen, sent*).

When you find such verbs—*was installed, has been reduced, will be chosen*—see if your meaning would be clearer and sharper if you wrote in the active voice instead.

"people," not "there" (which is never the real subject). Rewritten with the real subject at the beginning, the sentence would read "Over 40 people attended." As you can see, this sentence would be livelier—and shorter, too.

Here is another example:

Dummy subjects, weak verbs:

It is important for reports to be submitted by January 12 so that *there will be* sufficient time for the committee to review them.

Strong subjects and verbs:

Please *submit* your reports by January 12 so the *committee will have* sufficient time to review them.

You can also minimize your use of "to be" verbs and make your verbs more lively by using **active voice**. As the Communication Matters feature "Everything You Wanted to Know about Active and Passive Voice" explains, a sentence with a verb that can take a direct object (the recipient of the action) can be written either in a direct (active) pattern or an indirect (passive) pattern. Here are some examples:

Passive	Active
The results were reported in our July 9 letter.	We reported the results in our July 9 letter.
The new process is believed to be superior by the investigators.	The investigators believe that the new process is superior.
The policy was enforced by the committee.	The committee enforced the policy.
The office will be inspected on Tuesday.	Mr. Hall will inspect the office on Tuesday.
It is desired by the director that this problem be brought before the board.	The director wants the secretary to bring this problem before the board.

As you can see, the active versions are clearer and usually shorter.

You Make the Call

Sometimes using "there is" to start a sentence can be justified. Consider the following sentence: "There is no reason to wait until next year to find a replacement." If you were to rewrite this sentence to eliminate "there is," how would you do it? Would that effort be well spent? Can you formulate a guideline for when to use "there is" constructions?

Give your writing impact by using strong verbs.
© Fotosearch/Getty Images

The advice to prefer active voice does not mean that passive voice is incorrect or that you should never use it. Sometimes passive voice is preferable.

For example, when the doer of the action is unimportant to the message, passive voice properly deemphasizes the doer:

Advertising is often criticized for its effect on price.

The copier has now been repaired.

Passive voice may also enable you to avoid blaming your reader, as in these examples:

The damage was caused by exposing the material to sunlight.

The choice of color was not specified in your order.

And sometimes passive voice is unavoidable because the doer is unknown, as in this example:

During the past year, the equipment has been sabotaged seven times.

If none of these situations apply, try to write your sentences in the active "who does what" order.

Avoid Camouflaged Verbs

Another construction that should be avoided is the **camouflaged verb**. When a verb is camouflaged, it has been hidden inside a noun, as in this sentence: "The staff *effected an elimination of* the surplus." The sentence would be shorter and easier to understand if it read this way: "The staff *eliminated* the surplus." You'll find more examples in the Communication Matters feature "Will the Real Verb Please Stand Up?" Being sure the verbs express the real action in your sentences will help you avoid flabby, noun-heavy writing.

Writing Clear Sentences

When you sit down to write a given message, you have many bits of information at hand. How will you turn them into a clear, coherent message?

Your first task will probably be to plan the message's overall organization by figuring out what information should go where. But sooner or later, writing a successful message comes down to figuring out how to stitch your contents together in a series of sentences. How much information will you put into each sentence? And in what form and order will that information be?

The advice that follows will help you answer these questions.

Limit Sentence Content

LO5-7   Write short, clear sentences by limiting sentence content and economizing on words.

Having too much to do in too little time is a chronic problem in the workplace. No one, whether executive or entry-level employee, wants to read writing that wastes time. One way to help readers comprehend your messages efficiently is to avoid unduly long sentences.

Which of the following passages is easier to understand?

Version A

Once you have completed the online safety course, which will be available on the company portal until 29 June, your supervisor will automatically be notified, at which point he/she will authorize you to handle these materials, unless your score was below 90, in which case you will need to repeat the course.

Version B

You can access the safety course on the company portal any time between now and 29 June. You must score at least a 90 to pass it, but you can repeat the course as often as necessary. Once you have received a passing score, your supervisor will be automatically notified. He/she will then authorize you to handle these materials.

Sometimes writers try to be efficient by using as few sentences as possible, but as the examples above show, that can cause trouble. Having more sentences with less in them is often the better strategy.

Preferring short sentences does not mean making all sentences equally short, however. Combining some ideas into longer sentences will help you communicate clearly and add flow to your writing. The following examples illustrate. The first paragraph is an excerpt from an employee handbook. Obviously the use of one long sentence to convey the information was a poor decision.

> When an employee has changed from one job to another job, the new corresponding coverage will be effective as of the date the change occurs, unless, however, if due to a physical disability or infirmity as a result of advanced age, an employee is changed from one job to another job and such change results in the employee's new job rate coming within a lower hourly job-rate bracket in the table, in which case the employee may, at the discretion of the company, continue at the same level of insurance coverage that was in effect prior to such change.

So many words and relationships are in the sentence that it is almost impossible to follow.

Now look at the message written in all short sentences. The choppiness is confusing and irritating. Imagine reading a long document written in this style.

> An employee may change jobs. The new coverage is effective when this happens. But the job change could be because of physical disability or infirmity caused by age. This may put the employee in a lower pay bracket. The company has some discretion in such cases. It may permit the employee to continue at the same level of insurance coverage.

The following paragraph takes a course between these two extremes. It keeps the sentences a readable length but combines the contents in a way that conveys the two main points.

> When an employee changes jobs, the new corresponding insurance coverage becomes effective when the change occurs. If the change has occurred because of disability or infirmity caused by age and has put the employee in a lower pay bracket, the company may, at its discretion, permit the employee to continue at the same level of insurance coverage.

The upcoming sections on conciseness, management of emphasis, and sentence unity can help you decide how much content each sentence should carry.

Too many simple sentences create an elementary-sounding style, so combine ideas where appropriate for your adult readers.

© Â© travelib prime / Alamy Stock Photo

Communication Matters

Avoiding Stringy and See-Saw Sentences

If you try to pack too much information into a sentence, you can wind up with a stringy sentence like this:

> While we welcome all applications, we are particularly interested in candidates who have at least three years' experience, although we will consider those with less experience who have a degree in the field or who have earned a certificate from an industry-certified trainer, and we will also consider fluency in Italian a plus.

A see-saw sentence is one that goes back and forth between two points, like this:

> A blog can add visibility to a business, although it can be labor intensive to maintain, but the time spent on the blog could be worthwhile if it generates a buzz among our potential customers.

In these cases, edit the sentences down to readable size, use helpful transitional phrases (*in addition, on the other hand*) between them, and don't switch directions too often.

Here are more readable versions of the problem sentences:

> While we welcome all applications, we are particularly interested in candidates who (1) have at least three years' experience or (2) have less experience but have earned a degree or certificate in the field. Fluency in Italian is also a plus.

> A blog can add visibility to a business. True, maintaining a blog takes time, but if the blog generates a buzz among our potential customers, the time will be well spent.

From the Tech Desk

Readability Statistics Help Writers Evaluate Their Documents' Length and Difficulty

Microsoft Word's grammar and style checker gives writers the option of viewing the readability statistics for their documents. These statistics report the number of words, characters, paragraphs, and sentences in a document along with averages of characters per word, words per sentence, and sentences per paragraph.

The report you see here was generated for the blog post "How to Use Your Blog to Tell a Story."* It reports an average of 14 words per sentence, which might seem high, but the average sentences per paragraph (3.8) and average characters per word (4.5) suggest a very accessible document. The Flesch-Kincaid score, which puts this post at a reading grade level of 7.7, confirms that this writer's style is easy to follow. The Flesch Reading Ease score of 64.6 does so as well, since Microsoft recommends writing that falls within the 60–70 range.

To have Word calculate the readability statistics of your documents, select File > Options > Proofing and check "Show readability statistics." Then click Review > Spelling & Grammar. Your statistics will appear at the end of the review.

*Julie Neidlinger, CoSchedule Blog, July 24, 2014, accessed March 10, 2016, http://coschedule.com/blog/tell-a-story/.

Readability Statistics	? ✕
Counts	
Words	497
Characters	2,734
Paragraphs	17
Sentences	35
Averages	
Sentences per Paragraph	2.1
Words per Sentence	14.0
Characters per Word	4.5
Readability	
Flesch Reading Ease	64.6
Flesch-Kincaid Grade Level	7.7
	OK

Economize on Words

A second basic technique for shortening sentences is to use words economically. Anything you write can be expressed in many ways, some shorter than others. Wording your sentences efficiently will save your reader time and energy.

Watch out in particular for the following three sources of extraneous words.

Cluttering Phrases A **cluttering phrase** is a phrase that can be replaced by shorter wording without loss of meaning, as illustrated in this sentence:

> *In the event that* none of the candidates is acceptable, we will reopen the position.

Replacing the phrase *in the event that* with *if* would enable the sentence to make the same point more quickly:

> *If* none of the candidates is acceptable, we will reopen the position.

Similarly, the phrase that begins the following sentence adds unnecessary length:

> *In spite of the fact that* they received help, they failed to exceed the quota.

Although is an economical substitute:

> *Although* they received help, they failed to exceed the quota.

Here are additional examples of commonly used cluttering phrases:

Cluttering Phrase	Shorter Substitution
At the present time	Now
For the purpose of	For
For the reason that	Because, since
In the amount of	For
In the meantime	Meanwhile
In the near future	Soon
In the neighborhood of	About
In very few cases	Seldom, rarely
In view of the fact that	Since, because
With regard to, with reference to	About

Surplus Words To write economically, eliminate words that add nothing to sentence meaning. Eliminating these **surplus words** sometimes requires recasting a sentence, but often they can just be left out.

The following is an example of surplus wording from a business report:

> *It will be noted that* the records for the past years show a steady increase in the cost of tech support.

Now notice how dropping the opening words would enable the sentence to focus on the key point:

> The records for the past years show a steady increase in the cost of tech support.

Exhibit 5-3 Can Your Writing Pass the Monotony Test?

If your verbs are strong, your sentences vary in length, and you emphasize the right ideas, your writing will have an interesting and inviting rhythm.

So read your writing aloud. If you find your voice lapsing into a monotone, you probably need to apply one or more of the guidelines presented in this chapter.

Here's a second example:

> His performance was good enough to *enable him* to qualify for the promotion.

The words *to enable* add nothing and can be dropped:

> His performance was good enough to qualify him for the promotion.

The following sentences further illustrate how surplus words can be eliminated without changing the meaning.

Contains Surplus Words	Eliminates Surplus Words
There are four rules *that* should be observed.	Four rules should be observed.
In addition to these defects, numerous other defects mar the operating procedure.	Numerous other defects mar the operating procedure.
It is essential that the income be used to retire the debt.	The income *must* be used to retire the debt.
In the period between April and June, we detected the problem.	Between April and June we detected the problem.
He criticized everyone he *came in contact with*.	He criticized everyone he *met*.

Unnecessary Repetition of Words or Ideas Repeating words can sometimes add emphasis or create a desirable stylistic effect, but often it is unnecessary, as this sentence illustrates:

> We have not received your payment covering invoices covering June and July purchases.

It would be better to write the sentence like this:

> We have not received your payment covering invoices for June and July purchases.

Another example is this one:

> He stated that he believes that we are responsible.

The following sentence eliminates one of the *that*s:

> He stated that he believes we are responsible. [See the Communication Matters box "Is *That* a Surplus Word?" for more advice about *that*.]

Repeating ideas by combining different words that mean the same thing (*free gift, true fact, past history*) also add to sentence length. Known as **redundancies**, such repetitions rarely add anything of value, and sometimes they can be confusing, as in this sentence:

> The beginning of the speech will open with a welcome.

The beginning and *will open* are two ways to say the same thing. The following sentence is better:

> The speech will open with a welcome.

Exhibit 5-4 provides more examples of redundancies and ways to eliminate them.

Exhibit 5-4	Search Out and Destroy Needless Repetition

Needless Repetition	Repetition Eliminated
Please *endorse your name on the back* of this check.	Please *endorse* this check.
We must *assemble together* at 10:30 a.m. *in the morning*.	We must assemble at 10:30 a.m.
Our new model *is longer in length* than the old one.	Our new model *is longer* than the old one.
If you are not satisfied, *return it back* to us.	If you are not satisfied, *return* it to us.
One should know the *basic fundamentals* of clear writing.	One should know the *fundamentals* of clear writing.
The *consensus of opinion* is that the tax is unfair.	The *consensus* is that the tax is unfair.
As a matter of interest, I would like to learn more about your procedure.	I am *interested* in learning more about your procedure.

Manage Emphasis with Sentence Structure

All but the shortest documents contain multiple items of information. Some of these, such as the purpose of a message and the key facts, are especially important, while others, such as side points

LO5-8 Manage emphasis with sentence structure.

Now that businesspeople read so many of their messages on their phones and between tasks, sentences that communicate clearly and quickly are even more important.
© Maskot/Getty Images

or minor details, are not. Fortunately, the English language gives you ways to structure your sentences to convey the importance of each item.

Put the Main Ideas in the Main Clauses

Main (or independent) clauses are called **main clauses** for a reason: They express the main point of the sentence.

Compare these two sentences that might appear in an article for a company newsletter (main clauses are italicized):

> *Mr. Freshley,* who began working for Remington in 1952, *oversees all company purchases.*

> *Mr. Freshley,* who oversees all company purchases, *began working for Remington in 1952.*

The sentences contain exactly the same information, but the main clauses make them say different things. The first sentence focuses on Mr. Freshley's importance to the company, while the second sentence emphasizes how long he has been an employee. Which version is preferable? It would depend on what you wanted to emphasize and on what your readers would expect you to emphasize.

Use Coordination and Subordination Deliberately

When two or more pieces of information need to be included in one sentence, understanding **coordination** and **subordination** will help you decide how to structure the sentence.

When you coordinate ideas, you treat them as equal in importance by joining them with *and, but, or, so,* or *yet* (the coordinate conjunctions), or by setting them up as equals in a list. When you subordinate an idea, you treat it as less important than the main idea by putting it into a modifying clause or phrase. These examples illustrate:

> The company enjoyed record sales last year, *but* it lost money. [The two ideas are both in main clauses and are thus being treated as equally important.]

> *Although the company enjoyed record sales last year,* it lost money. ["Although" turns the first idea into a subordinate clause, making it less important than the second idea.]

> *Despite record sales,* the company lost money last year. [The first idea is now in a phrase, making it less important than the second idea.]

Use Short Sentences for Emphasis

Short sentences carry more emphasis than long, involved ones. They call attention to their content by conveying a single message without the interference of related or supporting information.

For example, notice the impact of the concluding sentence in the following excerpt from a fund-raising letter:

> Alumni like you have started a transformation that has increased our academic achievements, increased our enrollment, and created an internationally recognized campus landscape. But we have more to do.

Beginnings and endings of business messages are often good places for short sentences. A short opening enables you to get to the point quickly, and a short closing leaves the reader with an important final thought. Here are some examples:

Openings:

Yes, your insurance is still in effect.

Here are the new guidelines for requesting technical support.

Closings:

Thank you again for your generous contribution.

I'm looking forward to your presentation.

Give Sentences Unity

Good sentences have **unity**. This means that all the parts of the sentence work together to create one clear point.

Lack of unity in sentences is usually caused by one of two problems: (1) unrelated ideas or (2) excessive detail.

LO5-9   Keep sentences unified by omitting irrelevant points and unnecessary detail.

Unrelated Ideas The ideas in a sentence must have a reason for being together and convey one overall point. If they don't, you should separate them. If you believe they do go together, make clear how they're related.

The following sentences illustrate:

Unrelated	Improved
The brochure you requested is enclosed, and please let me know if you need any additional information.	The brochure you requested is enclosed. Please let me know if you need additional information.
Our territory is the southern half of the state, and our salespeople cannot cover it thoroughly.	Our territory is the southern half of the state, and it is too large for our salespeople to cover thoroughly.
Using the cost-of-living calculator is simple, but no tool will work well unless it is explained clearly.	Using the cost-of-living calculator is simple, but, like any tool, it will not work well unless it is explained clearly.
We concentrate on energy-saving products, and 70 percent of our business comes from them.	We concentrate on energy-saving products, which account for 70 percent of our business.

Excessive Detail Putting too much detail into one sentence tends to hide the central thought, and it also makes the sentence too long.

If the detail isn't necessary, remove it. If it is important, keep it, but divide the sentence into two or more sentences, as in the following examples:

Excessive Detail	Improved
In response to your email inquiry, we searched our records and confirmed your Oct. 1 order, so we are sending you a rush shipment of Plytec insulation immediately.	Thank you for helping us locate your order. We are sending you a rush shipment of Plytec insulation immediately.
In 2009, when I, a small-town girl from a middle-class family, began my studies at Bradley University, which is widely recognized for its business administration program, I set my goal as a career with a large public company.	I selected Bradley because of its widely recognized business administration program. From the beginning, my goal was a career with a large public company.
The fact that I have worked in the chemical industry for over 15 years holding a variety of positions in sales, marketing, and product management has provided me with a solid understanding of how to promote products in today's industry.	I have worked in the chemical industry for over 15 years and have held positions in sales, marketing, and product management. This experience has given me a solid understanding of how to promote products in the industry.

Word Sentences Logically

At some point, you've probably had a teacher write "awkward" beside one or more of your sentences. Often, the cause of such a problem is illogical wording. The paragraphs that follow will help you avoid some of the most common types of illogical sentences (see Exhibit 5-5).

LO5-10   Word sentences logically.

Mixed Constructions Sometimes illogical sentences occur when writers mix two different kinds of sentences together. This problem is called a **mixed construction**.

Exhibit 5-5 Common Types of Faulty Sentence Logic

- Mixed constructions
- Incomplete constructions
- Dangling or misplaced modifiers
- Faulty parallelism

For example, can you describe what's wrong with the following sentence about cutting costs?

First we found less expensive material, and then a more economical means of production was developed.

If you said that the first half of the sentence used active voice but the second half switched to passive voice, you're right. Shifts of this kind make a sentence hard to follow. Notice how much easier it is to understand this version:

First we found less expensive material, and then we developed a more economical means of production.

There's a similar problem in the following sentence:

The consumer should read the nutrition label, but you often don't take the time to do so.

Did you notice that the point of view changed from third person (*consumer*) to second (*you*) in this sentence? The following revision would be much easier to follow:

Consumers should read nutrition labels, but they often don't take the time to do so.

Sometimes we start writing one kind of sentence and then change it before we get to the end, illogically putting parts of two different sentences together. Here's an example:

Because the product release was delayed caused us to miss our sales quota.

Rewriting the sentence in one of the following ways would eliminate the awkwardness:

Because the product release was delayed, we missed our sales quota.

The delay in the product release caused us to miss our sales quota.

These sentences further illustrate:

Mixed Construction	Improved
Some activities that the company participates in are affordable housing, conservation of parks, and litter control. ["Affordable housing" isn't an activity.]	Some causes the company supports are affordable housing, conservation of parks, and litter control.
Job rotation is when you train people by moving them from job to job. [The linking verb "is" has to be followed by a noun or adjective, but here it's followed by an adverb clause.]	Job rotation is a training method in which people are moved from job to job.
My education was completed in 2009, and then I began work as a manager for Home Depot. [The sentence switches from passive voice to active voice.]	I completed my education in 2009 and then began work as a manager for Home Depot.
The cost of these desks is cheaper. ["Cheaper" can't logically refer to cost.]	These desks cost less. (*or* These desks are cheaper.)
The next graph looked into employees' attitudes toward the program. [This is an illogical subject-verb combination; a graph can't "look."]	The next graph shows how employees felt about the program.

Incomplete Constructions Certain words used early in a sentence signal that the rest of the sentence will provide a certain kind of content. Be careful to fulfill your reader's expectations. Otherwise, you will have written an **incomplete construction**.

For example, the following sentence, while technically a sentence, is incomplete:

She was so happy with the retirement party we gave her.

She was so happy . . . that what? That she sent everyone a thank-you note? That she made a donation to the library in the company's name? In a sentence like this, either complete the construction or leave "so" out.

Or consider the incomplete opening phrase of this sentence:

As far as time management, he is a master of multitasking.

You can rectify the problem in one of two ways:

As far as time management goes [*or* is concerned], he is a master of multitasking.

As for time management, he is a master of multitasking.

Dangling/Misplaced Modifiers

Putting modifiers in the wrong place or giving them nothing to modify in the sentence is another common way that sentence logic can go awry. Consider this sentence:

From reviewing the report, it is clear that the new schedule is saving money.

Who reviewed the report? The sentence doesn't say. This makes the opening phrase a **dangling modifier**, because what it is supposed to modify has been left out.

You can correct this problem in a couple of ways:

From reviewing the report, we learned that the new schedule is saving money. [With this method, you add what the phrase was intended to modify.]

The report makes clear that the new schedule is saving money. [With this method, you rewrite the sentence so that you can remove the dangling phrase.]

What makes this sentence hard to follow?

We have compiled a list of likely prospects using the information we gathered at the trade show.

Surely the "prospects" aren't really the ones using the information. The sentence would be clearer if the final phrase, a **misplaced modifier**, were more logically placed, as in

Using the information we gathered at the trade show, we have compiled a list of likely prospects.

Faulty Parallelism

Readers expect the same kinds of content in a sentence to be worded in the same way. **Faulty parallelism** violates this logical expectation.

How might you make the similar items in this sentence more parallel in wording?

They show their community spirit through yearly donations to the United Way, giving free materials to Habitat for Humanity, and their employees volunteer at local schools.

Here's one way:

They show their community spirit by donating yearly to the United Way, giving free materials to Habitat for Humanity, and volunteering at local schools.

Can you spot the faulty parallelism in this sentence?

To create a more appealing website, we can gather personal stories, create a new logo, as well as making the layout more readable.

Here's a corrected version:

To create a more appealing website, we can gather personal stories, create a new logo, and make the layout more readable.

Note that if you format your series as a bulleted list, you still need to keep the items parallel. This example has faulty parallelism:

The branding standards include

- The approved logos
- A style guide
- Using the approved color palette
- How to redesign existing materials

Communication Matters

Don't Make Me Laugh

Misplaced modifiers can have unintentionally humorous effects, as these examples show:

My mother told me that I would have gray hair when I was ten.

The company created a new toy for children made of plastic.

We saw several monkeys on vacation in Mexico.

Many people watched the Fourth of July fireworks in their cars.

To keep the joke from being on you, put the modifier next to what it modifies.

Source: "Misplaced Modifiers," *JamesBaquet.com,* January 15, 2012, accessed October 12, 2016, http://lessons.jamesbaquet.com.

A list has faulty parallelism when an item doesn't match the others in the list.
© Don Farrall/DigitalVision/Getty Images

This bulleted list has much better parallelism:

The branding standards include
- The approved logos
- A style guide
- The approved color palette
- Instructions for redesigning existing materials

Other rules of grammar besides those mentioned here can help you avoid illogical constructions and write clear sentences. See Reference Chapter A for more examples and advice.

Writing Clear Paragraphs

Skillful paragraphing is important to clear communication. Paragraphs show your readers where each topic begins and ends, thus helping them mentally organize the information. Strategic paragraphing also helps you make certain ideas stand out and achieve the desired response to your message. The following advice will help you use paragraphing to your best advantage.

Keep Paragraphs Concise

LO5-11   Keep paragraphs concise.

Skim the good examples in this book and you'll see that they all use short paragraphs. The opening paragraph quickly gets to the point and prepares the reader for what's coming. The body paragraphs typically have fewer than four sentences and take up fewer than seven lines, even in long reports and proposals. And the concluding paragraph is often just one or two sentences. Read on to see how and why to keep your paragraphs short.

Use Frequent Paragraph Breaks
If you're used to writing essays with long paragraphs, adjusting to the shorter paragraphs in business writing can take some practice. But there's good reason to make this adjustment. First, frequent paragraph breaks help make the look of your documents inviting. As Exhibit 2-4 points out, even one page of dense text is off-putting. Almost all businesspeople have too much to read, so a document with long paragraphs runs a risk of not being accurately understood or even read at all.

Breaking up the text with paragraphing also makes your text easier to comprehend because it divides the contents into digestible chunks and gives the reader little breaks between ideas. And third, short paragraphs aid comprehension by helping your reader see the structure of your ideas. Along with headings and lists, paragraph breaks enable readers to grasp the pattern of your content at a glance.

What if you're into your fourth sentence of a paragraph and you still have more to say? The solution is to look for a logical way to divide the paragraph into two or more paragraphs. It's fine to use more than one paragraph to convey a point as long as you divide the information in a logical place.

Omit Unnecessary Detail
You should include in your paragraphs only the information needed to achieve your purpose. To figure out what that information is, revisit the thinking you did as you planned your document. What information do you need to convey? What information does the reader need, and why? You can also be sensitive to how much effort it will take to read any given paragraph. If you would find the level of detail in a paragraph excessive and tedious, your reader probably would, too. Be as efficient as you can without giving too little information or being too curt.

How easy is it for you to follow this paragraph written by a human resources staff person to an employee?

> In reviewing the personnel records in our company database, I found that several items in your file were incomplete. The section titled "Work History" has blanks for three items of information. The first is for dates employed. The second is for company name. And the third is for type of work performed. On your record only company name was entered, leaving two items blank. Years employed or your duties were not indicated. This information is important. It is reviewed by your supervisors every time you are considered for promotion or for a pay increase. Therefore, it must be completed. I request that you log into the company portal and update your personnel record at your earliest convenience.

The excess detail makes it difficult for the reader to get to the key point, which is to update his or her personnel record. This revised message is better:

> In reviewing the personnel records in our company database, I found that the "Work History" section of your record is incomplete. Please log into the company portal at your earliest convenience to update it. This information will enable your supervisors to see all your qualifications when considering you for a promotion or a pay increase.

Give Paragraphs Unity

Like sentences, paragraphs should have unity. When applied to a paragraph, unity means that the paragraph sticks to a single topic or idea, with everything in the paragraph developing this topic or idea. When you have finished the paragraph, you should be able to say, "All the points in this paragraph go together."

A violation of unity is illustrated in the following paragraph from a job application letter. Most of the paragraph is about the applicant's coursework, but the sentence in italics is about the applicant's extracurricular activities. Moving this sentence into its own well-developed paragraph would correct the problem and probably make for a more persuasive letter.

Give every paragraph a clear focus.
© Natural Planet/Rich Reid/Media Bakery

> At the university I studied all the basic accounting courses as well as specialized courses in taxation, international accounting, and computer security. I also took specialized coursework in the behavioral areas, with emphasis on human relations. *Realizing the value of human relations in business, I also actively participated in organizations, such as Sigma Nu (social fraternity), Alpha Kappa Psi (professional fraternity), intramural soccer, and A Cappella.* I selected my elective coursework to round out my general business education. Among my electives were courses in investments, advanced business report writing, financial policy, and management information systems.

LO5-12   Make sure each paragraph has one main idea.

One good way to ensure the unity of your paragraphs is to use topic sentences. The **topic sentence** expresses the main idea of the paragraph, which the other sentences build around and support. In a sense, the topic sentence serves as a headline for the paragraph, and all the other sentences supply the story.

Not every paragraph must have a topic sentence. Some paragraphs introduce ideas, continue the point of the preceding paragraph, or wrap up the message with a goodwill comment. Even so, you should use topic sentences whenever you can, especially for the paragraphs in the body of your document. They force you to determine the purpose of each paragraph and help you check for paragraph unity.

Where the topic sentence should be in the paragraph depends on the subject matter and the structure you've planned for the document, but you basically have three choices: the beginning, end, or middle.

Option 1: Put the Topic Sentence First The most common practice is to begin with the topic sentence and continue with the supporting material. This arrangement has strong appeal because it enables the reader to see right away how all the sentences in the paragraph will be related.

Let's say, for example, that you're writing a paragraph reporting on economists' replies to a survey question asking their view of business activity for the coming year. The facts to be presented are these: 13 percent of the economists expect an increase; 28 percent expect little or no change; 59 percent expect a downturn; and 87 percent of those who expect a downturn think it will come in the first quarter. The conclusion the data point to is that over half of the respondents expect a decline in the first quarter. You might thus construct your paragraph like this:

> *Over half of the economists consulted think that business activity will drop during the first quarter of next year.* Of the 185 economists interviewed, 13 percent look for continued increases in business activity, and 28 percent anticipate little or no change from the present high level. The remaining 59 percent look for a recession. Of this group, nearly all (87 percent) believe that the downturn will occur during the first quarter of the year.

Option 2: Put the Topic Sentence at the End The second most common paragraph arrangement places the topic sentence at the end. Paragraphs of this kind present the supporting details first and lead readers to the conclusion, as in this example:

> Financial experts recommend that small organizations have enough cash reserves to cover three to six months of operating expenses. St. John's Community Fund has $112,000, or approximately four months, on hand. *Our cash reserves are thus well within the recommended guidelines.*

Option 3: Put the Topic Sentence within the Paragraph A third arrangement places the topic sentence somewhere within the paragraph. This arrangement is used least often, and for good reason: It doesn't put the topic sentence, which contains the main point, in a position of emphasis. Still, it is sometimes appropriate, as in this example:

> Kansas City is centrally located in our region, and hotels there are cheaper than in Chicago. *But Chicago is a more appealing destination.* Our members like to be in a vibrant downtown location. Flights to Chicago are also likely to be less expensive than those to Kansas City.

Make Paragraphs Coherent

Like well-made sentences, well-made paragraphs move the reader logically and smoothly from point to point. They clearly indicate how the different bits of information are related to each other in terms of logic and the writer's apparent purpose. This quality of enabling the reader to proceed easily through your message, without side trips and backward shifts, is called **coherence**.

The best way to give your message coherence is to arrange its information in a logical order. But logical organization is not enough. You also need to use **transitional devices** to tie your ideas together. The three main techniques for doing so are repeating key words and ideas, using pronouns, and using transitional words (Exhibit 5-6).

Repeating Key Words and Ideas By repeating key words and ideas from one sentence to the next, you can smoothly connect

LO5-13 Make paragraphs coherent.

Exhibit 5-6 Enhancing Coherence

After organizing your material logically, the three main ways to give your sentences and paragraphs coherence are

- repetition of key words.
- use of pronouns (to refer back to something earlier).
- use of appropriate transitional words.

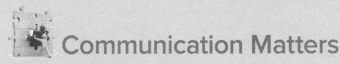

Communication Matters

Beware the Vague or Illogical *This*

When using *this* to add coherence to your writing, be careful to make the reference both clear and logical.

What does *this* refer to in the following example?

> I do not think the donors should be listed on the website. *This* may make some viewers feel uncomfortable or pressured to donate.

This almost refers to something clearly, but not quite. We can make the meaning sharp by revising the example in one of these two ways:

> I do not think the donors should be listed on the website. *Naming the donors* could make some viewers feel uncomfortable or pressured to donate.

> I think we should avoid naming the donors on the website. *This practice* could make some viewers feel uncomfortable or pressured to donate.

Here's another example:

> We need exposure to other markets. One of the easiest ways to do *this* is to advertise strategically.

"One of the easiest ways" to do what? There is nothing in the previous sentence that *do this* can refer to. Here's a possible correction:

> We need to gain exposure to other markets. One of the easiest ways to do this is to advertise strategically.

Now *do this* has something it can refer to: "gain exposure."

Any time you use the word *this* to refer to previous content, be sure the reference is clear. If it isn't, reword the content or write "this [something]" (e.g., "this practice").

---

successive ideas. The following sentences illustrate this transitional device (key words are in italics):

> I am a certified financial planner (CFP) and a member of the Financial Planning Association (FPA). Roughly 70 percent of the *FPA's 23,800 members are CFPs*. To earn this designation, we had to pass a difficult exam. In addition, about half the *members* have been in business at least 15 years. As an *organization,* we want to establish *planning* as a true profession, one seen in the same light as medicine, the law, and accounting.

Using Pronouns Because pronouns refer to words previously used, they make good transitions between ideas. The demonstrative pronouns (*this, that, these, those*) can be especially helpful. The following sentences (with the demonstrative pronouns in italics) illustrate this technique.

> During the three years that Easy Vac has been on the market, our customers have recommended only one improvement: making it more lightweight. The research department has devoted many hours to *this* improvement, and we are pleased to announce that *these* efforts have succeeded. Next year's model will weigh 3.2 pounds less while delivering the same powerful suction.

A word of caution, though: When using *this* or another demonstrative pronoun to refer to an earlier sentence, try to use it with a noun—for example, *this plan*—to make the reference clear (see the Communication Matters box "Beware the Vague or Illogical *This*").

Using Transitional Words When you talk in everyday conversation, you connect many of your thoughts with transitional words. But when you write, you may not use them enough. So be alert for places where providing such words will help move your readers through your paragraphs.

Some commonly used transitional expressions are *in addition, besides, in spite of, in contrast, however, likewise, thus, therefore, for example,* and *also*. A more extensive list appears in Chapter 11, which discusses transitions in reports. These words bridge thoughts by indicating the nature of the connection between what has been said and what will be said next. *In addition*, for example, tells the reader that what is to be discussed next builds on what has been discussed. *However* clearly signals that a contrasting idea is coming. *Likewise* indicates that what will be said resembles what has just been said.

Communication Matters

The Most Commonly Misused Transitional Expression?

One transitional expression seems to cause writers special trouble: "as such."

When is this transitional expression appropriate?

The answer is that it is appropriate *when it comes after a sentence about someone or something and comes before another statement about that person or thing*. Here are some examples:

Correct: Joe was just elected president. *As such*, he will chair the board meeting.

Correct: This computer program will be cloud based. *As such*, it will enable users to access it 24-7.

As you can see, the word that follows "as such" needs to rename something in the preceding sentence.

"As such" does not mean "therefore" or "as a result," so it is used incorrectly in this example:

Incorrect: The deadline has been moved up two weeks. *As such*, we will need to have our report completed by May 2.

The reader expects the next word after "as such" to be "it" (referring back to the deadline), so the word "we" is disorienting. You can correct the problem by using the more appropriate transitional expression for this sentence:

Correct: The deadline has been moved up two weeks. *Therefore*, we'll need to have our report completed by May 2.

Notice how the transitional expressions (in italics) in the following paragraph show the relations among the parts and move the reader steadily forward through the ideas:

> Three reasons justify shutting down the Crowton site. *First*, the building rock in the Crowton deposits is nearly exhausted. *Second*, the distances from the Crowton site to major markets make transportation costs unusually high. *Third*, the out-of-date equipment at the Crowton plant makes this an ideal time for relocation.

The transition words *first, second*, and *third* bring out the paragraph's pattern of organization and make it easy for the reader to follow along.

Here's another example:

> *In summary*, the survey results revealed that over half of our employees already volunteer in the community. *Moreover*, the remainder of the respondents indicated a largely positive attitude toward volunteering. *At the same time*, those who do not yet volunteer said that they felt too busy to do so. *Thus*, if the new program gave employees time off for volunteering or required a minimal time commitment, it would likely increase participation.

The transitional expressions convey that the paragraph summarizes what came before (*in summary*), that there's more good news (*moreover*), that there's an obstacle (*at the same time*), but that it can be overcome with the right program (*thus*).

Keep in mind that transitional devices can also be used between paragraphs—to tie thoughts together, to keep the focus of the message sharp, and to move the reader smoothly from point to point. Strive for coherence on both the paragraph and the document level.

Make Each Paragraph Serve a Strategic Purpose

LO5-14 Give each paragraph a strategic job to do.

Each paragraph needs to make a clear point. But it also needs to contribute to your overall communication strategy.

So ask yourself not only what each paragraph is saying but also what it is *doing*. Establishing rapport? Adding further support to a point? Explaining why something happened? Answering the reader's next question? Building the reader's confidence in your company? Awareness of each paragraph's strategic purpose will not only help you keep your paragraphs efficient and unified; it will also help you build an effective document overall.

One strategy for being mindful of each paragraph's purpose is to create a **says/does chart**. To fill out the chart, you go through your draft and describe, first, what each paragraph is about and, second, what role it plays in your communication strategy for the whole document. Exhibit 5-7 provides an example. As you can see, the chart is a great way to check that each part of your document advances your overall purpose. Even if you don't go so far as to fill out such a chart, you can use the basic idea to review and, if necessary, revise your paragraphs.

Exhibit 5-7   A Says/Does Chart for a Progress Report

Read the report below and then see how the student filled in a says/does chart to describe each paragraph's communication purpose.

Memo Report

Date: May 12, 2017

To: Professor Rodriguez

From: Sam Ellis SE

Subject: Group Four's Progress on the Report for Ms. Herbert

Our group consists of Bo Riddle, Ina Ward, Tiffany Paine, and me. We have made good progress on gathering information to help Ms. Herbert decide whether to include personality testing in her hiring process for Fashion Sense.

Research Topics and Methods

In our first group meeting, on May 3, we decided to investigate the following topics, assigned as shown:

- Types of personality testing available (Tiffany)
- Use of personality testing in the retail industry (Ina)
- Cost of personality testing (Bo)
- Possible legal risks of personality testing (me)

To research the types of testing available, we conducted mostly Internet research. We did both Internet and library research to investigate the remaining topics. We also interviewed Amy Loehmann, a professor in the law school, about possible legal issues.

Findings So Far

In the first week of work, we have gathered these main findings:

- Companies use many different kinds of personality tests, such as the Big Five personality test (see queendom.com) and tests based on four personality types (see MaximumAdvantage.com). But the most popular is the Myers-Briggs Type Indicator. Given its proven track record, Ms. Herbert is likely to want to use some version of this test if she adopts personality testing.
- Large retail stores such as Macy's do use personality testing, but we have not yet found much use of such testing for smaller businesses like Ms. Herbert's.
- Personality testing can be extremely expensive if the company hires a trained consultant to conduct the testing. For large-scale testing, these consultants charge thousands of dollars. However, many small testing outfits provide relatively simple, yet valid, tests. For example, for about $500, Proven Results will test a company's high-performing employees and develop a personality test based on those employees' traits (ProvenResults.com). This test can then be given to job applicants to determine their suitability for the work.
- Personality testing can definitely pose legal risks. Mainly, one must be sure not to ask questions that discriminate against the test takers on the basis of religion, race, or gender. If a company hires a consultant or firm like ProvenResults to do the testing, that person or firm will be the responsible legal party. If one doesn't hire a third party, it is advisable to have an attorney review the testing procedure before it is used.

Next Steps

We will continue to explore the kinds of tests that might be suitable for Ms. Herbert. Specifically, we will try to find out what kinds of personality tests the smaller retail companies use and which of these might be appropriate for Fashion Sense.

We will also try to determine the most cost-effective method for Ms. Herbert to adopt and acquire contact information for any testing services that look promising.

We are on track to have a complete draft of our report prepared by the May 22 deadline. This is an interesting project, and we believe we will be able to help Ms. Herbert make a well-informed decision.

Source: Kathryn Rentz and Paula Lentz, *M: Business Communication*, 3rd ed. (New York: McGraw-Hill, 2014).

Paragraph number	Says	Does
1 [Intro to the report]	Says who is in this student group and what their topic is; assesses their progress thus far.	Reminds the reader who's in the group and what its topic is so she doesn't have to consult her notes.
		Gives her an overall assessment that will help her comprehend what is to follow; saves the details for later sections.
		Conveys an image of the group as well organized and focused.
2 [Intro paragraph of the section "Progress Thus Far"]	Says how the group has divided up the work overall and introduces the list of individual assignments that follows.	Previews the list of individual areas of responsibility. Shows that the group has divided up the work in a logical, fair way and anticipated all important parts of the project.
3 [Bulleted list]	Says what each person is responsible for and what kind of progress he/she has made.	Shows that the work has been divided evenly and that there are no slackers.
		Includes concrete evidence of research thus far to attest to the groups' effort/research skills and to build confidence in their project.
4 [Intro paragraph of the section "Work Still to Be Completed"]	Provides a general statement of the main areas of information yet to be researched.	Helps the reader easily grasp what remains to be done. Builds the reader's confidence in the group's ability to direct/motivate itself.
5 [Bulleted list]	Lists the three most important kinds of information that are still needed; explains where/how the group will try to find them.	Helps the reader assess the likelihood of the project's success and advise the group if necessary. Builds confidence in the group's commitment/efforts/research skills.
6 [Concluding paragraph]	Says that the group is on track to complete a draft by the due date; states that they expect the findings to be useful.	Shows the reader that they are aware of and heeding the assigned deadlines.
		Displays convincing enthusiasm for the project and an awareness of its purpose, both of which bode well for its quality.

Power Charge Your Professionalism: Make Your Subjects and Verbs Agree in Number

Select the word that completes each sentence. Identify which subject–verb agreement guide from Reference Chapter A you used in making your choice.

1. A lot of time and energy (is/are) required for this project to succeed.
2. Sarah, along with several members of her staff, (support/supports) the policy change.
3. Neither the 20 vacation days nor the salary (was/were) enough to persuade Jorge to take the job.
4. Each of the interns (receives/receive) a monthly stipend and a parking permit.
5. The cost and the timeline of the project (makes/make) it unlikely that we will proceed.
6. The report on the costs associated with the technology updates (is/are) due next Friday.
7. The jury (is/are) expected to return with a verdict this afternoon.
8. Barr, Douglass, and Company (is/are) going out of business.

Making your subjects and verbs agree is important because . . .

- Readers become disoriented, and may have to reread the sentence, when they come to the verb and it does not match the subject. This wastes their time and distracts them from the message.
- Using the wrong verb makes it appear that you don't know what the subject of your own sentence is or weren't careful enough to avoid the error.

For further instruction on subject–verb agreement, see the exercises in the "Grammar and Common Sentence Problems" section of LearnSmart Achieve.

Key Terms

plain language 137
concrete words 139
abstract words 139
specific wording 139
denotation 140
connotation 140
two-word expressions
   (idioms) 140
dummy subject 141
active voice 142

camouflaged verb 143
cluttering phrase 146
surplus words 146
redundancies 147
main clauses 148
coordination 148
subordination 148
short sentences 148
unity 149
mixed construction 149

incomplete construction 150
dangling modifier 151
misplaced modifier 151
faulty parallelism 151
topic sentence 153
coherence 154
transitional devices 154
says/does chart 156

Critical-Thinking Questions

1. "Using short words makes the writing sound too simple and not very intelligent." Discuss. LO1

2. "It is important to use business clichés like *best practices* and *leveraging our strengths* to sound professional." Discuss. LO2

3. "Because technical language typically consists of acronyms and long, hard words, it can contribute to miscommunication. The best policy is to avoid such terms in business communication." Discuss. LO3

4. List synonyms (words with similar meanings) for each of the following terms. Then explain the differences in their shades of meaning. LO4
   a. salesperson
   b. co-worker
   c. old
   d. tell
   e. happiness
   f. customer
   g. boss
   h. misfortune
   i. inquire
   j. stop
   k. lie
   l. mistake

5. Explain what's wrong with this sentence: "This procedure is different than the one we use." What kind of error is this? Can you come up with other examples besides those provided in the chapter? LO5

6. Define and give examples of active and passive voice. Explain when each should be used. LO6

7. Take a look at this thank-you message to a new customer. Using the advice in this chapter, how would you revise it to make it more effective? LO1–LO6

   Dear [new customer],

   You are welcomed as a new customer and thanked for your business.

   It will be seen that we have a lot of wonderful products that have gained us notoriety in our industry. Plus, our CRM is second to none. If you ever have a complaint, our customer-service girls will take care of it ASAP.

   We are anxious to serve you further and look forward to a harmonious and mutually profitable collaborative experience.

8. Discuss this comment: "Long sentences tend to be difficult to understand. Therefore, the shorter the sentence, the better." LO7

9. Write a sentence with several parts that emphasizes one of the pieces of information and then rewrite the sentence to emphasize a different piece. What caused the change in emphasis? LO8

10. This chapter discusses two common causes of lack of unity in sentences: irrelevant points and unnecessary detail. Thinking about the writing process, why do you think these problems occur? LO9

11. Style experts advise against monotonous-sounding writing—that is, writing that has a droning, "blah-blah" effect when read aloud. What advice in this chapter might help you avoid this kind of style? LO1–LO9

12. This chapter discusses several kinds of illogical wording in sentences. Give an example of each, explain the problem, and correct it. LO10

13. Analyze the use of paragraph breaks in several different types of business writing (e.g., a sales letter, blog post, business article, report). In what ways do these examples use paragraph breaks differently? Can you think of reasons why the paragraphs would be longer in one type of document than in another? LO11

14. "Topic sentences are useful for reports and letters, but email messages don't need them." Discuss. LO12

15. Describe and illustrate the three main transitional devices. LO13

16. Fill in a says/does chart for a sample blog post, email message, or letter. What role does each paragraph seem intended to play in the overall communication strategy? Could any of the paragraphs do a better job of playing its role? LO14

Skills-Building Exercises

Using Familiar, Short Words LO1

Assume that your readers have about a 10th-grade education. Revise these sentences for easy communication to this audience.

1. Many creditable studies have ascertained that direct mail is still a viable sales technique.

2. We must endeavor to correct this problem by expediting delivery.

3. A proportionate tax consumes a determinate apportionment of one's monetary assets.

4. Many people believe that business has an inordinate influence on governmental operations.

5. It is imperative that the survey recipients be unrestrained in indicating their preferences.

6. Can we ascertain the types of customers that have a predisposition to utilize our instant-credit offer?

7. The preponderance of the advisory personnel we consulted envisioned signs of improvement from the current economic stagnation.

8. The company must desist from its deficit financing immediately.

Using Slang and Popular Clichés with Caution LO2

Revise the following sentences to eliminate slang and annoying popular expressions. Would any of them be acceptable under the right circumstances? If so, which and when?

1. We need a marketing strategy that will move us beyond the low-hanging fruit.

2. He doesn't have the bandwidth right now to take on another project.

3. This design is so not what I had in mind!

4. We are reaching out to you today to tell you about our new line of training products.

5. We should synergize our efforts to enhance our customer service.

6. The vendors we work with are super reliable.

7. Why don't you two take this discussion offline and bring a possible solution to the next meeting?

8. I would rank Tom Jenkins at the top of our list of candidates because he is crazy smart.

Using Technical Words and Acronyms Appropriately LO3

1. Select a paragraph from one of your textbooks that would be difficult for a student with no background in the subject matter to understand. Rewrite the paragraph so that this student can understand it easily.

2. Using examples other than those in the book, identify some terms that would probably need to be defined for those outside the profession or area of business in which these terms are used.

Selecting Concrete, Specific Words LO4

Revise these sentences to make them more precise and informative.

1. We are currently recruiting young people for internships.

2. She has a strong employment record as an accountant.

3. I spent a lot of time each week volunteering for nonprofit organizations.

4. If we don't receive the goods soon, we will cancel our order.

5. The cost of the online subscription was reasonable.

6. There is only a little time left on our copier's warranty.

7. The findings show that a lot of our employees are in favor of working from home one day a week.

8. Please donate your clothing to Dress for Success.

Avoiding the Use of Incorrect Similar Words LO5

Some of the following sentences are correct, and some are not. Indicate the correct sentences and correct the problem sentences.

1. We have less than 25 registrants so far.

2. I did not mean to infer that you had made a mistake.

3. He is not adverse to your suggestion; he simply wants more information.

4. The handbook offers advise on professional behavior.

5. Please except my apologies.

6. A complementary breakfast is included.

7. Write in such a way that you elicit the response you want.

8. This laptop needs its' battery replaced.

9. There is no reason why we should refund their money.

Using Two-Word Expressions Correctly LO5

These sentences misuse two-word expressions. Make the changes you think are necessary.

1. The purchasing officer has gone in search for a substitute product.

2. Based off of the auditor's report, I recommend that we invest more of our cash.

3. This strike was different than the one in 2000.

4. This letter is equally as bad.

5. She is an authority about mutual funds.

6. When the sale is over with, we will restock.

7. The service truck collided against the wall.

8. We have been in search for a qualified supervisor since August.

Limiting Use of Passive Voice and Dummy Subjects LO6

Revise the following sentences to give them action verbs.

1. It is expected that our competition will be taken by surprise by the new ad campaign.

2. It is believed by the typical union member that his or her welfare is not considered to be important by management.

3. There is interest among our customers in a less-expensive version.

4. The notes taken by the secretary will be posted on the website.

5. The union was represented by Cecil Chambers.

6. These reports are prepared by the salespeople every Friday.

7. If more information is needed, the customer service department can be contacted.

8. There are many obligations that we must meet.

Avoiding Camouflaged Verbs LO6

Revise the following to eliminate camouflaged verbs.

1. We will get back to you after we have made a determination of the damages.

2. Harold made a recommendation that we apply for a grant.

3. We will ask him to bring about a change in his work routine.

4. This new equipment will result in a savings in maintenance.

5. Will you please make an adjustment on this invoice?

6. The committee will begin implementation of the plan in January.

7. Approval of all orders must be made by the chief.

8. A committee performs the function of determining the award winner.

9. Verification of the amount is made daily by the auditor.

10. The president tried to effect a reconciliation of the two groups.

Making Sentences Economical LO7

Revise the following sentences for more economical wording.

1. Due to the fact that we financed the experiment, we received a share of the profits.

2. We should see the prime lending rate increase in the near future.

3. I will talk to him with regard to the new policy.

4. Mary is of the opinion that service has improved.

5. It is essential that we take the actions that are necessary to correct the problem.

6. We must keep this confidential information from being shared with others.

7. You should study all new innovations in your field.

8. In all probability, we are likely to suffer a loss this quarter.

9. The job requires a minimum of three years of experience.

10. In spite of the fact that they hadn't paid their previous bill, they placed another order.

Managing Sentence Content LO7–LO9

Make these sentences more readable, and the main points clear, by breaking them up, tightening the wording, and/or restructuring them.

1. Records were set Wednesday by both the New York Stock Exchange Composite Index, which closed at 8,001.40 up 27.08 points, topping its previous high of 7,986.50, and Standard & Poor's 500 Index, which finished at 1,264.03, up 6.90, setting a five-day high.

2. Reserving this property requires a $500 security deposit, which will be refunded unless there is damage to the property or evidence that there has been smoking in the cottage or a pet on the premises or if the reservation is canceled within 30 days prior to the rental period.

3. The Consumer Education Committee is assigned the duties of keeping informed of the qualities of all consumer goods and services, especially of their strengths and shortcomings, of gathering all pertinent information on dealers' sales practices, with emphasis on practices involving honest and reasonable fairness, and of publicizing any of the information collected that may be helpful in educating the consumer.

4. As you will not get this part of Medicare automatically, even if you are covered by Social Security, you must sign up for it and pay $88.50 per month, which the government will match, if you want your physician's bills to be covered.

5. Given our discussion yesterday, I have decided that you may choose either to take the final exam or to have the paper for which you received your highest grade count as an additional 15 percent of your course grade, but you must let me know in writing by May 1 which of these options you prefer or else the exam will be mandatory.

6. Although we have not definitely determined the causes for the decline in sales volume for the month, we know that during this period construction on the street adjacent to the store severely limited traffic flow and that because of resignations in the advertising department, our promotion efforts dropped well below normal.

Wording Sentences Logically LO10

Revise the following to eliminate illogical and awkward wording.

1. Because the Swift Company has a service-oriented culture is the reason it supports all forms of volunteerism.

2. Our staff is among the best as we strive for the highest level of customer service.

3. Thank you for your feedback that will help us continue to improve.

4. The meeting room you have reserved has a projector, Internet access, and will enable your attendees to hear the trainer easily.

5. As a five-star hotel, our guests' satisfaction is our top priority.

6. Upon reviewing the facts, the problem was a short in the wiring.

7. This streamlined process will save us so much money.

8. Depending on how you phrase your request will determine how the boss will respond.

9. In order to accommodate your request, please make your reservation by the end of October.

10. On behalf of the management team, I appreciate your extra work on the project.

11. We need to know how many will attend, and please indicate their choice of entrée.

12. As a member of the marketing staff, the best person to consult on this project is Allal.

13. As far as phone-call monitoring, I believe we should try other methods first.

14. Through our research of three local charities we feel that each one would be a good one to sponsor.

15. Each department will now have access to update your section of the website.

16. It is such a worthy cause, but I fear the organization's website will not attract many donors.

17. This is an important message, but by placing it in a long paragraph, it is unlikely that many people will read it.

18. As a 501(c)(3) organization, donations are tax deductible.

19. You can volunteer to help with publicity, set up, clean up, or you can bring refreshments.

20. From the results of the survey, it is clear that viewers preferred the second design.

Managing Emphasis, Focus, and Flow LO8, LO12, LO13

Write a topic sentence for each of the following, and reword any of the other sentences as needed to create a smooth, clear paragraph.

1. Jennifer has a good knowledge of office procedures. She works hard. She has performed her job well. She is pleasant most of the time, but she has a bad temper, which has led to many personal problems with the work group. I cannot recommend her for promotion. I approve a 5 percent raise for her.

2. Last year our sales increased 7 percent in California and 9 percent in Arizona. Nevada had the highest increase, with 14 percent. Although all states in the western region enjoyed increases, Oregon recorded only a 2 percent gain. Sales in Washington increased 3 percent.

3. I majored in marketing at Darden University and received a B.S. degree in 2011. Among the marketing courses I took were marketing strategy, promotion, marketing research, marketing management, and consumer behavior. These and other courses prepared me specifically for a career in retailing. I completed a one-semester internship in retailing with Macy's Department Stores.

4. Our records show that Penn motors cost more than Oslo motors. The Penns have less breakdown time. They cost more to repair. I recommend that we buy Penn motors the next time we replace worn-out motors. The longer working life offsets Penn's cost disadvantage. So does its better record for breakdown.

5. Recently China ordered a large quantity of wheat from the United States. Likewise, Germany ordered a large quantity. Other countries continued to order heavily, resulting in a dramatic improvement in the outlook for wheat farming. Increased demand by Eastern European countries also contributed to the improved outlook.

Managing Information in Sentences and Paragraphs LO8–LO13

Assume that you are the assistant manager of a hotel and are describing your hotel's meeting room to a prospective customer who is thinking of holding a seminar there. Turn the following choppy paragraph into coherent writing, making paragraph breaks where you think appropriate. Be ready to explain why you grouped the information and managed the emphasis the way you did. You may need to add some words or information to make the facts flow smoothly.

We have a meeting room. It will be available on the date you requested. It can seat 100 people. The seating can be arranged to your specifications. It is quiet. It is on the ground floor. It is not near the guest rooms. The lounge has live music on occasion. The lounge is at the opposite end of the hotel from the meeting room. The meeting room has a lectern. It has a projector. It has a screen. It has laptop hookup. We can rent additional equipment. We can rent it at no charge to you. The charge for the room is $300. This is the charge for one day.

Building Positive Relationships
through Communication

© Betsie Van der Meer/Getty Images

Chapter Six

As Chapter 1 points out, conveying information is not your only communication goal. Communication involves a human relations dimension, and if you neglect it, you will lose customers, alienate your co-workers, and lose the support of your superiors. The "people" content of your messages often needs as much attention as the informational content—and in some cases, it will be your primary consideration.

Sure, it's easier to fire off a curt email to a complaining customer or an annoying co-worker than to slow down and take that person's feelings into account. But messages written or spoken in haste have a way of coming back to haunt you. Think of a time you felt mistreated by someone in business. Perhaps you got an insensitive reply from an insurance company or an impersonal rejection letter from a company you were hoping to work for. Perhaps you even felt misled or lied to. Such interactions leave you with negative feelings about the company that will probably last a long time. Plus, you may spread those feelings to other potential customers or employees— or even go onto the Internet to broadcast your displeasure.

This chapter will help you see how to communicate in a way that elicits positive responses. In other words, it will help you build **goodwill** with your business associates and customers. Businesses cannot survive without goodwill, and you will not last long in business if you do not value it. Courteous, pleasant, ethical behavior is part of being a professional. Read on to see how to make your communications meet this professional standard.

Learning Objectives

LO6-1 Use the you-viewpoint to build goodwill.

LO6-2 Use a conversational style that has the appropriate level of formality and avoids "rubber stamps."

LO6-3 Describe ways to be courteous beyond using polite expressions.

LO6-4 Employ positive language to achieve goodwill and other desired effects.

LO6-5 Use the three major techniques for emphasizing the positive and de-emphasizing the negative.

LO6-6 Avoid unethical communication practices.

LO6-7 Cultivate personal qualities that promote ethical behavior.

LO6-8 Use professional codes of conduct and established approaches to ethical reasoning to help you make ethical decisions.

Problem-Solving Challenge

Affecting Human Relations through Writing

To prepare yourself for this chapter, play the role of Customer Service Director at a large office-supply company. You asked your latest hire, a new college graduate named Jason, to draft a reply to a complaint you received about one of your products. Here is the message he wrote:

> Dear Mr. Morley:
>
> Your December 3rd complaint was received and contents noted. After reviewing the facts, I regret to report that I must refuse your claim. If you will read the warranty brochure, you will see that the shelving you bought is designed for light loads—a maximum of 800 pounds. You should have bought the heavy-duty product.
>
> I regret the damage this mistake caused you and trust that you will see our position.
>
> Hoping to be of service to you in the future,
>
> Jason Abbott
> Customer Service

If this message were to go out, it would be a customer relations disaster. Jason's words are blunt, selfish, and unfriendly. Overall, they leave a bad impression—the impression of a writer and a business unconcerned about others' feelings.

After you read this chapter, play the role of Jason's manager and rewrite the message. Then plan how you would explain to Jason why your version is better.

Showing Consideration for Your Message Recipients

Every chapter in this book emphasizes considering your readers or audience, because doing so is essential for effective communications. The sections that follow will help you show your business associates and customers that you have considered their interests.

Use the You-Viewpoint

L06-1 Use the you-viewpoint to build goodwill.

Communicating from the **you-viewpoint** (also called **you-attitude**) is a powerful tool for building goodwill. It means thinking beyond your own goals to consider the communication situation from the recipients' perspective.

Using the you-viewpoint often means emphasizing *you* and *your* and de-emphasizing *I, we,* and *our,* but such is not always the case. *You* and *your* can appear in a selfish, harsh sentence—for example, "If you do not pay by the 15th, you must pay a penalty." Likewise, *we* and *our* can appear in a sentence that emphasizes the you-viewpoint, as in this example: "Our number-one goal is to protect your investment."

The you-viewpoint thus goes beyond choice of pronouns. It's an attitude of mind that places the recipient at the center of the message. Sometimes it just involves being friendly and treating people the way they like to be treated. Sometimes it involves skillfully managing people's response with carefully chosen words in a carefully designed order. How you apply it will depend on each situation and your own judgment.

The first step toward creating goodwill with your communication partners is to put yourself in their shoes.
© Claudiad/Getty Images

You-Viewpoint on the Sentence Level Although the you-viewpoint involves much more than word selection, you can often find opportunities for building goodwill by carefully considering your sentences.

For example, compare the wording in each pair of sentences below:

I-centered: I am happy to tell you that your proposal has been accepted.

You-centered: Congratulations! Your proposal for a professional development grant has been accepted.

We-centered: We are pleased that you have opened a charge account with Lowe's.

You-centered: Your new Lowe's charge account is now open!

Would the readers be offended if you used the less reader-centered wording in these examples? Probably not. But you would demonstrate more reader awareness by keeping the focus off yourself.

The following additional examples demonstrate the different effects that changes in viewpoint are likely to produce at the sentence level.

We-Viewpoint	You-Viewpoint
We are happy to have your order for Hewlett-Packard products, which we are sending today by UPS.	Your Hewlett-Packard printers were shipped by UPS today and should reach you by noon tomorrow.
Our policy does not permit outside groups to use our facilities unless they pay a rental fee.	Outside groups are welcome to rent our facilities. Your rental will ensure that your guests enjoy the park's full range of services.
We have been quite tolerant of your past-due account and must now demand payment.	If you are to continue to enjoy the benefits of credit buying, you must clear your account now.
We have received your report of May 1.	Thank you for your report of May 1.

You-Viewpoint on the Message Level Put yourself in the place of Jane Bryan. Her family, who are spread across the eastern, southern, and midwestern United States, put her in charge of finding a venue for a family reunion. After a great deal of Internet searching, she found two large, nice houses on Lake Michigan. The rest of the family approved the choice—though the cost for the week was quite steep ($10,600), and some of the family would have significant travel expenses. The representative of the rental company, though pleasant, was firm about receiving the fee in advance, so Jane also worked with the other family members to gather the money and make these payments on time.

Then, three weeks before the scheduled reunion, Jane received the following email message from her contact at the rental company:

You Make the Call
How would you have felt if you'd gotten this message? Why?

Good afternoon Jane,

I wanted to touch base with you because I visited the properties you are renting and noted that the private beaches for the properties are not as sandy as they are in the public beach area. As this is an act of nature and has only affected the *private* beaches, there will be no reimbursements, relocations, or other compensation applied as this is clearly outside of Lakeside Vacations' and the homeowners' control. Parking passes for the public beach will be provided in the homes.

I have attached a photo of the beach to give you a visual of what I observed.

As always, thank you for vacationing with Lakeside Vacations.

Beth

The attached photo showed a "beach" that was about 10 feet deep and completely covered with rocks. There was no sandy area anywhere.

This communication actually occurred (with the parties' names changed). Jane was not happy, but she decided to follow through with the reunion plans. However, she learned several months later that this rental company had gone out of business. She wasn't really surprised.

Consider the difference it might have made had the rental company's message gone like this:

Good afternoon, Jane,

I'm writing to let you know that severe spring storms in the St. Joseph area have eroded the beaches of the lakefront rental properties in the area. The attached photo shows the current condition of the beaches. The winds and currents can have this effect, and while they sometimes restore the sand, we can't guarantee that this will happen by the time of your family's visit.

Fortunately, St. Joseph has an extensive public beach that is only about a mile from your rental properties (click here to see beach photos). You will find complimentary parking passes for your family inside the homes. The beach has a jungle gym, a concessions stand, and umbrellas and chairs for rent. The boat and jet ski rental office is also there.

Of course, your magnificent view of the lake, your swimming pool, and the opportunity for walks along the beach have not been affected! You may also enjoy exploring the downtown area, taking one of the winery tours, or going on other excursions in this popular vacation spot.

Please let us know if we can assist you further with your planning. We look forward to your visit.

Beth

You Make the Call

Would you have revised the original message differently? For example, do you think the tone in the revised message is too positive?

As you can see from this example, using the you-viewpoint not only consists of using reader-centered pronouns when appropriate; it also means supplying helpful information and making the reader feel good about the decision to do business with you.

Ethical Use of the You-Viewpoint The you-viewpoint has been a matter of some controversy. Its critics argue that it can be insincere and manipulative, and, unfortunately, it is sometimes used this way. We've probably all encountered businesspeople—and others—who used flattery or fake friendliness to try to get their way.

To avoid being one of them, be sincerely interested in your reader. Develop an understanding of the importance of goodwill and an appreciation for the positive relationships that it helps build. Remember how you like to be treated, and treat others that way.

You can also keep in mind that the you-viewpoint helps readers see quickly in what ways a given message applies to them. This "translation" work supports both clarity and courtesy. When sincerely applied, the you-viewpoint benefits both the writer or speaker and the recipient.

LO6-2   Use a conversational style that has the appropriate level of formality and avoids "rubber stamps."

Use a Conversational Style

Another technique that helps build goodwill is to write in **conversational language**. Conversational language is warm, natural, and personable. It engages the reader, and it is also the language that is most easily understood.

In business, a conversational style does not always mean being colloquial. It does mean tailoring your language to your reader and avoiding stiff, impersonal wording.

Choose the Right Level of Formality

Business relationships are much more casual than they used to be. As recently as the early 20th century, routine business letters would contain such expressions as "beg to advise," "enclosed herewith," and "thanking you in advance, I remain. . . ." But companies have flatter organizational structures now, and the business world in general has a friendlier tone. Many top executives promote a relaxed company culture, and some wear t-shirts and blue jeans to work.

Still, a certain formality is expected in many business situations, just as many businesspeople still wear suits. When to be formal and when to be casual will depend on whom you're communicating with, what genre you're using, and what you're saying. If you choose the wrong **level of formality** for the situation, you run the risk of offending your reader. A too-formal style can sound impersonal and parental, but a too-informal style can make you sound unprofessional.

The more formal style is appropriate when you are

- Communicating with someone you don't know.

- Communicating with someone at a higher level than you.

- Using a relatively formal genre, such as a letter, long report, or external proposal.

- Preparing a ceremonial message, such as a commendation or inspirational announcement.

- Writing an extremely serious message, such as a crisis response or official reprimand.

When you are communicating in less formal situations, you can bring your formality down a notch. Co-workers and other associates who know each other well and are using an informal medium, such as texting, often joke and use emoticons (e.g., a smiley face) and initialisms (e.g., BTW) in their correspondence. When appropriate, such touches add goodwill.

Adjusting your level of formality can sometimes be as simple as substituting one word or phrase for another. Compare these examples of more and less formal wording:

More Formal	Less Formal
Studied, investigated, analyzed	Looked into
Rearranged	Juggled
Ensure	Make sure
Exceptional, superior	Great, terrific
As a result, therefore	So
Confirm	Double check
Consult with	Check with
Correct, appropriate	Right
Thank you	Thanks
We will	We'll
I am	I'm
Let me know	Keep me posted

A message using the wording on the left would convey a more formal image but would still sound like a person speaking naturally.

In your effort to sound more formal, do not use stilted or unnecessarily difficult words. You can sound conversational while also being respectful and clear, as these contrasting examples illustrate:

Stiff and Dull	Conversational
Enclosed please find the brochure about which you inquired.	Enclosed is the brochure you requested.
In reply to your July 11 letter, please be advised that your adherence to the following instructions will facilitate the processing of your return.	Here are the procedures for returning your purchase and obtaining a refund.
This is in reply to your letter of December 1, expressing concern that you do not have a high school diploma and asking if a GED would suffice as prerequisite for the TAA Training Program.	The GED you mention in your December 1 letter qualifies you for the TAA Training Program.
This is to acknowledge receipt of your letter dated 5 May 2016.	We received your May 5 letter and have forwarded it to the claims department for immediate attention.

Cut Out "Rubber Stamps" **Rubber stamps** are expressions used by habit every time a certain type of situation occurs. They're called "rubber stamps" because, like the wording on a rubber stamp, their wording is the same for all similar situations.

Because they are used routinely, rubber stamps communicate the effect of routine treatment, which is not likely to impress your recipients favorably. Such treatment tells them that the writer has no special concern for them—that the present case is being handled in the same way as any other. In contrast, words specially selected for the situation demonstrate the writer or speaker's interest in the specific recipient.

© Ingram Publishing

Chapter 5 discusses the problems that slang and popular clichés can cause. Here, we focus on the type of business clichés that are more routine and less colorful than those—the kind of wording that makes a message sound like a form letter. One common example is the "thank you for your letter" opening. Its intent may be sincere, but its overuse makes it a rubber stamp. Another is the closing comment "if I can be of any further assistance, do not hesitate to call on me." Other examples of rubber stamps are the following:

This is to inform you that . . .

Your cooperation is appreciated.

It has come to my (or our) attention that . . .

Thank you for your time.

Please let me know if you have any questions.

Thank you in advance.

Please respond at your earliest convenience.

Perhaps you are asking yourself, "What's wrong with thanking the reader for his or her time or offering to answer questions?" The answer is that such rubber stamps are not specific enough. They signal that you have quit thinking about *this* reader and his or her situation. A better ending is one that thanks the reader for something in particular or that offers to answer questions about a particular topic.

You do not need to know all the rubber stamps to stop using them. You just need to communicate in the language of good conversation, addressing your comments to a real person in a specific situation.

Be Courteous

LO6-3 Describe ways to be courteous beyond using polite expressions.

A major contributor to goodwill in business communication is courtesy. By **courtesy** we mean respectful and considerate treatment of others. Courtesy produces friendly relations between people, and the result is a better human climate for solving business problems and doing business.

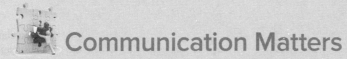

Communication Matters

Business Etiquette—It Depends on Where You Are

Most people are aware that certain unwritten rules for professionalism govern people's business interactions. Those with whom we do business expect us to show respect through our actions, words, and even appearance.

But what is considered appropriate will vary among situations, industries, and countries. For example, in a small informal company, relatively casual clothing and relaxed behavior would be expected, and anyone behaving too formally would be considered stiff and rude. In a more formal setting, such as a bank or the executive offices of a large organization, what one should wear, say, or even laugh at would be more constrained.

Doing business with those in or from another country requires additional considerations. For example, according to research conducted by MBA students at the University of Texas–Dallas, it is considered rude in China for women to wear high heels or wear short-sleeved clothing while doing business, or for men to wear anything besides a conservative business suit. The Chinese are also offended by large hand movements, being pointed at while spoken to, or any actions involving touching the mouth.*

To learn good business etiquette, consult such sources as Judith Bowman's *Don't Take the Last Donut: New Rules of Business Etiquette* (Pompton Plains, NJ: Career Press, 2009), the website *Kwintessential,* and Jeanette S. Martin and Lillian H. Chaney's *Global Business Etiquette: A Guide to International Communication and Customs* (Westport, CT: Praeger, 2012). And then adapt their advice to your specific situation.

*"China," *InternationalBusinessCenter.org*, accessed November 6, 2016, http://international-business-etiquette.com/besite/china.htm.

As with every other facet of your communications, how to be courteous depends on the situation. Including "please," "thank you," "we're sorry," and other standard expressions of politeness do not necessarily make a message courteous. Rather than focusing on stock phrases, consider what will make the recipient feel most comfortable, understood, and appreciated. A message with no overtly polite expressions whatsoever can still demonstrate great courtesy by being easy to understand, focusing on the recipient's interests, and conveying the author's feelings of goodwill.

Using the you-viewpoint and conversational language are two ways of being courteous. Below are three additional ways.

Avoid Blaming the Reader Customers, co-workers, bosses, and others you work with are going to make mistakes—just as you will. When they do, your first reaction is likely to be disappointment, frustration, or even anger. After all, their mistakes will cost you time, energy, and possibly even money.

But you must avoid the temptation to blame the reader when you are resolving a problem. No one likes being accused of negligence, wrongdoing, or faulty thinking. It is better to objectively explain the facts and then move on to a solution.

The following examples illustrate:

Blaming Language	More Positive Language
You failed to indicate which fabric you wanted on the chair you ordered.	To complete your order, please check your choice of fabric on the enclosed card.
If you had read the instructions that came with your cookware, *you would have known* not to submerge it in water.	The instructions explain why the cookware should not be submerged in water.
Your claim that we did not properly maintain the copier is *false*.	Listed below are the dates the copier was serviced and the type of service it received.
Your request for coverage is denied because *you did not follow* the correct appeals procedure.	We need additional information to be able to process your appeal. Please supply [the needed information] and resubmit your request to. . . .

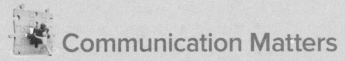

Communication Matters

Parent, Child, or Adult?

In the 1950s, psychologist Eric Berne developed a model of relationships that he called Transactional Analysis. It can be quite useful when applied to business communications.

At the core of this model is the idea that, in all our transactions with others, we occupy one of three positions: parent, child, or adult.

- A *parent* is patronizing, spoiling, nurturing, blaming, criticizing, and/or punishing.
- A *child* is uninhibited, emotional, obedient, whining, irresponsible, and/or selfish.
- An *adult* is reasonable, responsible, considerate, and flexible.

Obviously, using the "adult" tone will reflect best on you in the business world.

But being the adult is also important for another reason: It brings out the adult in your reader. People tend to play the role that your style invites them to play. If you sound parental, your readers will tend toward being childish, and vice versa. Communicating with courtesy and professionalism invites your readers to respond in kind.

Notice two helpful, related strategies in the better language above. One is to avoid using *you* when doing so would blame the reader. In these situations, you will actually have better you-viewpoint if you do not use *you*. The second strategy is to keep the focus on the facts rather than on the people. Sometimes these strategies will require using passive voice, but as Chapter 5 notes, doing so is not only acceptable but desirable in cases when it will keep you from assigning blame.

A more general strategy that can help you maintain good relations is to blow off steam before you handle a negative situation. Try never to send a message composed in anger. Tempting as it can be to do so, you will almost always regret it. Take the time to calm down and use a reasonable tone. A good relationship with your communication partner is worth much more than a moment's self-indulgence.

Refrain from Talking Down to Your Readers You can help make your communications courteous by avoiding any wording that might insult your readers' intelligence.

One type of insulting comment is to tell your readers something that they are already well aware of. The italicized middle sentence in the paragraph below makes this mistake. It is from the beginning of a report that a human resources director asked her assistant to write.

> As you requested, I surveyed the employees to assess their current level of engagement. *Employee engagement has been proven to reduce turnover and enhance performance.* The findings indicate that employees feel somewhat engaged in the company's goals but would be more engaged if there were better company-wide communication.

The writer's boss does not need to be told the business benefits of employee engagement. She obviously understands those benefits because she asked her assistant to survey employees on this topic.

Also potentially insulting are statements that tell the reader how to feel, such as "you'll be happy to know" and "you won't want to miss this." Likewise, statements that include such phrases as "you need," "you want," "you should," and "you must" suggest that the reader isn't an adult capable of making intelligent decisions. (See the Communication Matters feature "Parent, Child, or Adult?" for more advice about striking the right tone with your readers.)

Do More Than Is Expected One sure way to gain goodwill is to do more than you have to do for the recipient of your message. When we're in a hurry, it's tempting to communicate as tersely and quickly as possible, but such an approach can damage goodwill. Taking the time to give your reader a little extra help makes a lasting positive impression.

From the Tech Desk

Courtesy in the Age of Mobile Devices

In the United States, the name Emily Post has been synonymous with good manners for decades. With the publication of *Etiquette in Society, in Business, in Politics, and at Home* in 1922, Post became the undisputed authority on the topic, and she continued to be so the rest of her life. Her children, grandchildren, and great-grandchildren have carried on her tradition. *Emily Post's Etiquette* is now in its 18th edition, and it now includes a chapter about personal communication devices. Here are some excerpts from the chapter:

Cell Phones

- Without exception, turn your device off in a house of worship, restaurant, or theater; during a meeting or presentation; or anytime its use is likely to disturb others.
- If you must be alerted to a call, put your device on silent ring or vibrate, and check your caller ID or voice mail later. (Put it in your pocket; a vibrating phone, skittering across a tabletop, is just as disruptive as a ring.)

- Wherever you are, if you must make or take a call, move to a private space and speak as quietly as you can.
- Keep calls as short as possible; the longer the call, the greater the irritation to those who have no choice but to listen.
- On airplanes, it's a courtesy to everyone on board to quickly wrap up your call when the flight crew instructs passengers to turn off all electronic devices before takeoff. When cell phone use is permitted after landing, keep your calls short, limiting them to information about your arrival. Save any longer calls for a private spot in the terminal.
- Think about what your ring tone says about you. Is your frat boy hip-hop tone the right ring for your new job as a trainee at an accounting firm?

Text Messaging

- Text messaging is a strictly casual communication. You shouldn't use text messaging when informing someone of sad news, business matters, or urgent meetings unless it's to set up a phone call on the subject.

- Be aware of where you are. The backlight will disturb others if you text in a theater or house of worship.
- Keep your message brief. If it's going to be more than a couple of lines, make a call and have a conversation.
- Don't be a pest. Bombarding someone with texts is annoying and assumes they have nothing better to do than read your messages.
- Be very careful when choosing a recipient from your phone book; a slip of the thumb could send a text intended for a friend to your boss.
- Whenever you have a chance, respond to text messages, either by texting back or with a phone call.
- Don't text anything confidential, private, or potentially embarrassing. You never know when your message might get sent to the wrong person or forwarded.

Source: Based on Peggy Post, Anna Post, Lizzie Post, and Daniel Post Senning, *Emily Post's Etiquette: Manners for a New World*, 18th ed. (New York: HarperCollins, 2001), 240–248.

Here are some simple things businesspeople do to be considerate:

- Include an Internet link in an email message rather than making the readers find the site on their own or copy and paste the Web address into their browsers
- Offer an alternative solution when saying "no" to a request
- Tell readers about additional products or services that they might like
- Include tips on how to make the most of a product or service that they've just purchased
- Anticipate readers' questions and supply the information rather than waiting until the readers ask for it
- Attach a map, schedule, report, or other document that will come in handy when readers are trying to do or understand something
- Write a congratulatory note when a reader, or his or her company, has been in the news for a special achievement

Remember that your goal is both to communicate *and* to build positive human relations, and go the extra mile for your readers.

Communication Matters

Accentuating the Positive

LO6-4 Employ positive language to achieve goodwill and other desired effects.

As you know, one can say anything in many ways, and each way conveys a different meaning. In most cases, positive or neutral wording will succeed better than negative wording.

Use Positive Words

As Chapter 5 points out, all words have certain emotional associations. Because people generally prefer positive to negative feelings, **positive words** are usually best for achieving your communication goals. This is not to say that negative words have no place in business communication. Sometimes you must call a problem a problem or convey a negative message in no uncertain terms. But positive wording is usually more appropriate. It tends to put the reader in a receptive frame of mind, and it helps create the goodwill on which positive relationships depend.

Be particularly wary of strongly negative words, such as *mistake, failure, refuse, cannot, blame,* and *fault.* They have unpleasant associations that usually detract from your goal. If possible, use more positive alternatives.

Focus on What You *Can* Do

Oftentimes when we have to convey negative news, the fact that we must say "no" dominates our thinking. This reaction leads us to communicate in a style that is more negative and selfish than it actually has to be. In many cases, you will be able to help solve the reader's problem even if you cannot do exactly what he or she wants.

Let's consider the case of an employee who needs to respond to a local civic group's request to use the company's auditorium. The auditorium won't be available for their use, but the conference room will be. If the employee were unduly focused on the negative, he might write this response:

> We *regret* to inform you that we *cannot* permit you to use our auditorium for your meeting, as the Sun City Investment Club asked for it first. We can, however, let you use our conference room, but it seats *only* 60.

Look how the italicized words tilt the whole message toward the negative. The positively intended opening,

When you handle a sensitive situation in person, you can use body language and tone of voice to help convey goodwill. When you're writing, you can't. This makes careful word choice in written messages especially important.

© mentatdgt/Shutterstock

"We *regret* to inform you," is an unmistakable sign of coming bad news. "*Cannot* permit" is unnecessarily harsh. Even the good-news part of the message is hindered by the limiting word *only*. Because the writer focused only on the negative aspects of the situation, that is what the reader is being asked to focus on as well.

Had the employee considered the situation more positively, he might have written this instead:

> Although the SunCity Investment Club has reserved the auditorium for Saturday, we can offer you our conference room, which seats 60.

Not a single negative word appears in this version, even though it essentially says the same thing. The reader's response to this message would be much more likely to be positive.

Here are a few more examples that show what a difference positive wording can make (the negative words are in italics):

Negative	Positive
Smoking is *not* permitted anywhere except in the lobby.	Smoking is permitted in the lobby only.
We *cannot* deliver your order until Friday.	We can deliver your order on Friday.
We *regret* that we *overlooked* your coverage on this equipment and apologize for the *trouble* and *concern* it must have caused you.	You were quite right in believing that you have coverage on the equipment. We have now credited your account for. . .
We *regret* to inform you that the guest room is not available on the date you requested.	The guest room is already booked for the evening of August 7. Would August 8 be a possibility? We would be able to accommodate your party at any time on that date.

Manage Emphasis for a Positive Effect

Getting the desired response often involves giving proper emphasis to the items in the message. As Chapter 5 discussed, every message contains a number of facts and ideas that must be presented. Some of these items are more important than others, and some will be received more positively than others. A part of your job as a writer is to determine which items to emphasize in your message.

The three ways to manage **emphasis** for a positive effect are to use position, sentence structure, and space.

Emphasis by Position The beginnings and endings of your communications will carry more emphasis than the center parts. This rule of emphasis applies whether the unit is the message, a paragraph of the message, or a sentence within the paragraph (see Exhibit 6-1).

In light of this fact, you should put your more positive points in the beginning and ending and, if possible, avoid putting negative points in these positions. If you were to use this technique in a paragraph turning down a suggestion, you might write it like this (the key point is in italics):

> In light of the current budget crunch, we approved those suggestions that would save money while not costing much to implement. While *your plan is not feasible at this time,* we hope you will submit it again next year when we should have more resources for implementing it.

As you can see, putting information in the middle tends to de-emphasize it. Consider position carefully when organizing your positive and negative contents.

Sentence Structure and Emphasis Closely related to the technique of using position to manage emphasis is that of using sentence structure. As noted in Chapter 5, short, simple sentences and main clauses call attention to their content. To de-emphasize negative points, see if you can subordinate them by putting them into dependent clauses

LO6-5 Use the three major techniques for emphasizing the positive and de-emphasizing the negative.

Exhibit 6-1 Positions of Emphasis

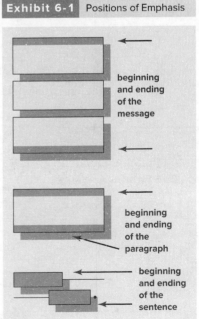

beginning and ending of the message

beginning and ending of the paragraph

beginning and ending of the sentence

Source: Kathryn Rentz and Paula Lentz, *M: Business Communication* (New York: McGraw-Hill, 2014).

and modifying phrases. This sentence from the previous example illustrates the point (the negative point is in a dependent clause):

While your plan is not feasible at this time, we encourage you to submit it again next year when we are likely to have more resources for implementing it.

Here's another example:

Your budget will be approved *if you can reduce your planned operating expenses by $2000.*

Space and Emphasis The less space you devote to a point, the less you emphasize it. You should therefore focus on the negative as little as possible. Look again at the ineffective message about the eroded beach in the section "You-Viewpoint on the Message Level." One reason the message is so negative is that the company's stern legal warning occupies more space in the message than any other topic.

When we say not to spend much space on negative news, we mean the actual negative point. As Chapter 9 will show, you will often need to preface such news with explanatory, cushioning words in order to prepare your readers to receive it as positively as possible. For this reason, it often takes longer to say "no" than to say "yes," as in these contrasting openings of a message responding to a request:

A Message That Says "Yes"

Your new A-level parking sticker is enclosed.

A Message That Says "No"

Your new University Hospital parking sticker is enclosed. As always, we had many more applicants for A-level passes than we had spaces. Your B-level sticker will enable you to park in the Eden Garage, which is connected to the hospital by a covered skywalk. If you would like to discuss additional options, please contact Ann Barnett, Director of Parking Services, at 555-6666 or ann.barnett@uh.com.

The "no" version certainly took longer. But notice that the space actually devoted to the negative news is minimal. In fact, the negative news isn't even stated; it is only implied in the positive second sentence ("Your B-level sticker . . ."). Look how much of the paragraph focuses on more positive things. That is the allocation of space you should strive for when minimizing the negative and emphasizing the positive.

Use Positive Emphasis Ethically

As with use of the you-viewpoint, emphasis on the positive, when overdone, can lead to fake and manipulative messages. The technique is especially questionable when it causes the recipient to overlook an important negative point in the message—the discontinuation of a service, for example, or information about an unsafe product.

Do not let your effort to please lead you to be dishonest or insincere. That would not only be morally wrong; it would also be a bad way to do business.

On the other hand, the topics we discuss in our communication—whether data, events, people, or situations—can be rightly perceived in multiple ways. In your quest to achieve your communication purpose, think before you let negative feelings make their way into your messages. You will often be able to depict the glass as half full rather than as half empty, and you will probably find that your own perspective has improved in the process.

Communicating Ethically

As Chapter 1 points out, people's trust in business is at a low point. At the same time, the Internet and social media make the risk of public scandal greater than ever. Many dedicated businesspeople are working hard to restore people's faith in business by ensuring that the behavior of their employees, suppliers, and contractors is above reproach. But no one's

When ethical and appropriate, view the glass as half full, not as half empty.
Source: Kathryn Rentz and Paula Lentz, *M: Business Communication* (New York: McGraw-Hill, 2014).

behavior can be thoroughly monitored. That is why employees who monitor their own behavior are highly prized. They can be depended on to do the right thing and bring credit to the organizations they work for.

Ethical dilemmas often arise in the area of business communication. This fact makes sense because communication requires human interaction, and **ethics** is about how people treat each other. It is the study of principles that guide, or should guide, human conduct.

Awareness of common ethical issues that arise, cultivation of certain personal qualities, and familiarity with resources for ethical reasoning will help you make ethical communication decisions.

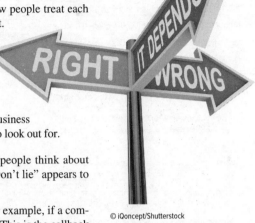
© iQoncept/Shutterstock

Communication-Related Ethical Issues

You won't be able to anticipate all the ethical issues you might face as a business communicator, but this section will familiarize you with some common ones to look out for.

Dishonesty Lying is probably the first topic that comes to mind when people think about unethical communication. We probably all agree that lying is wrong, and "Don't lie" appears to be a simple ethical rule to apply. Sometimes it is; sometimes it isn't.

A **lie of commission** (an outright falsehood) is usually ethically wrong. For example, if a company that sells back braces has its computer call potential customers to say, "This is the callback you requested regarding the ad you recently watched about back braces" when the customer did not request a call, this is a lie of commission (this example is real, by the way).

LO6-6 Avoid unethical communication practices.

But what if the "lie" is an edited photo of your company's building? Or a photo of someone who looks like a doctor but isn't? Now you'd be getting into territory where you need ethical reasoning.

A **lie of omission** (leaving out information) is often wrong as well. If an energy supplier were to sell you a year's worth of service at a low price and not make clear that the price would go up at the end of that year, this would be a lie of omission. (This is a real example, too.) But if you were selling a food slicer, would it be wrong not to mention that it doesn't work well with certain foods that people would likely want to slice (like cheese)? Here again, you'd be getting into a gray area.

Whatever course of action you decide is justified, you should keep in mind that it's bad for business, and for society as a whole, to undermine people's ability to trust each other's words. The more cynical and suspicious we become, the less good we can achieve together.

Discriminatory Wording As the workforce has grown more diverse, it has become increasingly important to avoid **discriminatory words**. These are words that refer negatively to groups of people because of their gender, race, nationality, sexual orientation, age, disability, or some other trait. Such words do not promote good business ethics or good business. The following advice will help you avoid them.

Use Gender-Neutral Wording Take care not to use words that discriminate by gender ("sexist" words). These guidelines will help:

- Avoid the use of masculine (or feminine) pronouns to refer to a group of people that can include both genders, as in this sentence: "The typical State University student completes his co-op in the junior year." Since some of the co-oping students are female, the use of *his* here is discriminatory. (See the Communication Matters feature "Three Ways to Avoid Sexist Pronouns" to see how to correct such sentences.)

In today's diverse workplaces, mutual respect between genders and across generations is key.
© Monkey Business Images/Shutterstock

Communication Matters

Three Ways to Avoid Sexist Pronouns

As the chapter says, the use of the gender-marked pronouns (*he, his, him, she, hers, her*) when discussing something that applies to both sexes—as in "The typical State University student completes his co-op in the junior year"—is considered unethical. You can use the following strategies to avoid this problem.

1. Reword the sentence to eliminate the offending word. Here are some examples:

Sexist	Gender-Neutral
If a customer pays promptly, *he* is placed on our preferred list.	A customer who pays promptly is placed on our preferred list.
If an unauthorized employee enters the security area, *he* is subject to dismissal.	An unauthorized employee who enters the security area is subject to dismissal.

2. Make the reference plural. The plural pronouns in English (*their, them, they*) refer to both sexes, so using these instead of the singular pronouns will correct the problem.

If customers pay promptly, *they* are placed on our preferred list.

If unauthorized employees enter the security area, *they* are subject to dismissal.

A word of warning, though: If you use this strategy, be sure to make all the references to the people plural. Otherwise, you'll have created an agreement error, as in this sentence: "If *a customer* pays promptly, *they are* placed on our preferred list" (the plural pronoun cannot be used to refer to the singular customer).

3. Substitute such gender-neutral expressions as *he or she, he/she, s/he, you, one,* and *person*. Using neutral expressions in the problem sentences, we have these revisions:

If a customer pays promptly, *he or she* is placed on our preferred list.

If *you* pay promptly, *you'll* be placed on our preferred list.

When an unauthorized employee enters the security area, *he/she* is subject to dismissal.

Anyone who enters the security area without authorization will be subject to dismissal.

- Avoid words derived from masculine words that leave out the other gender. Some examples are *man-made, manpower, chairman, fireman,* and *freshman.* The more inclusive alternatives are *manufactured, personnel, chair* or *chairperson, firefighter,* and *first-year student.*

- Avoid wording that calls undue attention to a person's gender or implies that one gender has more status than the other. Using first names to refer to female employees but not male employees would be an example of this type of discriminatory wording. So would expressions like *waitress, stewardess, male nurse,* and *female engineer.* Better wording would be *server, flight attendant, nurse,* and *engineer.*

Avoid Words That Stereotype by Race, Nationality, or Sexual Orientation Words that characterize all members of a group based on their race, nationality, or sexual orientation can be especially harmful because they frequently reinforce negative stereotypes about this group. Members of any minority vary widely in all characteristics. Thus, it is unfair to suggest that Jews drive a hard bargain, that Italians tend to work together to skirt the law, that Hispanics are best suited for manual labor, that gays are perfectionists, and so on. It is also inappropriate to call unnecessary attention to personal traits with such expressions as "a black police officer" or "the Indian CEO."

You probably will have no trouble avoiding this kind of wording in your writing because you know better. But it can sneak into your oral communication, especially your informal communication. Watch what you say, and be sure that calling attention to someone's racial or social group is warranted by the purpose of your communication. Otherwise, keep such references out of your remarks.

Avoid Words That Stereotype by Age You should also avoid wording that reinforces stereotypes based on age. Do not assume or imply that older workers are forgetful, slow,

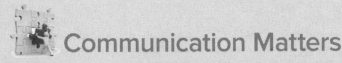

Communication Matters

Understanding the Different Generations in the Workplace

According to *Generations, Inc.,* five generations now comprise the U.S. workforce: the Traditional Generation (born between 1918 and 1945), the Baby Boomers (born right after World War II), Generation X (born between 1960 and 1979), Generation Y or the Millennials (born after 1979), and the Linkster Generation (born after 1995). Different social and historical forces have shaped these generations, with the result that their values and work habits are quite different.

The three main groups—Boomers, Gen Xers, and Gen Yers—have these major traits and preferences:

- The *Boomers* have the wisdom of experience that can provide historical perspective, have a "tenacity" that can help the organization meet new challenges, and "are team players who can enhance any group in which they participate." But they "need to be engaged," need to feel that they are still valuable, and need to feel free to use their knowledge to make decisions within reasonable limits (they shouldn't be "micromanaged").

- *Gen Xers* are happy working MTV style, meaning "they like activities that require intense bursts of energy and that challenge them to think quickly." They don't like "stupid rules," they do like "individual recognition," and they want to move ahead based on merit, not on schmoozing or seniority. They value work–life balance more than the Boomers did and are thus unwilling to work as hard, but they do value professional development. They want to be free to bring their own style to work but also want clear, fair, timely feedback on their performance.

- *Gen Yers* like to work in supportive environments like the ones that most of them grew up in. Thus, they react better to "coaching" than to being told what to do, and they like frequent reassurance that they are on the right track. Like Gen Xers, they are willing to work hard but not overly hard, they want to understand the value of the work, and they like creativity. They tend to be more fun-loving and less anxious than Gen Xers, though. They are also even more comfortable with communication technologies than Gen Xers are, so much so that they may need to be encouraged to use other forms of communication (e.g., face-to-face and phone conversations).

Source: Meagan Johnson and Larry Johnson, *Generations, Inc.* (New York: AMACOM, 2010).

technologically inept, or out of step with the times. Be careful how you refer to them as well. Think twice before using the words *senior citizen, mature,* and *elderly;* perhaps *senior, retired, experienced,* or *veteran* would be more acceptable. Likewise, do not assume or imply that young employees are impulsive, unduly ambitious, selfish, or afraid of hard work. And when tempted to refer to someone as *young (young accountant, accomplished young manager),* be sure that calling attention to the person's age is defensible.

Also be careful when using one of the popular generational labels in your writing. While it makes sense for the popular management literature to use such labels as *Baby Boomer* and *Millennial* as shorthand references to different generations, the same labels can seem discriminatory in business messages. Use such labels only when relevant and appropriate.

Avoid Words That Typecast Those with Disabilities Like those in other minority groups, people with disabilities run the risk of having others exclude them, treat them as strange, or minimize their abilities. But they are the largest minority group in the world; according to the latest census data, 19 percent—almost one in every five persons—of the noninstitutionalized population in the United States has a disability.[1] Plus, all of us have different levels of ability in different areas. It is important to keep these facts in mind when choosing your words.

For example, negative descriptions such as *crippled, confined to a wheelchair, wheelchair bound, handicapped,* and *mentally retarded* should be avoided. Instead, use *wheelchair user, developmentally disabled,* or whatever term the people with the disability prefer. In general, that also means saying "those with disabilities" rather than "the disabled" to avoid suggesting that the disability is the only noteworthy trait of people in this group.

Other Unethical Communication Practices Dishonesty and discrimination are the two main areas of unethical communication to watch out for, but there are many others. Unfortunately, some of them, like the ones listed below, are quite common.

- *Wasting others' time.* Perhaps you're surprised to see this item in this list, but think about it: When you waste people's time with unnecessary or unclear communications, you are robbing them of their most precious resource—a resource on which their own professional and personal success depends.

- *Playing political games.* There's nothing wrong with a desire for professional success, but when it comes at others' expense, it has been achieved unethically. "Throwing your colleagues under the bus" (unexpectedly changing sides to curry favor with your boss) and spreading harmful rumors (or letting them spread) fall into this category.

- *Undermining your employer.* Lots of people have issues with their bosses and/or the places where they work. But when you sign on to receive a paycheck in return for your labor, you owe a duty of care to the organization you work for, however imperfect it may be. Trashing your company (or even a company you worked for in the past) on Facebook or other social media, sharing company secrets, or spending hours on the Internet for personal reasons while you're on the job is unethical. If it is discovered, it will probably also get you fired.

- *Taking advantage of others.* Sometimes businesspeople use language that people won't understand, unduly emotional language, or other wording that keeps readers or listeners from being able to make a well-informed decision. In the previous example regarding the selling of back braces, it's likely that the company was hoping that the older people who answered the sales call would believe they'd actually asked for the call and just couldn't remember doing so. Be sure your communications give people a fair chance to determine what would actually be best for them.

Qualities to Cultivate

LO6-7 Cultivate personal qualities that promote ethical behavior.

To be an ethical communicator, you can cultivate certain personal qualities that make ethical behavior the natural choice. Four of the most important ones follow.

Trustworthiness Your **credibility**—the personal trait that inclines people to trust you—is arguably your most valuable business asset. Business relationships, and thus business itself, are impossible without it. Professional success requires taking a disciplined approach to telling the truth, saying what you mean, and doing what you say you'll do.

Cultivating the habit of reflection will help you behave ethically and appropriately.
© gstockstudio/123RF

Closely related to credibility is **integrity**. This is the quality of being true to your ethical principles in all situations (that is, aligning all your behaviors with your core values). It also means speaking the truth to yourself and being willing to admit your weaknesses and mistakes. Undercover Recruiter lists integrity as one of the top seven traits employers look for, calling it "probably the most important single quality for long-term success in life and at work."[2]

Restraint Successful businesspeople exercise **restraint**. Instead of acting impulsively or blurting out remarks, they take a moment to consider whether the behavior is appropriate. Doing so is certainly important for ethical behavior. When faced with an ethical challenge, you need to think before you act.

An infographic developed by psychologist Daniel Goleman, the inventor of the concept "emotional intelligence," identifies "self-regulation" as a crucial component of the soft skills managers are looking for in their young hires. The reflective attitude, impulse control, and openness to change that go along with restraint help keep your comments moderate and inoffensive.[3]

Ethical Bravery As important as restraint is, it is also important to speak up when your ethical principles require it. "Courage" and "inner strength" are also

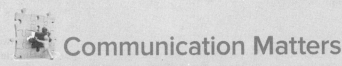

Communication Matters

How Much Self-Expression Is Allowed on the Job?

Can your employer tell you what to wear, outlaw decorated fingernails, or forbid the display of such body art as tattoos and piercings?

According to EmployeeIssues.com, a website about employee rights, the answer is yes—as long as the appearance policies are clearly stated in writing and are applied fairly to all employees.

Just as employers can require the use of uniforms, they can delineate what kinds of personal clothing will be acceptable on the job. For example, they might define "business casual" in a way that

explicitly excludes T-shirts, shorts, and flip-flops. And as long as tattoos and body piercings aren't required by your religion, they can be grounds for being disciplined or even fired—as long as the rules have been clearly laid out and communicated.

Looking professional need not mean selling out your cultural or ethnic heritage, argues Kali Evans-Raoul, founder of an image consultancy for minorities. Everyone must "balance self-expression with workplace realities," she asserts. Just as one doesn't wear a uniform at home, one

shouldn't expect to bring one's entire personal look to work.

To avoid conflicts over your on-the-job identity, your best bet is to try to choose an employer whose values align with your own. Then find and abide by that company's appearance policy.

Sources: "Dress Code Policy," *EmployeeIssues.com*, accessed November 3, 2016, http://employeeissues.com; Dan Woog, "Your Professional Image: Balance Self-Expression with Workplace Expectations," *Monster.com*, accessed November 3, 2016, http://www.monster.com.

on Undercover Recruiter's list of the top seven traits recruiters look for.[4] Sometimes you will need these to be able to do the right thing. But people will respect you for standing up for your principles, and you will develop a reputation as someone with strong integrity.

Communication Savvy Doing the right thing doesn't mean doing it in a dumb way. Use your communication problem-solving skills to figure out how to steer people in an ethical direction. Sometimes you may be able to show that the shady behavior being considered isn't likely to work, will cost money, or is potentially dangerous. Other times you may be able to help develop a new plan that is ethically sound. Confrontation and whistle blowing should be your last resorts, not your go-to strategies for helping your company avoid questionable behavior.

Resources for Ethical Reasoning

Fortunately, you do not have to start from scratch when trying to resolve an ethical dilemma. You can consult the code of conduct for your field or business as well as established models of ethical reasoning.

LO6-8 Use professional codes of conduct and established approaches to ethical reasoning to help you make ethical decisions.

Professional Codes of Conduct Almost every large company and professional organization has a **code of conduct**. Such codes typically describe the core values of the organization and behaviors that are and aren't considered ethical (see Exhibit 6-2).

Familiarity with the code of conduct for your profession and/or company can alert you to potential ethical issues that you hadn't even thought about, and many of them will be related to communication. To find the codes that apply to your situation, you can simply Google the name of your company or organization and "code of conduct" or "code of ethics."

Established Approaches to Ethical Reasoning You can also use popular models of ethical reasoning to inform your judgment. Three are particularly well known: **Aristotelian ethics**, **Kantian ethics**, and **utilitarian ethics**.[5] Even though businesspeople may be unaware of it, they

PREFACE

Because hundreds of thousands of business communicators worldwide engage in activities that affect the lives of millions of people, and because this power carries with it significant social responsibilities, the International Association of Business Communicators developed the Code of Ethics for Professional Communicators.

The Code is based on three different yet interrelated principles of professional communication that apply throughout the world.

These principles assume that just societies are governed by a profound respect for human rights and the rule of law; that ethics, the criteria for determining what is right and wrong, can be agreed upon by members of an organization; and, that understanding matters of taste requires sensitivity to cultural norms.

These principles are essential:

- Professional communication is legal.
- Professional communication is ethical.
- Professional communication is in good taste.

Recognizing these principles, members of IABC will:

- Engage in communication that is not only legal but also ethical and sensitive to cultural values and beliefs;
- Engage in truthful, accurate and fair communication that facilitates respect and mutual understanding;
- Adhere to the following articles of the IABC Code of Ethics for Professional Communicators.

Because conditions in the world are constantly changing, members of IABC will work to improve their individual competence and to increase the body of knowledge in the field with research and education.

ARTICLES

1. Professional communicators uphold the credibility and dignity of their profession by practicing honest, candid and timely communication and by fostering the free flow of essential information in accord with the public interest.

2. Professional communicators disseminate accurate information and promptly correct any erroneous communication for which they may be responsible.

3. Professional communicators understand and support the principles of free speech, freedom of assembly, and access to an open marketplace of ideas and act accordingly.

4. Professional communicators are sensitive to cultural values and beliefs and engage in fair and balanced communication activities that foster and encourage mutual understanding.

5. Professional communicators refrain from taking part in any undertaking which the communicator considers to be unethical.

6. Professional communicators obey laws and public policies governing their professional activities and are sensitive to the spirit of all laws and regulations and, should any law or public policy be violated, for whatever reason, act promptly to correct the situation.

7. Professional communicators give credit for unique expressions borrowed from others and identify the sources and purposes of all information disseminated to the public.

8. Professional communicators protect confidential information and, at the same time, comply with all legal requirements for the disclosure of information affecting the welfare of others.

9. Professional communicators do not use confidential information gained as a result of professional activities for personal benefit and do not represent conflicting or competing interests without written consent of those involved.

10. Professional communicators do not accept undisclosed gifts or payments for professional services from anyone other than a client or employer.

11. Professional communicators do not guarantee results that are beyond the power of the practitioner to deliver.

12. Professional communicators are honest not only with others but also, and most importantly, with themselves as individuals; for a professional communicator seeks the truth and speaks that truth first to the self.

Source: International Association of Business Communicators, accessed November 6, 2016, https://www.iabc.com/about-us/governance/code-of-ethics. Copyright © by International Association of Business Communicators British Columbia. All rights reserved. Used with permission.

Exhibit 6-3 The Three Main Approaches to Ethical Reasoning

- Aristotelian: What would the virtuous person do in this situation?
- Kantian: What if everybody did it?
- Utilitarian: What will yield the greatest good for the greatest number?

often rely on one or more of these approaches when deciding what to do (see Exhibit 6-3 for a quick summary).

Aristotelian Ethics The ethical philosophy of the ancient Greek philosopher Aristotle is still widely applied today in the form of "virtue ethics." His approach is based on the belief that the purpose of life is to achieve happiness through right acting. One must use one's reason to act the right way, and the more one does so, the more virtuous one's character becomes, which thus leads to more right acting. When faced with an ethical dilemma, a person attempting to use Aristotelian ethics would ask, "What would a virtuous person do?"

Aristotle granted that ethical decisions sometimes needed to be settled through debate, but he felt that, through reasoned argument, the innate goodness of one action over another would become clear. As idealistic as this sounds, he also believed that people needed to use their practical wisdom, or a wise interpretation of each situation, to determine how best to live by the moral ideals.

If you were sitting with other employees in the break room and they were criticizing a co-worker or boss unfairly, you might apply Aristotelian thinking to decide whether to speak up. Feeling that the comments were unjust, you might feel compelled to say something. But using your practical wisdom, you'd consider whether this was the right time to do so. If you decided it was, you'd speak up in a way that would help your co-workers develop a fairer attitude.

Kantian Ethics The Kantian approach, developed by Immanuel Kant during the Enlightenment (late 1600s–early 1800s), is similar to the Aristotelian approach, but with an emphasis on one's moral duty as a member of society rather than on promoting the good for its own sake. The assumptions supporting this approach are that human beings are rational, that we are rational in the same way, that we have a duty to act reasonably, and that, if we do so, we will all arrive at the same "right actions." This ethical approach leaves little room for consideration of specific circumstances.

Kant's most famous "categorical imperative" states that we should act a certain way only if the ethical principle behind our action could be made a "natural law"—that is, if it could be used to govern everyone else's behavior. In other words, you must apply the "What if everybody did it?" test. Let's say that you wanted to lie about something you did or said to make yourself look good in your boss's eyes. Would this be ethical? Kant would say no, because if everyone used lying to promote their own interests, the whole fabric of the business—and of society itself—would unravel, and in the long run their interests wouldn't be served. How about if you wanted to misrepresent your products in order to

The ethical approach developed by the Greek philosopher Aristotle (384–322 BC) is the foundation of many of today's codes of ethics.
© Panagiotis Karapanagiotis/123RF

You Make the Call
If you were in the situation described here, would you speak up? If so, how? If you wouldn't, why not? Would you handle it some other way?

Immanuel Kant.

German philosopher Immanuel Kant (1724–1804) developed his ethical approach during the Enlightenment, when the goal was to discover and live by universal natural laws.
© Shutterstock / Nicku

sell them? Again Kant would say no, because if everyone did that, it would cause a breakdown in the whole system of buying and selling, jeopardizing everyone's ability to make sales.

In reality, few people find it possible or desirable to live strictly by this code. There are often extenuating circumstances or potential drawbacks that they feel must be considered. But the Kantian approach is a good starting place for ethical reasoning. It can help you identify the core principles that apply and then consider why a departure from those principles might be justified.

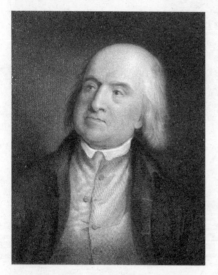

English philosopher Jeremy Bentham (1748–1832) helped develop the utilitarian approach, which was influenced by the Industrial Revolution.
© Photos.com/Getty Images

Utilitarian Ethics   A third popular approach to ethical reasoning, utilitarianism, was developed by Jeremy Bentham, John Stuart Mill, and others at the time of the Industrial Revolution (1800s). It takes a somewhat technical approach in that it asks, "What will yield the greatest good for the greatest number?" Faced with an ethical dilemma, a person would try to calculate the consequences of the available actions and then choose the action that would have the most desirable consequences for the most people.

Employers often use this type of reasoning when deciding to lay off employees. Certain individuals' welfare is sacrificed so the company can survive and the others will keep their jobs. But let's say that you're a salesperson who desperately needs to make your quota this quarter so you can keep your job and support your family. Would utilitarian ethics justify selling someone a product that you knew he or she didn't need or using a somewhat deceptive sales approach? Yes, it might.

This is why the utilitarian approach is rarely used all by itself. Calculating the consequences—which can be difficult to do—often runs people up against their sense of right and wrong.

A Process for Ethical Reasoning
Equipped with relevant codes of conduct and the three major approaches to ethical issues, you have a good chance of reasoning your way to ethically responsible communication. Note the word "chance" in the previous sentence. As with other messy, multifaceted problems, ethical problems cannot be solved with simple formulas that yield predictable results; ethical situations are too various, and have too many variables, for that. But the steps in Exhibit 6-4 will help you bring some order to your ethical problem solving.

While discussing ethical dilemmas with others can be helpful, it will ultimately be up to you to decide whether and how to act. Gather as much information as you can, reason as well as you can, and then be brave enough to do what you feel you must do. Even if you experience a setback, your integrity will serve you well.

Exhibit 6-4   A Three-Step Process for Ethical Reasoning

- **What makes me think this situation raises an ethical issue?**
  - The behavior in question may violate a professional code of ethics.
  - The behavior in question may violate a general ethical principle.
  - The behavior in question runs the risk of harming others.
- **What does the situation, in all its details, look like from the three main ethical perspectives?**
  - Aristotelian
  - Kantian
  - Utilitarian
- **Using one or more of these perspectives, what should I do or say—if anything—to help ensure an ethical outcome?**

Power Charge Your Professionalism: Make Your Pronouns and Antecedents Agree in Number

First identify the antecedent. Then select the pronoun that agrees with its antecedent. Identify which pronoun-antecedent agreement guide from Reference Chapter A you used in making your choice.

1. Each employee received (his or her/their) performance review last week.
2. The staff gave (its/their) recommendations.
3. Joe and Sam shared (his/their) thoughts on Facebook.
4. All staff members should focus (its/their) energy on attracting new clients.
5. Whenever an employee signs up for one of the company intramural sports teams, (he or she/they) must sign a form releasing the company from any liability.
6. If every member of the committee votes "yes," (it/they) will be the first committee to have a unanimous vote.
7. The membership dues and maintenance fees are two separate assessments; (it/they) must be paid for your membership to be activated.
8. The condominium association publishes (its/their) bylaws in the January newsletter.
9. Rogers and Associates, Inc. offers health and dental insurance to (its/their) employees.
10. When a businessperson gives a professional presentation, (he or she/they) should speak clearly and use visuals to maintain the audience's interest.

Making your pronouns and antecedents agree is important because . . .

- Readers become disoriented, and may have to reread the sentence, when they come to the pronoun and it does not match the antecedent. This wastes their time and distracts them from what you're trying to say.
- Using the right pronoun reflects well on you as a writer.

For further practice, see the "Pronoun and Antecedent Agreement" activity in LearnSmart Achieve, under the heading "Grammar and Common Sentence Problems."

Key Terms

goodwill 167
you-viewpoint 168
you-attitude 168
conversational language 170
level of formality 171
rubber stamps 172
courtesy 172

positive words 176
emphasis 177
ethics 179
lie of commission 179
lie of omission 179
discriminatory words 179
credibility 182

integrity 182
restraint 182
code of conduct 183
Aristotelian ethics 183
Kantian ethics 183
utilitarian ethics 183

Critical-Thinking Questions

1. Discuss this comment: "Using the you-viewpoint is ethically shady since the real purpose of business communication is to advance the writer or speaker's goals. Your communication should be honest about that." LO1

2. In what way, if any, could using the you-viewpoint when writing to someone you don't like (for example, someone who has complained unreasonably about something) be justified? LO1

3. "A message can't sound official unless it has an impersonal style and uses business jargon." Discuss. LO2

4. "If common business phrases apply to a situation, why not use them? Rubber stamps save time, and in business time is money. Plus, people are used to these expressions." LO2

5. "Please submit your payment at your earliest convenience." Is this a courteous sentence? Why or why not? LO3

6. What would be a way of doing more than would be necessary in the following situations? LO3
    1. You work as a sales clerk in a retail store. A customer asks you if your store carries a brand that it doesn't carry.
    2. You have invited someone to give a talk at your company, and he has just sent you an email in which he said yes. You email him back to say thank you.
    3. You've just finished doing a team project, for which you were the leader, and you were really impressed with the members' work.

7. "I'm nervous about deliberately employing positive wording. I think people like writers who shoot straight, and I worry that they'd think I was being deceptive." Discuss. LO4

8. You work for a mail-order business, and you're writing to tell the customer that the item he wants is not only out of stock but also discontinued. How might you use the three ways of de-emphasizing negative news in your message? LO5

9. Imagine that a customer has written to complain about the lack of attention that she received when visiting a paint store. The manager's responding letter explains why the sales staff was so busy, offers to make a special appointment with the customer to discuss her decorating needs, and then ends with the following paragraph:

    We do apologize again for any inconvenience that this situation caused you. We thank you for your understanding. Please do not hesitate to contact us again if we ever fall short of the superior service that you have come to expect from us.

    If the manager asked for your feedback on this letter, what would you say? It's full of polite expressions. Is it a good concluding paragraph? LO1–LO5

10. Consider each of the following communication-related behaviors and decide whether or not you think it is ethically defensible. Could any of the established approaches to ethical reasoning help you make your decision? Would the circumstances influence your answer? LO6–LO8
    1. Referring to a female staff person by her first name (e.g., "See Joan at the front desk") but to the higher-ranking employees by their first and last names (e.g., "Jim Smith in Tech Support can answer your question").
    2. Sending a male member of the sales team (or an Anglo-American) to give an important presentation because you know the client is gender (or racially) biased.
    3. Using your company email account to plan a family reunion.
    4. Using your company's instant messaging platform to comment on a co-worker.
    5. Boning up on hockey (even though you have no interest in it) before meeting with a potential client (or having a job interview with a potential boss) who loves the sport.
    6. Waiting to see how everyone else weighs in on a dicey issue (e.g., whether someone should be fired) before giving your opinion.
    7. Telling your boss that your co-worker held up her end on a team project when she really didn't.
    8. Complaining about the boss to your co-workers rather than discussing the issues directly with him or her.
    9. Criticizing your current or past workplace on Facebook, Twitter, or an Internet site.
    10. Letting others do more than their share on a group project (but still getting full credit) because you had unavoidable family issues to deal with.

Skills-Building Exercises

Using the You-Viewpoint LO1

Rewrite the following using the you-viewpoint. You may need to add additional material.

1. As required by company policy, I am denying your refund request because you needed to have submitted the warranty agreement within two weeks of your purchase.

2. We will be pleased to deliver your order by the 12th.

3. We have worked for 37 years to build the best lawn mowers on the market.

4. Today we are shipping the goods you ordered February 3.

5. Instead of stopping us in the hallway to ask for IT support, send us an email, or else we will have trouble keeping track of your service request.

6. (From an email to employees) We take pleasure in announcing that, effective today, the Company will give a 20 percent discount on all purchases made by employees.

7. We are happy to report approval of your application for membership in our club.

8. We do our best to provide the best customer service possible.

9. Since we no longer stock this item, we must give you store credit instead of a refund.

10. We give a 2 percent discount when payment is made within 10 days.

11. I am pleased to inform you that I can grant your request for payment of travel expenses.

12. We cannot permit you to attend classes on company time unless the course is related to your work assignment.

Using a Conversational Style LO2

Rewrite the following in a conversational style.

1. I hereby acknowledge receipt of your July 7 letter.

2. Please be so kind as to reply at your earliest convenience.

3. Attached please find the receipt requested in your May 1st inquiry.

4. In reply to your letter of July 13, permission to quote from our report is hereby granted.

5. I would deem it a great pleasure to accept your kind offer to serve on the committee.

6. Please be advised that, with regard to above invoice, a payment of $312 has been credited to your account.

7. Kindly advise the director as to your availability for participation in the program.

Using the Right Level of Formality LO2

Reword the following sentences to achieve a more appropriate level of formality. (You may need to recast the whole sentence.)

1. (In a report that several managers will read) The customers' evaluations of our service were pretty mixed, with some being really positive and others no so positive.

2. (In an email message to your division head—whom you do not know well—to congratulate her on receiving a prestigious award from a professional society:) Way to go, Melissa! You do us all proud!

3. (In a sales message:) Our products are awesome, and they don't cost a lot of money.

4. (In a response to a proposal from a vendor who wants to be your company's HR contractor:) I got your proposal. I'll give it a look-see and get back to you ASAP.

5. (In a complaint letter to your health-insurance provider:) No way should I have to pay this bill out of my own pocket!

6. (In an email to an employee about missing a deadline:) I need your information, Jane! Our project is gonna be a fail if we can't pull it together by the end of the month.

7. (In a thank-you message to a CEO for letting you interview him for a class project:) Thanks again, Mr. Adams, for the super-useful information.

Rewriting for Courtesy and a Positive Effect LO3–LO5

Underscore all negative words in these sentences. Then rewrite the sentences for a more positive effect. Use your imagination to supply contextual information when necessary.

1. Your misunderstanding of our January 7 email caused you to make this mistake.

2. We hope this delay has not inconvenienced you. If you will be patient, we will get the order to you as soon as our supply is replenished.

3. We regret that we must call your attention to our policy of prohibiting refunds for merchandise bought at discount.

4. Your negligence caused the damage to the equipment.

5. You cannot visit the plant except on Saturdays.

6. We were disappointed to learn from your July 7 email that you are having trouble with our Model 7 motor.

7. Our Stone-Skin material is less skimpy than the fabric used by the other brands.

8. Even though you were late in paying the bill, we still allowed the discount.

9. We were sorry to learn of the disappointing service you have had from our salespeople, but we feel we have corrected all mistakes by firing the incompetent personnel.

10. We have received your claim that our product was defective and have thoroughly investigated the matter.

11. We have received your undated letter, which you sent to the wrong office.

12. I regret to have to say that I will be unable to speak at your conference, as I have a prior commitment.

13. Do not walk on the grass.

Avoiding Unethical Communication Practices LO6–LO8

Prepare a short report for your instructor on a company or other type of organization that was recently involved in an ethical scandal. What behavior caused the scandal? What pressures, if any, were on the organization to behave this way? How easy/desirable would it have been for them to have avoided this behavior? Was this a cut-and-dried case of bad ethics, or do you think it was more complex than that? Be sure to cite your sources in the report.

Avoiding Discriminatory Language LO6

Change these sentences to avoid discriminatory language.

1. We are collecting money for a gift for our postman, who'll be retiring this month.

2. A successful writer adapts his communication style to different audiences.

3. The committee consisted of a businessman, a banker, and a female lawyer.

4. A good administrative assistant screens all telephone calls for her boss and manages his schedule.

5. If Ms. Adams is not in, Joe at the front desk can help you.

6. Any worker in violation of this rule will have a letter of reprimand put in his personnel file.

7. Two company representatives attended the conference: a Hispanic engineer and one of our younger managers.

8. Three people applied for the job, including a Baby Boomer and a Gen Yer.

9. These parking spaces are strictly for use by the handicapped.

10. He is one of the best gay designers in the city.

11. As a Gen Xer, she is very computer savvy.

12. The position was filled by a well-educated housewife who was returning to the workforce.

Using Resources for Ethical Reasoning LO8

Find the code of conduct for professionals who work in the area you hope to work in or the code of conduct for a company you'd like to work for. Read it carefully, and then write a short report for your instructor in which you summarize and comment on its contents. Did anything about it particularly impress or surprise you? Was anything left out that you thought should be included? Do you think it would actually help people in the field or the company behave in the right way? Attach a copy of the code of conduct to your report.

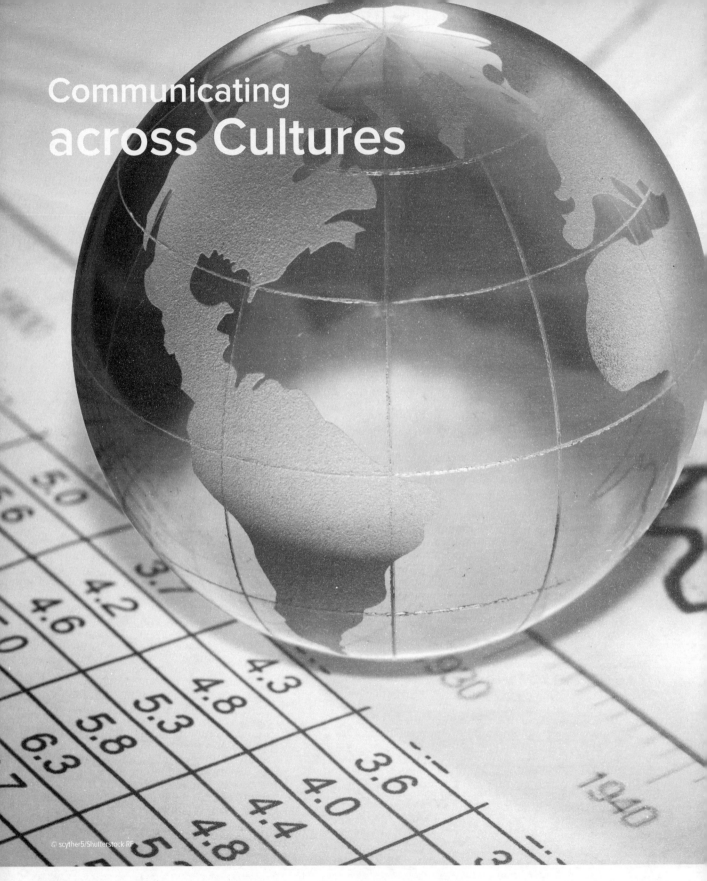

Communicating
across Cultures

© scyther5/Shutterstock RF

Seven

As Chapter 1 points out, increasing globalization is one of the major trends in business. The spread of the Internet, social media, and mobile devices has only fueled this trend.

In preparing to communicate with people from other cultures, you might well begin by heeding the advice throughout this book. Adapting your words, sentences, and overall messages to your audience is always important, and never more so than in cross-cultural situations. Clarity, courtesy, and correctness are appreciated everywhere. But how to achieve these goals can vary by culture. In one culture, for example, it might be appropriate to imply the main point, while in another you should state the point directly. Learning about the ways cultures differ is an important foundation for successful business communication. In addition, you must look at the special problems that our language presents to those who use it as a second language. This chapter will focus largely on these two topics.

Learning Objectives

LO7-1 Explain why effective cross-cultural communication is important for today's businesses.

LO7-2 Describe three major factors that influence a country or region's culture.

LO7-3 Describe cultural differences regarding body positions and movements and apply this knowledge when communicating across cultures.

LO7-4 Describe the impact of culture on views and practices concerning human relationships and apply this knowledge when communicating across cultures.

LO7-5 Describe language issues that can cause trouble for nonnative speakers.

LO7-6 Describe ways to prepare for effective cross-cultural communication.

Problem-Solving Challenge

Preparing for Cross-Cultural Communication

Assume that you're a recently hired trainer for a U.S. company that has a new branch office in Sweden. You've been sent to the office to facilitate the training of new employees.

After a fruitful brainstorming session with the leadership team, you ask the Swedish head manager, Andreas, to appoint a contact person in the group to help you launch the training project. Andreas turns to the HR manager, Prasan, who is from India, and says that he will be your key contact from here on out. You describe the process you want to follow and the documents you'll need in order to go forward.

Then you ask Prasan if you can expect the documents by the next day.

Hesitating, Prasan replies, "Yes, I can send everything to you by the end of the day tomorrow." His boss suddenly intervenes: "No, you can't. You have a lot of work right now and won't be able to meet that deadline." Turning to you, the Swedish manager continues, "You can expect the material you need in two weeks." Prasan looks somewhat embarrassed but nods in agreement.

Back in Andreas's office, you ask, "What just happened? Why did Prasan agree to an unrealistic deadline?" Andreas explains that Prasan wanted to save face by giving a pleasing answer. Such an answer would keep you from appearing to be demanding and would keep him from appearing to be slow. "He values face-saving more than accuracy," the Swede says—implying that he himself does not.

You wonder if such clashes of cultural preference could be handled more gracefully than the one you just witnessed. This chapter will introduce you to cross-cultural communication issues that may arise in business situations and help prepare you to meet them successfully.

LO7-1   Explain why effective cross-cultural communication is important for today's businesses.

© REX/Shutterstock

"Communication is the key to any global business."

—Anita Roddick, UK Entrepreneur, Founder of The Body Shop.

The Importance of Cross-Cultural Communication Skills

Globalization is one of the distinguishing traits of business in the 21st century. And it isn't just big businesses who are hiring people from other cultures and doing business around the world. According to Laurel Delaney, founder of GlobeTrade.com, "It's the small business owners of the world who are busting borders, discovering unlimited potential for growth and profit, and changing the shape of the world economy."[1]

Skillful cross-cultural business communication is important for several reasons. First, many businesses sell their products and services both domestically and internationally. Being able to communicate cross culturally will help you understand different customers' needs and persuasively explain how your company can meet these needs.

Another reason is that you will be a more effective employee within your company. According to the U.S. Bureau of Labor Statistics, over 16% of civilians in the U.S. workforce were born outside the U.S., and this number is on the rise.[2] If you can work harmoniously with those from other cultures, you will help create a more comfortable and productive workplace. Furthermore, if cultural barriers are minimized, your company will be able to hire a wider variety of good people. Also, you will minimize problems stemming from misinterpretations.

A final reason is that interaction with those from other cultures will enrich your professional and personal life. A full-time employee in the United States spends approximately 47 hours a week on the job.[3] This means that you're likely to spend a large percentage of your life at work. You'll want to be challenged, to grow, and to feel that your work has made a difference. Broadening your global perspective will help you with all these goals.

Dimensions of Cultural Difference

Dutch sociologist Geert Hofstede, probably the most respected expert on cross-cultural differences, defines **culture** as "the collective programming of the mind which distinguishes the members of one category of people from another," and national culture as "that component of our mental programming which we share with more of our compatriots as opposed to most other world citizens."[4] In other words, cultures are "shared ways in which groups of people understand and interpret the world."[5]

Our dominant culture affects almost everything about us—from the way we think and communicate to the way we hold our bodies or establish our personal space. Certainly the spread of capitalism, advances in technology and science, and the explosive growth of electronic media have eroded national differences. The title of a popular book on international business claims that "the world is flat,"[6] and many would agree that we have more in common globally than ever before. But cultural differences are still strong in many places and situations.

Of course, one culture can have many subcultures. With only a moment's reflection on regional, ethnic, and gender differences within your own culture, you'll realize that this is true. Plus, the person with whom you are communicating may be completely unrepresentative of his or her culture of origin. National borders are more permeable and workplaces more diverse than they have ever been. Still, an understanding of your communication partner's cultural roots will greatly enhance your interpretive and interaction skills.

Three Major Factors That Affect Culture

Following the advice of Canning, a UK-based communication consulting firm, we recommend starting your cross-cultural education with the big picture.[7] Instead of trying to memorize such isolated facts as a culture's typical greeting or attitude toward punctuality, try to gain a holistic understanding, starting with these basic questions:

- What is the *geography* of the country you are studying? In our Internet-influenced age, it may be difficult to believe, but location, weather, and features of the land still have a profound influence on what types of people live in a certain place. For instance, many natural borders around a country make for a more insular culture than changing, indistinct borders, and life under a broiling sun creates different habits and values than life in a darker, colder environment.

- What is the country's *history*? Have there been certain events or systems of government that have affected the national memory? And what is the country's history with your country?

- What role does *religion* play in the culture? Think for a moment about how religious values have shaped the Middle East, different Asian countries, or the United States. Even when many of a country's people have stopped observing traditional religious practices, the influence of religion can linger, surfacing in certain behaviors and attitudes.

These broad cultural factors can have a major effect on businesspeople's communication practices and preferences. If you know your audience is Islamic, for example, you will be prepared to interpret their behavior when they do not take notes at an important business meeting (they tend to favor oral communication and the use of memory rather than writing) or when they resist detailed planning of a project (since, in Islam, the success of human projects depends on God's will).

You Make the Call

In what ways is it good that communication technologies, ease of travel, and business alliances are reducing differences between cultures? Is there a downside to this trend? How are your thoughts on this topic likely to affect your cross-cultural behavior?

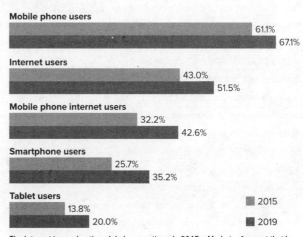

Select Digital Usage Metrics Worldwide, 2015 & 2019
% of population

Mobile phone users
61.1%
67.1%

Internet users
43.0%
51.5%

Mobile phone internet users
32.2%
42.6%

Smartphone users
25.7%
35.2%

Tablet users
13.8%
20.0%

■ 2015
■ 2019

The Internet is accelerating global connections. In 2015, eMarketer forecast that by the end of the year, 43% of people worldwide would use the Internet regularly through either a desktop/laptop or a mobile device. By 2019, one out of every two people across the globe is likely to be a regular Internet user.

Source: Adapted from Cindy Liu, "Worldwide Internet and Mobile Users: eMarketer's Updated Estimates for 2015," *eMarketer*, August 17, 2015, accessed March, 2016, http://totalaccess.emarketer.com.

LO7-2 Describe three major factors that influence a country or region's culture.

From the Tech Desk

Web Tools for Cross-Cultural Communication

The Internet offers many free tools to help you communicate across cultures. Three of the most useful are time-zone calculators, currency converters, and translation tools built right into your Web browser.

Time-zone calculators show you what time it is anywhere in the world, enabling you to plan your Skype sessions, phone calls, and live webinars accordingly. On Timeticker.com, for example, you can pick your country and see exactly what time it is there and where the time zone is (as in the example here, which shows the current time in Gaborone, Botswana).

Currency converters show you how one country's currency translates into another's. In the screen shot provided, you can see how the U.S. dollar compares to the British pound. Such converters are free, and they are programmed to use regularly updated exchange rates.

The Web also offers free **translation tools**. For example, right-clicking on a website in Internet Explorer will bring up the option to translate the site using Bing. In the screen shots provided, you can see how Bing translated a French website into English.

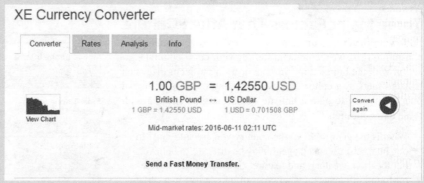

Keep in mind, though, that businesspeople the world over share many goals and problems. All are interested in keeping their businesses financially viable, hiring and retaining good employees, developing marketable products, finding reliable suppliers, and so forth. Your efforts to understand your cross-cultural audience—like those to understand communication partners from your own culture—can lead to many mutually beneficial relationships.

The next two sections will assist you in these efforts by discussing important dimensions of cultural difference, starting with physical differences and then moving to mental and social ones. Sensitivity to these dimensions will help you avoid **ethnocentrism**—the tendency to see only your own cultural programming as "normal"—and make you a better cross-cultural communicator.

Body Positions and Movements

One might think that the positions and movements of the body would be much the same for all people. However, physical behaviors differ by culture, and the differences can affect communication.

LO7-3   Describe cultural differences regarding body positions and movements and apply this knowledge when communicating across cultures.

For example, people from the United States who visit certain Asian countries may view the fast, short steps taken by the inhabitants as peculiar and their own longer strides as normal. And when people from those countries encounter U.S. natives who do not bow when meeting and leaving each other, they are likely to interpret the omission as rude. Similarly, people from the United States see standing up as the appropriate thing to do on certain occasions (as when someone enters the room), whereas people from some other cultures do not.

As you know, movements of certain body parts (especially the hands) are a vital form of human communication. Some of these movements have no definite meaning even within a culture. But some have clear meanings, and these meanings may differ by culture. In the United States an up-and-down movement of the head means "yes" and a side-to-side movement of the head means "no." These movements may mean nothing at all or something quite different to people from cultures in which thrusting the head forward, raising the eyebrows, jerking the head to one side, or lifting the chin are used to convey similar meanings.

Hand gestures can have many different meanings. The two-fingered sign that means "victory" or "peace" in the United States is considered vulgar in Australia, and the "OK" sign is insulting in such diverse countries as Russia, Germany, and Brazil.[8] Even the use of fingers to indicate numbers can vary by culture. In the United States, most people indicate "1" by holding up the forefinger, whereas in parts of Europe, "1" is the thumb, "2" is the forefinger, and so forth. To point to themselves, the Japanese point to their face, while the Chinese point to their nose and Americans point to their chest.[9] And holding up both hands with the palms facing outwards can mean either "ten," "I surrender," "I'm telling the truth," or "Up yours—twice!" depending on where you are.[10]

Even meanings of eye movements vary by culture. In North America, we are taught not to look over the heads of our audience but to maintain eye contact when giving formal speeches. In informal talking, we are encouraged to make eye contact but not to stare. In Indonesia, looking directly at people, especially those who are older or in higher positions, is considered disrespectful, whereas the British and the Germans tend to prefer sustained eye contact. Unless one understands these cultural differences, how one uses eye movement can be interpreted as being impolite on the one hand or shy on the other.

Touching and particularly handshaking differences are important to understand in cross-cultural communication. Some cultures, like the Chinese, do not like much touching. They will give a handshake that Westerners might

Remember that, despite cultural differences, businesspeople around the world share many of the same goals.
© SetsukoN/Getty Images

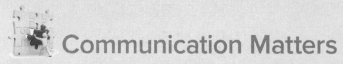

Carefully Present and Receive a Business Card in Japan

In Japan, it's considered bad manners to go to a business meeting without a business card, or *meishi*. There are a number of ways to present the card, but receiving it is an art, too. If you want to make a good impression on the presenter, receive it in both hands, especially when the other party is senior in age or status or a potential customer. Be careful not to fiddle with the card or put it in your rear pocket—that is considered crude. Put it in a distinctive case. Those who do business in both countries often have their business cards translated on the back, as the examples here show.

perceive as weak. Other cultures that like touching will give greetings ranging from a prolonged handshake to full embraces and kisses. Here are some additional examples:

Culture	Handshakes
Americans	Firm, three to five pumps
Germans	Brusque, firm, single pump, repeated upon arrival and departure
French	Light, quick, not offered to superiors, repeated upon arrival and departure, may include a double kiss
British	Soft, three to five pumps
Hispanics	Moderate grasp, repeated frequently
Latin Americans	Firm, long lasting
Middle Easterners	Gentle, repeated frequently
Asians	Gentle; for some, shaking hands is unfamiliar and uncomfortable (but not for Koreans, who generally prefer a firm handshake)
Arabs	Gentle, long lasting, sometimes with kisses on both cheeks

How people greet each other is a major indicator of their social norms. Instead of critically judging others because of their different greeting styles, seize the opportunity to gain insight into their cultures.

In our culture, smiles are viewed positively in most situations. But in some other cultures (notably African cultures), a smile is regarded as a sign of weakness in certain situations (such as bargaining). Receiving a gift or touching with the left hand is a serious breach of etiquette among Muslims, who view the left hand as unclean, but many cultures attach no such meaning to the left hand. And so it is with other body movements—arching the eyebrows, positioning the fingers, raising the arms, and many more. All cultures use body movements in communicating, but in different ways.

Communication Matters

High-Context versus Low-Context Cultures: Edward T. Hall

An extremely influential model of cross-cultural differences comes from U.S. anthropologist Edward T. Hall. With *Beyond Culture* (1976), as well as two earlier books (*The Silent Language* [1959], about perceptions of space and time, and *The Hidden Dimension* [1966], focusing on the use of space), Hall essentially launched the field of cross-cultural communication. His most lasting contribution to this field has been his dividing of the cultures of the world into low- and high-context communicators.

Low-context communicators, in Hall's model, tend to express themselves in concrete, direct, and explicit ways. The gist of the message and everything one needs in order to interpret it are all there in the message. American, German,

Scandinavian, Swiss, and Finnish people tend to fall into this category. They use and value a straightforward communication style.

High-context communicators use a more multimodal style. Rather than putting everything they mean into words, they use eye movements, body language, tone of voice, and other nonverbal elements to give interpretational cues. Though they communicate implicitly, they expect you to interpret their points by drawing on your knowledge of their cultural context. French, Japanese, Indian, Irish, British, and Arabic people tend to be high-context communicators—though of course their contexts can differ dramatically.

Lately Hall's model has come under fire for being unsupported by formal research. In an

extensive review of the topic, Peter Cardon has shown that Hall's generalizations arose from unsystematic observation and have often been contradicted. On the other hand, Cardon's study also shows that Hall's theory about low and high contexts is the most cited theory in cross-cultural communication. The fact that so many researchers, teachers, and consultants have found it useful suggests that, despite its flaws, the model has a certain tried-and-true appeal. So put it into your cross-cultural communication tool box—and apply it with caution.

Source: Peter W. Cardon, "A Critique of Hall's Contexting Model: A Meta-Analysis of Literature on Intercultural Business and Technical Communication," *Journal of Business and Technical Communication* 22, no. 4 (2008): 399–428.

Views and Practices Concerning Human Relationships

Probably causing even more miscommunication than differences in body positions and movements are the attitudes of different cultures toward various factors of human relationships. To illustrate, we will review six of these factors: time, space, frankness, social hierarchy, workplace values, and expression of emotions.

LO7-4 Describe the impact of culture on views and practices concerning human relationships and apply this knowledge when communicating across cultures.

Time In the United States, people tend to be **monochronic**. They regard time as something that must be planned in order to be used as efficiently as possible. They strive to meet deadlines, to be punctual, to conduct business quickly, and to work on a schedule.

In some other cultures (especially those of the Middle East and some parts of Asia), people are **polychronic**, viewing time in a more relaxed way. They see extensive planning as unwise and unnecessary. Being late to a meeting or a social function is of little consequence to them. In fact, some of them hold the view that important people should be late to show that they are busy. In business negotiations, the people in these cultures move at a deliberately slow pace, engaging in casual talk before getting to the main issue. It is easy to see how such different views of time can cause people from different cultures to have serious communication problems.

Space People from different cultures often vary in their attitudes toward space. North Americans tend to prefer about two feet of distance between themselves and those with whom they speak. But in some cultures (i.e., some Arabic and South American cultures), people stand closer to each other, and not following this practice is considered impolite. To take another example, North Americans view personal space as a right and tend to respect this right of others; thus, they stand in line and wait their turn. People from some other cultures view space as belonging to all,

Greetings vary among cultures, as do many other behaviors. Consult authoritative resources, including people with international experience, to learn the preferred ways of interacting in different cultures—and take a cue from your communication partner as well.
© Shutterstock/Rawpixel.com

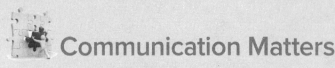

Communication Matters

Six Dimensions of Culture: Geert Hofstede

Between 1967 and 1973, Dutch sociologist Geert Hofstede collected 116,000 questionnaires about business practices and attitudes from IBM employees in over 50 countries. The result was the influential *Culture's Consequences* (1980), one of the most cited works on cross-cultural communication.

The book identified four dimensions of culture, to which a fifth was added in 1991. These became mainstays in the field of international business. In 2010, Hofstede added another dimension. Here's a brief description of each (with the last in the list being the newest):

• *Power distance.* To what extent do the less powerful members of a culture or organization expect that power will be distributed unevenly? If this is a normal expectation, it means that the company or culture exhibits "high power distance" and values hierarchy and obedience. If not, the company or culture has "low power distance."

• *Individualism vs. collectivism.* An individualistic culture is one in which people are expected to look after themselves and their families,

whereas a collectivist culture promotes strong identification with social groups.

• *Masculinity vs. femininity.* At the feminine end of the spectrum is a "modest, caring" attitude; at the masculine end is assertiveness and competitiveness.

• *Uncertainty avoidance.* This label refers to the extent to which "a culture programs its members to feel either uncomfortable or comfortable in unstructured situations." Uncertainty-avoiding cultures try to prevent such situations with strict rules and core values. Uncertainty-accepting cultures tend to be more relaxed, more tolerant of differences, and less rule-bound.

• *Long-term vs. short-term orientation.* This dimension was found in a study conducted by Chinese researchers. People with a long-term orientation look toward the future. They value persistence and thrift. Those with a short-term orientation value the past and present—respecting traditions, fulfilling social obligations, and saving face in social situations.

• *Indulgence vs. restraint.* An indulgent society allows relatively free gratification of basic human

drives to enjoy life and have fun. A restrained society suppresses gratification of needs and regulates it by means of strict social norms.

It is tempting to see whole cultures as falling at one end or the other on these dimensions. But as with other models for analyzing cultures, one must use this one only as a rough, preliminary guide. As one business executive puts it, "In my own practice, I look upon Hofstede's data as would an airplane passenger looking down upon mountain ranges. . . . These represent country cultures. Smaller ranges represent subcultures within countries. But to understand individuals, you have to land at the nearest airport and meet them at the ground level, taking into account their unique qualities."

Sources: Geert Hofstede and Jean-Claude Usunier, "Hoftstede's Dimensions of Culture and Their Influence on International Business Negotiations," in *International Business Negotiations*, eds. Pervez N. Ghauri and Jean-Claude Usunier, 2nd ed. (Amsterdam: Pergamon, 2003), 137–153; Geert Hofstede, Gert Jan Hofstede, and Michael Minkov, *Cultures and Organizations: Software of the Mind*, 3rd ed. (New York: McGraw-Hill, 2010); John W. Bing, "Hofstede's Consequences: The Impact of His Work on Consulting and Business Practices," *Academy of Management Executive* 18, no. 1 (2004): 80–87.

so they jostle for space when boarding trains, standing at ticket counters, or shopping. In encounters between people whose cultures have such different attitudes toward space, actions are likely to be misinterpreted.

Frankness North Americans tend to be relatively frank in their relationships with others, quickly getting to the point and perhaps being blunt in the process. Germans and Israelis are even more frank than Americans. Asians tend to be far more reticent or indirect and sometimes go to great lengths to save face or not to offend. The United States has a **low-context culture**, in which different traditions have come together and where individualism is highly valued. In this type of culture, the communicators explicitly share all relevant background information when communicating. Asian countries, on the other hand, tend to have a **high-context culture**, one with coherent, stable traditions and a strong group orientation.[11] In such a context, the communicators limit background information and rely on shared assumptions to provide the unspoken content (see the Communication Matters feature "High-Context versus Low-Context Cultures: Edward T. Hall"). Thus, Asians may appear evasive, roundabout, and indecisive to North Americans; and North Americans may appear harsh, impolite, and aggressive to Asians. Phone customs may be an exception, especially among the Chinese, who tend to end telephone calls abruptly after their purpose has been accomplished. North Americans, on the other hand, tend to move on to friendly talk and clearly prepare the listener for the end of the call.

Social Hierarchy

In many cultures, strict social classes exist, and class status determines how intimately people are addressed and treated in communication. For this reason, a person from such a culture might quiz a person from another culture to determine that person's class status. Questions concerning occupation, income, title, and origin might be asked. People from cultures that stress human equality are apt to take offense at such inquiries. This difference in attitude toward class status is also illustrated by differences in the familiarity of address. Some Americans are quick to use first names, but this practice is offensive to people from some other cultures, notably the English and the Germans, who expect such intimate address only from long-standing acquaintances.

Similarly, how people view superior–subordinate relations can vary by culture. Hofstede calls this dimension **power distance** (see the Communication Matters feature "Six Dimensions of Culture: Geert Hofstede"). The dominant arrangement in Latin America, for example, is a strong boss with weak subordinates doing as the boss directs. In other words, these cultures tend to exhibit "high power distance." In contrast, Israel, New Zealand, and Denmark have "low power distance," which means that authority is widely shared and decisions are often made by consensus. The United States falls somewhere in between.[12] These widely differing practices have led to major communication problems in joint business ventures involving people from these cultures.

Communicators from different cultures can bring their views of human relations to online communication, too. In one study, social networking preferences were found to line up with cultural differences. The U.S. users who were studied formed connections that were much broader and looser than those of their Chinese and South Korean counterparts, who cultivated online relationships more carefully and maintained them longer.[13] Another researcher found that Asians, fearful of overstepping their authority and reluctant to speak to strangers, can be hesitant to offer comments during online conversations.[14]

Workplace Values

Also differing by culture are our values regarding work. Americans, for example, have been steeped in the Protestant work ethic, believing that working hard is not only necessary for success but also essential to having a good character. The product of this thinking is an emphasis on planning, working efficiently, and maximizing production. Of course, not all of us subscribe to this ethic, but it is a strong force in our culture. The prevailing view in some other cultures is quite different. In Spain, for example, business is more relaxed because of the emphasis placed on interpersonal relationships and the view that planning can be futile.[15]

Views about the relationships of employers and employees also may differ by culture. North American workers expect to move freely from job to job, and they expect employers to hire and fire as their needs change. Expectations are quite different in some other cultures. In Japan, for example, employment tends to be for a lifetime. The company is viewed much like a family, with loyalty expected from employees and employer. Such differences have caused misunderstandings in American–Japanese joint ventures.

Expression of Emotions

From culture to culture, norms for personal expression differ. To illustrate, some Asian cultures strongly frown upon public displays of affection—in fact, they consider them crude and offensive. Westerners, on the other hand, accept at least a moderate display of affection. To Westerners, laughter is a spontaneous display of pleasure, but in some cultures (Japanese, for one), laughter also can be a controlled behavior, to be used in certain social situations. Even the display of sorrow is influenced by culture. In some Middle Eastern

You Make the Call
Do you think the different generations in the workplace have different attitudes toward hard work? If so, what do you think the differences are? How might people's definition of "work ethic" affect you in the workplace?

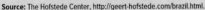

Get a Snapshot of Countries' Cultural Dimensions from the Hofstede Center

A great resource for learning the basics about any country's culture is the website of the Hofstede Center. Just go to the website (http://geert-hofstede.com/), click Cultural Tools > Country Comparison, and select the country you'd like to learn about. The website will bring up a graph of the country's ratings on the six cultural dimensions, followed by explanations of those ratings. The screen shot at left shows the information that came up for Brazil.

The site will even compare countries' ratings for you. The graph on the right shows what you'll see if you click in the "comparison country" box on the Brazil page and select the United States and then Vietnam.

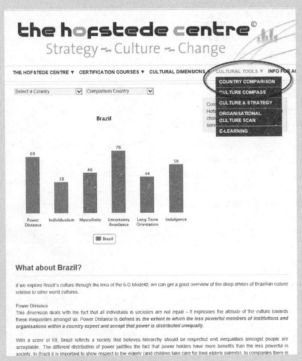

Source: The Hofstede Center, http://geert-hofstede.com/brazil.html.

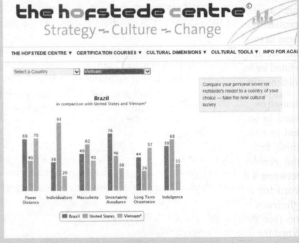

Source: The Hofstede Center, http://geert-hofstede.com/brazil.html.

cultures, sorrow is expressed with loud wailing. In similar situations, Westerners typically respond with more controlled emotions, which could be seen as cold and uncaring by Middle Easterners.

Many more such differences exist. It is common in some cultures to combine business and social pleasure; in others, the two are kept separate. Businesspeople in some cultures expect to engage in aggressive bargaining in business transactions; others prefer straightforward dealings. Some talk loudly and with emotion; others communicate in a more subdued manner. Some communicate with an emphasis on efficiency; others communicate with many more words than are necessary to get the point across.

There are countless differences between cultures. You do not need to learn them all. But you do need to recognize their existence, respect them, and study them when necessary. Only then can you adapt your communication style accordingly.

Problems of Language

The people on earth use more than 3,000 languages. Because few of us can learn more than one or two other languages well, problems of miscommunication are bound to occur in international communication.

Lack of Language Equivalency

The different concepts, experiences, and values of different cultures are reflected in their languages. This means that precise translations can be difficult. Even a word that may seem the same in two languages may have different meanings. For example, we think of a *florist* as someone who sells flowers and related items in a flower store, but in some cultures, flowers are sold mostly by street vendors.

Sometimes a word in one language has no corresponding word in another. For example, *supermarket* has no equivalent in some languages. The French have no word to distinguish between *house* and *home, mind* and *brain,* and *man* and *gentleman.* The Spanish have no word to distinguish between a *chairman* and a *president,* while Italians have no word for *wishful thinking.* And Russians have no words for *efficiency, challenge,* and *having fun.* It goes the other way, too (see the Communication Matters feature "They Have a Word for That!").

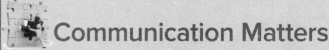
Another explanation for the lack of language equivalency is that there are grammatical and syntactic differences among languages. Some languages (Urdu, for example) have no gerunds, and some have no adverbs and/or adjectives. Not all languages deal with verb mood, voice, and tense in the same way. The obvious result is that even the best translators often cannot find literal equivalents between languages.

LO7-5 Describe language issues that can cause trouble for nonnative speakers.

Adding to these equivalency problems is that of multiple word meanings. Like English, other languages have more than one meaning for many words. Think, for example, of our numerous meanings for the simple word *run* (to move fast, to compete for office, a score in baseball, a break in a stocking, a fading of colors, and many more). Unless one knows a language well, it is difficult to know which of the meanings is intended.

Within a culture, certain manners of expression may be used in a way that their dictionary translations and grammatical structures do not explain. Those within the culture understand these expressions; those outside may not. For example, we might say, "Business couldn't be better," meaning business is very good. Someone from another culture might understand the sentence to mean "Business is bad" (impossible to improve). Or we might say, "We could never be too nice to our customers," meaning that try as we may, we couldn't be overly nice. To someone from another culture, the sentence might mean "We cannot be nice to our customers."[16]

Similarly, words can be used in different ways in different cultures. For example, as one business communication scholar explains, "The Chinese *yes,* like the Japanese *yes,* can often be

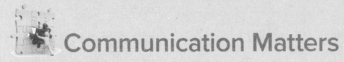
Communication Matters

Blundering with Words

Companies can make blunders in international business through their products, practices, and words. Here are some of those where words were the culprit.

- When Coca-Cola first attempted to market its drink in China, the characters representing it sounded like Coca-Cola but translated to *a wax-flattened mare*. Now the characters that represent it translate to *happiness in the mouth*.
- Olympia tried to introduce a copier in Chile under the name Roto, which is the Spanish word for *broken*.

- American Motor Company's Matador translated into *killer* in Puerto Rico, clearly not a good name in a place with high traffic fatality rates.
- Toyota's MR2 did well in most countries, but in France it was often pronounced *merde*, meaning *human waste*.
- Ford encountered problems when it introduced a low-cost truck it named *Fiera* into Latin American countries. The name translates to *ugly old woman*.
- Bacardi developed and launched a fruity drink, calling it Pavian. In German it means *baboon*.

- When Nike attempted to place a graphic of flames on its shoes, it discovered that the illustration resembled the Arabic script meaning *Allah,* the word for God. The Council on American–Islamic Relations demanded an apology and withdrawal of the shoes from the market.

Source: David A. Ricks, *Blunders in International Business*, 4th ed. (Malden, MA: Blackwell Publishing, 2006).

understood by Americans and British as their English *yes*. But the Chinese *yes* often means 'I am listening.' Or it may be understood in English as the opposite. For example, when an American says to a Chinese counterpart, 'I see you don't agree with this clause,' the Chinese will usually reply 'Yes,' meaning a polite agreement with the negative question: 'Yes, you are right. I do not agree with the clause.'"[17]

Overcoming such language problems is difficult. The best way would be to learn your partner's language well, but when this is impractical, you can be aware that translation problems exist and ask questions to determine what the other person means or understands you to mean. For very important messages, you might consider using a procedure called **back translating**. This procedure involves using two translators, one with first-language skills in one of the languages involved and one with first-language skills in the other language. The first translator translates the message into his or her language, and the second translator then translates the message back into the original. If the translations are good, the second translation matches the original.

Difficulties with English

English is the primary language of international business. This is not to say that other languages are not used. For example, an executive from Iraq and an executive from Saudi Arabia would communicate with each other in Arabic, while an executive from Venezuela would use Spanish in dealing with an executive from Mexico. However, when executives have no common language, they are likely to use English. The members of the European Free Trade Association conduct all their business in English. In the words of one international authority, "English has emerged as the *lingua franca* of world commerce in much the same way that Greek did in the ancient world of the West and Chinese did in the East."[18]

We must keep in mind, though, that English is not the primary language of many of those who use it. Since many of these users have had to learn English as a second language, they are likely to use it less fluently than native speakers and to experience comprehension problems. Two of the more troublesome areas of difficulty are reviewed here.

Two-Word Verbs One of the most problematic traits of English for nonnative speakers is its heavy use of two-word verbs. By **two-word verbs** we mean a phrase consisting of (1) a verb and (2) a second element that, combined with the verb, produces a meaning that the verb alone does not have. For example, take the verb *break* and the preposition *up*. When combined, they have a meaning quite different from the meanings the words have alone. And look how the meaning changes when the same verb is combined with other words: *break away, break out, break in, break down*. Exhibit 7-1 lists additional examples.

Of course, nonnative English speakers will have learned some of these word combinations, but many of them are not covered in language textbooks or listed in dictionaries. For this reason, you

Exhibit 7-1	Some Two-Word Verbs That Confuse Nonnative Speakers		
Verb Plus *Away*	**Verb Plus *In***	**Verb Plus *Out***	**Verb Plus *Up***
give away	cash in	blow out	blow up
keep away	cave in	clean out	build up
lay away	close in	crowd out	call up
pass away	dig in	cut out	catch up
throw away	give in	die out	cover up
Verb Plus *Back*	run in	dry out	dig up
cut back	take in	even out	end up
feed back	throw in	figure out	fill up
keep back		fill out	get up
play back	**Verb Plus *Off***	find out	hang up
read back	break off	give out	hold up
take back	brush off	hold out	keep up
turn back	buy off	lose out	look up
win back	check off	pull out	mix up
	clear off	rule out	pick up
Verb Plus *Down*	cool off	tire out	save up
calm down	cut off	wear out	shake up
die down	finish off	work out	shut up
hand down	let off		slow up
keep down	mark off	**Verb Plus *Over***	wrap up
let down	pay off	check over	
lie down	run off	do over	**Verb Plus Miscellaneous Words**
mark down	send off	hold over	bring about
pin down	show off	pass over	catch on
play down	shut off	put over	get across
put down	sound off	roll over	pass on
run down	start off	run over	put across
shut down	take off	stop over	put forth
sit down	write off	take over	set forth
wear down		talk over	
		think over	
		win over	

may need to substitute one-word alternatives when communicating with nonnative speakers of English, as in these examples:

Two-Word Verbs	Suggested Substitutes
give up	surrender
speed up, hurry up	accelerate
go on, keep on	continue
put off	defer, delay
take off	depart, remove
come down	descend
go in, come in, get in	enter
go out, come out, get out	exit, leave
blow up	explode
think up	imagine
figure out	solve
take out, take away	remove
go back, get back, be back	return

Additional problems result from the fact that some two-word verbs have noun and adjective forms. Fortunately, some of these words appear in standard dictionaries (e.g., *hookup, feedback, breakthrough, lookout,* and *takeover*). But since some do not, you'll need to watch out for these expressions as well.

Slang and Colloquialisms

As Chapter 5 points out, slang and colloquialisms can cause problems when your reader or listener is unfamiliar with them. The odds of this being the case are dramatically increased in cross-cultural communication.

For example, will non-U.S. communicators understand the expressions *nerd, control freak, 24/7, pumped,* or *basket case*? How about words derived from U.S. sports, such as *kickoff, over the top, out in left field, strike out, touch base,* and *get the ball rolling*? Such expressions are sometimes defined on English as a Second Language (ESL) websites but rarely in dictionaries. They would be risky to use except with those very familiar with U.S. English. (See Exhibit 7-2 for more colloquialisms to avoid.)

Exhibit 7-2 Examples of Colloquialisms to Avoid with Nonnative Speakers

head for home	shoot from the hip	in a rut
seal the deal	over the top	blow things out of proportion
grasp at straws	on the same page	make heads or tails of it
slap on the wrist	back to the drawing board	six of one, half dozen of the other
on target	start at square one	countdown
in the ballpark	a flop (or bust)	shortcut
do the trick	call it a night	educated guess
learn the ropes	a toss-up	all ears
pitch in	twist someone's arm	add fuel to the fire
between a rock and a hard place	in the ballpark	break the ice

In the United States we tend to use colloquial expressions often in our everyday communicating. They are colorful, and they can communicate clearly to those who understand them. But when you are communicating with nonnative English speakers, try to replace them with words that are clearly defined in the dictionaries that these people are likely to use to understand your message. Following are some examples:

Not This	**But This**
This is just off the top of my head.	Here's a quick idea.
He frequently shoots from the hip.	He frequently acts before he thinks.
We would be up the creek without a paddle.	We would be in a helpless situation.
They couldn't make heads or tails of the report.	They couldn't understand the report.
The sales campaign was a flop.	The sales campaign was a failure.
I'll touch base with you on this problem in August.	I'll talk with you again about this problem in August.
I'll share our research with the committee so they won't have to start from scratch [or reinvent the wheel].	I'll share our research with the committee to save them some work.
We will wind down manufacturing operations in November.	We will end manufacturing operations in November.
Your prediction was right on target.	Your prediction was correct.
Don't let him get to you.	Don't let him upset you.

Advice for Communicating across Cultures

LO7-6 Describe ways to prepare for effective cross-cultural communication.

As the preceding sections make clear, cross-cultural communication is fraught with potential barriers and misunderstandings. And even with the best effort on your part, not every act of cross-cultural communication will succeed. Like other kinds of communication, cross-cultural communication involves people—and people are unpredictable. In every culture, some persons are uncooperative, deceitful, prejudiced, or insensitive, while others are respectful, welcoming, sincere, and harmony seeking. You can only make sure that you are as prepared as possible. Keeping in mind the following advice will help.

Do Your Research

This chapter cites many helpful resources on different cultures and their communication practices, and Exhibit 7-3 lists additional websites and books. Before any international business encounter, be sure to do your homework. Learn something about the topography, climate, and location of your potential partners' countries of origin. Learn something about their language—and learn to speak it if you can. Study descriptions of their history, their ways of life, their religious traditions, their values, their manners, and even their food and recreation.

Besides doing library and online research, talk with people who have had experience with those in other cultures, and if they have writing samples, ask to see them. Take an intercultural business course or even a course designed for those preparing to do business in a specific country. Pursue opportunities to socialize or do teamwork with nonnatives in your own country. Attend cultural festivals and other such events. The more effort you make to reach out beyond your own world, the better your cross-cultural relations will be.

Look for opportunities, such as attending cultural festivals, to broaden your world.
© Chon Kit Leong/123RF

Websites:

www.state.gov. The U.S. government's main diplomatic website. The "Countries and Regions" tab on the main menu bar gives you access to the site's Background Notes. These provide extensive, frequently updated information on all countries with which the United States has relations.

https://www.cia.gov/library/publications/resources/the-world-factbook/index.html. Resources from the U.S. Central Intelligence Agency. The site "provides information on the history, people, government, economy, geography, communications, transportation, military, and transnational issues for 267 world entities."

http://trade.gov/index.asp. Website of the International Trade Administration, U.S. Department of Commerce, whose purpose is to promote international trade. Through the "Publications" tab on the main menu bar, you can access the agency's latest publications, including its monthly newsletter, as well as previous articles and reports.

www.export.gov/. Website of the U.S. Commercial Service (under the International Trade Administration), offering assistance of all types on international trade. Of particular value are its Country Commercial Guides, regularly updated for each country (access these through Opportunities > Market Research > Market Research Library).

www.sba.gov/aboutsba/sbaprograms/internationaltrade/exportlibrary/index.html. Resources from the U.S. government for small businesses interested in doing international trade.

www.oecd.org/home/0,3305,en_2649_201185_1_1_1_1_1,00.html. Website for the Organisation for Economic Co-operation and Development (OECD)—originally the Organisation for European Economic Co-operation (OEEC)—an organization of 34 member countries that share their knowledge and resources on over 200 countries (click the "Countries" tab).

www.fita.org/index.html. Site of the Federation of International Trade Organizations, a nongovernmental organization promoting international trade. Has links to over 8,000 international trade-related websites on such topics as maps and geography, international business terms, trade law, and many more. (A good place to start is "Really Useful Links" in the "Tools of Trade" section of the lefthand main menu bar.) Some links lead to free resources; some are for paying members only.

www.NationMaster.com. A popular educational website started by an Australian statistics enthusiast. Offers maps, flags, and country profiles, but its greatest strength is statistics on many countries, which the site will graph for you.

www.kwintessential.co.uk/etiquette/doing-business-in.html. Site of a UK consulting firm that offers free guides for doing business in 46 countries.

Selected Books:

Jag Bhalla, *I'm Not Hanging Noodles on Your Ears and Other Intriguing Idioms from Around the* World (Washington, DC: National Geographic, 2009). A compilation of colorful expressions in different languages.

Mary Murray Bosrock, *Asian Business Customs & Manners: A Country-by-Country Guide* (Minnetonka, MN: Meadowbrook, 2007). Other books in this popular series focus on Europe, United States, Mexico/Canada, Russia, and the Middle East.

Martin J. Gannon and Rajnandini Pillai, *Understanding Global Cultures: Metaphorical Journeys Through 30 Nations, Clusters of Nations, Continents, and Diversity*, 5th ed. (Los Angeles: Sage, 2013). An insightful, innovative approach that interprets cultures through their popular metaphors, such as "the Japanese garden" and "the Finnish sauna."

Jeanette S. Martin and Lillian H. Chaney, *Global Business Etiquette: A Guide to International Communication and Customs* (Westport, CT: Praeger, 2012). Comprehensive guide to world business communication and behavior.

Terri Morrison and Wayne A. Conaway, *Kiss, Bow, or Shake Hands: How to Do Business in Sixty Countries*, 2nd ed. (Avon, MA: Adams Media, 2006). An alphabetically arranged country-by-country guide describing the overall culture, behavioral styles, negotiating techniques, protocol, and business practices of each country.

Mike Nicks and Barry Tomalin, *The World's Business Cultures and How to Unlock Them*, 3rd ed. (London: Thorogood, 2014). Provides an introduction to culture and covers 12 important business cultures in depth.

Kirk St. Amant and Sigrid Kelsey, *Computer-Mediated Communication across Cultures: International Interactions in Online Environments* (Hershey, PA: IGI Global, 2012). A collection of studies on such topics as different cultures' use of social networking sites, international gaming communities, and cultural influences on online conversations.

Fons Trompenaars and Charles Hampden-Turner, *Riding the Waves of Culture: Understanding Diversity in Global Business*, 3rd ed. (New York: McGraw-Hill, 2012). A great introduction to cultural differences and their likely impact on doing business and managing cross culturally.

Know Yourself and Your Company

As several books by international communication experts point out, a frequent mistake made by those preparing to do business abroad is that they focus all their research on people in the culture they're about to engage with and forget to research themselves. Yet knowing yourself is a good way to anticipate and prevent likely frustrations. For example, if you know you tend to be a "low-context," "low power distance," "individualistic," "masculine," "long-term goals" kind of person, you will be less caught off guard by people at the opposite ends of these spectrums. You can remind yourself to watch and listen carefully for visual and vocal cues, to be patient, to show respect, and to act with due dignity yourself.

It is also important to understand the business you represent. Is yours a rule-bound, procedure-governed operation or one that is more loose and trusting? Do you solve problems by leaving them to management, by hiring an expert, or by pooling everyone's ideas? Does your company avoid mixing business with pleasure? Do employees socialize only with their peers, or does everyone in the company feel free to relax together? Does your company tend to take a straight, efficient route to its goals or learn and adjust as it goes? Just as you will view your international business partner as representative of his or her company, so he or she will view you. Be sure you send accurate signals.

Be Aware—and Wary—of Stereotypes

One of the most sensitive issues in cross-cultural communication is the extent to which generalizing about a culture perpetuates **stereotypes**. We have come to regard stereotyping as negative, with good reason: Stereotyping can prejudice us and blind us to others' true natures. But the reason stereotypes are powerful is that they are based to some degree on observable likenesses within groups of people. They appeal because they are tempting mental shortcuts. But as the international business consultants at Canning point out, that is also their downside. They "are fixed and conventionalized" and for that reason "suggest a failure to learn from experience." Well-researched cultural stereotypes can be useful as basic models that you then adjust as you accumulate additional information. The generalizations can be a beginning point of reference, but you should quickly let them go when someone clearly doesn't represent the general type.[19]

Another reason it is important to be aware of stereotypes is that your prospective international business partners are likely to see *you* through the lens of a cultural stereotype. The more familiar you are with the way people from your culture or country are seen by those in another, the better prepared you will be to show them the ways in which you differ from the stereotype.

You Make the Call

Stereotyping affects people's views of those in their same country, too. What comes to mind when you think of a New Yorker? Or someone from Georgia? Or Los Angeles? Or Idaho? What do you think has given rise to our national stereotypes, and what evidence have you seen that they are often false?

Adapt Your English to Your Audience

The nonnative English speakers you meet will vary widely in their skill. Some may speak better English than you do, while others may have only the barest grasp of the language. As we have suggested, erring on the side of simplicity is your best bet for clear communication. Write or talk simply and clearly. Talk slowly and enunciate each word. Remember that because most nonnative speakers learned English in school, they are acquainted mainly with primary dictionary meanings and are not likely to understand slang words or words with subtle connotations.

You also will communicate better if you carefully word your questions. Be sure your questions are not double questions (for example, avoid a question like "Do you want to go to dinner now or wait until after the rush hour is over?"). Also, avoid the yes/no question that some cultures may have difficulty answering directly. Use more open-ended questions, such as "When would you like to go to dinner?" And avoid negative questions, such as "Aren't you going to dinner?" If the respondent says "Yes," it could mean either "Right, I am not going to dinner," or "Yes, I'm going."

Finally, try to confirm that you understand and are being understood correctly. Even in Britain, whose culture is similar to ours in the United States, similar words can have different meanings. For example, we use a billion to mean 1,000,000,000, whereas the British use it to mean 1,000,000,000,000. If a Brit asks to *table* an item, an American will probably interpret that as a request to put it off, when the real request is to bring it to attention.[20] Continually checking for shared meaning can help ensure the accuracy of the communication process.

Be Open to Change

International communication can be a broadening experience if you approach it with openness and tolerance. In addition to learning about new and better ways to do business, you can also grow personally and enlarge your world.

Is adapting to the practices of one's international partners always feasible? No. You may find that the culture of the company you represent will simply not mesh with those of some potential business partners. Is adapting to others' practices always ethical? Here, too, the answer is no. For example, Jean-Claude Usunier lists several practices to avoid in international negotiations, including bribing, buying information, buying influence, giving misleading information, exploiting the other party's ignorance, undermining the competition by buying out their people, and negotiating without intending to keep any promises.[21] Unfortunately, these practices are all fairly widespread, even though some have been made expressly illegal by such acts as the U.S. Foreign Corrupt Practices Act. And other ethical problems—racism, sexism, homophobia, disregard for the environment, exploitation of labor, and so forth—may arise.

If put in a situation where you must choose between making a deal or behaving ethically and legally, seek advice from others in your company. You are likely to be advised to do the ethical thing—not only because most businesspeople are honorable but also because, in the Internet age, news about scandalous company dealings travels fast, often with disastrous results.

If approached patiently, humbly, and sincerely, forming international business relations can be incredibly exciting. Be ready to make and acknowledge mistakes, and to forgive them in others. Mutual respect is key—perhaps *the* key—to successful cross-cultural communication.

Power Charge Your Professionalism: Use the Right Pronoun

Use Reference Chapter A to help you select the word that correctly completes each sentence below. Then explain why you chose the word you did.

1. The representatives from our company will be Janet, Tom, and (me/I/myself).
2. The Chinese have signed off on the deal proposed by Jim and (me/I/myself).
3. Allison was a coauthor of the report, so (she/her) and I will present it.
4. The agreement (which/that) we reached will be beneficial to both parties.
5. The international vendors (whose/who's) proposals we read all looked capable and competitive.
6. The CEO with (who/whom) we met seemed skeptical.
7. The Indian service representatives (who/whom) we hired speak excellent English.
8. The Danish executives (that/who) attended the conference would like to join our organization.

Using the right pronoun is important because . . .

- Most of your international business associates will speak English, which means that they will have studied English grammar extensively. You do not want them to catch you making mistakes in your own language!
- Errors involving the personal pronouns (e.g, *I*, *me*, *he*, *him*, *they*, *them*) are especially damaging to your professional image because they suggest a low level of literacy.

For further practice using the right pronoun, see the activities on using the right pronoun case and using the right relative pronoun in LearnSmart Achieve, under "Grammar and Common Sentence Problems."

Key Terms

Critical-Thinking Questions

1. If you were trying to persuade your boss to implement some form of cross-cultural training in the company, what kinds of evidence might help you make a convincing case? **LO1**

2. Put yourself in the shoes of the trainer described in this chapter's Problem-Solving Challenge. What might have been a better way to handle the situation? How might the trainer have prepared better for such a situation? **LO2–LO6**

3. What are the prevailing attitudes in our culture toward the following, and how can those attitudes affect our communication with those from other cultures? **LO3**
   a. Handshakes
   b. When/where people sit and stand
   c. Use of head and hand gestures
   d. Laughter

4. What are the prevailing attitudes in our culture toward the following, and how can those attitudes affect our communication with those from other cultures? **LO4**
   a. Negotiation methods
   b. Truth in advertising
   c. Company–worker loyalty
   d. Women's appropriate roles in society
   e. The Protestant work ethic

5. Assume that you've just been made manager of a team of young employees that includes a recent hiree from Asia. Many people from Asian countries feel that it is inappropriate to bother their boss or express dissatisfaction. How might you encourage your Asian team member to ask you questions, let you know when he/she is having difficulties, and bring any concerns to your attention? (If you're an Asian student, what would encourage you to communicate more with your boss?) **LO4**

6. Is a conversational style as appropriate in cross-cultural communication as it is in the United States? Discuss. **LO4–LO5**

7. On a recent trip to India, Mr. Yang, a prominent Chinese executive, dined with his client, Himanshu Jain. Mr. Yang commented that the food was spicy, which Mr. Jain interpreted as an opportunity to discuss Indian cuisine. After lengthy explanations, Mr. Yang commented again that the food was spicy. What's happening here? What barrier is likely getting in the way of clear communication? (Adapted from Danielle Medina Walker, Thomas Walker, and Joerg Schmitz, *Doing Business Internationally: The Guide to Cross-Cultural Success* [New York: McGraw-Hill, 2003], 237.) **LO4**

8. Think of English words or U.S. expressions (other than this chapter's examples) that probably do not have precise equivalents in some other culture. How would you attempt to explain each of these to a person from that culture? **LO5**

9. Compare the two email messages below. Both were written to inform the reader that the writer's company had been charged too much for an ad published in the reader's magazine. The first (with both Japanese and English versions displayed) was written by a Japanese author to a Japanese reader. The second was written by a U.S. author to a U.S. reader. What differences in the two approaches do you see? What cultural differences might account for these writing differences? **LO4–LO5**

   Japanese version in Japanese:

   料金についての問い合わせ

   トラベルジャパン雑誌広告部

   吉田一郎様

   この度は貴誌トラベルジャパンの4月号32ページに弊社の広告を掲載して頂き、ありがとうございました。

   本日広告料37万円引き落としの連絡を受取りました。しかしこの金額はフルページ用のもののようです。弊社の広告は2／3ページでしたので、貴社の広告料リストによれば29万円のはずです。

   御参照のため注文書の写しを添付いたしました。ご確認のうえ、ご対応頂けますよう、お願い申し上げます。

   多摩リゾート　経理部

   鈴木美智子

Japanese version in English:

Subject: Inquiry about the charge

Dear Mr. Yoshida,

Thank you for putting our advertisement on page 32 in the April issue of your magazine, *Travel Japan*.

We received today a notice that \370,000. was charged to our account for the ad. However, this amount seems for a full-page ad. Since our ad covers 2/3 of the page, the amount should be \290,000. according to your list of the advertising rates.

I have attached a copy of the purchase order for our 2/3 page ad for your reference. We would appreciate your checking into the matter and making a necessary adjustment as soon as possible.

Sincerely,

Michiko Suzuki

U.S. version:

Subject: Adjustment needed for the Hocking Hills account

Dear Mr. Dugan,

As the attached purchase order shows, The Hocking Hills Resort & Spa submitted a request for a 2/3 page ad to run in the March issue of *Travel Ohio*. Our 2/3 page appeared on page 32 of that issue, but the receipt we just received indicates that we were charged for a full-page ad.

Will you please credit our account for $800, the difference between the two ad rates?

Thank you,

(Source for Japanese message: Yukie Aoyagi, Language Education Center, Seitoku University, Japan.)

10. Following is a real message written from a U.S. marketing professional to a potential client in Germany. After researching German business communication on the Internet, explain why the U.S. author wrote the message the way she did for this audience. (Consider how the message might have been different had she written it to a prospective client in the United States.) LO4–LO6

Dear Herman:

Meeting you and the other members of the product selection team last Friday was a sincere pleasure. We are honored not only that you took the time to explain the current dynamics and structure of General Telekom but also that you gave us your entire day. Thank you for your generosity.

I understand that you have graciously offered to share some of United Plorcon's key product qualities with the other executives in your company. We are most appreciative that you have offered to help in this way. Based on our discussions at the meeting, we will summarize the main points of interest and send them to you.

To make the cost-benefit charts more self-explanatory, I will slightly condense the material and add some notes. They will not be confidential, so please share them if you wish. I will send the revised charts to you by the end of the week. After I send them, I will follow up with you to ensure that you have all the material you need to explain who we are and what we offer.

Finally, thank you for your hospitality. Staying in an ideally located hotel, having coffee at a beautiful castle, viewing some of the world's best art, and sharing an exquisite meal made my first visit to Stuttgart a most memorable one. I hope that between our two companies, we can create many opportunities for our United Plorcon team to return to your beautiful city.

I look forward to talking with you again soon.

Respectfully yours,

Skills-Building Exercises

Understanding Cultural Differences LO2–LO4

1. Research Denmark or another country and analyze the likely impact of its geography on its culture.

2. Research France or another country to assess the likely impact of its history on its culture.

3. Research India or another country and analyze the likely impact of its religious background on its culture.

4. Research how U.S. geography, history, and religious background have influenced its culture.

5. Study a country's culture and then infer its people's likely attitudes toward American values and behaviors.

6. You're chair of an important committee in your professional organization, and the committee has just acquired its first non-U.S. member, a citizen of the United Arab Emirates. What factors should you be aware of as you conduct your communications with the committee? (Or, do this exercise substituting Japan, Romania, or another country your instructor assigns.)

7. Compare the use of smiling or gift-giving in three countries from different parts of the world and explain why this knowledge is important.

8. Research the differences in government and culture between North and South Vietnam, Northern Ireland and the Irish Republic, North and South Korea, or mainland China and Hong Kong. Explain how the differences would likely affect business communication practices.

9. Research the extent to which the younger adults in a country are breaking away from its traditional cultural values and practices. What accounts for the changes, and what are the implications for business communication?

10. Interview a student or business professional whose country of origin is not the United States about differences between his/her country and the United States. Use this person's insights, as well as the information and references in this chapter, to write a short report on your findings and their implications for business communication.

Adapting Your Language for Cross-Cultural Communication LO5

1. From a newspaper, magazine, or website, find and bring to class eight sentences containing words and expressions that a nonnative English speaker might have difficulty understanding. Rewrite the sentences for this reader. LO5

2. What word choices in the following email message might give a nonnative speaker trouble? Rewrite the memo to avoid such wording.

   Dear conference-planning team,

   High-fives to you for an awesome conference! I heard tons of compliments from the participants. You've definitely set a new high for our annual conferences!

   The schedule you set up couldn't have worked out better. The seven-minute downtime between sessions gave people plenty of time to get to the next session without having to hustle.

   The receptions were great icebreakers, and the catered food was out of this world. The sushi bar was an especially big hit—I saw many people coming back for seconds at that table.

   Sincere thanks to you for all the time and effort you invested in this labor of love. Your organization is in your debt.

3. Review the cross-cultural thank-you message in the last item listed in the Critical-Thinking Questions and rewrite it as if it were going to an executive at Verizon in New York City. LO4–LO5

Exploring Ethical Issues in Cross-Cultural Business LO6

Choose a country quite different from your own and, after studying its culture and business practices, write a short report on the kinds of ethical issues that might arise in doing business with those from this country. (For starters, you might read the article "Building Ethical Business Cultures: BRIC by BRIC" at http://www.europeanbusinessreview.com/?p=1930.) Which of these issues might be relatively easy to deal with? Which would be more difficult? Which might be deal-breakers?

Writing Good-News
and Neutral Messages

© iStockphoto.com/teekid

Chapter Eight

Most business messages address neutral or good-news situations that arise in the course of conducting business. As a result, most business messages are constructed using a **direct organizational pattern**. That is, the message leads with its main point or objective and then moves to additional or supporting information. Businesspeople need to know immediately what to do, why, and how upon reading a message. When external audiences interact with companies, they also expect information presented as quickly as possible in routine situations.

Learning Objectives

LO8-1 Assess the reader's likely reaction to your message.

LO8-2 Describe the general plan for direct-order messages.

LO8-3 Write clear, well-structured routine inquiries.

LO8-4 Write direct, orderly, and favorable answers to inquiries.

LO8-5 Write order acknowledgments and other thank-you messages that build goodwill.

LO8-6 Write claim messages that address errors while building goodwill.

LO8-7 Write clear and effective internal-operational communications.

Approaches to Good-News and Neutral Messages

As we discuss in Chapter 2, writing business messages requires careful thinking about the situation, your readers, and your goals. A good way to begin is to analyze your audience and assess your reader's probable reaction to your message. If the reaction is likely to be positive or neutral, you will generally use the direct organizational plan—that is, you will present your objective right away. If your reader's reaction is likely to be negative, you may need to use the indirect organizational plan, which is discussed in Chapter 9. This chapter outlines the general direct plan and then illustrates how you can apply it to common types of good-news and neutral business messages.

The General Direct Plan

Beginning with the Objective

The opening of your message should contain your **objective**. If you are seeking information, ask for it. If you are giving information, give it. Whatever you need your reader to know, think, feel, do, or believe, put it at the beginning of your message.

Sometimes you can put the objective in the first sentence of your message. Other times, however, your audience may think you are too direct or demanding if you put the objective in the first sentence. If you think your audience will find you too blunt, you can include some background information or a short phrase, clause, or sentence that orients your reader to your objective. Then you can present to your objective and end the first paragraph. Use the rest of the message to fill in the details.

Covering the Remaining Part of the Objective

The paragraph or paragraphs that follow the introduction are the body of the message. The body contains the detailed information the reader needs to fulfill the objective of the message. In this section you can ask questions, answer questions, or provide information by topic, in order of importance, or as steps in a sequence. You want to include any descriptions or explanations that will help your reader understand your message. As you write, be sure that your information is arranged systematically and logically so that the organization of your document makes sense to your reader.

Keep in mind that if you cover all of your objectives in the beginning (e.g., you ask your reader a single question), you may not have a body for your message. In this case, you can simply move from your opening paragraph to your goodwill ending.

Showing goodwill in writing is as important as showing goodwill in interpersonal situations.

© Digital Vision/Getty Images RF

Ending with Goodwill

End the message with a friendly, professional statement that is relevant to the topic of your message. Include any important deadlines and a reason for a deadline so that the reader understands the importance of a timely response. General closings such as "Thank you," "If you need further information, please ask," or "Please return these forms as soon as possible" are polite, but they are clichés. Furthermore, phrases such as "as soon as possible" are vague and may have different meanings for you and your reader.

You will build more goodwill with a closing that helps your reader respond to your message or, when no response is needed, lets your reader know that the discussion has concluded; for example, "Your answers to these questions by December 1 will help us fill the accounting position before our busy tax season" or "Thank you for submitting your travel forms. If I need anything else regarding your trip, I will contact you."

Now let's see how you can adapt this general direct plan to fit the most common types of neutral and good-news business messages.

Problem-Solving Challenge

Searching for New Regional Headquarters

Introduce yourself to routine inquiries by assuming you are the assistant to the vice president for administration of White Label Industries (WLI). WLI is the manufacturer and distributor of an assortment of high-quality products.

You and your boss were recently chatting about WLI's plans to relocate its regional headquarters. Your boss tells you that she and other top management have chosen the city but have not been able to find the perfect office space. She says that they have not been happy with what realtors have found for them or with what they have found in their own searches of classified ads and realty agencies' websites. When you suggest that they expand their search to something a little less traditional, such as LoopNet.com, your boss says, "Great idea! I don't think any of us have used LoopNet, though. Could you find some locations and show them to us at our Friday meeting?"

You're a bit intimidated by the prospect, but you know that this is a great chance to demonstrate your professional skills. You visit LoopNet and find what you believe would be the perfect office headquarters. You know you could just show the executives the ad at the meeting, but having read the ad and having analyzed your audience, you know the executives will need more information. To present your best professional image at Friday's meeting and help the executives make a good decision, you need to write a routine inquiry seeking additional details about the office space.

Routine Inquiries

Beginning Directly

The opening of the **routine inquiry** should focus on your main objective: getting an answer to your question(s). Routine inquiries can open with either the main question or a brief statement to provide background information or orient the reader, followed by the request or question.

LO8-3   Write clear, well-structured routine inquiries.

In making your request, you can ask one broad question that sets up other questions you'll ask in the body of the message, or you can ask one specific question and then use the body of your message for any explanatory material.

For example, if your objective is to get more information about the office space described in the Problem-Solving Challenge, you might ask a general question:

> The 3,200-square-foot Riverdale office space you advertised on LoopNet seems like a great fit for our regional headquarters. To help us decide on a new office space, could you please answer a few questions about the terms of the lease for the Riverdale offices?

The body of your message would then present a list of the specific information you are seeking.

On the other hand, if you have only one piece of information you are seeking, you could ask a specific question:

> The 3,200-square-foot Riverdale office space you advertised on LoopNet seems like a great fit for our regional headquarters. Could you please send me the terms of the lease for the first- and second-floor office suites?

You might then offer some explanation of what you're looking for, or you might conclude your message. Regardless of how you begin, be sure your reader has a clear sense of your purpose.

Providing Information and Explanations

To help your reader answer your questions, you may need to include an explanation or information. If you do not explain enough or if you misjudge the reader's knowledge, you make the reader's task of responding difficult. For example, answers to your questions about the terms of the lease for WLI's office space may depend on characteristics or specific needs of the company. Without knowing how WLI will use the space, even the best realtor or property manager may not know how to answer your questions or direct you to other office space that better meets your needs.

Answering inquiries that do not include adequate explanation can be frustrating.
© fizkes/Shutterstock

Where you include the necessary explanatory information depends on the nature of your message. Usually, a good place for general explanatory material is after the direct request in the opening paragraph. In messages that ask more than one question, include any necessary explanation after each question.

Asking the Questions

After you ask your initial question, you will take one of two directions. If your inquiry involves only one question, then you have achieved your objective, and you may move to a goodwill ending. If you have to ask several questions, then you will develop an organized, logical list in the body of your message.

First, if you have two or more questions, make them stand out by asking each question in a separate sentence. Combining two or more questions in a sentence deemphasizes each and invites the reader to overlook some. You can call attention to your questions in a number of ways. First, you can make each question a separate sentence with a bullet (e.g., ●, ○, ■) to call attention to it.

Second, you can give each question a separate paragraph if your explanation and other comments about each question justify having a paragraph.

Third, you can order or rank your questions. By using words (*first, second, third*, etc.), numerals (*1, 2, 3*, etc.), or letters (*a, b, c*, etc.), you emphasize the questions. You also provide the reader with a convenient checklist for answering.

Fourth, you can structure your questions in **true question form**. Sentences that hint at a need for information may not attract the reader's attention. The statements "It would be nice if you would tell me . . . " and "I would like to know . . . " are really not questions. They just hint that you want information. The questions that stand out are those written in question form: "Will you please tell me . . . ?" and "How much would I save . . . ?" and "How many contract issues have you had . . . ?"

Avoid questions that can be answered with a simple *yes* or *no* unless you really want a simple *yes* or *no* answer. For example, the question "Is the lease an annual one?" may not be what you really want to know. Better wording might be "What are the options for the length of a lease?" Often, combining a yes/no question with its explanation yields a better, more concise question; for example, "Is a monthly lease available? We need to have the flexibility to lease additional space in the building as our company expands."

Ending with Goodwill

The goodwill ending described in the general plan is appropriate here, just as it is in most business messages. Remember that the closing creates the most goodwill when it fits the topic of the message and includes important deadlines and reasons for them. A generic statement such as "Thank you for your help" shows less goodwill than a specific statement such as "Thank you for helping us find a new office for our growing company."

Reviewing the Pattern for Routine Inquiries

In summary, the plan recommended for the routine inquiry message is as follows:

- Depending on your audience's anticipated reaction, begin with your objective or orient the reader and then ask either a specific question that sets up the entire message or make a general request for information.
- Include any necessary explanation.
- If two or more questions are involved, make them stand out with bullets, numbering, paragraphing, and/or question form.
- End with a goodwill conclusion adapted to the topic of the message.

Comparing Examples of a Routine Inquiry

Two routine inquiry messages illustrate bad and good approaches to requesting information about office space for a new WLI regional headquarters (see the Problem-Solving Challenge at the beginning of the discussion of routine inquiries). The first example follows an indirect pattern, while the second is direct and more appropriate for this neutral message.

As you read the first example, note that it is marked by a icon in the side panel. We use this icon throughout the book wherever we show bad examples. The good examples will be indicated by a ⊚ icon.

An Indirect Message
The less effective message begins slowly and gives obvious information. The writer gets to the point of the message in the second paragraph but does not ask questions; the writer just hints for information. Important information does not stand out but is listed in rapid succession in one sentence. The closing is vague.

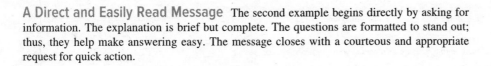

Mr. Piper:

We saw the advertisement for 3,200 square feet of Riverdale office space that you posted a couple of weeks ago on LoopNet. As we are interested, we would like additional information.

Specifically, we would like to know the interior layout, annual cost, availability of transportation, length of lease agreement, escalation provisions, and any other information you think pertinent.

If the information you give us is favorable, we will inspect the property. Please send your reply as soon as possible.

Sincerely,

A Direct and Easily Read Message
The second example begins directly by asking for information. The explanation is brief but complete. The questions are formatted to stand out; thus, they help make answering easy. The message closes with a courteous and appropriate request for quick action.

Dear Mr. Piper:

The 3,200-square-foot Riverdale office suite advertised March 24 on LoopNet may be suitable for the new regional headquarters we are opening in November. Could you please answer the following questions about the space?

- Is the layout of these offices suitable for a workforce of 10 executives, 2 receptionists, and 22 office employees? (If possible, please send us a diagram of the space.)
- What are the dimensions of the office suites on the first and second floors?
- Are housekeeping, maintenance, and utilities included?
- What type of flooring and walls does the office space have?
- Does the location provide easy access to mass transportation and the airport?
- What is the length of the lease agreement?
- What escalation provisions are included in the lease agreement?

We look forward to learning more about your property. Your response by April 1 will help us secure a space that meets our needs by April 30.

Sincerely,

You Make the Call
On the surface, it might seem as though the conclusion is self-serving, but how does the reader benefit by meeting the writer's deadline?

You can also study the following annotated examples. The margin comments in the annotated examples help you see how these sample inquiries follow the advice in this chapter.

Annotated Example
Routine Inquiry (Getting Information about a Training Program)

This email message is from a company training director to the director of a management-training program. The company training director has received literature on the program but needs additional information. The message asks for this information.

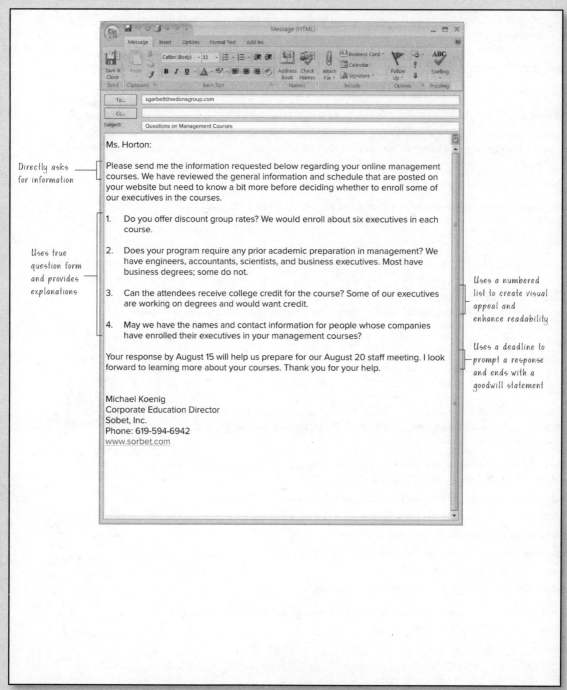

Directly asks for information

Ms. Horton:

Please send me the information requested below regarding your online management courses. We have reviewed the general information and schedule that are posted on your website but need to know a bit more before deciding whether to enroll some of our executives in the courses.

Uses true question form and provides explanations

1. Do you offer discount group rates? We would enroll about six executives in each course.

2. Does your program require any prior academic preparation in management? We have engineers, accountants, scientists, and business executives. Most have business degrees; some do not.

3. Can the attendees receive college credit for the course? Some of our executives are working on degrees and would want credit.

4. May we have the names and contact information for people whose companies have enrolled their executives in your management courses?

Your response by August 15 will help us prepare for our August 20 staff meeting. I look forward to learning more about your courses. Thank you for your help.

Uses a numbered list to create visual appeal and enhance readability

Uses a deadline to prompt a response and ends with a goodwill statement

Michael Koenig
Corporate Education Director
Sobet, Inc.
Phone: 619-594-6942
www.sorbet.com

Source: Kathryn Rentz and Paula Lentz, *M: Business Communication*, 3rd ed. (New York: McGraw-Hill, 2014). Microsoft Outlook.

Annotated Example

Routine Inquiry (An Inquiry about Hotel Accommodations)

This letter to a hotel inquires about accommodations for a company's annual meeting. In selecting a hotel, the company's managers need answers to specific questions. The message covers these questions. While it is true that the writer could have asked these questions in an email, the letter format conveys a formality that is consistent with the size and scope of the event and invites further communication via email or the phone.

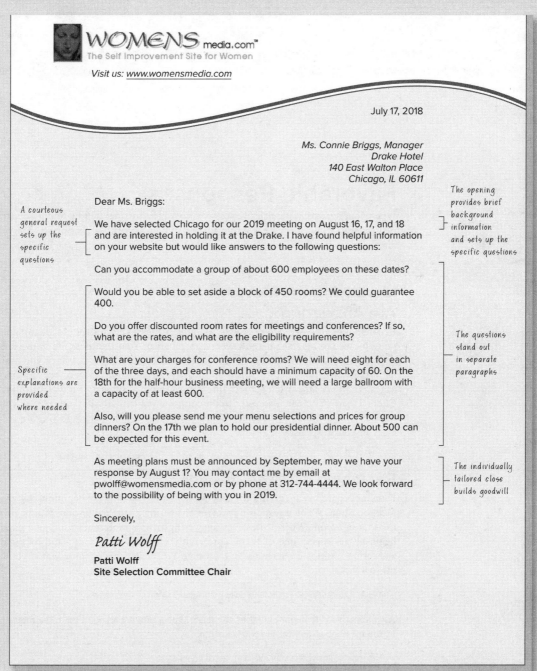

WOMENS media.com
The Self Improvement Site for Women

Visit us: *www.womensmedia.com*

July 17, 2018

Ms. Connie Briggs, Manager
Drake Hotel
140 East Walton Place
Chicago, IL 60611

Dear Ms. Briggs:

A courteous general request sets up the specific questions

We have selected Chicago for our 2019 meeting on August 16, 17, and 18 and are interested in holding it at the Drake. I have found helpful information on your website but would like answers to the following questions:

The opening provides brief background information and sets up the specific questions

Can you accommodate a group of about 600 employees on these dates?

Would you be able to set aside a block of 450 rooms? We could guarantee 400.

Do you offer discounted room rates for meetings and conferences? If so, what are the rates, and what are the eligibility requirements?

Specific explanations are provided where needed

What are your charges for conference rooms? We will need eight for each of the three days, and each should have a minimum capacity of 60. On the 18th for the half-hour business meeting, we will need a large ballroom with a capacity of at least 600.

The questions stand out in separate paragraphs

Also, will you please send me your menu selections and prices for group dinners? On the 17th we plan to hold our presidential dinner. About 500 can be expected for this event.

As meeting plans must be announced by September, may we have your response by August 1? You may contact me by email at pwolff@womensmedia.com or by phone at 312-744-4444. We look forward to the possibility of being with you in 2019.

The individually tailored close builds goodwill

Sincerely,

Patti Wolff

Patti Wolff
Site Selection Committee Chair

Source: Kathryn Rentz and Paula Lentz, *M: Business Communication*, 3rd ed. (New York: McGraw-Hill, 2014). Microsoft Outlook.

Problem-Solving Challenge

Answering a Potential Customer's Questions

Continue in your role as assistant to the vice president for operations of White Label Industries (WLI). This time, your task is to respond to a customer's message.

In your email inbox this morning, you have an inquiry from Dr. Motley, a veterinarian who wants to know more about WLI's Chem-Treat paint. In response to an advertisement, this prospective customer asks a number of specific questions about Chem-Treat. Primarily, she wants to know whether the paint is safe to use around the animals (and their owners) who visit her clinic. Do you have supporting evidence? Do you guarantee the results? Does the paint resist dirt and stains? How much does a gallon cost? Will one coat do the job?

You can answer all but one of the questions positively. Of course, you will include this one negative point that two coats are needed to do most jobs, but you will de-emphasize it. The response will be mostly a good-news message. Because the reader is a potential customer, you will work to create goodwill.

Favorable Responses

LO8-4 Write direct, orderly, and favorable answers to inquiries.

When your answer to inquiries is positive, your primary goal will be to tell your readers what they want to know. Because your message will be a **favorable response**, you want to use a direct approach.

Identifying the Message You Are Answering

Because this message is a response to another message, you should identify the message you are answering so that the reader can recall or find the message being answered. Of course, in an email message, your subject line will identify the message you are answering, and your reader may see the original message in the email thread, but in hard copy messages, you may also use a subject line; for example, "Subject: Your April 2 Inquiry about Chem-Treat." You can also refer to the message incidentally in the text ("as you requested in your April 2 inquiry"). Ideally, you want to identify the message you are responding to early in your response.

Beginning with the Answer

Directness here means giving the readers what they want at the beginning by answering the main question. When a response involves answering a single question, you begin by answering that question. When it involves answering two or more questions, one good plan is to begin by answering one of them—preferably the most important—and then moving on to answering additional questions. In the Chem-Treat case, this opening would get the response off to a fast start:

Yes, WLI's Chem-Treat acrylic latex paint is among the safest on the market.

An alternative is to begin by letting the reader know you are responding to the request and setting up the message to answer several questions:

Here are the answers to your questions about Chem-Treat.

Logically Arranging the Answers

If you are answering just one question, you have little to do after handling that question in the opening. You answer it completely and present whatever explanation or other information is needed. Then you are ready to close the message.

If, on the other hand, you are answering two or more questions, the body of your message becomes a series of answers. You should order them logically, perhaps answering the questions in the order your reader used in asking them. You may even number your answers, especially if your reader numbered the questions. Or you may decide to arrange your answers by paragraphs so that each stands out clearly.

Skillfully Handling the Negatives

When your response will include some bad news along with the good news, you need to handle the bad news with care so that it does not receive more emphasis than it deserves.

In properly emphasizing the good- and bad-news information, you should use the techniques discussed in Chapter 5, especially positioning. That is, place the good news in positions of high emphasis at paragraph beginnings and endings and at the beginning and ending of the message as a whole. Place the bad news in a secondary position.

In addition, you can use space emphasis to your advantage. This means giving less space to bad news and more space to good news. You also want to select positive words and build sentences that put bad news in modifying phrases or subordinate clauses rather than in main clauses. Your overall goal should be to present the information in your response so that your readers feel good about you and your company.

Considering Extras

To create goodwill, as well as future business, you should consider including extras with your answers. Extras are the things you say and do that are not required and go beyond a routine response. Examples are a comment or question showing an interest in the reader's situation, some additional information that may prove valuable, or a suggestion for use of the information you have provided. For instance, in responding to the Chem-Treat issue described in the Problem-Solving Challenge, you might provide additional information Dr. Motley would find helpful in purchasing paint for her clinic (e.g., how much surface area a gallon covers). These extras encourage readers to build a business relationship with you.

Closing Cordially

As in the other types of direct messages, your ending should be specific to your topic and build goodwill. For example, you might close the Chem-Treat message with these words:

If I can help you further in deciding whether Chem-Treat will meet your needs, please let me know.

Reviewing the Pattern for Favorable Responses

To write a favorable response message, you should use the following plan:

- Identify, either incidentally or in the subject line, the message being answered.

- Begin with the answer or state that you are complying with the request and answering several questions.

- Continue to respond in a way that is logical and orderly.

Using Function Keys in Microsoft Word

Have you ever wondered what the F1–F12 keys are for on your computer keyboard? These function keys enable you to work quickly and more efficiently as you perform many tasks, whether you use the key alone or in combination with the FN, Ctrl, Alt, or Shift keys. Although the keys may perform differently depending on your computer and keyboard, common functions include the following:

- F1: Opens Word Help
- F2 + Ctrl + Alt: Opens Windows Explorer so that you can search for files
- F2 + Ctrl: Opens Print Preview
- F3 + Shift: Toggles text from uppercase to lowercase
- F4 + Alt: Closes Word
- F7: Checks spelling and grammar

- F7 + Alt: Opens the Thesaurus
- F10: Presents keyboard options for accessing menu options in Microsoft Office programs
- F11: Opens and closes the full-screen mode
- F12: Opens a "Save as . . ." dialog box in Microsoft Office programs
- F12 + Ctrl: Opens an existing document in a Microsoft Office program

- De-emphasize any negative information.
- Consider including extras.
- End with a friendly comment adapted to your topic and your reader.

Comparing Examples of a Favorable Response

The contrasting email messages illustrate two strategies for answering routine inquiries using the Chem-Treat paint example in the Problem-Solving Case at the beginning of this section. The first message violates much of the advice in this and earlier chapters. The second meets the reader's needs and supports the writer's business goals.

An Indirect and Hurried Response The ineffective example begins indirectly with an obvious statement referring to receipt of the inquiry. Though well intended, the second sentence continues to delay the answers. The second paragraph begins to respond to the reader's request, but it emphasizes the most negative answer by discussing it first and by using negative wording. This answer is followed by hurried and routine answers to the other questions asked. Only the barest information is presented. The message contains no goodwill closing.

Subject: Your Inquiry of April 3

Dear Dr. Motley:

I have received your April 3 message, in which you inquire about the availability of our Chem-Treat paint. I want you to know that we appreciate your interest and will welcome your business.

In response to your question about how many coats are needed to cover new surfaces, I regret to inform you that two are usually required. The paint has been well tested in our laboratories and is safe to use as directed.

Ray Lindner
Customer Service Representative

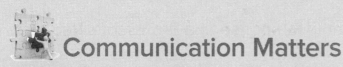
How Routine Responses Were Written in the Late 1800s

The following model letter for answering routine inquiries appears on page 75 of O.R. Palmer's *Type-Writing and Business Correspondence*. Published in 1896, the book was a leader in its field.

Dear Sirs:

The favor of Dec 18th, enclosing blue prints for tank, received. In reply thereto we beg to submit the following:

[Here was a listing of materials for the tank.]

Trusting that our price may be satisfactory to you, and that we shall be favored with your order, we beg to remain,

Very truly yours,

Many phrases in this document are so formal that the message sounds impersonal and stiff. Other popular phrases from that era include

"Assuring you of our continued cooperation, we remain . . . ," "Herewith enclosed please find . . . ," "Kindly advise at an early date . . . ," "The undersigned deems it advisable . . . ," and "Reference is made to your May 7 letter, in which. . . ."

Over the last century, these phrases have fallen out of use, and the language of direct messages has become more personal, direct, and focused on building goodwill.

A Direct and Organized Message The good message begins directly with the most favorable answer. Then it presents the other answers, giving each answer the emphasis and positive language it deserves. It subordinates the one negative answer by position, use of space, and positive wording. More pleasant information follows the negative answer. The message closes with goodwill and subtle product promotion.

Subject: Your April 3 Inquiry

Dear Dr. Motley:

Yes, Chem-Treat's low-odor, low-VOC acrylic latex paint is among the safest, most environmentally friendly paints.

Chem-Treat's latex formula also makes it ideal for high-traffic areas. Cleaning usually requires only a little soap and water.

One gallon of Chem-Treat is usually enough for one-coat coverage of 500 square feet of previously painted surface. For the best results on new surfaces, you will want to apply two coats. For new surfaces, you should figure about 200 square feet per gallon for a long-lasting coating.

We appreciate your interest in Chem-Treat, Dr. Motley. You can view Chem-Treat's safety ratings and customer reviews on our website: www.wli.com/chemtreat/features. If I can help you further in deciding whether Chem-Treat will meet your needs, please let me know.

Ray Lindner
Customer Service Representative

Favorable Response (Favorable Response to a Professor's Request)

This email message responds to a professor's request for production records that will be used in a research project. The writer is sending the information requested but attaches restrictions to the use of the information. Notice that the message emphasizes the positive points.

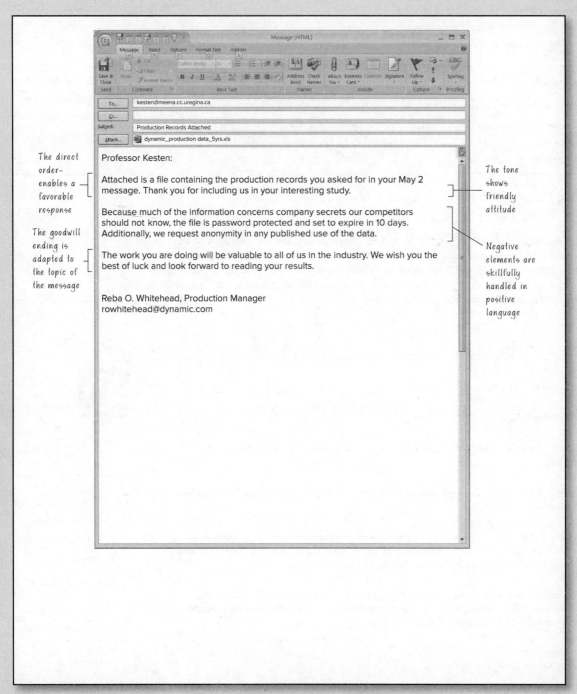

The direct order enables a favorable response

The goodwill ending is adapted to the topic of the message

The tone shows friendly attitude

Negative elements are skillfully handled in positive language

To: kesten@meena.cc.uregina.ca

Subject: Production Records Attached

Attach: dynamic_production data_5yrs.xls

Professor Kesten:

Attached is a file containing the production records you asked for in your May 2 message. Thank you for including us in your interesting study.

Because much of the information concerns company secrets our competitors should not know, the file is password protected and set to expire in 10 days. Additionally, we request anonymity in any published use of the data.

The work you are doing will be valuable to all of us in the industry. We wish you the best of luck and look forward to reading your results.

Reba O. Whitehead, Production Manager
rowhitehead@dynamic.com

Source: Kathryn Rentz and Paula Lentz, *M: Business Communication,* 3rd ed. (New York: McGraw-Hill, 2014). Microsoft Outlook.

Annotated Example
Favorable Response (Answering a Request for Detailed Information)

Answering an inquiry about a company's experience with executive suites, this letter numbers the answers as the questions were numbered in the inquiry. The opening appropriately sets up the numbered answers with a statement that indicates a favorable response. As with many routine responses, the writer could have chosen to send this message as an email. It is possible, though, that the reader requested a formal written response to use to support her case for using temporary executive suites.

Merck & Co., Inc.
One Merck Drive
P.O. Box 100, WS1A-46
Whitehouse Station NJ 08889

MERCK

August 7, 2018

Ms. Ida Casey, Sales Manager
Liberty Insurance Company
1165 Second Ave.
Des Moines, IA 50318-9631

Dear Ms. Casey:

The direct opening makes the purpose clear

Here is the information about our use of temporary executive suites that you requested in our August 3 phone conversation.

1. Our executives have mixed feelings about the effectiveness of the suites. At the beginning, the majority opinion was negative, but it appears now that most believe the suites meet our needs.

2. The suites option definitely has saved us money. Rental costs in the suburbs are much lower than downtown costs; annual savings are estimated at nearly 30 percent.

The list format aids comprehension

3. We began using executive suites at the request of several sales representatives who had read about other companies using them. We pilot tested the program in one territory for a year using volunteers before we implemented it companywide.

4. We are quite willing to share with you the list of facilities we plan to use again. Additionally, I am enclosing a copy of our corporate policy, which describes our guidelines for using executive suites.

Answers are complete yet concise

The friendly close is adapted to the one case

If you have questions after reviewing this information, please contact me at earpdm@merck.com or 908-423-3333. I wish you the best of luck in using these suites in your operations.

This extra builds goodwill

Sincerely,

David M. Earp

David M. Earp
Office Manager

Enclosure

Source: Kathryn Rentz and Paula Lentz, *M: Business Communication*, 3rd ed. (New York: McGraw-Hill, 2014). Microsoft Outlook.

Problem-Solving Challenge

Building Goodwill with a "Thank-You" Message

The next work you take from your inbox is an order for paints and painting supplies. It is from Mr. Tony Li of Central City Paint Company, a new customer whom White Label Industries (WLI) has been trying to attract for months. You usually acknowledge orders with routine messages, but this case is different. You feel the need to welcome this new customer and to cultivate future business with him.

After checking your current inventory and making certain that the goods will be on the way to Mr. Li today, you are ready to write him a special acknowledgment and thank him for his business.

Order Acknowledgments and Other Thank-You Messages

LO8-5 Write order acknowledgments and other thank-you messages that build goodwill.

As a business professional, you will find yourself in situations where business and social etiquette require thank-you messages. Such messages may be long or short, formal or informal. They also may be combined with other purposes such as confirming an order. In this section we focus on one specific kind of thank-you message—the **order acknowledgment**—as well as more general thank-you messages for other business occasions.

Writing Order Acknowledgments

Acknowledgments are sent to let people who order goods know the status of their orders. Most acknowledgments are routine. They simply tell when the goods are being shipped. Many companies use form or computer-generated messages for such situations. Some use printed, standard notes with check-boxes or write-in blanks. But individually written acknowledgments are sometimes justified, especially with new accounts or large orders.

Skillfully composed acknowledgments can do more than acknowledge orders, though this task remains their primary goal. These messages can also build goodwill through their warm, personal tone. They can make the reader feel good about doing business with a company that cares.

Being Direct and Building Goodwill in Order Acknowledgments

Like the preceding direct message types, the acknowledgment message begins with its good news—that the goods are being shipped—and it ends on a goodwill note. Except when some of the goods ordered must be delayed, the remainder of the message is devoted to building goodwill by emphasizing the customer's receipt of the goods rather than merely the shipment of them:

> The Protect-O paints and supplies you ordered April 4 should reach you by Wednesday. They are leaving our Walden warehouse today by Arrow Freight.

It can also include a warm expression of thanks for the order, especially when a first order is involved. Anything else you can say that will be helpful to the reader is appropriate—information about new products, services, or opportunities for the reader. You can then close with a forward-looking note about continued business relations.

Being Tactful in Order Acknowledgments

Sometimes acknowledging an order is complicated by your inability to send the goods requested right away. You could be out of them, or perhaps the reader did not give you all the information you needed in order to send them. In some cases, delays are routine and do not pose a serious problem. In these situations, you can use the direct approach. However, you still want to minimize negative news so that your routine message does not become a negative-news message. You can do this by using positive language that focuses on what *can* or *will* happen rather than what *didn't* or *won't* happen.

Tables Help Writers Organize Data for Easy Reading

Setting up tables within a document is an easy task thanks to computer tools. In both instances, information can be arranged in columns and rows. Headings can be formatted, and formulas can be entered to generate data in the cells. The table you see here could be one the writer created for use in a favorable response to an inquiry about possible locations for a meeting in Chicago.

Organizing information with tables makes it easier for the reader to get the information quickly and concisely. A careful writer will include column and row labels as needed, helping the reader extract information both quickly and accurately.

Hotel Name	Address	Convention Room Rate for Standard Rooms	Guest Rating
Chicago Marriott Downtown	540 North Michigan Avenue, Chicago, IL 60611-3869	$409	4.2
Drake Hotel	140 East Walton Street, Chicago, IL 60611-1545	$309	4.3
Palmer House Hilton	17 East Monroe Street, Chicago, IL 60603-5605	$252	4.4

In the case of a vague order, for example, you should request the information you need without appearing to accuse the reader of giving insufficient information. You risk offending the reader by writing "You failed to specify the color of phones you want," but you gain goodwill by writing "So that we can send you the phones you want, please check your choice of colors on the space below."

Similarly, you can handle back-order information tactfully by emphasizing the positive part of the message. For example, instead of writing "We can't ship the tablets until the 9th," you can write "We will rush the tablets to you as soon as our stock is replenished by a shipment due May 9." If the back-order period is longer than the customer expects or longer than the 30 days allowed by law, you may want to build goodwill by giving your customer an alternative, such as a substitute product or service.

In some cases delays will lead to major disappointments, which means you will have to write a bad-news message. A more complete discussion of how to handle such negative news is provided in Chapter 9.

Using Strategies for Other Thank-You Messages

One of the first thank-you messages you write will be the one for a job interview, which is discussed in Chapter 15. Once you are employed, you may send thank-you messages after a meeting or when someone does a favor for you or gives you a gift, when you want to acknowledge others' efforts that have somehow benefited you, when you want to thank customers for their business, or perhaps when someone has donated time or money to your organization or a cause it supports. The possibilities for situations when you might send thank-you notes are many, and sending a message of sincere thanks is a great way to promote goodwill and build your and your company's professional image.

Thank-you messages are often brief and written directly. You can begin with a specific statement of thanks:

Thank you for attending the American Cancer Society fundraiser lunch for Relay for Life last week and for donating money to the cause.

Communication Matters

Personalizing Form Letters

Many businesses use form letters to acknowledge customer orders or to respond in other routine and frequently recurring situations. Often these letters follow a template so that they are standardized in their form and content and expedite communication between the business and its customers. You have likely received a form letter upon placing an order for a product.

While form letters help businesses communicate consistently and efficiently, form letters have a reputation as impersonal formalities. You, however, have some options for personalizing these letters to build goodwill and still be quick and efficient in your communication. For example, writing a short note on a form letter or signing your name in ink rather than sending only a typed document lets the reader know you at least saw the letter and thought about him or her.

If notes are not possible, you can still personalize your communication by using the reader's name and other personal information such as a mailing address or account number. Microsoft Word's Step-by-Step Mail Merge Wizard feature guides you through quick and easy steps to send a personalized form message to individuals already in your email contact list or in a list that you create.

This feature also works if you are sending form letters or emails that require some customizing. For example, let's say you are sending usernames and passwords to individual clients who need to access their accounts for the first time. All clients receive essentially the same letter with the only difference

being the username and password. The Mail Merge Wizard saves you the time of having to create individual messages for each recipient.

Given how quick and easy the process is, why not take the opportunity to build goodwill by adding your personal touch to the next form letter you send?

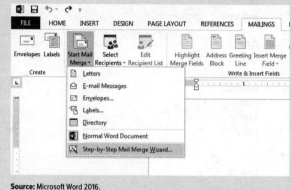

Source: Microsoft Word 2016.

Follow with a personalized comment relevant to the reader:

> With your support, the 2018 Relay for Life will be our most successful yet. You can find details regarding the event on our website at https://secure.acsevents.org/site/SPageServer/?pagename=relay.

Conclude with a forward-looking statement:

> I hope you are able to join us for the running of the relay on June 12.

Your tone should be informal and friendly. If you are on a first-name basis with the reader, you may omit a salutation or use the reader's first name, but if your relationship with the reader is a formal one, do not use the reader's first name to create a contrived sense of closeness.

Whether you hand write the thank-you, send an email, or use company stationery depends on the audience. If you have poor handwriting or believe your handwriting does not convey a professional image, you may want to type your message. Though you should always check your own spelling, grammar, and punctuation before sending any message, doing so is especially important in handwritten notes when you have no computer spell check to alert you to possible errors.

Reviewing the Pattern for Order Acknowledgments and Other Thank-You Messages

To write an order acknowledgment or thank-you message,

- Begin by thanking the reader for something specific (e.g., an order).
- Continue with your thanks or with further information.
- Use positive, tactful language to address vague or delayed orders.

- If appropriate, achieve a secondary goal (e.g., reselling or confirming a mutual understanding).
- Close with a goodwill-building comment that you adapt to the topic of the message.

Comparing Examples of an Order Acknowledgment

These two messages illustrate two strategies for sending the thank-you note discussed in the Problem-Solving Case at the beginning of this section. The first message violates much of the advice in this and earlier chapters. The second meets the reader's needs and supports the writer's business goals.

An Indirect Message That Delays the Good News The bad example begins indirectly, emphasizing receipt of the order. Although intended to produce goodwill, the second sentence further delays what the reader wants most to hear. Moreover, the letter is written from the writer's point of view.

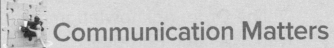

Communication Matters

A Workplace without Email? One Company's Strategy

French tech company Atos discovered that its nearly 80,000 employees were spending a disproportionate amount of time using email to communicate with their co-workers.

The company's solution to making communication more productive was to phase out email as an internal communication tool through its Zero email™ program. Instead, employees used the company's bluKiwi social network, Sharepoint, or Lync for their internal communication. In addition to reducing the volume of email, the company says moving to communication technologies such as instant messaging creates higher levels of employee engagement and social interaction.

Initially, responses to the Zero email program ranged from enthusiasm to skepticism. However, Gartner, Inc., an information technology research firm, reported that Atos saw a 60% drop in email volume in the first year and shifted its culture to one that centered on social collaboration.

Source: "Gartner Report: Atos No-Email Initiative Provides Valuable Lessons on Driving Big Change Through Social Collaboration," *Atos,* August 4, 2014, accessed November 14, 2016, http://na.atos.net/en-us/home/we-are/zero-email/zero-email-insights-and-stories/gartner-report-atos-no-email-initiative-provides-valuable-lessons-on-driving-big-change-through-social-collaboration.html.

Dear Mr. Li:

Your April 4 order for $1,743.30 worth of Protect-O paints and supplies has been received. We are pleased to have this nice order and hope that it marks the beginning of a long relationship.

As you instructed, we will bill you for this amount. We are shipping the goods today by Blue Darter Motor Freight.

We look forward to your future orders.

Sincerely,

You Make the Call
Could you do without email? In what situations might a business find email necessary or beneficial?

A Direct Acknowledgment That Builds Goodwill The better message begins directly, telling Mr. Li that he is getting what he wants. The remainder of the message is a customer welcome and subtle selling. Notice the good use of reader emphasis and positive language. The message closes with a note of appreciation and a friendly, forward look.

Dear Mr. Li:

Your selection of Protect-O paints and supplies was shipped today by Blue Darter Freight and should reach you by Wednesday. As you requested, we are sending you an invoice for $1,743.30, including sales tax.

Welcome to the Protect-O circle of dealers. Our representative, Ms. Cindy Wooley, will call from time to time to offer whatever assistance she can. She is a highly competent technical adviser on paint and painting.

We also will do our best to give you the most efficient service. In addition, we'll continue to develop the best possible paints—such as our new Chem-Treat line. As you will see from the enclosed brochure, Chem-Treat is a real breakthrough in mildew protection.

Thank you for your order, Mr. Li. We are determined to serve you well in the years ahead.

Sincerely,

Annotated Example
Online Order Acknowledgment (Order Confirmation with a Second Purpose)

This email message thanks the reader for her order and follows with details regarding shipment and managing the order. While the email is a form message, it addresses the customer by name, the tone is polite, and the details are specific to the topic of the order, which helps the reader find sources of help or answers to questions.

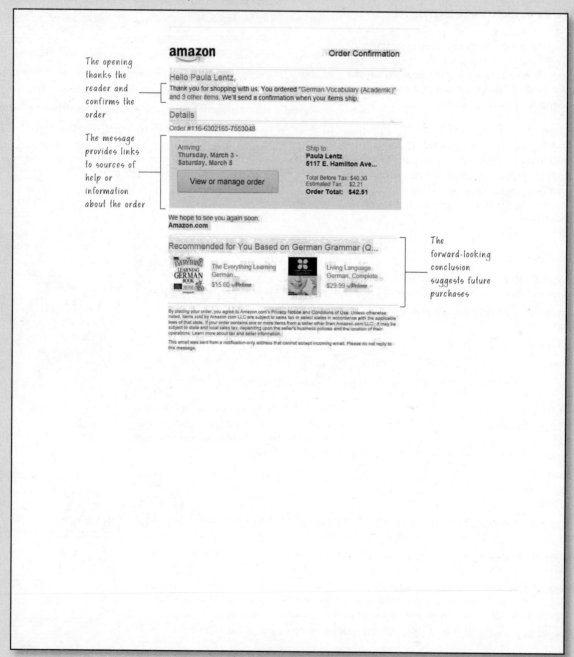

The opening thanks the reader and confirms the order

The message provides links to sources of help or information about the order

The forward-looking conclusion suggests future purchases

amazon Order Confirmation

Hello Paula Lentz,

Thank you for shopping with us. You ordered "German Vocabulary (Academic)" and 3 other items. We'll send a confirmation when your items ship.

Details

Order #116-6302165-7553048

Arriving:
Thursday, March 3 -
Saturday, March 5

[View or manage order]

Ship to:
Paula Lentz
5117 E. Hamilton Ave...

Total Before Tax: $40.30
Estimated Tax: $2.21
Order Total: $42.51

We hope to see you again soon.
Amazon.com

Recommended for You Based on German Grammar (Q...

The Everything Learning German...
$15.60 *Prime*

Living Language German, Complete...
$29.99 *Prime*

By placing your order, you agree to Amazon.com's Privacy Notice and Conditions of Use. Unless otherwise noted, items sold by Amazon.com LLC are subject to sales tax in select states in accordance with the applicable laws of that state. If your order contains one or more items from a seller other than Amazon.com LLC, it may be subject to state and local sales tax, depending upon the seller's business policies and the location of their operations. Learn more about tax and seller information.

This email was sent from a notification-only address that cannot accept incoming email. Please do not reply to this message.

Source: Amazon.com

Annotated Example

Order Acknowledgment (Acknowledgment with a Problem)

This email letter concerns an order that cannot be handled exactly as the customer would like. Some items are being sent, but one must be placed on back order, and another cannot be shipped because the customer did not give the information needed. The message skillfully handles the negative points.

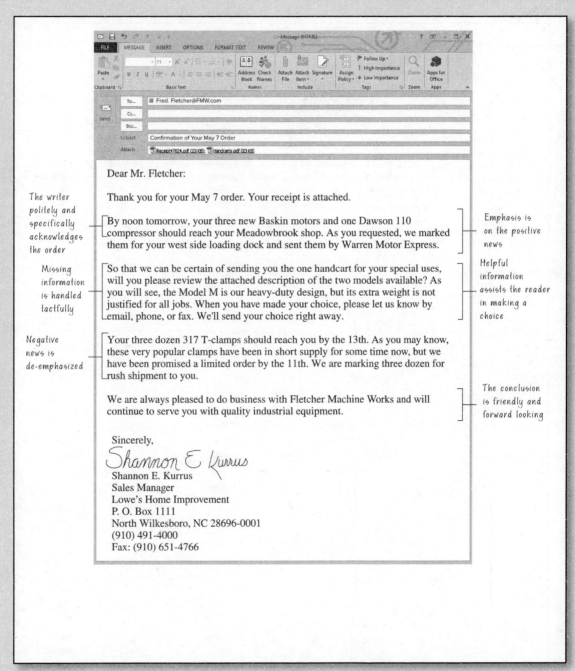

The writer politely and specifically acknowledges the order

Missing information is handled tactfully

Negative news is de-emphasized

Emphasis is on the positive news

Helpful information assists the reader in making a choice

The conclusion is friendly and forward looking

To... Fred.Fletcher@FMW.com
Cc...
Bcc...
Subject Confirmation of Your May 7 Order
Attach Receipt#7824.pdf (23 KB); Handcarts.pdf (23 KB)

Dear Mr. Fletcher:

Thank you for your May 7 order. Your receipt is attached.

By noon tomorrow, your three new Baskin motors and one Dawson 110 compressor should reach your Meadowbrook shop. As you requested, we marked them for your west side loading dock and sent them by Warren Motor Express.

So that we can be certain of sending you the one handcart for your special uses, will you please review the attached description of the two models available? As you will see, the Model M is our heavy-duty design, but its extra weight is not justified for all jobs. When you have made your choice, please let us know by email, phone, or fax. We'll send your choice right away.

Your three dozen 317 T-clamps should reach you by the 13th. As you may know, these very popular clamps have been in short supply for some time now, but we have been promised a limited order by the 11th. We are marking three dozen for rush shipment to you.

We are always pleased to do business with Fletcher Machine Works and will continue to serve you with quality industrial equipment.

Sincerely,

Shannon E Kurrus

Shannon E. Kurrus
Sales Manager
Lowe's Home Improvement
P. O. Box 1111
North Wilkesboro, NC 28696-0001
(910) 491-4000
Fax: (910) 651-4766

Source: Kathryn Rentz and Paula Lentz, *M: Business Communication*, 3rd ed. (New York: McGraw-Hill, 2014). Microsoft Outlook.

Annotated Example

Thank-You Message (A Follow-Up to an Informational Interview)

This email is a thank you to a businessperson from a student. The writer is thanking the reader for taking the time to meet for an informational interview. In the interview, the reader shared her thoughts about her profession and offered advice to the student to help him be successful in pursuing a similar career.

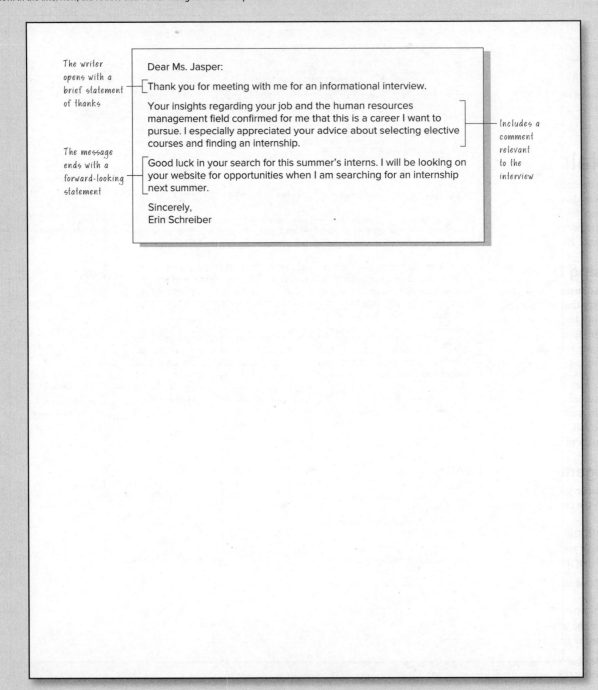

The writer opens with a brief statement of thanks

Dear Ms. Jasper:

Thank you for meeting with me for an informational interview.

Your insights regarding your job and the human resources management field confirmed for me that this is a career I want to pursue. I especially appreciated your advice about selecting elective courses and finding an internship.

Includes a comment relevant to the interview

The message ends with a forward-looking statement

Good luck in your search for this summer's interns. I will be looking on your website for opportunities when I am searching for an internship next summer.

Sincerely,
Erin Schreiber

Problem-Solving Challenge

Requesting a Correct Shipment and Revised Invoice

Continue in your role with White Label Industries (WLI). As the assistant to the vice president of operations, you manage the supervisors on the paint production line. Today, one of the team leaders came to you for some feedback on his writing. Last week, he ordered some safety equipment (goggles and face masks) for employees on the production line; however, he received gloves instead of goggles and only half the masks he ordered. He looked at the invoice and noticed he received someone else's order. He just wants the correct order shipped and his bill adjusted accordingly.

He called his sales representative but got her voice mail. He left her a quick message to call him about the order, but this is an urgent message, so just in case she is online and checking her email, he also wants to send her an email explaining the situation. He asks for your feedback on the email, and you are surprised at the indirect language and unnecessarily negative and harsh tone. You need to use what you know about writing a direct claim to help him write a message that not only resolves the issue but also builds goodwill.

Claims

Occasionally, things go wrong between a business and its customers (e.g., merchandise is lost or broken during shipment, customers are inaccurately billed for goods or services). Such situations are not routine for a business; for most businesses, the routine practice is to fulfill their customers' expectations. Whether claims are written directly or indirectly depends on the audience and context. Both approaches are discussed in this section.

LO8-6   Write claim messages that address errors while building goodwill.

Using Directness for Claims

Most businesses want to know when something is wrong so they can correct the matter and satisfy their customers. Many times the easiest and quickest way to address these claims is simply to call the company directly. Sometimes, though, you want a written record of the claim. In addition, depending on a company's phone options for accessing customer service, sending a written claim via email or the company website may be more efficient than making a phone call.

You may use the direct approach in cases where you anticipate that the reader will grant an adjustment of your claim (e.g., adjusting an incorrect charge to an invoice). When you write the claim, you want to keep your tone objective and professional so that you preserve your reader's goodwill. If you use words such as *complaint* or *disappointment,* you will compromise your chances of receiving an adjustment quickly.

Organizing the Direct Claim

Because you anticipate that the reader will willingly grant your request, a **direct claim** begins with the claim, moves to an explanation, and ends with a goodwill closing.

Beginning a Direct Claim   The direct claim should open with a polite but direct statement of what you need. If the statement sounds too direct, you may soften it with a little bit of explanation, but the direct claim should be at the beginning of your message, as in this example:

> Please adjust the invoice (# 6379) for our May 10 order to remove the $7.50 shipping charge.

Explaining the Issue   The body of the direct claim provides the reader with any information he or she might need to understand your claim. To continue with the same example, you might write the following brief middle paragraph:

> Because our order totaled $73.50, we were able to take advantage of your offer for free shipping on orders of $50 or more and should not have been charged a shipping fee.

From the Tech Desk

Quick Parts Makes Quick Work for Business Writers

If you don't already do so, you may someday find yourself frequently using the same text in multiple email messages. For example, perhaps you have a standard message you send to customers who request information from you. Or maybe you frequently send reminder emails to your staff.

Whatever the scenario, if you find yourself typing the same information repeatedly, you may want to take advantage of Outlook's Quick Parts feature. Its use is simple:

1. Type your text in the message area of your email.
2. Select your text.
3. Go to Insert » Quick Parts » Save Selection to Auto Parts Gallery.

From there you can label and save the text you selected. As you create a library of Quick

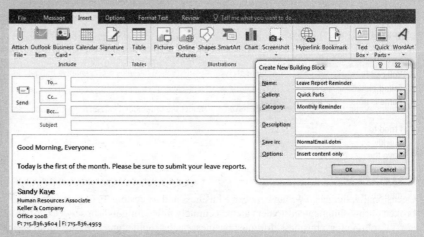

Source: Microsoft Outlook 2016.

Parts features, you can also organize your texts by category. Then, whenever you need to use that text in an email, just go to the Quick Parts feature and select your text from your library. It will be automatically inserted in your message.

Providing a Goodwill Closing Your close should end with an expression of goodwill such as the following:

> Please send a corrected copy of the invoice to me at jsmith@americanmortgage.com. We look forward to continued business with National Office Supplies.

Reviewing the Pattern for Direct Claims

To write a direct claim message, you should use the following plan:

- Begin with a direct but polite statement of your claim.

- In the body of the message, give the reader the information he or she needs to adjust the claim.

- Close with an expression of goodwill.

Comparing Examples of a Direct Claim Message

The following two email messages show contrasting ways of handling the erroneous shipment described in the Problem-Solving Challenge presented at the beginning of this section.

An Indirect and Harsh Message The first message starts slowly with a long explanation of the situation. Some of the details in the beginning sentence are helpful, but they do not deserve the emphasis that this position gives them. The problem is not described until the second paragraph, and the wording here is clear but much too strong. The words are angry, insulting, and threatening, and the writer talks down to the reader. Such words are more likely to produce resistance. The negative writing continues into the close, leaving a bad final impression.

Subject: Problem with Our Order #2478

Beth,

As you know, White Label Industries has been ordering our safety supplies from you for over 15 years. We have always depended on you for quick and accurate service, which, unfortunately, looks like it didn't happen this time. When our orders are not accurate and our safety gear is not what we ordered, you put our employees in jeopardy, and WLI loses money if employees don't have safety gear and can't work.

You can imagine how shocked I was when I opened the order expecting face masks and goggles but found gloves and half the face masks I ordered. The address on the invoice is correct but the company name is not ours, so I'm guessing you shipped someone else's order to our address.

I tried to call you, but you didn't answer, so I left a voice message. I'm guessing you'll want to fix this quickly, so please call me or email me and let me know what you are going do. If my employees do not have the masks and goggles by tomorrow, they can't work, and we will have to shut down our production line, which will cost us a lot of money. This was really disappointing service, but I'm sure it won't happen again, as you have always been accurate in the past. We would hate to think that we need to go with a different supplier. Thank you.

Ken

A Firm yet Courteous Message The second message follows the plan suggested in the preceding paragraphs. A subject line quickly and neutrally identifies the situation. The message begins with a clear statement of the claim. Next, it uses objective language to tell what went wrong. The ending is rational and shows that the writer is interested in resolving the issue, not placing blame.

Subject: Need Correct Order Shipped (Invoice 2478)

Beth,

Please send 50 safety goggles and 100 face masks, as well as a new invoice, to replace the incorrect order that arrived this morning.

On Monday, I placed the order for the safety goggles and face masks, but today I received only 50 face masks and 15 boxes of safety gloves. The invoice indicates that this order was supposed to go to J&M Medical Supplies but was shipped to our address.

If you send the order today, we should receive it tomorrow. Our employees will need the safety equipment in order for us to keep the production line running.

Please confirm the shipment of our correct order and let me know how you want to handle the return of J&M's order.

Thanks,

Ken

Problem-Solving Challenge

Seeking an Adjustment for a Subpar Experience

Play the role of Jeff Sutton, owner and president of White Label Industries (WLI). You've just received a bill from Regal Banquet Center for the party you held there last week. It's for $2,410, which you had agreed to pay for an elegant three-course meal, plus drinks, for your 27 employees.

The food was as good as its reputation, but there were two problems. First, the room for the party was much too warm. You complained to the servers but to no avail. You would have opened windows to correct the problem yourself, but the room you were given did not have any windows (something you weren't happy about, either). Second, there was apparently a shortage of servers on the night of your event. Some of your employees had to wait a long time for their food, while those who had their food first either had to start eating before the others or let their food get cold while waiting for all to be served. This ragged timing ruined the dinner, and it also threw off the timing of the program you had planned.

You were embarrassed by these problems. They reflected poorly on you and your efforts to thank your employees for their work. While you understand that unexpected problems can arise, you just don't think you should have to pay the full amount for a subpar experience. You'll need to write a claim message asking for an adjustment to your bill.

Using Indirectness in Claims

Sometimes you may anticipate that your audience's reaction to your claim may be negative or that your claim involves a sensitive topic. Of course, in these situations a phone call or in-person conversation may be most appropriate, but if these channels are not possible or if you want a written record of your exchange, you want to write an **indirect claim**. The indirect approach is the focus of Chapter 9, but we discuss the indirect claim here to contrast it with the direct claim.

Choosing the Right Tone Your goal in a claim message is to convince your recipient that you deserve some kind of compensation or remedy for a situation that has occurred. When writing this kind of message, project an image of yourself as a reasonable person. Just as importantly, project an image of the reader as a reasonable person. Give the reader a chance to show that, if presented with the facts, he or she will do the right thing. Keep your tone as objective as you can while also making sure that the reader understands the problems caused by the situation. Focus as much as possible on facts, not feelings.

Leading into the Problem in the Beginning A claim message needs to identify the transactions involved. This you can do early in the message as a part of the beginning. One way is to put the identification in the subject line of an email message or in the subject line of a letter, as in this example:

> Subject: Quick Time Microwave Warranty

Another way is just to include a neutral but relevant buffer:

> On May 29 we purchased a new Quick Time microwave for use in our company break room (Order# C13144).

Whether you use a subject line and your first paragraph or the first paragraph alone to introduce the problem, choose your words carefully. Such negatively charged words as *complaint* or *disappointment* can put your readers on the defensive before you've even had a chance to make your case.

Describing the Problem Clearly In the body of your message, explain what happened. The words describing the problem should be courteous yet firm. They should cover the problem completely, giving enough information to permit the reader to judge the matter. Present your case using facts and logic. If there were consequences to what happened, include them:

> When we purchased a Quick Time microwave (Serial No. 713129), we were told that even with heavy use, the quality of the microwave is such that we needed only the six-month warranty rather than the three-year extended warranty. We have had the microwave for only seven months, but it suddenly quit working.

Customizing Your Word or Outlook Toolbar

As a writer, you repeatedly use some features in Word and Outlook (e.g., Print, Save, Undo). Word and Outlook let you customize your toolbar (the space above the ribbon) so that you can more quickly access these options you use frequently.

As shown here in Word, you can choose File > Options > Quick Access Toolbar. Once there, you simply click a command in the "Choose commands from" list and then click "Add." You can see that the items in the "Customize Quick Access Toolbar" list now appear in the Word document toolbar. Whenever you need to use one of those commands, just select it from your toolbar.

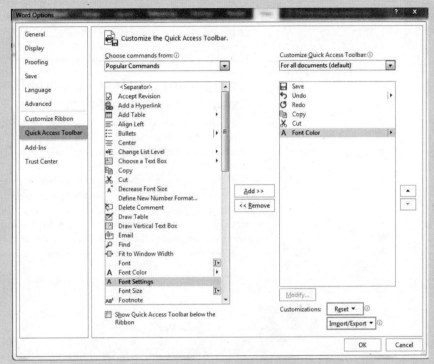

Source: Microsoft Word 2016.

Notice that this example uses the passive voice ("were told") to avoid accusing or blaming language. You should follow these statements with any other evidence that supports your eventual request to replace the microwave.

Requesting the Correction The facts you present should prove your claim, so your next step is to follow logically with making the claim. How you handle the claim, however, is a matter for you to decide. You have two choices: You can state what you want (money back, replacement), or you can leave the decision to the reader. You choose which, based on the situation. In our example with the microwave, you might say

> We ask that you replace the microwave at no charge to us.

Building Goodwill with a Fair-Minded Close Your final friendly words should leave no doubt that you are trying to maintain a positive relationship. You could express appreciation for what you seek. However, you want to avoid the cliché "Thanking you in advance." Instead, say something like:

> I would be grateful if you could send the new microwave this week, as our employees rely on it for their meals.

Whatever final words you choose, they should clearly show that yours is a firm yet cordial and fair request.

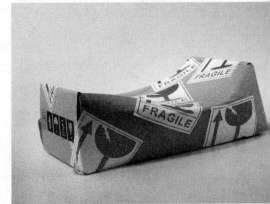

Unanticipated problems occur in business, but writing a clear, complete, and fair-minded claim will usually solve them.
© focal point/Shutterstock

Reviewing the Strategy for the Indirect Claim Message

To write an indirect claim message, you should use the following plan:

- Identify the situation (invoice number, product information, etc.) and lead into the problem.

- Present enough facts to be convincing.

- Seek corrective action.

- End positively—friendly but firm.

Comparing Ineffective and Effective Examples of an Indirect Claim

The two messages show contrasting ways of handling Jeff Sutton's problem with the Regal Banquet Center described in the Problem-Solving Challenge. The first is blunt and harsh. The second is courteous, yet clear and firm.

A Blunt and Harsh Message From the very beginning, the first message includes the writer's insulting refusal to pay. "To whom it may concern" is impersonal, generic, and outdated. The opening paragraph is a blurts out the writer's stance in angry language. The middle of the message continues along this negative path, accusing the reader with *you* and *your* and using emotional language. The negative writing continues into the close, leaving a bad final impression. Such wording is more likely to produce resistance than acceptance.

Subject: Bill Adjustment

To Whom It May Concern:

I just received a bill for $2,410 for the winter party that I held for my employees at the Regal Banquet Center. I absolutely refuse to pay this amount for the subpar job you did of hosting this event.

First, you put us in an unpleasant room with no windows even though we had made our reservations weeks in advance. The room was also much too warm. I asked your staff to adjust the temperature, but apparently they never did. Since the room didn't have any windows, we just had to sit there and swelter in our dress clothes. As if this weren't bad enough, it took the servers so long to bring all our food out that some people had finished eating before others were even served. This made a complete mess of the nice dinner and the scheduled program.

I had heard good things about your center, but now regret that I chose it for this important company event. The uncomfortable and chaotic experience reflected poorly on me and on my appreciation for my employees. Enclosed is my payment for $1,000, which I feel is more than fair.

Sincerely,
Jeff Sutton, Owner and President
White Label Industries

A Firm yet Courteous Message The second message follows the recommended plan. A subject line quickly identifies the situation. The first paragraph leads into the problem. Next, in a tone that shows firmness without anger, it tells what went wrong. Then it requests a specific remedy. The ending uses subtle persuasion by implying confidence in the reader. The words used here leave no doubt about the writer's interest in a continued relationship. This more tactful but honest claim invites the reader to do what is fair, and it retains goodwill.

Subject: Invoice #3712 (Sutton Party on December 12, 2018)

Dear Ms. Sanchez:

As you know, Sutton Creative Services held its winter-holiday party at Regal Banquet Center on December 12. While the food was exceptional, I have some concerns regarding our experience.

When I booked the party last August, I requested that we have the party in Salon A because of its size and view of the city. The room we were given for the event was Salon C. As you know, the room is small and has no windows. In addition, the location also had the drawback of making the temperature hard to control. The servers were sympathetic but were unable to keep the room from getting too warm for my 27 employees. I know that you book many parties during the holiday season; however, as the attached copy of our contract shows, we agreed that Sutton Creative Services would be in Salon A.

It also appeared that more servers were needed for our party. The fare was elegant, but with only two servers, some guests had finished eating before others had even started. As a result, we had to start the after-dinner program in the middle of the meal, requiring the speaker to talk while people were eating. This made it difficult for people to pay attention to his presentation.

Overall, the event was not the impressive "thank-you" to my hard-working employees I had in mind when we drew up the contract. In light of these circumstances, I am requesting a revised invoice of $1,000. I believe this is a fair amount for an experience that I am sure did not represent the Regal's typical level of customer service.

I would be grateful for your response by the end of the month so that I can forward the adjusted bill to my accountant for payment.

Sincerely yours,
Jeff Sutton, President and Owner
White Label Industries

Problem-Solving Challenge

Reminding Employees of the Shipping Policy

As the administrative assistant for the vice president of operations at White Label Industries (WLI), you have been asked by your boss to send a note on her behalf to all employees reminding them of the company's shipping policy. Whether customers pay shipping charges depends on the products they order. However, some customers who repeatedly order the same product are sometimes charged for shipping but other times are not, which, of course, leads to unhappy customers and is costly for WLI. Your challenge is to write a note that clearly and concisely explains the policy.

Internal-Operational Messages

As Chapter 1 explains, **internal-operational communications** are those messages that stay within a business. They are messages to and from employees that get the work of the organization done. The memorandum discussed in Chapter 2 is one form of operational communication. Internal email messages and instant messages are others, and so are the various documents posted on bulletin boards, mailed to employees, uploaded on intranets, or distributed as handouts.

The formality of such messages ranges widely. At one extreme are the casual memorandum, email, or instant message exchanges between employees concerning work matters. At the other

LO8-7 Write clear and effective internal-operational communications.

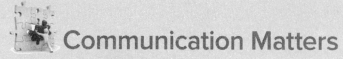

Communication Matters

Gmail's Smart Reply

Gmail's Inbox app offers Smart Reply, which allows you to use auto responses in email messages.

According to Gmail's blog, the app uses "machine learning" to recognize routine inquiries and then generates three possible responses. For example, if someone sends you a message such as "Do you have the documentation for how to use the new software?" then Smart Reply will give you three options for a reply: "I don't, sorry," "I will have to look for it," or "I will send it to you."

What does this mean for business writers? Of course, Smart Reply will save writers time, as it is quicker to select a routine response than it is to type it on a phone. Good business writers, though, will always consider their audience and purpose and choose whatever message best builds goodwill, communicates the message, and projects a professional image, whether that is a Smart Reply or their own unique reply.

You Make the Call
In what situations might you not want to use auto text such as Smart Reply?

Source: Bálint Miklos, "Computer, Respond to This Email: Introducing Smart Reply in Inbox by Gmail," *Official Gmail Blog*, November 3, 2015, accessed November 6, 2015, gmailblog.blogspot.com/2015/11/computer-respond-to-this-email.html.

---

are formal documents communicating company policies, directives, and procedures. Then, of course, various stages of formality exist in between.

Writing Casual Operational Messages

Casual operational messages typically resemble casual conversation. Usually they are quick responses to work needs. Careful construction and wording are not required. The goal is simply to exchange the information needed to conduct the company's work.

The tone of these casual operational messages as well as many of the messages at more formal levels is straightforward, even blunt. The participants exchange information, views, and recommendations forthrightly. They write with the understanding that all participants are working for a common goal—what is best for the company—and that people working together in business situations want and need straightforward communication.

For example, in a message to a co-worker, you might write,

> How about those numbers by tomorrow morning? I need them first thing for my meeting with Jeff. Thx.

Writing Moderately Formal Messages

Moderately formal messages tend to resemble the routine messages discussed earlier in this chapter. Usually they require more care in construction and often follow a direct pattern.

The message begins with the objective and then systematically and clearly covers the vital bits of information. It ends with a forward-looking statement. Your message should be clear, concise, and courteous and have a somewhat formal tone. The following example demonstrates a moderately formal message:

> Hello, Everyone:
>
> I am looking forward to our retreat next Friday. To make sure we accomplish our goals for the meeting, let's all be sure to do the following:
>
> • Read the information packets that Rick sent earlier this week.
>
> • Come prepared to share your ideas and vision for the coming year. Brainstorming is key, so all ideas are welcome.
>
> • Send any special meal requests by tomorrow.
>
> This promises to be an exciting discussion. See you there!

Writing Formal Messages

The most formal operational messages are those presenting policies, directives, and procedures. Usually written by executives for their subordinates, these administrative messages are often compiled in manuals, perhaps kept in loose-leaf form and updated as new material is developed, or stored on a company intranet and updated as needed. Their official status accounts for their formal tone.

Formal operational messages usually follow a direct order, although the nature of their content can require an indirect order. The goal should be to arrange the information in the most logical order for quick understanding. Because the information frequently involves a sequence of steps or topics, numbering them can be helpful; and because these documents must be clearly understood and followed, the writing must be clear to all, including those with low verbal skills. This example about energy conservation illustrates these qualities:

DATE: June 10, 2018

TO: All Employees

FROM: Terry Boedeker, President

SUBJECT: Energy Conservation Measures

To help us keep costs low, the following conservation measures are effective immediately:

- Thermostats will be set to maintain a temperature of 72 degrees Fahrenheit throughout the air-conditioning season.

- Air conditioners will be shut off in all buildings at 4 p.m. Monday through Friday.

- Air conditioners will be started as late as possible each morning so that buildings are at the appropriate temperature within 30 minutes after the start of the workday.

- Lighting levels will be reduced to approximately 80 to 100 watts in all work areas. Corridor lighting will be reduced to 50 watts.

- Outside lighting levels will be reduced as much as possible without compromising safety and security.

In addition, please conserve energy by doing the following:

- Turn off lights not required in performing your work.

- Keep windows closed when the cooling system is operating.

- Turn off all computer monitors and printers at the end of the day.

I am confident that these measures will reduce our energy use significantly. Not only is this a cost-saving measure, but it also helps us do our part to be an environmentally friendly company.

Even though this message is straightforward, note the writer's courtesy and his use of *us* and *our*. When writing direct messages, skillful managers make use of such strategies for maintaining good relations with employees. Remembering this goal becomes especially important in situations where managers have news to convey or requests to make that employees may not be ready to accept. In fact, in these situations an indirect order will be more appropriate, as Chapter 9 will discuss. For most internal-operational communication, however, the direct order will be both expected and appreciated.

Reviewing the Pattern for Internal-Operational Messages

To write an internal-operational message, you should use the following plan:

- Organize in the direct order.

- Choose the appropriate tone (casual, moderately formal, or formal).

- Be clear and courteous.

- Order the information logically and in a way that is visually appealing.

- Close in a way that builds goodwill.

Comparing Examples of an Internal-Operational Message

The following messages illustrate two possible ways to address the Problem-Solving Challenge above regarding WLI's shipping policy. The ineffective message is confusing not only in its content but also in its visual presentation of the information. The effective message delivers the content and takes advantage of visual formatting to make the information clear.

A Wordy, Confusing, and Indirect Message The ineffective example is wordy, long, and disorganized and lacks visual appeal. In addition, the message is not accurate because it says the shipping policy is new, even though the purpose of the message is to remind readers of the existing policy.

Subject: Inconsistent Shipping Policies

WLI has been incurring increasing freight expenses and a decline in freight revenue over the last two years, impacting our ability to achieve our financial goals. The warehouse team has done a lot of research into the reasons behind this increase, and it has come to our attention that a very considerable number of shipments are going out of Cedar Rapids (1) as unbillable to the customer and/or (2) as overnight shipments rather than ground.

WLI has only one product for which shipping is not billed to the customer—the Chem-Treat paint. In all other cases, product shipments are supposed to be billed to the customer. ***Therefore, effective immediately, except for Chem-Treat shipments, which by contract provide for free overnight (weekday delivery) shipping, WLI will bill the customer for all shipments of products. Finance will screen all orders to ensure that they indicate billable shipping terms.***

WLI's overnight shipping falls into a few categories, including shipments of products to customers and shipments of marketing materials to prospects and customers. There are no customer programs or marketing programs for which WLI offers overnight shipping (except Chem-Treat). **Therefore, effective immediately, except for Chem-Treat shipments, which by contract provide for overnight (weekday delivery) shipping, WLI will not ship products overnight to customers unless the overnight shipping is billed to the customer. Also effective immediately, shipments of sales/marketing materials are to be shipped ground, not overnight.**

This policy change will impact some of your work processes, requiring you to be more planful in getting products shipped to customers in a businesslike and timely manner, and challenging you to prevent last-minute rush situations. I suspect that much of the freight performance situation, from a financial point of view, is an awareness issue for our Cedar Rapids team. I thank each of you in advance for adherence to this policy. We are fortunate to have an excellent distribution team in Cedar Rapids. That team needs all of our help so that their high-quality shipping and inventory control performance becomes matched by strong financial performance.

Exceptions to the billable shipping-only and no overnight shipping policies must be brought to me for approval prior to entering the order.

Dean Young
VP Operations

A Direct, Concise, and Visually Appealing Message The effective example is written directly and accurately because it communicates the point that this is a reminder of an existing policy, not an announcement of a new policy. This message is also more concise and gives the reader only the information he or she needs to know to comply. In addition, headings, bullets, and other text formatting create visual appeal that aids reading.

Subject: Refresher on Our Shipping Policy

Please remember that our shipping policy is as follows:

Shipping Charges:

- Chem-Treat paint is the only product for which shipping is *not* billed to the customer.
- All other product shipments (including sales/marketing materials) *are* billed to the customer.

Overnight Shipping:

- Sales/marketing materials are to be shipped ground, not overnight.
- Chem-Treat paint may be shipped overnight at *no charge* to the customer, as provided by contract.
- All other overnight product shipments *are billed* to the customer.

Billing our customers accurately and consistently for shipping improves customer satisfaction with our service. In addition, the increased freight revenue will help us achieve our financial goals and control our shipping and inventory costs.

To ensure that your customers receive their products quickly, refer to the shipping and mailing timeline on WLI's intranet.

The Finance Department will be screening all shipment invoices to ensure shipments are billed accurately. If you have questions regarding the shipping policy or require an exception, please contact me at Ext. 555.

Dean Young
VP Operations

Other Direct Message Situations

In the preceding pages, we have covered the most common direct message situations. Others occur, of course. Using the strategies we've discussed should help you write effective direct messages for any routine business situation.

In handling good-news and neutral messages, remember that whenever possible you should get to the goal of the message right away and cover any other information in a logical order. As in the good examples discussed in this chapter, you should end your message with appropriate and friendly goodwill words. In addition, be sure to pay attention to your word choice, positive language, and you-viewpoint, to convey the correct meaning in both your content and your tone. If you follow this advice, you will likely not only build goodwill with your audience but also enhance your professional image and that of your company.

Power Charge Your Professionalism: Use Commas with a Series, Phrases, and Clauses

Insert commas as needed in the sentences provided. Indicate which comma guide you used from Reference Chapter A to determine the punctuation for each sentence. If the sentence is correct, leave it as is.

1. Our company was founded on the principles of trust honesty and ethical business practices.
2. Our employees volunteer because they believe in serving their community.
3. The shareholders asked several questions at the annual meeting and they seemed happy with the answers they received.
4. All employees who are interested in health savings accounts should attend the information session at 3:00.
5. After we talk to our representatives we should know the reasons for the drop in sales.
6. Ramone remembered to contact the vendor about our order but forgot to confirm the new delivery date.
7. At our advisory board breakfast we will launch our new corporate sustainability program.
8. The new printers which were purchased last May are much faster than our old printers.

Commas are important because . . .

1. With clauses and phrases, commas indicate when ideas are coordinated (of equal importance) or subordinated (of unequal importance).
2. With items in a series, a comma indicates which items in a series are separate from one another or whether items simply rename what came before. For example if we say "managers, Greg, and Ruidong," we are talking about several people. If we say "managers, Greg and Ruidong," we are talking about two people.

The number of guides for comma use can be overwhelming. You may find it helpful to think of commas as a means of creating sentence patterns. For example, a sentence with a dependent clause (DC) followed by an independent clause (IC) requires a comma to subordinate the dependent clause to the independent clause: DC, IC. A sentence with two independent clauses joined by a coordinating conjunction (e.g., *and, but, or*) requires a comma to coordinate the ideas: IC, coordinating conjunction IC.

When you start seeing these patterns you will realize that commas are not random marks you put wherever you sense a pause. Instead, you will see your sentences as opportunities for coordinating and subordinating your ideas. And as we've discussed throughout the text, your ability to properly emphasize or de-emphasize ideas—to coordinate and subordinate—is critical to clear communication and to building goodwill with your audience.

For further instruction on using commas, see "Phrases, Clauses, and Fragments" in the "Grammar and Common Sentence Problems" module and "Commas" in the "Punctuation and Mechanics" module of LearnSmart Achieve.

Key Terms

Critical-Thinking Questions

1. When is the direct order appropriate in inquiries? When would you use the indirect order? Give examples. LO1, LO2

2. "Explanations in inquiries merely add length and should be eliminated." Discuss. LO3

3. Discuss why just reporting truthfully may not be a sufficient strategy for handling negative information in messages answering inquiries. **LO4**

4. Defend a policy of doing more than asked in answering routine inquiries. Can the policy be carried too far? **LO4**

5. What can acknowledgment messages do to build goodwill? **LO5**

6. Discuss situations where the following email forms of an order acknowledgment would be preferred: form message and a special message. **LO5**

7. Discuss how problems (vague orders, back orders) should be handled in messages acknowledging orders. **LO5**

8. When would you use the direct approach to write a claim? When would you use the indirect approach to write a claim? **LO6**

9. Discuss the use of directness in internal-operational communications. Why is it desirable? Can it be overdone? When might indirectness be appropriate? **LO7**

Skills-Building Exercises

1. Point out the shortcomings in this email response to an inquiry about a short course in business communication that Casey Webster's company offered to its employees. The course was taught by a local college professor. Mr. Braden's initial inquiry included five questions: (1) How did the professor perform? (2) What was the course format (length, meeting structure)? (3) What was the employee evaluation of the instruction? (4) Was the course adapted to the company and its technical employees? (5) Was homework assigned? **LO1, LO2, LO4**

> Subject: Course evaluation
>
> Mr. Braden:
>
> Your January 17 inquiry addressed to the Training Director has been referred to me for attention since we have no one with that title. I do have some training responsibilities and was the one who organized the in-house course on clear writing. You asked five questions about our course.
>
> Concerning your question about the instructor, Professor Alonzo Britt, I can report that he did an acceptable job in the classroom.
>
> Some of the students, including this writer, felt that the emphasis was too much on grammar and punctuation, however. He did assign homework, but it was not excessive.
>
> We had class two hours a day from 3:00 to 5:00 p.m. every Thursday for eight weeks. Usually the professor lectured the first hour. He was a good lecturer but sometimes talked over the heads of the students. This was the main complaint in the evaluations the students made at the end of the course, but they had many good comments to make also. Some did not like the content, which they said was not adapted to the needs of a technical worker. Overall, the professor got a rating of B– on a scale of A to F.
>
> We think the course was good, but it could have been better adapted to our needs and our people. I also think it was too long—about 10 hours (five meetings) would have been enough. Also, we think the professor spent too much time lecturing and not enough on application work in class.
>
> Please be informed that the information about Professor Britt must be held in confidence.
>
> Casey Webster

2. List your criticisms of the following email message inquiring about a convenience store advertised for sale. **LO1, LO3**

   Subject: Store details needed

   Mr. Meeks:

   This is in response to your advertisement in the May 17 Daily Bulletin in which you describe a convenience store in Clark City that you want to sell. I am very much interested since I would like to relocate in that area. Before I drive down to see the property, I need some preliminary information. Most important is the question of financing. I am wondering whether you would be willing to finance up to $50,000 of the total if I could come up with the rest, and how much interest you would charge and for how long. I also would like to have the figures for your operations for the past two or three years, including gross sales, expenses, and profits. I also need to know the condition of the building, including such information as when built, improvements made, repairs needed, and so on.

   Hoping that you can get these answers to me soon so we can do business.

3. Criticize the following thank-you message from a college student to a professor who has sent her a job lead. **LO1, LO5**

   Subject: Thanks

   Dear Prof. Smith,

   Thanks for the hot tip on the job! I'm interviewing there tomorrow!

   Sarah

4. Point out the shortcomings in this claim message for a scanner received in damaged condition. The box was damaged when it arrived in Ms. Nelson's office, but she has no proof that Mr. Hicks's company is at fault. Think about whether the direct or indirect approach would be appropriate. **LO1, LO6**

   Dear Mr. Hicks:

   The Rigo Scanner Model 391 was in damaged condition when I received it on November 2. I doubt that the damage was the result of anything that happened here because our shipping employees treat each package with care. I can only assume that you sent the damaged package from your office.

   I'm guessing you stand behind product and will replace it. I will return the damaged unit.

   This has caused me a great deal of inconvenience, so I am sure you will do what you can to make things right and assure me that problems like this rarely occur in your shipping department.

   Molly Nelson

5. Critique the following direct claim message. **LO1, LO6**

   I wonder if you would consider reducing the bill I recently received for repair work that Tom, one of your men, performed last week. I did not realize that he would charge me for the time he spent going to Home Depot to get the parts he needed because the charge did not appear on the itemized estimate along with the other charges for his time. If I'd known this, I probably wouldn't have chosen your company to do the work.

   Please let me know your reply as soon as possible.

   Kim Keeley

6. Criticize the following operational message from a restaurant manager. **LO1, LO8**

   Wait staff:

   It has come to my attention that our customer service is substandard. We will therefore hold mandatory training sessions over the next three weeks. See your shift supervisor to plan your work schedule so that you can attend.

Problem-Solving Cases

Routine Inquiries

1. **Contacting a Mentor:** You recently learned about Mentors for Majors, a campus service program that pairs students with mentors. Mentors are alumni or other working professionals who have agreed to field student inquiries about the nature of their jobs and strategies for career success.

   You've been thinking about a career and would like to get more information about it from an experienced professional. Checking over the list, you find that there's a mentor in your area. Write an email to the person in which you ask questions about this field of interest. Show consideration for the reader and demonstrate your own serious interest in that type of career. (If your instructor directs, use either someone you know or someone you've researched on the Internet and through other resources. Turn in a one-paragraph profile of this person along with your email of inquiry.)

2. **Learning More about Google Drive:** You are a sales manager (you choose the company), and you just attended a professional meeting where the featured speaker extolled the virtues of using Google Drive in her organization. Intrigued, you'd like to learn more about how Google Drive might enhance collaboration among your sales staff or in your company in general.

   First, do some Internet research on Google Drive. You might also set up a Google account of your own to explore the Google Drive features more thoroughly. Then email the speaker you heard—who welcomed follow-up questions—and ask her what you most want to know about setting up a collaborative project and using Google Drive in your company or department. Review Google Drive's website carefully to ask intelligent questions regarding the product and how a company can use it.

3. **Finding the Right Market Research Firm for Your Company:** You are the new assistant to a marketing manager at Verbarg Home Furnishings, a national chain of furniture stores. You and your boss have been studying the stores' sales data from the last 10 years, and it appears that the post-Baby Boomer generations have somewhat different furniture needs and preferences than their elders did. For one thing, young adults are waiting longer to buy a home than the Boomers did, and you wonder what impact that is having on their furniture buying. Young homeowners also seem to want different products and different qualities in their products than their predecessors did, but you're not sure what their tastes are.

   "We need to get into the minds of these buyers and find out what their world is like," your boss says. "I think it's time we did some focus group research to learn more about this demographic. Look into having one of our local marketing research firms conduct a couple of focus groups for us. See what process they'd recommend to help us understand our younger customers. Find out what strategies they use, how much they'd charge—you know, everything that would be involved in having them conduct some focus groups for us."

   You do an Internet search to identify some potential firms. To be methodical about your research and have a written record of what you learn, you decide to submit your inquiries in writing. Your first one will go to DataPro, Inc. The company's website provides an email address for "general inquiries," and that looks like your best bet. After thinking carefully about what you need to find out and what would make one research firm better than another for Verbarg's needs, write your inquiry. (You may need to learn more about market research firms in general to figure out what to ask—and also flesh out the facts about Verbarg.)

4. **Exploring the Possibility of Using Personality Testing:** You work in Human Resources at Argot Products, a large local company that makes employee uniforms and other workplace gear. Your boss, HR Director Jack Aldridge, recently read a report from the Society for Human Resource Management on how companies are using personality testing to get the right people into the right positions. According to the report, almost 20% of the companies who were surveyed use personality tests as part of their hiring/promotion process, and the industry that uses them the most is manufacturing. Also, the primary way the tests are used is to assess the candidates' potential for middle-management positions. Jack wonders if Argot should use personality testing, especially for assessing employees' managerial potential. He asks you if you'll take the first steps toward exploring this question.

You do a bit of informal research on personality testing, and you learn that there are several different kinds, that there may be legal issues involved, and of course that it comes with a cost. To learn more about how Argot might benefit from personality testing, you decide to call JobFit, a local HR consulting group. The receptionist puts you through to Nan Dawkins, one of the consultants, but you get her voice mail. Thinking quickly, you simply leave the message that you're calling to discuss the possible adoption of personality testing at Argot and that you'll follow up with an email providing your specific questions.

Now write that email to Ms. Dawkins. Tell her enough about your company and ask her enough on-target questions to help her prepare a helpful response for you. (Doing some quick research on issues surrounding personality testing will help you do a good job on this assignment.)

5. **Choosing an Online Meeting Platform:** You're part of the management team at Rena's, a trendy restaurant with five locations in your metropolitan area. Each month, the management—everyone from the five restaurant location managers up to the president/owner—has a breakfast meeting in which they discuss any issues that have arisen, the financial health of the business, progress on current initiatives, any ideas for creating new business, and various other topics. You think such meetings are a great idea, and you understand the advantages of face-to-face communication (especially in this company's culture, which is close knit and family oriented)—but you wonder if these meetings are really worth the time and expense involved. You recently attended a Young Professionals Network meeting where you learned that many of your peers are conducting business meetings online, using platforms such as WebEx, GoToMeeting, or MeetingBurner. Curious, you checked out these products' websites, viewed the demos, and studied the fact sheets. You are thinking that one of these products just might be a viable alternative to Rena's monthly management meetings.

The research you've done so far has let you know what each platform does, but you need to know more about which of the platforms is best for facilitating the types of interactions that your meetings require (e.g., answering and asking questions). You decide to consult Brendan Huang, whom you met at the Young Professionals meeting, and who works for a company whose online meetings sound similar to what you envision for your company. Prepare your questions in the form of an email of inquiry. As you prepare your questions, think carefully about what types of interactions might occur during a business meeting.

6. **Securing Convenient Parking for a Guest Speaker:** Parking is tight at your university, especially near certain buildings. The campus has two large parking garages, and both of them are far away and downhill from the University Student Center where your student group is planning to hold a special event featuring a guest speaker. As the president of the student group, you find yourself needing to reserve one of the few surface spaces close to the center. You have invited the guest speaker (a local businessperson, politician, researcher, or other accomplished person) to come speak at the chapter meeting on May 3 from 4:00 to 5:30 p.m. This guest will be rushing to the meeting from work and will be carrying a laptop as well as various print materials to distribute. You think it would be impractical as well as rude to force this guest to park in a garage and then trudge up a long hill to get to the event.

The parking services website at your school informs you that you will need to submit an online request for your special parking permit, but the form has apparently been designed for campus personnel only (staff with purchase-order numbers and billing addresses). You call parking services to find out how you, a student, can request the special permit you need, and the parking-services representative says to send your request to its office using the "Contact Us" email address on their website. Write the message to get permission for the reserved parking space you need. While you're at it, find out if there will be a charge and, if so, what it will be.

7. **Researching a Venue for a Company Retreat:** As a new intern at a real estate firm in Columbus, Ohio (or a city of your choice), you've been given an important assignment from the VP of sales: to explore a possible venue for a weekend retreat for the sales staff. The boss is wondering whether a nearby state park, the Salt Fork State Park Lodge and Conference Center, might be a good choice (you can pick a different venue to explore).

He'd like to hold the retreat during the _____ season (you decide which). He's thinking that, counting the 25 employees and their families, about 75 people would attend. He'd anticipate having a welcome party on Friday evening, meetings for the staff during the day on Saturday, a dinner and some kind of entertainment on Saturday evening, and one last business meeting on Sunday morning. Are the Salt Fork facilities the appropriate size for this gathering? How long does it take to get there? Does the center have the meeting room and technology you'd need? Would it offer sufficient leisure activities for the employees and their families? What would the price tag likely be? He leaves it to you to figure out what else might be good to know.

Of course, you began your research by studying the center's website. But it doesn't provide answers to some of your questions, so you decide to email the manager of the center, whose address is on the website. Craft a well-organized email message to her to get the information you need, and ask her to mail you any conference-planning materials and price lists she has. Be sure to tell her what she needs to know about your event in order to give you helpful answers.

8. **Scheduling Software Training:** You work for a large credit union that is upgrading the software it uses to manage and maintain members' account and personal information. Everyone who works with or has access to members' information (tellers, customer service representatives, financial officers, loan representatives, department supervisors and managers, employee trainers, technical writers, marketing specialists, clerical staff, and information systems specialists) will need training on the upgraded software. Your boss has asked you, as the lead corporate trainer, to coordinate training sessions.

   You discover that the makers of the software (Financial Software Systems, Inc.) can provide training on site or at its corporate headquarters, which happen to be in your town. You need to know which of these options is both feasible and practical. You have 500 employees who will need training. You have a corporate training room with 20 computers, a reliable Internet connection, and a data projector. The software will be installed in six months. Ideally, you would like to train all of your employees in the two months before the installation. That way they can continue to practice on the software installed in the corporate training room if they would like.

   Although you have thought about calling for the information, you decide to write so that you have a permanent record of the answers to your questions. Write to Ms. Whitley Freeman, training coordinator, to inquire about Financial Software Inc.'s availability to provide training during the time period you require and for information that will help you decide whether to train onsite or at company headquarters.

9. **Requesting Automatic Payments:** You took out your car loan with First National Bank because of its low interest rates. Every month, you make your loan payment using your credit card issued by Tri-County Credit Union where you also have your savings and checking accounts. You then pay your credit card by transferring funds from your savings account to your credit card account each month.

   You earn a few rewards points by paying with your credit card, but the points you earn are not worth the inconvenience of remembering and making the payment. You notice on First National Bank's website that you can pay your loan through automatic monthly deductions from any account, even an account that is not at First National Bank. The website says that setting up the deduction requires a voided check from the financial institution from which you want the payment deducted as well as the financial institution's routing number. You're not sure where to find the credit union's routing number, and you still have questions about the process. You decide to click the link to "Contact Us" and ask your questions in the text box that appears. Though you'll want to think of more questions, you will at least want to know if you pay a fee for this service and how long it takes to set up this payment option.

10. **Inviting Contest Submissions:** You are an intern for Canon City's recently formed Downtown Area Development Commission. The commission promotes downtown businesses, markets the downtown area as a great place for businesses to locate, and encourages citizens to shop downtown stores and enjoy local entertainment and dining. To build community spirit, the commission has decided to hold a contest to find its logo. Artists who are Canon City residents

are encouraged to submit their designs for the commission to use on all of its work. The artists agree to be photographed and have their names used in the commission's publicity. The winning artist will receive $2,500 and a year of free advertising in the commission's monthly newsletter and on the commission's website.

All the artists need to do is submit a logo in .jpg format, proof of residency (think of what this might be as you write your document), and the legal agreement relinquishing rights to royalties or profit from their work if the commission chooses their logo. The logo can be sent by email or in the mail on a DVD, but it's not your fault if the DVD is damaged in the mail. The other forms can be completed online or downloaded and sent in the mail. Add any other details you think would be helpful.

Your job is to write a request to local artists asking that they submit a design. The announcement will be posted on the commission's website. You can format it in Microsoft Word as you want it to appear on the site. As you format your request, consider what you learned in Chapter 4 about designing documents for the Web. Your company's webmaster will take care of the online formatting; he just needs to know how you want it to look. Artists must know that if they violate any of the steps in submitting their logo, they will be immediately disqualified from the contest.

11. **Inquiring about an Apartment:** You and a friend have decided to move off campus next year into an apartment. Together, you have narrowed down your list of requirements: The apartment needs to be within a 15-minute walk of campus and on the bus line, have two bedrooms, allow pets, have onsite laundry facilities, and cost no more than $550 per month including rent and utilities.

You plugged this information into the online form on your school's webpage for off-campus housing and received the following hit: "2-bedroom apartment within walking distance of campus. Laundry nearby. Cost: $535/month, escrow $35/month. Available June 1. Contact Casey at cvenit@ecrealestate.com for more information." Taking into account your needs, write an email to Casey to find out if this apartment will meet all of your requirements.

Remember, this correspondence could be the start of a yearlong professional relationship.

Favorable Responses

12. **Agreeing to Create a Student Internship at Your Organization:** You are an alum of (your school). You currently work as the assistant director of a local nonprofit organization (you pick the organization). Recently, your school's Professional Development Program contacted you to ask if you would be willing to provide an internship for current students at your school. These students would be juniors and seniors who are participating in the program, which requires a professional-development course and an internship. They would represent a wide range of majors. If you agree to participate, your internship opportunity will be listed on the program's internships webpage as one of the options the students can pursue.

You are willing to provide the internship. You can offer 15 hours a week to someone who would be willing to help with marketing, public relations, social media advertising, and general office tasks. The intern would assist in writing grant proposals and perhaps presenting reports orally and in writing to the organization's board of directors. What you cannot offer, though, is financial compensation. You're a nonprofit organization that is not, nor is ever likely to be, in a position to pay an intern.

Write a response to the program's director explaining what you can do and what kinds of students would be appropriate and minimizing any negative news.

13. **Agreeing to Let a Student Shadow You:** You're a _____ (you choose the job title) at _____ (you choose the company), and you've just received an email from a student at the local university asking if she can shadow you for a day to learn more about what the work in her major will be like. Write the student and tell her she can shadow you; tell her which day of the ones she suggested is best for you and when she should arrive; tell her where to park and enter the building and where/how to meet you; and cover any additional questions she's likely to have. Drawing upon your knowledge of the job you're pretending to have and the kind of company

it's in, write a cordial, clear, well-organized, and thorough email that sets the visit up and prepares the student to have an educational, enjoyable day.

14. **Explaining a Vacation Policy:** You assist the operations manager at a manufacturing company, and one of your jobs is to ensure that you always have enough staff to maintain your production schedule.

    In the last week, you've heard from several of your supervisors that your newer employees, as well as some of the more experienced ones, are asking you to clarify how to request vacation time during the summer. They want to know when they can take vacation, how soon they need to let you know, where they can go to use the online vacation leave forms (which are new since last summer when employees had to print forms and fill them out), and how they can check online to see how much vacation they've accrued (also new since last summer when they had to contact their supervisors directly). Summer is a slow time for your company except for the first two weeks in June, the last week in July, and the first week in August, when no one is allowed to take vacation. Other times of the year are fine as long as you have enough staff and as long as requests for more than three consecutive vacation days are made two months in advance. When an employee needs only a day or two, a month's notice is fine. All vacation requests will be honored on a first-come-first-served basis to ensure sufficient staffing. All forms and personal vacation hours earned can be found on the "Employees" page of the company website.

    Creating realistic details as needed, write a response to these employees explaining the vacation request policy and process.

15. **Suggesting YouTube Videos:** You are an intern for Kaya Asher, director of corporate communications at Argus, a management consulting firm. Kaya has been asked to lead a seminar to help the sales representatives use more persuasive oral communication, including formal presentations. Because she wants to do more than just tell her audience about oral communication skills, she plans to use YouTube videos to make her presentation more interesting and engaging. She has asked you to find four YouTube videos, two that illustrate effective oral communication and two that illustrate poor oral communication. You find four videos that you think will work for her as well as some alternatives. Write a response to her request. Provide links to the videos as well as a brief summary of what each video contains and why you think it is appropriate for Kaya's presentation.

16. **Granting a Customer's Refund Request:** You're an assistant manager at the Seattle Marriott Waterfront. You've just fielded a phone call from Joline McCracken, who was a guest at your hotel last week. She checked out without carefully reviewing her bill, so she didn't realize that she'd been charged for her use of the hotel's Wi-Fi. As an attendee of a conference hosted by the hotel, she was supposed to have had free use of the Internet, but apparently she'd clicked on the wrong connection option each time she used it, which caused her to be charged. She's requested a refund of $38. You've checked your records and confirmed what she said. Now email her to let her know that you've processed the refund. Attach a copy of the adjusted bill. While you're at it, you'll thank her for her business, of course. You'll also take advantage of this opportunity to invite her to join Marriott Rewards. Study the program's website and select the details that you believe will be most appealing to her.

17. **Agreeing to Conduct an Employee-Enrichment Session:** You just got off the phone from speaking with the assistant to Hugh Evers, the director of training and development at a large insurance provider in your city. One of Hugh's most recent achievements was setting up Power Fridays, a program that enables employees to get together for an hour each Friday afternoon to learn something that will help them conduct their work more effectively and enjoyably. The sessions have addressed such topics as handling difficult conversations, thinking creatively, and understanding the different generations in the workplace. Hugh's assistant called to ask if you'd be willing to be a speaker at one of these sessions since you are something of an authority about the value of _____ (yoga, martial arts training, mindfulness, nutrition, or some other topic of your choosing). You agreed to so do, thanking the assistant for the invitation. Now you need to confirm this agreement by email and indicate as well what topics you'll be covering and/or activities you'll be doing, since the assistant will need to forward this information to Hugh.

18. **Providing Items for a College Fundraiser:** Recently, you received a letter from Jana Perkins, president of Midway University's Beta Upsilon Sigma (BUS) business fraternity. BUS is holding a silent auction to raise money for Special Olympics, and Jana has contacted you to see if your company, Backwoods Outfitters, could supply some items for the auction. Your company sells camping gear, hunting and fishing equipment, biking gear, skis, snowshoes, clothing, nonperishable food and dry goods, canoes, and kayaks—anything anyone would need for an outdoor venture no matter how large or how small. In addition, Backwoods Outfitters offers weekend rental packages that include a tent, canoe, backpacks, and supplies for $300 per weekend. The store also rents canoes, kayaks, bikes, skis, snowshoes, and additional camping gear separately.

    As the manager for Backwoods Outfitters, you are happy to grant Jana's request and see this as a great opportunity to advertise your company and do something for the students and community. Respond to Jana's letter, telling her which item or items you will provide for the auction.

19. **Staffing a Marathon:** Great news! As president of your school's Rowing Club, you've just received an offer from Michael Selzer, the manager of a local grocery store and an alum of your school, to pay your student organization $500 to staff his store's table at the city marathon and half-marathon. Considering that your student organization is currently fundraising to pay for a cross-country trip to attend a competition, the timing of this offer couldn't be better.

    The water and sports drinks will be provided by the marathon, and Mr. Selzer will handle the setup of the table and promotional banner. Your club is being asked to provide the person power—a minimum of seven people to staff the table from 7:00 a.m. to 3:00 p.m. This time commitment may be an issue for some of your members, given that the race is being held the weekend before finals week.

    Write an email to Mr. Selzer thanking him for the opportunity and agreeing to participate. Find out how many people have to be at the table at any given time, and ask any other questions you may have. Be sure you make him feel good about choosing your organization for this fundraising opportunity.

20. **Granting a Customer's Request for Free Shipping:** You're a customer service representative at CarParts.com, a mail-order retailer, and you recently received an email message requesting that you pay the shipping for the return of a part that was incorrectly represented on your website. The customer makes a good case, and the purchase records confirm his order. Also, the website does list the wrong number for the part (a problem that you have the webmaster correct immediately). The purchase records also show that this customer buys from you quite often.

    You'll be glad to pay the return shipping for the wrong part (you will send him a prepaid UPS label) and will credit his account once you receive it. You will also encourage him to purchase the correct part from you. Overall, you'll do your best to restore any goodwill that the incident may have cost you and make the customer feel good about ordering from you again.

Order Acknowledgments and Other Thank-You Messages

21. **Saying "Thank You" for a Job Shadowing Opportunity:** You're a student who just shadowed a professional in your area of study. You had a great day at the company. Sure, there was some down time when she was answering email and doing paperwork, but she made an effort to tell you what she was doing and why. (Plus, for those down times, she'd given you some good reading material about the company and its industry.) She also included you in a meeting with her team and in chats with other employees on her breaks. She treated you to lunch and went to the trouble of inviting a couple of entry-level employees—with jobs like the one you hope to get after you graduate—to join you. All in all, she really outdid herself. Thank her in a way that acknowledges the effort she went to for you. (Fill in the realistic details that your message will need in order to be effective.)

22. **Revising an Order Acknowledgment:** You've just been hired as a marketing intern for a large online auto parts dealership Anytime Autos. Your boss drops by your desk and asks you to look at the order acknowledgment email message that the company currently uses. Here's what it says:

This email was sent from a notification-only email address. Please do not reply to this message. Dear [Customer]: You have received this message because you have ordered a product from Anytime Autos. If you'd like to be removed from our mailing list, reply with a blank message to sales@anytimeautos.com. Please be advised that you may not change or cancel your order, as we begin processing orders as soon as they are placed. We are currently checking your credit information and inventory availability. You will receive a Sales Invoice once your order has been assembled and packaged. If you do not receive a Sales Invoice within 24 hours, please contact us. Your invoice number is: 11-38520. All orders are shipped, no signature required. Please be aware that orders only ship on business days, we do not offer weekend or holiday delivery. All orders placed after 5 p.m. EST will ship the following business day. A tracking number will be emailed to you within 1–2 business days. Frequently asked questions: Visit our website and click on Customer Service. Thank you for buying from Anytime Autos.

"Think you can do better?" your boss asks. "Absolutely," you answer. Go for it. (If your instructor permits, you may choose another type of business for this case.)

23. **Welcoming New Members:** As the president of your college's DECA chapter, write the welcome message that you will send to new members. The message will include a receipt for their first-year dues, their member number, a reminder about the next meeting, and of course contact information for the organization. Highlight any other benefits of membership you think new members would enjoy. Add any other opportunities for members to become active in the DECA. Just as importantly, though, make readers feel good about the investment they've just made in their professional development. Remember that the more they take advantage of what the organization has to offer, the more likely they'll be to renew their membership next year.

24. **Acknowledging Donors' Support:** Recently, your student organization attended a national conference and competition in Anaheim, California. You did a considerable amount of fundraising from both campus departments and businesses in the local community prior to the trip to defray costs for your members.

After a lot of hard work and determination, your group placed fourth out of 25 teams from all over the United States. It was a great experience—and clearly it would not have been possible without the financial help from your supporters.

Now that the competition is over and you are back on campus, write a thank-you letter to your supporters. Let them know how much you appreciate their contributions. Make sure that your letter is professional so that you can keep them on your donor list for the future.

25. **Thanking a Businessperson for Participating in Your Research Project:** You are currently completing your senior year of college and are in the middle of your capstone project: a study of the different management styles of U.S. and Asian restaurant managers in your city (or substitute a research project of your choice). You've just conducted one of the in-depth personal interviews that will be your main source of information, and now you need to write the interviewee, one of the managers, to thank him for his time and information. Write your message in the form of a letter, and make this busy person feel good about helping you with your project.

Claims

26. **Getting a Refund for an Invoicing Error:** You're a clerk in the accounting office of Hocking Hills Resort and Spa, which recently placed a 2/3-page advertisement in *Travel Ohio* magazine. Today's email brought a notice from the magazine that Hocking Hills's account had been charged $3,700—the amount that a full-page ad costs.

You check with Lizzie Adams, the assistant director of sales and marketing for the resort, and she informs you that this amount is wrong. She proves it by showing you a list of the magazine's advertising rates and a copy of the purchase order, which clearly states the amount for a 2/3-page ad. Obviously, the accounting office for *Travel Ohio* has made an error.

Write *Travel Ohio* to request a credit to Hocking Hills's account. Use the medium and any supporting evidence that you think will do the best job of getting the results you seek.

27. **Requesting a Refund for a Vendor Error:** Remington Textiles is hosting a welcome dinner for a delegation of German executives who are interested in learning about Remington's products and possibly pursuing some contracts. You really want to make a good impression, so you have paid close attention to the details for the dinner. You even contracted with a local design company, Ridge Water Designs, to make an elegant, tasteful welcome banner (in German, no less!) to place above the doorway of the private room at the restaurant where the dinner will take place.

When you ordered the banner, Robin Heinze, the designer, told you that Ridge Water Designs could do the banner but could not deliver it until the afternoon of the dinner. Though you were nervous about getting the banner so close to the time of the dinner, you agreed after you were assured everything would be fine. The banner arrived two hours before the dinner. It looked great, but Ridge Water Designs spelled the German company's name incorrectly. Obviously, you could not use the banner, which cost $225, and you were incredibly disappointed, as you had sent Ridge Water Designs an email with the spelling of the company's name and even spelled it over the phone when you ordered the banner. On the day of the dinner, Ridge Water Designs sent you a quick email to confirm that the banner was sent but indicated that no one would be in the office for the rest of the day.

Write to Robin Heinze and request that you not be charged $225 for a sign that you obviously could not use.

28. **Addressing an Unacceptable Cleaning Job:** You are the building manager for Schneider Enterprises. After a recent construction project at the company, you contracted Custom Cleaning Services, a commercial cleaning company, to clean the office. According to the contract, you would pay $3,000 once the job was completed. When you drew up the contract for the cleaning, you and Beth Menendez, manager of Custom Cleaning Services, developed a checklist of cleaning jobs that needed to be done. The cleaning crew worked throughout the weekend. Though you let them in the building on Saturday morning and Sunday morning, you only checked in the evening that the building was locked after the crew left. You did not check the crew's work.

When you arrive for work on Monday morning, you notice that the cleaning crew missed some of the items on the checklist, and the cleaning job is sloppy. There are streaks on the windows. The walls also have streaks of dust, dirt, and fingerprints. Some of the light fixtures have not been cleaned or dusted, and the floor seems to have a film of some kind on it—like the cleaner did not quite cut through all of the dirt. You know that Beth would not find this cleaning job acceptable and would want you to be a satisfied customer.

Contact Beth and request what you think is reasonable for addressing this situation. You'll use email rather than the phone so that you can attach a few telling photos.

29. **Requesting Reimbursement for a Canceled Flight:** Assume the role of Carla Reyes. You arrived at the airport last Saturday only to find that Cross Country Airlines canceled your 1:00 p.m. flight because of a severe thunderstorm. You thought about renting a car and driving the seven hours to your home, but several other stranded passengers with canceled flights had the same idea, so no cars were available for one-way rental.

Although you were at a major airport, you live in a small town where there are only two flights to your hometown each day. You were rebooked on the only later flight available that day, at 9:50 p.m. You waited all day in the airport and were just 25 minutes from boarding your flight when you were told that your 9:50 p.m. flight had been canceled because a flight crew was unavailable. The agent at the Cross Country Airlines service counter said that the 1:00 p.m. flight the following day was already booked and that you had been assigned to Sunday's 9:50 p.m. flight.

The airline offered to put you up in a hotel for the evening and transport you to the airport on Sunday. This was unacceptable. First, you were flying home to attend your grandfather's 80th birthday celebration on Sunday. You would have missed the party if you had taken that 9:50 p.m. Sunday flight. Second, the hotel checkout is at 11:00 a.m., which means you would have had to spend almost 12 hours at the airport on Sunday.

Fortunately, by 10:00 p.m. on Saturday, you were able to secure a one-way car rental to your hometown, so you decided to cancel your seat on the Sunday, 9:50 p.m. flight. The car rental cost $96. As you made the seven-hour drive to your home, you decided that you should be refunded the $112 cost of the ticket that you were not able to use through no fault of your own. In addition, to compensate for the seven hours you had to spend driving through the night to reach your grandfather's party, you believe the airline should pay for your rental as well.

Write to Cross Country Airlines and request that the company pay for your rental and refund the money for your ticket. Be sure to provide details the reader needs to know to act quickly on your request.

30. **Requesting Reimbursement for a Faulty Repair:** After your flight lands around midnight, you make your way to your car only to find that the brakes on your 2009 Hyundai Sonata are not working. You know you cannot make the two-hour drive home, so you decide to rent a hotel room for the night and have the car towed and repaired in the morning. After investigating, the mechanic tells you that the brake caliper on the rear driver-side tire is not attached to the rest of the braking mechanism. You mention to the mechanic that you find this odd because you just had new brakes installed. The mechanic speculates that during the repair the bolts attaching the caliper were not sufficiently tightened; the bolts fell off, leaving the caliper unattached. He fixes the brakes and sends you on your way, but when you arrive home, you decide to contact the dealer to request reimbursement for the brake repair ($285.47) and for the hotel room you had to pay for because you couldn't drive home ($124.18).

You've always received excellent service from the dealership that installed the new brakes, so you call to request reimbursement. However, you learn that no one is available to talk, so you decide to submit your request for reimbursement via the email address the receptionist provided for you. Send the email to the dealership's service manager requesting reimbursement. Attach any relevant documentation to support your request.

31. **Asking a Gym to Honor the Terms of Your Membership:** When Ultimate Fitness Gym opened in your town, you were thrilled. You took advantage of the grand opening deal of a lifetime membership fee of $25 per month. That was five years ago. The gym is building a new facility. You are a little surprised when you receive a letter four months before the new gym's grand opening offering you a new lifetime membership of $49.99 per month. The letter says that previous lifetime memberships will not be valid once the new facility opens and encourages you to take advantage of this great deal. You're thinking that $49.99 per month is definitely not as great a deal as your current lifetime membership of $25 per month, and you wonder why you would pay the increased price when you've already bought what is supposed to be a lifetime membership.

You called the gym and were told, "The 'lifetime' in 'lifetime membership' refers only to the life of your membership in this building. A new building means a new membership, and our new lifetime memberships are $49.99 per month." Your brother, who is an attorney, reads the contract and says that even though it does not specify that "lifetime" means the life of the membership in a particular building, it is worded in such a way that the gym can change the terms. This seems like a flimsy explanation for raising your membership. In fact, it seems as though the gym is desperate for a way to raise revenue to cover the cost of the new building and is targeting lifetime memberships of loyal members. You also feel you were misled about the terms of your contract when you were told you had purchased a "lifetime" membership for $25 per month.

You have talked with the employees at the front desk and to the gym's manager, but they refuse to waive the new lifetime membership fee for current lifetime members, citing corporate policy as their reason. Frustrated with the employees' lack of sympathy, understanding, and action, you decide to write a letter to the CEO at corporate headquarters asking that he reconsider the new lifetime membership fee and allow yours to remain at $25 per month.

32. **Requesting an Adjustment to a Restaurant Bill:** You're a manager at Becker Plumbing, a successful local company. Zelda Miller, your office manager, is retiring after 35 years with the firm. To celebrate her years of service, you've organized a lunch outing at Walt's, a local steakhouse, for the entire office staff. Everyone in the office is looking forward to the outing, especially since the last two months have been very busy. When you get to Walt's, you are told by

the hostess that your tables are not ready, and your party winds up having to wait 20 minutes before being seated. Once you're seated, the harried server gives your group minimal attention and also gets some of the orders wrong. You feel bad for Zelda and also embarrassed because it was your idea to choose Walt's. At the very least, you feel that your company deserves a partial refund. You decide to write to the restaurant's management to express your displeasure.

33. **Requesting an Adjustment for Lunches You Never Ate:** The small company that you work for, InFocus Solutions of Washington, D.C., is busy prepping for its annual board meeting. As the junior member of the team, you were asked to order lunch from Breadline and pick up the order on the day of the meeting. Abiding by Breadline's catering policy, you paid for half of the lunch when ordering and will pay the rest of the bill upon pickup.

Sandwiches and salads for 20 people, plus chips, drinks, and dessert, came to $235.84. You paid $117.92 over the phone with your company credit card when you placed the order.

After weeks of preparation, the day of the meeting is finally here. As you board the Metro on your way into the office, you receive an "Urgent Alert" on your cell phone from the city. An unidentified package has been spotted on the White House grounds; consequently, until further notice, no one except emergency personnel are allowed within a five-block radius of the White House. Your office is outside of the locked down area . . . but then you remember that Breadline is only a block away from the White House! Thankfully, you are able to make other lunch reservations, and the board meeting is an all-around success. However, Breadline still owes InFocus Solutions $117.92 for the lunch you were unable to pick up. You're worried because of a clause in the contract saying "deposits are nonrefundable except in extreme cases (e.g., a natural disaster)." You may not get your deposit back.

You understand that Breadline likely purchased the food for your lunch before you cancelled it and would lose money if it returned your deposit; but you also think that especially in Washington, D.C., a suspicious package is the equivalent of a natural disaster. Send the manager a message requesting an adjustment to your account.

34. **Requesting a Free Yard Service:** Your yard is big and hilly, and you just don't have the time and energy right now to maintain it yourself. You finally sprang for a professional lawn-mowing service, but the first visit from BeautyLawn did not go well. Yes, the grass looks nice, and the crew trimmed nicely around the edges—but they also mowed over the very area you asked them not to mow, the hill where your daffodils were just starting to come up. The crew chief, while respectful and hard working, did not seem to understand English very well. You suspect that even though he wanted to be accommodating, he simply didn't understand the instructions you gave him. Write BeautyLawn a persuasive claim in which you explain what happened and request that this first yard service be at no charge. You think that's a pretty fair request, given that you won't be enjoying your daffodils this year.

35. **Requesting a Refund for Missing Amenities:** You and your family have just returned from five days (four nights) at SunFun Resort at Wrightsville Beach, North Carolina. Your room was nice, the staff was friendly, and the beach was great. What was disappointing was that the pool was closed during your whole stay because of "mechanical problems." When you expressed your disappointment to the young people staffing the front desk, they clearly hadn't been advised on how to handle the situation and simply said, with apologies, that there was nothing they could do. You didn't want to make an angry fuss about it since you were there to relax, so you let the matter drop.

But now that you're back home, you think you'll write the management of the resort to request a partial refund. After all, the room rate was over $370 per night, plus tax, and the big, beautiful swimming pool was one reason you chose SunFun instead of another resort. You live in Michigan, and it's not likely that you'll return to Wrightsville any time soon, so you definitely want a refund, not a coupon for a discounted future stay. (You may make up additional details as long as they are realistic and do not change the basic facts of the case.)

Internal-Operational Messages

36. **Improving an Internal Message about the Security System:** Revise the poorly written message below so that it will be clear and direct and have an appropriate tone and style. You may add information if you need to for the message to make sense. Be sure to fix any grammar, mechanics, punctuation, or word choice errors.

    From: Jim Hannigan

    Sent: Tuesday, June 2, 2018

    To: All Employees

    Subject: Security System

    As many of you have noticed the security system is not working at this time, we are aware of this problem and are awaiting repair parts to correct the issue. In response, the outer doors are unlocked and you will not need to use your badge until we are repaired. Later this evening we will be falling back to keyed door locks for the evening. If you are going out the front door, you will need to use the handle to get out the exterior doors after 5 p.m.

    Thank you for your patients, Jim Hannigan

    Building Supervisor

    Ext. 5555

37. **Improving an Internal Message about Employee Breaks:** Revise the following poorly written message so that the message will be clear and direct and have an appropriate tone and style. You may add information if you need to for the message to make sense. Be sure to fix any grammar, mechanics, punctuation, or word choice errors.

    Employees are taking to long of breaks. This must stop immediately so that we don't lose productivity.

    If we loose productivity, we could lose customers, and you could lose your job.

    Remember that you get 15 minutes in the morning and 15 in the afternoon. You get 30 minutes for lunch. This means you don't leave early, and it doesn't mean you take 30 minutes to eat and then take another

    5 or 10 to get back to work. This means you get back to work after 30 minutes. Also, this means that when you are working, you are not allowed to be on Facebook or email for personal reasons. This has lead to alot of waste time, to. I know all of you care about your jobs. If their is any questions, please do not hesitate to contact me. Thank you for all of your hard work. It is appreciated.

38. **Informing Company Employees about the Leave Donation Program:** As a company that has more than 50 employees living in or near the city where it is located, your company is covered by the U.S. Family Medical Leave Act (FMLA). This means that employees who meet certain criteria, as outlined by the U.S. Department of Labor (www.dol.gov/whd/regs/compliance/whdfs28.pdf), may take up to 12 weeks of unpaid leave if they have a baby, an extended illness, or an impaired relative to assist.

    Many companies have started "leave donation" programs that enable employees to donate some of their accumulated sick leave or vacation time to fellow employees who have taken unpaid leaves. As office manager for your company, you periodically remind employees of this opportunity to help their colleagues. You think the time has come around again for this reminder, especially since you're aware of at least two employees who might need their co-workers' donations.

    Write the employees, some of whom have never heard of this program, about the leave donation program. You will direct them to the FMLA website and to your own company's intranet for the full, official details; however, you will include the basics in your message: how much leave employees need to have accumulated in order to donate, the minimum and maximum amount of hours they can donate, the irreversibility of the donation, what recipients may use it for, how to donate, the fact that donating is strictly voluntary, and whatever else you think readers need to know in order to decide whether to pursue the matter further. (To generate such details, you can visit the FMLA website and the website at your school or business that describes this kind of policy.)

39. **Reporting on a Possible Venue for a Company Retreat:** Play the role of the intern described in Problem 7 ("Researching a Venue for a Company Retreat"). You've now gathered all the information you can reasonably obtain without traveling to the site itself, so now it's time to share it with your boss. Send him an email message to do so, and impress him with your research, and writing skills.

40. **Sharing the Maintenance Schedule:** You are the facilities and grounds supervisor for AVG Enterprises. It's now April 1. Every summer you clean the office carpeting and polish and wax the floors. Employees can also request that their offices be painted, but their supervisors need to justify and approve the request. Those who have had their offices painted in the last five years can forget having them painted again, as you do not have the time or the budget. You do the floors one department at a time. You have to schedule cleaning for accounting, human resources, education and training, facilities and grounds, communications, sales, marketing, and information systems departments. Usually, it takes a week to do one department, as you have to do this early in the evening so that the floors are dry by the time employees arrive the next morning. If any offices need to be painted, the job needs to be done before the floors are done; you need three weeks' notice so that you can pick colors, order paint, and schedule the work. The floor maintenance will begin June 1. Develop a cleaning schedule that you'll send to all employees and department supervisors. Remind employees of the approval process for getting their offices painted. Because not everyone in the building has access to email, you'll write this as a memo.

41. **Announcing a Professional-Development Program:** You are the human resources manager for a public relations company. Your company employs people in many types of positions (e.g., communication, marketing and sales, creative services, accounting, customer service and support, clerical). You were talking with a colleague at a recent Society for Human Resource Management meeting and learned that your colleague's company offers professional development activities for its employees. These activities are generally workshops in which an expert shares his or her knowledge on a particular topic such as conflict resolution or email etiquette. Workshops are held on site. Most are only an hour or so and are held once a month during the workday. Of course, employees are paid to attend these sessions and are not required to attend all of them—only the ones that interest them.

    You think this kind of professional development program is just what your company needs. You present such a program to your CEO and receive permission to try the program for six months, so you develop a list of topics, set a schedule, and contact experts who agree to lead the workshops.

    Send a message to the employees of your company in which you describe the program, present a schedule, invite them to attend, and include a brief list of the topics the program offers in the next six months. Be sure you think about what information might motivate readers to participate in this program.

42. **Announcing the Creation of a New Company Policy:** Fifteen years ago, you and three male college buddies started an environmental engineering company, Water Works. You're proud that the company now has over 50 employees, including several female engineers. The time has finally come to hire a human resources professional rather than contracting out the payroll and benefits services. So you hire Janet Bloom, who brings extensive knowledge and experience to the position. After working there a couple of months, Janet comes to you with a concern. "We don't have a sexual harassment policy," she says. "I see a lot of friendly teasing going on between the male and female employees, but sometimes the females seem a bit offended. To have a welcoming company culture and to ensure that you don't run into legal trouble, I think you really need a sexual harassment policy. It doesn't have to accuse anyone of anything. But it should make clear what constitutes sexual harassment and emphasize that any such forms of behavior are grounds for reprimand or even dismissal."

To help you develop such a policy, she sends you some Web links to other companies' policies and also directs you to the U.S. Equal Employment Opportunity Commission's (EEOC's) website. In consultation with an attorney, you and Janet craft a policy. Now it's time to tell the employees about it. Thinking carefully about the kind of response you want from your employees, send out a memo in which you announce that the company now has a sexual harassment policy, which is fully described on the company's intranet.

43. **Educating Employees about Personnel Files:** Continue on as the executive in the problem above. The new sexual harassment policy you announced two months ago seems to have been well received, but recently you had to use it as grounds for a written warning to an employee whom two employees had complained about. This warning went into the offending employee's personnel file.

Perhaps as a result of this action, news of which no doubt made its way around the company grapevine, other employees seem to have become curious about exactly what goes into a personnel file and how that information can be used.

After doing some research on this topic, send the employees an email in which you enlighten them. In preparing your email, consider the kinds of questions they're likely to have. For example, what kinds of documents get put into a personnel file? Which, if any, of these can be shared and with whom? Are the contents of personnel files ever shared with those who are considering hiring Water Works's former employees? Can employees read their own personnel files? You may well think of additional questions that you should address.

44. **Inviting Employees to a Meeting about a Company Volunteer Event:** Each year your company organizes a team to participate in your city's Making Strides Against Breast Cancer walk, one of a series of walks sponsored by the American Cancer Society. This year you are the coordinator of your company's team. Your first task is to invite all employees to an informational meeting. Send a message to everyone in the company regarding the meeting and include an agenda for the meeting. A little research on the Making Strides Against Breast Cancer website will help you decide what to include in your message. Of course you want your message to start generating enthusiasm for the cause right away—but be sure you make clear that coming to the meeting won't obligate anyone to participate in the walk. You just want to spread the word about it and be sure that anyone looking for a worthy cause to support (and an inspiring team experience) knows about this opportunity. Those who want to be on the team can sign up at the end of the meeting or let you know by August 3.

Writing Bad-News Messages

© Shutterstock / fizkes

Chapter Nine

Like all human resource professionals, Joan McCarthy, senior director of human resources communication for Comcast Cable, sometimes has to deliver negative news to employees, whether it's about health care coverage, organizational change, or other issues. Her advice? "Balance, not spin, is the key. Frequent, candid communication that balances the good with the bad will go much further toward restoring and maintaining employee trust than the most creative 'spin.'"

Sometimes McCarthy will state negative news directly, while other times she takes a more gradual approach. Whichever pattern you use, "it's important to communicate openly and honestly," she advises. But you should also balance out the negative by "reinforcing the positive, putting the news in perspective, and showing what the organization is doing to help." In these ways you can "communicate bad news in a way that preserves your company's credibility and keeps employee trust and morale intact."

Many times, you will give bad news in person because doing so shows respect and sensitivity and because you can take advantage of verbal and nonverbal cues to communicate sympathy, empathy, and understanding. Other times, though, you will have to deliver the message in writing. This chapter contains strategies for minimizing the negative impact of bad news, whether you're delivering it to internal or external readers. Much of what is discussed can be applied to both written and face-to-face messages.

Learning Objectives

LO9-1   Determine which situations require using the indirect approach.

LO9-2   Write messages following the general plan for an indirect approach.

LO9-3   Use tact and courtesy when refusing a request.

LO9-4   Write adjustment refusals that minimize the bad news and overcome negative impressions.

LO9-5   Write negative announcements that maintain goodwill.

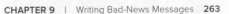

Approaches to Writing Bad-News Messages

LO9-1 Determine which situations require using the indirect approach.

Research supports the idea that the indirect approach is effective when you must say "no" or convey other disappointing news.[1] Using the **indirect approach**, which requires that you preface the bad news with an explanation, can convince the reader that your position is correct or at least that you are taking a logical and reasonable position, even if the news is bad for the reader. In addition, an explanation cushions the shock of bad news and shows sensitivity to the reader's situation.

However, research also indicates that the direct approach is warranted for communicating negative news in some contexts.[2] In one study of "data breach notification letters" (letters a company uses to alert readers when the security of their personal information has been compromised), the researcher concluded that when "writers must convince readers that a potential problem exists and encourage them to act," a direct approach may be more appropriate.[3]

In addition, if you think that your negative news will be accepted routinely, you might choose directness. For example, in many buyer–seller relationships in business, both parties expect back orders and order errors to occur now and then. Thus, messages reporting this negative information would not really require indirectness. You also might choose directness if you know your reader well and feel that he or she will appreciate frankness. Although such instances are less common than those in which indirectness is the preferable strategy, you should always analyze your audience and business goals to choose the most appropriate organizational approach to delivering negative news.

Chapter 8 shows you how to write direct and indirect claim messages, which are a common type of bad-news message where you have to carefully consider your audience and context to choose the right approach.

As in Chapter 8, we first describe a general plan. Then we adapt this plan to specific business situations—three in this case. First is the refusal of a request, a common task in business. Next we cover adjustment refusals. Lastly, we cover negative announcements.

The General Indirect Plan

LO9-2 Write messages following the general plan for an indirect approach.

As with direct messages, indirect messages follow a general pattern. In fact, as you learn about the general indirect plan, you will see that the objectives of the direct and indirect plan are similar: Both require that you communicate your main point, project a professional image, and build or preserve the reader's goodwill. The main difference is in the strategy you use to achieve these objectives.

Using a Strategic Buffer

Indirect messages presenting bad news often begin with a strategic buffer. A **buffer** is an opening that identifies the subject of the message but does not indicate that negative news is coming.

One characteristic of the buffer is that it is relevant to the topic of the message. Another characteristic of a buffer is that it is neutral—it does not give away the bad news. A relevant but neutral buffer might simply acknowledge your receipt of the reader's earlier message and indicate your awareness of what it said. Buffers are also generally positive but not so positive that they lead readers to believe they are about to receive good news. For instance, a positive buffer might thank the reader for bringing a situation to your attention or for being a valued customer or employee.

Some may argue that not starting with the good news is a clear indication that bad news is coming. They argue that if this is the case, then why not just start with the bad news? The answer is that a buffer gives readers a chance to prepare for the news—and even if they suspect the news will be negative, the use of a buffer indicates consideration for their feelings.

Setting Up the Negative News

Because you have to say "no" or present some other kind of negative news, you have to figure out how to construct the message so the reader views your news objectively. You want your reader to see the news as a reasonable business decision that the reader would have made were he or she in your situation, so you have to think of the information that best supports your case.

Your strategy might be to explain the fairness of a certain action. It might be to present facts that clearly make the decision necessary. Or you might cite the expert opinion of authorities whom both you and your reader respect. It might even be possible to show that your reasons for the negative decision will benefit the reader.

Whatever explanatory strategy you choose, these reasons should follow your buffer and precede the negative news itself. In other words, the paragraph after the buffer should start explaining the situation in such a way that by the time the negative news comes, the reader is prepared to receive it in the most favorable light possible.

Presenting the Bad News Objectively

Next, you present the bad news. If you have developed your reasoning convincingly, this bad news should appear as a logical outcome. You should present it as objectively and positively as the situation permits. In doing so, you must make certain that the negative message is clear.

Remember that you are not trying to figure out how to turn this into a good-news situation. If you could do so, you would not be writing a bad-news message. At the same time, you do not want to make a negative situation worse by using unnecessarily negative language or ignoring any positive or forward-looking news associated with the bad news. For example, you do not need to make the situation even more unpleasant by using words such as "unfortunately," "disappointed," or "upset." Likewise, instead of using words such as "cannot" or "will not," you can focus on what you "can" do or "will" do rather than reinforce the negative news.

One useful technique for achieving an objective or positive tone is to present your reasoning in first and third person, avoiding second person. To illustrate, in a message refusing a request for a refund for a returned product, you could write these negative words: "Since you have broken the seal, state law prohibits us from returning the product to stock." Or you could write these words emphasizing first and third person: "State law prohibits retailers from returning to stock all products with broken seals."

Sometimes, you can soften the negative news by linking it to a reader benefit. For example, if you preface a company policy with "in the interest of fairness" or "for the safety of our guests," you are indicating that all of your patrons, including the reader, get an important benefit from your policy.

Your efforts to present this part of the message objectively and positively should employ the suggestions for subordination,

Communication Matters

You Think Saying "No" in the United States Is Tricky. . .

Maintaining goodwill with negative messages is often difficult with U.S. readers, even if one uses the indirect approach recommended in this chapter. But it can be even more difficult if you are corresponding with readers in other countries.

As intercultural business communication experts Linda Beamer and Iris Varner point out, "Asian cultures are renowned for saying yes. In fact, in Japan, Westerners have heard *yes* and gone home happy even though the Japanese really meant *no.*"

Why does this happen? Beamer and Varner explain:

Saying *no* is more difficult for people in high-context cultures (cultures where communicators depend heavily on contextual cues to interpret words' meanings) because when they communicate about problems, they would rather not actually have to put a refusal into words. In Chinese, a *no* may reside in the words "That may be difficult."

No in high-context cultures is frequently couched in an expression that turns the situation around. For example, a person who has to refuse an invitation to dine out with a business associate may say by way of refusal, "You must be very tired and want to have a quiet evening." This way, the refused person does not lose face, although the refusal is clearly understood in a high-context culture.

Be sure to learn about such communication preferences on the part of your readers when preparing cross-cultural negative-news messages.

Source: Iris Varner and Linda Beamer, *Intercultural Communication in the Global Workplace*, 5th ed. (New York: McGraw-Hill/Irwin, 2011), 194–195.

Setting up your bad news indirectly helps your reader receive the news more easily.
© Triangle Images/Digital Vision/Getty Images

When you deliver an apology, make sure the apology is sincere.
© JGI/Blend Images LLC RF

emphasis, and sentence construction presented in Chapter 5 and positive communication described in Chapter 6. In subordinating the bad news and using positive words, however, you must make certain your words truthfully and accurately convey your message.

Offering an Alternative Solution

For almost any negative-news situation, you can do something to help the reader with his or her problem.

If someone wants to hold an event on your company grounds and you must say "no," you may be able to suggest other sites. If someone wants information you do not have, you might know of another way that he or she could get similar information. If you cannot volunteer your time and services, perhaps you know someone who might, or perhaps you could invite the reader to make the request again at a later, better time. If you have to announce a cutback on an employee benefit, you might be able to suggest ways that employees can supplement this benefit on their own. Taking the time to help the readers in this way is a sincere show of concern for their situation. For this reason, it is one of your most powerful strategies for maintaining goodwill.

Ending on a Positive Note

Since even a skillfully handled bad-news message can be disappointing to the reader, you should end the message on a forward-looking note. Your goal here is to shift the reader's thoughts to the future—perhaps what you would say if you were in face-to-face conversation with the person. Your comments should fit the topic of your message, and they should not recall the negative message. They should make clear that you value your relationship with the reader and still regard it as a positive one.

Apologizing

Many times when a writer must deliver bad news, the first thought is to apologize. After all, if a customer or co-worker is unhappy—regardless of the reason—somehow apologizing seems a good strategy for making a situation better.

Sometimes an apology can make a bad situation better, but other times it can make a bad situation worse. If the bad news is something you had no control over (e.g., a customer broke an item because he or she did not follow instructions), apologizing can make you appear in the wrong even when you are not. A reader may also wonder why, if you are so sorry, you cannot do what the reader wants you to do. Apologies may even have legal implications if they can be construed as admissions of guilt.

On the other hand, if a customer incurs finance charges because you forgot to credit a payment to the customer's account, an apology, along with a credit to the account and removal of the finance charge, may help restore goodwill.

If you do apologize in a bad-news message, do so early in the message as you explain the reasons and deliver the bad news. Then move beyond the apology just as you move beyond the bad news and toward your forward-looking conclusion. If you think your apology may have legal implications, you can have your message reviewed by a supervisor or your company's legal department before sending it.

This general plan for writing indirect messages can be used in several situations in which you have to deliver bad news in business. The rest of this chapter focuses on common bad-news scenarios and shows you how to adapt your messages to them.

Problem-Solving Challenge

Denying a Request for a Donation

As in Chapter 8, assume the role of assistant to the White Label Industries (WLI) vice president. Today your boss assigned you the task of responding to a request from the local chapter of the National Association of Peace Officers. This worthy organization has asked WLI to contribute to a scholarship fund for children of police officers who were killed in the line of duty.

The request is persuasive. It points out that the scholarship fund is terribly short. As a result, the association is not able to take care of all the eligible children. You have been moved by the persuasion and would like to comply, but you cannot because WLI policy does not permit it.

Even though you do not like the effects of the policy in this case, you think the policy is good. Each year WLI earmarks a fixed amount—all it can afford—for contributions. Then it donates this amount to the causes that a committee of its executives considers the most worthy.

Unfortunately, all the money earmarked for this year has already been given away. You will have to say no to the request, at least for now. You can offer to consider the association's cause next year.

Your response must report the bad news, though it can hold out hope for the future. Because you like the association and because you want it to like WLI, you will try to handle the situation sensitively and tactfully.

Refused Requests

A **refused request** is definitely bad news. Your reader has asked for something, and you must say no. Your primary goal, of course, is to present this bad news. You could do this easily with a direct refusal; however, opening with the bad news that you are refusing the reader's request could make you and your company appear insensitive. As a courteous and caring businessperson, you have another goal of maintaining goodwill. To achieve this goal, you must convince your reader that the refusal is fair and reasonable before you break the bad news.

LO9-3 Use tact and courtesy when refusing a request.

Developing the Strategy

Finding a fair and reasonable explanation involves carefully thinking through the facts of the situation. First, you want to consider why you are refusing the reader's request and your reader's likely reaction to the refusal. Then you must find the best way of explaining your reasons to your reader. To do so, you might think of how you would like to receive the news if you were the reader. What comes out of this thinking is the strategy you should use in constructing your message.

In some situations company policy forbids compliance. Using company policy as a reason for a refusal works only if you can defend and clearly explain the policy. In other situations, you must refuse simply because the facts of the case justify a refusal—that is, you are right and the reader is wrong. In such cases, your best course is to review the facts and to appeal to the reader's sense of fair play.

In any situation, you may have multiple ways to offer a fair and reasonable explanation. Your job is to analyze your audience and communication goals and select the strategy that best fits your message.

Setting Up the Buffer

Having determined the explanation, you begin the message with a buffer that sets up the discussion. For example, in the case of WLI's refusal to donate to the National Association of Peace Officers' worthy cause (see the Problem-Solving Challenge at the beginning of this section), you could say the following:

> Your organization is doing a commendable job of educating needy children. Like many other worthy efforts, it well deserves the support of our community.

Telling people news they don't want to hear requires careful communication.
© Olix Wirtinger/Corbis RF

This buffer is relevant because it clearly marks the message as a response to the inquiry. It is neutral because it implies neither a "yes" nor a "no" answer. This buffer puts the reader in an agreeable or open frame of mind—ready to accept the explanation that follows.

Presenting the Reasons for the Refusal

As with the general indirect plan, you next present your reasoning. To do this, you use your best persuasion techniques: positive wording, proper emphasis, sound logic, and convincing details. The reason for the refusal in WLI's message to the National Association of Peace Offices is that the company has already given its allotted donation money to other worthy organizations.

Handling the Refusal Positively

If your reasons are sound, your refusal of the reader's request should be a logical conclusion and come as no surprise. Your reader may not be happy about the refusal, but if you have done your job well, the reader should accept the reasons behind it. Because the refusal is the most negative part of your message, you should not give it much emphasis. You should state it quickly, clearly, and as positively and objectively as possible; and you should keep it away from positions of emphasis, such as paragraph endings.

You might even be able to make the message clear without stating the negative news explicitly. For example, if you are refusing the request from the National Association of Peace Officers, you could simply say that you have recently awarded this year's recipients your company's allotted funds for charitable giving and that you encourage the reader to apply again next year. You must be sure, though, that your message leaves no doubt about your answer. Being unclear the first time will leave you in the position of writing an even more difficult, more negative message later.

To state the refusal positively, you should carefully consider the effects of your words. Harsh words such as *refuse, will not,* and *cannot* stand out. So do apologies such as "I deeply regret to inform you . . ." and "I am sorry to say . . ." You can usually phrase your refusal in terms of a positive statement of policy. For example, instead of writing "your insurance does not cover damage to buildings not connected to the house," write "your insurance covers damage to the house only." Or instead of writing "We must refuse," a wholesaler could deny a discount by writing "We can grant discounts only when. . . ." In some cases, your job may be to educate the reader. Not only will this be your explanation for the refusal, but it will also build goodwill.

Offering an Alternative When Possible

If the situation justifies an alternative, you can use it in making the refusal positive. More specifically, by saying what you can do (the alternative), you can clearly imply what you cannot do. For example, if you write "What we can do is to (the compromise), . . ." you clearly imply that you cannot do what the reader requested, and you do so without using negative words.

Closing with Goodwill

Your goal in the conclusion is to move beyond the bad news and leave your reader with a feeling of goodwill and a good impression of you as a business professional.

Because you want to end on a positive note, you should not apologize or reinforce the bad news with something such as "Again, I regret that we must refuse your request." You also do not want to assume you know how the reader feels with something such as "Thank you for understanding why we must make this decision." In addition, you do not want a general conclusion such as "Thank you for your time" that could be applied to any message. These general conclusions show that you are not thinking about your reader in this specific case.

The best closing should be positive and relevant to your topic. In the case of the National Association of Police Officers, for example, the positive news is that the organization can apply again next year. You could say something positive about the subject of the request as long as it does not remind the reader of the bad news.

Reviewing the Pattern for Refusing a Request

To adapt the general plan to refuse a request, you want to do the following:

- Begin with a neutral buffer that references a response to the request.

- Present your justification or explanation, using positive, objective language.

- Refuse clearly, objectively, and positively.

- Include an alternative or compromise when appropriate.

- Use an end comment that is relevant to your message and promotes goodwill.

Comparing Examples of a Refused Request

The advantage of the indirect order in refusal messages is illustrated by contrasting examples of WLI's possible response to the request from the National Association of Peace Officers described in the Problem-Solving Challenge for this section. Both examples are clear in refusing the request, but only the one that uses the indirect order is likely to maintain the reader's goodwill.

You Make the Call
Can you make the case for delivering this message using a direct approach?

The Direct Refusal The first example states the bad news right away and is so blunt that it leaves an immediate negative impression. The result is that the reader is less likely to accept the explanation that follows. The explanation is clear, but note the unnecessary use of negative words (*exhausted, regret, cannot consider*). Note also how the closing words leave the reader with a strong reminder of the bad news.

Subject: Your request for a donation

Ms. Cangelosi:

We regret to inform you that we cannot grant your request for a donation to the association's scholarship fund.

So many requests for contributions are made of us that we have found it necessary to budget a definite amount each year for this purpose.

Unfortunately, our budgeted funds for this year have been exhausted, so we simply cannot consider additional requests.

We won't be able to consider your request until next year.

We deeply regret our inability to help you now and trust that you understand our position.

Mark Stephens

Communication Matters

Delivering Bad News: A Sign of Leadership

Erika Andersen, author of *Leading So People Will Follow*, says that most leaders will likely identify delivering bad news as the hardest part of their job. At the same time, she says delivering bad news well demonstrates a leader's courage because "it shows that [he/she] will do things that are personally uncomfortable or difficult for the good of the enterprise." However, the act of delivering bad news is only courageous if the news is delivered effectively. Andersen offers the following suggestions for being courageous in bad-news situations:

1. Speak up: Hiding the bad news or ignoring it only makes a bad situation worse.
2. Be accurate: Andersen says leaders should be "simple, clear, true, and balanced." If leaders minimize the importance of an issue or lose their objectivity, audiences cannot trust them.
3. Take responsibility: Leaders must acknowledge that as the face of the company, they are responsible both for what they do and for what the company does. Good leaders do not try to distance themselves from their actions or the consequences of them.
4. Listen: People naturally are going to be angry, frustrated, or afraid upon hearing bad news. Good leaders will let people work through their emotions rather than try to talk people out of them or make people feel as though their reactions are inappropriate.
5. Say what [they will] do next: People expect that once leaders have taken responsibility, leaders will know how to make a bad situation better.
6. Do what [they] say—and repeat as needed: Leaders must follow through on their plans to remedy bad situations, which may mean addressing the concerns of several audiences individually or simultaneously. And leaders who do not follow through on their plans are viewed more negatively than if they never had any plans at all.

Source: Erika Anderson. "How Great Leaders Deliver Bad News," *Forbes*, March 6, 2013, accessed September 6, 2016, http://www.forbes.com.

The Indirect Refusal The second example skillfully handles the negative message. Its opening words are relevant and neutral. They set up the explanation that follows. The clear and logical explanation ties in with the opening. Using no negative words, the explanation leads smoothly to the refusal. Note that the refusal is also handled without negative words and yet is clear. The friendly close is specific to the topic of the message.

Subject: Your Scholarship Fund Request

Ms. Cangelosi:

Your efforts to build the scholarship fund for the officers' children are commendable.

White Label Industries assists worthy causes whenever we can. That is why every January we budget in the upcoming year the maximum amount we believe we are able to contribute to such causes. Then we distribute that amount among the various deserving groups as far as it will go. Since our budgeted contributions for this year have already been made, we are placing your organization on our list for consideration next year.

We wish you success in your efforts to improve the lives of the children in our city.

Mark Stephens

Annotated Example
Refused Request Message to an External Audience
(Denying an Artist's Request)

A regional medical facility displays local artists' work at its various satellite locations. Artists submit applications to have their work displayed. This message shows a good strategy for denying a request to an artist who applied to have her work displayed in the Lake Superior Family Medicine Clinic's reception area.

Lake Superior Family Medicine Clinic
4546 Burger Lane
North Concord, WI 54746
Web: www.lsfm.org
phone: 715-987-4958
fax: 715-567-7684

Lake Superior Family Medicine Clinic

Visit us: Web: https://www.lsfm.org

June 15, 2018

Ms. Jane Burroughs
2942 County Highway J
North Concord, WI 54746

Dear Ms. Burroughs:

A relevant, neutral buffer gains the reader's favor by thanking her

Thank you for submitting your artwork for display at Lake Superior Family Medicine Clinic. The jury's deliberation process took more time than expected due to the number of submissions. Such a delay is a rare occurrence, so your patience was appreciated.

A reasonable, convincing explanation is supported by a fact

The Medical Center's art wall and case is a free service open to local artists like you. This exhibit area has been embraced by not only artists but also community members because of the beauty it showcases. In fact, it's so popular that we had 75 requests from local artists last month. Due to the limited wall space available and the large number of art submissions, your artwork was not chosen for display at this time.

An alternative creates a positive tone

The jury enjoyed your pieces and noted that your art "personified light." We encourage you to submit up to 10 pieces from your collection once again in 120 days. As outlined in the initial request letter dated May 22, 2018, artists can submit up to 10 submissions every 120 days.

A relevant, forward-looking conclusion builds goodwill

If you have any questions, please contact me. Again, thank you for submitting your artwork. We look forward to your next submission.

Sincerely,

Samantha Kennedy

Director, Marketing/Community Relations
Lake Superior Family Medicine Clinic
Email: sakennedy@lsfmc.org
Phone: 715-456-7890

Annotated Example
Refused Request Message to an Internal Audience (Saying "No" to an Employee)

This message denies a hard-working employee's request. Showing appreciation for his work and citing the CEO's directive are likely to keep the employee's goodwill. In addition, the writer shows respect for the employee's request by remaining logical and objective and offers a positive alternative.

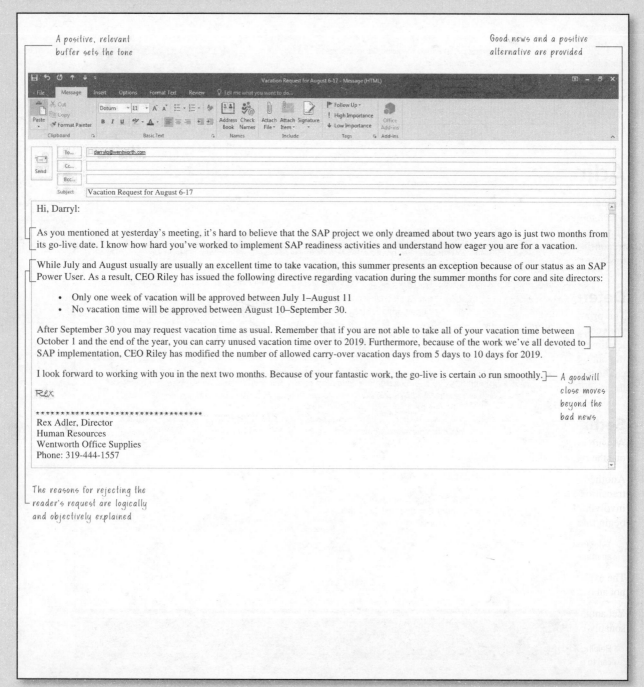

A positive, relevant buffer sets the tone

Good news and a positive alternative are provided

Vacation Request for August 6–17 - Message (HTML)

To... darrylg@wentworth.com

Subject: Vacation Request for August 6–17

Hi, Darryl:

As you mentioned at yesterday's meeting, it's hard to believe that the SAP project we only dreamed about two years ago is just two months from its go-live date. I know how hard you've worked to implement SAP readiness activities and understand how eager you are for a vacation.

While July and August usually are usually an excellent time to take vacation, this summer presents an exception because of our status as an SAP Power User. As a result, CEO Riley has issued the following directive regarding vacation during the summer months for core and site directors:

- Only one week of vacation will be approved between July 1–August 11
- No vacation time will be approved between August 10–September 30.

After September 30 you may request vacation time as usual. Remember that if you are not able to take all of your vacation time between October 1 and the end of the year, you can carry unused vacation time over to 2019. Furthermore, because of the work we've all devoted to SAP implementation, CEO Riley has modified the number of allowed carry-over vacation days from 5 days to 10 days for 2019.

I look forward to working with you in the next two months. Because of your fantastic work, the go-live is certain to run smoothly.

Rex

****
Rex Adler, Director
Human Resources
Wentworth Office Supplies
Phone: 319-444-1557

A goodwill close moves beyond the bad news

The reasons for rejecting the reader's request are logically and objectively explained

Problem-Solving Challenge

Denying a Customer's Claim

Sometimes your job at White Label Industries (WLI) involves handling a complaint. Today, that is one of your tasks because the morning email has brought a strong claim for adjustment on an order for WLI's Do-Craft fabrics. The writer, Ms. Arlene Sanderson, explains that a Do-Craft fabric her upholstering company used on some outdoor furniture has faded badly in less than 10 months. She even includes photographs of the fabric to prove her point. She contends that the product is defective, and she wants her money back—all $2,517 of it.

Inspection of the photographs reveals that the fabric has been subjected to strong sunlight for long periods. Do-Craft fabrics are for indoor use only. Both the WLI brochures on the product and the catalog description stress this point. In fact, you have difficulty understanding how Ms. Sanderson misread it when she ordered from the catalog.

Anyway, as you see it, WLI is not responsible and should not refund the money. At the same time, you want to keep Ms. Sanderson as a repeat customer. Now you must write a message that will do just that. This section will help you write your message.

Adjustment Refusals

Adjustment refusals are a special type of refused request. Your reader has made a claim, which means he or she is asking you to adjust (fix) something that has gone wrong. Usually, you grant these claims. Most are legitimate, and you want to correct any error for which you are responsible. The facts require that you say no. The following section shows you how to handle this type of message. To learn more about writing a claim, see Chapter 8.

LO9-4   Write adjustment refusals that minimize the bad news and overcome negative impressions.

Determining the Strategy

The primary difference between this and other refusal messages is that in these situations your company will probably have clear, reasonable guidelines for what should be regarded as legitimate requests for an adjustment. You will not, therefore, have to spend much time figuring out why you cannot grant the reader's request. You will have good reasons to refuse. The challenge will be to do so while still making possible an ongoing, positive relationship with the reader.

Setting Up Your Buffer and Strategy

As with any bad-news message, you will begin with a buffer. Since this message is a response to one the reader has sent, a logical buffer is an acknowledgment of the reader's claim.

Another way to begin is to state a point of common agreement, which allows you to then transition to your explanation of reasons why this case is an exception. To illustrate, a case involving a claim for adjustment for failure of an air conditioner to perform properly might begin this way:

> You are correct in believing that an 18,000 BTU window air conditioner should cool the ordinary three-room apartment.

The explanation that follows this sentence might be one that shows the apartment in question is not an ordinary apartment.

Yet another strategy is to build the case that the claim for adjustment goes beyond what can reasonably be expected. A beginning such as this one sets it up:

> Helping our customers find the perfect appliances is one of our most satisfying goals. We do all we reasonably can to reach it.

The explanation that follows this sentence will show that the requested adjustment goes beyond what can be reasonably expected.

Making Your Case

In presenting your reasons for refusal, explain your company's relevant policy or practice. Without accusing the reader, call attention to the relevant facts—for example, that the item in question was damaged, that the printed material warned against certain uses, or that the warranty has expired. Putting together the policy and the facts should lead logically to the conclusion that the adjustment cannot be granted.

> The product literature for the window unit indicates air conditioner you purchased is best suited for spaces of approximately 1,400 square feet; your message indicates that you are using the air conditioner for a three-room apartment of approximately 2,200 square feet, which may explain why the air conditioner is not performing as you expected. Before you purchased your Super Air 2000, the manufacturer began producing larger window units with more features, so we discontinued this model and sold our remaining stock on clearance, including this unit to you in April.

Refusing Positively and Closing Courteously

As in other refusal messages, your refusal is derived from your explanation. It is the logical result. You word it clearly, and you make it as positive as the circumstances permit. For example, this one is clear, and it contains no negative words:

> As your receipt notes, the sales of all discontinued clearance items are considered final. This policy helps us have the space to provide our customers with the newest, most technologically up-to-date models.

If a compromise is in order, you might present it in positive language like this:

> You may be interested in a new model, which comes with a one-year unlimited warranty. I have attached a coupon for a 30% discount, which you can use either in the store or online.

As in all bad-news messages, you should end this one with some appropriate, positive comment. You could reinforce the message that you care about the reader's business or the quality of your products. In cases where it would not seem selfish, you could write about new products or services that the reader might be interested in. You do not need to apologize or remind the reader of the bad news. Your goal is to move beyond the bad news and toward future business.

> I invite you to view the latest models on our website at www.acerappliances.com/air_conditioners and am happy to answer your questions about any of the products.

Reviewing the Pattern for Refusing an Adjustment

To apply the indirect plan to writing an adjustment refusal, you will want to do the following:

- Begin with a relevant, neutral buffer that sets up your strategy.
- Present the strategy that explains or justifies the refusal, being factual, objective, and positive.
- Refuse clearly and objectively, perhaps including an alternative.
- End with positive, forward-looking, friendly words.

Comparing Examples of an Adjustment Refusal

These examples illustrate effective and ineffective ways to address the Problem-Solving Challenge at the beginning of this section. The ineffective example, which is blunt and insulting, destroys goodwill. The good one, which uses the techniques described in the preceding paragraphs, will do a better job of goodwill.

The Direct Refusal This example begins bluntly with a direct statement of the refusal. The language is negative (*regret, must reject, claim, refuse, damage, inconvenience*). The

You Make the Call
Would you apologize to this customer?

explanation is equally blunt. In addition, it is insulting ("It is difficult for me to understand how you failed . . ."). It uses little tact and little you-viewpoint. Because the closing is negative, it recalls the bad news.

Subject: Your May 3 claim for damages

Ms. Sanderson,

I regret to report that we must reject your request for money back on the faded Do-Craft fabric.

We must refuse because Do-Craft fabrics are not made for outside use. It is difficult for me to understand how you failed to notice this limitation. It was clearly stated in the catalog from which you ordered. It was even stamped on the back of every yard of fabric. Since we have been more than reasonable in trying to inform you, we cannot possibly be responsible.

We trust that you will understand our position. We regret very much having to deny your request.

Marilyn Cox, Customer Relations

An Indirect Refusal This example begins with a point of agreement that sets up the explanation. Without accusations, anger, or negative words, it reviews the facts of the case, which absolve the company from blame. The refusal is clear, even though it is implied rather than stated. It uses no negative words, and the bad news does not receive undue emphasis. The closing shifts to helpful suggestions that are relevant to the topic of the message—suggestions that may actually result in a future sale.

Subject: Your May 3 Message about Do-Craft Fabric

Ms. Sanderson:

Certainly, you have a right to expect the best possible service from Do-Craft fabrics. Every Do-Craft product is the result of years of experimentation. We are determined that our products will do for you what we say they will do.

We carefully inspected the photos of Do-Craft Fabric 103 that you sent us. It appears that each sample has been subjected to long periods in extreme sunlight. Because Do-Craft fabrics cannot withstand exposure to sunlight, our advertising, the catalog, and a stamped reminder on the back of every yard of the fabric advise customers that the fabric is meant for indoor use only.

As you can see from our catalog, the fabrics in the 200 series are recommended for outdoor use. You may also be interested in the new Duck Back cotton fabrics listed in our 500 series. These plastic-coated cotton fabrics are economical, and they resist sun and rain remarkably well.

If we can help you further in your selection, please contact us at service@wli.com.

Marilyn Cox, Consumer Relations

An out-of-town customer bought an expensive dress from the writer and mailed it back three weeks later asking for a refund. The customer explained that the dress was not a good fit and that she did not like it anymore. But stains on the dress proved that she had worn it. This letter skillfully presents the refusal.

MARIE'S
Fashions

103 BREAKER RD. HOUSTON, TX 77015 713-454-6778 Fax: 713-454-6771

February 19, 2019

Ms. Cherie Ranney
117 Kyle Avenue E.
College Station, TX 77840-2415

Dear Ms. Ranney:

A neutral, relevant buffer opens the message

We understand your concern about the elegant St. John's dress you returned February 15. As always, we are willing to do as much as we reasonably can to make things right.

The explanation is set up

A review of the facts supports the writer's position

Negative language is minimized in the refusal

What we can do in each instance is determined by the circumstances. With returned clothing, we generally give refunds. Of course, to meet our obligations to our customers for quality merchandise, all returned clothing must be unquestionably new. As you know, our customers expect only the best from us, and we insist that they get it. Thus, because the perspiration stains on your dress would prevent its resale, we must consider the sale final. We are returning the dress to you. With the proper alterations, it can be an elegant addition to your wardrobe.

Objective language maintains a neutral tone—no blaming or accusing

The writer emphasizes what can be done, which helps restore goodwill

A friendly goodwill close promotes future business

Please visit us again when you are in the Houston area. It would be our pleasure to serve you.

Sincerely,

Marie O. Mitchell
Marie O. Mitchell
President

dm

Problem-Solving Challenge

Announcing an Increase in Health Insurance Costs

As the assistant to the human resources director at White Label Industries (WLI), you have been given the difficult assignment of writing a bad-news message for your boss. She has just returned from a meeting of the company's top executives in which the decision was made to deduct 25% of the employees' medical insurance premiums from their paychecks.

Until now, WLI has paid it all. But declining profits are forcing the company to ask employees to contribute more. Something has to give if WLI is to remain competitive while also avoiding layoffs.

The administrators decided on a number of cost-cutting measures including this reduction in the company's payment for medical insurance. The message you will write to WLI employees is a negative announcement.

Negative Announcements

Occasionally, businesses must announce bad news to their customers or employees. For example, a company might need to announce that prices are going up, that a service or product line is being discontinued, or that a branch of the business is closing. Or a company might need to tell its employees that the company is in some kind of trouble, that people will need to be laid off, or, as in the Problem-Solving Challenge in this section, that employees will contribute more to the cost of their health insurance. These **negative announcements** usually follow the general indirect plan discussed in this chapter.

LO9-5 Write negative announcements that maintain goodwill.

Determining the Strategy

When faced with the problem of making a negative announcement, your first step should be to determine your overall strategy. Will you use direct or indirect organization?

In most cases the indirect arrangement will be better. This route is especially recommended when it is reasonable to expect that the readers would be surprised, disappointed, or even angered by a direct presentation. When planning an indirect announcement, you need to think about what kind of buffer opening to use, what kind of explanation to give, how to word the news itself, and how to leave your readers feeling that you have considered their interests and made a good decision.

You Make the Call
In what situations would you make sure to deliver a negative announcement in person?

Setting Up the Buffer

As with the preceding negative message types, you should plan your indirect beginning (buffer) carefully. You should think through the situation and select a buffer that will set up or begin the explanation that justifies the announcement. Perhaps you will begin by presenting justifying information. Or maybe you will start with complimentary or cordial talk focusing on the good relationship that you and your readers have developed. Choose the option that will most likely prepare your reader to accept the coming bad news.

Presenting the Justification and Bad News

In most cases, the opening paragraph will enable you to continue with background reasons or explanations in the next paragraph, before you present the bad news. Doing so will help you de-emphasize the bad news by locating it in the middle of the paragraph rather than at the beginning.

As in other negative situations, you should use positive words and an objective tone and avoid unnecessary negative comments when presenting the news itself. Since this is an announcement, however, you must make certain that you cover all the facts. People may not be expecting this news. They will therefore want to know the reasons for the situation. They also want to know that you have done all you can to ease the effects of the bad news, so you will need to provide evidence that this is true. If the readers must do something, the steps must be clearly covered as well. All questions that may come to the readers' minds should be anticipated and covered, too.

When making a negative announcement, remember that an indirect, tactful approach is usually better than a blunt or aggressive approach.

© JGI/Jamie Grill/Getty Images RF

Focusing on Next Steps or Remaining Benefits

In many cases negative news will mean that things have changed. Customers may no longer be able to get a product that they have relied upon, or employees may have to find a way to pay for something that they have been getting for free. For this reason, a negative announcement will often need to help people solve the problem that your news just created for them. In situations where you have no further help to offer—for example, when announcing certain price increases—you can still help people feel better about your news by calling attention to the benefits that they will continue to enjoy. You can focus on the good things that have not changed and perhaps even look ahead to something positive or exciting on the horizon.

Closing on a Positive or Encouraging Note

The ending should cement your effort to cover the matter positively. The ending should not include an apology or continued discussion of the bad news. Instead, you can use a positive look forward, a sincere expression of gratitude, or an affirmation of your positive relationship with your readers.

Reviewing the Pattern for Negative Announcements

To write a negative-news announcement, you will do the following:

- Start with a buffer that sets up justification for the bad news.

- Present the justification for the bad news.

- Give the bad news objectively, positively, and clearly.

- Help solve the problem that the news may have created for the reader.

- End with appropriate goodwill.

Comparing Examples of a Negative Announcement

Effective and ineffective techniques in negative announcements are illustrated in these messages that announce WLI's plan to have employees contribute more to the cost of their health insurance (see the Problem-Solving Challenge at the beginning of this section). The ineffective example is written in a direct pattern, which in some circumstances may be acceptable but clearly is not in this case. The effective example follows the indirect pattern.

A Direct Message That Causes Panic The following example will clearly alarm readers with its abrupt announcement in the beginning. The readers aren't prepared to receive the negative message. They probably don't understand the reasons behind the negative news. The explanation comes later, but the readers are not likely to be in a receptive mood when they see it. The message ends with a repetition of the bad news.

To Our Employees:

WLI management sincerely regrets that effective February 1 you must begin contributing 25% of the cost of your medical insurance. As you know, in the past the company has paid the full amount.

This decision is primarily the result of the continued high cost of medical insurance and declining profits over the last several quarters. Given our tight financial picture in general, we needed to find ways to reduce expenses.

We trust that you will understand why we must ask for your help with cutting costs to the company and thank you for helping us save money.

Sincerely,

A Courteous and Logical Indirect Message The better example follows the recommended indirect pattern. Its opening words begin the task of convincing the readers of the appropriateness of the action to be taken. After more convincing explanation, the announcement flows logically. Perhaps it will not be received positively by all recipients, but it represents a reasonable position given the facts presented. After the announcement comes an offer of assistance to help readers deal with their new situation. The last paragraph reminds readers of remaining benefits and reassures them that management understands their interests. It ends on an appreciative, goodwill note.

To All Employees:

Even though the Affordable Care Act has increased competition among insurance providers, the cost of medical coverage has increased for most companies.

Such is the case at our company. The premiums that we pay to cover our health benefits have increased by 34% over the last two years, and they now represent nearly a third of our expenditures. Meanwhile, as you know, our sales have been lower than usual for the past several quarters.

For the short term, we must find a way to cut overall costs. Your management has considered many options and rejected such measures as cutting salaries and reducing personnel. Of the solutions that will be implemented, the only change that affects you directly concerns your medical insurance. On **March 1** we will begin deducting 25% of the cost of the premium from your paycheck.

Jim Taylor in the Personnel Office will soon be announcing an informational meeting about your insurance options. Switching coverage, choosing a less expensive plan with higher deductibles, or setting up a flexible spending account may be right for you. You can also see Jim after the meeting to arrange a personal consultation. He is well versed in the many solutions available and can give you expert advice for your situation.

Our health care benefits are some of the best in our city and in our industry, and those who continue with the current plan will not see any change in their medical coverage or their copays. Your management regards a strong benefits program as critical to the company's success, and we will do all we can to maintain these benefits while keeping your company financially viable.

Sincerely,

Annotated Example
Negative Announcement (Decreasing Work Hours)

Shop employees are told of the effects a slow economy will have on their work hours. The message is friendly and empathetic but clearly conveys the negative news. The goodwill close looks forward to better economic times.

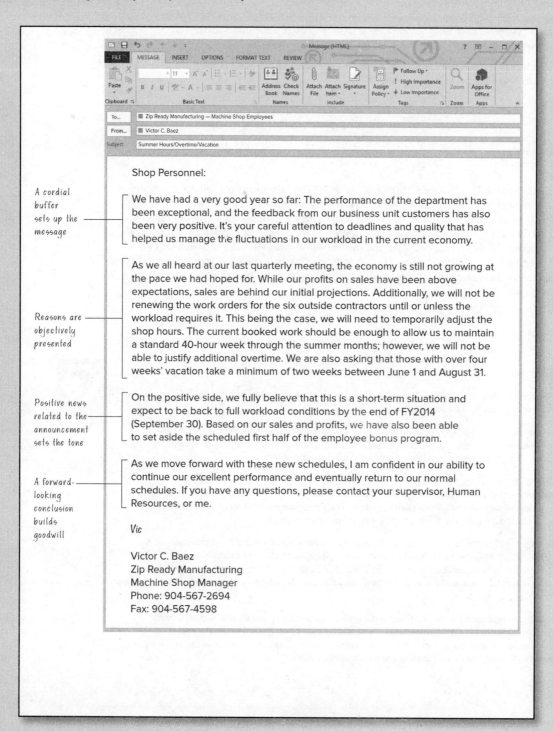

A cordial buffer sets up the message

Reasons are objectively presented

Positive news related to the announcement sets the tone

A forward-looking conclusion builds goodwill

To... Zip Ready Manufacturing — Machine Shop Employees
From... Victor C. Baez
Subject Summer Hours/Overtime/Vacation

Shop Personnel:

We have had a very good year so far: The performance of the department has been exceptional, and the feedback from our business unit customers has also been very positive. It's your careful attention to deadlines and quality that has helped us manage the fluctuations in our workload in the current economy.

As we all heard at our last quarterly meeting, the economy is still not growing at the pace we had hoped for. While our profits on sales have been above expectations, sales are behind our initial projections. Additionally, we will not be renewing the work orders for the six outside contractors until or unless the workload requires it. This being the case, we will need to temporarily adjust the shop hours. The current booked work should be enough to allow us to maintain a standard 40-hour week through the summer months; however, we will not be able to justify additional overtime. We are also asking that those with over four weeks' vacation take a minimum of two weeks between June 1 and August 31.

On the positive side, we fully believe that this is a short-term situation and expect to be back to full workload conditions by the end of FY2014 (September 30). Based on our sales and profits, we have also been able to set aside the scheduled first half of the employee bonus program.

As we move forward with these new schedules, I am confident in our ability to continue our excellent performance and eventually return to our normal schedules. If you have any questions, please contact your supervisor, Human Resources, or me.

Vic

Victor C. Baez
Zip Ready Manufacturing
Machine Shop Manager
Phone: 904-567-2694
Fax: 904-567-4598

Using Directness in Some Cases

As we mentioned at the beginning of this chapter, in some cases it is likely that the reader will not have a strong negative reaction to the bad news. If, for example, the negative news is expected, its impact may be viewed as negligible. There is also a good case for directness when the company's announcement will contain a remedy or announce new benefits that are designed to offset the effects of the bad news. As in all announcements with some negative element, this part must be worded as positively as possible. Also, the message should end on a goodwill note. The following sample message, announcing the end of a store's customer reward program, illustrates this situation.

Dear Ms. Cato:

Effective January 1 Frontier Designs is discontinuing its Preferred Customer program to offer several new promotions.

Your accumulated points will be converted to a savings coupon worth as much as or more than your points total. Your new points total is on the coupon enclosed with this letter. You may apply this coupon in these ways:

• When shopping in our stores, present your coupon at the register.

• When shopping from our catalogs, give the coupon number to the telephone service agent, enclose your coupon with your mail order, or enter it with your online order at www.frontierdesigns.com/catalog.

In all these cases we will deduct your coupon value from your purchase total. If you have any questions, please call us at 1-800-343-4111.

We thank you very much for your loyalty. You'll soon hear about exciting new opportunities to shop and save with us.

Sincerely,

Power Charge Your Professionalism: Use Colons and Semicolons

Insert colons, semicolons, and commas as needed in the following sentences. Indicate which punctuation guide you used from Reference Chapter A to determine the punctuation for each sentence. If the sentence is correct, leave it as is.

1. Many companies allow employees to work from home however other companies question whether these employees can be productive if they are not working from the office.
2. As we moved through the review process we never lost sight of our goal We needed to identify our best employees and gain their support for culture change across our organization.
3. Our customers tell us their favorite features of our Internet service are its speed reliability and cost.
4. We have hired four new staff members Brenda Stevens a human resources generalist Joe Kingsley an IT specialist Thomas Dorsett an accountant and Zoe Hinz a purchasing agent.
5. Over 300 patients visited our office last week this this week however only 225 patients scheduled appointments.
6. Rick Allie Yu and Lou are scheduled to lead four of the training sessions on Tuesday and Robert Julie Evelyn and Leslie are schedule to lead the sessions on Wednesday.
7. Dale Carnegie is known for this quote "Success is getting what you want. Happiness is wanting what you get."
8. Over a million copies of our fitness app have been downloaded making it the most popular app among our customers ages 20–40.

Using colons and semicolons correctly is important because . . .

• Semicolons and colons help show relationships between and among ideas. You can use the semicolon and colon, along with commas, to show coordination, subordination, and emphasis.
• Good use of punctuation helps your reader follow the logic of your thoughts and ensures your messages are clear.

For further instruction, see "Colons" and "Semicolons" in the "Punctuation and Mechanics" module of LearnSmart Achieve.

Key Terms

Critical-Thinking Questions

1. Give examples of times (or situations) when indirectness or directness would be appropriate for responses giving negative information. LO1

2. Writing in the indirect order usually requires a buffer, making indirect messages longer than direct messages. Since conciseness is a virtue in business writing, how can the indirect order be justified? LO2

3. What strategy is best in a message refusing a request when the reasons for the refusal are in the writer's best interests and not in the reader's? LO3

4. "Apologies in refusals are negative because they call attention to what you are refusing. You should avoid using them." Discuss. LO3

5. Some business writers explain an adjustment refusal simply by saying that company policy did not permit granting claims in such cases. Is citing company policy adequate? Discuss. LO4

6. Negative announcements usually need to include much more than the announcement. Explain. LO5

7. Give examples of negative announcements that would be appropriately written in the direct order. LO5

Skills-Building Exercises

1. Point out the shortcomings in the following email message from a sports celebrity declining an invitation to speak at the kickoff meeting for workers in a fundraising campaign for a charity. LO3

   Subject: Your Request for Free Lecture

   Ms. Chung:

   As much as I would like to, I must decline your request that I give your membership a free lecture next month. I receive many requests to give free lectures. I grant some of them, but I simply cannot do them all. Unfortunately, yours is one that I must decline.

   I regret that I cannot serve you this time. If I can be of further service in the future, please call on me.

   Sincerely yours,

2. Criticize the following message refusing the claim for a defective riding lawn mower. The mower was purchased 15 months earlier. The purchaser has had difficulties with it for some time and submitted with the claim a statement from a local repair service verifying the difficulties. The writer's reason for refusing is stated in the email. LO4

   Subject: Your May 12 Claim

   Mr. Skinner:

   Your May 12 claim of defective workmanship in your Model 227 Dandy Klipper riding mower has been reviewed. After considering the information received, I regret to report that we cannot refund the purchase price.

   You have had the mower for 15 months, which is well beyond our one-year guarantee. Even though your repair person says that you had problems earlier, he is not one of our authorized repair people. If you will read the warranty you refer to in your letter, you will see that we honor the warranty only when our authorized repair people find defects. I think you will understand why we must follow this procedure.

   If you will take the machine to the authorized service center in your area (La Rue Lawn and Garden Center), I am confident they can correct the defect at a reasonable charge.

   If I can be of additional service, please contact me.

   Sincerely,

3. You work for an online mail-order company, Nonsensicals, which sells such novelty items as T-shirts with clever sayings, unique toys and games, and such household accessories as framed posters and retro table lamps. Most of the employees are young, somewhat quirky, and very Internet savvy. Now consider the following email sent to everyone from the company president. **LO5**

   Subject: No More Social Networking during Work Hours

   It has become obvious to me that people are spending too much time doing social networking and not enough time actually working while on the job. From now on, you must do your networking (whether on Facebook, LinkedIn, Twitter, Instagram, Snapchat, or any other such network) on breaks or during other personal time. Anyone found using these websites on company time will receive an official reprimand.

   Considering the advice in this chapter, what would be the main ways to improve this negative announcement?

4. You own a small new- and used-book store and café with free wireless Internet access. You enjoy the calm, quiet atmosphere of your store and like that your customers choose your store to conduct business, socialize with friends, or just enjoy a good book and a cup of coffee. Increasingly, many customers are talking on their cell phones—very loudly and in places where they shouldn't be. They hold up the order line by talking on the phone when they should be talking to the cashier. They disrupt others who are enjoying the quiet atmosphere to work or read. Sure, customers who are working on the computer may need to talk on the phone, but must these customers be so loud and disruptive that those across the room who are trying to read can hear their conversations? Many customers have actually complained. You want to make these customers happy but not at the expense of making your cell phone users unhappy. Write a cell phone use policy to post in your store. **LO5**

Problem-Solving Cases

Refused Requests

1. **Saying "No" to Community Service:** You have just started your career in an entry-level _____ position (you pick the position). Your company encourages employees to do community service and considers this service in annual performance reviews, which impact salary increases, and when promoting employees. Rim Ridge Community Arts Association, a nonprofit organization that promotes art, music, theater, and dance in your town, has asked you to be on its board of directors. The board's main job is raising funds to support the arts, but the board also relies on its members' various professional expertise in marketing, grant writing, management, Web design, social media, law, and other fields to run the organization. At first, this seems like a great opportunity for you to use your expertise to do some philanthropic work and maybe impress your boss, but as you think about being a board member, you really wonder whether you want to work all day at your job and then do the same type of work on the evenings and weekends for the board. Plus, you really don't have much interest in the arts. Fundraising isn't something that excites you, either. After thinking about it, you realize this just isn't the right opportunity for you.

   Respond to Rim Ridge's request, turning down the offer to serve on the board. As you explain your reasons for turning down the request, be sure your tone is respectful of the work that Rim Ridge does for the arts in your community.

2. **Rejecting an Employee's Suggestion:** As the HR director at Vanguard Industries, you couldn't be happier with how your efforts to establish an employee volunteer program have worked out. Thanks to the employees' donations of their time and expertise, the community where you live has been improved, and the company has gained a more positive public profile. But there are still some bumps in the road, and today you're dealing with one of them.

   Part of the program you set up is a database of company-approved schools, foundations, and other nonprofit organizations for which employees may volunteer. In order to get approved time off work for their contributions, employees must choose one of these organizations. There are over 30 organizations on the list, and more are added each month as employees propose new causes for the company to support.

Janet Robbins, one of the administrative assistants, has just sent you an email requesting that the Pregnancy Care Center be approved as one of Vanguard's nonprofit partners. You check out the organization's website, and what you suspected is confirmed: Even though the center isn't affiliated with any particular denomination, it has a Christian focus (the words "ministry" and "God-given right to life" appear in its mission statement; and "prayer partner" is listed as one of the volunteer opportunities there, along with other religion-related roles). In advocating right to life, it also takes a firm stand on an extremely controversial issue.

To help protect Vanguard from charges of bias, the guidelines for proposing an addition to the list of supported organizations state that the organization can have no religious or political affiliations. Thus, you simply cannot grant Janet's request.

You worked very hard to get the employees behind the new volunteer program, and you don't want Janet, a key player in the company grapevine, to start any negative talk about it. Refuse her request in such a way that you do not lose her support for the program.

3. **Refusing a Sponsorship Request:** Today you've received a solicitation from a well-meaning service organization, Building Caring Communities (BCC). BCC is inviting your company, Dennison Wealth Management, to be a featured sponsor of its annual Fix It Fair, which has volunteers from all over the city contributing one day's labor to helping their less fortunate neighbors with yard work, home repairs, and other tasks. Your contribution of $1,000 will help pay for the volunteers' T-shirts (on which your company's name will appear), the supplies, and the picnic that will follow the day's work. Any employees who volunteer will have the satisfaction of knowing they helped make someone's home safer or more comfortable.

Although this $1,000 doesn't sound like much for a successful business, you've given over $5,000 to such causes this year, and that's all you can afford right now. And even if you could afford the $1,000 donation, you're not sure that the publicity opportunity BCC offers would be the best use of your money. Those helped by BCC aren't likely to become your customers since one reason they're being helped is that they can't afford to pay for services like yours. Write the BCC chair a letter turning down the request for a sponsorship while building goodwill and promoting a positive image of your company as a supporter of BCC's efforts. In fact, if BCC could use more volunteers, you and another employee might be interested in helping with some yard work during the Fix It Fair.

4. **Rejecting a Meeting Location:** As executive director of the Northwest Human Resources Institute, you have been gathering information to help the organization's board of directors decide where to hold its annual meeting three years from now. Specifically, the board has asked you to investigate two possible sites: Seattle, Washington, and Portland, Oregon. In both cities you received good help from representatives of the chamber of commerce, but Collin Mallard of Seattle was particularly helpful. He went out of his way to show you the city and give you insider information on its attractions and restaurants. He also took you to the hotels with appropriate facilities for your event and introduced you to the managers. Overall, he was a delightful tour guide. You were hoping to send your organization's business his way.

Unfortunately, the board has decided on Portland for the meeting. Now it is your job to inform Mr. Mallard that Seattle's bid has been turned down. Certainly, you will express your thanks for his help. You can also report that the decision was a close one and that Seattle will be considered for later years. Send your message to Mr. Mallard via letter. Remember that the board will see a copy of it. (If your instructor directs, research the two cities and come up with plausible reasons why Portland was chosen.)

5. **Turning Down a Job Offer:** As a new college graduate, you're delighted that not one but two companies have offered you a position in their _____ (you decide which) department. You met representatives of both companies at your university's job fair. From this first contact came an invitation for an onsite job interview with each company. You really enjoyed

learning more about the operations of both companies and meeting their friendly employees. Both companies have great employee benefits, and the salaries they're offering are comparable.

After careful thought, you've decided to go with Company B. You sense a little better match between their values and yours, and you think the opportunity for advancement might be better there as well. Write the recruiter at Company A to reject its offer. Of course you will convey your appreciation for the company's consideration, and the things you learned on your visit will enable you to give some well-deserved compliments. What will be stickiest is figuring out how to explain why you're choosing another offer. The explanation won't need to be long, but the company does deserve one. You certainly don't want to close the door on future employment or business relations with this company, so the time you spend crafting this message will be time well spent. (If your instructor directs, research two companies to use for this assignment.)

6. **Declining an Offer to Advertise:** You're responsible for marketing communications at MyBiz.com, a midsized company that makes software specially designed for managing small businesses. Today you've received an email from Rachel Lundemeyer, who works for the Association for Small Business Owners, asking if your company would like to purchase an ad to run in the association's quarterly magazine, *Small Business Today*. She informs you that the magazine has a circulation of around 3,500; and she has included the prices for 1/4-, 1/2-, and full-page ads. You've actually been cutting back on print ads. They're expensive, and you believe that your promotional webinars are a much more effective way to generate sales leads. Plus, your advertising money has already been earmarked for other purposes for this year. It's possible that you'd be interested in purchasing an ad next year. You'd need more information, though. Do readers pay for this magazine (e.g., with their membership dues), or is it distributed free to prospects on a mailing list? You'd be more inclined to advertise in the magazine if readers paid for it since that would indicate a certain level of interest on their part. And are there other promotional opportunities available in the magazine—for example, could you publish a promotional article about your company, or is there a "highlighted vendors" section that you could be listed in? Does the magazine include QR codes so readers can easily visit the advertisers' websites?

Respond to Rachel to refuse her request for now and to gather the additional information you'll need to be able to consider future requests from her.

7. **Denying an Employee's Request:** The professional development program at MediTech has been restructured (see "Negative Announcements," case 18). However, you, the budget director, have received a proposal from Victor Ramos, one of your four senior sales managers, to attend the annual United Professional Sales Association's annual conference. Mr. Ramos knows that the conference, which is in a city 330 miles away, does not fall within the new guidelines for reimbursement, but he has an idea. As a senior sales manager, he (along with all employees in the sales department) earns a bonus when the sales department exceeds corporate sales goals. These bonuses have not been cut because MediTech sees these bonuses as an incentive for the sales staff and senior management to work harder to attract new customers, and during these tough economic times, MediTech needs all of the customers it can get. Mr. Ramos proposes, though, that instead of paying him the money for his sales bonus, the company use the money to pay for his trip to the annual sales conference.

Initially, you think this is a great idea. As long as an employee is motivated to do well, you don't think it should matter to the company what the incentive is. Granted, the company could just pay Mr. Ramos the bonus money and let him use it as he wishes, but then Mr. Ramos would have to pay income tax on the bonus. Mr. Ramos has even agreed to take vacation time to attend the conference.

You take Mr. Ramos's proposal to the others on your executive management team (the president, CEO, and vice president) and are surprised when they reject Mr. Ramos's proposal. If Mr. Ramos is allowed to do this, then all of the other 25 senior managers will be allowed also, which would create an administrative nightmare for the people in your accounting department.

Furthermore, even though Mr. Ramos is willing to take vacation time to attend the conference, the company must pay him if he is on company business—which he seemingly would be if the company pays him his sales bonus to attend the conference—and there is no way you can just let him have the time off. The other senior managers may be angry and think Mr. Ramos is getting special treatment.

Your job is to write a response to Mr. Ramos on behalf of the executive management team refusing his request. You think his initiative and creative thinking in finding another funding source for professional development are commendable. Be sure you retain his goodwill so that he is motivated to continue doing such a wonderful job for MediTech.

8. **Rejecting a Request for a Deadline Extension:** You are a supervisor in the marketing department at Plytec Plastics. You and four others have been working on a campaign for a company product that will be released in three months. Today is Wednesday. Because your boss, the manager of the marketing department, needs a week to prepare the presentation of the campaign to the board of directors, she has asked for the campaign materials by Monday of next week. You and the rest of your team have known about the deadline for three months. This morning you received a message from Mary, the graphic artist, saying that there is no way she can finish her portion of the project by Monday. She says she can have the project finished by Thursday and is requesting an extension. In her message she says she has been swamped with work for two other projects. In addition, her children have been sick this week with colds, so she has had to take time off to care for them, and she is hosting a birthday party for one of her children on Sunday, so she cannot work over the weekend to finish her part of the project.

You talk to your boss, who says she cannot wait until Thursday for Mary's work. To be honest, neither can you, as it reflects poorly on your leadership and supervisory abilities if you cannot deliver a team project on time. Your boss's calendar is so busy that she really needs a full week to get her presentation ready for the board, and if her presentation is not excellent, the entire department appears incompetent. Mary has had three months to get her work done, and many times—just yesterday, as a matter of fact—you have seen her on Facebook or on personal phone calls when she should have been working on the project. She was also late with her work for the last project you worked on together, and you are a bit annoyed that this is happening again.

You are thinking that since you have two other graphic artists in the department, you will ask one of them to work with you on future projects. You know for sure that if Mary does not have her material ready by Monday, you will be talking about Mary's inability to meet deadlines in her performance and salary review next month. Though you plan to talk with Mary in person, you also want a permanent record of your decision, so you decide to write a message to Mary denying her request for an extension and offering at least one suggestion for what she might do to meet her deadline.

9. **(Partially) Rejecting a Request from Neighborhood Leaders:** You work directly under the founder/owner of Premium Properties, a local apartment-rental company that does millions of dollars of business in the University Heights neighborhood of your city. The latest and most ambitious project your boss has undertaken is to purchase a group of worn-out-looking, 1960s-era apartment buildings and replace them with expansive, modern-looking buildings that will rent out at about $1,200 per month per apartment. Things are going well, and the new buildings are shaping up to be really impressive. They'll certainly look better than what used to be there.

Today your boss comes into the office and says that there's a bit of a problem. "I got this letter from the president of the University Heights Community Council. They're complaining about the trash that the construction workers are leaving on the sidewalks outside the property and on the way to and from their cars. They also don't like having all the extra cars and trucks on the streets, so they want us to use the lot of an empty grocery store that's about three blocks from the construction site. I get the feeling that they think the look of the buildings clashes with the historic look of the rest of the neighborhood, and they don't like the noise, either—but they didn't complain about those things.

He sighs. "I'm too busy and too mad to write this letter. I mean, don't they appreciate how much better looking the new complex will be? And that it'll bring a lot more professionals into the neighborhood—folks who have money to spend and will make good neighbors? Heck, I'm a neighbor myself. How about they support me a little?!" He takes a deep breath and then asks if you'll write something he can send back to the president—something that can be read at the next Community Council meeting and that will keep the relationship between the community and Premium Properties as cordial as possible. "I'll certainly advise the construction company to tell their employees not to drop their trash around. But I'm not going to ask that they be made to walk three blocks to the site—that's just unreasonable. With building come growth pains—that's just the way it is. You've gotta expect some inconvenience. Besides, the construction will go on for only about another month." You assure your boss that you'll tackle this thorny PR issue. Now give it your best shot.

10. **Protecting Company Property:** Brian Kerry is the public relations director for Billings Industries, a company that has a large campus with beautiful gardens and a parklike setting. Falling Water Sounds, a local arts organization, wants to host a summer concert series on the company's campus where people can bring their friends and families, enjoy a picnic, and listen to a variety of music groups. Falling Water Sounds wanted to have the concert series in city parks, but people cannot bring alcohol into city parks, and Falling Water Sounds wants people to be able to enjoy whatever food and drink they want to bring to the concert and does not anticipate a rowdy crowd or illegal activity. The goal is to get families and friends together for an evening of music.

Brian envisions families enjoying a concert on the company's campus; he thinks this is a great opportunity for the company to be a good citizen and to promote the company's presence in the community. However, Brian decides to deny the request. Think of at least three reasons why Brian might deny the request. Then, assume the role of Brian and write a letter to Falling Water Sounds denying the request to hold the summer concert series on the company's property.

Adjustment Refusals

11. **Refusing a Refund Request:** You have worked for three months at The Right Image, an online company that owns and licenses images and videos. Although you do have some content that is available at no charge, most of your content must be purchased by users. Customers can purchase a single image or video and sets of images and videos and then download them, or they can purchase subscriptions that let them download a certain amount of content per month or per year. Recently, Somaya Sodi, a student at Southeastern State University, purchased an image for $100 that her student organization planned to use on hats, t-shirts, mugs, and other merchandise. This fee for images that are used for merchandising purposes is much higher than the usual $20 fee per image, because the image is being used for commercial profit. You can't get a share of the commercial profits, but charging more for the images and videos ensures you benefit somewhat from the commercialization of your content.

Somaya has just contacted you stating that she has found an image from another company that she can use for free, so she wants a refund for the image she purchased. She does like your image better than the free one, so she asks if you would instead be willing to charge her only $20. You do not give refunds for content unless the image or video itself is damaged or flawed. The reason for your refund policy is simple: Once an image or video is downloaded, there really is no way for customers to return the product or to ensure that they won't use it, so essentially returning the money gives customers the content for free.

You understand students are on tight budgets, but you need to refuse Somaya's request for a refund and her request to charge her only $20 for the image.

12. **Refusing a Return and Refund:** As a customer service representative for a major retailer, you have to refuse Lisa Hornung's request for a refund. Lisa used your website's Contact Us form to ask about returning a treadmill she purchased four months ago. She says the treadmill motor is much louder than she anticipated and that the noise disrupts her workouts. She ordered the treadmill online and had it shipped to her house, but she wants to know if she should return it to the nearest retail store or ship it back to you, and she wants you to remove the $879 charge from her credit card. The problem is that Ms. Hornung has waited too long to make this return. As your website clearly states, customers can return merchandise for any reason within 60 days of the purchase. After that, there is nothing you can do except recommend an authorized repair center. Any repairs would not be covered because the 60-day warranty has also expired, and she did not purchase the extended warranty that would have protected her for a full year. You have a good reason for your return policy. Many people buy fitness equipment thinking they will be motivated to work out but then quickly lose interest and regret their purchase. People will then say "it doesn't work" as an excuse to get a refund.

Write to Ms. Hornung to give her the bad news. See if you can figure out how to keep her goodwill and her future business. You'll also need to resolve what to do about the loud motor.

13. **Denying a Claim for an Unused Plane Ticket:** Jeremy Ellison is upset. He recently purchased a plane ticket to fly home for his parents' 50th wedding anniversary. When he arrived at the airport, he learned that his flight had been canceled due to a rain storm. The next flight out was the following evening, which would have caused him to miss the anniversary party. He opted to rent a car and drive seven hours through the night to get home in time for the party. Now, however, he wants a $392 refund ($292 for the one-way plane ticket he did not use and $100 for the car rental).

Unfortunately, your hands are tied. The ticket receipt does clearly state that tickets are not refundable because air travel is sometimes affected by factors beyond the control of Cross Country Airlines. Cross Country Travel reimburses the cost of a missed flight only if the airline has made an error it could have avoided, if the passenger has a documented medical emergency, or if the passenger has paid a $150 flight insurance fee. And you never reimburse a rental vehicle—renting a vehicle is the customer's choice. Though you can understand Jeremy's desire to get home for his parents' anniversary, the truth is that Cross Country Airlines did all it could to get people on flights. You simply are not allowed to give refunds in such cases. However, you are allowed to give a coupon toward the customer's next flight with you.

Respond to Mr. Ellison's complaint, trying to the best of your ability to restore good relations with him.

14. **Rejecting a Late-Charge Claim:** You are a branch manager for a large bank. On July 1 the bank began assessing a $15 surcharge to all debit cards that had not been used in six months. The $15 fee was deducted from cardholders' checking or savings accounts. Eight weeks before the July 1 deadline, the bank's customer service department sent letters to all debit cardholders whose cards had been inactive telling them that if they didn't use their cards by July 1, they would be assessed the $15 fee. Customers were also told that if they no longer wished to have the card, they were to call an 800 number to deactivate it. In addition, all cardholders were reminded that after July 1, they had to use their cards at least once every six months to avoid the fee. The notice was also placed on cardholders' monthly statements, posted on the bank's website, included in the bank's quarterly newsletter, and advertised in branch office lobbies.

After July 1 customers with unused cards were assessed the $15 fee. Many customers who somehow missed the notices of the policy change called customer service to express their anger and disappointment. Once the customer service representatives reminded these customers of the multiple notices regarding the fee, most grudgingly accepted that they should have paid more attention.

One particularly angry customer, though, was not satisfied with this explanation. After her phone call to customer service, Laura Nelson wrote a letter to you, the branch manager, saying that the bank had done an insufficient job in informing customers of the fee. She said a phone call would have been the best way to let her and others know, and she wants the $15 fee returned to her account. She says that if you don't give her the $15, she will take her accounts elsewhere.

You believe that the bank did all it could do to inform the customers. Making phone calls to all of them would have been unreasonable and inefficient. Besides, in a society where phone scams and financial fraud are becoming common, would she have thought a voice message about a $15 fee on a debit card was credible? Write a response to Ms. Nelson denying her request to return the $15 to her account. Retain her goodwill so that she does not take her accounts to another bank.

15. **Rejecting a Claim for a Registration Refund:** You are a manager for Renata's, a large upscale bar and grill. During the summer months, you sponsor a 10K charity fun run. Each year you donate the proceeds to a different charity. This year the proceeds go to the United Way and the Waite City Free Clinic. Runners pay a $50 registration fee to participate in the event. The fee covers Renata's costs: insurance, liability, security, water, and promotional materials. Though you'll let people register for the run at any time, including the day of the event, you do not refund the registration fee after March 15 for any reason. You need to know your budget,

and adjusting credit card charges or handling cash for anyone who wanted a refund would be too time consuming.

Today (May 5) you received an email from Oliver Shand. He paid the $50 registration fee on February 2. He broke his ankle on February 24. He thought he would be healed in time to participate, but he just has not had time to do the rehabilitation and training he will need to participate in the run. He wants his card credited for $50. You're a runner, and you empathize with him, but he should have requested the refund when he broke his ankle. Besides, you think it's pretty cheap and a little tacky that he would want a refund for what is essentially a charitable donation (which, by the way, he will still get a receipt for so that he can claim a tax deduction). You are going to deny his request, using critical thinking and problem-solving skills to explain why the fee is nonrefundable after March 15 and to help him feel more positive about your keeping his money.

16. **Denying a Claim for Damages:** You work in customer service at the headquarters of Petro Company, a large chain of gas stations. Today you must answer a complaint that you received from a customer whose car was damaged by the automatic car wash at one of your stations. When the car went through the wash, the whirling brush on the driver's side broke the mirror. The customer says that when he complained to the manager on duty at the station, she called his attention to the sign at the entry to the car wash stating that Petro would not be responsible for any damage to the cars. She also noted that the sign says to fold in the mirrors of the car before entering the car wash. When the customer explained that his mirrors do not fold in, the manager said she was sorry but that there was nothing she could do. Using a link on your company's website, the customer has written the company an email message. He feels that your car washes should be safe for cars like his, and he wants you to pay $100 toward repairing the damaged mirror. Write a response in which you refuse his request. The best you can do in cases like this is attach a coupon good for $10 at any of your stations' stores.

17. **Writing a Form Letter for Denying Refund Requests:** You're a new hire in the customer service office at the headquarters of a large bookstore that sells both online and in brick-and-mortar stores. Your boss comes into your office to discuss a situation with you. "We just got another return and refund request from a customer who has waited too long to get her money back. We try to make sure people know that they have only 14 days to return an item for refund or credit—I mean, the policy is on all our receipts and on our website. And if they ask for the refund within the time limit, they can even return their purchase to a nearby store rather than having to pay for shipping it back to us. But we still get these tardy returns from some people. Then we have to figure out what to do with the returned merchandise. We've been giving store credit, which is easier than mailing back the return, but I've had it. From now on, when we receive late returns, we're going to send these customers an email message (if the merchandise was purchased online) or a letter (if we don't have an email address) saying that they should have read the policy and that we have no choice but either to keep what they sent, for no credit, or to send it back to them with a charge for the return shipping, which will have to be paid in advance by credit card."

You correctly guess what's coming next. "Will you draft a form letter that we can send to people when this happens? Of course, you should say everything nicely. But they don't understand that our refund policy helps us save money, which then lets us offer benefits like free two-day shipping for members and discounted products. It's all been carefully costed out, and absorbing the cost for returns made after 14 days is not part of the plan." This task is certainly a challenge—but you believe you're up for it. Draft a message that will convey the negative news, convince customers that your policy is reasonable, and impress your boss.

Negative Announcements

18. **Changing the Rules for Professional Development:** Your company, MediTech, is an industry leader in manufacturing cardiac medical devices. MediTech lets its 20 senior management staff attend one professional development activity a year (e.g., an annual professional conference, continuing education) anywhere in the United States for up to five days. The senior managers really enjoy this program because it provides a break in their routine and lets them travel, network, and build their knowledge of the latest industry trends and products.

However, business has not been good this past year, so the company has decided to save money by limiting travel for these activities to within 150 miles of the office. The company also will not pay for hotel stays or any registration fees over $100. When the alternatives are layoffs, increased employee contributions toward health insurance, switching to an employee health insurance plan with less coverage, or eliminating sales performance bonuses, cutting this policy seems like one way to save money without affecting everyone in the company. If senior managers want to take vacation time or pay for activities beyond what the company covers, they certainly may.

As MediTech's budget director, you know senior managers will be upset. The policy has been around so long that some even see this policy as a right and a status symbol rather than a privilege. Some others may wonder how they will maintain their skills or network with others in their fields. They certainly won't want to pay for these activities themselves. Write a message to your senior management staff explaining why the new professional development restrictions are in place. Appeal to their management expertise so that they see this as a good business decision. Provide alternatives for networking and developing their skills.

19. **Curbing Expenses When Thanking Clients:** You're a regional manager for Arch Insurance, Inc., whose specialty is corporate travel and personal accident policies. Most of your company's revenue comes from selling policies to businesses and other organizations that need to cover their employees when they're at work or traveling. Just now you were reprimanded by your boss for excessive expenditures for wining and dining clients. She says that the seven agents who work for you spent over $9,000 last quarter taking representatives of companies, hospitals, and other organizations out to lunch and dinner, either to thank them for their business or attract them as customers. Sure, landing even one good contract with a large organization can mean thousands of dollars for the company, and representatives of a company that caters to businesses can't afford to look "cheap." But you have to agree that things have gotten out of hand. Your boss says that many of the receipts are for the most expensive restaurants in the area and for such extravagant purchases as $150 bottles of wine. This has got to stop. There are plenty of elegant ways to say "thank you" or to appeal to a client besides spending money excessively.

Using your good problem-solving skills, think about how to advise your employees. Then write the negative announcement that will change their behavior but also maintain their goodwill and their drive to succeed.

20. **Addressing Social Networking at Work:** Assume that you are the _____ (you choose the supervisory position) of a small (you choose the type) company or department. More and more, you've noticed, when walking past employees' cubicles and offices that a social networking site such as Facebook, Instagram, or LinkedIn is up on the screen. You've read some articles pointing out that social networking on the job can be quite a drain on employees' productivity, and you worry that this is happening in your company (have you noticed any lapse in performance lately?). You think the time has come to send an email to the employees advising them to limit their use of social networking on the job.

The thing is, you know that social networking does also bring certain company benefits. You don't want to have the IT person block or monitor the use of social networking sites, nor do you want a strict policy that will actually be counterproductive. So you're going to try to get people to monitor themselves. Think carefully about what you want the employees to do and why (for example, instead of doing social networking, what should they be doing?). Then write the message that will get them to change their behavior.

21. **Announcing That Employees Must Now Buy Their Own Smartphones:** You're an employee-relations specialist in the HR department of a large hospital. Until now, all employees who need to be able to check their email on the go—administrators and managers, physicians, nurse practitioners (NPs), physician's assistants (PAs), and tech services—have been able to have their cell phones covered in one of two ways:

1. Use a cell phone provided by the company (an iPhone or an Android-based phone) for their business messages and have the company pay the bill each month.

2. Use their own smartphones and get reimbursed for their total phone usage by emailing their bills to someone in the accounting office each month.

An attractive feature of the first option is that employees are given free phone upgrades and tech support, but the downsides are that they have to use one of the two models being offered, and they have to carry two phones (one for work; one for personal use). The attractive features of the other option are that people can use phones of their choice and they can get reimbursed for their whole phone bill. But to protect the security of work messages, they have to download an app to their personal phones that locks the phone and requires them to use a password to unlock it, as well as have their phones encrypted by IT; and submitting the phone bill for reimbursement each month is a bit of a hassle. Plus, not everyone wants to have their work messages mixed in with their personal messages.

The hospital is now eliminating the first option. Having everyone on the same plan will be simpler, and the hospital will save money by not having to buy expensive phones and by recovering some of the employee hours that it's taking to offer two options. Now you must send a message to all the affected employees to let them know.

22. **Enforcing a Three-Strikes Policy:** You are the office manager at Marion Dental Health Center. (With your instructor's permission, choose a different business or organization that serves its customers through scheduled appointments.) The center's policy is "three strikes and you're out"—that is, if a patient breaks three appointments without advance notice, the patient is not allowed to make any further appointments.

While most people will call in advance to reschedule an appointment, others just don't show up. Until now, you have dealt with patients informally when they skip an appointment, and you have never held them accountable. You know issues arise that prevent people from attending their appointments. When these issues arise, you understand that canceling a dental appointment is not something the patient thinks about first. However, you have started to feel as though some patients are taking advantage of your goodwill. You also think patients don't understand that not canceling an appointment in advance means you lose revenue and cannot give the appointment to someone who could use it. The dentists and hygienists, too, are tired of dealing with these no-shows. You and the clinic staff have decided to let patients know you will start enforcing your three-strikes policy.

Think carefully about the facts you'll need to include in order to justify your policy. You do not want to alienate the patient; you want patients to understand that this policy helps you be more efficient and serve them better. As your instructor directs, write this message as a form letter and as an announcement on your website. Chapter 3 can help you address special considerations for electronic messages.

23. **Announcing a Reduction in Staff:** You were recently promoted to a managerial position in the technology services department of a large manufacturing company that operates around the clock. Now you're facing your first real challenge in this position: You've been told that, for cost-cutting purposes, the two positions that were recently vacated in your work group (one employee moved away and another left to work for a different company) will not be filled in the foreseeable future, so the group will have to make do with its three remaining members, whose responsibilities will increase. It's your job to tell them so.

Before two employees left, each employee in the group would be on call one week out of every five weeks. Now the remaining three employees have had to be on call for two weeks, off call for three weeks, and then back on call again. This presumably temporary schedule will become the norm. Another issue is that the five-person group had sufficient work to do, so the three employees who are left have experienced an increase in their workloads that will continue.

At least you can tell them that they'll each be receiving a 4% salary raise and that some of their work will be offloaded to other groups. Plus, in light of their increased responsibilities, you'll now act as gatekeeper to their services. Until now, anyone in the company with a technology issue or question could contact the group members directly, and this would go on constantly. Now, all tech requests for your group will need to go through you for prioritizing and screening. Also, each department that uses your services will be asked to collect and prioritize their tech needs each week and submit them all at once, rather than having the requests constantly trickling in (exceptions will be granted for emergencies). You'll also tell your employees that they should let you know if they become overworked or are having other difficulties so that you can address these issues as they arise.

24. **Making Do with Old Computers:** You work as an administrative intern for Peck and Briggs, a small but well-respected public accounting firm located in Cleveland, Ohio. Traditionally, Peck and Briggs has replaced its employees' computers on a rotating schedule every three years.

But the recession has required some cost-cutting measures, and those who are waiting for replacement computers will now need to wait another year before receiving their upgraded computers. In addition, everyone in the firm will need to be advised that computers will now be replaced on a four-year, not three-year, schedule. This means that they will need to make do with the Microsoft Office suite that is on their current computers, since that software is upgraded only when the computers are replaced. (This issue will not affect the accounting software, since the firm uses Intact.com, a cloud-based software service, rather than software on their own computers.) Your task is to draft a message for Mr. Peck, senior partner, to send to all employees informing them of the new policy.

25. **Borrowing Equipment:** You work for Edwards Manufacturing, a large company that makes parts for heating and cooling systems. Lately, you have been having a seemingly small but incredibly irritating problem: People cannot seem to remember (or take the time) to return the things they borrow from various conference rooms scattered throughout your building. For example, you attended a meeting in one where people didn't have a place to sit because someone moved chairs to another conference room and didn't put them back. And then the leader of the meeting went to use the whiteboard only to find all of the working markers gone; only the ones that didn't work were left. The meeting was delayed 15 minutes while people roamed the halls and traveled to other floors to locate chairs and markers. Finding borrowed chairs or other equipment when it is scattered throughout the company is time consuming and inefficient, especially when the people who borrowed it could much more easily return it.

You also see this as an issue of consideration and good manners. If everyone would just return what they borrow, you could all be happier and more efficient in your work.

You have talked to your facilities manager, who agrees that this has become a serious issue. She asks you to draft an announcement for her to send to employees explaining the issue and announcing a new policy. If people absolutely need to borrow equipment from a room, they need to check the room reservation calendar (available in Outlook) to see if anyone is using the room. If someone is using the room, people need to check with that person before borrowing any equipment. Regardless of whether anyone is using the room, people who remove equipment from a room must use a signout sheet available in each conference room; they also need to return the equipment after they use it.

As you write the message, remember some of your co-workers do not use the room or are good about returning what they borrow. Also think about the reasons your co-workers may not return what they borrow. Are you sure it is because they are inconsiderate or lack manners?

26. **Explaining a Delayed or Canceled Order:** You're a communications intern at J. J. Brown's, a mail-order clothing and camping gear store, and you've been asked to revise the messages the company sends to customers whose orders have been delayed or canceled. When a customer calls to place an order, the call center representative checks to see that each item being ordered is available, but if other customers are requesting the same item at around the same time, the computer shows the items to be in stock even though an item is sold out. Sometimes when this happens, you can tell customers that more of the desired item is being ordered and give them an estimated delivery date. Other times, when the item is gone, it's permanently gone, which is especially likely with clearance items.

Your boss feels that the current form emails informing customers of canceled or delayed orders are too stiff and impersonal. After all, the goods your company sells are associated with fun and adventure. The revised messages shouldn't be too cheerful (after all, they are bad-news messages), but they should convey a more positive image.

Write the two messages that are needed, one for canceled orders and one for delayed orders. In your messages, leave blanks where information specific to each order will be included and indicate in brackets what kind of information that will be.

27. **Getting Rid of Unlimited Vacation:** About 10 years ago your company adopted an unlimited vacation policy for all of its salaried employees. The terms of the policy are simple: As long as employees get their work done and as long as the work is of excellent quality, they can work whenever they wish.

Initially, this policy worked great! People were happy that for the most part they could basically set their own schedules. Employees felt trusted and empowered and as a result seemed to be highly motivated and productive. They also felt they had a better balance between their work and personal lives.

Ten years into the policy, however, you've noticed a change. Some employees never take time off. Others are taking more time off than ever, and while most work seems to get done, it does not always get done, nor does it get done with a high quality. In fact, the balance between work and personal lives seems to have become skewed in favor of employees' personal lives. Plus, with so many people taking unlimited vacation, it is hard for managers to schedule and manage the workload.

In short, the employees you have today do not seem to be able to handle the same responsibility of unlimited vacation as your employees 10 years ago had. Regardless of whether this is a change in your employees or a change in the nature or volume of work, you know the time has come to change the policy. Employees will now have to request vacation time. The amount of vacation they are allowed in a year will depend on the number of years they have worked for the company and whether they work full or part time.

Having a vacation policy does have its benefits. Because such policies are somewhat governed by law, employees can get paid for unused vacation time if they leave the company. In addition, you hope a formalized policy will encourage those who rarely use vacation to take time to recharge and relax. And as many employees know, when they take unlimited vacation time, many are still responding to work emails, calling in to the office, or doing some work at home. You think having a set vacation time will let employees take real vacations, as the office will be able to plan better for their absence.

Draft an announcement to employees that explains the policy change. Announce, also, that there will be information sessions in the coming weeks to explain the policy, the amount of vacation employees receive, and the procedure for requesting vacation time.

28. **Discontinuing a Double Coupon:** Revise the following negative announcement to improve the organization, content, tone, grammar, punctuation, and mechanics.

> Dear Valued Quality Food Mart Customers; Due to the fact that some customers have recently abused our coupon policy, effective immediately we are prohibiting the use of double coupons, this includes any use of any coupon with another coupon or using any coupon with sale items that do not require a coupon.

> What this does mean is you using only one coupon on an item or getting only the sale price for your grocery items. Not using more than one coupon or using a coupon with an item already on sale. We will still take all manufacturers coupons and store coupons. Just not more than one at a time and not for an item on sale.

> We are doing this because people use coupons in a manor for which they are not intended. Due to the popularity of reality shows such as "Coupon Frenzy" where people compete using coupons to see how much groceries they can get for free or not a lot of cost. We cannot do this and remain in business, we must manage how we and customers use coupons so that we can serve you better.

> Thank you for your understanding. Please feel free to contact us if you have any questions. We apologize for any inconvenience this may cause you

Writing Persuasive Messages and Proposals

© Stockbyte/Getty Images

Chapter Ten

Everything you write on the job will have some kind of persuasive purpose—to convince the reader of your professionalism, convey an appealing company image, promote good relations, or all of these. But in some situations, persuasion will be your central goal. In these cases, your readers will hold a certain position, and your task will be to move them from this position to one that is more favorable to you and/or your company. Meeting this challenge requires careful analysis, strategic thinking, and skillful writing.

But the rewards of persuasive communication are many. Read on to see how to boost your persuasion savvy.

Learning Objectives

LO10-1 Describe important strategies for writing any persuasive message.

LO10-2 Write skillful persuasive requests that begin indirectly, develop convincing reasoning, request action, and close with goodwill.

LO10-3 Show awareness of common ethical concerns regarding sales messages.

LO10-4 Describe the planning steps for direct mail or email sales messages.

LO10-5 Compose sales messages that gain attention, present persuasive appeals, use appropriate visual elements, and effectively call for action.

LO10-6 Integrate the Internet and social media into your sales efforts.

LO10-7 Write well-organized and persuasive proposals.

Approaches to Writing Persuasive Messages and Proposals

In the broadest sense, **persuasive messages** are intended to get readers or listeners to part with some of their resources—whether time, money, attention, an emotional investment, or something else they would have done—in exchange for something we're offering them. According to research conducted by entrepreneur and sales guru Daniel Pink, about one in nine people identify as salespeople in the United States (based on the U.S. Bureau of Labor Statistics), but the rest of us spend about 40% of our time "persuading, influencing, and convincing others in ways that don't involve selling." In other words, "Whether it's selling's traditional form or its non-sales variation, we're all in sales now."[1]

Photo courtesy of Daniel Pink. Photo by Rebecca Drobis.

"We're all in sales now."

Daniel H. Pink
Former speechwriter for Al Gore
Author of five books on business trends

This is an important insight to keep in mind as you read this chapter. The content will focus on the main types of persuasive writing in the workplace. But as you learn about these, you can also pick up tips about how to persuade or influence in more ordinary, spontaneous ways.

We begin by discussing **overtly persuasive messages**. By definition, these are messages that are written to potentially uncooperative readers, people who need to be convinced to do as you ask. For this reason, it is often best to organize these persuasive messages in an **indirect order**. Preparing the reader to accept your idea is a much better strategy than announcing the idea from the start and then having to argue uphill through the rest of the message. Ideally, you should organize each persuasive message so that, from the title or subject line to the end, your readers will agree with you. If you try to have them on your side from start to finish, you'll have your best chance of success.

Another form of persuasion is even more indirect: **content marketing**. This is a relatively new but hugely popular kind of selling, and it actually does no overt selling at all. Instead, the goal is to build awareness of and respect for a company's brand by sharing interesting, helpful information. The reader may thus be motivated to go to where the company *is* selling, such as on its website, to learn more and perhaps make a purchase.

Although indirectness is appropriate for many persuasive messages, sometimes you will want to use the **direct order**. Such will be the case if you believe your reader is already inclined toward doing what you're requesting (for example, joining the Relay for Life team when they've done so for several years) or if the reader has been previously prepared to receive the request. Proposals that are written in response to specific invitations fall into this latter category.

In the following pages we first provide general advice for effective persuasion of any kind. We then discuss two common types of overtly persuasive messages: the persuasive request and the sales message. Next we look at how companies are using multiple media in their marketing efforts, including content marketing. Lastly, we cover another important category of persuasive writing: proposals.

General Advice about Persuasion

LO10-1 Describe important strategies for writing any persuasive message.

All our previous advice about adapting your messages to your readers comes into play with persuasive messages—only more so. Moving your reader from an uninterested or even resistant position to an interested, cooperative one is a major accomplishment. To achieve it, keep the following advice in mind.

Know Your Readers

For any kind of persuasive message, thinking about your subject from your readers' point of view is critical. To know what kind of appeals will succeed with your readers, you need to know as much as you can about their values, interests, and needs. Companies' marketing departments sometimes spend a great deal of money to acquire this kind of information. Using a variety of research techniques, they gather **demographic information** (such as age, gender, income, and geographic location) and **psychographic information** (such as social, political, and personal preferences) about their target audience. They also develop mailing lists based on prior shows of interest from consumers and purchase mailing lists from other organizations that have had success with certain audiences.

If you don't have these resources, you can use other means to learn as much as possible about the intended readers. You can talk with customer service about the kinds of calls they're getting, study the company's customer database, chat with people around the water cooler or online, and run ideas past colleagues. Good persuasion depends on knowledge as well as on imagination and logic.

Choose and Develop Targeted Reader Benefits

No one is persuaded to do something for no reason. Sometimes their reasons for acting are related to **tangible** (or measurable) **rewards**. For example, they will save money, save time, or acquire some kind of desired object. But often, the rewards that persuade are **intangible**. People may want to make their lives easier, gain prestige, or have more freedom. Or perhaps they want to identify with a larger cause, feel that they are helping others, or do the right thing. In your quest for the appeals that will win your readers over, do not underestimate the power of intangible benefits, especially when you can pair them with tangible rewards.

When selecting the **reader benefits** to feature in your persuasive messages, bear in mind that such benefits can be built into what you're selling, added on as an incentive, or both. **Product benefits** are benefits that readers will get automatically by complying with your request. For example, if you are trying to persuade people to attend your company's awards dinner, the pleasure of sharing in their colleagues' successes will likely be the main built-in benefit. Door prizes would be an **added-on benefit**. We might classify the meal itself as a combination—not really the main feature of the event but definitely central to it. In most cases, the product benefits should do the main persuasive work because they build more loyalty to your product. Added-on benefits are more short lived, and relying too much on them can actually cheapen your product or service in the readers' eyes.

When presenting your reader benefits, be sure the readers can see exactly how the benefits will help them. The literature on selling makes a useful distinction between **product features** and reader benefits. If you say that a wireless service uses a certain kind of

Knowing your readers enables you to target their interests.
© Brand X/Stockbyte/Getty Images

Added-on benefits like giveaways can add incentive, but the product benefits are usually stronger.
© David Zalubowski/AP Images

Painting a vivid scene of the reader enjoying the benefits can help you persuade.
© Ralph Henning/Alamy

technology, then you're describing a feature. If you say that the technology results in fewer missed or dropped calls, then you're describing a benefit. Benefits persuade by enabling readers to envision the features of the recommended product or action in their own worlds.

One common technique for achieving this goal is to use what we call **scenario painting**—a description that pictures the reader in a sample situation enjoying the promised benefits. Here is an example of scenario painting from a website promoting a tour of Warner Brothers Studio:

> Led by our top tour guides, this exclusive tour takes you into the craft shops where artisans create sets, props, costumes and more. You'll visit working production sets to talk to key crew people, watch as Foley artists create sound effects for film and TV, and get an up close and personal look at the magic of movie making. In addition, your private group will dine in the studio commissary where you have the real opportunity to dine with the stars.

Scenario painting is common in sales messages, but you can also use it to good advantage in other persuasive messages—even internal ones. Whatever your persuasive situation or strategy, be sure to provide enough detail for readers to see how they will benefit from what you are asking them to do.

Make Good Use of Three Kinds of Appeals

The first acknowledged expert on persuasion, the Greek philosopher Aristotle, lived almost 2,500 years ago, but many of his core concepts are still widely taught and used. Of particular value is his famous categorizing of persuasive appeals into three kinds, summarized in Exhibit 10-1: those based on **logic (*logos*)**, those based on **emotion (*pathos*)**, and those based on the **character (*ethos*)** of the speaker. All three kinds come into play in every persuasive message—in fact, one might say, in every kind of message. But as the writer of a persuasive message, you will need to think especially carefully about how to manage these appeals and which ones to emphasize given your intended audience.

Exhibit 10-1	The Three Main Types of Persuasive Appeals

- Logical (*logos*)—makes a rational argument
- Emotional (*pathos*)—arouses certain feelings and values
- Character based (*ethos*)—projects appealing traits of the writer or speaker

As you plan your message, consider what kind of logical appeals you might use. Saved money? Saved time? A more dependable or effective product? How about emotional appeals? Higher status? More sex appeal? Increased popularity? And don't neglect appeals based on character. What kind of image of yourself and your company will resonate with the reader? Should you get a celebrity or expert to endorse your product or to serve as the spokesperson? Not only when planning but also when revising your persuasive message, assess your appeals. Be sure to choose and develop the ones most likely to persuade your audience.

Make It Easy for Your Readers to Comply

Sometimes writers focus so much on creating persuasive appeals that they put insufficient thought into making the requested action as clear and easy to perform as possible. If you want people to give money or buy your product, tell them where and how to do it, and supply a preaddressed mailing envelope or a Web address if applicable. If you want employees to give suggestions for improving products or operations, tell them exactly where and how to submit their ideas, and make it easy for them to do so. If you want people to remember to work more safely or conserve on supplies, give them specific techniques for achieving these goals and include reminders at the actual locations where they need to remember what to do. Making the desired action specific and easy to perform is a key part of moving your readers from resistance to compliance with your request.

With this general advice in mind, we now turn to the four main types of persuasive writing in business: persuasive requests, sales messages, multimedia selling, and proposals.

Persuasive Requests

At many points in your career—starting with your job search—you will need to make **persuasive requests**. Perhaps, as in the Problem-Solving Challenge "Raising Funds for a Worthy Cause," you will be asked to write a fundraising message. Perhaps you will need to ask your management for another staff position or for special equipment. You may need to persuade a potential client to join you in a meeting so that you can demonstrate the benefits of your products. Or maybe you will be trying to persuade your employees to change their behavior in some way.

Whether written to internal or external readers, requests that are likely to be resisted require an indirect, deliberate approach. In essence, you must persuade the reader that he or she should grant your request before you actually state it. Such an achievement requires that you carefully plan your persuasive strategy.

LO10-2 Write skillful persuasive requests that begin indirectly, develop convincing reasoning, request action, and close with goodwill.

Problem-Solving Challenge

Raising Funds for a Worthy Cause

You're a mid-level manager for Arslan, one of the largest custodial services companies in your city. Like many others in the company, you devote some of your personal time to serving the community. Arslan wants you to do this volunteer work for the sake of good public relations, and you want to do it because it is personally and professionally rewarding.

Currently, as chair of the fundraising committee of the city's Junior Achievement program, you head all efforts to get financial support for the program from local businesspeople. The committee can contact some of these potential donors by phone, but there are too many for you to be able to reach all of them this way.

At its meeting today, the Junior Achievement board of directors discussed various solutions. One director suggested using a fundraising letter. The board accepted the idea with enthusiasm.

Because you're the fundraising chair, the job of writing this letter fell to you.

You'll need to think carefully about your approach. Although the local businesspeople are probably generous, they are not likely to part with money without good reason. In fact, their first reaction to a request for money is likely to be negative. So you will need to overcome their resistance in order to persuade them. Your task is indeed challenging.

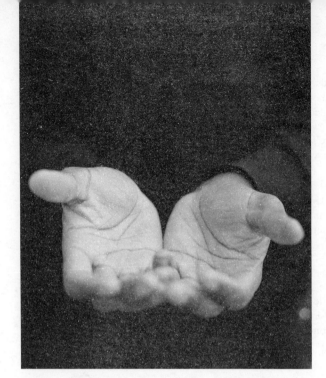

Many times in your career you will need to ask for something, whether for yourself, your company, or a cause you support. The techniques in this chapter will help you get a positive response.

© Image Source/Getty Images

Determining Your Strategy

Figuring out the best persuasive approach involves three interrelated tasks: determining what you want, figuring out your readers' likely reactions, and deciding upon a persuasive strategy that will overcome reader objections and evoke a positive response.

Think carefully about your actual goals for your persuasive request. A request for a one-time-only donation might be written very differently from a request that is intended to create a long-time, multiple donor. If you were convincing employees to leave the parking places next to the building for customers' use, you would write a very different message if it were the third rather than the first request. Your goals, considered in the context of your organization's goals and your relationship with your readers, are key shapers of your persuasive message.

To anticipate how your readers will react to your request, consider everything you know about them and then put yourself in their shoes. Look at the request as they are likely to see it. Figure out what's in it for them and how to overcome any objections they may have.

For example, you may be able to show that your reader stands to gain in time, money, or other tangible benefits. Or you may be able to show that your reader will benefit in goodwill or prestige. In some cases, you may persuade readers by appealing to their love of beauty, excitement, serenity, or other emotions. In different cases, you may be able to persuade readers by appealing to the pleasant feeling that comes from doing a good deed.

A special kind of persuasive request is one that casts the request as a problem–solution message. With this strategy, you first present a problem that you and the readers share—called the **common-ground persuasion technique**—and then show how doing as you propose will solve the problem for all concerned.

Many fundraising letters use this technique; they begin with striking facts about the current economic climate, the environment, or living conditions in a certain area of the world and then go on to say how we can help. But this strategy can also be a powerful one for internal audiences who might not be receptive to a straightforward proposal for action but who share your opinion that something needs to be done. If you begin with a description of the need for action, your readers will be better prepared to hear what action you recommend.

A persuasive request situation is a special opportunity for analysis, creativity, and judgment. With careful use of all three, you can plan messages that will change your readers' minds and move them to action.

Gaining Attention in the Opening

The opening of a persuasive request has two main goals: to gain attention and to lead into your central strategy.

You need to draw your reader in with the opening of your persuasive message because you are writing to a person who has not invited your message and may not agree with your goal. An interesting beginning is a good step toward getting this person in a receptive mood.

Determine what your reader will find compelling. It might be a statement that arouses curiosity, such as the following examples.

You Make the Call

Read the first Annotated Example at the end of this section (the persuasive internal request). If you were writing to your fellow employees as an employee who is in charge of the blood drive rather than as the company president, what would you do differently? Why? For example, would you still use the letter format? Would you use a different beginning and ending? Would you change anything in the middle?

From a letter raising money for an animal shelter:

> Thanks to SPCA, the holidays will be much brighter for a little guy named Dasher.

From a message asking readers to donate to a social cause:

> It's not fair!

From a message asking people to renew their membership with an athletic club:

> Sitting is the new smoking.

Because questions get people thinking, they are often effective openings. The following examples indicate the possibilities.

From the cover message of a questionnaire seeking the opinions of medical doctors:

> What's your preferred method for meeting your continuing education requirements each year?

From a message requesting that young alumni serve as mentors to current students:

> Do you remember how hard it was to figure out what you wanted to do when you grew up?

From a message seeking the cooperation of local businesses in promoting a fair:

> How could your business benefit if 300,000 visitors came to Metroville during a single week?

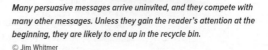

If writing your request in the form of a problem–solution message, you should start with a goal that you and the readers share. For example, let's say that a project manager in your company has retired and you want to recommend his capable administrative assistant as his replacement. Since no member of the support staff has ever broken into the managerial ranks, any direct proposal to promote your candidate will likely be resisted. To get readers on your side from the beginning, you could start your message with facts that everyone can agree upon: that someone has retired, that his or her duties are important, and that someone capable needs to be found quickly. Your subject line for an email along these lines might be something like, "Reassigning Jim Martin's Duties" (which everyone supports), not "Promoting Kathy Pearson" (which your readers would resist).

Many persuasive messages arrive uninvited, and they compete with many other messages. Unless they gain the reader's attention at the beginning, they are likely to end up in the recycle bin.
© Jim Whitmer

Whatever the case, the form of indirectness that you choose for your opening should engage your readers right away and get them thinking along the lines that will lead to their approval of your request.

Developing the Appeal

Following the opening, you present a compelling case for the readers to do as you ask. What you present will depend on the careful planning you've done.

As with any argument intended to convince, you'll need to develop your points with logical, engaging details. You'll also need to make good use of the you-viewpoint, of course, because readers will need to see why they should comply. You'll need to use logic and emotion appropriately and project an appealing image (see the Communication Matters feature "The Ingredients of Successful Fundraising" for a list of persuasive personal qualities). And because your reader will easily become impatient, you'll need to make every word contribute to your persuasive effort.

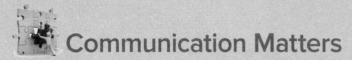

Making the Request Clearly and Positively

After you have done your persuading, it's time to move to the action you seek. If you have prepared the readers well, they should be ready to accept your request. But you need to word it carefully. Avoid words that suggest reasons for refusing, as in this example:

> I know that you are very busy, but will you please consider accepting an assignment to the board of directors of the Children's Fund?

Note how much more effective this positive wording will be:

> Your organizing skills and stature in the community would make you an ideal board member for the Children's Fund.

Whether your request should end your message will depend on the situation. In some cases, you may want to follow the request with additional persuasive material. In cases where your request is relatively simple, won't cost the reader much, and isn't likely to be resisted, you can end your message with the request. Whatever wording your choose, the ending should make the readers feel good about doing as you ask.

Reviewing the Strategy for Persuasive Requests

The general plan for persuasive requests can be summarized as follows:

• Open with words that (1) gain attention and (2) set up the strategy.

• Develop the strategy using persuasive language and the you-viewpoint.

• Make the request clearly and without negatives either (1) at the end of the message or (2) followed by words that continue the persuasive appeal.

Comparing Bad and Good Examples of a Persuasive Request

The persuasive request is illustrated by the following contrasting letters that ask businesspeople to donate to Junior Achievement. The first message is direct and bland. The second message, which follows the indirect approach and provides convincing details, is much more likely to succeed.

A Selfish, Blunt Approach   The weaker letter begins with the request. Because the requested action is something the reader probably doesn't want to do, the direct beginning is likely to get a negative reaction. In addition, the comments about how much to give tend to lecture rather than suggest. Some explanation follows, but it is weak and scant. In general, the letter is poorly written and makes little use of the you-viewpoint.

Dear Mr. Williams:

Will you please donate to the local Junior Achievement program? We have set $50 as a fair minimum for businesses to give. But larger amounts would be appreciated.

The organization badly needs your support. Currently, about 900 young people will not get to participate in Junior Achievement activities unless more money is raised.

If you do not already know about Junior Achievement, let me explain. Junior Achievement is an organization for high school students. They work with local business executives to form small businesses and then operate the businesses. In the process, they learn about our economic system. This is a good thing, and it deserves our help.

Hoping to receive your generous donation,

Jane Monroe

Skillful Persuasion Using the Indirect Order The following message uses the recommended indirect pattern. Its opening generates interest and sets up the persuasive strategy. Not until the reader has been sold on the merits of the request does the message make the request. It is followed by final words that leave the reader thinking about the benefits that a *yes* answer will give. Also note the effective use of the you-viewpoint throughout.

Dear Mr. Williams:

Right now—right here in our city—620 teenagers are running 37 corporations. The kids run the whole show; their only adult help comes from business professionals who work with them.

Last September these young people applied for charters and elected officers. Then they created plans for business operations. One group planned to build websites for local small businesses. Another elected to conduct a rock concert. Yet another planned to publish electronic newsletters for area corporations. After determining their plans, the kids issued stock—and sold it, too. With the proceeds from stock sales, they began their operations. This May they will liquidate their companies and account to their stockholders for their profits or losses.

What's behind these impressive accomplishments? As you've probably guessed, it's Junior Achievement. Since 1919, this nonprofit organization has been teaching school kids of all ages about business, economics, and entrepreneurship. Thanks to partnerships between volunteers and teachers, these students gain hands-on experience with real business operations while learning the fundamentals of economics and financial responsibility. They also learn cooperation and problem solving. It's a win–win situation for all involved.

To continue to succeed, Junior Achievement needs all of us behind it. During the 13 years the program has been in our city, it has had enthusiastic support from local business leaders. But with over 900 students on the waiting list, our plans for next year call for expansion. That's why, as a volunteer myself, I ask that you help make the program available to more youngsters by contributing $50 (it's deductible). By helping to cover the cost of materials, special events, and scholarships, you'll be preparing more students for a bright future in business.

Please make your donation now by completing our online contribution form at www.juniorachievement.org. You will be doing a good service—for our kids, for our schools, and for our community.

Best regards,

Jane Monroe

A Persuasive Internal Request (Asking Employees to Donate Blood)

The writer wants employees to participate in the company's annual blood drive. He needs to convince them of the importance of the drive and overcome their likely objections. This message will be embedded in an email message to the employees.

Department of Community Relations
Edison, Colorado 80864
(719) 777-4444
CommunityRelations@Amberly.com

February 27, 2017

Opens with an attention-getting, you-focused question

Did you help save Brad Meyer's life?

Uses a character-based appeal: invites the reader to identify with these "lifesavers"

A few years ago, an employee of Amberly was driving to a friend's wedding when an oncoming car, operated by a drunk driver, swerved across the center line. Brad doesn't remember the crash. But he does remember two months spent in the hospital, two months of surgery and therapy.

Tells an engaging story with specific details

Without the help of people like us, Brad would not have lived. Some Amberly employees save lives regularly. We're blood donors. Please be a lifesaver and join us on Friday, March 19, for Amberly's annual blood drive.

Your help is needed for a successful drive.

Avoids words such as "draw blood" or "needle" that would bring unpleasant thoughts to mind

Giving blood is simple. The entire process will take less than 45 minutes.

Giving blood is safe. Experienced health professionals from the Steinmetz Blood Center will be on site to conduct the procedure exactly as they would in a clinical setting.

Giving blood is convenient. The Steinmetz staff will be in Room 401, Building B, between 9:00 a.m. and 3:00 p.m. To save time, make an appointment to donate. Call the Steinmetz Blood Center at 569-1170.

Giving blood is important. Nobody knows who will need blood next, but one thing is certain—it will be available only if healthy, caring people take time to give it. Brad's accident required 110 units—more than 12 gallons—of blood. Because 110 people set aside 45 minutes, Brad Meyer has a lifetime of minutes to be grateful.

Addresses likely reader objections

Recalls the emotion-based opening and links it to a logical appeal: You or someone in your family might benefit

Take a few moments now to make your pledge on the reverse side of this letter. Then return it to the Community Relations department, Mail Location 12, by March 15.

Makes the requested action clear and easy

From Brad and from other families—like yours and mine—who might need it in the days to come,

Thank you,

John M. Piper

John M. Piper
President, Community Relations

Annotated Example

A Persuasive External Request (Asking Music Fans to Contribute to the Public Radio Station)

The writer of this message wanted the reader to renew her annual gift to the city's classical public radio station. The use of appealing details and a focus on emotional benefits are the main persuasive strategies here. The message came with a renewal card and a return envelope.

CINCINNATI PUBLIC RADIO

91.7 WVXU CINCINNATI   **WGUC 90.9**   **88.5** WMUB OXFORD

9 ************AUTO**3-DIGIT 452
Ms. Wendy Beckman
73 Thrall Street
Cincinnati, OH 45220-1916

Dear Ms. Beckman,

Paragraph uses emotional appeal and evidence that the station is popular.

This is the time of year when WGUC *sparkles*. Cincinnati Symphony concert broadcasts are back, last season's Cincinnati Opera performances make Friday nights more glamorous, and *Tunes from the Crypt* officially kicked off the season on Halloween.

Sensory details and examples of popular musical broadcasts create an appealing opening paragraph.

Every year we receive dozens of letters and emails from happy listeners who tell us WGUC's music selection makes November and December brighter:

Others' words add authenticity and concrete details.

"I am often awake in the wee small hours of the night, but I am never alone. There is that beautiful music that keeps me company. Thank you from the bottom of my heart..."
"I must tell you how fabulous your music leading up to Christmas & the week after was. It's nice that you play hymns as well as carols. I listened every day!"
"After a long day it was so relaxing to get into my car and listen to a soothing arrangement of "O Holy Night" on my drive home. Thanks!"

WGUC's music helps you relax after a long day; 90.9 keeps you company throughout the night; and classical music makes every morning better.

Paragraph makes good use of intangible benefits and the you-viewpoint.

Your annual renewal gift makes all of this possible.

Request comes after appealing details have done their work.

As you begin to prepare for the months ahead and your year-end contributions, I hope you will include WGUC at the top of your list. *Please renew your support now, while you are thinking about it.* Use the enclosed envelope to return a check, or if you prefer, you can renew online or become a sustaining member at www.wguc.org <http://www.wguc.org>.

Readers are urged to act now and given a reason to do so.

Options for responding are clear and convenient.

We wish you a wonderful Thanksgiving with family and friends. Be sure to tune in for Mark Perzel's *A Feast for the Ears* on Thanksgiving morning at 10am - and *Giving Thanks* with John Birge at 6pm.

Ending fits the feel-good mood and add one last persuasive detail.

Sincerely,

Sherri V. Mancini
Vice President of Development

Problem-Solving Challenge

Generating More Customers for Your Business

Play the role of Zach Miller, a student in your university's college of business. You've had your own house-painting business ever since you started college. So far, you've gained your customers through word of mouth only, but you think it's time to expand.

You've got two buddies willing to come on board if you can generate enough business for them to work full time in the summer months and part time in the spring and fall. You've decided that your first step in growing the business will be to advertise your services to the faculty and staff of your school. After getting permission to post your message to the listservs of several offices and academic departments, you sit down to think through what you want to say.

Considering your audience, you decide to reveal to them that you're a student. Given the line of work they're in, your readers obviously like the feeling of helping young people succeed. On the other hand, you'll need to overcome any concern that the job you'll do will be less than professional. As you start figuring out your persuasive details, you realize that it may be a good idea to include links to other information. Hmmm . . . this message is going to take some careful planning in order to be effective. The following sections will help you think through your options.

Sales Messages

One of the most widely disseminated forms of business communication is the **sales message**. It is such an important component of most businesses' sales strategies that it has become an elaborate, highly professionalized genre, shaped by extensive consumer research. Think about the typical sales letter that you receive. Careful attention has been paid to the message on the envelope, to the kinds of pieces inside, and to the visual appeal of those pieces, as well as to the text of the letter itself. You can also see a professional's hand in many of the sales emails that appear in your in-box and in other sales communications, such as blog posts, Facebook pages, and white papers.

Even if you're not going into marketing, you will often find yourself in the position of helping to shape a major sales campaign or contribute to its success through social networking. You may also have valuable insight to share about your product's benefits and your potential customers.

In addition, as we've said, knowledge of selling techniques can help you in many of your other professional activities. There will be an element of "selling" in much of the communicating you do.

Questioning the Ethics of Sales Messages

Sales messages are a controversial area of business communication, for two main reasons: They are often unwanted, and they sometimes use ethically dubious persuasive tactics. You probably know from your own experience that sales letters are not always received happily. Called "junk" mail, these mailings often go into the wastebasket or recycle bin without being read. They are still heavily used, though, because, especially when combined with other sales strategies or sent to certain kinds of readers, they work. (See the Communication Matters feature "Are Sales Letters Becoming Extinct? Absolutely Not!")

Email sales messages are often unwelcome, too. Referred to as **spam**, unsolicited email sales messages have generated strong resistance among email users. They clutter up people's in-boxes, waste people's time, and invade their personal space. They also place a heavy burden on Internet providers, driving up costs to the users.

Fortunately, a more acceptable form of email selling has developed. Called **permission-based email**, it permits potential customers to sign up for email promotions on a company's website or provide their email addresses to an email or phone marketer. The potential customers may be asked to indicate the products, services, and specific topics of their interest, or the company may be able to track those interests based on what the customer has searched for or ordered in the

Communication Matters

Are Sales Letters Becoming Extinct? Absolutely Not!

You might be wondering if digital media are making sales letters obsolete. While the overall volume of sales mailings has declined, print sales messages still justify big spending, as these sources explain:

- According to the results of a survey conducted by the Direct Marketing Association (DMA), 42% of those who receive direct mail either read or scan it. Those between 45 and 54 are most likely to respond, but the older groups and those between 18 and 21 also have strong response rates. The response rate is better when the mail comes from a business where the recipients were previously customers, and people tend to now favor postcards over letters. ("6 Significant Statistics from the DMA on the Current State of Direct Mail," Eleventy Marketing Group, June 10, 2015, accessed March 21, 2016, http://eleventygroup.com/site/2015/06/10/significant-statistics-dma-direct-mail/.)

- According to the DMA's 2015 Response Rate Report, the direct mail response rate continues to outperform digital channels. Direct mail achieves a 3.7% response rate with a house list and a 1% response rate with a prospect list, whereas all digital channels combined only achieve a 0.62% response rate. (Debora Haskel, "2015 DMA Response Rate Report: Direct Mail Outperforms All Digital Channels Combined By Nearly 600%," IWCO Direct, accessed March 21, 2016, http://www.iwco.com/blog/2015/04/14/dma-response-rate-report-and-direct-mail/#sthash.GMFsGnQ4.dpuf.)

- An article in *Forbes* magazine reports that physical mail has certain advantages over electronic mail. It "leaves a 'deeper footprint' in the brain because it involves more emotional processing, connects better with readers' feelings, and evokes more emotionally vivid memories."

(Steve Olenski, "In This Land of Digital, Let's Not Forget the Physical," October 18, 2011, accessed March 21, 2016, http://www.forbes.com/sites/marketshare/2011/10/18/in-this-land-of-digital-lets-not-forget-the-physical/#5ec4d7e139fc.)

- A study by the marketing firm Epsilon found that "a majority of consumers still prefer postal mail for a large portion of their multichannel communication." Interestingly, their preferences for physical mail are stronger in some industries than in others, as shown in the chart below.

To be effective, though, sales mailings should be part of an integrated multichannel communication plan. Marketers continue to embrace multichannel marketing, with 44% of those who participated in the DMA survey saying that they use three or more channels period. (Haskel, "2015 DMA Response Rate.")

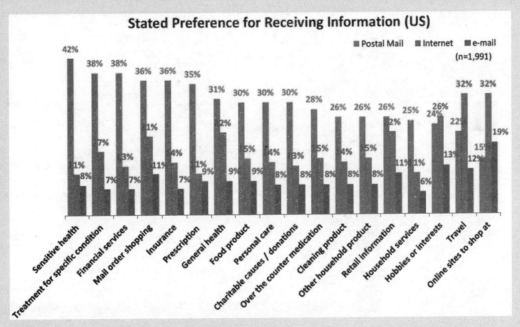

Source: Epsilon, *Channel Preferences for Both the Mobile and Non-Mobile Consumer, Print in the Mix,* December 3, 2012, accessed March 21, 2016, http://printinthemix.com/Fastfacts/Show/644.

LO10-4   Describe the planning steps for direct mail or email sales messages.

past. The marketers can then tailor their messages to the customer, and the customer will receive only what he or she wants.

As for the charge that persuasive messages use unfair persuasive tactics, this is, unfortunately, sometimes the case. The unfair tactics could range from deceptive wording and visuals to the omission of important information to the use of emotional elements that impair good judgment.

In a Missouri court case, Publishers Clearing House was found guilty of deception for direct mail stating that the recipients were already winners, when in fact they were not.[2] One linen supply company sent a letter to parents of first-year students at a university telling them that the students would need to purchase extra-long sheets, offered by this company, to fit the extra-long beds on campus—but omitted the fact that only one dorm out of four had such beds. And it is well documented that images, because they work on an emotional level, persuade in ways that tend to bypass the viewers' reasoned judgment, leading some to question the ethics of such elements.[3]

Certain kinds of online sales messages are particularly obnoxious, such as giant pop-ups that obscure the screen. Some of these trap readers in a loop that they can't exit without restarting their computers or, in extreme cases, paying for technical service.

Any persuasive message is, by its very nature, biased. The writer has a favored point of view and wants to persuade the reader to adopt it. Let your conscience be your guide as you consider how to influence your reader.

Preparing to Write a Sales Message

Before you can begin writing a sales message, you must know all you can about the product or service you are selling. You can't sell well unless you can tell your potential customers what they need to know.

It is especially important these days to know your product inside and out because many of your prospects will have already researched it themselves. The "information asymmetry" that used to characterize the seller-buyer conversation (the seller has more knowledge than the buyer) has shifted toward "information symmetry" (both parties are well informed). A positive effect of this

We've all encountered this unethical form of selling: the spyware ad that pops up and gives you no way to close it besides rebooting your computer . . . or sometimes even having the pesky malware removed by a tech expert.

Learn about e-Selling from Chief Marketer and MailChimp

The use of digital media for sales campaigns has grown enormously over the last several years because of the increased popularity of these media and the devices people use to access them. If you'd like to learn more about the complex art and science of e-marketing, read on.

Chief Marketer's website (www.chiefmarketer.com) has great information about using technology to conduct effective email, Web, social, and mobile campaigns. Their researchers have gathered statistics about consumer behavior regarding each medium and developed marketing strategies based on that behavior. If you've been wanting to go behind the scenes and see how the pros design electronic messages to sell through different channels, Chief Marketer is for you.

Chief !Marketer

Source: www.chiefmarketer.com

If you're particularly interested in writing effective sales emails, let MailChimp show you how. This company specializes in conducting email sales campaigns. You can access excellent material on their "Resources" page (mailchimp.com/resources), such as their guide to designing for mobile devices, mobile-friendly templates, and an "Email Marketing Benchmarks by Industry" report. Check out their "Subject Line Comparison," which examined the open rates of 40 million emails and compared the subject lines of the best and worst performers.

Source: mailchimp.com

---

trend is that many sellers now focus on showing how the product solves a prospect's problem rather than using gimmicky, high-pressure sales techniques.[4] In effect, they help the product sell itself.

As we have stressed, you must also study your readers. You should gather demographic, psychographic, and any other kind of information that will help you understand why they might want or need your product. The more you know about them, the better you will be able to adapt your sales message to them. (Read about consumers' media preferences by industry in the graphic at the bottom of the Communication Matters feature "Are Sales Letters Becoming Extinct? Absolutely Not!")

In large businesses, a marketing research department or agency typically gathers information about prospective customers. If you do not have such help, you will need to gather this information on your own, perhaps by purchasing an email list from another company or a market-research report.

But two of your best resources will be your own logic and imagination. Given what you know about your product, who would be likely to need or want it? In what ways would it make their lives better or

Begin work on a sales message by thoroughly studying the product or service you're selling.
© Juice Images / Alamy Stock Photo

solve a problem for them? Being able to imagine how they live now and how they'd live if they had your product is perhaps your best tool of all, because that is what will enable you to help them see how the product's benefits would play out in their own worlds. (See the Communication Matters feature "Take It from Web Developers: Personas Rock!" for a great tool to help you imagine your customer's perspective.)

To be able to choose the most persuasive channel for your message, familiarize yourself with all the sales media that are now available. As discussed later in this chapter, most companies use several media working together. Sales emails are often linked to websites, and websites often link to social networking sites and customized apps. You may even decide that the best approach is to start with an email and follow up with a phone call, or speak face to face with a prospect and then hand him or her some sales literature. There have never been so many media available, and the more you know about them, the better your selling can be.

Determining the Central Appeal

With your product or service, your prospects, and your medium or media in mind, you are ready to create the sales message. This involves selecting and presenting your persuasive appeals, whether emotional, logical, character based, or a combination. But for most sales messages, one appeal should stand out as the main one—mentioned in the beginning, recalled in the middle, and reiterated at the end. While other benefits can be brought in as appropriate, the message should emphasize your central, best appeal.

Emotional appeals—those based on our senses and emotions—can be found in almost any sales message, but they predominate in messages promoting intangible benefits, as in the following example:

> This special exhibit, 14 years in the making, features the works of Charles François Daubigny, a central figure in the development of 19th-century French landscape painting. He captured unique qualities of light and atmosphere, launched a floating studio that changed the way artists could frame their compositions, and became a mentor, colleague, and friend to the Impressionists. The 40 masterpieces in the exhibit showcase the full range of the artist's achievement, and a selection of 15 Impressionist and Post-Impressionist paintings by Claude Monet, Vincent Van Gogh, and Camille Pissarro attests to his influence.

Logical appeals are useful for selling products that help readers save money, do a better job, or get better use from a product. Illustrating a rational appeal (saving money) are these words from a message selling magazine subscriptions:

> And now you can subscribe for only $28, saving $40 off the newsstand price. That's 12 information-filled issues of *Science Digest* for only $2.33 a copy—and you can save even more by subscribing for 2 or 3 years.

Character-based appeals can enhance any kind of sales message. They persuade by stating or implying "I use this product, so you should, too" or "I am an authority, so you should do what I recommend." Ads that employ sports figures, film stars, or experts to sell their products are relying heavily on character-based appeals. Companies themselves often project an appealing "character" in their sales campaigns. Note how the following excerpt from a sales letter for *Consumer Reports* magazine uses the company's identity to persuade:

> *Consumer Reports* is on your side. We're a nonprofit consumer protection organization with no commercial interests whatsoever. To put it bluntly, we don't sell out to big companies and private interest groups—we're accountable to no one except to consumers. And when you're not beholden to advertisers (like other so-called consumer protection publications), you can tell it like it is.

People may also buy a certain product because they want to identify with, and be identified with, a certain successful, socially responsible, or "cool" company as projected in the company's sales messages.

A well-known spokesperson can add character appeal.
© Leonard Zhukovsky/Shutterstock

Communication Matters

Take It from Web Developers: Personas Rock!

A valuable tool in nearly every website developer's toolbox is the *persona*: a fictional character who represents an important segment of the developer's target population. To plan a website, a developer might create two, six, ten, or more personas, depending on the site's anticipated scope and purposes. Many others in marketing communications have also adopted this planning strategy.

Below is a sample persona that a delivery service for gourmet foods might use to capture one segment of its target audience.

As you can see, there's enough information here—including names and a photo—for the marketing team to think of these characters as real people. Taking the time to create such realistic representations of your readers can really pay off in the form of more compelling, on-target sales messages.

Carolyn and Mark Herbert: Young-Professional Foodies

AGE:	**Late 20s**
MARITAL STATUS:	**Married one year after living together for three years**
JOBS:	**Communications director for a local foundation (Carolyn); IT advisor for a hospital network (Mark)**
COMBINED ANNUAL INCOME:	**$120,000**

EDUCATION:
BA in English and MA in creative writing (Carolyn); BS in computer science (Mark)

HOBBIES:
Cooking, partying with friends, travel, playing with their cats, watching hip series and food shows on TV.

FOOD PREFERENCES:
Fresh ingredients, international cuisine, everything from beef tenderloin to sushi and vegetarian as long as it's delicious. Tend toward low-calorie ingredients but with the occasional dessert splurge. Prefer quality over quantity and stay away from "junk food." Want all the calories they consume to have a tasty pay-off.

BEVERAGE PREFERENCES:
Usually keep lite beer as well as specialty brands on hand. Enjoy a good glass of wine and will sometimes spend over $30 on a bottle.

GROCERY-SHOPPING QUOTE:
"We like to try new recipes from *Cooking Light* and *Bon Appetit* and invents ones like them on our own. We usually like dishes that don't take long to fix, but we'll go to considerable trouble to make things in the tastiest way. Fresh herbs are a must. We like to grill nice cuts of meat, fish, and handmade gourmet burgers, too—along with fresh veggies."

© Hero Images/Getty Images RF

In any given case, many appeals are available to you. You'll need to use those that fit your product or service and your readers best.

Determining the Makeup of the Mailing

When you write a sales message to be sent by mail or email, a part of your effort is to determine the makeup of the mailing. To know what you want to say in your main message, you'll need to decide what kinds of additional pieces will be included or linked to and the job each one should do.

Direct-mail messages can include many extras beyond the main message, as in this example from the National Audubon Society. Each piece needs to be carefully planned so that it will achieve its goal and work well with the other pieces.

Courtesy of Kathryn Rentz

For example, the letter featured in this section's second Annotated Example (the direct-mail message selling a management-training seminar) came with a second page that included a detailed agenda for the workshop as well as a list of management skills the attendees would learn. Moving this material to a second page enabled the writer to keep the letter itself relatively short and fast moving. Many sales and fundraising mailings are even more elaborate, including brochures, giveaways, order forms, and more. Even if you won't be designing the pieces yourself, you should plan, or work with others to plan, what should be included and why.

Email sales messages can use all the publishing features available on the computer. Like the Annotated Example featuring a sales email, the message can be presented creatively with color, font variations, box arrangements, artwork, and more. It may include links to the seller's website as well as to other supporting material and to the ordering procedure. And it may have attachments. As with a direct-mail package, the email sales package can use many elements to persuade and to provide all the information a reader will need in order to make a purchase.

Gaining Attention before the Message Begins

LO10-5 Compose sales messages that gain attention, present persuasive appeals, use appropriate visual elements, and effectively call for action.

Sales messages must gain the reader's attention right away; otherwise, they won't be read. For this reason, the sales effort often begins before the actual message does.

Many mailed messages have an attention getter on the envelope. It may be the offer of a gift ("Your gift is enclosed"). It may be a brief sales message ("12 months of *The Smithsonian* at 60 percent off the newsstand price") or even something as simple as "For a limited time only" or "A special offer for you." It may be a bit of art with a message (a picture of a cruise ship and the words "Your ship is waiting . . ."). Sometimes the envelope has a distinctive shape or color.

With email, the effort to gain attention begins with the *From* and *Subject* information. To reduce the chances of having the readers or their spam filters regard your message as spam (see Exhibit 10-2), write from an email address that identifies you and your company, and send your message to

---

Exhibit 10-2   Subject Lines That Sent These Emails to the Spam Folder

Here's a selection of subject lines for emails that a spam filter kept out of a recipient's in-box. What general guidelines for how *not* to write a sales subject line might you come up with by reading this list?

- Save Big $$$ on Every Home Warranty
- 7 Seconds to Get Your Libido Back!
- A Natural Solution without the Serious Side Effects
- ATTN: Your Reply (Business Proposal)
- ENCORE: BY POPULAR DEMAND!
- Avoid Costly Invasion of Privacy Suits
- Your Selection as a Top Female Executive: Confirm Today
- Lift Saggy Skin Without Surgery!
- [Name:] You may qualify for a reverse mortgage
- [Name:] Get Your $100 Gift Card! Expires Soon . . .

- Urgent Credit Card Debt Notice
- Auto Warranty Money Saving Coupons Enclosed
- Free Roof Coverage for You!
- [Name:] Extreme Grocery Savings: Just a Click Away
- Loan Offer: Apply Now
- CONQUER YOUR LIFE!
- Re:
- Hello.
- Mailbox helpdesk

each individual's address rather than to a large group of addresses (your e-marketing team can use a merge tool to help you do this).

Your subject line should be specific and short. It can be clever, but avoid such sensational wording as "How to earn $60,000 the first month" as well as all capital letters, exclamation points, dollar signs, and "free" offers. If you don't, you'll risk having spam filters block your message or send it to the recipient's junk folder. An email with the subject line "How to Make Your Kitchen More Efficient" that is sent to a researched list of restaurant managers and owners is much more likely to be opened and read than a message with the subject line "You have to read this!" that is sent to thousands of readers.

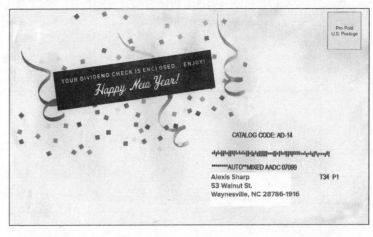

The envelope often begins the persuasive effort. A timely appeal and/or a giveaway can be especially effective.
Courtesy of Kathryn Rentz

Gaining Attention in the Opening of the Message

The first words of your message must also gain attention and motivate the reader to keep reading. What you do here can be creative, but the method you use should help set up the rest of your content. Sure, "Free chocolate for the rest of your life!" would gain attention, but you'd be unlikely to be able to deliver on such an offer. You don't want to say anything in your opening that might make your reader feel tricked.

One of the most effective attention-gaining openings is a statement or question that introduces a need the product will satisfy, such as this one for a cleaning service:

Juggling work, kids, dinner, housework—sometimes it just gets to be too much.

A different tack is illustrated by the following example. It attracts interest by telling a story and using character-based appeal:

In 1984 three enterprising women met to do something about the lack of accessible health information for women.

And here's an opening that uses a question to arouse interest:

Were you overcharged for your last tree service?

Whatever opening strategy you choose, it should lead into your central selling point.

Building a Persuasive Case

With the reader's attention gained, you proceed with the sales strategy you've planned.

If your main appeal is emotional, your opening has probably established an emotional atmosphere that you should continue to develop. You might describe the appearance, texture, aroma, and taste of your product so vividly that your reader will mentally see and feel it. If you selected a rational appeal as your central theme, you might write about such qualities as durability, savings, and ease of operation. When using character-based appeals, you might emphasize comments from a well-known, carefully selected spokesperson or provide evidence that your company is expert and reliable.

Be sure to answer the readers' likely questions and overcome any objections they may have. For example, if you're promoting a gym to young women, you should mention any child care that's available on site; or if you're selling a museum membership to an older demographic, you could mention the nearby parking and the accessibility features of the museum.

With an emphasis on character-based appeals, this attractive letter and separate insert build a central argument: Only the experts at TruGreen can give you the results you want. Note how the envelope begins the persuasive effort.

Live life outside.

<BARCODE>
<Seq_Num>
<Lot_Num>
<Full_Name>
<Address_Main>
<Address_2nd>
<City> <State> <ZIP5> <ZIP4>

An eye-catching bargain helps overcome cost-based resistance and urges the reader to act now.

SAVE NOW
ONLY
$29.95*
FIRST LAWN APPLICATION

Dear <Name>,

This bold and simple opening promotes timely action and links the service to a beautiful lawn in summer.

Now's the time to prepare your lawn for summer.
It's the season for backyard brunches, naps in the hammock and touch football on the lawn. It's also the time to prepare for summer with a special offer on a tailored TruGreen® plan. We're ready to help your lawn win the fight against weeds for space and nutrients, so you'll have a lush, green stage for outdoor living this summer.

The evocative emotional details here . . .

Start your TruGreen lawn plan now and get your first application for ONLY $29.95.
We begin with a Healthy Lawn Analysis,✦ exploring your climate, soil condition, grass type and lawn usage. From there, your TruExpert℠ certified lawn specialist tailors a year-round plan to provide the right help at the right time, like now—when your grass is battling weeds like dandelions and crabgrass in their own growing season. And it's all backed by our Healthy Lawn Guarantee,®✦ so you can leave the hard work to us and spend more time enjoying life on your lawn.

. . . are supported by these rational appeals.

Sincerely,

Mel Oliver

Science-based details and guaranteed customer satisfaction also build trust in the company's expertise and dependability.

Mel Oliver, *TruGreen Customer Care*

TruGreen will gladly visit your property as often as needed between scheduled visits to make any necessary adjustments and to ensure your satisfaction.

<XXX> of your neighbors have TruGreen lawns. What are you waiting for?

"Act now" strategies are followed by an easy-to-find phone number and web address.

Start your TruGreen plan today.

<800_PHONE>
<TruGreen.com/LandingPage>

TRUGREEN | PGA
Live life outside.
The Official Lawn Care Provider of the PGA of America

Photos evoke summer fun on a nice lawn, promoting the letter's central theme.

This part makes effective use of a negative situation to be avoided.

Something other than grass may be emerging from your lawn.

HEALTHY LAWN ANALYSIS

The first step toward a tailored year-round plan is checking these key aspects of your lawn:

- climate
- soil condition
- grass type
- lawn usage

Weeds are awakening.

From late spring to early summer, a variety of weeds are trying to carve out a piece of your lawn. And to deal with them, you need to understand your lawn's conditions.

That's why TruGreen® starts with our detailed Healthy Lawn Analysis.® It helps us design a tailored year-round plan to provide exactly the help your lawn needs to overcome threats like weeds and remain healthy throughout the year.

TruGreen reiterates its main rational appeal: a science-based approach to each customer's lawn.

<XXX> of your neighbors have TruGreen lawns. What are you waiting for?

Live life outside.®

Start today and get your first application for ONLY $29.95.*

<800_PHONE>

<TruGreen.com/LandingPage>

Repeating the phone number and website makes it easy to see how to receive these appealing reader benefits.

Get expert care for your trees and shrubs, too.

*Requires purchase of annual plan. Special price of $29.95 is for first application only, for new residential EasyPay or PrePay customers only, and applies to lawns up to 5,000 square feet. For lawns more than 5,000 square feet or for the regular lawn application price for a lawn of any size, please call for estimate. Valid at participating TruGreen locations. Availability of services may vary by geography. Not to be combined with or used in conjunction with any other offer or discount. Additional restrictions may apply. Consumer responsible for all sales tax. ⁺Purchase of full lawn plan required for Healthy Lawn Analysis, which is typically performed at the first visit. ⁺Guarantee applies to full plan customers only. The PGA name, logos, and marks are trademarks of The Professional Golfers' Association of America. ©2016 TruGreen Limited Partnership. All rights reserved.

<SOURCE_CODE> Tennessee Charter #448, #439, #185, #443, #422, #3883. In Connecticut, B-0153, B-1380, B-0127, B-0200, B-0151.*

TRUGREEN
Live life outside.®

PRSRT STD
U.S. POSTAGE
PAID
TRUGREEN

The main reader benefit—having a beautiful lawn for summer fun—first appears here.

Address lawn threats now.
Love your lawn this summer.

Window = 738" w X 1.5"h
.875" from Left
1.125" from Bottom

The slogan ties into the main reader benefit.

TRUGREEN
Live life outside.®

PGA

An impressive credential helps build a strong ethos.

The Official Lawn Care Provider of the PGA of America

Annotated Example

A Direct-Mail Message (Selling a Management Seminar)

This sales letter uses all three types of appeals (logical, emotional, and character based). The mailing included a second page that provided a detailed outline of the seminar and a longer list of likely reader benefits.

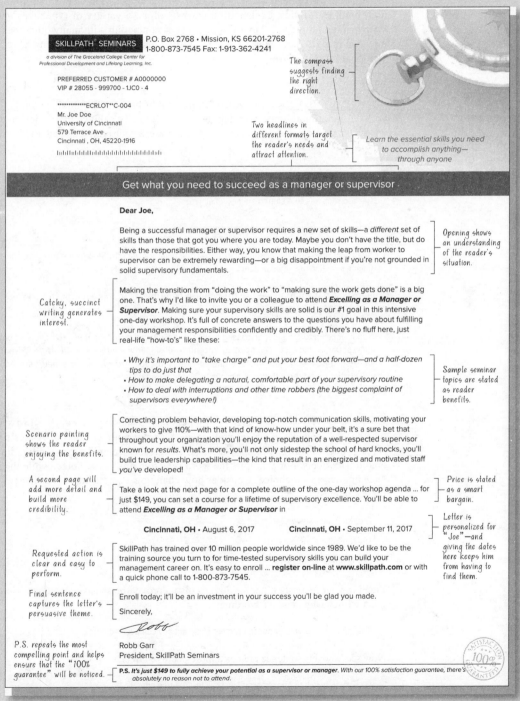

SKILLPATH® SEMINARS
P.O. Box 2768 • Mission, KS 66201-2768
1-800-873-7545 Fax: 1-913-362-4241
a division of The Graceland College Center for Professional Development and Lifelong Learning, Inc.

PREFERRED CUSTOMER # A0000000
VIP # 28055 - 999700 - 1JC0 - 4

*************ECRLOT**C-004
Mr. Joe Doe
University of Cincinnati
579 Terrace Ave .
Cincinnati , OH, 45220-1916

The compass suggests finding the right direction.

Two headlines in different formats target the reader's needs and attract attention.

Learn the essential skills you need to accomplish anything— through anyone

Get what you need to succeed as a manager or supervisor

Dear Joe,

Being a successful manager or supervisor requires a new set of skills—a *different* set of skills than those that got you where you are today. Maybe you don't have the title, but do have the responsibilities. Either way, you know that making the leap from worker to supervisor can be extremely rewarding—or a big disappointment if you're not grounded in solid supervisory fundamentals.

Opening shows an understanding of the reader's situation.

Making the transition from "doing the work" to "making sure the work gets done" is a big one. That's why I'd like to invite you or a colleague to attend **Excelling as a Manager or Supervisor**. Making sure your supervisory skills are solid is our #1 goal in this intensive one-day workshop. It's full of concrete answers to the questions you have about fulfilling your management responsibilities confidently and credibly. There's no fluff here, just real-life "how-to's" like these:

Catchy, succinct writing generates interest.

- *Why it's important to "take charge" and put your best foot forward—and a half-dozen tips to do just that*
- *How to make delegating a natural, comfortable part of your supervisory routine*
- *How to deal with interruptions and other time robbers (the biggest complaint of supervisors everywhere!)*

Sample seminar topics are stated as reader benefits.

Correcting problem behavior, developing top-notch communication skills, motivating your workers to give 110%—with that kind of know-how under your belt, it's a sure bet that throughout your organization you'll enjoy the reputation of a well-respected supervisor known for *results*. What's more, you'll not only sidestep the school of hard knocks, you'll build true leadership capabilities—the kind that result in an energized and motivated staff *you've* developed!

Scenario painting shows the reader enjoying the benefits.

Take a look at the next page for a complete outline of the one-day workshop agenda ... for just $149, you can set a course for a lifetime of supervisory excellence. You'll be able to attend **Excelling as a Manager or Supervisor** in

A second page will add more detail and build more credibility.

Price is stated as a smart bargain.

Cincinnati, OH • August 6, 2017   **Cincinnati, OH** • September 11, 2017

Letter is personalized for "Joe"—and giving the dates here keeps him from having to find them.

SkillPath has trained over 10 million people worldwide since 1989. We'd like to be the training source you turn to for time-tested supervisory skills you can build your management career on. It's easy to enroll ... **register on-line** at **www.skillpath.com** or with a quick phone call to 1-800-873-7545.

Requested action is clear and easy to perform.

Enroll today; it'll be an investment in your success you'll be glad you made.

Final sentence captures the letter's persuasive theme.

Sincerely,

Robb

Robb Garr
President, SkillPath Seminars

P.S. repeats the most compelling point and helps ensure that the "100% guarantee" will be noticed.

P.S. It's just $149 to fully achieve your potential as a supervisor or manager. With our 100% satisfaction guarantee, there's absolutely no reason not to attend.

Skillpath Seminars, Direct Mail Letter. Copyright © by Skillpath Seminars. All rights reserved. Used with permission.

Using a Persuasive Writing Style

Sales writing can be quite different from other kinds of business writing. It is usually highly conversational and fast moving. It even uses techniques that are incorrect or inappropriate in other forms of business writing, such as sentence fragments or catchy slang. As the Annotated Examples show, it also uses visual emphasis devices (underlining, capitalization, boldface, italics, exclamation marks, color), a variety of type sizes and fonts, and many paragraph breaks. Any sales message is competing with many other messages for the intended readers' attention, so snappy writing and enhanced formatting have become conventional for this genre.

Stressing the You-Viewpoint In no area of business communication is the use of the you-viewpoint more important than in sales writing. To achieve the reader involvement you want, you should use the second person and present your product's benefits from the reader's perspective.

For example, consider the following sentence from a sales message:

> Our zoo shop has cute stuffed animals of all types.

Now look how much more appealing this version is:

> Need a birthday present for someone special or a baby-shower gift? Stop by the zoo shop and choose from our unique selection of stuffed animals.

You may also want to make use of scenario painting, as in this excerpt from a sales letter for *The New York Times*:

> You'll wake up to the most discussed news stories and widely anticipated exclusive sections in our Sunday newspaper, including the compelling, recently redesigned magazine *Arts & Leisure*, covering a wide array of exciting new work and artists on the cultural landscape; *Travel*, for our expert perspectives on alluring destinations; and the influential, always fascinating *Book Review*.

Choosing Words Carefully In persuasive messages, every word can influence whether the reader will act on your request, so put yourself in your reader's place as you select your wording. Some words, while closely related in meaning, have different emotional effects. For example, the word *selection* implies a choice, while the word *preference* implies a first choice. Consider how changing a single adjective changes the effect of these sentences:

> The NuPhone's *small* size . . .
>
> The NuPhone's *compact* size . . .
>
> The NuPhone's *sleek* size . . .

Framing your requests in the positive is also a proven persuasive technique. Here's a positive point written with negative wording:

> Switching to Apex Energy doesn't require filling out any complicated forms.

Now see how this sentence creates a more positive effect:

> It's easy to switch to Apex Energy—just call this toll-free number.

Communication Matters

Current Trends in Promotional Writing: A Q&A with a Young PR Professional

Kelly Croslin is an employee of LPK Brands Inc. Here she shares her view of today's promotional writing landscape.

Courtesy of Kelly Gadd Croslin

Q: How do current promotional strategies differ from those of, say, 10 years ago? What has changed?

A: Certainly one significant change is the move toward digital promotions. Now, many consumers view promotional material exclusively through social media channels, websites, and email. Many companies make certain offers, events, or products available only to their loyal digital audiences to entice them to engage with their brands more frequently over these channels. Brands need to be wherever their customers want them whenever they need them.

An increase in experiential promotional tactics has also become popular. With consumers receiving more than 5,000 marketing messages each day, it's hard for brands to stand out with traditional promotions. Whether through special events, street teams, or a traveling display, companies want to create an experience that consumers can't ignore.

Q: What persuasion principles and strategies are still important, no matter what the medium?

A: While the communication channels have changed, people still have the same basic needs, so persuasive appeals are still based on credibility, logic, and emotion. If anything, consumers' sensibilities have been heightened by the overwhelming access to information. In particular, the credibility of the communicator or company has become more important. Since anyone can post whatever he/she likes online and call it accurate, consumers have had to become more skeptical and discerning—but they also are quicker to make decisions and less likely to fact check.

Q: What advice would you give other young business professionals about promoting their companies' products or services?

A: Familiarity with digital media is certainly a strength. However, I would caution today's young employees not to discount promotional and marketing strategies that have worked well for decades. Well-planned strategy is still the key to successful execution, and professionalism and good, solid writing skills are still very important. But be aware that information about your products/company will be available quickly, good or bad, so be as prepared as possible and put problem-solving skills to work when things do not go as planned.

Consider using other people's words—for example, the comments of satisfied customers or praise from published material. Here's a quote from *Esquire* magazine that appeared in a sales letter for *Cook's Illustrated*:

> "There's no more authoritative food magazine. When Cook's Illustrated endorses a cheesecake, it's because its editors made 45 of them."

Enhancing Your Message with Visuals

The Web has made today's readers more visually oriented than any before in history. When preparing any kind of sales message, be sure to consider whether photos, tables, boxes, word art, borders, or other graphical elements would enhance your message's appeal.

Email sales messages have become just as visually appealing as print mailings, if not more so. Many that sell products are almost all pictures, while others are at the opposite end of the spectrum. Probably most fall somewhere in between these two extremes, like the Annotated Examples of email sales messages in this chapter. Cultivate your visual-rhetoric skills so that you can advise your publications staff or design inviting messages yourself.

Annotated Example

An Email Sales Message (Persuading Readers Who Used a Trial Version of an Application to Purchase It)

This message, with the subject line "Use Your Snagit Captures Anywhere," uses logical appeals and a variety of visual elements to make the product's benefits stand out.

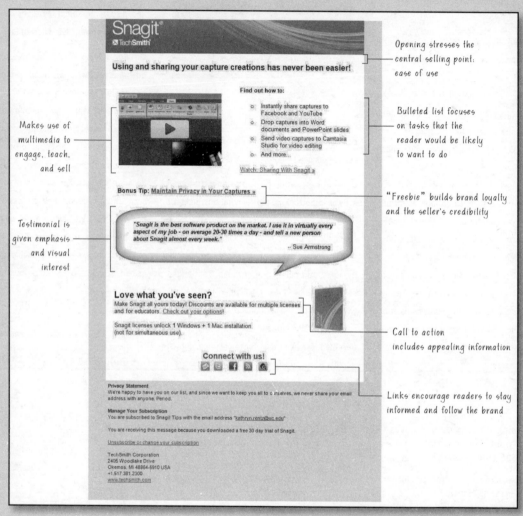

Makes use of multimedia to engage, teach, and sell

Testimonial is given emphasis and visual interest

Opening stresses the central selling point: ease of use

Bulleted list focuses on tasks that the reader would be likely to want to do

"Freebie" builds brand loyalty and the seller's credibility

Call to action includes appealing information

Links encourage readers to stay informed and follow the brand

Source: SnagIt.

Communication Matters

Persuasive Strategies Vary across Cultures

When writing persuasive messages, be especially careful to adapt them to the culture of the intended readers.

For example, while U.S. and Chinese sales letters use many of the same core elements, there are also these crucial differences:

- U.S. sales letters often use attention-getting headlines and postscripts that pressure readers to act, while Chinese sales letters do not use these aggressive strategies.
- Both types of letters contain a salutation, but it is more formal in Chinese letters (for example, "Honored Company" instead of "Dear Mr. Smith"). Furthermore, Chinese letters follow the salutation with polite words of greeting, whereas U.S. letters go directly into sales talk.
- U.S. letters tend to describe the product's benefits by using "you," whereas the Chinese, finding the use of "you" disrespectful, tend to use "we" (as in "Our consistent goal is to produce comfortable luxury cars of high standard and good quality").
- Both types of letters extol the benefits of the product, but Chinese letters use fewer details, especially about price.

- When making the actual request, Chinese letters are less pushy than U.S. letters, favoring such mild language as "If you are interested in our products, please contact us."
- Both types of letters use a complimentary close, but instead of "Sincerely yours," the Chinese attempt to promote cooperation and mutual respect with such closings as "Wishing good health."

Source: Yunxia Zhu, "Building Knowledge Structures in Teaching Cross-Cultural Sales Genres," *Business Communication Quarterly* 6, no. 4 (December 2000): 49–69.

Making the Sales Request

After you have developed your reader's interest in your product or service, you're ready to invite the reader to buy. This is what the previous paragraphs have been leading to and is, of course, the goal of the message.

Your request for action should be specific and clear, like these:

> Just complete the enclosed order card and drop it in the mail today, or visit www.eatlean.com to subscribe online.

> To start enjoying *House and Garden*, just call 1-888-755-5265. Be sure to have promo code 3626 handy to receive your 40% discount.

Similarly, in email selling you should make the action easy by including an easy-to-see link to an order form or to the first part of the ordering process. For example, you might say "Just click here to order your customized iPhone case" or "You can download our free catalog of business gifts at http://thankyoutoo.com." Many sales emails make the desired action easy by including multiple links to the target page on the company's website.

Join 1 — Join Angie's List today for $30 off. Use promo code **30USAToday**.
View email online | No longer interested in Angie's List "Great Deals" Emails? Unsubscribe

Join 2 —

Angie's list.
Educate your guess.™
Quick Tour | About the List | Praise | Press | FAQ | Join

SAVE $30
Join 3 — Join Angie's list now ▶
Join Angie's List with promo code 30USAToday by 4/10/08 and get $30 off your annual membership.

Angie's list. is in **USA TODAY** March 31, 2013

"Considering a new doctor? Hoping to learn more about a doctor you already see? Or maybe you'd like to praise or pan one.

You could do it the old-fashioned way and talk to friends and relatives or even the doctor in question. Or you could do this...read and write doctor ratings at Angie's List, the site where members in 120 metropolitan areas rank their plumbers, roofers and landscapers." Read more

Join 4 — Join Angie's list.

Courtesy of Angie's List

This email sales message makes the desired action easy.
Source: Reprinted with permission.

Because readers sometimes put things off, you should give them a reason to act now. Here are some examples:

> . . . to take advantage of this three-day offer.

> . . . so that you can be ready for the Christmas rush.

> . . . so that you can immediately begin enjoying. . . .

Another effective technique for the close of a sales message is to briefly recall the central strategy of the message. For example, if you began your sales message for a local auto repair shop by talking about the stress of dealing with an unreliable shop, you might end with the following:

> And enjoy the peace of mind that comes with getting dependable care for your car—every time.

Adding a Postscript

Unlike other business messages where a postscript (P.S.) appears to be an afterthought, a sales message can use a postscript as a part of its design. It can be used effectively in a number of ways: to urge the reader to act, to emphasize the major appeal, to call attention to other enclosures, or to suggest that the reader pass along the sales message. Here are some examples:

> P.S. Hurry! Save while this special money-saving offer lasts.

> P.S. Our magazine makes a distinctive and appreciated gift. Know someone who's having a birthday soon?

> P.S. Click now to order and you'll automatically be entered into a contest for a 5G Android smartphone.

Offering Name Removal to Email Readers

Until January 1, 2004, it was a courtesy to offer the recipients of commercial email the option of receiving no further emails from the sender. Now, thanks to the so-called CAN-SPAM Act, it is a legal requirement as well (see Exhibit 10-3). Consider placing this invitation in a prominent place—perhaps even before the main message. Wherever it is, the link should be easy to identify. See the Guidelines from the Online Trust Alliance for more about acceptable opt-out practices.

Reviewing the Strategy for Sales Messages

The basic strategy for sales messages can be summarized as follows:

- Gain favorable attention.

- Create desire by presenting the appeals, emphasizing supporting facts, emphasizing the reader's viewpoint, and enhancing the message with appropriate visual elements.

Exhibit 10-3	CAN-SPAM: It's the Law

The CAN-SPAM Act applies not only to bulk email but also to all commercial email messages whose purpose is to promote a product or service. Here are its main requirements:

1. Don't use false or misleading header information.
2. Don't use deceptive subject lines.
3. Identify the message as an ad.
4. Tell recipients where you're located (i.e., a physical postal address).
5. Tell recipients how to opt out of future email from you.
6. Honor opt-out requests promptly.
7. Be sure your email sales contractor (if you've hired one) is following the law.

- Include all necessary information—using a coordinated sales package (brochures, leaflets, links, and other appended parts).
- Make a clear request for prompt action.
- Possibly add a postscript.
- In email writing, offer to remove the reader from your email list to comply with legal requirements.

Comparing Bad and Good Examples of a Sales Message

The following two email sales messages show bad and good efforts to promote Zach Miller's painting business (described in the Problem-Solving Challenge in this section).

A Weak, Self-Centered Message The following ineffective example begins with a dull, vague subject line. The first sentence talks only about the writer and delays answering the reader's obvious question, "What's the offer?" The second sentence begins to hint at the topic, but it is still writer focused. The middle paragraph contains some potentially good logical points, but the general, bland language won't generate much enthusiasm. Also, the character appeal is weak. Zach comes across as just another struggling student trying to pay his way through school; he does not make a convincing case that he and his friends would actually do a good job. The final sentence doesn't tell the reader what information to include in a response—and no final selling ends the message.

Subject: Offer from a Student

Hello,

My name is Zach Miller, and I'm a business student here at North Rapids University. I've been learning about business not only in the classroom but on the job, by running my own house-painting operation.

If you'd like to have your house painted this summer, I can do it for considerably less than what you'd pay a professional service. I would carefully prepare your house for painting, and I use good-quality paint. My two friends and I will also guarantee to complete the job within three days (weather permitting).

Please email me if you'd like an estimate.

Sincerely,

Zach Miller

Skillful Use of Character and Rational Appeals The better message follows the advice presented in the preceding pages. The subject line contains concrete reader benefits and states right away that the job will be professionally done. The opening sentence is an engaging question and is again focused on key benefits. The second paragraph builds confidence in the writer and his co-workers, and it ends by allaying any worries that the homeowner will be held liable if one of the students is injured. The third paragraph provides convincing logical details about the job. In the final paragraph, the writer uses a Web link to make it easy for readers to submit an estimate request, and he directs them to an attachment that contains further information and one last reader benefit.

Subject: A Professional-Quality Paint Job for Less

Would you like a great deal on having your house painted this summer while supporting North Rapids University students?

My name is Zach Miller, and I'm a junior business major here at NRU, in the Honors Plus program. I'm a graduate of St. Xavier High School and have been running my own house-painting business for three years. I employ two other NRU students, Jeff Barnes and Alex Wilson, who are also business students. We are all fully licensed and insured.

We use only 100% acrylic paints from top manufacturers like Benjamin Moore, Porter, and Sherwin Williams. Our specialty is careful preparation. We will scrape or power wash all surfaces of your house and do any needed minor repairs before we paint. The work comes with a two-year guarantee and, combined with our low rates, is an excellent value.

If you'd like a free estimate, just fill out the online estimate request form. The attached flyer tells more about me and also includes a coupon for 10% off if you schedule your paint job the day you receive your estimate.

Zach Miller
millerzs@mail.nru.edu
cellular: (431) 445-5560

Multimedia Selling

LO10-6   Integrate the Internet and social media into your sales efforts.

It is the rare company these days that doesn't do **integrated marketing communications**— that is, coordinate its selling across several media. There are over 3 billion people online around the world. They now buy more tablets than laptops or PCs, and the sales of smartphones have now exceeded those for all other types of phones.[5] Within the United States, 88.5 percent of the population is on the Internet,[6] and 78 percent have at least one social-media profile.[7] They spend more than half of their online time on apps.[8] And as the previous section pointed out, sales mailings are still very much in the mix. There have never been so many ways to reach so many consumers.

Even if you aren't planning on becoming a marketing professional, you need to be aware of your company's multimedia marketing efforts because you may well play a role in them. Below we discuss two ways that you might be involved: linking your communication to other communications and posting material on different social-media platforms.

Problem-Solving Challenge

Blogging for Your Employer

You've just landed an internship as marketing assistant with S&G Publications, which publishes one of your favorite magazines, *Horse & Rider*. You've been a horse lover all your life, and you're majoring in communications, so this is the perfect opportunity for you to learn how to prepare for work you'll love.

S&G regularly posts informative pieces on their website about subjects of reader interest. Yesterday your boss approached you and said, "How about writing a blog post for us about horses? It'd

be a content-marketing piece—no selling, just fun advice for the readers of *Horse & Rider*." You give it some thought and decide there's no time like the present to break into blogging.

You own a horse yourself, so you could write about any number of things. But many people are more knowledgeable about horses than you are. What's an area that you're especially qualified to write on? Hmmm . . . how about why students should keep their horses during college? You

know you wondered about this yourself, but you decided to keep your horse, Sierra, and you're really glad you did. You run this idea past your boss, and she loves it.

So now it's time to create your piece. But first you've got to bone up on content marketing and blogging. What should you title your piece? What should it look like? What tone of voice should you use? How much and what kind of content should it have? You'd better get busy!

Linking Your Communication to Other Communications

Given today's focus on integrated marketing, you should consider linking any persuasive message you write to other sources of information and opportunities for action.

Linking to Other Communications in Mailings Mailed sales messages can't include live links, of course, but they can definitely include various ways to buy or learn more. You might include an address and phone number, the company's Web address, and even an invitation to visit the company on Facebook or follow it on Twitter. Exhibit 10-4 shows how the writer of a recent GEICO sales message included multiple ways for the reader to respond.

Exhibit 10-4   A Sales Letter from GEICO Offering Several Ways for the Reader to Respond

Note how many options for responding this second page of a sales message provides.

So take a look at what you're getting from your current insurer, then contact GEICO. After all, it's no coincidence 97% of our customers report being satisfied, and that's why you should become a GEICO policyholder today.

Sincerely,

Ted Ward

Ted Ward
Vice President

P.S. Don't get left out in the cold this winter! Go to geico.com, call 1-800-947-AUTO (2886), or contact your local GEICO agent for a fast, free, no-obligation rate quote. See how much you could save on car insurance. And be sure to ask about our Emergency Road Service program. We can help you with problems like a flat tire, dead battery and more for pennies a day per car.

With GEICO, you get:

- **Money-saving discounts** for good drivers, your car's safety items and more.
- **Coverage** for your motorcycle, ATV, off-road bike, RV and boat.
- **Homeowners, renters and PWC insurance** through the GEICO Insurance Agency.
- **Convenient payment options** to fit your budget needs, including Electronic Funds Transfer (EFT) and Recurring Card Payments (RCP).
- **Online convenience** with our secure, easy-to-use website geico.com. Once you're a policyholder, you can make a payment, change drivers or vehicles — even report or track the status of a claim from the convenience of your home computer or mobile app.
- **Claim repairs guaranteed** for as long as you own your car when you use a GEICO-recommended repair facility.

Get a free quote on your smartphone or tablet!

In just 15 minutes you could save $500 or more on car insurance. Scan this code to get your free, no-obligation rate quote directly on your mobile device.

A bar code reader app and a camera are required to scan code.

Annotated Example

An Email Sales Message (Promoting Visits to a Museum)

This message was sent to previous visitors of the museum to encourage them to return. It was sent in early April—right when readers might be wanting to enjoy a spring break with their families. Notice how the appeals and the links work together to promote further reading and action.

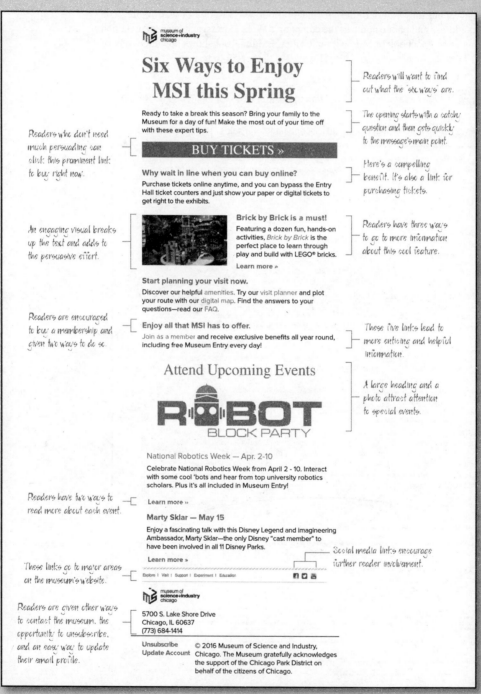

Readers who don't need much persuading can click this prominent link to buy right now.

An engaging visual breaks up the text and adds to the persuasive effort.

Readers are encouraged to buy a membership and given two ways to do so.

Readers have two ways to read more about each event.

These links go to major areas on the museum's website.

Readers are given other ways to contact the museum, the opportunity to unsubscribe, and an easy way to update their email profile.

Readers will want to find out what the 'six ways' are.

The opening starts with a catchy question and then gets quickly to the message's main point.

Here's a compelling benefit. It's also a link for purchasing tickets.

Readers have three ways to go to more information about this cool feature.

These five links lead to more enticing and helpful information.

A large heading and a photo attract attention to special events.

Social media links encourage further reader involvement.

Museum of Science + Industry, Chicago

Six Ways to Enjoy MSI this Spring

Ready to take a break this season? Bring your family to the Museum for a day of fun! Make the most out of your time off with these expert tips.

BUY TICKETS »

Why wait in line when you can buy online?
Purchase tickets online anytime, and you can bypass the Entry Hall ticket counters and just show your paper or digital tickets to get right to the exhibits.

Brick by Brick is a must!
Featuring a dozen fun, hands-on activities, *Brick by Brick* is the perfect place to learn through play and build with LEGO® bricks.

Learn more »

Start planning your visit now.
Discover our helpful amenities. Try our visit planner and plot your route with our digital map. Find the answers to your questions—read our FAQ.

Enjoy all that MSI has to offer.
Join as a member and receive exclusive benefits all year round, including free Museum Entry every day!

Attend Upcoming Events

ROBOT BLOCK PARTY

National Robotics Week — Apr. 2-10
Celebrate National Robotics Week from April 2 - 10. Interact with some cool 'bots and hear from top university robotics scholars. Plus it's all included in Museum Entry!

Learn more »

Marty Sklar — May 15
Enjoy a fascinating talk with this Disney Legend and imagineering Ambassador, Marty Sklar—the only Disney "cast member" to have been involved in all 11 Disney Parks.

Learn more »

Explore | Visit | Support | Experiment | Education

Museum of Science + Industry, Chicago

5700 S. Lake Shore Drive
Chicago, IL 60637
(773) 684-1414

Unsubscribe
Update Account

© 2016 Museum of Science and Industry, Chicago. The Museum gratefully acknowledges the support of the Chicago Park District on behalf of the citizens of Chicago.

Courtesy Museum of Science and Industry, Chicago

Linking to Other Communications in Email

Email sales messages enable the reader to connect to the company even more efficiently because live links can be included right there in the message. Every sales email should include at least one link (probably to a page on the company's website) because links engage people and drive them to special offers and places to buy.[9] "Share," "Like," "Tweet," and other links can also be included, depending on the audience and the campaign.[10] According to a recent study by Movable Ink, 76% of the marketers who were surveyed include social-media buttons in emails.[11]

Some graphics-rich emails, like the one from Hilton Honors shown in Exhibit 10-5, consist almost completely of links. This kind of email message is easy to interact with on a smartphone, and it basically acts as a portal to more in-depth information on the company's website. There's some research to suggest, though, that people prefer email that uses text to convey the main points.[12] The Annotated Example shown opposite "An Email Sales Message: Promoting Visits to a Museum" illustrates this more common kind of message. Notice, though, how many ways this text-based message still uses links to promote sales and further reading.

Linking to Other Communications from Your Website or Social-Media Posts
Google any company or check out its website these days and you're likely to see an array of social-media buttons that you can click to view the company's presence on those sites (Exhibit 10-6). You may also find a button enabling you to have the site's contents fed to your RSS reader and/or a link enabling you to subscribe to the company's newsletter or emails.

As the following section discusses, social media platforms offer many ways to connect readers to additional information, whether through links to the company's website, buttons for sharing posts on other platforms, or linked photos and videos. When preparing any kind of promotional material, consider how it might profitably be coordinated with your company's other marketing channels.

Posting Material on Social Media

Businesses large and small attract customers and employees through social media. A 2014 study of the 500 fastest-growing companies in the United States found that 94% used LinkedIn, 80% used Facebook, and 79% used Twitter; and approximately 50% used blogging, YouTube, and Google+ (the platforms with the next three highest percentages of use).[13] Eight of 10 small-business owners also use social media to grow their businesses.[14]

Evidence of integrated marketing communications is nowhere more evident than on companies' websites, where you're likely to see an array of buttons that link to the company's social media pages (as in the first example below, the banner for Business News Daily's website). Google also displays the buttons in a brief profile of the company on the search-results page (second visual). Lots of people are needed to create all this online content. Maybe you will be one of them!

Source: https://www.google.com. Google and the Google logo are registered trademarks of Google Inc.; © Pixtal/AGE Fotostock RF.

Rather recently, companies have added a new sales strategy to their social media marketing efforts: content marketing. As defined by the Content Marketing Institute, "Content marketing is a strategic marketing approach focused on creating and distributing valuable, relevant, and consistent content to attract and retain a clearly-defined audience—and, ultimately, to drive profitable customer action.[15] Translated, this means that, rather than using traditional sales tactics, companies give away useful, interesting information to those whom they hope to turn into customers or more loyal customers.

Even though content marketing avoids overt selling, it is an effective strategy for building **brand equity,** which is the value of your company's positive image and name recognition. The goal is to make customers and prospects aware of your brand and impress them with your knowledge so that, if and when they're ready to buy, they will choose you. For this reason, it's critical to enable them to make the connection between your free content and your company, usually by adding a brief bio that includes your company's name, using your company's Twitter handle, or posting the content on your company's website. Exhibit 10-7 shows an email message linking to a recent content-marketing post

Exhibit 10-7 An Example of a Content-Marketing Email/Blog Post

Marketers often use email to drive consumers to their content-marketing material. Here, you can see an email message that readers received from TMR Direct, a direct-mail company, about the advantages of using postcards rather than sales letters. Readers can click the link at the top or the bottom of the message to go to the full blog post. No overt selling whatsoever occurs in the post. But the helpful information may help turn readers into better marketing strategists . . . and perhaps new or repeat customers!

7 Reasons Postcard Marketing Can Be a Great Choice

By Spencer Powell, Jun 29, 2016 10:00:00 AM

At TMR Direct, we've noticed an increase in the number of our clients who are successfully using postcards as part of their overall direct marketing strategy. What is it about this type of mailing that makes them so attractive to so many customers? Here are seven reasons why postcard mailings can be a good choice for your marketing efforts.

Read more »

Source: TMR Direct; Image © Charles Taylor/Shutterstock RF

Rogue Marketing: When Going Social Gets Out of Hand

The more social media accounts a company has, the better—right? Think again. As Rebecca Lieb, content-marketing expert, says in a recent blog post, the more accounts you have, the more likely it is that difficulties will arise. Businesses with 1,000 or more employees have an average of 178 social media accounts! Having too many accounts managed by people who know too little can cause these problems:

- *Inconsistency.* While the personal voice is often a virtue in social media posts, the author still needs to support the company's brand and follow its guidelines for posting. Otherwise, the company will be sending mixed messages about itself—and some of those messages might be embarrassing or otherwise harmful.

- *Scattered energy, untrackable results.* It might seem cool to create a Pinterest, Twitter, or Facebook account to promote your company, but you need to think it through. Are your customers or potential customers using that medium? What do you want to achieve with it? How will you know if it's successful? Who will post to it, and how often? These are the kinds of strategic questions that need to be answered in the company's social-media plan—which those who are tempted to create new accounts need to follow.

- *Neglected accounts.* Leib warns against "digital detritus": "The Twitter account that's been tweet-less for two years now. The site promoting the event that happens last July. The photo account with three shots on it. The

Facebook page that was frequently updated the week it launched, then abandoned." Such abandoned sites make organizations appear "unplanned, unfocused, undedicated and uncaring."

- *Transitory owners.* What happens when Julie from marketing quits *and* no one can get into that account she maintained? The more social-media accounts there are, the more likely such headaches will exist.

So before creating that new Twitter account and tweeting away for your company, be sure you've worked out the goal and the details with your company's marketing team.

Source: "Why Content Marketing Goes Rogue and How to Rein It In," *Marketing Land,* July 9, 2013, accessed November 1, 2016, http://marketingland.com.

You Make the Call

A 2013 study by Gallup found that about half of the polled employees were posting work-related material on social media, and about a third of these were doing so without any encouragement from the company. What do you think is the right amount of freedom for a company to allow for this kind of activity? What kinds of things should employees feel free to post on their own?

on a direct-mail company's website. You can find literally thousands of content-marketing pieces on the Web and social media, ranging from thoughtful articles on LinkedIn, cool visuals on Pinterest and Instagram, and tweets that link to valuable or interesting information.

Below we review four popular and distinctly different social media platforms in business. You may well have opportunities to contribute content to any of these or to other ones, whether you're overtly promoting your company or doing content marketing. Your participation, though, should be aligned with your company's **social media plan** or at least approved by your company (see the From the Tech Desk feature "Rogue Marketing: When Going Social Gets Out of Hand"). To see what's involved in social media planning, read Julie Neidlinger's post "How to Create a Social-Media Strategy (with Three Steps and a Template)" or similar advice on other social-marketing sites.

Blogs

While blogging has lost ground a bit in recent years, it is seeing a resurgence with the growing popularity of content marketing, especially among entrepreneurs. As Corey Wainwright at HubSpot points out, blogging generates many benefits:

- With each blog post, you have created another page for your company's website, which means one more opportunity for search engines to find you and drive traffic to your site.

- The increased activity that blogging brings to your site makes the site show up higher in search results.

- The content of your posts can be shared via links in tweets, LinkedIn conversations, Facebook posts, and in other social media messages, reaching new audiences.

- Blogging promotes your company's authority. You can show that you are good at what you do and understand your customers' (and potential customers') needs. If you spark enough interest and comments, you can become a "thought leader" in your industry.[16]

Blog posts are fun to write because they use a somewhat casual, more personal tone and require both clever thinking and creativity. Be sure to keep the paragraphs short, use headings and/or lists to break up the text and maintain interest, and add some visual appeal (one appropriate photo and some color are usually sufficient).

Facebook You are probably well aware of the promotional opportunities offered by Facebook—which is by far the most popular social media platform in the world. To promote their brands, companies can do the following:

- Create appealing profile pages.

- Post interesting visuals, text, and videos (whether sales posts, content marketing, or both) on their news feeds.

- Promote their products, as well as worthy causes, by holding and publicizing "events."

- Link viewers to their other social media outlets and to other businesses or organizations they want to support.

- Attract "likes" and followers, which then generates a larger following.

- Conduct polls, message viewers, offer coupons, and otherwise interact with their fan base.

- Create ads and purchase ad space on Facebook to have their ads reach the desired market.

Once you're on the job, you may have some great ideas for leveraging your company's Facebook presence (Exhibit 10-8). Being able to make such suggestions, and to write compelling content yourself, will definitely be an asset.

Twitter According to *Business News Daily,* Twitter has more than 320 million active users worldwide and is one of the top 10 websites in the United States.[17] Twitter is famous for its tight space restrictions (140 or fewer characters per post), but you can get around this constraint by posting links, video, photos, polls, and more. Plus, the brevity is part of the appeal; it's what enables subscribers to read a lot of little interesting tidbits each day.

You can easily interact with other users by mentioning their usernames in your posts, so Twitter is unparalleled for enabling quick connections and dialog. If you're lucky, some of your interesting content might get retweeted by your readers and perhaps go viral. You can, and should, also retweet other posters' interesting content, which is another way to build connections. In addition, you can tweet about posts you've made on other media—your blog, for example—and thus stretch the reach of your good material.

Twitter is also a great way to dialog with your customers. A particularly useful way to find out what your customers and potential customers are thinking is to arrange Twitter chats. These are conversations that occur on Twitter at a predetermined time on a predetermined topic. You can think of a Twitter chat as "a casual networking event"—one that can yield a great deal of useful information.[18]

The downside to Twitter is that it must constantly be fed. If you go too long between posts, posts from others that come in after yours will push your posts down in a long list of "old" tweets, making it almost pointless for you to have posted them in the first place. In one study, 95% of the 98 brands being researched published a tweet at least once a day, and 82% published

Exhibit 10-8   Making a Business Splash on Facebook

There is some evidence that fewer young people are on Facebook these days, in part because so many parents and grandparents are using it. But young adults are still heavily into Facebook; they're just using it more as a research tool. So, for example, they might check out Green Bean Delivery's Facebook page to learn more about them, see if others like their services, consider signing up, and perhaps spread the word to their friends.

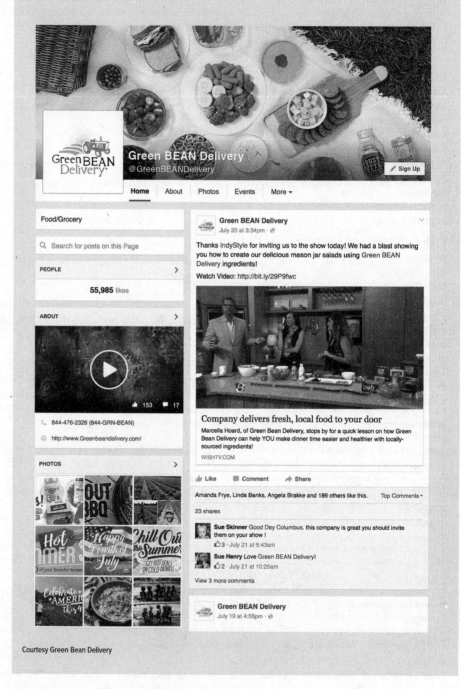

Courtesy Green Bean Delivery

between one and six tweets a day. (Only 6% were tweeting more than 10 times per day, indicating that most marketers felt this was too many.[19])

This means that if you or your company decides to use Twitter, someone needs to be ready with the time and ideas to do so. If you're not in charge of your company's Twitter account, make yourself useful by sending ideas and contents for tweets to the person who is. He or she will be grateful, and such efforts will enhance your value to the company.

Instagram Some social media tools are all about visuals. Instagram is one of them. Like Pinterest, it is a platform for photo and video posts. It was first created in 2010, but it already has more than 400 million active users, and this number is on the rise. Now owned by Facebook, Instagram is especially useful for global businesses and those targeting young people; 70% of its users come from outside the United States, and American teens rate it as the most popular social network.[20] But eMarketer also predicts that by 2019, at least 111.6 million Americans, or more than 4 in 10 Internet users, will be on Instagram.[21]

Instagram is a relatively young social media platform, but its popularity is growing fast.
© bloomua/123RF

Unlike the other social media tools discussed here, this is an entirely mobile platform (if you want to post rather than just view). With their smartphones, users download the user-friendly app and start shooting away. But there's much more to Instagram than Snapchat. With Instagram, you create lasting posts, as you do with Twitter and Facebook, whereas Snapchat's material disappears within 10 seconds of being viewed. Plus, Instagram has much more robust social networking and photo-editing options. Compared to Pinterest, Instagram is less good for directing viewers to your company's website; while you can share Instagram posts to Facebook, Twitter, and a few other social media platforms, the only place you can put a clickable link is in your bio. But Instagram has a more real-time feel than Pinterest, and it appeals to males and females alike, whereas 70% of Pinterest's users are female.[22]

Instagram is especially useful for businesses that would likely want to share photos, such as restaurants, fashion designers, and real estate firms. But almost any business could find Instagram useful. You could post photos of new items you're selling, coupon codes, promotional videos, and more.

To find and build followers on Instagram, you can do the following:

- Use the "Search" tab to find interesting content and users to follow. You just type in your keywords and then look for people or hashtags that contain those keywords. Or, you can look at the "Trending Tags" or click the "Explore Posts" feed. When you find posts you like, you can tap them to see who posted them and read their captions. This will give you an idea of who your likely followers might be and how to word your own hashtags (topic identifiers). Plus, if you follow photo-posters you like, they will likely follow you back.

- Use the "You" tab to see who has liked your photos, commented on them, or otherwise referenced you, and use the "Following" tab to see this information for people you're following.

- Tag particular users on particular posts to be sure they see your post.

- "Like" or comment on others' posts. If others comment on yours, be sure to comment back, or use the Direct Messaging feature to reply to them personally.

As with any other social platform, be sure to get the go-ahead from your marketing team before you start using Instagram for business purposes. You need to have an eye for detail and decent photography skills to be able to use this tool creditably. But even if you don't use it yourself, you might be able to feed ideas to those who are promoting your company through Instagram.

Comparing Bad and Good Examples of a Content-Marketing Blog Post

The following two blog posts show contrasting ways of handling the content-marketing task described in the Problem-Solving Challenge for this section.

An Impersonal, Uninteresting Content-Marketing Post The first effort misses the mark in several ways. The writer has no distinctive voice and makes no personal connection with the reader. The writing (starting with the title) is bland, and the content is only marginally worth the reader's time. Plus, there is no visual interest.

Why College Students Shouldn't Sell Their Horses

College is a busy time, so when high-school graduates are getting ready to go off to school, they may wonder if they should let their parents sell their horses. After all, horses are expensive to keep and require considerable attention. Plus, life would certainly be simpler if the student didn't have a horse to think about and tend to.

But there can be some good reasons not to sell that horse. Here are a few:

1. The student will have a buddy. College can get lonely, especially during that first year. A student who needs a little love and companionship can find comfort by spending some time with her horse.

2. The student will have an excuse for getting away from it all for a while. The academic and social strains of college can sometimes be too much. If the student has a horse, he can visit his buddy in a quiet barn and get recharged.

3. The student will be able to enjoy nature and some physical exercise. It is easy to lose perspective when one is coping with college life. A horse will give a student a chance to get outside and do physical things instead of living inside her head most of the time.

So before deciding to end your horse-owning days, give the matter some careful thought. It's definitely an issue with two sides to it.

A Personable, Entertaining, and Well-Designed Post The second message immediately engages the reader with its title. Throughout the post, the writer continues to talk to the reader in an entertaining personal style, and she provides tips that are both useful and interesting. The photos add to the appeal, and an interesting bio at the end adds to the writer's credibility.

Five Reasons Why You Should Own a Horse in College

By Martha Jones | March 15, 2016

Have you ever wondered why you should keep your horse instead of selling it when you start college? After all, you know the time required to take care of a horse and continue its training. But before you decide to ship off your Black Beauty and lock away your riding boots, you might want to pause for a second.

I'm a junior in college and have owned my horse for two years now, because, well, I just couldn't wait until I graduated. But as I've traveled through the emotional trauma of exams and grades, I've come to realize there are benefits to owning a horse in college.

1. You have a study buddy.

The barn is actually a great place to study, because it's removed from the chaos of the school campus. But even better, instead of suffering through your homework alone, you have a great study buddy who will be right there for you as you navigate your classes. A horse won't be a know-it-all or tell you that you need better grades. This animal just lets you work through your problems at your own pace and supports you as you figure it out. Of course if you let your horse have grass or treats, it'll be more than ready to spend time with you.

2. You have an excuse for a caffeine break.

Your friends can't argue with you when you say you have to go ride your horse. They may not know that what you really need is a place to kick up your feet and recharge on some caffeine. On your way to the barn, swing by to get your favorite flavor of coffee. Then when you ride, sit in a comfortable positon and enjoy the drug that's allowed you to make it this far in college. Not only will you get a moment to relax, but you'll also be sharing a moment with your horse.

3. You get your exercise time in.

You don't have to feel the pressure of going to the school's crowded gym, where the students next to you are doing 50 burpees and running two laps compared to your one. The barn itself is a gym, where you can do every type of exercise you need to do to get in shape. Want to become a faster runner? You'll be able to notch up your speed when your horse is running loose on the property. Feel like you don't have any arm strength? Filling water buckets will sculpt your arms in no time. You don't even have to tell your friends that you're working out; they'll see the results in no time and will most likely ask you what your secret is.

4. You're never alone on a Friday night.

When you own a horse, you no longer have to worry about the fear of being alone on a Friday night as your friends hit the town with their baes. There is always the option of heading to the barn to spend quality time with your horse. Your date will be quiet, listen to you, and will always be there for you no matter what. So next time your friends ask you if you have plans on Friday night, don't hang your head in shame as you think of spending the evening alone in your apartment. Instead, tell them that you have a date they could only dream of.

5. You build a friendship that goes beyond college.

Unlike the semesters in college, you don't just have your horse for a couple months and then exchange it for a new one. Your horse is there for you when you've had a long week of exams and you need time to relax. Your horse is also there on the days you don't have time to drive to the barn and visit it. And when you graduate from college and receive the slip of paper you've been dreaming of, well, your horse will be there for you then, too. So the next time you're thinking of resigning from being a horse owner, remember that your horse will outlive the time you spend at college and maybe, just maybe, you need it to get through those years.

Martha Jones attends the University of Cincinnati, where she is juggling her equine passion and degree in Communication. In her nonexistent free time, she heads to the barn to see her Paint mare, Sierra.

Courtesy Martha Jones

Courtesy Martha Jones

Courtesy Martha Jones

Courtesy Martha Jones

Courtesy Martha Jones

Problem-Solving Challenge

Selling Your Services through Proposal Writing

Play the role of Evan Lockley, vice president of account management at Whitfield Organizational Research. Your company collects internal information for businesses that want to improve their management techniques, information flow, employee morale, work processes, or other parts of their operations. To keep a steady stream of clients coming in, Whitfield must write numerous proposals for performing this kind of research.

As the manager of client accounts and the lead proposal writer at Whitfield, you now sit down to write a proposal to submit to RT Industries. This company is about to implement an enterprise

resource planning (ERP) system. This implementation will require employees in every functional area of the business—from purchasing to inventory to design, manufacturing, and shipping—to learn the system and enter the data for their area. If the implementation is successful, the management at RT Industries will be able to tell, with the click of a few buttons, exactly how every facet of the business is doing. But implementing such a system is a major and potentially disastrous organizational change, and RT knows it. That's why they want to pay an organizational research firm to track the implementation and make sure it's as

successful as possible. RT has invited Whitfield, along with other firms, to bid on this job.

You and one of your principal researchers have visited with the implementation team at RT Industries to learn more about the system they've chosen and their particular concerns. Whitfield has experience tracking such organizational changes, so you feel your odds of winning this client are good. But now you need to make your case. How can you craft a proposal that will make as positive an impression as possible? How can you make sure the readers at RT Industries will choose you over the competition? Read on to see how to write a persuasive proposal.

Proposals

LO10-7 Write well-organized and persuasive proposals.

Proposals are serious business. The livelihood of many companies and nonprofit organizations depends on them. Since they are carefully researched and written for high stakes, they don't exhibit the playfulness and creativity that sales and social-media messages often do.

In fact, proposals resemble reports. Both genres require that information be carefully gathered and presented. Visually, they can seem quite similar; at their most formal, they use the same kinds of prefatory material (e.g., title page, letter of transmittal, table of contents). And proposals frequently use the direct pattern that most reports use. But proposals differ from reports in one essential way: Proposals are intentionally *persuasive*. Proposal writers are not just providing information in an orderly, useful form. They are writing to get a particular result, and they have a vested interest in that result. Whether they use the direct or indirect approach, their purpose is to persuade. The following sections provide an introduction to the main types of proposals and offer guidelines for preparing them.

Types of Proposals

Proposals can vary widely in purpose, length, and format. Their purpose can be anything from acquiring a major client to getting a new copier for your department. They can range from one page to hundreds of pages. They can take the form of an email, a memo, a letter, or a report. They are usually written, but they can be presented orally or delivered in both oral and written form. As with other kinds of business communication, the context will determine the specific traits of a given proposal. But all proposals can be categorized as either internal or external and either solicited or unsolicited (Exhibit 10-9).

Exhibit 10-9   The Main Categories of Proposals

Answer these two questions to start your proposal planning:

- Is it an *internal or external* proposal? That is, will it go to readers inside or outside my organization?
- Is it a *solicited or unsolicited* proposal? That is, am I responding to a request for proposal or "selling" my idea to someone who doesn't expect it?

How you answer will help shape your proposal's contents, format, and tone.

Internal or External Proposals can be either **internal** or **external**. That is, they may be written for others within your organization or for readers outside your organization.

Web Resources for Proposal Writing

You can find excellent free advice about proposal writing—along with examples and templates—on the Internet.

Here are just a few useful sites to check out:

• CapturePlanning.com is perhaps the best all-around site for learning about proposal writing. The site is full of freebies—from examples to articles to templates—that you can access just by registering.

• The team at learntowriteproposals.com offers such useful articles as "Our Top Ten Proposal Writing Tips," "10 Ways to Make Your Proposal Easier to Understand," and "11 Things Not to Do When You Write a Business Proposal."

• Debra Klug, author of ProposalWriter.com, discusses a wide range of relatively specific topics, such as getting a government grant to start a business, and provides a huge assortment of links to proposal-related resources.

• At fedmarket.com, Richard White provides links to his free webinars and publications about how to win government contracts.

The reasons for internal proposals differ, but you will almost surely find yourself having to write them. They are a major means by which you will get what you need in order to do your job better or change your organization. Whether you want a computer upgrade, an improved physical environment, specialized training, travel money, or additional staff members, you will usually need to make your case to management. Of course, much of what you need as an employee will already be provided by your company. But when resources are tight, as they almost always are, you will have to persuade your superiors to give you the money rather than allocating it to another employee or department. Even if your idea is to enhance company operations in some way—for example, to make a procedure more efficient or cost effective—you may find yourself having to persuade. Companies tend to be conservative in terms of change. The management wants good evidence that the trouble and expense of making a change will pay off.

In addition, as the practice of outsourcing has grown, many companies have adopted a system in which departments have to compete with external vendors for projects. As the director of technical publications for a company, for example, you may find yourself bidding against a technical-writing consulting firm for the opportunity, and the funding, to write the company's online documentation. If you are not persuasive, you may find yourself with a smaller and smaller staff and, eventually, no job yourself. Clearly, the ability to write a persuasive internal proposal is an important skill.

External proposals are also written for a variety of reasons, but the most common purpose is to acquire business for a company or a grant for a nonprofit organization. Every consulting firm—whether in training, financial services, information technology, or virtually any other business specialty—depends upon external proposals for its livelihood. If such firms cannot persuade companies to choose their services, they will not be in business for long. Companies that supply other companies with goods they need, such as uniforms, computers, or raw materials, may also need to prepare proposals to win clients. Business-to-business selling is a major arena for external proposals.

But external proposals are also central to other efforts. A company might propose to merge with another company; a city government might propose that a major department store choose the

Whether solicited or unsolicited, proposals must do an effective job of presenting what is being proposed. You must work hard to meet the needs of your audience to win their business.
© Hero Images/Getty Images RF

city for its new location; a university professor might write a proposal to acquire research funding. Because most nonprofit and community organizations depend on grant money to support their work, they often write proposals to philanthropic foundations, to wealthy individuals, to businesses, or to government funding agencies. Depending on the nature of the organization that you work for, proficiency in external proposal writing could be critical.

Solicited or Unsolicited Another way to categorize proposals is **solicited** versus **unsolicited**. A solicited proposal is written in response to an explicit invitation offered by a company, foundation, or government agency that has certain needs to meet. An unsolicited proposal, as you can probably guess, is one that you submit without an official invitation to do so.

The primary means by which organizations solicit proposals is the **request for proposals**, or **RFP** (variations are requests for quotes—RFQs—and invitations for/to bid—IFBs or ITBs—both of which tend to focus only on price). These can range from brief announcements to documents of 50, 100, or more pages, depending upon the scope and complexity of the given project. As you might expect, their contents can also vary. But a lot of thought and research go into a good RFP. In fact, some RFPs—for instance, a company's request for proposals from IT firms to design and implement its technology infrastructure—need to be just as elaborately researched as the proposals being requested. Whatever its topic or purpose, the RFP needs to include a clear statement of the organization's need, the proposal guidelines (due date and time, submission process, and proposal format and contents), and the approval process, in addition to such helpful information as background about the organization.

When responding to an RFP, you should be careful to heed its guidelines. With some firms, your proposal gets eliminated if it arrives even one minute late or omits a required section. This is particularly true for proposals to the federal government, whose proposal guidelines are notoriously, and perhaps understandably, regimented (see Exhibit 10-10). On the other hand, most RFPs give you some latitude to craft your proposal in such a way that your organization can put its best foot forward. You will want to take advantage of this maneuvering room to make your proposal the most persuasive of those submitted. Of course, you will decide in the first place to respond only to those RFPs that give your organization (or, if it is an internal RFP, your department) a good chance to win.

In business situations, solicited proposals usually follow preliminary meetings between the parties involved. For example, if a business has a need for certain production equipment, its buyers might first identify likely suppliers by considering those they already know, by looking at industry material, or by asking around in their professional networks. Next they would initiate meetings with these potential suppliers to discuss the business's needs. Some or all of these suppliers would then be invited to submit a proposal for filling the need with its particular equipment. As you can see, the more relationships you have with companies that might use your goods or services, the more likely it is that they will invite you to a preliminary meeting and then invite you to bid. One expert, in fact, asserts that "winning starts with pre-RFP relationships," which "provide the intelligence you need to design and execute a winning plan."[23] Another advises that "proposals can be won (or lost) before the RFP hits the streets."[24]

Many nonprofit organizations depend upon grant writing for their survival.
© Jonathan Fredin/AP Images

Even if you are preparing a proposal for a government or foundation grant, it is wise—unless the RFP specifically forbids it—to call the funding source's office and discuss your ideas with a representative.

When writing unsolicited proposals, your job is harder than with solicited proposals. After all, in these scenarios, the intended reader has not asked for your ideas or services. For this reason,

Exhibit 10-10 First Page of a Government RFP

At FedBizOpps.gov, the U.S. government issues hundreds of opportunities for businesses, large and small, to bid on government jobs. Following are the first two pages of a 15-page RFP inviting recipients to bid on the job of planning a conference for the National Endowment for the Arts. The second page lists the kinds of contents the respondents must submit in their proposals.

As the Small Business Administration's guidelines for proposal writing advise, be sure to follow the request for proposal's specifications, or else your proposal will instantly be deemed "non-responsive" (that's government lingo for "goes in the trash").

March 10, 2016

Reference: Convening Consultant for the Future of the Arts & Creativity in America

Subject: Request for Proposal
                  Solicitation Number NEARFP16-11

Dear Offeror:

The National Endowment for the Arts (NEA) invites contractors to submit proposals for the services described in the attached statement of work, under the authority of Part 12 of the Federal Acquisition Regulation.

Enclosed you will find a Statement of Work that requests proposals for a Consultant with extensive experience in shaping large conferences (for approximately 200 people) to help the NEA and the John F. Kennedy Center for the Performing Arts (Kennedy Center) produce a convening by developing and managing 1) the agenda, 2) the participant/attendee list, and 3) the convening deliverables. The Consultant will work closely with the Chairman's Office at the National Endowment for the Arts (NEA) and production staff at the Kennedy Center.

Questions concerning this proposal shall be submitted via email to HARRISL@ARTS.GOV by **6:00 p.m. (EST) March 24, 2016**. Please **submit** your **proposals** by **April 6, 2016** at **6:00 p.m.** (EST). This RFP in no way obligates the U.S. Government to award a contract, nor does it commit the U.S. Government to pay any cost incurred in preparing and submitting your proposal.

The Government will award a contract resulting from this solicitation to the responsible offeror whose offer conforms to the solicitation and is most advantageous to the Government, price and other factors considered. In order to select the winning offeror, NEA will rank offerors from best to worst. In addition to the narrative assessments prepared by the Evaluation Team for each evaluation factor, a point scoring system will be used to rank all technical proposals. The point scoring system uses a rating scale of 100%. NEA, however, will not select an offeror for award on the basis of a superior capability without consideration of price. NEA intends to make one award under this solicitation.

This procurement is a small business set-aside. The North American Industry Classification Systems (NAICS) code for this acquisition is **541611** with a small business size standard of $15.0M. The actual period of performance will be determined at the time of award through December 1, 2016.

Proposals submitted in response to this RFP must be delivered via **email**.

Proposals that are **mailed, hand-carried, or faxed will not be accepted.** Proposals must be received by the <u>closing date and time stated above</u>. Please refer any questions concerning this request to Latonca M. Harris at (202) 682-5476 or by email at HARRISL@ARTS.GOV.

Sincerely,

Latonca M. Harris

Latonca M. Harris
Contracting Officer
Grants & Contracts Office

Continued

Exhibit 10-10 *Continued*

Enclosures:

Section B, Supplies/Service and Prices
Section C, Description/Specifications/Statement of Work
Section D, Preservation, Packaging and Marking
Section E, Inspection and Acceptance
Section F, Deliveries or Performance
Section G, Contract Administration Data
Section H, Special Contract Requirements
Section I, Contract Clauses
Section J, List of Attachments
Section K, Representations, Certifications and Other Statements of Offerors
Section L, Instructions, Conditions and Notices to Offerors
Section M, Evaluation Factors for Award

your proposal should resemble a sales message. It should quickly get the readers' attention and bring a need of theirs vividly to mind. It should then show how your product or services will answer the need. And from beginning to end, it should build your credibility. For example, if you want to provide training for a company's workforce or persuade a company to replace its current insurance provider with your company, you will need to target your readers' need in the opening, use further details to prepare them to receive your plan, lay out the benefits of your proposal quickly and clearly, and get the readers to believe that yours is the best company for the job. Careful and strategic preparation of unsolicited proposals can result in much success.

As with solicited proposals, you should try, if at all possible, to make prior contact with a person in the organization who has some power to initiate your plan. All other things being equal, a proposal to someone you know is preferable to a "cold" proposal. It is best to view the unsolicited proposal as part of a larger relationship that you are trying to create or maintain.

Proposal Format and Contents

While each proposal is unique, every successful one is designed with the key decision makers in mind, emphasizes the most persuasive elements, and presents the contents in a readable format and style.

Format and Formality The simplest proposals are often email messages. Internal proposals usually fall into this category. The more complex proposals, especially those for external parties, may take the form of long reports, including prefatory pages, extensive text, and an assortment of appended parts. Most proposals fall somewhere between these extremes.

Because of the wide variations in the makeup of proposals, you'll need to investigate the situation carefully before designing a particular proposal. Try to find out what format the readers will expect and what other proposal writers have submitted in similar situations. In the case of an invited proposal, review the request thoroughly, looking for clues concerning the preferences of the inviting organization. If you have minimal guidance, design a format based on your analysis of the audience and your knowledge of formatting strategies. Your design should be the one that you think is best for the one situation.

The same advice applies to your decisions about formality. Let your reader and the circumstances be your guide. Internal proposals tend to be less formal than external ones because the parties are often familiar with each other and because internal documents, in general, are less formal than external ones. If you are proposing a major initiative or change, however, using a formal presentation—whether oral, written, or both—may be in order. Likewise, external

Annotated Example

An Internal Unsolicited Proposal (Asking for Funding for a Professional Membership)

This email proposal asks a company to sponsor an employee's membership in a professional organization. Starting with the subject line, the writer tries to avoid saying anything that the reader—in this case, the head of a corporate communications department—would disagree with. When enough background and benefits are given, the writer states the request and then describes the cost in the most positive terms. Offering to try the membership for one year helps the proposal seem relatively modest.

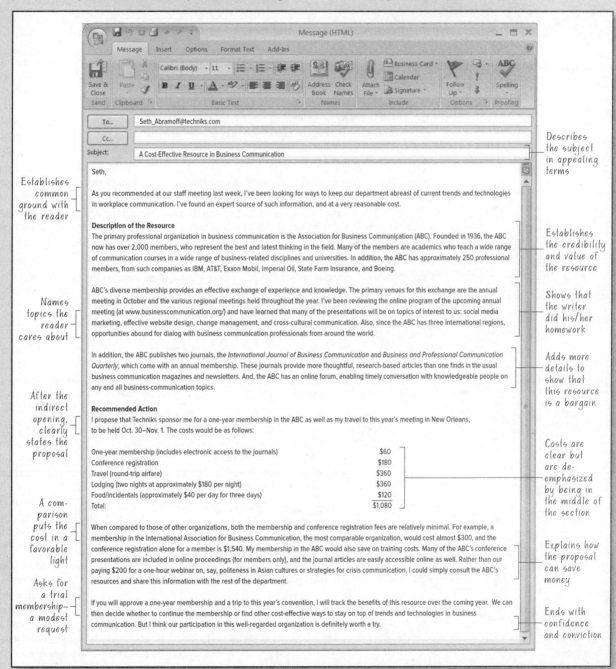

Establishes common ground with the reader

Names topics the reader cares about

After the indirect opening, clearly states the proposal

A comparison puts the cost in a favorable light

Asks for a trial membership—a modest request

Describes the subject in appealing terms

Establishes the credibility and value of the resource

Shows that the writer did his/her homework

Adds more details to show that this resource is a bargain

Costs are clear but are de-emphasized by being in the middle of the section

Explains how the proposal can save money

Ends with confidence and conviction

To... Seth_Abramoff@techniks.com

Subject: A Cost-Effective Resource in Business Communication

Seth,

As you recommended at our staff meeting last week, I've been looking for ways to keep our department abreast of current trends and technologies in workplace communication. I've found an expert source of such information, and at a very reasonable cost.

Description of the Resource

The primary professional organization in business communication is the Association for Business Communication (ABC). Founded in 1936, the ABC now has over 2,000 members, who represent the best and latest thinking in the field. Many of the members are academics who teach a wide range of communication courses in a wide range of business-related disciplines and universities. In addition, the ABC has approximately 250 professional members, from such companies as IBM, AT&T, Exxon Mobil, Imperial Oil, State Farm Insurance, and Boeing.

ABC's diverse membership provides an effective exchange of experience and knowledge. The primary venues for this exchange are the annual meeting in October and the various regional meetings held throughout the year. I've been reviewing the online program of the upcoming annual meeting (at www.businesscommunication.org/) and have learned that many of the presentations will be on topics of interest to us: social media marketing, effective website design, change management, and cross-cultural communication. Also, since the ABC has three international regions, opportunities abound for dialog with business communication professionals from around the world.

In addition, the ABC publishes two journals, the *International Journal of Business Communication* and *Business and Professional Communication Quarterly*, which come with an annual membership. These journals provide more thoughtful, research-based articles than one finds in the usual business communication magazines and newsletters. And, the ABC has an online forum, enabling timely conversation with knowledgeable people on any and all business-communication topics.

Recommended Action

I propose that Techniks sponsor me for a one-year membership in the ABC as well as my travel to this year's meeting in New Orleans, to be held Oct. 30–Nov. 1. The costs would be as follows:

One-year membership (includes electronic access to the journals)	$60
Conference registration	$180
Travel (round-trip airfare)	$360
Lodging (two nights at approximately $180 per night)	$360
Food/incidentals (approximately $40 per day for three days)	$120
Total:	$1,080

When compared to those of other organizations, both the membership and conference registration fees are relatively minimal. For example, a membership in the International Association for Business Communication, the most comparable organization, would cost almost $300, and the conference registration alone for a member is $1,540. My membership in the ABC would also save on training costs. Many of the ABC's conference presentations are included in online proceedings (for members only), and the journal articles are easily accessible online as well. Rather than our paying $200 for a one-hour webinar on, say, politeness in Asian cultures or strategies for crisis communication, I could simply consult the ABC's resources and share this information with the rest of the department.

If you will approve a one-year membership and a trip to this year's convention, I will track the benefits of this resource over the coming year. We can then decide whether to continue the membership or find other cost-effective ways to stay on top of trends and technologies in business communication. But I think our participation in this well-regarded organization is definitely worth a try.

Wise Words from a Professional Proposal Writer

A proposal or grant is the beginning of a relationship. Essentially, the readers are interviewing your company or organization, trying to determine whether a basis for a positive, constructive alliance exists. Your proposal is the face you are presenting to the client or funding source. If they feel comfortable with your proposal, they will feel comfortable with your company or organization.

Source: Richard Johnson-Sheehan, *Writing Proposals*, 2nd ed. (New York: Pearson/Longman, 2008), 232–233.

proposals, while they tend to be formal, can be quite informal if they are short and the two parties know each other well. Many successful business proposals are pitched in letter format. As with every other kind of message, adaptation to your reader is key.

Content

Whether you are writing an external or internal proposal or a solicited or unsolicited one, your primary goal is the same: to make a persuasive argument. Every element of your proposal—from the title to the cover letter to the headings and organization of your content to the way you say things—needs to contribute to your central argument.

To be able to design your proposal according to this principle, you need to know your readers and their needs (which may be represented in an RFP). You also need to know how you can meet those needs. From these two sets of facts, you can develop your central argument. What is your competitive edge? Value for the money? Convenience? Reliability? Fit of your reader's needs or mission with what you have to offer? Some or all of the above? How you frame your argument will depend on how you think your proposal will be evaluated.

The reader of a business proposal will bring three basic criteria to the evaluation process:

- Desirability of the solution (Do we need this? Will it solve our problem?)

- Qualifications of the proposer (Can the author of the proposal, whether an individual or company, really deliver, and on time and on budget?)

- Return on investment (Is the expense, whether time or money, justified?)

If you can answer these questions affirmatively from the point of view of your intended recipient, you have a good chance of winning the contract or your management's approval.

When you have figured out what to propose and why, you need to figure out how to propose it. If the RFP provides strict guidelines for contents and organization, follow them. Otherwise, you have considerable latitude when determining your proposal's components. Your reader is likely to expect some version of the following eight topics, but you should adapt them as needed to fit the facts of your case. (See the Annotated Examples for two very different proposals.)

1. *The writer's purpose and the reader's need.* An appropriate beginning is a statement of your purpose (to present a proposal) and the reader's need (such as reducing the turnover of sales staff). If the report is in response to an invitation, that statement should tie in with the invitation (for example, "as described in your July 10 announcement"). The problem and your purpose should be stated clearly. This proposal beginning illustrates:

   As requested at the July 10 meeting with Alice Burton, Thomas Cheny, and Victor Petrui in your Calgary office, Murchison and Associates present the following proposal for studying the high rate of turnover among your field representatives. We will assess the job satisfaction of the current sales force, analyze exit interview records, and compare company compensation and human resource practices with industry norms to identify the causes of this drain on your resources.

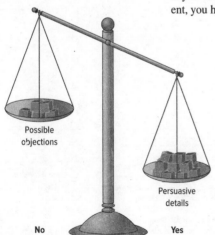

Possible objections

Persuasive details

No   Yes

Give your readers enough information to tip them toward Yes.

If a proposal is unsolicited, its beginning must gain attention in order to motivate the recipient to read the proposal. An effective way of doing this is to begin by briefly summarizing the highlights of the proposal with emphasis on its benefits. This technique is illustrated by the beginning of an unsolicited proposal that a consultant sent to prospective clients:

> Is your social marketing strategy working?
>
> Twitter, blogs, Facebook, LinkedIn—such tools have become essential to building your brand. Are you making the best use of them?
>
> Using a three-step social media audit, Mattox and Associates can find out. With access to your media and just one day of onsite interviews, our experts will tell you . . . [the rest of the proposal follows].

Your clear statement of the purpose and problem may be the most important aspect of the proposal. If you do not show right away that you understand what needs to be done and have a good plan for doing it, you may well have written the rest of your proposal in vain.

2. *The background.* Reviewing relevant background information can help lay the groundwork for your argument and demonstrate your full knowledge of the situation. For example, a college's proposal for an educational grant might review the relevant parts of the college's history. A company's proposal of a merger with another company could discuss industry developments that make the merger desirable. Or a chief executive officer's proposal to the board of directors that a company be reorganized might discuss key points from the change-management literature.

3. *The specific need.* Here is here you zero in on the recipient's specific problem or goals. Your purpose in this important section is to paint a picture of the problem or goal in such a way that the reader feels a keen need for what you are proposing.

You might wonder if this section applies in situations where an RFP has been issued. In such cases, won't readers already know what they need? In many cases the answer is no, not exactly. They may think they know, but you may see factors that they've overlooked. Plus, restating their problem in ways that lead to your proposed solution helps your persuasive effort. And whatever the situation, elaborating on the receiving organization's needs enables your readers to see that *you* understand those needs.

4. *The description of your plan.* The heart of your proposal, and its longest section, will be a description of what you propose to do. Using headings and subheadings as needed, this section should give sufficient detail to convince the reader of the plan's logic, feasibility, and appropriateness. It should also identify the "deliverables," or tangible products, of the proposal.

5. *The benefits of the proposal.* Your proposal should make it easy for your readers to see how your proposed action will benefit them. A brief statement of the benefits should appear at the front of your proposal, whether in the letter of transmittal, executive summary, opening paragraph, or all of the above. But you should elaborate on those benefits in the body of your proposal. You might do so in the section describing your plan, showing how each part will yield a benefit. Or, you might have a separate section detailing the benefits. As with sales writing, the greater the need to persuade, the more you should stress the benefits.

As an example of benefits logically covered in proposals, a college's request for funding to establish a program for retraining the older worker could point to the profitability that such funding would give local businesses. A proposal offering a consulting service to restaurants could stress such benefits as improved efficiency, reduced employee theft, savings in food costs, and increased profits.

6. *Cost and other particulars.* Once you have pitched your plan, you need to state clearly what it will cost. You may also need to cover time schedules, performance standards, means of

(text continued)

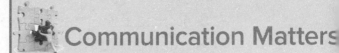

Communication Matters

The Seven Deadly Sins of Proposal Writing

Expert proposal writer Tom Sant warns against seven ways to put your proposal on the fast track to the trash can or delete folder:

1. Failing to qualify the deal (i.e., bidding on jobs that you can't win)
2. Not focusing on what the customer cares about
3. Not structuring the document persuasively
4. Not differentiating your offer and your company
5. Not offering a compelling value proposition
6. Not making it easy to understand and use
7. Not editing carefully to remove mistakes and credibility killers

Source: Tom Sant, *The Seven Deadly Sins of Proposal Writing: How to Write Proposals that Help Win Deals,* Qvidian, accessed November 13, 2016, http://info.qvidian.com.

Annotated Example

A Solicited External Proposal (Proposing to Track a Big Organizational Change—for a Fee)

A design and manufacturing company has invited research firms to propose plans for tracking its implementation of an enterprise resource planning (ERP) system—information technology that integrates all functions of the company, from job orders to accounting to customer management. The midlevel formality of this proposal responding to the RFP is appropriate given the proposal's relative brevity and the two parties' prior meeting.

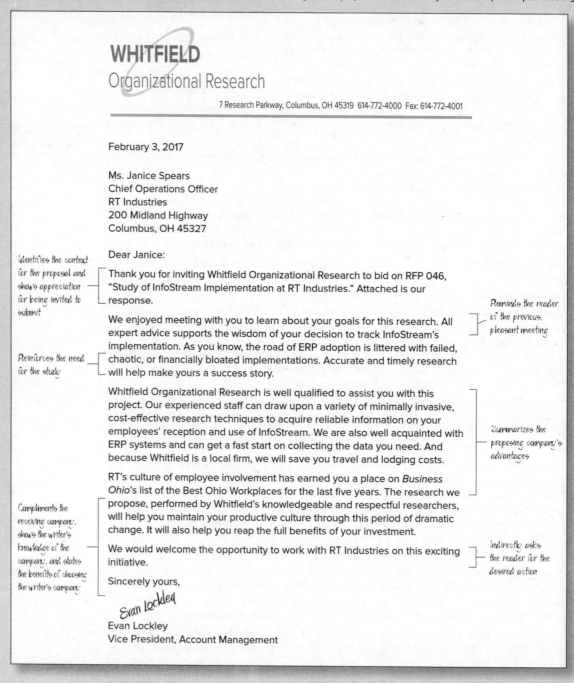

WHITFIELD
Organizational Research

7 Research Parkway, Columbus, OH 45319 614-772-4000 Fax: 614-772-4001

February 3, 2017

Ms. Janice Spears
Chief Operations Officer
RT Industries
200 Midland Highway
Columbus, OH 45327

Dear Janice:

Identifies the context for the proposal and shows appreciation for being invited to submit

Thank you for inviting Whitfield Organizational Research to bid on RFP 046, "Study of InfoStream Implementation at RT Industries." Attached is our response.

Reminds the reader of the previous, pleasant meeting

We enjoyed meeting with you to learn about your goals for this research. All expert advice supports the wisdom of your decision to track InfoStream's implementation. As you know, the road of ERP adoption is littered with failed, chaotic, or financially bloated implementations. Accurate and timely research will help make yours a success story.

Reinforces the need for the study

Whitfield Organizational Research is well qualified to assist you with this project. Our experienced staff can draw upon a variety of minimally invasive, cost-effective research techniques to acquire reliable information on your employees' reception and use of InfoStream. We are also well acquainted with ERP systems and can get a fast start on collecting the data you need. And because Whitfield is a local firm, we will save you travel and lodging costs.

Summarizes the proposing company's advantages

RT's culture of employee involvement has earned you a place on *Business Ohio*'s list of the Best Ohio Workplaces for the last five years. The research we propose, performed by Whitfield's knowledgeable and respectful researchers, will help you maintain your productive culture through this period of dramatic change. It will also help you reap the full benefits of your investment.

Compliments the receiving company, shows the writer's knowledge of the company, and states the benefits of choosing the writer's company

We would welcome the opportunity to work with RT Industries on this exciting initiative.

Indirectly asks the reader for the desired action

Sincerely yours,

Evan Lockley

Evan Lockley
Vice President, Account Management

Annotated Example (continued)

Response to RFP 046:
Study of InfoStream Implementation at RT Industries

Proposed by
Whitfield Organizational Research
February 3, 2017

Executive Summary

Provides a clear overview of the problem, purpose, and benefits

RT Industries has begun a major organizational change with its purchase of InfoStream enterprise resource planning (ERP) software. To track the effect of this change on personnel attitudes and work processes in the company, RT seeks the assistance of a research firm with expertise in organizational studies. Whitfield Organizational Research has extensive experience with personnel-based research, as well as familiarity with ERP software. We propose a four-part plan that will help ensure the success of your implementation.

Our methodology will be multifaceted, minimally disruptive, and cost effective. The results will yield a reliable picture of how InfoStream is being received and used among RT's workforce. With this information, RT's change leaders can intervene appropriately to effectively manage this companywide innovation.

Project Goals

RT Industries has so far invested over $1.6 million and over 1,000 employee hours in the purchase of and management's training on InfoStream's ERP system. As RT integrates the system fully into its company of 800+ employees over the next 12 months, it will invest many additional dollars and hours in the project, with the total investment likely to top $2 million. Adopting such a system is one of the most wide-ranging and expensive changes a company can make.

Shows knowledge of the company; reminds readers of the investment they want to protect

Reinforces the need for the study

As Jeri Dunn, Chief Information Officer of Nestle USA, commented in *CIO Magazine* about her company's troubles with its ERP adoption, "No major software implementation is really about the software. It's about change management." An ERP system affects the daily work of everyone in the company. The most common theme in ERP-adoption failure stories—of which there are many—is lack of attention to the employees' experience of the transition. Keeping a finger on the pulse of the organization during this profound organizational change is critical to maximizing the return on your investment.

Our research will determine

- How well employees are integrating InfoStream into their jobs.
- How the new system is changing employees' work processes.
- How the system is affecting the general environment or "culture" in the company.

States the benefits, supported by clear logic

Whitfield has designed a four-part, multimethod research plan to gather these data. Through our periodic reports, you will be able to see how InfoStream is being integrated into the working life of the company. As a result, you will be able to make, and budget for, such interventions as strategic communications and additional training. You will also find out where employee work processes need to be adjusted to accommodate the new system.

Whitfield Organizational Research 2

Instituting a change of this magnitude *will* generate feedback, whether it is employee grumbling or constructive criticism. Whitfield associates will gather this feedback in a positive, orderly way and compile it into a usable format. The findings will enable RT's management to address initial problems and ward off future problems. The research itself will also contribute to the change management efforts of the company by giving RT's employee stakeholders a voice in the process and allowing their feedback to contribute to the initiative's success.

Deliverables

The information you need will be delivered as shown below. All dates assume a project start date of July 1, 2017.

Readers can see the products of the proposed research up front

Approximate Date:	Deliverable:
October 1, 2017	Written report on an **initial** study of 12–14 employees' work processes and attitudes and on a companywide survey.
February 1, 2018	Written report at **midyear** on the same employees' work processes and attitudes and on a second companywide survey.
June 30, 2018	**Year-end** report (written and oral) on employees' work processes and attitudes and on a final companywide survey.

Anticipated Schedule/Methods

The research will take place from July 1, 2017, the anticipated go-live date for InfoStream at RT, to approximately June 30, 2018. As shown below, there will be four main components to this research, with Part III forming the major part of the project.

Research Part and Time Frame	Purpose	Methods
Part I (July '17)	Gather background information; recruit research participants	Gather data on RT (history, products/ mission, organizational structure/ culture, etc.). Interview personnel at RT and at InfoStream about why RT is adopting an ERP system, why RT bought InfoStream, and how employees at RT have been informed about InfoStream. During this period we will also work with the COO's staff to recruit participants for the main part of the study (Part III).

Gives details of the project in a readable format

Whitfield Organizational Research 3

Research Part and Time Frame	Purpose	Methods
Part II (July '17):	Obtain the perspective of the InfoStream launch team	Conduct a focus group with the launch team, with emphasis on their goals for and concerns about the implementation. Anticipated duration of this interview would be one hour, with participants invited to share any additional feedback afterward in person or by email.
Part III (July–Sept. '17; Nov. '14–Jan. '18; Mar.–June '18):	Assess the impact of InfoStream on employee work processes and attitudes	Conduct three rounds of 1–2 hour interviews with approximately 12–14 RT employees to track their use of InfoStream. Ideally, we will have one or two participants from each functional area of the company, with multiple levels of the company represented.
Part IV (September '17, January '18, May '18)	Assess companywide reception of InfoStream	Conduct three Web-based surveys during the year to track general attitudes about the implementation of InfoStream.

This plan yields the following time line:

	7/17	8/17	9/17	10/17	11/17	12/17	1/18	2/18	3/18	4/18	5/18	6/18
Initial research	▓	▓										
Focus group	▓											
1st round of interviews	▓	▓	▓									
1st Web survey			▓									
Initial report				▓								
2nd round of interviews					▓	▓	▓					
2nd Web survey							▓					
Midyear report								▓				
3rd round of interviews									▓	▓	▓	
3rd Web survey											▓	
Year-end report												▓

Timeline makes it easy to see what will happen at each point

Annotated Example (continued)

Interview Structure and Benefits

While Parts I, II, and IV will provide essential information about the project and its reception, the most valuable data will come from Part III, the onsite interviews with selected RT employees. Gathering data in and about the subject's own work context is the only reliable way to learn what is really happening in terms of the employees' daily experience. Following is a description of our methodology for gathering these kinds of data:

Initial interview:

- Gather background information about the participants (how long they have worked at RT, what their jobs consist of, what kind of computer experience they've had, how they were trained on InfoStream).
- Ask them to show us, by walking us through sample tasks, how they use InfoStream.
- Ask them to fill out a questionnaire pertaining to their use of InfoStream.
- Go back over their answers, asking them to explain why they chose the answers they did.
- Ask them either to keep notes on or email us about any notable experiences they have with InfoStream.
- Take notes on any interruption, interactions, and other activities that occur during the interview.

From data gained in these interviews, we will assess how well the participants' current work processes are meshing with InfoStream. We will also document how use of InfoStream is affecting the participants' attitudes and their interactions with other employees and departments. We will check our findings with the participants for accuracy before including these data in the initial report.

Midyear interview:

- Ask the participants if they have any notable experiences to relate about InfoStream and/or if any changes have occurred in the tasks they perform using InfoStream.
- Have the participants fill out the same questionnaire as in the first interviews.
- Discuss with participants the reasons for any changes in their answers since the first questionnaire.
- Observe any interactions or other activities that occur during the interview.
- Check our findings with the participants for accuracy before including these data in the midyear report.

Year-end interviews:

- Will be conducted in the same fashion as the second interviews.
- Will also include questions allowing participants to debrief about the project and about InfoStream in general.

Benefits of this interview method:

- Because researchers will be physically present in the employees' work contexts, they **can gather a great deal of information**, whether observed or reported by the employee, **in a short amount of time**.
- Because employees will be asked to elaborate on their written answers, the researcher **can learn the true meaning of the employee's responses**.

Special section elaborates on the company's unique methodology; helps justify the most expensive part of the plan

Whitfield Organizational Research   **5**

- Asking employees to verify the researcher's findings **will add another validity check and encourage honest, thorough answers**.

Specific Knowledge Goals

We will design the interviews and the companywide surveys to find out the extent to which

- InfoStream is making participants' jobs easier or harder, or easier in some ways and harder in others.

- InfoStream is making their work more or less efficient.

- InfoStream is making their work more or less effective.

- They believe InfoStream is helping the company overall.

- They are satisfied with the instruction they have received about the system.

- InfoStream is changing their interactions with other employees.

- InfoStream is changing their relations with their supervisors.

- InfoStream is affecting their overall attitude toward their work.

The result will be a detailed, reliable picture of how InfoStream is playing out at multiple levels and in every functional area of RT Industries, enabling timely intervention by RT management.

A tantalizing list of what the readers most want to know whets their desire to hire the proposing company

Cost

Opening sentence notes cost savings.

Because we are a local firm, no travel or lodging expenses will be involved.

Research Component	Estimated Hours	Cost
Part I (background fact finding)	6 hours	$300
Part II (focus group with launch team)	3 hours (includes preparation and analysis)	$300
Part III (3 rounds of on-site interviews)	474 hours	$18,960
Part IV (3 rounds of Web-based surveys)	48 hours	$1,920
Preparation of Reports	90 hours	$3,600
		Total: $25,080

Cost breakdown justifies the expense but is not so detailed that the readers can nitpick specific items

Credentials

Efficient credentials section focuses only on relevant qualifications

Whitfield Organizational Research has been recognized by the American Society for Training and Development as a regional leader in organizational consulting. We have extensive education and experience in change management, organizational psychology, quantitative and qualitative research methods, and team building. Our familiarity with ERP software, developed through projects with such clients as Orsys and PRX Manufacturing, makes us well suited to serve RT's needs. Résumés and references will be mailed upon request or can be downloaded from www. whitfieldorganizationalresearch.com.

appraising performance, and equipment and supplies needed. Remember that a proposal is essentially a contract. Anticipate and address any issues that may arise, and present your requirements in the most positive light.

7. *Evidence of your ability to deliver.* The proposing organization must sometimes establish its ability to perform. This means presenting information on such matters as the qualifications of personnel, success in similar cases, the adequacy of equipment and facilities, operating procedures, and environmental consciousness. With an external proposal, resist the temptation to include long, generic résumés. The best approach is to select only the most persuasive details about your personnel. If you do include résumés, tailor them to the situation.

8. *Concluding comments.* In most proposals you should urge or suggest the desired action. This statement often occurs in a letter to the readers, but if there is no cover letter or the proposal itself is not a letter, it can form the conclusion of your proposal. You might also include a summary of your proposal's highlights or provide one final persuasive push in a concluding section.

Whatever you're writing—whether a proposal, request, sales message, content-marketing post, tweet, or some other kind of message—the art of persuasion can be one of your most valuable assets. Adding the tips in this chapter to your general problem-solving approach will help you prepare for all those times in your career when you will need others' cooperation and support.

Power Charge Your Professionalism: Make Logical Comparisons

When making comparisons in your writing, be sure they are logically worded. Keep these points in mind:

Be sure your comparison is complete. If you use a word like "more," "faster," or "easiest," be sure to say or clearly imply the rest of the comparison ("more" or "faster" than what? "Easiest" out of what group of things?).

Be sure your comparison is logical. Things being compared must be the same kinds of things. Consider this sentence: "Unlike Gap's Facebook page, Coldwater Creek uses models of many different ages." It contains an illogical comparison because it compares Gap's *page* to the *company* Coldwater Creek. The sentence should read "Unlike Gap's Facebook page, Coldwater Creek's (or "Coldwater Creek's page") uses models of many different ages."

Make comparisons that use more/less/-er and most/least/-est correctly. The rule is to use "more," "less," or "-er" when comparing only two things. When comparing more things, use "most," "least," or "-est."

Assess the comparisons in the following sentences. If the sentence contains a comparison error, correct it. If you think the sentence can be left as is, explain why.

1. This smartphone, offered only by Verizon, is the fastest.
2. CrudAway will clean your engine better, and at a fraction of the cost.
3. In a blind taste test with the other leading brand, consumers rated Tums the highest.
4. This campaign was less successful than last year.
5. Our toothpaste now has even more whitening power!
6. Our technicians and service managers are the most honest and ethical auto-repair shop in the city.
7. Our competitive pricing makes us one of the more popular landscaping firms.
8. We will need more donations to be able to create the child care center.

Being sure your comparisons are logical is important because . . .

• Faulty comparisons can be confusing.
• They can make it sound like you are making empty or exaggerated claims.
• They can make you appear to be poorly educated and/or careless—neither of which is an impression you want to convey.

For additional instruction and practice, see "Faulty Comparison" under "Style and Word Choice" in LearnSmart Achieve.

Key Terms

persuasive messages 296
overtly persuasive
    messages 296
indirect order 296
content marketing 296
direct order 296
demographic information 297
psychographic
    information 297
tangible rewards 297
intangible rewards 297
reader benefits 297

product benefits 297
added-on benefits 297
product features 297
scenario painting 298
logic (*logos*) 298
emotion (*pathos*) 298
character (*ethos*) 298
persuasive requests 299
common-ground persuasion
    technique 300
sales message 306
spam 306

permission-based email 306
integrated marketing
    communications 324
brand equity 328
social media plan 330
proposals 336
internal proposal 336
external proposal 336
solicited proposals 338
unsolicited proposals 338
requests for proposals
    (RFPs) 338

Critical-Thinking Questions

1. Explain why a persuasive request is usually written in the indirect order. In what kinds of situations might the direct order be appropriate? LO2

2. What does it mean to use the you-viewpoint in persuasive requests and sales messages? LO2, LO5

3. Compare persuasive requests and sales messages. What traits do they share? Can you point to some general differences? LO2, LO5

4. Consider ads that you have seen on television, in magazines, or on the Internet. Which ones rely heavily on emotional appeals? Which on logical appeals? Which on character-based appeals? Do the chosen appeals seem appropriate given the product, service, or cause that is being promoted? LO1, LO5

5. Think of or find a television, radio, print, email, or Web-based sales message or persuasive request that you regard as especially effective. Explain why you think it was well designed. LO2, LO5

6. What appeals would be appropriate for the following products when they are being sold to consumers? How might the appeals differ depending on the age and/or gender of the target audience? LO1, LO4
    a. Shaving cream or razors
    b. Home repair tools
    c. Frozen vegetables
    d. A wireless service provider
    e. Lubricating oil
    f. Tires
    g. Women's jeans
    h. Candy
    i. Breakfast cereal
    j. Video games
    k. Medicine for a health condition

7. Assume that you're preparing a sales mailing that won't use the reader's name. Would you still use a salutation (e.g., "Dear Neighbor")? If so, what would you use? If not, how would the message begin? LO5

8. "Any fundraising or sales message that is longer than a page won't be read." Discuss this statement. LO2, LO5

9. If you were helping to design an email message to sell solar panels, would you include visual elements? If so, what kind? If not, why not? LO5

10. Discuss the relationship between the main sales message and its accompanying support information in an example you've seen. What was the persuasive purpose of each piece? LO4–LO6

11. Examine the call for action in a persuasive request or sales message you've received. Do you think it would get results? Why or why not? LO2, LO5

12. Think of a sample persuasive request or sales message that you regard as ethically questionable. Discuss the nature of the ethical problems. LO3

13. Many fundraising messages show pictures of children in poverty or with obvious health problems. In what way can the use of such emotional visuals be justified? In what way might they be ethically questionable? **LO3**

14. Both fundraising and sales mailings are often "signed" with a signature that looks handwritten. Sometimes there even appear to be handwritten personal notes in the mailings. What do you think of this practice? Does it add to the messages' effectiveness? Could it be considered ethically shady? **LO1–LO5**

15. For what kinds of situations would you prepare email sales messages that have a fair amount of text versus messages that are almost all graphics? Why? **LO5–LO6**

16. How does the need to be persuasive make a proposal different from a report? **LO7**

17. Discuss the differences between solicited and unsolicited proposals. **LO7**

18. For what kinds of situations might you select email format for your proposal? Letter format? A longer, report-like format? **LO7**

19. "I don't need to discuss my readers' needs in my proposal. They know what their needs are and don't want to waste time reading about them." Discuss. **LO7**

Skills-Building Exercises

1. Assume that, as a volunteer for a nonprofit organization in your town, you have been asked to write the next fundraising letter for the organization. In what ways might you gather enough information about the intended readers to write a successful message? **LO1, LO2**

2. List the tangible and intangible benefits that you might describe when promoting the following items or services. **LO1**
   a. Membership in a health club
   b. High-speed Internet service or digital cable service
   c. A certain line of clothing
   d. Car insurance

3. List some added-on benefits you might use as an extra push if you were promoting the items in exercise 2. **LO1**

4. For each item in exercise 2, list two likely product features and then turn them into reader benefits. **LO1**

5. Choose one of the items in exercise 2 and write a paragraph that uses scenario painting to promote the item. **LO1**

6. Critique the following persuasive request message. It was written by the membership chairperson of a chapter of the Service Corps of Retired Executives (SCORE), a service organization consisting of retired executives who donate their managerial talents to small businesses in the area. The recipients of the message are recently retired executives. **LO1, LO2**

   Dear Ms. Petersen:

   As membership chair it is my privilege to invite you to join the Bay City chapter of the Service Corps of Retired Executives.

   We are a volunteer, not-for-profit organization. We are retired business executives who give free advice and assistance to struggling small businesses. There is a great demand for our services in the Bay City area, which is why we are conducting this special membership drive. The work is hard and the hours can be long, but it is satisfying to be of help to others.

   Please find enclosed a self-addressed envelope and a membership card. Fill out the card and return it to me as soon as possible. We meet the first Monday of every month (8:30 at the Chamber of Commerce office). This is the fun part – strictly social. A lot of nice people belong.

   I hope we can count on you.

   Sincerely yours,

7. The following request was sent to faculty who had at least one university athlete in their classes. The response wasn't very good (few recipients replied, and a few who did reply declined to participate). Why do you think it was so unsuccessful? What advice would you have given the writer of this email if he/she had shown you a draft? LO1, LO2

> Subject: Invitation to Participate in a Pilot Project
>
> The Center for Excellence in eLearning, in partnership with Student-Athlete Support Services (SASS), is conducting an opt-in pilot during Spring Semester 2016 to determine whether assigning the Observer role to academic advisors in Blackboard can improve learning outcomes for the student athletes they advise. The goal is to encourage open and honest discussions between students and their advisors and to ensure that the athletes are compliant with NCAA regulations and university policies.
>
> In addition to counseling student athletes, SASS advisors confirm that their advisees are meeting academic requirements through frequent and proactive contact with instructors. The current process requires student athletes authorize the release of their records by presenting a paper form to each of their instructors at the start of each term. It also requires instructors respond to individual inquiries from athletic advisors.
>
> As Observers, advisors can monitor their students directly in Blackboard, eliminating the administrative overhead of the current process. Originally created for parents to monitor the progress of K-12 students, we are repurposing the Observer role to provide athletic advisors with a limited, read-only view of an advisee's course.
>
> Observers can:
>
> - Read the Course Overview, Announcements, and the syllabus.
>
> - Access select course content areas, like Learning Modules, Course Documents, embedded videos, and learning objects.
>
> - See the course calendar and upcoming due dates.
>
> - Review graded items, including Assignment comments with any annotations and written feedback from the instructor.
>
> - Optionally receive email messages sent through the Retention Center.
>
> Observers *cannot*:
>
> - Access content areas or items unavailable to students.
>
> - Connect to publisher tools like McGraw Hill Connect, Wiley Plus, Web Assign, or Echo360's Active Learning Platform.
>
> - Read or post messages in discussion boards, blogs, wikis, or journals.
>
> - Access the Grade Center, see the grades of other students, or send email messages from the course.
>
> - View rubrics, open an exam, or review test answers.
>
> Observers can see most content areas by default, but instructors can override these settings, selectively choosing which content areas and tools are accessible to Observers.
>
> We would like to invite you to participate in this pilot project by completing the form at https://www.surveymonkey.com/pilotproject and selecting which courses to include in the pilot project. Please complete the form before the close of business on Wednesday, February 24.
>
> Thank you for your consideration. Please let me know if you have any additional questions or concerns.

8. In almost any situation requiring persuasion, the writer can choose from several promising strategies. For one of the Annotated Examples in the sections on persuasive requests and sales messages, plan how you might rewrite the message using a completely different approach. LO1–LO5

9. Evaluate each of these parts of sales messages. LO5

Email Subject Line

a. Earn BIG profits NOW!!!
b. Reduce expenses with an experienced consultant's help
c. Free trial offer ends this week!
d. Your coupons are about to expire (from a store where you shop)
e. This week's travel deals (from a discount travel site you've used)
f. Tell us about your service experience with us (from your cable provider or the tech help of a major computer company)
g. Evaluate our service (from a mail-order company where you've shopped)
h. The best electric razor on the market!
i. Your opinion needed (from a charity you're familiar with)
j. Your account needs to be updated now.
k. Inquiry
l. An irresistible offer . . . (from a store where you shop)

Openings

Product or Service: A Credit Card That Gives Bonus Points toward Multiple Airlines

a. Where would you like to go? How would you like to get there?
b. With a Blue Horizons credit card, you'll get 5,000 sky points just for opening an account.
c. How does "no annual fee" sound?

Product or Service: A Financial Consulting Service

d. Would you hire yourself to manage your portfolio?
e. Are you satisfied with the income your portfolio earned last year?
f. Dimmitt-Hawes Financial Services has helped its clients make money for over half a century.

From the Body of the Message

Product or Service: A Pest-Control Company

a. If your home gets hit by termites while you're covered by our plan, you won't pay a dime for any future treatments or repairs—guaranteed.
b. Our guarantee covers all future treatments and any needed repairs.
c. Once you purchase our guarantee, all treatments and repairs will be covered for as long as your plan is active.

Product or Service: A Mail-Order Food Company

d. Our pasta assortment makes a great gift for your family, friends, and colleagues.
e. Treat your friends and business associates to a true taste of Italy with this elegant and affordable gift.
f. The aroma will remind you of walking into a neighborhood ristorante in Milano or Rome.

Product or Service: A Unique Mattress

g. Control Comfort's unique air support system lets you control the feel and firmness of your bed simply by pushing a button.
h. The button control adjusts the feel and firmness of Control Comfort's air support system.
i. Just by pushing a button you can get your choice of feel and firmness in Control Comfort's air support system.

Action Endings

Product or Service: An Alumni Directory

a. To receive your personal copy, just sign and return the enclosed order form along with your check or credit card information.
b. To find out what your classmates are doing now, just fill out and return the enclosed card along with your payment.
c. Don't put it off! Now, while it's on your mind, sign and return the enclosed card.

Product or Service: A News Magazine

d. To begin receiving your copies of *Today's World*, simply fill out and return the enclosed card or subscribe online.
e. For your convenience, a subscription card is enclosed. It is your ticket to receiving *Today's World*.
f. If you agree that *Today's World* is the best of the news magazines, just check "yes!" on the enclosed form and drop it in the mail.

Postscripts

a. You can also monogram items you order before November 1.

b. If you order before November 1, you can have your items monogrammed.

c. All orders placed before November 1 are eligible for monogramming.

10. Study the visual dimension (including the logo) of a company's online sales messages. In what ways do the visuals add to the persuasion? What image of the company do they convey? LO5, LO6

11. Find a series of tweets or blog posts from a spokesperson for an organization. What kind of voice does this person use? What image of the company is being conveyed? LO6

12. Evaluate a content-marketing blog post in an area you know something about or are interested in. How effective do you think it is? Why? LO6

13. Choose a company or nonprofit organization and study how it presents itself across several media. In what ways is a consistent brand projected? In what ways does the company present itself differently depending on the medium? LO6

14. Find and study the guidelines for applying for an undergraduate research grant at your school (or study the ones at the University of Connecticut). What are the criteria (both explicit and implied) for a successful proposal? When reviewing a set of proposals that all meet these criteria, what kinds of facts might lead the selection committee to fund certain projects and not others? LO6

15. Pretend you are writing an unsolicited internal proposal to request funding for a trip to a major professional meeting in your area of expertise. What kinds of information will you need to include? What arguments might your supervisors or management find convincing? What kinds of objections might you need to overcome? LO6

Problem-Solving Cases

Persuasive Requests

1. **Helping to Recruit Faculty and Staff for a Service Event:** As a student employee in your school's community relations department, you've attracted positive attention with your strong communication skills. As a result, the assistant director has asked you on several occasions to critique news releases, Web content, and other information from this office. That business communication course you took last semester must have really paid off!

Today your boss drops by your desk with a printout of an email that he's frowning over. "We're not getting the participation we want in our yearly Tech U Serves event," he complains. Handing you the email, he says, "Here's what we sent out this year. I think this invitation may be part of the problem." You read what it says:

Subject: Sign up for Tech U Serves

All Tech U faculty and staff are invited to participate in this year's Tech U Serves event, which will take place on May 6. To register, click here. You can indicate on the form what kind of work you want to do and what kind of organization you want to help. Be sure to get your supervisor's permission, if applicable, since there is a limited number of volunteer spots available.

You'll need to come to the kick-off event on the Commons on May 3 between 11:00 a.m. and 1:00 p.m. to pick up your registration materials. You can also meet your service team. Raffle prizes will be awarded to those in attendance.

Tom Huber

Community Relations

572-3382

You agree that the invitation is not appealing, nor does it answer some of the readers' likely questions. To learn more about the event, you visit the Community Relations website. There you find a list of places where Tech U Serves volunteers have served in the past (see the list below). Using your best problem-solving strategies for persuasive requests, rewrite the invitation for your boss. (Your instructor may substitute a different campus event.)

Examples of past clients/projects for Tech U Serves:

—Westwood School: Painting and Updating Walls/Adding Color

Description: We have really "blah" walls in the school and it is really hard to get things to hallway or in the cafeteria to add some color to the building . . . but we were thinking of maybe doing it on a canvas versus the wall itself. . . . just thoughts. This would be a great thing for our school.

Type of Service: Environmental

—Corryville Catholic: Painting Student Bathroom

Description: This bathroom has high ceilings. Some of the younger girls are frightened of the boiler noises that come from this bathroom. By refreshing it up, we hope to eliminate the fear of using the bathroom.

Type of Service: Environmental

—WordPlay Cincy: Read the Day Away

Description: Volunteers would come to local primary school(s) to read with children in class. Volunteers may also assist WordPlay with organizing and transporting books for children. There will be a brief introduction to WordPlay, lunch, reading with children, then assisting around WordPlay with various tasks.

Type of Service: Working with People

—Retirement Village at Long Cove Point

Description: Card playing, sing-a-long, assist in gardening with residents

Type of Service: Working with People

—Friends of the Public Library

Description: In preparation for our big 43rd annual used book sale in June, volunteers are needed to help pack hundreds of boxes of books at our book warehouse in Hartwell.

Type of Service: Physical

—Cincinnati Community Toolbank

Description: Volunteers will assist staff with prepping tools to be repaired or painted and possibly helping staff pull tools for upcoming orders.

Type of Service: Physical

—WH Community Garden

Description: We have 25 beds now with drawings for an additional 50 beds. We would love to get an additional 25 done in 2015. I think two people can build and set into place one bed in an hour. We will procure the wood and the screws, all we need are people handy with power tools. We are working hard to make Walnut Hills a healthier community!

Type of Service: Physical

—Habitat for Humanity of Greater Cincinnati

Description: Join with Habitat for Humanity of Greater Cincinnati to build homes, communities, and hope. Participants will help build a home for a deserving family from 9:00 a.m.–4:00 p.m. Zero Experience is required. All tools and safety gear will be provided. Training will take place onsite. Specific duties will depend on the status of the build project.

Type of Service: Physical

—Summerside Elementary School: Outdoor Classroom/Go Green Courtyard

Description: Summerside Elementary is part of the West Clermont School District and we are looking to begin work on an outdoor classroom with trails that will be used by classroom teachers. Also, we are looking to develop our courtyard into an area where our go green club could grow plants and flowers for our school grounds.

Type of Service: Environmental, Physical

—Avondale Every Child Succeeds: Avondale ECS/Carmel Church Community Clean Up

Description: Paint front doors of church; clean chairs and tables; clean and organize small kitchen. Thank you for helping us organize our space for the Avondale families. We need things like paintbrushes, rollers, tarp, and some cleaning supplies.

Type of Service: Environmental, Physical

—Clovernook Center for the Blind and Visually Impaired: Make Clovernook Center Beautiful

Description: Volunteers will be working outside to help landscape the grounds of the Clovernook Center for the Blind and Visually Impaired. Tasks included weeding, gardening, laying down mulch, etc. Volunteers are asked to bring gloves, shovels, rakes, edgers, and any other gardening supplies they might have.

Type of Service: Environmental, Physical

—American Cancer Society Cincinnati Hope Lodge: Hope Lodge Spring Cleaning

Description: Shampoo carpets in common areas of lodge with lodge shampooer. Clean & sort the four kitchens. Dust & polish the woodwork in Hope Lodge.

Type of Service: Environmental, Physical

2. **Revising a Membership Renewal Message:** In many cities, each neighborhood has its own elected community council that looks after the neighborhood, responds to (and often acts on) neighbors' concerns, oversees projects, and represents the neighborhood to City Council. Pretend that you were recently elected to one of these community councils and have volunteered to serve on the membership committee. One of the other committee members has volunteered to write this year's membership-renewal request, and this is the email message she proposes to send out:

Subject line: SC is missing you.

Happy New Year from Southview Council.

Our Membership Committee has been pondering what they did wrong in 2015. They have you on a list of good members that renewed your membership in 2014, but chose not to renew in 2015. We respect your decision to not renew, but we are curious about what caused you to make this choice. We would like to work our way back into your good graces again. We represent you and do many good works, programs, and events to support you—our Southview neighbor. As we wrote in our emails to you previously, a lot of our efforts are possible through your membership dues. Memberships are the second largest fundraising activity the Southview Council performs.

We would appreciate your sharing your thoughts and concerns on this matter. We will reflect upon them in an effort to improve & change what we are doing. Please email us with a reply, or feel free to come to one of our monthly meetings to speak to all our Trustees.

Kind regards,

SC Membership Committee

Given what you know about making persuasive requests, you're sure there's a better approach. Rewrite the message to make it more effective. To gather convincing details, read the websites of some community councils to see the kinds of good work they do for their neighborhoods.

3. **Persuading Alums to Participate in a Survey:** Assume that you're on a student team that is doing a project for a marketing, information technology, business communication, or other business-related course. Your project will involve conducting an online survey to find out _____ about alums of your school's business college (you decide the topic/purpose of the survey).

With the support of your instructor, you were able to persuade the administrators of the college to share with your team the email addresses of its graduates from the last five years (to the extent that the graduates have kept their contact information updated). You've designed the survey—but now you need to write the email cover message that, you hope, will persuade people to participate. Think carefully about the kinds of appeals that might work well for this audience and write the message. (With your instructor's permission, you can choose a different college or a certain major.)

4. **Persuading a Professional to Let You Shadow Him/Her:** Assume that an instructor is requiring you to "shadow" a professional in your field for half a day so that you can use your observations as the basis of a short report. Find someone in your field whose job you want to learn more about and write him or her a persuasive email requesting that you be allowed to tag along for a morning or afternoon. Do not choose someone you know. Think carefully about the reader's possible objections and include the information that will make your request successful.

5. **Using an Announcement to Promote Your Nonprofit:** The Metroville Cultural Arts Center (or women's shelter, or animal-rescue organization, or another nonprofit of your choosing) has exciting news: It has just been awarded a grant worth $____,000 (you choose the amount) from The ____ (you fill in the name of the funder) to ____ (you fill in what the money will be used for).

Seize this opportunity to email current and past supporters of your organization not only to tell them the good news but also to encourage them to make a donation and/or volunteer. Make your announcement visually appealing, and use what you know about logical, emotional, and character-based appeals to stir your readers to action. (Even if they don't act now, though, this message will definitely help build your brand equity with them.) Think carefully, too, about other material that this message could/should be linked to.

6. **Raising Funds for Your Team:** As a member of a sports (or some other kind of) team at your school that doesn't get sufficient (or any) funding to operate, you've noticed that some of the other teams have raised money by conducting clever fundraising campaigns. For example, the women's crew team ran a "Rent-a-Rower" campaign that invited university personnel and those living near campus to hire one or more rowers for various jobs. You've been working with your coach and teammates to figure out how your team can raise money, and you've come up with this great idea: (you decide what it is!). Write the message that will make the campaign a success. Think carefully about what will be in your message, how you'll design it, how you'll distribute it, and who will receive it.

7. **Publicizing a Charitable Event:** A student organization to which you belong has chosen ____ (you decide what) as its main charity event this year. Your job is to write a persuasive message to attract donations or paying supporters.

You'll need to tell the recipients of your message when, where, and how to participate. Think about their likely questions and about the kinds of details that might prompt them to actually participate. Once you've worked out the logistics and your persuasive strategy, write the message. You might want to design it as an attractive flyer or poster.

8. **Recruiting People to Serve on Your Business Advisory Board:** You work as the director of the Job Service Office in your town. You help the unemployed search for work, take required employment exams or software competency tests, write résumés and application letters, fill out applications, prepare for interviews, and practice interview skills. You've read about similar agencies in other states where local offices have a business advisory board made up of business people in the community. You think this is just what you need—an advisory board that informs you of trends in various industries, gives advice on skills employers are looking for, and provides general input regarding jobs in your community.

You decide that you are going to create such a board. You envision that the business advisory board will meet formally twice a year. Two or three other times a year, you may survey them to learn about employment trends in your community. You also would like board members to be available informally to provide input regarding the services you offer and how you might improve your work. You're guessing that being a board member would require 10–15 hours per year, and you'd like for each member to agree to a two-year term.

Your first step in recruiting members is to think about the types of businesses in your community: manufacturing, industry, technology, law, medicine, finance, retail, food service, and hospitality. You'll also need to think about why these businesses might benefit from having a member of their staff on your business advisory board.

Prepare a letter of invitation to send to the human resources directors at these businesses. Persuade them to recruit a representative from their company to serve on your board.

9. **Recruiting People to Serve on Your Email Advisory Panel:** You work at the company head-quarters for a chain of retail stores (you decide what kind). One of your jobs is to recruit customers for your email advisory panel. Customers who join this panel receive approximately eight surveys a year on such topics as product selection, customer service, and the general shopping experience. Essentially, the panel is a group of loyal customers who make it easy for you to get feedback that helps your stores remain competitive. For each survey they complete, the panel members are automatically entered into a drawing for $1,000. They do need to complete every survey in order to continue to be panel members.

Your first step in recruiting members is to include on customers' receipts an invitation for them to visit the company website, take a survey, and have their names entered into a drawing for $1,000. Anyone who takes this first step then receives an email inviting him or her to join the panel.

Write the email invitation, persuading those who have already shown interest in the store to join the panel and become regular survey respondents.

10. **Recruiting Volunteers for Your Health Fair:** The nonprofit organization you work for coordinates an annual health and wellness fair for residents of your city. Each year, professionals from the community (e.g., physicians, dentists, cosmetologists, mechanics, lawyers, and social workers) volunteer their time, services, and supplies to help the underserved in your community. For example, dentists offer free cleanings. Physicians and nurses offer blood pressure, immunization, and diabetes screenings and refer patients to the town's free clinic as needed. A social worker might provide resources to someone in danger of losing his or her home. Someone who cannot afford car repairs can get them at your fair and then be able to get to his or her job. The fair provides much needed services for around 400 people each year. It's really heartwarming to see a community come together in this way.

As your instructor directs, write to a member of one group of professionals (e.g., a physician, a mechanic) and persuade him or her to volunteer for this year's fair.

11. **Persuading Employees to Get a Professional Headshot:** You are an intern in the human resources department at a financial services firm. When new employees are hired, they have their photo professionally taken for use in company publications and on the company website. Other employees are supposed to have their photos updated every three years, though this rule is not enforced. However, because your company is undergoing a major redevelopment of its website and social media outlets, your boss has decided that everyone should have his or her photo updated, regardless of the last time the picture was taken, so that the photos all have the same background and look. A couple of weeks ago, your boss sent a message to the staff letting them know that at some point in the next three weeks, each person should arrange to have a photo taken at Littrelle Photography, which is about five minutes from your office. Evening and weekend appointments are available. There is no cost to employees.

Unfortunately, you are in the last week of that three-week window and only 5 of the 75 employees have had their photos taken. In reading his original message, your boss realizes that he assumed everyone would get a photo taken and didn't realize he would have to be so persuasive. Your boss is now counting on you to write a persuasive announcement to the employees requesting that they get the photo taken. You have extended the time period by an additional two weeks, but you really cannot extend it further because your new sites go live soon. As you write, think about why these photos might be important to the firm and to its clients. Think, too, about why people should care that they have an updated photo.

12. **Persuading Employees to Use Writing Guidelines:** You were recently hired in the training and development department for an accounting firm with offices throughout the country. As in all professions, accountants must communicate clearly, concisely, and correctly with their audiences. Recently, though, the manager for your local office has been receiving complaints about emails your accountants and other staff are sending. Emails appear to be written quickly and are often incomplete, making a number of exchanges necessary for the audience to understand the message. In addition, they appear poorly edited. One client received an email where

the accountant typed "principle" rather than "principal." All staff in your office have been made aware of the issue, but no one seems inclined to do anything about it. Many cite a lack of time as a reason for not writing well, but because you know these people to be extremely professional, you also wonder if individuals think they communicate better than they do or do not know how to write any better than they already are. The complaints are still coming.

Your boss suggested you develop some training opportunities to encourage good business writing. Because employees cite time as a reason they do not proofread or edit their work, you know that asking them to attend writing workshops will not be popular. Instead, you decide to write a series of quick guides on organizing, writing, and formatting emails; proofreading; and recognizing common errors. These guides are online documents employees can access through the company intranet. The trick, however, is persuading people to use them. You need to write a persuasive message that compels employees to use your quick guides. If people do not use these quick guides to improve their emails, they will be forced to attend workshops, so it is in employees' best interest to use these guides. You have found some Internet research suggesting that poor communication is costly. You may decide to use this research in your message.

13. **Encouraging Patients of a Clinic to Use the Online Patient-Information Tool:** You work in the employee relations department at Northwoods Clinic. Two years ago, the clinic was dealing with such a high volume of patient communication that it couldn't keep up. Some of the communication was, of course, essential (e.g., a patient talking to a nurse about symptoms), but other communication (e.g., reordering contact lenses for patients, sending bills in the mail and processing payments, or checking on a patient's test results) was causing a backlog and taking employees' time away from patients who needed them. The clinic's solution was to develop MyNorthwoods.com, a website where patients could order contacts, pay bills, check test results, schedule appointments, update their contact information, update insurance information, and receive their health profiles from their annual exams. It seemed like an ideal solution except for one thing—few people signed up for it.

You think the patient response is slow for a few reasons: People are wary of having their health information available online, they think the process for signing up will take too much time, or they may have missed previous letters informing them of this online service. You've looked at previous mailings sent to patients and determined that they were not very persuasive (you didn't write them). You decide you will create a well-written persuasive message to get people to sign up. Write a persuasive letter to patients to sell them on the idea of using MyNorthwoods.com.

14. **Lining Up a Guest Speaker for Your Student Group or Employees:** Choose or invent a student group or company that holds special informative events from time to time and write a persuasive message inviting an expert on an appropriate topic to come speak at one of these events. Put some thought into what kind of event this is, what kind of person to invite, what topics to cover, and how to get him or her to say yes. (Sample speech topics include doing business in foreign countries, being more productive, managing one's time, professional networking, using appropriate body language, negotiating, and handling difficult conversations.)

Sales Messages

15. **Persuading Seniors to Rejoin a Gym:** As a member of the management team for FitBody Gym, located downtown in your city, you've just attended a strategy session in which the team generated ideas for increasing memberships. Your boss presented data about current memberships broken down by demographic categories. One group that stood out for its low number of memberships was older adults. "We're doing well attracting people in their 20s, 30s, and 40s," your boss says, "but we're not attracting enough senior citizens. In fact, our data show that many members let their gym memberships lapse once they reach a certain age." The team decides that one strategy to remedy this problem will be to send a letter to those aged 50 and over who have let their club membership lapse to point out the benefits of continuing to work out. You've been assigned the task of creating this mailing.

Studying the websites of several athletic clubs and, using realistic facts as well as your imagination, write the letter that will persuade these former members to rejoin. Consider carefully how to turn features of the club into benefits for your readers. (Your instructor may require you to create certain additional pieces for this mailing, or may allow you to choose a different kind of business and/or audience.)

16. **Selling a Subscription or Membership:** As you know, many types of businesses depend on memberships or subscriptions to generate income—zoos, symphonies, playhouses, museums, gyms and rec centers, airline clubs, fruit (or wine or whatever)-of-the-month clubs, member-based wholesalers (e.g., Costco, Sam's Club), country clubs, airport parking services, and more. Your task is to write a letter to sell a membership with one of these organizations to prospective members.

    Pick a type of business you know something about and then either choose a real company/organization or invent one to write your letter for. Analyze the needs and values of your audience, identify the features/advantages of the membership (or different levels of membership), and then write the text that will get your readers to buy. Create a blurb to go on the envelope, too.

    Keep your letter to one page, and make it visually appealing (incorporate some kind of graphic, and use some color). You can refer to an enrollment form if you want, but you don't have to actually create the form. You should refer to other information about the organization besides what's in your letter. But your letter should do the main selling job.

17. **Writing a cover message for a catalog:** Research shows that, when mailed to well-chosen recipients, print catalogs can significantly increase sales. Assume that your company (you choose what it sells and to whom) is planning to send its latest catalog to promising prospects and that you've been asked to write the cover letter for it. What should you highlight about your products? What kind of tone should you use and character should you project? What image of the reader will you paint so that the recipients will want to identify with your company and its customers? What action do you want your readers to take? You have a lot of things to decide—so you better get busy! (Alternative assignment: Assume that the catalogs are being sent to prior customers who haven't bought from you in a while.)

18. **Conducting an FAQ Postcard Campaign:** Take a page from TMR Direct's direct-mail play-book and create an "FAQ Campaign" for a company of your choosing. The campaign will consist of five postcards. Each should ask one of the customers' five most frequently asked questions on the front and then answer that question on the back—but then of course direct the reader to more information on the company's website. Don't forget to make your post-cards visually appealing.

19. **Enticing Customers to Buy Your Fitness Shakes:** You work for the marketing director for Fitology, a company that sells and delivers online fitness and nutrition plans for customers. As part of customers' online fitness programs, you encourage (but don't require) them to pur-chase your nutritional shakes. With 210 calories, 2 grams of fat, 21 grams of carbs, 29 grams of protein, and 25 flavors, they are a great meal substitute or post-workout snack. The prob-lem is that sales of the shakes have declined each month for the last six months. You suspect the decline is the result of your competition's recent promotion saying their customers eat "real" food at each meal, which implies your shakes are not an adequate meal.

    To encourage Fitology customers to purchase the shakes, you'll email them an offer of 20% off their next shake order with a minimum purchase of a 30-serving supply (current price: $120 or $4/shake; you do the math to figure out the sale price) and throw in four free shake packets. To get the discount, they'll need to use the promotional code Fit-Shake when they submit their online order. Tell them where/how they can make their purchase, reacquaint them with the shake, emphasize its value as a meal replacement, and give them a reason to act now. (You can assume that legal language about not combining this offer with any other offer, not using the offer to pay for taxes and processing/shipping charges, and a few other caveats will be typed in small print at the bottom of the letter. You can also assume a disclaimer regard-ing food allergies and weight-loss guarantees.)

20. **Recruiting Customers to Your Rewards Program:** Like other large restaurant chains, Urban Grille has a customer rewards club. Customers who join this program can take advantage of special deals just by signing up on the company's website and having coupons sent to their email in-boxes. Customers can print the coupons or just present the coupon and bar code on their phones when they pay for their food. In addition, club members receive a special dis-count on their birthdays.

    Lately, some of the chain's franchisees have been grumbling that they are not getting enough business through this program. So your boss, marketing director of Urban Grille, directs you to write two messages—one for the company's website and one for Facebook—persuading readers to become members of the customer-rewards program. To encourage them to sign up, you may want to provide an incentive.

Carefully consider the persuasive, logistical, and visual elements to include and then write the messages.

21. **Selling Ad Space on Your Business's Website:** You and three other students decide to start a business. You are going to create an ad-supported online service listing local apartment-rental options for students and providing advice on leases, security deposits, and other issues tenants may face. Not only will you be listing properties, but you'll also let students rate properties and give feedback on landlords, rental agencies, and the rental units themselves.

You need to craft a message you can use when you approach potential advertisers and ask them to buy ad space. You will target advertisers from businesses throughout your community that serve the student population. You also think that landlords and rental agencies might benefit from buying ad space, even though you know some landlords and properties are likely to get poor ratings. As you think about these two audiences (general businesses; landlords and rental agencies), you realize you need two messages, one for each audience.

When you create these two messages, consider what information would be persuasive to each. For the audience of landlords and rental agencies, you will need to think carefully about why landlords and rental agencies would still want to advertise on your site if your readers might give them bad ratings. You'll sell ads for $25 per month and automatically bill the advertiser's account unless he or she cancels the ad.

22. **Persuading Customers to Shop in Your New Location:** Your upscale clothing store—part of a national chain—recently moved from a location downtown to one in an affluent suburb north of town. You'd like for those customers who patronized your store in its previous location to continue to shop with you. Write all the local customers for whom you have mailing addresses and invite them to visit you at your new location. You can offer them a limited-time-only coupon to sweeten the invitation—but your message should also remind them of why they like to shop at your store. Plus, your new location has some benefits: The store is bigger, and it's in a nicer area with other appealing businesses around. Think of the verbal and visual contents that will entice your customers to continue to shop with you. Of course, they also have the option of shopping at your online store. (Your instructor may allow you to choose a different kind of store.)

23. **Selling Fans (or Other Products) by Email:** You're part of the management team of a business that manufactures and sells ceiling fans. Even though your operation is small, your fans are popular, and you sell them online to customers across the United States. Unfortunately, the tight economy has taken its toll on your business; sales are down considerably, even though it's summer. In response, the management team has decided that they will purchase a targeted email distribution list and send an email sales message to all those on the list.

You've been put in charge of drafting a sample message, which the team will discuss at its next meeting. Create an email message to sell your company's fans. What is distinctive about your products? Why should readers spend their limited discretionary money on a ceiling fan? Study the websites of various fan sellers to generate the details that will make your message persuasive. Should you use any visuals in your message? Links to additional information? Carefully think through the whole selling effort. You think you'll design the message in Word and save it as a PDF to show how the email will actually look once your IT person prepares it for delivery. (Or, choose a different product that is appropriate for this case.)

24. **Upselling to Your Current Customers:** You're part of the marketing communications team for Global Airways, a major airline that flies to airports all over the world. Periodically, you send the members of your frequent-flyers program "upselling" emails that are intended to get these people to enroll or re-enroll in your more exclusive, costly programs. You've been assigned the task of designing the latest message intended to promote the Global Crowne Club, a for-fee service (involving both an initial fee and a monthly fee) whose subscribers are allowed access to a comfortable, quiet lounge at over 50 airports around the world. This sales campaign will offer an extra month at no charge to those who purchase or renew a one-year Crowne Club membership within a certain period and use the designated promo code. In addition, 10% of their purchase will be donated to a worthy foundation.

Study the websites of various airlines and various foundations to generate the contents for your message. Think carefully about what information to include in the message and what links to provide. (At your instructor's discretion, you may plan an upselling sales message for a different company's current customers.)

Multimedia Selling

25. **Persuading Customers to Write Reviews of Your Products:** Design an email message that will persuade the customers of your mail-order company to review the products they recently purchased. You want this information not only because it's helpful feedback but also because having customer comments on your website indicates that there's a "social buzz" about your products. (Before you draft your message, figure out what kind of company you'll be representing, what they sell, and to whom. You'll also need to decide what products a sample customer recently bought, since the messages will be personalized in terms of showing what each recipient purchased.)

    To supply their reviews, readers will click on the photos of each item they bought, which will take them to a web page where they can select a rating (one to five stars), describe the pros and cons, and add other comments. They'll also be asked to give themselves a nickname and indicate what area of the country they come from. Unless the review is inappropriate in some way, it will be put on the "reviews" page for that product for other shoppers to see. Each time a customer writes a review, his/her name will be entered into a monthly drawing for a $500 shopping spree.

    While you're at it, think carefully about the other visuals and links that could appear in this message. You have the opportunity to do more selling and to build a more informed, loyal customer base, so take advantage of it!

26. **Promoting an Online Food-Delivery Service:** Study the websites of Grubhub, OrderUp, UberEATS, and one or two other online food-delivery services. Then assume that you work for a business like that in your town or area. Design a promotional email message that will get prospective customers to . . . do what? Try it? Sign up? Download the app? Make clear in your message what this business is and how it works. You can assume that the large majority of the recipients will be reading the email—and, you hope, using your service—on their phones.

27. **Planning a Twitter Promotion for a Special Event:** Plan and write a series of tweets to promote a special event that will be taking place at your school (e.g., the senior recital for music majors, the annual fashion show by the fashion designers, a job fair, a community-service event) or be sponsored by your company (e.g., a community-service event, the opening of a new branch, the launch of a new product, an international festival, a special exhibit). Put careful thought into the hashtag for these promotional messages. Work with your instructor to determine how many tweets you need and the period of time during which they will be posted. Don't forget to use links and photos to your advantage!

28. **Writing a Facebook Page to Promote an Event:** Do the same as in #27 but, instead of preparing a series of tweets, design and write a Facebook event page.

29. **Promoting an Event through Instagram:** Do the same as in #27, but instead of planning a Twitter promotion, plan a series of Instagram posts, with captions, to promote your event. Include sample photos to illustrate the kinds of photos you'll be hoping to use in the promotion, and plan when each will be sent.

30. **Create a Mock-Up of a Facebook Page for Your Employer:** You've just begun working for a mom-and-pop business in your neighborhood as an office helper, marketing person, shelf stocker, cashier, and jack/jill of all trades. When you asked the owners if they had a Facebook page, they looked at each other and said yes . . . but you could tell by the way they answered that it wasn't much. You took a look, and you were right: There's almost nothing on it.

    Looking at other businesses like theirs and using what you know about what Facebook users like, design an enhanced page for the business, complete with sample content (you can piece together screenshots and other material in a Word document if you don't want to create an actual Facebook page). Be ready to explain (either to your class or to your instructor) why you designed the page the way you did.

31. **Creating a Mock-Up of a LinkedIn Page for Your Company:** Same as #30, but choose a different company and write the company's LinkedIn page instead. To prepare, read about the main purposes behind companies' pages and then be sure that your page meets those goals as well.

32. **Writing a Content-Marketing Blog Post:** For this assignment, you're going to choose a topic and write a compelling blog post about it. You'll first need to figure out what (real or fictional) company you work for, what your (real or fictional) area of expertise is, and what kind of people you're trying to sell to. Choose a topic you already know something about and are interested in! It does not have to be about business; it just needs to be on a topic related to something that your company sells and can be assumed to have some special knowledge about—e.g., purchasing the right gear for a hike (if you're an outdoor equipment or fitness company) or keeping your energy bills as low as possible (if you're a windows-replacement or heating and cooling company).

Once you've made your decision, research your topic to come up with an original, interesting, informative post that your intended readers will find valuable and impressive. Be sure to include at least one photo to add interest.

33. **Creating a Short Promotional Video:** Videos are an increasingly popular sales medium, especially with younger consumers. For this assignment, you're going to work with some of your classmates to design a video to promote something of interest (e.g., your major, a club, a non-profit, your neighborhood or city, a sports team or arts organization, a company). It does not have to be professional quality—in fact, its amateurism can be part of its appeal. But every aspect of the video should be deliberately planned and be appropriate for the topic and your audience.

To get started, watch a few promotional videos on YouTube and other sites to get ideas. Then plan the contents, which will include choosing the setting(s), the "characters," and the "plot." Once your team has a plan it likes, write the script and the storyboard (a description of what will be on screen at each point during the video). Then shoot the video using a smartphone. Keep your video to about one minute. Write a brief cover document for your instructor that describes your intended audience, your video's purpose, and the place(s) you would post it (or maybe even *will* post it!).

Proposals

34. **Proposing a Multimedia Ad Campaign:** Assume that there's an "ad campaign" competition at your school funded by the local chapter of the American Marketing Association. Either individuals or teams can enter, and they can be from any major.

Choose a company whose products you know well and create a multimedia campaign to promote its products or services. Then write up your ideas in the form of a proposal that contains these parts (unless your instructor assigns a different structure):

- Overview (why the campaign is needed; a summary of what you're proposing and how it will fulfill the need)

- Goal of the Campaign (more about whom the campaign is intended to reach and, thus, what its main persuasive theme/goal will be)

- Target Audience(s) (more demographic and psychographic information about your intended readers/viewers)

- Proposed Media and Content (the form the campaign will take on different media, with sample content provided)

- Required Resources (what resources will be needed to conduct the campaign)

- Tracking Methods (how the company will be able to tell if the campaign is working)

- Conclusion (a brief, positive wrap-up of what you've proposed and why you think it will work)

You should wind up with a proposal of 8–10 pages, not counting the title page. Use footnotes to document any research that supports your proposal, and be sure your proposal recommends the use of at least three different media (other media besides those discussed in this chapter—such as billboards and promotional events—can be included). Or, if your instructor prefers, you can prepare an oral presentation that pitches your plan. In either case, your assumed audience will be the marketing team for the company you've chosen.

35. **Proposing That a Company Adopt Instagram, Pinterest, or YouTube:** Choose a company that does not currently have an Instagram account, a Pinterest page, or a YouTube channel—or make up a fictitious company (perhaps one similar to a company you're familiar with)—and write a proposal that the company begin using one of these new channels. Assume that you are preparing this proposal for a client that your instructor recruited, a client who is genuinely considering adopting the new medium but doesn't know much about it. Think carefully about what the client needs to know. For example, how does the medium work exactly, and how does one get started? What can you do with it? What are the advantages of this medium? Can it be integrated with the company's other media? What kind of upkeep does it need? What are its limitations or drawbacks? Be sure to include helpful screen shots and other visuals, as needed, to educate the client and encourage him/her to take the plunge into this new medium.

36. **Proposing the Adoption of Branding Guidelines:** As the lead communications specialist at Littleton Advertising and Creative Services, you and your team are tired of the amount of editing you need to do whenever someone submits material to your department for publication in the company newsletter, press releases, annual report, and website. There is no consistency in formatting, punctuation, mechanics, writing style, colors, or the use of the company logo. While these items are always edited to conform to company styles, you worry that the employees' submissions suggest they do not understand branding or the importance of it to a company.

You think that if employees understood the concept of branding, they could write better and more consistent content. Furthermore, it is reasonable to expect that everyone in your department have some consistency in their initial drafts so that your final editing and revising are not so time consuming. Plus, you worry that the documents you don't see (e.g., letters, emails) may not be written or edited as well as they could be and want employees to be empowered to write independently of your editing and represent your company's brand well.

You think an online corporate style guide housed on Littleton's intranet is your answer and decide to propose to your CEO that Littleton have one. You and your team will develop and implement it. Because this is summer, it's your slow time anyway, so you have the time to create it. In your proposal, make the case for creating and using a style guide as a means of coroporate branding, include a timeline for developing it, and propose a plan for implementing the style guide at your company. Be sure to show, too, how a style guide makes work more efficient for everyone. An Internet search for corporate style guides will help you gather information for your proposal.

37. **Proposing a Team-Building Activity:** Due to budget cutbacks, the morale at your company has dropped to an all-time low. Employees are not excited about going to work, and it's beginning to show in productivity rates: As a whole, sales are down 9% from last quarter.

You serve on the company's Quality Circle, which recently met to brainstorm ideas for improving morale. The group agreed that everyone needs a little more fun. Toward that end, they decided that the company should consider sponsoring various team-building activities. You volunteered to look into the options and come back to the committee with a proposal for the first of these activities.

Using research and your own creativity, come up with a relatively inexpensive, fun activity for lightening everyone's mood and building camaraderie. When you've got all the information you need, write up your ideas in a well-written, persuasive email proposal that the Quality Circle—and your bosses—will like.

38. **Proposing to Be Allowed to Work from Home:** You work as an instructional designer at Birchwood Hills, a company specializing in long-term care, memory care, and assisted-living facilities. Your company has over 2,000 full- and part-time employees in 30 locations of various sizes in five states. Your job is to develop and create online learning, training, and continuing education opportunities for the company's staff.

You love almost everything about your job—your fun co-workers, the interesting work, using your creative and technical abilities . . . everything! You love working with content experts such as nurses, administrators, therapists, and physicians to develop training materials. In fact, you spend much of your days talking with these people. Some days, though, all you need is to carve out some quiet time and space to work, but that is not likely to happen in your busy office. Someone always needs you, and it's convenient for them to stop by your desk for help or for a quick chat. It's also hard to be working intently on a project and then leave at your most inspired moment to attend a meeting.

Upon visiting the Instructional Design Professionals group on LinkedIn, you notice how many instructional designers work full or part time from home; you think this might be just what you need. You could structure your work week to be at the office two days a week for meetings and other face-to-face contact and then spend three days a week working from home to do your instructional design work. Of course, you would be available by phone or email at home, but you would have more control over interruptions with phone and email than you would with interruptions at the office.

To pitch your idea to your supervisor, you prepare a proposal. You research the advantages and disadvantages of working from home, figure out the equipment you would need, estimate the cost of setting up a home office and consider how to convince Birchwood Hills to cover it, and determine any other costs your employer might incur. Address why this is a good idea not just for you but for Birchwood Hills as well. Be sure your proposal adequately addresses any resistance your supervisor might have.

39. **Proposing That Your Employer Switch to Square.** You were recently hired as an assistant manager for a local restaurant (or bar, or farmer's or crafts market, or coffee shop, or bakery, or . . .). Since the owners are seldom onsite, you are often in charge of making the schedule, ordering supplies, and keeping the enterprise in good running order. Business is doing well, but you think it could do better if it switched from cash registers and multiple credit-card fees to Square. As far as you know, all the employees have smartphones, and any future employees are likely to have them as well. Using Square's mobile credit-card processing system would be very convenient for both the employees and the customers, and it could also make good sense financially.

You have mentioned the idea to one of the owners, and she's intrigued. In fact, she's glad to have a young, tech-savvy person like yourself to explore the idea. She asks you to do the necessary research and then email your proposal to her and the other owner. You're pleased to have this opportunity to help the business and impress your bosses with your research, analysis, and writing skills. Be sure to include in your proposal what would be necessary to switch the business over to Square.

40. **Proposing that Your Organization Create a Sexual Harassment Policy:** You are the office manager for a small nonprofit or company that has done quite well over the 10 years it has been in existence. It now has over a dozen employees and regularly serves several hundred members/clients/customers per year. It still isn't large enough to justify the cost of a full-time HR professional, so the executives contract out the HR services it needs. But they also pay for you to belong to the Society for Human Resource Management (SHRM) so you can stay on top of current HR practices and help keep the organization abreast of them.

From studying the SHRM website and following its listserv, you've realized that your organization really should have a sexual harassment policy. You're read about the problems that can arise when no such policy is in place, and you think your organization should protect itself against those. Plus, the organization will be better off if it has a clear policy for employees to follow.

You ran this idea past one of the executives, and he agreed with you. Now he wants you to present your thoughts and information in a document that you'll attach to an email to the organization's executive team. You'll do sufficient research to be able to motivate the readers to act and advise them on how to go about developing the policy (for example, should they seek the assistance of an attorney?). Convince them that this effort is worth the time and any expense involved. (Alternative topics: social media policy; nondiscrimination policy)

41. **Proposing a Corporate Philanthropy Program:** As director of corporate communications and public relations for Noland Construction, a popular company in a large metropolitan area, you think the time has come to create a more formal, robust corporate philanthropy program. Your company is a good community citizen; it already gives time, money, and supplies on a random basis to charities that request help. But that's the problem: These donations are random, and it's hard to use random acts of kindness as a basis for compelling publicity for your company.

You decide to write a proposal in which you (1) convince the owners of the benefits of a better organized corporate philanthropy program, and (2) propose the type of program that you think the company should create. Research the benefits of corporate philanthropy programs, think carefully about the logistics of your plan, and do any additional planning that will enable you to decide exactly what you want to propose and why. Then write the proposal. Send it as an email attachment to VP Jack Yount, who is interested in your idea and has agreed to share it with the other four company executives. Invent any additional details that will not significantly alter the challenge before you. Be sure your readers can see the connections between what you are proposing and its potential company benefits.

42. **Proposing That Your Company Cover the Cost of an Online Course, Webinar, or Series of Webinars:** You work for the _____ company (you decide what kind) as a (you decide what position). You want to take an online course or attend a webinar or webinars on _____ (you decide what topic) and have the company cover the cost. You've run the idea past your supervisor, who is basically supportive but will need to get the OK from his/her boss. For this you'll need to make your case persuasively and in writing.

Write an email proposal to your supervisor requesting that the company cover the cost of the course/webinar(s). Convince the decision maker that the content will be worth paying for (perhaps the fee will even enable more than one employee to "attend"). Remember to think of the major objections he/she might have and be sure to account for these as you build your argument. To ensure that your proposal has a sufficient level of detail, you may want to base it on a real course, webinar, or series of webinars that is being offered by a college, professional organization, or business (for example, see training/webinars being offered by IconLogic).

43. **Proposing a Fundraising Event for Your Organization:** As head of the fundraising committee for your organization (e.g., a church, a philanthropic society, or a club), you've been reading about silent auctions, and you believe that this kind of event would be perfect for your organization. The others on the fundraising committee agree. Now you need the approval of the organization's leaders. To get that, you'll need to do more research, work out all the details about the event you have in mind, and then write it all up as a persuasive proposal. You'll email your proposal (attached as a Word document) to the president of the organization for him/her to share with the rest of the leaders so they can discuss it at their next monthly meeting.

44. **Proposing an App for Your Company:** You just read on the Internet that over half the time that people spend on their phones is spent on apps! Wouldn't it be cool if the company you work for had one? The more you think about it, the more you think the answer is "yes!" You mention the idea in an email to your boss, and before you know it, you're being invited to share your thoughts with the head of marketing!

So, go for it. Research the benefits of having a company app. Research what it would cost the company to have one developed and what the implementation and maintenance cost, if any, would be (would there be a labor cost?). Then plan out your app! What features will it have? What will the interface look like? What kinds of audience-participation activities will it enable? Overall, how will it enhance the company's business? And how/where should the company promote it? Work out the answers to these questions and more and then prepare the proposal that will get you known as the employee who came up with the app idea! Don't forget to include a cool visual in your proposal that shows your vision for the app.

45. **Proposing a Community-Improvement Project:** You were having lunch with a friend of yours, a small-business owner, the other day, and she mentioned that, with the blessing of the city parks board, she has taken over the maintenance of the triangle across from her business where several streets come together. She has planted hardy plants there, she mows it regularly, and she keeps any trash picked up. Not only is she helping out the city, but she's also helping to make the area around her business attractive. Hmmm . . . you've been looking for a proposal topic for your business communication class, and you think this might be the kernel of a great idea. You do a bit of Web research and see that many cities have well-organized adopt-a-park programs.

Do sufficient additional research and thinking to develop a proposal for your city or town to adopt such a program. You know, you're really getting into this. . . . Maybe you'll actually send your proposal to the mayor or the parks director. (Or, if your instructor permits, choose a different kind of program or project.)

Researching and
Writing Reports

© Mark Adams/123RF

Information is what enables businesses and other kinds of organizations to operate. Without information, they wouldn't know what products or services to provide, how to design them, whom to design them for, how to market them, and how to keep track of their performance. They wouldn't know who their competitors were or what market or social niche to fill. They wouldn't know whether to expand or shrink, how to invest their assets, or which supplier or contractor to use. They wouldn't know whether to hire, fire, or promote someone. They wouldn't even know how much money they have, how much debt they're in, where they're spending their money, or where their money is coming from. Reports are the primary vehicle for gathering and sharing all these kinds of information.

Successful reports and effective research go hand in hand. Caroline Molina-Ray, an expert on research-based business communications, explains why:

"Business leaders must base their decisions on relevant facts—not just on intuition. Effective research provides leaders with facts they can use to plan, evaluate, and improve business performance. To be most useful, research reports must not only include pertinent data but also explain what the data mean and how a decision maker might act on this information."[1]

In class, a report-writing task might be just an assignment—but in the workplace, the need for the information is real. It can be exciting and rewarding to fulfill that need. Plus, working on report projects gives you more of an insider's view into how the business is run and greater participation in its success. The better you are at gathering and sharing useful information, the more successful you will be in your career.

Learning Objectives

LO11-1	Write clear problem and purpose statements.
LO11-2	List the likely factors involved in a problem.
LO11-3	Explain the difference between primary and secondary research.
LO11-4	Use Internet search engines to gather information.
LO11-5	Use other Web resources to gather information.
LO11-6	Evaluate websites for reliability.
LO11-7	Use social networking sites to gather information.
LO11-8	Use the library to gather information.
LO11-9	Use sampling to conduct a survey.
LO11-10	Construct a questionnaire and conduct a survey.
LO11-11	Design an observational study for a business problem.
LO11-12	Conduct an experiment for a business problem.
LO11-13	Explain the uses of focus groups and personal interviews.
LO11-14	Discuss important ethical guidelines for research.
LO11-15	Interpret your findings accurately.
LO11-16	Organize information in outline form using time, place, quantity, factors, or a combination of these patterns.
LO11-17	Turn an outline into a table of contents whose format and wording are logical and meaningful.
LO11-18	Write reports that are focused, objective, consistent in time viewpoint, smoothly connected, and interesting.
LO11-19	Prepare reports collaboratively.

Problem-Solving Challenge

Researching User-Testing Methods for Your Boss

Introduce yourself to the subject of report writing by assuming the role of management intern at Mockbee's Ice Cream and Bakery, a popular confectionery in your city. Mockbee's began 96 years ago as one mom-and-pop store and has now grown into a thriving business with 17 stores across the city. You've worked part time for Mockbee's ever since you were in high school, and you were thrilled when they agreed to create a management internship for you. All the vibes indicate that you are being groomed for a career with this great local company.

You report to Betsy Tippett, an operations analyst for the company. As you've watched her over the last few weeks, you've been amazed at the amount of research and report writing she has to do. Yesterday, for example, you worked with her to determine whether the company should switch to a new cellular-service provider. Last week, she worked on determining the causes of a problem at one of the stores. The week before that, she researched online document storage and sharing platforms and identified the one she felt would suit Mockbee's best. For each of these activities, she prepared a written report.

Now it's your turn. Betsy dropped by your desk yesterday and explained what she needed. "As you know," she said, "we chose Box as our new document-storage platform, and it's scheduled to go live in three weeks. To get ready for the roll-out, I've been working with Jim Ash, our tech, to create a Web-based tutorial that will explain to the office staff and store managers what Box is and how to use it. We have drafted the tutorial, and we know we should user-test it, but neither of us is experienced in this area. Can you research the different user-testing options out there and recommend the method we should use? This would be really helpful—especially since, if this tutorial gets a good response, we might want to create more."

Of course you say yes. But inside, you're full of questions. How will you find out what options there are? How will you figure out which one would be best for Mockbee's? And how will you prepare your findings? You're sure Betsy wants a written report, but what kind? When you press her for answers, she begins to look a little impatient. Then you get it: *She's* not quite sure what she's looking for—and you get the feeling that she's curious to see what you'll come up with. So this is something you're going to need to work out on your own. It's time to get resourceful.

Defining Reports

How often you will write reports and the types you will write will depend on the size and nature of the organization you work for. If you work for an organization with fewer than 10 employees, your reporting might consist only of entering information into forms or preparing short informative messages. But larger, more complex organizations will require longer, more complex reports. The kind of organization you work for will also influence the amount of report writing you might do. For example, financial firms, publicly traded companies, consulting companies of all types, and nonprofits with a variety of stakeholders must routinely report on their operations and achievements.

Whether the report is a filled-in form, a brief email, a short document, a long research paper, or an oral presentation, it contributes to the organization's business intelligence.

What Is a Report?

A **report** is an orderly and objective communication of factual information that enables key decision makers to make informed decisions.

As an *orderly* communication, a report is prepared carefully. This care in their preparation distinguishes reports from short, more casual exchanges of information. As an *objective* form of communication, reports are unbiased. They "tell it like it is," presenting all the relevant facts and interpreting them without advancing any particular agenda. Reports differ significantly from proposals in this way, because proposals inform in order to persuade. As *communication,* reports may use oral, written, and/or visual media to convey their content, but, like all effective communications, they must serve a clear purpose and be adapted to the readers' needs. The basic ingredient of reports is *factual information.* Factual information is based on events, statistics, and other data. Finally, a report *must enable key decision makers to make informed decisions,* whether those decision makers are the management in one's own company, the management in a client company, or citizens who must choose a course of action.

A written report has several advantages over other communication forms. Written reports are a good medium for conveying detailed findings. They also make permanent records, so readers who need the information contained in these reports can study them as needed. Plus, written reports are a convenient and efficient means of distributing information because they can be easily routed to a number of readers. But oral reports can be appropriate, too, depending on the circumstances—for example, when presenting information to a board of directors or some other group that will want to ask questions and discuss your findings.

Harnessing data can be exciting—and it's critical to business success.

Who Writes Reports?

Almost everyone in a professional role prepares reports. Every area represented by the majors in your business school—from accounting and finance to management and marketing—brings with it an array of report-writing needs. Professionals with expertise in many other areas, such as information technology, e-learning and Web design, engineering, social work, architecture, political science, communication, and health services, often write reports as well.

Reports in any of these areas can be internal or external, depending on their purpose. Those that are circulated among internal audiences are intended to help the organization correct problems, adapt to changing circumstances, or try new ventures. Reports written to external audiences can also serve various purposes. If the organization is a consulting firm, reports to the client may be its primary product. If the company is publicly traded, it is required by law to publish financial reports to the government and to shareholders. Depending on the nature of its business, a company may have to research and write reports for various agencies about its impact on the environment, its hiring practices, or its compliance with quality standards.

Sometimes reports are written by individuals. Increasingly, however, they are prepared in collaboration with others. Even if one person has primary responsibility for a report, he or she will often need contributions from many people. Indeed, preparing reports draws on a wide variety of communication skills, from getting information to working with others to designing a helpful and creditable finished product.

Sometimes the report-writing needs in a certain area have become so consistent that standardized forms have been developed, like the one for a standard audit report shown in Exhibit 11-1. But many times, there will be no such form. In such cases, you will need to assess what information is needed and then organize and format it yourself. This chapter and the following chapter describe how to meet such challenges with written reports. Chapter 13 will advise you on preparing oral reports.

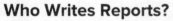

You Make the Call

What kinds of reports do you anticipate needing to write in your profession? Why? Which of these, if any, do you think will be written collaboratively?

LO11-1 Write clear problem and purpose statements.

Report writing requires curiosity and clear thinking. To understand the problem, to identify your report's purpose, and to prepare the report that will solve the problem, you may need to consult many sources of information.

© Ingram Publishing/SuperStock RF

Determining the Report Problem and Purpose

Your work on a report logically begins with a need, which we refer to in the following discussion as the **problem**.

Someone or some group in your organization (usually your superiors) needs information to make a decision. Perhaps the need is for information only; perhaps it is for information and analysis; or perhaps it is for information, analysis, and recommendations (see the Communication Matters feature "How Far Should Your Report Go?"). Whatever the case, someone with a need will ask you to do the work or, if the investigation is your idea, authorize you to do it. How you define this need (problem) will determine your **report's purpose**.

The Preliminary Investigation

Your first task is to understand the problem. To do this well, you will almost always have to gather additional information beyond what you've been given. You may need to study the company's files or query its databases, talk over the problem with experts, search through external sources, and/or discuss the problem with those who authorized the report. You should do enough preliminary research to be sure you understand the problem that your report is intended to address.

Communication Matters

How Far Should Your Report Go?

All business reports should help solve business problems. But how far they should go in solving these problems will depend on what your reader wants.

Does your reader want *orderly information* only? Or *orderly information* followed by *interpretations*? Or *orderly information* followed by *interpretations* and *recommendations*?

Let's say a hardware chain is considering a site for a new store. The report you write to help the management determine the appropriateness of the site might take one of the forms in the table below.

When determining your report's purpose, be sure you ask yourself what the reader has asked for and what your data will support. Then deliver exactly that—no more and no less.

Informative Report	Analytical Report	Recommendation Report
A report that lists all the competition within a 5-mile radius, grouped according to location or type of company.	A report that lists all the competition within a 5-mile radius **and** draws conclusions about the likely demand for a new hardware store in the area.	A report that lists all the competition within a 5-mile radius **and** draws conclusions about the likely demand for a new hardware store in the area **and** recommends a decision or further action.

The Need for Clear Problem and Purpose Statements

Your next task is to clearly state your understanding of the problem and your report's purpose.

The **problem statement** provides a clear description of the situation that created the need for your report. Problem statements are generally written as descriptive statements. For example, a simple one might read, "Sales are decreasing at Company X." The problem statement for the Problem-Solving Challenge at the start of this chapter might be a little more complicated; it might read, "Betsy and Jim have drafted a tutorial to teach Mockbee's staff and managers about Box. They now need to figure out how to user-test this tutorial and any additional tutorials they might create."

You should then write a **purpose statement** (also called the research or report objective). This statement is often written in the form of an infinitive phrase or a question. Thus, if your problem is that Company X wants to know why sales are decreasing, your purpose statement would be "to determine the causes of decreasing sales at Company X" or "What are the causes of decreasing sales at Company X?" For the Problem-Solving Challenge, the purpose statement would be "to find an appropriate, effective user-testing method for the Box tutorial and any future tutorials" or the question form of this purpose.

Sometimes, as in the preceding examples, the purpose will be clearly implied in the problem statement. Other times, though, the problem will be so complex or general that you will need to put some thought into your report's purpose. For example, the purpose of a report intended to help a company reduce employee turnover could be "to find out why employee turnover is so high," "to find out how other companies have addressed employee turnover," "to find out what makes loyal employees stay," a combination of these, or some other purpose. Consider carefully what approach your report should take.

Also keep in mind that no matter how clearly you try to frame the problem and purpose at the beginning of your investigation, your conception of them may change as you conduct your research. As with other types of business writing, report writing often involves revisiting earlier steps (recursivity), as discussed in Chapters 1 and 2.

In your completed report, the problem and purpose statements will be an essential component of the report's introduction and such front matter as the letter of transmittal and executive summary. They will convey to your readers what they're reading and why.

Determining the Factors

LO11-2 List the likely factors involved in a problem.

Once you've defined the problem and identified your purpose, you determine what **factors** you need to investigate. That is, you determine what subject areas you must look into to solve the problem.

What factors a problem involves can vary widely. Here, we'll discuss three common types: sub-topics of the overall topic, possible causes of a problem, and points of comparison between things that are being evaluated.

Use of Subtopics in Informative Reports

If the problem is a relatively straightforward lack of information, you will need to figure out the sub-areas where information is needed. Illustrating this type of situation would be the problem of preparing a report that helps a team of company employees prepare for their first business trip to China. After consulting resources on Chinese culture and considering the activities the team will be engaged in, you might come up with a plan like this:

Purpose statement: To help the team prepare for successful cross-cultural negotiations in Shanghai, China.

Subtopics:

1. The influence of Chinese history and government on its culture

2. The special role of Shanghai in Chinese history and culture

3. Business etiquette in China

4. Negotiating and bargaining in China

5. Socializing in China

6. Building a long-term relationship with the Chinese

Possible Causes for Problems Requiring a Solution

Some problems concern why an undesirable situation has occurred. In analyzing problems of this kind, you should search for possible explanations or solutions. Once you've formulated these, you research each one to see if it applies to the situation you're investigating.

To illustrate, assume that you have the problem of determining why sales at Company X have declined. In preparing to investigate this problem, you would think of the possible explanations for the decline. You might identify such possible reasons as these:

Purpose statement: To find out why sales at Company X have declined.

Possible causes:

1. Activities of the competition have caused the decline.

2. Changes in the economy of the area have caused the decline.

3. Merchandising deficiencies have caused the decline.

4. Changes in the environment (population shifts, political actions, etc.) have caused the decline.

You would then conduct the necessary research to evaluate each possible cause. You might find that one, two, or all apply. Or you might find that none is valid. If so, you would have to generate additional explanations for further evaluation.

Bases of Comparison in Evaluation Studies

When the problem concerns evaluating something, either by itself or in comparison with other things, you will need to identify the bases for the evaluation—that is, the characteristics you will evaluate and the criteria you will use to evaluate them.

Report-Writing Tools Help Businesses Succeed

To survive and thrive, businesses must have timely, accurate data about their operations. For many businesses, that means investing in software that will generate the informational reports they need.

The most powerful report-writing tools are those that are integrated with enterprise resource planning (ERP) software, which allows managers real-time access to data about the different facets of the company. These products' report-writing tools make it easy to get a snapshot of any part of business operations, whether it be the current financial picture, the sales history of a certain product, or the status of customers' accounts.

But even small businesses can find electronic assistance for generating reports. Shown here is the title page of a sample home-inspection report created with Horizon software. The software enables home inspectors to create all the necessary components—from transmittal letter to contract to results and recommendations—and then generates a professional-looking report for the customer.

While you may not be able to find software to support your report writing to this extent, you will almost surely use electronically generated reports when preparing your own reports. Be sure to familiarize yourself with any report-writing tools your organization uses so that you do not overlook important data or leave out information that your reader expects to see in your report.

Source: "Sample Home Inspection Reports," Carson Dunlop, 2016, accessed April 15, 2016, http://www.carsondunlop.com/wp-content/documents/pdfs/Professional-Home-Inspection-Report.pdf. (top-left) © OJO Images/SuperStock RF; (top-center) © Denise McCullough RF; (top-center) © Martin Wahlborg/Getty Images RF; (top-right) © Martin Barraud/Caia Image/Glow Images RF; (bottom) © David Buffington/Getty Images RF

For example, if a company needs to know which of three cities would be best for a new production facility, the bases for comparing the cities would be the factors that would be likely to determine the new facility's success. After considering such factors, you might come up with a plan like this:

Purpose statement: To determine whether Company Y's new plant should be built in City A, City B, or City C.

Comparison bases:

1. Availability of skilled workers

2. Tax structure

3. Community attitude

4. Available transportation methods

5. Nearness to markets

In any of these three types of reports, each of the factors you decide to investigate may have factors of its own. Subdivide them as much as you need to in order to be able to provide a thorough, useful report.

Gathering the Information

You can collect information you need for a project by using two basic forms of research: primary and secondary. **Primary research** (also called *empirical research*) involves firsthand data gathering. It produces new information through the use of experiments, surveys, interviews, and other methods of direct observation. **Secondary research** uses material that someone else has published in resources such as periodicals, brochures, books, digital publications, and websites. To be an effective report writer, you should be familiar with the techniques of both primary and secondary research, because both types will often be needed.

Conducting Secondary Research on the Internet

One of the most accessible research tools we have is the Internet. That makes the Web a good place to start a research project. Using search engines, other Web-based tools, and online social networks, we can often find all the secondary information we need.

Using Search Engines Internet search engines compile indexes of information about websites, such as the meta tags (hidden keywords) they use, how often they're visited, and other sites they link to. When you use a **search engine**, you are actually searching its index,

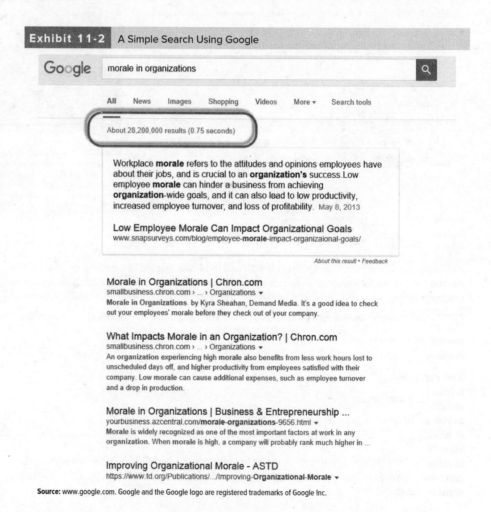

Exhibit 11-2 A Simple Search Using Google

Source: www.google.com. Google and the Google logo are registered trademarks of Google Inc.

Exhibit 11-3   A Google Search Using a Filter to Narrow the Results

Source: www.google.com. Google and the Google logo are registered trademarks of Google Inc.

not the Web itself. According to eBizMBA, the top five search engines are Google, Bing, Yahoo!, Ask, and AOL, with Google being the most popular.[2] Google, whose simple, clean screens you see in Exhibits 11-2 and 11-3, provides the ability to do a simple search or a more advanced search.

As you can see in Exhibit 11-2, even a simple Google search includes ways to filter the information you are searching. In this case the search words "morale in organizations" pulled up 28,200,000 results. If you use the categories across the top of the screen (such as "News," "Images," or options under the "More" pull-down menu), you can limit your results to those sources, as shown in Exhibit 11-3. Another way to limit the results is to put your search phrase in quotation marks. Then Google will look for that actual phrase.

You can use another Google tool, Google Scholar (http://scholar.google.com/), to search scholarly literature, which includes journals from academic publishers, conference papers, dissertations, academic books, and technical reports. You perform a simple search in Scholar just as you would in Google's regular search. A sample search with the phrase "conducting surveys at work" brought up the resources shown in Exhibit 11-4. For any given resource, you can view "Related articles" (circled in blue), and you can use the "Cite" feature (circled in green) to retrieve a citation for the source in the citation format you prefer (as shown). The bottommost option, "Create alert" (circled in red), lets you sign up to receive email alerts when new items are posted on this topic.

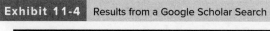
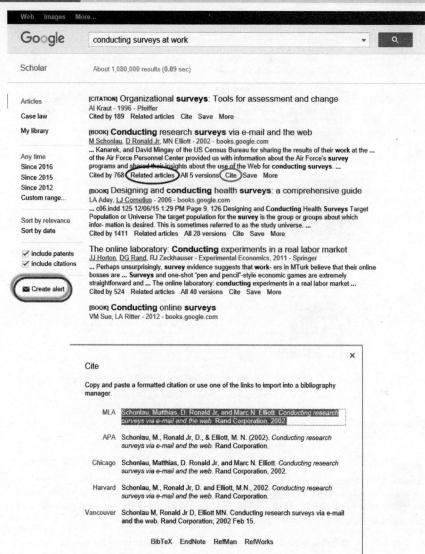

Source: http://scholar.google.com. Google and the Google logo are registered trademarks of Google Inc.

You can use the filters on the left side of the screen to filter out resources you don't want. You can further refine your research by using the Google Scholar Advanced Search option (Exhibits 11-5 and 11-6).

Whatever search engine you are using, a good command of **Boolean logic** will help you find the information you need quickly and accurately. Boolean logic uses three primary operators: AND, NOT, and OR. As explained in the From the Tech Desk feature "Use Search Operators to Manage Your Search," AND and NOT will narrow your search, and OR will expand it.

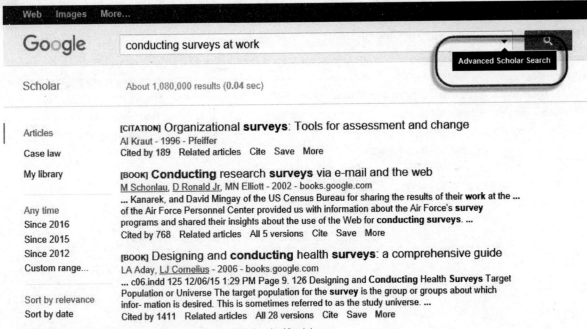

Web   Images   More...

Google   conducting surveys at work   ▼   🔍

Advanced Scholar Search

Scholar   About 1,080,000 results (0.04 sec)

Articles

[CITATION] Organizational **surveys**: Tools for assessment and change
Al Kraut - 1996 - Pfeiffer
Cited by 189   Related articles   Cite   Save   More

Case law

My library

[BOOK] **Conducting** research **surveys** via e-mail and the web
M Schonlau, D Ronald Jr, MN Elliott - 2002 - books.google.com
... Kanarek, and David Mingay of the US Census Bureau for sharing the results of their **work** at the ...

Any time
Since 2016
Since 2015

of the Air Force Personnel Center provided us with information about the Air Force's **survey**
programs and shared their insights about the use of the Web for **conducting surveys**. ...
Cited by 768   Related articles   All 5 versions   Cite   Save   More

Since 2012
Custom range...

[BOOK] Designing and **conducting** health **surveys**: a comprehensive guide
LA Aday, LJ Cornelius - 2006 - books.google.com
... c06.indd 125 12/06/15 1:29 PM Page 9. 126 Designing and **Conducting** Health **Surveys** Target

Sort by relevance
Sort by date

Population or Universe The target population for the **survey** is the group or groups about which
infor- mation is desired. This is sometimes referred to as the study universe. ...
Cited by 1411   Related articles   All 28 versions   Cite   Save   More

Source: http://scholar.google.com. Google and the Google logo are registered trademarks of Google Inc.

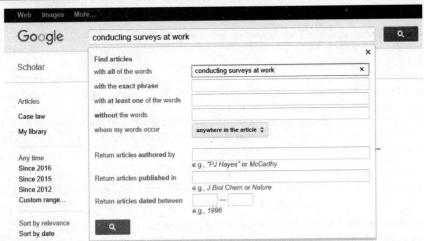

Web   Images   More...

Google   conducting surveys at work   🔍

Scholar

Articles

Case law

My library

Any time
Since 2016
Since 2015
Since 2012
Custom range...

Sort by relevance
Sort by date

Find articles   ✕
with **all** of the words   conducting surveys at work   ✕
with the **exact phrase**
with **at least one** of the words
without the words
where my words occur   anywhere in the article ⬍

Return articles **authored by**
                              e.g., "PJ Hayes" or McCarthy
Return articles **published in**
                              e.g., J Biol Chem or Nature
Return articles **dated between**   —
                              e.g., 1996

🔍

Source: http://scholar.google.com. Google and the Google logo are registered trademarks of Google Inc.

Use Search Operators to Manage Your Search

The terms AND, OR, and NOT can help you zero in on helpful resources.

Here's how they work:

- AND is a narrowing term. Putting AND between your search terms will bring up *only* those resources that match all the search terms you used, as shown in the shaded area below. (Google automatically adds "AND" between your search terms unless you tell it to do otherwise.)

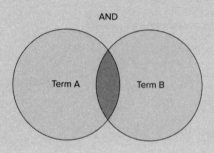

- NOT (or, in the case of Google, the minus sign) is also a narrowing operator. With this term, you tell the search engine what terms to *exclude* (the unshaded area below).

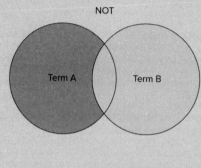

- OR is an expanding term. You'd use OR if you were unsure which search terms to use or wanted to broaden your search. This kind of search brings up *all resources that have at least one* of the terms (so the whole area covered by each of the search terms is shaded below).

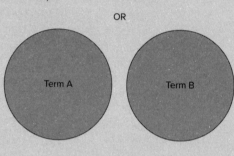

Becoming skilled at using Boolean logic will not only help you get the Internet-based information you need; it will also help you search online databases (discussed in a later section) more efficiently.

If you want to look for Web resources using more than one search engine, you can use a **metasearch engine**. With this tool, you enter the search terms once, run the search simultaneously with several search engines, and view a combined results page. One of the earliest, and still one of the most popular, metasearch tools is Dogpile. Exhibits 11-7 and 11-8 illustrate how Dogpile searches various search engines for the search term "employee morale" and then combines the results and presents them in an easy-to-view form. As with Google, you can also search for an exact phrase or use one of the specialized search tabs. Other popular metasearch engines are Mamma, Metacrawler, and Search.com. When using these tools, be sure to look down below the ads for your search results.

Another type of search tool that has emerged is the **specialized search engine**. Three popular examples are Yahoo People Search (for finding people's contact information), Edgar (for finding corporate information), and FindLaw (for gathering legal information).

While these tools help you find relevant Web documents, it is crucial to remember that the tools are limited: Not all of the documents published on the Web are indexed, and no search tool covers the entire Web. Also, as discussed in "Evaluating Websites" later in this section, you'll need to assess the accuracy and completeness of the retrieved sources.

Exhibit 11-7 | Illustration of the Metasearch Tool Dogpile

Source: www.dogpile.com

Using Other Web-Based Resources Many other Web-based resources besides those gathered by a search engine can help you with your research.

LO11-5 Use other Web resources to gather information.

You may have been advised by some of your college instructors not to use **Wikipedia** as a reference when you write essays or other papers. The reason is that Wikipedia is written and maintained by volunteers, and virtually anyone can post and edit articles. Since its launch in 2001, though, Wikipedia has become a more credible and useful resource. While we do not advise you to use its articles as your main source of information, it can be a useful place to start learning about a subject, especially if you take advantage of the citations that are listed at the end of most articles.

Blogs (short for "Web logs") started out as personal diaries or pages in 1994, but they soon became a journalism tool, and today, many companies and entrepreneurs maintain blogs, too. Like Facebook and LinkedIn, blogs can be a useful tool for finding information on a business problem.

There used to be special search engines, such as Technorati or Google Blog Search, for searching the blogosphere, but Google's main search engine has become so powerful that these tools have become obsolete. If you search a topic like "employee morale" on Google, many of the hits you get will actually be blog posts, especially now that content marketing has become so popular. If

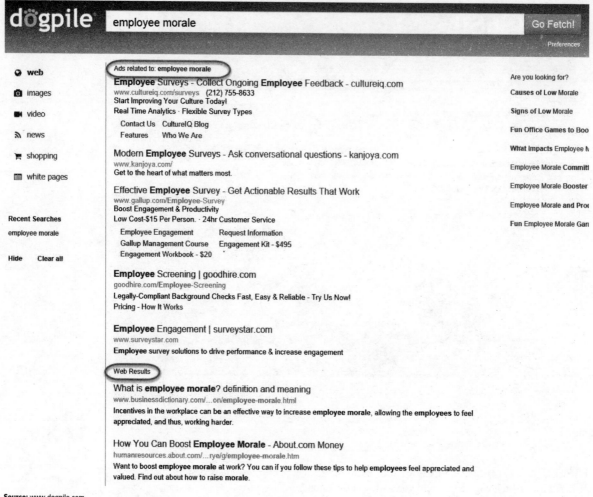

Source: www.dogpile.com

you want to look specifically for blog posts on your topic, simply add "blog" to the end of your search term. Exhibit 11-9 shows an article retrieved this way. If you find a blog you like, you can usually search it or click on links or categories in a menu pane on the right to find other posts you might like from this resource.

RSS (Really Simple Syndication) feeds and **email subscriptions to websites and blogs** can be useful research tools as well. News outlets such as *The New York Times* and *CNN* offer RSS feeds on their websites, and scholarly journals also offer RSS feeds for their tables of contents. When you subscribe to an RSS feed, the site pushes its new content to your chosen RSS reader or app (such as Feedly, NewsBlur, or Microsoft Outlook). You can then browse the news you care about all in one place and easily stay current on certain topics. There's some indication that the use of RSS has declined now that people can receive instant updates via Twitter and other social media.[3] If a site you want to keep up with doesn't have an RSS button, it will

VendHQ   Sign In

vend· Blog   Events   Customers   Tips

⌂ Home ▸ Retail Tips & Trends

5 Proven Ways to Boost Employee Morale, Increase Productivity, and Drive Sales

Francesca Nicasio · August 12, 2014 · 5 Comments

Who you have in your store is nearly as important as what you have in it. Your staff has a direct effect on sales, customer satisfaction, and the overall success of your store, which is why it's important that you should not only invest in finding and hiring the right people but also put in the effort to keep them happy and motivated.

Source: https://blog.vendhq.com; image © Ai825/Shutterstock RF.

probably offer a way to sign up for an email subscription. Subscribers receive an email message whenever a new article or newsletter is posted to the site.

Many industry leaders' websites have become treasure troves of information now that content marketing has become so popular. They also conduct their own research on timely topics. To get to their best resources, you may need to register for a free membership (which you can opt out of later if you wish). To learn how companies are using direct mail, you could search the resources at TMR Direct. You could visit Copyblogger to get the latest posts on content marketing. MailChimp has statistics and advice on e-marketing, and Chief Marketer looks at the whole marketing scene. To get a sense of larger business trends, you could read the research and commentary at such management-consulting sites as McKinsey & Company and The Future of Work.

Likewise, many professional associations' websites share free information with their members and the public. The American Institute of CPAs, for example, posts information from the *Journal of Accountancy* and other resources. The websites of the American Marketing Association, the American Management Association, the International Association of Business Communicators, the National Association of Realtors, and many more associations offer reports, white papers, and articles, often with more timely information than you'd find in a library's database.

You Make the Call

Some research indicates that people can assess the trustworthiness
of a website in seconds. What indicators do you think they're picking
up on?

Evaluating Websites   Websites can be an invaluable source of useful information. But
as you know, all are not equally creditable. Some may be biased; others may be inaccurate.
So it's important to know how to evaluate websites for completeness, accuracy, and
reliability.

To gauge the trustworthiness of the sites you visit, assess them on the following criteria:

- *Purpose.* Why was the information provided? To explain? To inform? To persuade? To sell?
  To share? What are the provider's biases? Who is the intended audience? What point of
  view does the site take? Could it possibly be ironic, a satire, or a parody?

- *Qualifications.* What are the credentials of the information provider? What is the nature
  of any sponsorship? Is contact information provided? Is it accurate? Is it complete—name,
  email address, street address, and phone number? Is the information well written, clear,
  and organized?

- *Validity.* Where else can the information provided be found? Is the information from the
  original source? Has the information been synthesized or abstracted accurately and in the
  correct context? Is the information timely? When was it created? When was it posted? How
  long has the site existed? Is it updated regularly? Do the links work? Has the site received
  any ratings or reviews?

- *Structure.* How is the site organized, designed, and formatted? Does its structure
  provide a particular emphasis? Does its coverage sufficiently meet the needs of its
  intended audience?

By critically evaluating the websites you use, you can ensure that the Web-based information in
your reports will reflect well on your research.

Taking Advantage of Social Networks   As you know, many of today's businesses take
advantage of social media like Facebook and Twitter for marketing purposes, but such networks
can also be useful for researching a business problem.

Facebook was launched as a personal social networking service in 2004, but businesses large and
small have adopted it as a key marketing venue. According to recent statistics gathered by digital-
marketing clearinghouse DMR, 41% of small businesses (accounting for 50 million sites) have
Facebook pages, while 75% of U.S. brands promote their Facebook posts—and 99% of U.S.
fashion brands are on Facebook.[4]

Because of its pervasiveness, Facebook also makes an excellent research tool. It is especially useful for surveys (which we discuss later in this chapter). You can also go to company Facebook
pages to research company-specific information.

Twitter started out as a personal communication tool, but organizations and companies now
liberally populate the "Twitterverse." As of 2014, 67% of Americans were using social
media, and one in six of those were on Twitter.[5] According to one study, 51% of active
Twitter users follow companies, brands, or products on social networks.[6] The two main
ways to use Twitter as a research tool are to search its contents and to follow certain topics
or people.

Several search tools are available for searching topics on Twitter. A sample search in one of
these, Twazzup, is shown in Exhibit 11-10. You can also search for a company or topic within
Twitter itself. Exhibit 11-11 shows what a search on the same topic as in the previous exhibit,
"employee morale," brought up. As you can see, the Twazzup results are more numerous and
easier to scan, while the Twitter results are more in depth.

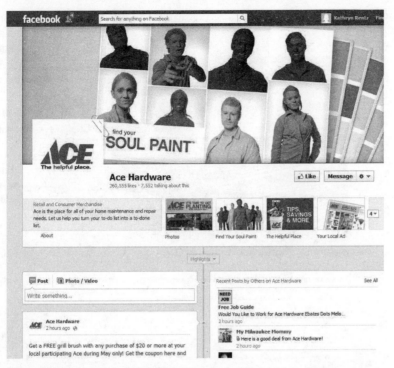

Companies' Facebook pages, like this one for Ace Hardware, can tell you a lot about the companies and their customers. You can read the company's profile, see what their customers are saying, learn about products and special promotions, and more.

Source: http://www.facebook.com/#!/acehardware

Exhibit 11-10   Illustration of a Twitter Search Using Twazzup

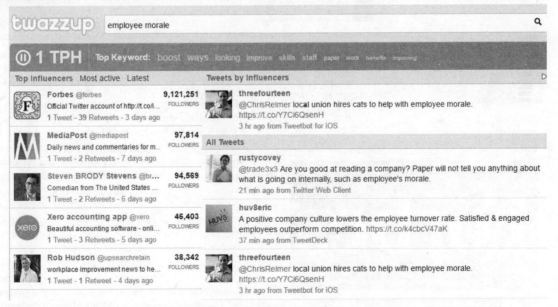

Source: www.twazzup.com; (a) © John Lund/Drew Kelly/Blend Images LLC RF; (b) © Dougal Waters/Getty Images RF; (c) © Monashee Frantz/age fotostock RF; (d) © Sam Edwards/age fotostock RF

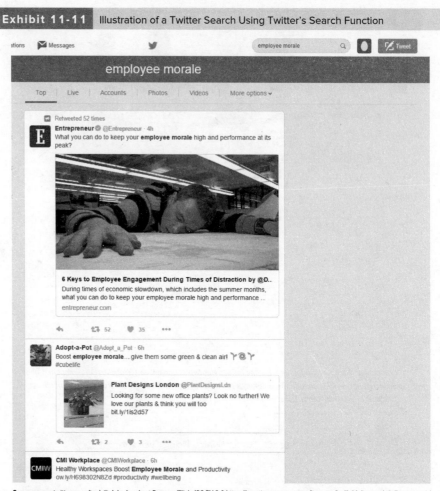

Source: www.twitter.com; (top) © John Lambert Pearson/Flickr/CC BY 2.0 https://creativecommons.org/licenses/by/2.0/; (bottom) © Exactostock/SuperStock RF

Exhibit 11-12   Illustration of a Twitter Hashtag in a Tweet

Source: https://twitter.com

To get more information relevant to your particular business problem, you should consider following topics by following specific **hashtags**. Hashtags are created by using the symbol # to mark keywords or topics. These marked topics are then easier to find in Twitter Search. If you find a hashtag you want to follow to learn more about a certain topic, you can click on that link and be taken to all the other tweets in that category. In the example in Exhibit 11-12, @Th1nkchange used the hashtag #EmployeeEngagement. If you click on the link for the hashtag, you can see all the latest posts that use this hashtag, as shown in Exhibit 11-13.

LinkedIn can also be useful for researching a business problem. To take full advantage of LinkedIn as a research tool, use the various Search options, particularly People, Companies,

Exhibit 11-13 | Illustration of the Results of Following a Hashtag

(top left): © Syda Productions/Shutterstock RF, (top right): © Jacob Ammentorp Lund/Getty Images RF, (bottom left): © Fuse/Getty Images RF
(bottom middle): © Jirsak/Shutterstock RF, (bottom right): © Blend Images/SuperStock RF

Source: https://twitter.com

Groups, and Posts (Exhibit 11-14). If, for example, you want to see what types of employee morale issues other companies are having, you can search with the Companies search. You could use the Groups search function to research groups that focus on human resources, training, or motivation. The Posts option will bring up articles that people have posted on your topic. You can also message another LinkedIn user—perhaps someone who has posted several articles on a topic—to discuss that topic one on one.

In addition to offering useful content and ways for you to connect with people, social-media sites show you what readers like and don't like, what's trending, and how other companies are using these media.

Listservs of Professional Organizations

As we've mentioned, professional organizations are another good and sometimes overlooked research tool for business problems. Members

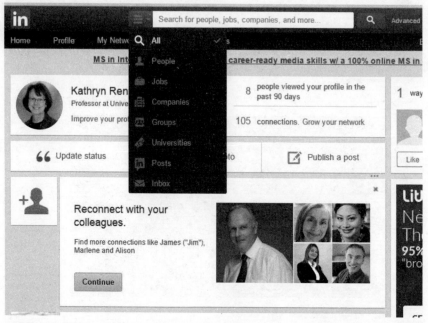

Source: www.linkedin.com; images (tl) Courtesy Kathy Rentz; (b, clockwise from left) © Image Source RF, all rights reserved.; © John Lund/Sam Diephuis/Blend Images LLC RF; ©Andersen Ross/Blend Images LLC RF; ©John Lund/Sam Diephuis/Blend Images LLC; © Ingram Publishing RF

of most professional organizations have benefits that include access to a member directory, salary surveys, conferences, industry information, and educational opportunities. Many such organizations also maintain one or more **listservs** (electronic mailing lists). Using these listservs, you can send a question out to the membership and tap the wisdom of the group. You can even survey the members on a given topic.

There are many organizations to consider joining, including the Association for Business Communication, the Association for Financial Professionals, the Sales and Marketing Professional Association, and the Society for Human Resource Management, among others.

Conducting Secondary Research in a Library

LO11-8   Use the library to gather information.

With so much information available on the Web, it is tempting to think that libraries have become obsolete. But libraries contain a wealth of information that is unavailable anywhere else or available elsewhere only for a fee. You will often find your best information in a library—and probably save money in the process.

Searching the Catalog   Today most libraries use online catalogs to list their holdings. You can locate sources in these catalogs by using the standard Keyword, Title, Author, and Subject options as well as a few other options. Becoming familiar with such catalogs is essential, especially for the libraries you use frequently. Effective and efficient searching techniques can yield excellent information.

Two search options you need to understand clearly are **Keyword** and **Subject**. When you select the Keyword option, the system will ask you to enter search terms and phrases. It will then search for those exact words in several of each record's fields, as illustrated in Exhibit 11-15. If you wanted to find resources on similar topics, you might think you'd use Subject—but Subject searches use only those topics that are recognized by the Library of Congress, so you can come up empty if you don't know how the Library of Congress labels the categories related to your topic.

Exhibit 11-15 | Results from a Keyword Search in a Library Catalog

Source: http://uclid.uc.edu

If your school's online library catalog doesn't show you the relevant Subject headings when you do a Subject search, you can find them by visiting the Library of Congress Authorities Web page at http://authorities.loc.gov and clicking "Search Authorities." Exhibit 11-16 shows possible headings for a search on "intercultural communication." If you click the red button to the left of the main heading, the search engine will sometimes suggest additional Subjects to search.

Searching by Subject will make your search more orderly and thorough than searching by Keyword because you'll find all the resources that the Library of Congress librarians think are related to your topic. On the other hand, you'll miss any resources related to your topic that haven't been tagged with those Subject headings, so your best bet is to do both Keyword and Subject searching.

Exhibit 11-16 Sample Library of Congress Subject Search

Source: http://authorities.loc.gov

Exhibit 11-17   Illustration of a Search Using the *ABI/Inform* Database

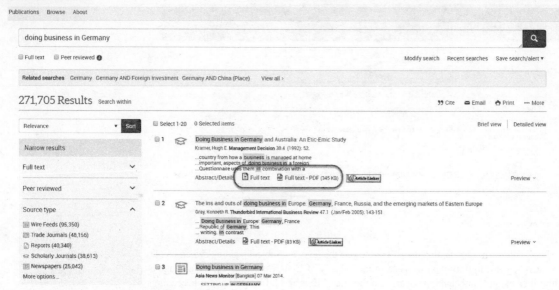

Source: http://search.proquest.com.proxy.libraries.uc.edu/abicomplete

Searching Databases
The online catalog helps you identify books and other holdings in your library, and it may help you find some articles. But to do a good job of searching the periodical literature—that is, articles published in newspapers, magazines, and journals—you will need to use an online **database**, such as *ABI/Inform* (Exhibit 11-17). Thanks to databases, you can search hundreds or even thousands of publications at once rather than having to search journals or other publications one by one. You can refine your search by using the filtering options on the left or advanced search options. Better yet, the material you like will often be available right there in full-text format for you to download (as shown in Exhibit 11-17), and some databases will create a citation for the source for you in the citation format your readers prefer.

ABI/Inform and *Business Source Premiere* are two of the most complete business databases, providing access to hundreds of business research journals as well as important industry and trade publications.

Factiva provides access to current business, general, and international news, including access to various editions of *The Wall Street Journal*. It also includes current information on U.S. public companies and industries. Similarly, *LexisNexis* offers access to current business and international articles, providing them in full text. Additionally, it includes legal and reference information.

If you need information on a particular company, you could use *LexisNexis® Company Dossier*. This database provides complete pictures of companies' financial health, brands, and competitors for both U.S. and international companies. *Hoover's Online* is also an excellent resource for company-specific information, and others include *Business & Company Resource Center, Business Source Complete,* and *D&B's Million Dollar Database.*

Consulting Reference Materials
Along with database sources, you may want to investigate other print and Web-based reference materials for information (Exhibit 11-18). To conduct research on a particular industry, for example, you could use *BizMiner,* which offers industry statistical reports and industry financial analysis benchmarks for over 5,000 lines of business and industries. Other industry-specific sources include *Plunkett Research Online* and *Standard & Poor's Industry Surveys.* To find out about international trade you can use the *(CIA) World*

Exhibit 11-18   Useful Reference Materials

Type of Source	Description	Examples
Encyclopedias	Offer background material and other general information. Individual articles or sections of articles are written by experts in the field and frequently include a short bibliography.	*Encyclopedia Americana* *Encyclopaedia Britannica* *World Book* *Encyclopedia of Banking and Finance* *Encyclopedia of Business and Finance* *Encyclopedia of Small Business* *Encyclopedia of Advertising* *Encyclopedia of Emerging Industries*
Biographical Directories	Supply biographical information about leading figures of today or of the past.	*Who's Who in America* *Who's Who in the World* *Who's Who in the East* *Who's Who in the South and Southwest*
Almanacs	Offer factual and statistical information.	*The World Almanac and Book of Facts* *The Time Almanac* *The New York Times Almanac*
Trade Directories	Compile details in specific areas of interest. Variously referred to as *catalogs, listings, registers,* or *source books*.	*The Million Dollar Directory* *Thomas Register of American Manufacturers* *The Datapro Directory* *America's Corporate Families* *Who Owns Whom* *Directory of Corporate Affiliations* *Directories in Print*
Government Publications	Include surveys, catalogs, pamphlets, and periodicals from various governmental bureaus, departments, and agencies.	*Annual & Quarterly Services* (service-industry data) *Census of Wholesale Trade* *Census of Mineral Industries* *Statistical Abstract of the United States* *Survey of Current Business* *Monthly Labor Review* *Occupational Outlook Quarterly* *Federal Reserve Bulletin*
Dictionaries	Provide definitions, spellings, and pronunciations of words or phrases. Electronic dictionaries add other options such as pronunciation in audio files.	*American Heritage Dictionary* *Funk & Wagnalls Standard Dictionary* *Random House Webster's College Dictionary* *Merriam-Webster's Collegiate Dictionary*
Additional Statistical Sources	Provide statistical data.	*Statistical Abstract of the United States* *Standard & Poor's Statistical Service* *Statistical Reference Index*
Business Information Services	Supply a variety of information to business practitioners.	*Corporation Records* *Moody's Investors' Advisory Service* *Value Line Investment Survey* *Gale Business Insights: Global* *Hoover's Online Factiva*
International Sources	Supply international corporate information.	*Principal International Businesses* *Major Companies of Europe* *Japan Company Handbook* *International Encyclopedia of the Social Sciences* *International Business Dictionary and References* *International Brands and Their Companies* *Foreign Commerce Handbook* *Index to International Statistics Statistical Yearbook*

How do I find business news and trends?

ABI Inform Complete on ProQuest

Business Source Complete

Factiva (includes Dow Jones, Reuters Newswires and *The Wall Street Journal*, plus more than 8,000 other sources from around the world)

LexisNexis Academic, News and Business sections

Proquest Business Insights

Wilson OmniFile Full Text Mega

How do I find information about companies?

Business & Company Resource Center

Business Source Complete

Companies' own websites

Company Dossier (on *Lexis/Nexis*)

D&B's (Dunn & Bradstreet's) *Million Dollar Database*

Datamonitor 360

Factiva

Hoover's Online

Mergent Online

ORBIS

SEC Filings (on Edgar) at www.sec.gov/edgar/

Standard & Poor's NetAdvantage

Thomson One Banker

Value Line Research Center

How do I find information about particular industries?

ABI/INFORM Complete

BizMiner

Datamonitor 360

Freedonia Focus Market Research

Decision Support Database

Global Market Information Database

IBISWorld

ICON Group International

MarketLine

MarketResearch.com Academic

Mergent Industry Reports

Mintel Market Research Reports

Plunkett Research Online

Standard & Poor's Industry Surveys

How do I find biographical and contact information for businesspeople?

Biographical Dictionary of American Business Leaders

Biography in Context (Galegroup)

Biography Reference Bank (Wilson)

D&B's Million Dollar Database

LexisNexis Academic, Reference/Biographical Information section

Standard & Poor's NetAdvantage (Register of Executives)

How do I find data provided by the U.S. government?

American Community Survey (U.S. Census Bureau) at www.census.gov/acs/www/

American FactFinder at http://factfinder2.census.gov/

Business USA at http://business.usa.gov/

FRED (Federal Reserve Economic Data) at http://research.stlouisfed.org/fred2/

Bureau of Labor Statistics Data at www.bls.gov/home.htm

How do I find out about other countries and international trade?

Country Studies (Library of Congress) at http://lcweb2.loc.gov/frd/cs/cshome.html

(CIA) World Factbook at www.cia.gov/library/publications/the-world-factbook/

Country Reports (from the Department of State) at www.state.gov/countries/

Europa World Yearbooks

Global Market Information Database WDI Online (World Bank's World Development Indicators)

How do I find information about cities?

American FactFinder at http://factfinder2.census.gov/

Cities' own websites

Complete Economic and Demographic Data Source: CEDDS (Woods & Poole Economics)

State and County

QuickFacts at http://www.census.gov/quickfacts/table/PST045215/00 (can search for cities)

SimplyMap (a Web-based mapping application that lets users create maps and reports using demographic, business, and marketing data for the United States)

Source: Compiled with the assistance of Senior Business Librarian Wahib Nasrallah, University of Cincinnati.

Factbook, which offers information on different countries' histories, governments, economies, geographical traits, and interactions with other countries. *Country Reports* from the Department of State also provides general information, region-specific information, and travel information.

The library materials you choose will be determined by your research question. Exhibit 11-19 lists helpful resources for common research tasks in business. A reference librarian can recommend additional resources to help you with your research task.

Conducting Primary Research with Surveys

When the information you seek can't be found in secondary sources, you will need to conduct primary research. One of the most popular primary research tools in business is the **survey**.

The premise of the survey as a method of primary research is simple: You can best acquire certain types of information by asking questions. With surveys, you can gather demographic information as well as information about people's opinions, behaviors, and beliefs. A survey can also be a preliminary step toward conducting an experiment or an observation, or a way to help you understand what the data gathered by these other methods mean.

Once you have decided to conduct a survey, you'll need to make a number of decisions, including what questions to ask and how to ask them. But none of these decisions will be more important than whom to survey. Except for situations in which a small number of people are involved in the problem under study, you won't be able to reach all the people involved. Thus, you'll need to select a **sample** of respondents who represent the group as a whole as accurately as possible. You can select that sample in several ways.

Choosing Your Sampling Technique

The type of sampling technique you use will be determined by the purpose of your research. While all samples have some degree of sampling error, you can reduce the error through techniques used to construct representative samples. These techniques fall into two groups: **probability** and **nonprobability sampling**.

Probability samples are based on chance selection procedures, which means that every element in the population, or a subgroup of the population, has the same probability of being selected for the sample. These techniques include **simple random sampling**, **stratified random sampling**, **systematic sampling**, and **area** or **cluster sampling**.

LO11-9   Use sampling to conduct a survey.

- *Simple random sampling.* By definition, this sampling technique gives every member of the group under study an equal chance of being included. To ensure equal chances, you must identify every member of the group and then, using a list or some other convenient format, record all the identifications. Next, through some chance method, you select the members of your sample.

  For example, if you are studying the job attitudes of 200 employees and determine that 25 interviews will give you the information you need, you might put the names of all 200 workers in a container, mix them thoroughly, and draw out 25. Since each of the 200 workers has an equal chance of being selected, your sample will be random and can be presumed to be representative.

- *Stratified random sampling.* Stratified random sampling subdivides the group under study and makes random selections within each subgroup. The distribution of a particular group in the sample should closely replicate the distribution of that group in the entire population. Assume, for example, that you are attempting to determine the curriculum needs of 5,000 undergraduates at a certain college and that you have decided to survey 20% of the enrollment, or 1,000 students. To construct a sample for this problem, first divide the enrollment list by academic concentration: business, liberal arts, nursing, engineering, and so forth. Then draw a random sample from each of these groups, making sure that the number you select is proportionate to that group's percentage of the total undergraduate enrollment. Thus, if 30% of the students are majoring in business, you will randomly select 300 business majors for your sample; if 40% of the students are liberal arts majors, you will randomly select 400 liberal arts majors for your sample; and so on.

- *Systematic sampling.* In systematic sampling you decide what percentage of a population you are interested in sampling, such as 10% of 10,000. Then, going down a list of the population's members, you select your participants at regular intervals (e.g, every ninth person).

  If you use this method, your sample will not be strictly random because by virtue of their designated place on the original list, items do not have an equal chance of being selected. Therefore, it is important to make sure your source list for the sample is not organized in a way that would create a biased sample.

- *Area or cluster sampling.* Researchers use area sampling when no master source list of a population is available. For example, if you want to survey employees in a given industry, it is unlikely there is a list of all these employees. An approach you may take in this situation is to randomly select a given number of companies from a list of all the companies in the industry. Then, using organization units and selecting randomly at each level, you break down each of these companies into divisions, departments, sections, and so on until you finally identify the workers you will survey.

Researchers frequently survey a sample of the group that is being studied.
© wdstock/Getty Images RF

Nonprobability samples are based on an unknown probability of any one member of a population being chosen for the sample. These techniques include **convenience sampling**, **purposeful sampling**, and **referral sampling**.

- *Convenience sampling.* A convenience sample is one whose members are convenient and economical to reach. When professors use their students as subjects for their research, they are using a convenience sample. Researchers generally use this sample to reach a large number quickly and economically. This kind of sampling is best used for exploratory research. A form of convenience sampling is *judgment* or *expert* sampling. This technique relies on the judgment of the researcher to identify appropriate members of the sample. Illustrating this technique is the common practice of predicting the outcome of an election based on the results in a bellwether district.

- *Purposeful sampling.* With purposeful sampling you look for a sample that has certain characteristics. Let's say you want to find out students' attitudes about a new tool for searching the university's online library collections. It would be more logical to draw your sample from the students who use the system rather than from all the students at the university.

- *Referral sampling.* Referral samples are those whose members are identified by others. This technique is used to locate members when the population is small or hard to reach. For example, you might want to survey Six Sigma Black Belt certification holders. To get a sample large enough to make the study worthwhile, you could ask those from your town to give you the names of other Black Belt holders. Or perhaps you are trying to survey the users of a project management application. You could survey a user group and ask those members for names of other users. You might even post an announcement on a listserv, LinkedIn, or some other online platform asking for names.

Constructing the Questionnaire

Once you have determined whom you will survey, you will need to construct your survey instrument, or **questionnaire**. A questionnaire is simply an orderly arrangement of the survey questions with appropriate spaces provided for the answers. But simple as the finished questionnaire may appear, it is the result of careful planning. You must word your questions so that the results will be **reliable**; a test of a questionnaire's reliability is its ability to generate similar results when used in similar circumstances. You also want your questionnaire to be **valid**, measuring what it is supposed to measure.

Keeping these guidelines in mind will help you achieve reliable, valid results:

LO11-10 Construct a questionnaire and conduct a survey.

- *Avoid leading questions.* A **leading question** is one that in some way influences the answer. For example, the question "Is Dove your favorite bath soap?" may lead the respondent to favor Dove. Some people who would say "yes" would name another brand if they were asked, "What is your favorite brand of bath soap?"

- *Avoid absolute terms.* Try not to include words like *always* and *never* in your questions. Using these terms may make respondents unlikely to choose these answers, and the wording of the question could skew your data toward middle selections like *sometimes* or *frequently*.

- *Focus on one concept per question.* **Double-barreled questions** combine multiple questions and lead to inaccurate answers. An example of such a question is "To what extent do managers and co-workers affect your perception of the company?" This question asks a respondent two questions. If the respondent feels that managers do impact their perception but co-workers do not, the answer the respondent provides will not be an accurate reflection of his or her beliefs, and the question will not lead you to reliable data.

- *Make the questions easy to understand.* Questions that not all respondents will clearly understand will generate faulty data. Unfortunately, it is difficult to determine in advance just what respondents will not understand. As will be discussed later, the best means of detecting such questions in advance is to test the questions before using them, but you can catch many problematic questions yourself.

One kind of problem is vague wording, which is illustrated by the question, "How do you bank?" This could mean any number of things. Another is using words that respondents may not understand, as in the question, "How reliable is your Web router?" Some respondents won't know exactly what their Web router is, and "reliable" means different things to different people.

- *Avoid questions that might trigger personal prejudices or pride.* People are reluctant to give accurate answers to questions about their age, income status, morals, and some personal habits. How many people, for example, would answer "no" to the question "Do you brush your teeth daily?" How many people would give their ages correctly? How many citizens would admit to fudging a bit on their tax returns?

If such information is essential to the solution of the research problem, use a less direct means of inquiry. To ascertain age, for example, you could ask for dates of high school graduation. Or you could provide an age range for a respondent to choose from, such as 20–24, 25–34, 35–44, 45–54, and 54 and older. This technique works well with income questions, too. People are generally more willing to answer questions that provide ranges instead of asking for specifics.

- *Ask only for information that can be remembered.* If asking questions about the past, be sure to ask only for information that the respondents can be expected to remember. Being aware of three traits of human memory can help you. First, people remember recent events better than older events. They can remember insignificant events that occurred within the past few hours, but by the next day, they will have forgotten some of the details, and a month later, they may not remember any. You might well remember, for example, what you ate for lunch on the day of the survey, and perhaps you might remember what you ate for lunch a day, two days, or three days earlier. But you would be unlikely to remember what you ate for lunch a year earlier.

When conducting a survey, ask only for information that is likely to be remembered accurately.
© Hill Street Studios/Blend Images/Getty Images

The second principle regarding memory is that people tend to remember significant events. You may long remember minor details about the first day of school, your wedding, or an automobile accident. People readily remember events such as these because in each event there was an intense stimulus—a requisite for retention in memory.

A third principle of memory is that fairly insignificant facts may be remembered over long time periods through association with something significant. Although you would not normally remember what you ate for lunch a year earlier, for example, you might remember if the day in question happened to be Christmas Day or your first day at college.

Designing the Questionnaire and Planning Its Delivery
Overall, the questionnaire should be designed to gather useful information that can be easily tabulated and meaningfully analyzed.

Be sure to enable the respondents to provide the demographic information you need. In some instances, such information as the age, sex, and income bracket of the respondent is vital to the analysis of the problem.

When practical, enable the respondents to check an answer. Easy-to-answer questions will encourage participation, and providing choices will make numerical analysis easier, too. Such questions must always provide for all possible answers, including conditional answers. For example, a direct question may provide for three possible answers: Yes ＿＿, No ＿＿, and Don't know ＿＿.

Consider using **scaling** when appropriate. It is sometimes desirable to measure the intensity of the respondents' feelings about a given topic, such as a product or company process. In such cases, some form of scaling is useful. The most common forms are ranking and rating.

The **ranking** technique consists of asking the respondent to rank a number of alternative answers to a question in order of preference (1, 2, 3, and so on). For example, in a survey to determine consumer preferences for toothpaste, the respondent might be asked to rank toothpastes A, B, C, D, and E in order of preference. The **rating** technique provides a scale showing the complete range of possible attitudes on a topic and assigns number values to the positions on the scale. The

Web-Based Survey Tools Help Writers Design, Analyze, and Report Results of Questionnaires

Web-based survey tools, such as those offered at SurveyPlanet and SurveyMonkey.com, can help you design professional-looking questionnaires as well as compile and analyze the results.

When preparing your questions, you can choose from several question types, as shown in the sample SurveyMonkey screen below. You can also select your preferred design or theme (e.g., color and layout). You can move the questions to change the order, and you can enable respondents to skip parts of the survey based on their answers to certain questions.

Such tools are useful for many business purposes, such as conducting training program evaluations, gathering employee feedback on policies and procedures, conducting marketing surveys, and assessing customer satisfaction.

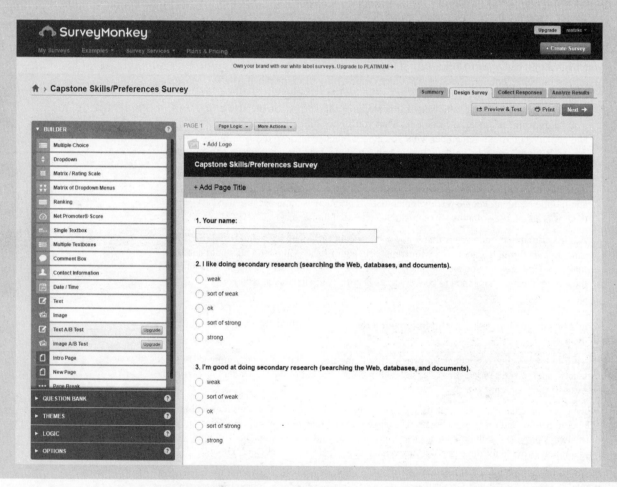

respondent must then indicate the position on the scale that corresponds to his or her attitude. Typically, the numeral positions are described by words, as Exhibit 11-20 illustrates.

Think carefully about how to order the questions on your survey. For example, starting with a question about a topic of keen interest to your recipients can motivate them to respond to the survey; on the other hand, it can also trigger emotional reactions that will lead to poorly considered answers. Frequently, some questions must come after other questions because they follow

Exhibit 11-20 Illustration of a Rating Question

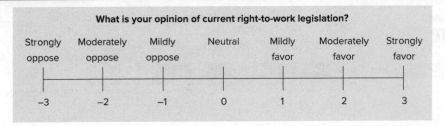

What is your opinion of current right-to-work legislation?

Strongly oppose	Moderately oppose	Mildly oppose	Neutral	Mildly favor	Moderately favor	Strongly favor
−3	−2	−1	0	1	2	3

up or build on the previous questions. Use whatever order will encourage participation, move respondents smoothly through the survey, and gather the most reliable data.

Fairly early in the planning process, you should choose your **survey channel**. You can get responses to your questions in four primary ways: by personal (face-to-face) contact, by phone, by mail (print or digital), or through websites (e.g., Facebook). You should select the way that in your unique case yields the best sample and the best results at the lowest cost.

All these decisions should be recorded in a **survey plan**. Your plan should include such logistics as when and where you'll conduct your survey, how many times it will be sent out, and when it will close. It should also include any additional materials you'll need. If you are conducting a mail or Web survey, for example, you'll need to develop an explanatory message that motivates the subjects to respond, tells them what to do, and answers all the questions they are likely to ask (see Exhibit 11-21). If you are conducting a personal or phone survey, you'll need to develop a script and/or instructions for the surveyors.

Conducting a Pilot Study Before conducting the actual survey, you should, if at all possible, conduct a **pilot study** on your questionnaire and survey plan. A pilot study is a small-scale version of your survey; in essence, it is a form of user testing (described later in the section). You select a few people to use as testers and have them take your survey to identify unclear questions, technological glitches, or other problems. Based on the results, you modify your questionnaire and working plan. Including this step in your survey planning will help you avoid the disappointment (and cost) that results from administering a flawed survey.

LO11-11 Design an observational study for a business problem.

Conducting Observations and Experiments

Two types of primary research that involve watching and/or recording what happens are **observations** and **experiments**.

Observations Simply stated, observation is seeing with a purpose. It consists of watching the events related to the problem you're investigating and systematically recording what you see. With this technique, you do not manipulate the details of what you observe; you take note of situations exactly as you find them.

To see how observation works as a business technique, consider this situation. You work for a

Systematically observing what happens can be a useful form of primary research.
© The McGraw Hill Companies/Mark Dierker, photogtapher

Exhibit 11-21 A Sample Cover Message for an Online Survey

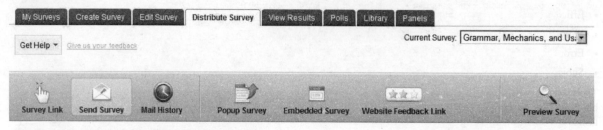

Source: University of Wisconsin Eau Claire; Paula Lentz.

fast-food chain, such as McDonald's, that wants to check the quality and consistency of some menu items throughout the chain. By hiring observers, sometimes called mystery shoppers, you can gather information on the temperature, freshness, and speed of delivery of various menu items. This method may reveal important information that other data collection methods cannot.

The observation procedure can be any system that ensures the collection of complete and representative information. But every effective observation procedure includes a clear focus, well-defined steps, and provisions for ensuring the quality of the information collected. For example, an observation procedure for determining the courtesy of employees toward customers when answering the phone might include counting the number of times each employee used certain polite expressions, checking for the use of other courtesy techniques (e.g., offering further help), and recording how long it took for the employee to solve the customer's problem. In other words, you would have to identify observable courteous behaviors to be able to record them.

One particular observation technique that can be used in business research is **user testing**. Also called **usability testing**, this research technique captures a person's experience when interacting with a product such as a document, a mobile device, a website, a piece of software, or any number of other consumer products.

In general, user testing measures how well users can learn and use a product and how satisfied they are with that process. When engaging in user testing, a researcher will measure the following factors:[7]

- Intuitive design
- Ease of learning
- Efficiency of use
- Memorability
- Error frequency and severity
- Subjective satisfaction

There are many ways to perform a user test. The most common method is to select a small number of testers (5 to 15) who represent the targeted users or customers and have them perform a task. To set up a user test of a new tablet your company is developing, for example, you would create a situation (a scenario) in which a person performs a task using the product while observers watch and take notes. While the tester worked on this task, you would watch what he or she did to determine how successfully the tester could use the device and what kinds of reactions it generated. After the testing session, you would administer a questionnaire to get additional feedback from the tester.

Experiments Conducting an experiment can be a useful technique for researching a business problem. Experiments test the effects of a particular variable on some existing situation or activity. Therefore, to conduct an experiment, you systematically manipulate one factor of a problem while holding all the others constant. You then measure any changes resulting from your manipulations.

LO11-12 Conduct an experiment for a business problem.

For example, suppose you want to determine whether a new package design will lead to more sales. You might start by selecting two test cities, taking care that they are as alike as possible on all the characteristics that might affect the experiment. Then you would secure information on sales in the two cities for a specified time period before the study. Next, for a second specified time period, you would use the new package design in one of the cities and continue to use the old package in the other. During that period, you would keep careful sales records and check to make sure that advertising, economic conditions, competition, and other factors that might have some effect on the experiment remained unchanged. At the end of the study period, you could be relatively confident that any differences you found between the sales in the two cities were caused by the difference in package design.

The simplest experimental design is the **before–after design**. In this design, illustrated in Exhibit 11-22, you select a test group of subjects, measure the variable in which you are interested, and then introduce the experimental factor. After a specified time period, during which the experimental factor has presumably had its effect, you remeasure the variable in which you are interested. If there are any differences between the first and second measurements, you may assume that the experimental factor, plus any uncontrollable factors, is the cause.

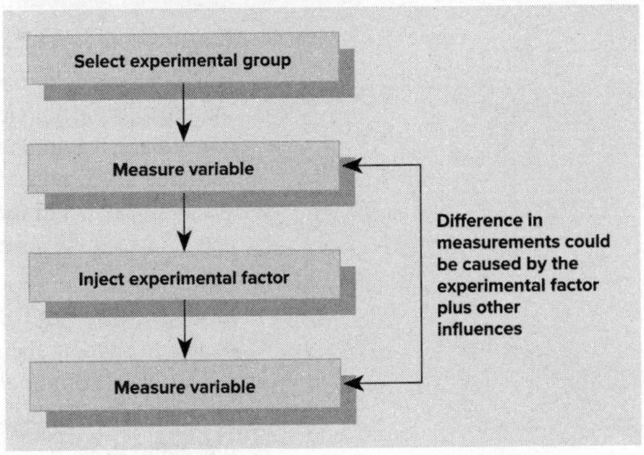

You can probably recognize the major shortcoming of this research method: The experimental factor may not explain the change. Your results could have been caused by other factors (e.g., changes in the weather, holiday or other seasonal influences on business activity, or advertising for other products). At best, you have determined only that the variable you were testing *could* have had an effect.

To control for influences other than the experimental factors, you need a more complex method, such as the **controlled before–after design**.

Exhibit 11-22

The Before–After Experimental Design

Select experimental group

↓

Measure variable

↓

Inject experimental factor

↓

Measure variable

Difference in measurements could be caused by the experimental factor plus other influences

Exhibit 11-23 The Controlled Before–After Experimental Design

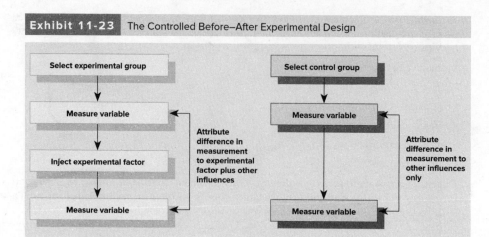

With this method, you select not one group, but two: the experimental group and the control group. Before introducing the experimental factor, you measure the variable to be tested in each group. Then you introduce the experimental factor into the experimental group only. When the period allotted for the experiment is over, you again measure the variable being tested in each group. Any difference between the first and second measurements in the experimental group can be explained by two causes: the experimental factor and other influences. But the difference between the first and second measurements in the control group can be explained only by other influences because this group was not subjected to the experimental factor. Thus, comparing the "afters" of the two groups will give you a good idea of how much the experimental factor affected the results for the experimental group (Exhibit 11-23).

Conducting Qualitative Primary Research

LO11-13 Explain the uses of focus groups and personal interviews.

The techniques for primary research that we've discussed thus far are (largely) quantitative. That is, they are designed to gather useful numbers. But some primary research methods are qualitative. Qualitative researchers take a more interpretive approach to research. They begin with a more general question about what they want to learn and then study natural phenomena to gather insights into the phenomena or even to learn to ask different questions. Accordingly, they are likely to use such research tools as **focus groups** and **personal interviews**, and they will collect mostly verbal data. **Qualitative research** does not enable statistical analysis or the application of the findings to larger populations; rather, it enables you to interpret what the data mean at a more localized level.

Whether you conduct a personal interview or convene a focus group, you need to decide how you will record the interactions since you cannot rely on your memory. Sometimes, simply taking notes is sufficient. Other times, you may want to record the session so that you can note nonverbal behaviors (e.g., tone, facial expressions, gestures) that influence the interpretation of a participant's response. Then you would transcribe the notes using a system for coding these nonverbal behaviors in the text of the transcript. Bear in mind that you must always ask the participants for their permission to record focus groups or interviews.

Conducting Focus Groups The purpose of a focus group is to bring together a group of people to find out their beliefs or attitudes about the topic of a research project. For instance, if you want to learn how one of your company's products could be improved, you might gather a group of people who currently use your product and have them discuss what they like or don't like about it.

Focus groups can help you learn not only what the target population prefers but why.
© Spencer Grant/PhotoEdit

As the moderator of the discussion, you can structure the conversation and ask questions that will elicit useful data from the participants, or you can simply allow participants to voice their ideas. As you may have experienced, when people discuss a topic in a group, they often generate more or better ideas than they would have working alone. The focus group thus becomes a sort of brainstorming session, which can yield rich data. Of course, as the moderator you also have to make sure that all participants can freely share their ideas. Some of the tips discussed later in this chapter and in Chapter 14 for encouraging participation in group projects and meetings may also help you facilitate focus groups. Because of advances in technology, focus groups can be conducted face to face, online with technologies such as Skype, or even over the phone.

Conducting Personal Interviews If you decide that talking with people one on one is the best way to gather data to answer your research question, you will likely conduct face-to-face interviews or phone interviews. People may be willing to share stories and opinions in a personal interview that they might not be comfortable sharing in a larger group.

Preparing for a personal interview is much like preparing for a survey. First, you need to decide whom to interview (your sample). Then you need to construct questions, as you would for a survey. However, the nature of the questions for a face-to-face interview will be a bit different. Researchers conducting surveys prefer to use **closed-ended questions** because these force the participants to give only one possible response (e.g., answering a yes/no question, choosing an age range from a list provided by the researcher, or selecting a rating on a scale) and allow for quick data analysis. However, when conducting interviews, many researchers favor **open-ended questions** because the conversational nature of the interview setting enables participants to provide detailed, rich, and varied responses. Furthermore, open-ended questions in personal interviews give researchers the opportunity to ask follow-up questions that they would not be able to ask participants taking a written survey.

Conducting Ethical Business Research

Throughout the research process, you need to be sure you are conducting research in an ethical manner. In particular, you should adhere to guidelines for treating research participants ethically, and you should report your research accurately and honestly.

LO11-14 Discuss important ethical guidelines for research.

Treat Research Participants Ethically Many companies, academic institutions, and medical facilities have guidelines for conducting research with human subjects and have institutional review boards (IRBs) to ensure that employees comply with the laws and policies that govern research. Be sure that you are familiar with these policies before conducting primary research that involves people.

The main principle behind such policies is that participants in a research study have the right to informed consent. That is, they have the right to know the nature of their participation in the study and any associated risks. In addition, their participation must be voluntary, and they must be able to discontinue their participation at any time during the study; just because they agreed to participate at one point does not mean they are obligated to finish the project. Furthermore, participants need to know whether their participation and the data associated with them in the study will be **confidential** (known only to the researcher and participant) or **anonymous** (known only to the participant). If protecting participants' rights will require you to develop a proposal to an IRB, an informed consent letter to the participants, and an informed consent form, be sure you build this process into the planning stage of your project.

Report Information Accurately and Honestly When researching and writing business documents, do not ever lose sight of your main goal: to provide decision makers with reliable information. You will defeat this purpose if you misrepresent your findings.

As you interpret and present secondary information, assess its quality. Does the author draw conclusions that can be supported by the data presented? Are the sources reliable? Are the data or interpretations biased in any way? Are there any gaps or holes in the data or interpretation? You need to be a good judge of the material, and if it has limitations, you should note them in your document.

Also, be sure to cite your sources. The whole point of including citations is to allow your readers to check your sources for themselves. Any mistakes in your citations may not only frustrate your readers but also make you look inept or dishonest. Be particularly careful to give credit where credit is due. **Plagiarism**, which is submitting another person's published work as your own without properly crediting it, is especially damaging to your credibility. Be sure to follow the guidelines in Reference Chapter B for correctly citing your sources.

As for primary research, once you have good data to work with, you must interpret them accurately and clearly for your reader. Here, too, you should acknowledge any limitations of your research. Be careful as well to avoid misleading visuals, as dicussed in Chapter 4.

Interpreting the Findings

LO11-15 Interpret your findings accurately.

The next major stage of the report-writing process is to interpret the information you've gathered.

Actually, you will have done a lot of interpreting already by the time you reach this stage. You had to interpret the elements of the situation to understand the problem and determine your research purpose. You also had to interpret your data as you were gathering them to make sure that you were getting appropriate and sufficient information. But when your research is finished, you will need to formulate the interpretations that will guide the shape and contents of your report.

To do this, keep both your problem and your readers in mind. Your findings will need to apply clearly to the given problem in order to be viewed as logical solutions. But they will also need to meet the readers' needs in order to be viewed as relevant and helpful. If you have kept your reader-based problem and purpose statements in mind while doing your research, making logical, reader-based analyses of your data should follow naturally.

How you interpret your data will vary from case to case, but the following general advice can help you with this process.

Avoiding Errors in Interpretation

Certain human tendencies lead to error in interpretation. The following list explains how to minimize them:

1. *Report the facts as they are.* Do nothing to make them more or less exciting. Adding color to interpretations to make the report more interesting compromises objectivity.

2. *Do not think that conclusions are always necessary.* When the facts do not support a conclusion, you should just summarize your findings and conclude that there is no conclusion. All too often, report writers think that if they do not conclude, they have failed in their investigation.

3. *Do not interpret a lack of evidence as proof to the contrary.* The fact that you cannot prove something is true does not mean that it is false.

4. *Do not compare noncomparable data.* When you look for relationships between sets of data, make sure they have enough similarities to be comparable. For example, you might be able to draw conclusions about how two groups of employees differ at Company X, but you probably would not be justified in comparing Group A from Company X to Group B from Company Y.

Interpreting facts requires not only analytical skills and objective judgment but consideration of ethical issues as well.
© Steve Cole/Getty Images RF

5. *Do not draw illogical cause–effect conclusions.* The fact that two sets of data appear to affect each other does not mean they actually do. They may be only **correlated** (strongly associated for an undetermined reason). Use research and good logic to determine whether a cause–effect relationship is likely.

6. *Beware of unreliable and unrepresentative data.* Much of the information to be found in secondary sources is incorrect to some extent. The causes are many: collection error, biased research, recording mistakes. Beware especially of data collected by groups that advocate a position (political organizations, groups supporting social issues, and other special interest groups). Make sure your sources are reliable. And remember that the interpretations you make are no better than the data you interpret.

7. *Do not oversimplify.* Most business problems are complex, and it can be tempting to settle for easy answers. Avoid conclusions and recommendations that do not do justice to the problem.

8. *Tailor your claims to your data.* There's a tendency among inexperienced report writers to use too few facts to generalize far too much. If you have learned about a certain phenomenon, do not assume that your interpretations can automatically be applied to similar phenomena. Or if your research has revealed the source of a problem, do not assume that you can also propose solutions; finding solutions can be a separate research project altogether. Make only those claims that are well supported by your evidence, and when you are not sure how strong to make them, use such qualified language as "may be," "could be," and "suggest."

Contextualizing the Data

The data you collect won't mean anything in a vacuum. They turn into information only when you translate them into something that is meaningful to your readers. For this to happen, you must consider your data in context and try to see patterns in it that are relevant to your readers' interests.

Let's say that you've been asked to find out how satisfied the customers are at a health clinic, and you conducted a survey for this purpose. The seventh question, "How accurate are the bills you receive from the billing office?" yielded the results shown in the graph.

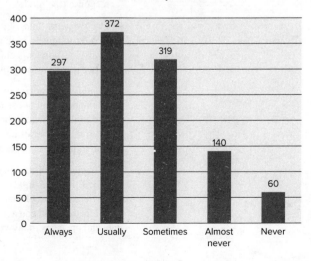

Accuracy of Bills

Always	297
Usually	372
Sometimes	319
Almost never	140
Never	60

At first glance, you might think, "Oh, we're doing pretty well—most of the answers are toward the positive end." But think again! How accurate should people's bills be? A good billing office would shoot for 100%. And how many billing errors would it take to send a customer to a competitor? Maybe only two or three. And think how many phone calls the billing staff has to respond to because of so many erroneous bills. In context, these data point to a very serious problem.

As with every other facet of business communication, interpreting data means factoring in everything you know about the situation to determine the most helpful findings.

Interpreting Numerical Data

"You can't manage what you can't measure" is a common business expression, and while non-numerical data, such as descriptions of customers' experiences or comments by employees, are also extremely valuable, the popularity of this expression rightly suggests that businesses need accurate numbers in order to succeed. Bar code systems and other "smart machines" are producing what people refer to as "big data," which is essentially huge amounts of numerical information. To use such data intelligently, you must find ways of simplifying them so that your reader can grasp their general meaning.

If you're planning on using your data to predict how the larger population from which your sample was drawn will behave, you'll need to use **inferential statistics**. There are several different methods for crunching numbers this way, and you would be wise to learn enough about statistics to be able at least to interpret the results that these methods produce. Possibly of greater use to you in writing simple reports, though, are **descriptive statistics**. You can describe helpful patterns in the data just by using ordinary math—and you should, for your readers' sake.

Here are simple ways to help your readers understand what your numbers mean:

- *Calculate percentages.* Often it's easier for readers to wrap their minds around percentages rather than raw numbers. So, instead of saying "245 strongly agreed" (out of 400), say "61.2% (245) strongly agreed." (Formula: Divide the number of responses by the total number of participants.)

- *Use "majority" correctly.* It means "more than half." It doesn't mean "those who chose the most popular response" (unless those who voted for the most popular response account for more than half of the respondents). Better yet, try to use more specific wording, such as "just over half" or "the large majority."

- *Use "average" accurately.* "Average" means the median response. (Formula: Add all the responses or ratings and then divide them by the total number.) You cannot say "the average response was 'sometimes'" when what you really mean is that it was the most common response (the mode).

- *Use the word "most" with care.* "Most" doesn't really have a uniform meaning, but it needs to refer to quite a high percentage of the responses. You would not be justified in saying that "most" respondents chose an answer if only 61% of the respondents chose it. If 85% or more chose it, your use of this word would probably be acceptable.

- *Combine categories of responses when that will be helpful.* For example, if you've asked respondents to choose an answer on a five-point scale, with the two positive answers at one end of the scale and the negative ones at the other end, it may be more helpful to compare the total number of positive responses to the total number of negative ones than to call attention to just the most positive and most negative answers.

As Chapter 4 points out, visuals are a powerful way to communicate detailed information clearly. But they can also greatly aid your own interpretation of data. Such programs as SPSS and Microsoft Excel make it easy for you to translate different combinations of numbers into visual form so you can actually see patterns and comparisons. Take as many different looks at the data and create as many visuals as you need to be able to analyze your findings thoroughly.

When presenting your interpretations, explain any statistical methods you used, and make clear what your tables and charts mean. Remember that statistics and visuals are not an end in themselves: Their ultimate purpose is to help you give readers the findings they need in a form they can understand.

Organizing the Report Information

When you have interpreted your information, you will know your report's main points. Now you are ready to organize this content for presentation. Your goal here is to arrange the information in a logical order that meets your reader's needs.

LO11-16 Organize information in outline form using time, place, quantity, factors, or a combination of these patterns.

The Nature and Benefits of Outlining

An invaluable aid at this stage of the process is an **outline**. A good one will show what things go together (**grouping**), what order they should be in (**ordering**), and how the ideas relate in terms of levels of generality (**hierarchy**) (see Exhibit 11-24). Although you can outline mentally, a written plan is advisable for all but the shortest reports. Time spent on outlining at this stage is well spent because it will make your drafting more efficient and orderly. For longer reports, your outline will also form the basis for the table of contents.

If you have proceeded methodically thus far, you probably already have a rough outline. It is the list of topics that you drew up when planning how to research your problem. You may also have added to this list the findings that you developed when interpreting your data. But when it's time to turn your research plan into a report plan, you need to outline more deliberately. Your goal is to create the most logical, helpful pattern of organization for your readers.

In constructing your outline, you can use any system of numbering or formatting that will help you create a logical structure for your contents. If it will help, you can use the conventional or the decimal symbol system to mark the levels. The **conventional outlining system** uses Roman numerals to show the major headings, and letters of the alphabet and Arabic numbers to show the lesser headings, as illustrated here:

Conventional System

I. First-level heading

   A. Second level, first part

   B. Second level, second part

      1. Third level, first part

      2. Third level, second part

         a. Fourth level, first part

            1. Fifth level, first part

               a. Sixth level, first part

II. First-level heading

   A. Second level, first part

   B. Second level, second part etc.

Exhibit 11-24 The Three Kinds of Thinking Involved in Outlining

- Grouping (putting similar kinds of content together to create the different topics)
- Ordering (deciding what order the topics will be in)
- Creating a hierarchy (deciding what main topics you will use and what subtopics will go under them)

The **decimal outlining system** uses whole numbers to show the major sections, with decimals and additional numbers added to show subsections. That is, the digits to the right of the decimal indicate each successive level in the outline, as shown here:

Decimal System

1.0 First-level heading

    1.1 Second level, first part

    1.2 Second level, second part

       1.2.1 Third level, first part

       1.2.2 Third level, second part

          1.2.2.1 Fourth level, first part

2.0 First-level heading

    2.1 Second level, first part

    2.2 Second level, second part, etc.

Bear in mind that in the drafting state, the outline is a tool for you even though it is based on your readers' needs. Unless others will want to see an updated outline as you work, spend minimal time on its appearance. Allow yourself to change it, scribble on it, depart from it—whatever seems appropriate as your report develops. The time to labor over the outline's format and exact wording will be when you use it to create the headings and the table of contents for your finished report.

Basic Guidelines for a Logical, Clear Structure

As mentioned many times in this book, your readers' needs should influence how you organize your documents. But *all* readers like documents that are organized logically and legibly. Be sure your report follows these structural guidelines:

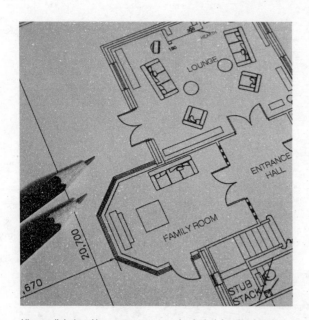

Like a well-designed house, your report needs a logical, functional structure. Figure out what kind of report you're going to build and then be sure that the layers are clear and the supporting "rooms" are in the right place.
© Image Source/SuperStock

- The overall *structure should be appropriate* for the report's content and purpose (see more about logical patterns in the next section).

- The *structure should be discernible and consistent*. The headings shouldn't look random, and the report should stick to the main structural pattern.

- All *sections on the same level of importance should be about the same size*. (So you shouldn't have two large major sections and one tiny one, or four subpoints that vary radically in length. If you seem to be heading toward this problem, find a different way to group or divide up the information.)

- You *must have at least two headings on each level* (so, if you have a subsection within a major section, you need to have at least one more subsection there).

- The *sections should be discrete*. That is, they shouldn't overlap in terms of the topics they're covering (it's fine, though, for two sections to be closely related).

- *Each section should be unified*. That is, it should cover only one identifiable main topic.

- Headings, indentations, and perhaps lists should be used to *break up the text and highlight the document's structure*—but they shouldn't be used so often that the text is too chopped up to be easily comprehended.

Common Patterns of Organization

When planning your report's structure, think about what overall pattern would suit your contents best. There are several common patterns you could choose from. Here, we'll discuss four of them: time, place, quantity, and factor. Others that might be appropriate, depending on your topic, are general-to-specific, most-to-least-important, criteria for evaluation, classification, cause/effect, problem/solution, and question-and-answer (which arranges the topics in the order of the readers' likely questions).

When you're reporting on information across certain time periods, consider using a **time-based pattern**. Your main sections would be periods of time, and they would follow a logical sequence, such as past to present or present to past. The periods you select do not need to be equal in duration, but they should be about equal in importance.

For example, a report on the progress of a research committee might be divided into the following comparable subperiods:

Orientation: May–July

Project planning: August

Implementation: September–November

Within each section, you could use either a time-based pattern (e.g., going through the orientation schedule) or a different pattern if it were appropriate (e.g., what the three main groups of attendees did at the orientation).

If the information you have collected has some relation to geographic location, you may use a **place-based pattern**. Ideally, this division would also yield sections that were roughly equal in length and importance.

A report on the sales of a U.S. manufacturer might be broken down by these major geographic areas:

New England

Atlantic Seaboard

South/Southwest

Rocky Mountains

Pacific Coast

Another illustration of organization by place would be a report on the productivity of a company with a number of customer service branches. A major division of the report might be devoted to each of the branches. The information for each branch might be broken down further, this time by sections, departments, or divisions.

A **quantity-based pattern** is possible for information that has quantitative values. To illustrate, an analysis of the buying habits of potential customers could be divided by such income groups as the following:

Under $30,000

$30,000 to under $45,000

$45,000 to under $60,000

$60,000 to under $85,000

$85,000 to under $100,000

$100,000 and over

As mentioned in the discussion of report problems, some problems require that certain factors, or information areas, be investigated. A report investigating the appropriateness of a proposed location for a new office might use this **factors-based pattern**:

Desirability of the neighborhood

Available properties

Rent

Convenience to current and new customers

Parking

Combined Patterns

In some instances, combinations of two or more structural patterns are possible. In a report on a company's sales, for example, the information could be arranged by a combination of quantity and place:

Areas of high sales activity

Areas of moderate sales activity

Areas of low sales activity

A report on sales of cyclical products might use the following combination of time and quantity:

Periods of low sales

Periods of moderate sales

Periods of high sales

When you're writing a report comparing two or more things, you can choose one of two patterns. You can *base your main structure on the things being compared* and, within each main section, assess each thing according to your chosen criteria. Or, you can *use the evaluation criteria as your main structuring logic* and discuss the things being compared within each section.

For example, take a report that addresses the problem of determining the better of two locations for an annual sales meeting. It could be organized by site or by the evaluation criteria. Organized by sites, the evaluation criteria would probably be the second-level headings:

Site A	Site B
Airport accessibility	Airport accessibility
Hotel accommodations	[and so on]
Meeting facilities	
Favorable weather	
Costs	

Organized by the evaluation criteria, the two possible sites would probably be the second-level headings:

Airport accessibility	Hotel accommodations	Meeting facilities	[and so on]
Site A	Site A	Site A	
Site B	Site B	Site B	

In most cases, the second method would be better because it makes it easier for readers to see how the things being evaluated compare on each criterion. But such is not always the case. Sometimes you might prefer to convey a complete, coherent picture of each thing being compared, one at a time, and then provide a summary section that compares them. You'll need to decide which is better, given the situation.

LO11-17 Turn an outline into a table of contents whose format and wording are logical and meaningful.

From Outline to Table of Contents

When you are ready to prepare the table of contents for your report, you will be, in essence, turning the outline that helped you write into an aid for the reader. Because it will be your public outline, the table of contents needs to be carefully formatted and worded.

True, you will probably design the table of contents late in the report-writing process. We discuss it here as a logical conclusion to our discussion of outlining. But if others involved in the project want to see a well-prepared outline before your report is done, you can use the following advice to prepare that outline.

Note also that what we say about preparing the headings for the table of contents also applies to writing the headings for the report sections. The two sets of headings, those in the table of contents and those in the report itself, should match exactly. Using Word's Styles to format your headings and its Table of Contents generator to create your table of contents will ensure this consistency.

Choosing Your Outline's Format

Whatever format you used for your personal outline, you now need to choose one that your reader will find *instructive, readable,* and *appropriate*.

To create an instructive format, clearly indicate the hierarchy of the information. You should use form (font selection, size, style, and color) and placement (location and indentation) to distinguish among the levels of your contents, as illustrated by the table of contents of the sample long report in Chapter 12.

Make the format readable by using ample vertical white space between topics and enabling readers to see at a glance how the report is organized. Using leaders (dots with intervening spaces) between your topics and your page numbers can also enhance readability.

An appropriate format is the one that your reader likely expects. These days, most business readers view the conventional outlining system (Roman numerals, letters, and Arabic numbers) and the decimal system (as in 1.2.1) as adding unnecessary clutter to the table of contents. Instead, they prefer the cleaner look of the form-and-placement (formatting) method to show them how the parts relate to each other. However, in the military and some technical environments, the decimal system is expected, and in other contexts, your readers may want the full numerals and letters of the conventional system. In our examples, we use format rather than numbering to indicate levels of information, but be sure to use whatever format your readers will prefer.

Using Parallel Construction for Your Headings

As a rule, you should write headings at each level of the table of contents in the same grammatical form. In other words, equal-level headings should be **parallel** in structure. For example, if the first major heading is a noun phrase, the rest of the major heads should be noun phrases. If the first second-level heading under a major head is an *-ing* phrase, all second-level headings in the section should be *-ing* phrases.

This rule is not just an exercise in grammar; its purpose is to show similarity. As you will recall from Chapter 5, parallelism helps your readers understand which topics are alike and go together. If you state similar topics in different forms, your logic will become blurry, and your reader will have trouble following you.

It is usually considered acceptable to vary the form from one section and level to another; that is, the second-level heads in one section need to match, but they do not need to match the second-level heads in the other sections, and the third-level heads do not need to match the second-level heads. Just be sure that the headings on each level of each section are parallel.

The following headings illustrate violations of parallelism:

Programmer Output Is Lagging (sentence).

Increase in Cost of Labor (noun phrase)

Unable to Deliver Necessary Results (adjective phrase)

Making the headings all noun phrases would fix the problem:

Lag in Programmer Output

Increase in Cost of Labor

Inability to Deliver Necessary Results

Or you could make all the headings sentences, like this:

Programmer Output Is Lagging.

Cost of Labor Is Increasing.

Information Systems Cannot Deliver Necessary Results.

Here's a different kind of faulty parallelism:

Managers Prefer an Intranet

U.S. Employees Prefer a Social-Media Site

A Newsletter Is Preferred by Overseas Employees

The third heading is "off." Can you see why? If you answered that it switches from active to passive voice, you're right.

Writing Concise—but Informative—Headings

Your headings should be as concise as possible while still being clear and informative. Although the following headings are informative, they're much too long:

Personal Appearance Enhancement Is the Most Desirable Feature of the NuSee Lenses.

The Drawback Mentioned by Most People Is That They Are Difficult to Put In.

More Comfort Is the Most Desired Improvement for NuSee Lenses.

Here is one possible revision:

Most Desirable Feature: Enhanced Personal Appearance

Prime Criticism: Difficult to Insert

Most Desired Improvement: Comfort

In your effort to be concise, should your headings omit *a, an,* and *the,* as some of the examples above do? Authorities on readability recommend including these words in body text, but there appears to be no consensus on whether to use or omit them in headings and titles. See what your teacher or boss prefers, and whichever way you choose, be consistent throughout your report.

Avoiding Monotonous Repetition in Your Headings

In the wording of headings, as in all other forms of writing, you should use some variety of expression. Repeating words too frequently makes for monotonous writing. The following outline excerpt illustrates this point:

Oil Production in Texas

Oil Production in California

Oil Production in Louisiana

If the lead-in to these sections makes clear that they will talk about oil production, you can simply remove "Oil Production in" and keep the states' names. If that seems too terse for your purposes, you can vary the headings like this:

The Leader: Texas

Runner-up: California

Third Place: Louisiana

The table of contents is an important preview of your report. Your goal is to use headings that are interesting, precise, and logically structured.

Writing the Report

By the time you write your report, you will have already done a good deal of writing. You will have written—and probably rewritten—problem and purpose statements to guide you through your research. You will have collected written data or recorded your findings in notes, and you will have organized your interpretations of the data into a logical, reader-centered structure. Now it is time to flesh out your outline with clearly expressed facts and observations.

When you draft your report, your first priority is to get the right things said in the right order. As Chapter 2 advises, you should not strive for a perfect draft the first time around. Understand that some pieces will seem to write themselves, while others will be much more difficult. Allow yourself to move along, stitching together the pieces. Once you have a draft to work with, you can perfect it.

When revising, your goal is to make your report communicate as clearly and quickly as possible. Your readers' time is valuable, and you risk having your report misread or even ignored if you do respect this fact.

You can increase your report's chances of success by writing a reader-centered beginning and ending. Such characteristics as objectivity, consistency in time viewpoint, coherence, and interest can also enhance the reception of your report. We'll review these topics next.

LO11-18   Write reports that are focused, objective, consistent in time viewpoint, smoothly connected, and interesting.

Beginning and Ending

Arguably the most critical parts of your report will be the beginning and ending. In fact, researchers agree that these are the most frequently read parts of a report.

Whatever other goals it may achieve, the opening of your report should convey what problem you studied, how you studied it (your purpose), and (at least generally) what you found out. Why? Because these are the facts that the reader most wants to know when he or she first looks at your report.

Here is a simple introduction that follows this pattern:

> In order to find out why sales were down at the Salisbury store, I interviewed the manager, observed the operations, and assessed the environment. A high rate of employee turnover appears to have resulted in a loss of customers, though the deteriorating neighborhood also seems to be a contributing factor.

In a formal report, some brief sections may precede this statement of purpose (for example, facts about the authorization of the study), and there might be extensive front matter (as discussed in the next chapter). What follows this introduction can also vary depending on the size and complexity of the report (for example, you may need to go into more detail about the research methods and limitations or to preview how the report is organized). But whatever kind of report you are writing, make sure that the beginning gets across why you did the report, how you approached the report's topic, and why the results are of significance to the reader.

Your ending will provide a concise statement of the report's main payoff—whether facts, interpretations, or recommendations. In a short report, you may simply summarize your findings with a brief paragraph, since the specific findings will be easy to see in the body of the report. In a longer report, you should make this section a more thorough restatement of your main findings, formatted in an easy-to-read way. Both the gist ("So what did you find out?") and the significance ("Why should I care?") of your report should be clear.

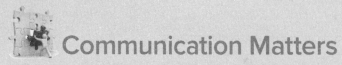
Formal, Informal, or Somewhere in Between?

As the next chapter points out, the format and makeup of your report will signal its level of formality. But you will also need to decide how formal your report will be on the stylistic level. Compare the following three versions of the same point:

- The study revealed that 20% of the participants were unaware of Jacob's Foods.
- Our study revealed that 20% of the participants were unaware of your store.
- We found out that 20% of your market had never heard of your store.

Did you notice the decreasing level of formality? What accounts for the differences? Be sure to choose a style that matches the relationship you have with your readers and their preferences. But whatever style you choose, write clearly and professionally.

Being Objective

As we have said, a good report is objective; it presents all relevant facts and interprets them logically, without bias. Your objectivity should be evident in both your content and your writing style.

Objectivity as a Basis for Credibility

An objective report has an ingredient that is essential to good report writing—**credibility**. Powerful assertions made in emotionally charged language may at first glance appear to strengthen your report. But if bias is evident at any point in a report, the reader will question the trustworthiness of the entire report. Maintaining objectivity is, therefore, the only sure way to make report writing believable.

Personal versus Impersonal Writing

Perhaps to sound scientific or impartial, report writers in business developed an impersonal style in the mid-20th century that was common until around the 1980s. This **impersonal writing** avoided the first and second person (*I, we,* and *you*) and used only third person. Taking the human beings out of reports in this way does perhaps convey an impression of objectivity. We expect news reporting to use this style, for example.

The problem is that this kind of writing, in unskillful hands, can be boring and difficult to follow. In the early 1980s, a group of researchers in Washington, D.C., collected research on how readers read. Their findings, published in the ground-breaking booklet *Guidelines for Document Designers,* advocated the use of personal pronouns, because **personal writing** is easier to comprehend than impersonal writing.[8] In addition, personal writing is more conversational and therefore more interesting, and such writing need not compromise the objectivity of the writer.

Still, some report readers will prefer the impersonal style, especially in formal situations. If they do, you will need to use it.

Here are contrasting examples of the personal and impersonal styles:

Personal

Having studied the advantages and disadvantages of using coupons, I recommend that your company not adopt this practice. If you used coupons, you would have to absorb their cost. You would also have to hire additional employees to take care of the increase in sales volume.

Impersonal

A study of the advantages and disadvantages of using coupons supports the conclusion that the Mills Company should not adopt this practice. The coupons themselves would cost extra money. Also, use of coupons would require additional personnel to take care of the increase in sales volume.

Notice that both versions are active, clear, and interesting. Strive for these effects no matter which style you choose.

Being Consistent with Time

A report that has illogical time shifts—for example, one that says "The managers responded . . ." (past tense) in one place but "The employees say . . ." (present tense) in another place—confuses the reader. Thus, it is important that you maintain a **consistent time viewpoint**.

If you adopt the **past-time viewpoint**, you treat the research, the findings, and the writing of the report as past. Thus, you would report the results of a recent survey in past tense: "Twenty-two percent of the managers *favored* a change." You would write a reference to another part of the report this way: "As Part II *indicated*, ..." Your use of the past-time viewpoint would have no effect on references to future or current happenings. It would still be proper to write "If the current trend *continues,* 30% *will favor* a change by 2018." It would also be acceptable to phrase your final interpretations and/or recommendations in present tense, as in "The findings *indicate* that managers are not adequately trained."

Writing in the **present-time viewpoint** presents as current all information that can logically be assumed to be current at the time of writing. All other information is presented in its proper place in the past or future. Thus, you would report the results of a recent survey in these words: "Twenty-two percent of the managers *favor* a change." You would refer to another part of the text like this: As Part II *indicates*, ..." But in referring to an earlier survey, you would write: "In 2009 only 12% *held* this opinion." And in making a future reference, you would write, "If this trend continues, 30% *will hold* this opinion by 2018."

Including Transitions

A well-written report reads as one continuous story, with the parts smoothly connected. Much of this flow is the result of logical organization. But transitions are needed, too, especially in long reports.

As Chapter 5 explains, transitions are words or sentences that show the relationships between parts of a sentence, paragraph, or document. In reports, they may appear at the beginning of a part as a way of relating this part to the preceding part. They may appear at the end of a part as a forward look. Or they may appear within a part as words or phrases that help move the flow of information.

Sentence Transitions Throughout the report you can improve the connecting network of thought by using sentence transitions. They are especially helpful between major parts of the report.

In the following example, the sentences first summarize what has been said thus far. The last sentence then transitions to the next topic.

> These data show clearly that alternative fuel cars are the most economical. Their operation by gas and hydrogen and their record for low-cost maintenance give them a decided edge over gas-fueled cars. Before a definite conclusion about their merit can be reached, however, one more vital comparison should be made.

The reader now knows to expect the next part of the report to discuss one more comparison.

Here is another example of a forecasting sentence:

> At first glance the data appear convincing, but a closer observation reveals a number of discrepancies.

The reader knows to expect a discussion of the discrepancies next.

Transitions provide important bridges from one report section to the next.
© PhotoAlto/Alamy

Topic sentences (discussed in Chapter 5) can also be used to link the various parts of the report. Note in the following example how the topic sentences (in italics) maintain the flow of thought by emphasizing key information.

The Acura accelerates faster than the other two brands, both on a level road and on a 9% grade. According to a test conducted by *Consumer Reports,* Acura reaches a speed of 60 miles per hour in 13.2 seconds. To reach the same speed, Toyota requires 13.6 seconds, and Volkswagen requires 14.4 seconds. On a 9% grade, Acura reaches the 60-miles-per-hour speed in 29.4 seconds, and Toyota reaches it in 43.3 seconds. Volkswagen is unable to reach this speed.

Because it carries more weight on its rear wheels than the others, Acura also has the best traction of the three. Traction, which means a minimum of sliding on wet or icy roads, is important to safe driving, particularly during the cold, wet winter months. Since traction is directly related to the weight carried by the rear wheels, a comparison of these weights should give some measure of the safety of the three cars. According to data released by the Automobile Bureau of Standards, Acura carries 47% of its weight on its rear wheels. Nissan and Toyota carry 44 and 42%, respectively.

Transitional Words If the writing is to flow smoothly, you will also need to connect clause to clause, sentence to sentence, and paragraph to paragraph, as Chapter 5 advises.

The following list includes some of the most common transitional expressions and when to use them.

Relationship	Word Examples
Listing or enumeration of subjects	In addition
	First, second, . . .
	Besides
	Moreover
Contrast	On the contrary
	In spite of
	On the other hand
	In contrast
	However
Likeness	Also
	Likewise
	Similarly
Cause–effect	Thus
	Because of
	Therefore
	Consequently
	For this reason
Explanation or elaboration	For example
	To illustrate
	For instance
	Also
	Too

Helpful as transitions are, you should use them only when they are needed—when including them would provide a useful preview or leaving them out would produce abruptness. For example, avoid such boring, unnecessary transitions as "This concludes the discussion of Topic X. In the next section, Y will be analyzed."

Maintaining Interest

Like any other form of writing, report writing should be interesting. Actually, interest is as important as the facts of the report, because communication is not likely to occur without it. Readers cannot help but skip over parts of the report if their attention is allowed to stray.

To write interestingly, avoid business clichés and unnecessarily abstract language. Remember that behind every fact and figure there is life—people doing things, machines operating, a commodity being marketed. A technique of good report writing is to bring that life to the surface by using concrete words and active-voice verbs as much as possible. Keeping your wording efficient also helps maintain the reader's interest.

But you can overdo efforts to make report writing interesting. Such is the case whenever your reader's attention is attracted to how something has been said rather than to what has been said. Effective report writing simply presents information in a clear, concise, and interesting way. Report-writing style is at its best when the readers are prompted to say "Here are some interesting facts" rather than "Here is some interesting writing."

Writing Reports Collaboratively

LO11-19   Prepare reports collaboratively.

There's a reason why so many of your instructors assign group projects: You are likely to participate in numerous team projects on the job. The shift from hierarchical to flatter, more flexible organizations over the last few decades has generated a more collaborative workplace. Often, the specialized knowledge of different people is needed to tackle a project. Plus, a team approach can enable a company to respond to a problem or opportunity more quickly than it could if someone had to pull together the information from various isolated sources. The availability of many computer tools that allow groups to collaborate easily and well from different places has also helped fuel this trend.

Because of their length and complexity, reports are often researched and prepared by teams. The rest of this section offers advice for team report writing, but much of that advice can apply to other kinds of team projects as well.

Determining the Group Makeup

The first step is to decide who will be in the group. In professional settings, participants will be chosen based on their availability and the relevance of their expertise to the report problem. In the classroom, either the class or the instructor will create the groups based on the nature of the project and the skills of the students. At a minimum, a group can consist of two people, but it is better to have three to five members for a substantial project.

In most business situations, the highest ranking administrator in the group serves as leader. In groups made up of equals, a leader is usually appointed or chosen by the group because someone needs to be the main conduit between the group and those who assigned or need the report. For class projects, it is also a good idea to have one person in charge of overseeing the entire process.

Creating the Ground Rules

In organizations where teamwork is common, the **ground rules** for participation in a group may be understood. But students and working professionals alike may find it helpful to establish explicit guidelines for the participants.

Some rules may govern the members' interactions. For example, a rule might be, "Listen to what others are saying, without interrupting." Or it might instruct members to frame their comments in terms of the report's purpose and audience when critiquing what others think or

You Make the Call

Have you ever worked on a team project that didn't go well? If so, what were the causes? What could have been done differently to have prevented or corrected the problems?

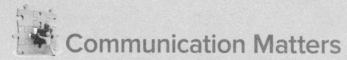

Communication Matters

Does Your Group Have Emotional Intelligence?

Ever since the 1995 publication of Daniel Goleman's *Emotional Intelligence: Why It Can Matter More Than IQ*, companies have been looking for ways to cultivate the emotional intelligence (EI) of its members.

But groups can enhance their collective EI, too. According to Vanessa Urch Druskat and Steven B. Wolff of the *Harvard Business Review*, "Group EI norms build the foundation for true collaboration and cooperation—helping otherwise skilled teams fulfill their highest potential."

What kinds of things should a group do to channel its members' insights and emotions into positive results? Here's a partial list from Druskat and Wolff:

- Encourage all members to share their perspectives before making key decisions.
- Handle confrontation constructively. If team members fall short, call them on it by letting them know the group needs them.
- Regularly assess the group's strengths, weaknesses, and modes of interaction.

- Let the group express its emotions.
- Cultivate an affirmative environment.
- Encourage proactive problem solving (looking ahead to anticipate the needs of the company or client).

Source: "Building the Emotional Intelligence of Groups," *Harvard Business Review*, March 2001, accessed November 4, 2016, https://hbr.org.

---

have written. Others might cover more logistical issues, such as conscientiously doing one's share of the work, keeping the group informed if problems arise, and being on time with one's contributions.

Ideally, the group will help generate the team ground rules. Some instructors find that having each group draw up a contract or collaboration plan is a good way to get group work off to a good start and prevent problems down the line (see Exhibit 11-25).

Exhibit 11-25	A Sample Planning Document for a Group Project

Report Topic:

Client/Intended Audience:

Format and Approximate Length:

Contact Information for Group Members:

- x
- x
- x

Role Each Member (Tentatively) Plans to Play: [one must be the leader, in addition to whatever else he/she will do]

- x
- x
- x

Milestones in the Project: [should align with project due dates]

- x
- x
- x
- x

Dates and Locations for Face-to-Face Meetings:

Main Method of Collaborative Writing: [e.g., sending drafts by email; Google Drive; a wiki]

Ground Rules: [here are some examples]

1. Everyone must participate in group meetings (whether in person or online). If for some reason a member can't attend, he/she must let the rest of the group know immediately and find out what he/she must do to get caught up.

2. Everyone will be copied on everyone else's emails and, if a response is needed, answer as soon as possible. While we have a project leader, it is up to all of us to stay informed and keep the project rolling.

3. Everyone will deliver his/her work on time, and the work will show good effort.

4. If the group cannot get a member to do his/her fair share of the work, the leader will let Dr. Rentz know. She will have a conference with the student to see if he/she can be brought back on track.

5. The quality of the final product is everyone's responsibility, so everyone needs to give suggestions and evaluative feedback. The feedback should be honest but courteous, and the suggestions should be aligned with the audience and purpose for the report and/or the grading standards for the project.

Choosing the Means of Collaboration

Not that many years ago, groups needed numerous face-to-face meetings in order to get their work done. Today there are many other venues for group interactions. Your group should put careful thought into the choice of media that will enable effective collaboration while taking into account members' time constraints, distance from each other, and technological preferences.

If possible, you should have at least two face-to-face meetings—one at the start of the project and another near the end (for example, when doing the final revisions). You can meet either physically or virtually. But the bulk of the collaborating may take place by email, by discussion board, or through such online collaborative authoring tools as Google Drive or wikis. Whatever tools you use, it is important to choose them consciously and create any ground rules that will apply to their use. (See the From the Tech Desk feature for a list of useful collaboration tools.)

From the Tech Desk

Tools for Collaborative Writing

Many electronic tools are available for supporting a group writing project. Here are some of the most useful ones for the different parts of the process.

Brainstorming and outlining tools. When you're gathering your ideas and generating the topics to be investigated, you can simply type them into Word. Once you have a substantial amount of content, you can use Word's Outline view to create a logical structure for your ideas. Or, you could also use a concept-mapping tool, such as Edraw, to generate and link ideas (see Exhibit 2-9).

Scheduling tools. A Gantt chart or Microsoft Outlook's calendar (see Exhibits 2-5 and 2-6) can be useful for planning and tracking your project. A table in Word or a spreadsheet in Excel can work fine, too. If you use Google Drive's Google Sheets to create your schedule, it can live in the cloud, where people can easily access it, edit it, and comment on it. To find out when everyone will be available for a meeting, you can create a Doodle poll and have Doodle send it to the team members by email.

Dialoguing tools. Emailing, phoning, and texting can all be useful communication tools, but sometimes your group needs to meet virtually. Skype and Google hangouts are excellent platforms for video and/or audio-based communications.

Document-sharing tools. Instead of trying to share files by email, set up a team folder in Dropbox or Box. This is an especially good idea if the files you'll be sharing will be large or you have quite a few files to collect.

Drafting and revising tools. You have a lot of choices here.

- For drafting, Word is hard to beat because of all the writing and formatting options it provides. But the Word-like version available on Google Drive, Google Docs, is fairly good, and it enables more than one group member to work on the draft. (Ditto for Google Slides if you're preparing an oral report.)
- For group revising, Google Docs (or Google Slides) is excellent. Team members can easily access the document and revise and/or comment on it. Google Docs will assign each writer's contributions a different color and keep track of the revision history—and if you don't

like some changes that were made, you can go back to an earlier version. A downside is that files uploaded from Word to Google Docs are likely to lose some of their formatting.

- Word's Track Changes and Commenting tools are also extremely useful (see Exhibit 2-14). When "Track Changes" is turned on, Word will keep track of all changes made to the document and assign different colors to the reviewers so that others can easily determine who made which edits. The commenting tool identifies each reviewer, too. Clicking on "Reviewers" in the drop-down menu will show which people have reviewed the document.
- If you're using Dropbox or Box for file sharing, you might also want to use it for collaborative revising. Both tools enable team members to comment on a document by clicking the file and then entering comments, which are saved in the "Comments" pane. Those with editing rights can open the document directly and edit it using Word Online. Both companies also recently announced a real-time editing function for Office Online users.

Making a Project Plan

To produce a coherent, effective report on deadline, the group should structure its tasks to meet the project's goals. Using the steps discussed in the next section and any additional considerations, the group should prepare a timeline that clearly states or shows the deadline for each task. A Gantt chart can be very useful along these lines (see Exhibit 2-5), but even a simple list or table can suffice. Your plan should make clear who is responsible for what and by when.

Your plan can also describe in some detail the desired form and style of the final document, such as which template it will use or whether or not it will use "you." The more the group determines such matters up front, the less scrambling it will need to do at the end to generate a coherent, consistent-looking report.

Researching and Writing the Report

However the group decides to operate, the following activities typically occur, usually in the sequence shown.

Many reports written in business are produced in collaboration with others. Although you will do some work individually, you can expect to plan, organize, and revise the report as a group.
© Stockbyte/Getty Images RF

1. *Determine the problem and purpose.* As in all report projects, the participants must determine just what the report must do. It is a good idea for everyone to help draft the problem and the purpose statements for the report. That will help ensure a shared sense of the intended readers' needs and the report's goal.

2. *Plan the makeup of the report.* Here, the team considers the formality of the situation, the anticipated length of the report, and intended audience's likely preferences (see Chapter 12) to plan what kind of report they will write. In addition, the team can discuss what writing style to use (e.g., whether to use personal pronouns; how formal to make the report).

3. *Identify the factors.* The group next determines what needs to be studied in order to achieve the report's purpose. This step involves determining the factors of the problem, as described earlier in the chapter. Here, too, it is good to bring everyone's thinking to bear on identifying the factors of the problem.

4. *Gather the needed information.* This activity can include any of the types of research discussed in this chapter. It is probably a good idea to divide up this work in some logical way to minimize duplication of effort.

5. *Interpret the information.* Determining the meaning of the information gathered is the next logical step for the group. In this step, the participants apply the findings to the problem and select the appropriate information for the report. If the research tasks have been divided among the participants, each individual should prepare preliminary interpretations of his or her information. But when the pieces come together, the group as a whole should think through all the facts, identify their significance, and interpret them from the readers' points of view.

6. *Organize the material.* Using a logical structure based on time, place, quantity, factor, or other relationships in the data, the group next organizes the material. Earlier discussions about

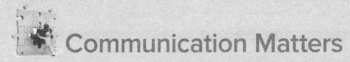

Communication Matters

Three Methods of Collaborative Writing

In her book *Team Writing: A Guide to Working in Groups*, Joanna Wolfe describes three main collaborative-writing methods. Each has advantages and drawbacks, so any group is likely to use all three at various points in the project.

Face-to-Face Collaboration

As the label indicates, this method consists of everyone working together in one place.

Pros: This is a great method for launching the project, drafting plans and schedules, and reviewing the visual design of the document.

Cons: Unless the instructor allots an enormous amount of class time to the project, this method isn't feasible for actually getting the report written. It's also difficult for all members to contribute equally.

Divided Collaboration

With this method, the team divides up the work according to sections, and each member prepares one or more sections.

Pros: This is the fastest means of collaboration since individuals prepare the different sections. It also has the advantage of giving each person a clear area of responsibility.

Cons: Members can bring in sections that are weak, wildly different in terms of tone and writing quality, and/or difficult to incorporate with the other sections.

Layered Collaboration

With this method, each piece of the report goes through layered revising, with each group member's revisions constituting a layer.

Pros: This method can be excellent for the revision stages. It ensures that everyone has a stake in the quality of the report and feels ownership for the project.

Cons: If everyone has multiple opportunities to critique the project at every step, this method is too slow.

Use these labels to be sure that everyone in the group understands what process the team will be using at each stage of the project.

Source: Wolfe, Joanna, *Team Writing: A Guide to Working in Groups* (Boston: Bedford/St. Martin's, 2010).

---

which factors to investigate may have already determined the main structural pattern for the report, but the subtopics and their structure will now need to be determined.

7. *Draft the report.* After the planning has been done, the group next turns its attention to the writing. The length of the report and the amount of face-to-face time available can help the group decide whether to divide up this task, make one person responsible, or try to do it together (see the Communication Matters feature "Three Methods of Collaborative Writing").

8. *Revise collaboratively.* Now the group reviews the draft to improve its effectiveness and quality. Ideally, each team member will participate in this process. Everyone should offer courteous but meaningful criticism and suggestions for improving the report.

9. *Edit the final draft.* After the group has done its work, one member is usually assigned the task of editing the final draft. This editor gives the document a consistent style and serves as the major proofreader. However, since the document reflects on all members, they should assist with the final proofreading.

If all the work has been done with care and diligence, this final draft should be a report better than anyone in the group could have prepared alone.

In a sense, you will never write any report by yourself, even if you are the sole author. You will likely have input from others (including the person who requested the report), and you can consult many different kinds of resources. If you analyze the problem carefully, aggressively seek the information you need, and take pride in preparing a well-structured, well-written product, you can meet any report-writing challenge successfully.

Power Charge Your Professionalism: Avoid Faulty Parallelism

As discussed in Chapter 5, a common grammatical problem is faulty parallelism. This problem occurs when you indicate that items are alike by putting them in a pair, a series, a bulleted list, or the same level/group of headings—but then don't word the items with the same grammatical structure. Items that are being set up as equals need to be worded that way as well.

Catch and correct the faulty parallelism in the following examples (some may be correct).

1. This report will first examine the causes of the problem and then ways to address them.
2. The patient-information pamphlet needs these additional components:
   - Definitions of key medical terms
   - A list of patient support groups
   - Where to find additional information
3. [These are the main headings in the body of a report evaluating a company website:]
   Visual Appeal
   How the Information Is Structured
   Are There Sufficient and Appropriate Navigation Methods?
   Does the Content Meet the Viewers' Needs?
   The Quality of the Writing
4. The survey explored how many students give blood, why they give blood, and how to increase their donations.
5. The client asked us to gauge the demand for a new events facility by assessing the competition and would nearby companies be likely to use a new facility.
6. We compared the three applications on the following criteria:
   - How well they meet the company's needs
   - How intuitive they are
   - Information security
   - Cost
7. The Japanese tend to value indirectness, building long-term relationships, and they expect to give and receive gifts.
8. The appendix lists the focus-group participants, their occupations, and provides the discussion prompts.

Avoiding faulty parallelism is important because . . .

- If you word similar topics in different forms, your logic will become blurry, and your readers will have trouble following you.
- Faulty parallelism shows your inability to distinguish between different types of sentence components.

For further instruction and practice, go to the "Parallelism" activities under "Style and Word Choice" in LearnSmart Achieve.

Key Terms

Critical-Thinking Questions

1. Generate a hypothetical situation relevant to your field in which a research report would be needed. Write realistic problem and purpose statements for the report. LO1

2. What are three to five subtopics for your hypothetical research problem (Question 1)? LO2

3. Which of the following are secondary research sources and which are primary? Why? LO3
    a. Information from *The Wall Street Journal* about the unemployment rate
    b. Information from a focus group of potential customers about a new online ordering system
    c. Information about an industry's use of social media collected by following a blog
    d. Information about salaries collected from members of the listserv of a professional organization
    e. Information about the courtesy of the service staff gathered from a survey of the customers

4. Assume that you've been given the task of writing the report on the topic you generated in Questions 1 and 2. What kinds of Internet research could you do to gather relevant information? What search terms would you use? LO4, LO5

5. Find an article on the Internet that gives advice about conducting some aspect of business operations (e.g., improving teamwork, managing employees, communicating with potential customers). Using the advice in the book, evaluate the credibility and usefulness of the article. LO6

6. Explore a business-related topic on Twitter or LinkedIn. What kinds of information can you find that might help solve a business problem? LO7

7. Which databases or other resources would be good sources of information for each of the following subjects? LO8
    a. A certain company's market share
    b. Whether or not a company is being sued
    c. Trends in a certain industry
    d. Strategies for a successful job interview
    e. The job outlook in a certain industry
    f. Recent trends in business-related technology
    g. The potential world market for a certain product
    h. Government regulations for incorporating your business
    i. The qualifications of a new CEO of a company
    j. The negotiation style used in a certain culture

8. Explain the difference between quantitative and qualitative research, and describe a sample situation in which each would be appropriate. LO9–LO13

9. Explain the difference between random sampling and convenience sampling. Give an example of when each type of sampling would be feasible and appropriate. LO9

10. Point out the problems in the following sample survey questions. LO10
    a. How often do you shower?
    b. (First question in a phone survey) Which Democratic candidate do you favor, Jean Adams or Seth Rubins?
    c. Do you consider the ideal pay plan to be one based on straight commission or straight salary?
    d. What kind of gasoline did you purchase last time?
    e. How much did you pay for clothing in the past 12 months?

11. What is scaling? What is the difference between rating and ranking? LO10

12. Define observation as a research technique and give an example of a business problem that might warrant observational research. LO11

13. Define experiment as a research technique and give an example of an experiment a company might conduct. LO12

14. Why does the controlled before–after design give more helpful information than the before–after design? LO12

15. When would you use a focus group or personal interview to gather information? What are the advantages and disadvantages of each? LO13

16. Explain the difference between closed-ended and open-ended survey questions. LO13

17. What are the basic ethical guidelines for conducting business research? Why are such guidelines important? LO14

18. Jim's boss asked him to investigate why sales for the last quarter were low. Jim interviewed one of the sales managers about the problem, and she complained that the new people didn't know how to sell. Jim then wrote a report in which he identified the new people's deficient skills as the problem and recommended that more training be provided for them. What errors in interpretation do you see in Jim's report? LO15

19. You are writing a report on the progress of your local cable company's efforts to increase the sales of five of its products through different advertising media: print and online newspapers and magazines, television, radio, email, and social media. Plan the headings for this report and explain why you'd organize the information this way. LO16

20. In what ways can the format of the table of contents ease readers' comprehension of a report? Find an example of a helpfully formatted table of contents and explain what makes it effective. LO17

21. Explain the difference between personal and impersonal writing. Which is "better"? LO18

22. Explain the difference between the present-time viewpoint and the past-time viewpoint. Is it incorrect to have different tenses in the same report? Give examples to make your point. LO18

23. Evaluate this statement: "Reports are written for people who want them, so you don't have to be concerned about holding their interest." LO18

24. Evaluate this statement: "Collaborative reports are always better than reports written by an individual because they use many minds rather than one." LO19

25. "Disagreements in groups are counterproductive and should be avoided." Discuss. LO19

Skills-Building Exercises

1. For each of the following report situations, write a clear problem statement and list what factors could or should be explored. LO1, LO2
   a. A manufacturer of breakfast cereals wants to attract a new demographic of consumers.
   b. The manufacturer of a toothpaste wants a bigger share of the toothpaste market.
   c. A company wants to give its stockholders a summary of its operations for the past calendar year.
   d. A building contractor engaged to remodel an office for Company X submits a report summarizing its weekly progress.
   e. The supervisor of Department X must prepare a report about the need for a new staff member.
   f. Baker, Inc. is experiencing higher than normal employee turnover.
   g. An executive must rank three subordinates on the basis of their suitability for promotion to a particular job.
   h. A restaurant manager must compare two possible suppliers of fresh seafood.
   i. An investment consultant must advise a client on whether to invest in the development of a lake resort.
   j. A consultant needs to help a wine shop improve its profits.

2. Find a company whose website features a section on its role as a community or world citizen (e.g., its principles and practices for corporate social responsibility). How persuaded are you that the information there is complete and accurate? Check the information there against other Internet resources to see if your assessment was accurate. LO6

3. Search the relevant research databases in your school library to gather information about a current business topic, practice, or technology. Using the citation style preferred by your instructor, construct an annotated bibliography that presents and briefly describes your findings. (See Reference Chapter B for citation formats and advice.) LO8

4. Using your imagination to supply any missing facts you may need, develop a plan for conducting a survey to research these problems. LO9, LO10
   a. Pizza Marketplace, a resource for people in the pizza business, wants to give its subscribers a profile of carry-out pizza customers. It needs such information as what kinds of people do carry-out, how often, why, and about how much they spend. Likewise, it will seek to determine who does not carry out and why.
   b. The editor of your local daily newspaper wants to learn who reads what in both the print and online editions of the paper.
   c. Your boss wants to hire an experienced computer webmaster for your company. Because the company has not ever hired anyone for such a position, you were asked to survey experienced webmasters to gather likely salary figures.
   d. A professional organization that you belong to wants to find out how its members are using social media in their work, what types they are using, and how much they are using each type.
   e. You work in the human resources department of a company. The director needs to make changes to the company's health care plan for the coming year and wants you to find out which of the three current plans employees are using, why they selected it, and how satisfied they've been with it.

5. Using your imagination to supply any missing facts you may need, develop a plan for conducting an observation to help solve each of these problems. LO11
   a. A chain of department stores wants to know what causes differences in sales in a certain department across its stores.
   b. Your university wants to know the nature and extent of its parking problem.
   c. The management of an insurance company wants to determine the effectiveness of its customer-service representatives.

d. The director of a community library wants a detailed study of the patrons' use of its facilities (what facilities are used, when, by whom, and so on).

e. The management of a restaurant wants a study of its workers' efficiency in the kitchen.

6. Using your imagination to supply any missing facts you may need, develop a plan for conducting an experiment to help solve the following problems. LO12

   a. The Golden Glow Baking Company has for many years manufactured and sold cookies packaged in attractive boxes. It is considering packaging the cookies in recyclable bags and wants to conduct an experiment to determine consumers' likely response to this change.

   b. A producer of expensive cosmetics wants to know whether using quick response (QR) codes in its print ads would significantly increase its profits.

   c. The Marvel Soap Company has developed a new cleaning agent that is unlike current soaps and detergents. The company wants to determine the optimum price for the new product.

   d. National Cereals, Inc. wants to determine the effectiveness of advertising to children. Until now, it has been aiming its appeal at parents.

7. Using your imagination to supply any missing facts you may need, develop a plan for conducting focus groups to help solve these problems. LO13

   a. A brand of work boots has for years sold its products through conventional retail outlets. It now wants to examine the possibility of selling through catalogs or online.

   b. The International Association of Publishers wants to gauge the current attitude toward electronic textbooks.

   c. Sizemore Rentai Car Company would like to add a line of hybrid cars for its business customers, but the CEO is not sure whether such cars would appeal to these customers.

8. Using your imagination to supply any missing facts you may need, develop a plan for conducting interviews to help solve these problems. LO13

   a. Grow More Company sells children's clothes. The company has seen an increased rate of employee turnover this year, and your supervisor want to know why.

   b. Jacob's Hardware Store recently sent out a survey to get feedback on its customer service. The management would like to follow this up with some interviews to get a better sense of what happened on one particular Saturday when customers said they'd received very poor service.

9. Think of a hypothetical problem that would involve gathering information across several time periods. How might you organize this information besides using a time-based pattern? Compare and evaluate the two possibilities as the main bases for organizing the report. LO16

10. Assume that you are writing up the results of a survey conducted to determine what kinds of groceries are purchased by female college students in the United States. What organizational patterns could work here? Which would you recommend? LO16

11. For the problem described in the preceding exercise, use your imagination to construct topic headings for the outline. LO17

12. Improve the parallelism of these headings. LO17

    a. Lagging Sales in Region I

    b. Moderate Increase Seen for Region II

    c. Sales in Region III

13. Improve the parallelism of these headings in a report evaluating a piece of production equipment. LO17

    a. High Cost of Operation

    b. Good Production Efficiency

    c. Maintenance Cost Is Low

14. Select an editorial, feature article, book chapter, or other relatively lengthy document that has no headings. Write headings for it. LO17

15. Assume you are writing a report that summarizes a survey you have conducted. Write a paragraph of the report using the present-time viewpoint; then write the paragraph using the past-time viewpoint. Base the paragraph on the following information. LO18

    Answers to the question about how students view the proposed Aid to Education Bill in this survey and in a survey taken a year earlier (last year's results are in parentheses):

    For, 39% (21); Against, 17% (43)

    No answer, undecided, etc., 44% (36)

16. List the advantages and disadvantages of each of these different media for writing collaboratively. LO19
    a. Face-to-face meetings
    b. Email
    c. Discussion board
    d. Online writing tool (e.g., Google Drive)
    e. Live online interaction (e.g., chat or Skype)

Creating the Right
Type of Report

© Mutlu Kurbas/Getty Images

Chapter

Twelve

With a general understanding of what reports do, how to research report problems, and how to organize and write reports, you are ready to consider the many varieties of reports you may need to prepare.

Report-writing situations are infinitely varied, so there are hundreds or even thousands of different kinds of reports, many of them specific to certain industries or professions. Here, we cover only some of the most common types. But the guidelines in this and the preceding chapter can help you meet any report-writing challenge. Just remember to learn all you can about your readers, their needs, and their expectations. If possible, find a report like the one you're about to write. Then use your good business-writing judgment to prepare an attractive, easy-to-read report that delivers exactly what your readers need.

Learning Objectives

LO12-1 Explain the makeup of reports relative to length and formality.

LO12-2 Discuss the four main ways that the writing in short reports differs from the writing in long reports.

LO12-3 Choose an appropriate form for short reports.

LO12-4 Adapt your general knowledge of report writing when preparing routine operational reports, progress reports, problem-solving reports, and minutes of meetings.

LO12-5 Write longer reports that include the appropriate components, meet the readers' needs, and are easy to follow.

Problem-Solving Challenge

Figuring Out What Kind of Report to Prepare

Continue in your role as a management intern for Betsy Tippett, an operations manager for Mockbee's Ice Cream and Bakery (as introduced in Chapter 11).

You've now finished researching why and how to do usability testing, and it's time to write up your findings for Betsy. But how should you do it? A number of questions arise:

• What format should you use? For example, should you create a title page? Or just send Betsy all your information in a long email? Or do something else?

• How should you deliver the report to her? Drop it on her desk? Email it as an attachment? Both?

• Should you address the report to Jim Ash, too, since he helped create the tutorial and will be user-testing it?

• How formal should your language be? Is it okay to use "I" and "you"?

• Should you say up front what you found out or save that until the end?

• Should you just present the information or also make recommendations?

• Do you need to cite your sources? If so, how should you do it?

If this were a class assignment, you'd ask your teacher, but Betsy clearly wants you to take care of this task yourself, and these don't seem like questions you should bother her with. There's no way around it: You're going to have to use your best judgment. Fortunately, those who have gone before you have created some helpful rules of thumb. You'll need to make a lot of decisions, but at least you won't have to start from square one.

An Overview of Report Components

As you prepare to write any report, you will need to decide on its makeup. Will it be a simple email? Will it be a long, complex, and formal report? Or will it fall somewhere between these extremes?

To a great extent, your decisions will be based on the report's anticipated length and formality. The more complex the problem and the more formal the situation, the more elaborate the report is likely to be. Adjusting your report's form and contents based on its likely length and formality will help you meet the reader's needs in each situation.

In the subsections that follow, we first explain how to decide which components to use for a given report. We then briefly review the purpose and contents of each of these components.

The Report-Components Grid

LO12-1 Explain the makeup of reports relative to length and formality.

The diagram in Exhibit 12-1 can help you construct reports that fit your specific need. The topmost horizontal line of the grid shows what to include in the most **formal reports**. Such reports have a number of pages that come before the report itself, just as this book has pages that come before the first chapter. Typically, these **prefatory pages**, as they are called, are included when the situation is formal and the report is long. The exact makeup of the prefatory pages may vary, but the most common parts, in this order, are title fly, title page, letter of transmittal, table of contents, and executive summary. Flyleaves (blank pages at the beginning and end that protect the report) may also be included.

As the need for formality decreases and the scope of the problem becomes smaller, the makeup of the report changes. Although the changes that occur are not universally agreed upon, they tend to follow the order represented in the grid. First, the title fly drops out. This page contains only the report title, which also appears on the next page. Since the title fly is used primarily for reasons of formality, it is the first component to go.

On the next level of formality, the executive summary and the letter of transmittal are combined. Here, the report problem and findings are simple enough to be summarized in a short space. As shown in the grid, a report at this stage has three prefatory parts: title page, table of contents, and combined transmittal letter and executive summary.

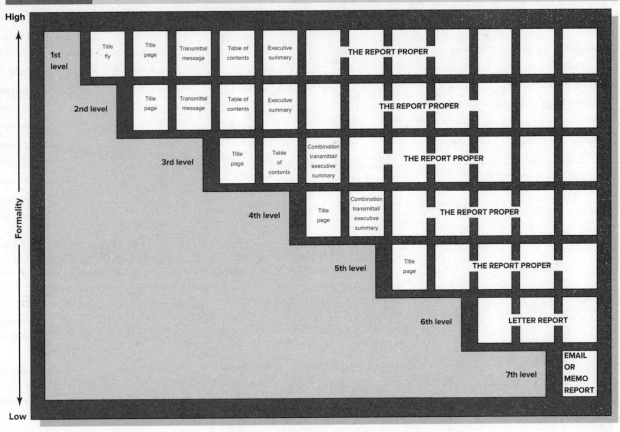

At the fourth step, the table of contents drops out. Another step down, as formality and length requirements continue to decrease, the combined letter of transmittal and executive summary drops out. The report at this level, commonly called the **short report**, now has only a title page and the report text. The title page remains because it serves as a useful cover page and contains the most important identifying information.

Below the short-report form is a form that presents the information as a **letter report**. This form is short but still somewhat formal because the report is being sent to external or especially important internal readers. Finally, for short problems of less formality, the **email** or **memo** form is used.

This is a general analysis of how reports are adapted to the problem and situation. Although it won't cover every report, it can be relied upon for most reports you will write.

The Report Components

To be able to decide which parts of a long, formal report to include in your reports, you'll need to understand the purpose and expected contents of each component represented in Exhibit 12-1. The sample long report that ends this chapter contains examples of these.

Title Pages The first two pages of a long, formal report—the **title fly** and **title page**—contain identification information. As we have said, the title fly contains only the report title; it is

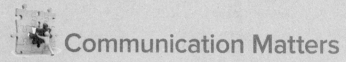
included simply to give a report the most formal appearance. The title page provides additional information.

Although constructing title pages is easy, composing the title is not. In fact, on a per-word basis, the title may require more time than any other part of the report. A good title efficiently and precisely covers the contents. That is, in condensed wording, it captures what the report is about and, if possible, the report's purpose. Consider building your title around some or all of the "five Ws and one H" (see the Communication Matters feature on this topic) to make it as informative as possible while still being concise. A subtitle can help you be both complete and efficient, as in this example: "Employee Morale at Florida Human Resource Offices: An Analysis and Recommendations."

In addition to displaying the report title, the title page identifies the recipient and the writer (and usually their titles and company names). The title page also contains the date unless it is already in the title of the report. You can find attractive designs for title pages in report templates on the Internet and within Word, Google Docs, and other word processing programs.

Transmittal Message As the label implies, the **transmittal message** is a message that transmits the report to the reader. In formal situations, it usually takes letter form. In less formal situations (e.g., when delivering a report to internal readers whom you know fairly well), the report can be transmitted orally or by email. Whatever the case, you should think of the transmittal as a personal message from the writer to the reader, with much the same contents you would use if you were handing the report over in a face-to-face meeting. Except in cases of extreme formality, you should use personal pronouns (*you, I, we*) and conversational language.

The transmittal letter in the sample long report in this chapters illustrates the usual structure for this component. Begin with a brief paragraph that says, essentially, "Here is the report." Identify the report's contents and purpose and, if appropriate, its authorization (who assigned the report, when, and why). Focus the body of the message on further explanation of its purpose, the key parts of the report, or on any other facts about the report that could be useful to your readers. If you are combining the transmittal message with the executive summary, as represented by the third and fourth levels of Exhibit 12-1 and illustrated in Exhibit 12-5, here is where you will include that summary. At the end of the message, you should provide a pleasant and/or forward-looking comment. You might express gratitude for the assignment, for example, or offer to do additional research or help implement the recommendations.

Table of Contents If your short report goes much over five pages (or 1,500 words), you might consider including a **table of contents**. As Chapter 11 points out, this is the report outline in finished form, with page numbers to indicate where the parts begin. The formatting should reflect the report's structure, with main headings clearly differentiated from subheadings. The section titles should state each part's contents clearly and match the report's headings exactly. The table of contents may also include a list of illustrations (or, if long, this list can stand alone). If a separate table of contents would be too formal, you can use the introduction of your report to list the topics the report will cover.

Executive Summary The **executive summary** is the report in miniature. For some readers it serves as a preview to the report, but for others—such as busy executives who may not have time to read the whole report—it's the only part of the report they will read. Because of this latter group of readers, the summary should be self-explanatory; that is, readers shouldn't have to read other parts of the report in order to make sense of the summary. As pointed out previously, whether the executive summary is one of the prefatory parts, is included in the transmittal message, or is part of the report proper depends on how long and how formal the report is.

You Make the Call
If you were writing a report on how a company could improve its sales, would you use the direct or indirect order in the executive summary and the report? Why? What kinds of factors might influence your decision?

You construct the executive summary by summarizing the parts of the report in order and in proportion. You should clearly identify the topic, purpose, and origin of the report; state what kind of research was conducted; present the key facts, findings, and analysis; and state the main conclusions and recommendations. If you include these parts in this order, which usually matches the order of the report contents, your summary will be written in the indirect order. But sometimes writers use the direct order by starting with the conclusions and recommendations and then continuing with the other information. Exhibit 12-2 shows the difference between these two structures, and Exhibit 12-3 gives examples. Whichever order you choose, the executive summary will need to be a masterpiece of economical writing.

It may be desirable to include other report components not discussed here—for example, a copy of the message that authorized the report, various appendices containing supplementary material, a glossary, or a bibliography. As with any writing task, you will need to decide what parts to provide given the facts of the situation and your readers' preferences.

Exhibit 12-2 Diagram of the Executive Summary in Indirect and Direct Order

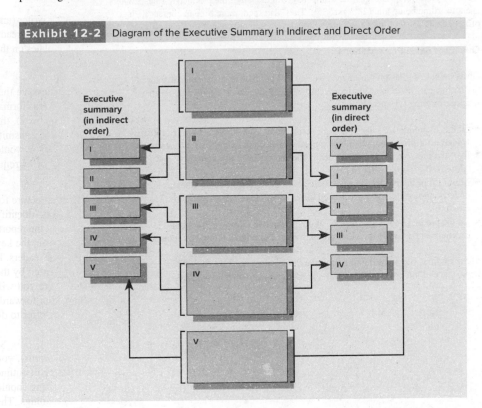

Direct Order

EXECUTIVE SUMMARY

To enhance the performance of Nokia's salespeople, this report recommends adding the following topics to Nokia's sales training program:

- Negative effects of idle time
- Projection of integrity
- Use of moderate persuasion
- Value of product knowledge

Supporting these recommendations are the findings and conclusions drawn from a five-day observational study of 20 productive and 20 underperforming salespeople. The study also included an exit interview and a test of each salesperson's product knowledge.

Productive Use of Time

The data show that the productive salespeople used their time more effectively than did the underperforming salespeople. Compared with the latter, the productive salespeople spent less time being idle (28% vs. 53%). They also spent more time in contact with prospects (31.3% vs. 19.8%) and more time developing prospects (10.4% vs. 4.4%).

Quality of Sales Presentations

Observations of sales presentations revealed that productive salespeople displayed higher integrity, used pressure more reasonably, and knew the product better than underperforming salespeople.

- Of the 20 productive salespeople, 16 displayed at least "moderately high integrity." Underperforming group members ranged widely on the integrity scale, with 7 in the "questionable" group and 5 each in the "moderately high integrity" and "deceitful" groups.
- Most (15) of the productive salespeople used moderate pressure, whereas the underperforming salespeople tended toward extremes (10 high pressure, 7 low pressure).
- On the product knowledge test, 17 of the productive salespeople scored excellent and 3 fair. In the other group, 5 scored excellent, 6 fair, and 9 inadequate.

These findings support a training program that covers productive use of time and the importance of integrity, moderate sales pressure, and product knowledge.

Exhibit 12-3 (*continued*)

Indirect Order

EXECUTIVE SUMMARY

Midwestern Research Associates was contracted to study the performance of Nokia's salespeople. A team of two researchers observed 20 productive and 20 underperforming salespeople over five working days. The study also included an exit interview and a test of each salesperson's product knowledge.

Productive Use of Time

The data show that the productive salespeople used their time more effectively than did the underperforming salespeople. Compared with the latter, the productive salespeople spent less time in idleness (28% vs. 53%). They also spent more time in contact with prospects (31.3% vs. 19.8%) and more time developing prospects (10.4% vs. 4.4%).

Quality of Sales Presentations

Observations of sales presentations revealed that productive salespeople displayed higher integrity, used pressure more reasonably, and knew the product better than underperforming salespeople.

- Of the 20 productive salespeople, 16 displayed at least "moderately high integrity." Members of the underperforming group ranged widely on the integrity scale, with 7 in the "questionable" group and 5 each in the "moderately high integrity" and "deceitful" groups.
- Most (15) of the productive salespeople used moderate pressure, whereas the underperforming salespeople tended toward extremes (10 high pressure, 7 low pressure).
- On the product knowledge test, 17 of the productive salespeople scored excellent and 3 fair. In the other group, 5 scored excellent, 6 fair, and 9 inadequate.

Recommendations

On the basis of these findings, this report recommends adding the following topics to Nokia's sales training program:

- Negative effects of idle time
- Projection of integrity
- Use of moderate persuasion
- Value of product knowledge

Coverage of these topics will help bring the underperforming salespeople up to the level of Nokia's high-performing sales staff.

Characteristics of the Shorter Reports

LO12-2 Discuss the four main ways that the writing in short reports differs from the writing in long reports.

The shorter report forms (those toward the bottom of the grid) are by far the most common in business. These are the everyday working reports—those used for the information reporting that is vital to an organization's communication. Because of their comparative brevity and informality, these reports tend to differ from long reports in the four ways described in this section.

Little Need for Introductory Information

Most of the shorter, more informal reports require little or no introductory material, especially if their title or subject line states the report's topic and purpose. Because they are intended for only a few readers and these readers are likely to be expecting the report, a brief reminder of the report's problem and purpose usually suffices.

Determining what introductory material to provide is simply a matter of answering one question: What does my reader need to know before reading the information in this report? In very short reports, an incidental reference to the problem or to the authorization of the investigation will be sufficient. In some cases, however, you may need a detailed introduction comparable to that of a more formal report.

Reports need no introductory material if their very nature explains their purpose. This holds true for personnel actions, weekly sales reports, inventory reports, and some progress reports.

Predominance of the Direct Order

Because shorter reports usually address routine problems, they are likely to be written in the direct order. That is, the report will begin with its most important information—usually the conclusion and perhaps a recommendation (see Exhibit 12-4). Business writers use this order because they know that busy readers typically want the key point quickly.

The form that the direct order takes in longer reports is somewhat different. The main findings will be somewhere up front—either in the letter of transmittal, executive summary, or both—but the report itself may be organized indirectly. The introduction will present the topic and purpose of the report, but the actual findings will be brought out in the body sections, and their fullest statement will usually appear in the conclusions or recommendations section.

As you move down the grid toward the shorter and more informal reports, the need for the direct order in the report itself increases. In the simplest reports, the direct order is more the rule than the exception.

Here's an example of a short report that uses the direct pattern:

> The hiring committee recommends appointing Sue Breen as our new Corporate Communications Officer.
>
> We interviewed three candidates for the position . . . [*The rest of this paragraph describes the candidates.*]

Exhibit 12-4   A Refresher: Direct vs. Indirect Order

- **Direct order:** Leads with your main point (after a brief introduction). Then provides the details/reasons.
- **Indirect order:** Gives facts and reasons before stating the main point (that is, leads up to it).

A message in the direct order is *more like an announcement*. A message in the indirect order is *more like a narrative (story)*.

While all three candidates had strengths, Ms. Breen emerged as the top candidate, for these reasons:

- She was the most experienced of the three candidates, with 27 years' experience in corporate communication.

- She had the most expertise with the widest variety of communication media, from annual reports to blog posts to intranets and social networking, and she understood the advantages and disadvantages of each.

- She has an impressive track record. At Gemini Web Conferencing, she launched a corporate communications program that . . . [*The report continues to make the case and then reiterates its recommendation at the end.*]

As you can see, this report states its main point first and then supplies the supporting information.

In contrast, a report written in the indirect order presents the supporting information before stating its main conclusion or recommendation, like this:

The hiring committee interviewed three candidates for the position of Corporate Communications Officer: . . . [*The opening paragraph briefly describes the candidates.*]

While all three candidates had strengths, Ms. Breen emerged as the top candidate, for these reasons:

- She was the most experienced of the three candidates, with 27 years' experience in corporate communication.

- She had the most expertise with the widest variety of communication media, from annual reports to blog posts to intranets and social networking, and she understood the advantages and disadvantages of each.

- She has an impressive track record. At Gemini Web Conferencing, she launched a corporate communications program that . . . [*The list continues to make the case.*]

In light of these assets, we recommend that Sue Breen be appointed as our new Corporate Communications Officer.

Whether to use the direct or indirect order depends on your readers' needs and their likely reactions to your content. If your readers need the report conclusion or recommendation as a basis for an action that they must take, directness will speed their effort by enabling them to quickly receive the most important information. If they have confidence in your work, they may choose to skim or not even read the rest of the report before acting on your information. Should they desire to question any part of the report, however, the material will be there for their inspection.

On the other hand, if there is reason to believe that it would be better for your readers to arrive at the conclusion or recommendation only after a logical review of the analysis, you should organize your report in the indirect order. This arrangement is especially preferable when you will be recommending something that you know your readers will not favor or want to hear. For example, in the preceding illustration, if you suspect that one of the executives to whom you're making your hiring recommendation prefers another candidate to Sue Breen, you'll want to make your case before stating the committee's decision. Presenting the supporting data before the recommendation prepares resistant readers to accept your solution to the report problem.

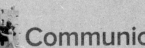

Using a Report Template for a Polished Look

When preparing a report, consider using a predesigned template to give your report a professional, consistent design.

In Word, you can access the available report templates by clicking File > New and entering *report* in the "Search for online templates" field. When you find a template you like, such as the one shown here, you can download it to your computer for your current and future use.

If you're not pleased with the color scheme, you can click on Colors and choose a new scheme—or, if you want both different colors and different fonts, you can click Design > Themes to change them.

For most business reports, you'll want to choose a relatively conservative design like the one shown here. The more visually elaborate designs are better for special publications, such as annual reports and sales proposals.

Source: Microsoft Word 2016.

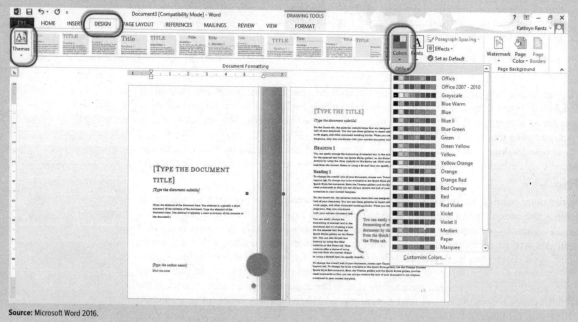

Source: Microsoft Word 2016.

A More Personal Writing Style

The writing in shorter reports tends to be more personal than in long reports. That is, the shorter reports are likely to use the personal pronouns *I, we,* and *you* rather than only the third person.

Several factors account for this tendency toward personal writing in shorter reports. First, such reports tend to be from and to people who know each other and who normally address each other informally when they meet. In addition, shorter reports are apt to be prepared by individuals rather than those representing a team or an organization, so it is natural for the writer to use "I" when stating his or her observations and analyses and presenting his or her opinion. Finally, shorter reports tend to deal with day-to-day problems, which are informal by their very nature. It is logical, then, to report them somewhat informally.

As explained in Chapter 11, your decision about whether to write a report in personal or impersonal style should be based on the situation. Convention favors using impersonal writing for the most formal situations. For most short reports, personal writing is likely to be preferable because of their relatively routine nature.

Less Need for Coherence Helpers

In short reports, a quick overview at the beginning, clear headings, brief transitions, and clearly marked conclusions are usually sufficient to help the reader comprehend the purpose, structure, and contents of the report.

Readers of a long, formal report need more help. They need a detailed preview of the report's structure (e.g., in the report's table of contents and introduction), reminders of what they just read (e.g., section summaries), and clear transitions that indicate how each new section will build on the previous ones. In effect, they need a road map that will enable them to know at every point where they are in the report and how each section is related to the overall goal of the report.

Readers of long reports need navigation aids to help them anticipate what's coming, remember where they've been, and arrive at the end with a clear sense of the report's contents and purpose.
© Matthew Benoit/123RF

Forms for Short to Mid-Length Reports

LO12-3 Choose an appropriate form for short reports.

Because you'll be writing mostly the shorter report forms, let's take a closer look at how those forms differ in terms of format and content.

The Short Report

One of the more popular of the less formal report forms is the short report. Representing the fourth and fifth steps in the formality stairway, this report consists of only a title page and the text, or a title page, combined transmittal message/summary, and the text. The short report is ideally suited for the short but somewhat formal problem.

Like most of the less formal report forms, the short report may be organized in either the direct or indirect order. If the report is addressed to an internal audience, it will likely use the direct order unless there is reason to believe that readers will resist the conclusions or recommendations. Reports written to external audiences may or may not state the main conclusions or recommendations in the opening paragraphs, but it is customary to include these in the transmittal message since it doubles as an executive summary (see Exhibit 12-5).

You Make the Call

Think of a situation in which you would use the impersonal instead of the personal style in a short report. Why would you use this more formal style in a relatively short report?

UNIVERSITY

November 13, 2017

Ms. Valerie Ott, Manager
Hampton Inn–Blue Ash
2601 Reed-Hartman Highway
Cincinnati, OH 45219

Dear Ms. Ott:

As you requested, our report-writing team in Dr. Brevard's Writing for Business class conducted a study to determine if there was strong local demand for a meeting space within a 5-mile radius of the hotel. This report provides the results.

In order to find out how strong the local demand is, we collected information from a variety of nearby businesses, colleges, hospitals, and restaurants. We contacted these establishments through email and phone and conducted a four-question survey.

From our research we found that there is indeed a very strong local demand for a new meeting space. The respondents felt that the available options in the area were either too large or too expensive. We also learned that most of the respondents would like for the new facility to have its own food service rather than having to arrange a caterer for their events.

Thank you for allowing us the opportunity to do this real-world project. We hope this information will be valuable when determining whether to build a mid-sized meeting facility.

Sincerely,

Tiffany Jones, Amanda Chapman,
and Grant Cole

When you open your short report with the main findings or recommendations, the next section usually provides background on the report problem and what you did to investigate it. In other words, a fuller description of your problem and purpose comes after the opening statement of the findings, as described in Chapter 11. When your report uses the indirect order, a coherent statement of your problem and purpose open the report. The findings then come out as the reader reads the text, and they are gathered together at the end of the report in a helpful summary. The indirect pattern is illustrated by the sample long report in this chapter.

Even if you have provided your recommendations up front, you should reiterate and perhaps expand on them at the end of your report. Readers do not mind this kind of redundancy as long as the recommendations are helpfully restated, not just copied and pasted from the front of the report. Plus, stopping short of your main points at the end of your report would end it too abruptly.

The mechanics of constructing the short report are much the same as the mechanics of constructing the more formal, longer types. The short report uses the same form of title page and page layout. Like the longer reports, it uses headings, though usually only one or two levels because of its brevity. Like any other report, the short report uses visuals, footnotes, a bibliography, and/or an appendix when these are needed.

Letter Reports

Another common short-report form is the letter report—that is, a report in letter form. Letter reports are used primarily to present information to people outside the organization. For example, a company's review of the performance of a particular product may be presented in letter form and sent to the person who requested it. An outside consultant may deliver his or her analyses and recommendations in letter form. If the report is internal but still requires a certain degree of formality, the letter format is also appropriate. For example, an officer of an organization may report certain information to the membership in a letter.

Though missing certain components of long, formal reports, short reports require many of the same analytical and organizational skills used to develop longer reports.
© Comstock/Stockbyte/Getty Images

Typically, letter reports are three to four pages, but they may be longer or shorter. Because letters are traditionally personal form of communication, letter reports are usually written in the personal style, with *I, you*, and *we* references—though there are exceptions, such as letter reports for a company's board of directors or other important readers.

Letter reports may use either the direct or the indirect order. Those in the direct order begin with the main findings or recommendations. Sometimes they use a subject line to announce the topic of the report so the first paragraph of the letter can get right to the main point. The subject line usually appears just above the salutation. It commonly begins with the word *subject* followed by a description of the report's contents, as in the following example:

> Subject: Requested Review of Association Members' Travel Expenses
>
> Association members spent 11% more on travel to association meetings in 2016 than they did in 2015, and they expect another increase in travel expenses this year.

Next would come a brief section indicating why the study was undertaken and how. Then the report would present the findings in more detail. Finally, it would close with a summary of the findings and perhaps their implications.

Indirect-order letters tend not to use a subject line, and they open with brief background information, such as who authorized the report and the topic. A letter report written to the executives of an organization, for example, might use the following indirect opening:

> As requested by the board of directors January 6, the Membership Committee reviewed members' expenditures for travel for 2015 and 2016 to determine whether increasing travel expenses may be causing a decline in attendance at association meetings. To gather our data . . . [says whatever research was performed].

Following the introduction would be a logical presentation and analysis of the findings. After this presentation would come a summary of these findings and any implications. (See the Annotated Example of a letter report.)

Whether written in the direct or indirect order, a letter report needs a brief closing paragraph. This should be a pleasant, forward-looking comment that fits the situation.

Annotated Example
A Letter Report with Footnotes

For this assignment, the instructor asked students to find real clients who would be interested in receiving an evaluation report on a facet of their company's social media practices. Because the reports would be short, would be addressed to external audiences, and would need a certain degree of formality, students were advised to use the letter-report format. As with many business reports, this report relies on footnotes to cite the sources. A references list could be added if the report were longer and/or in short-report format.

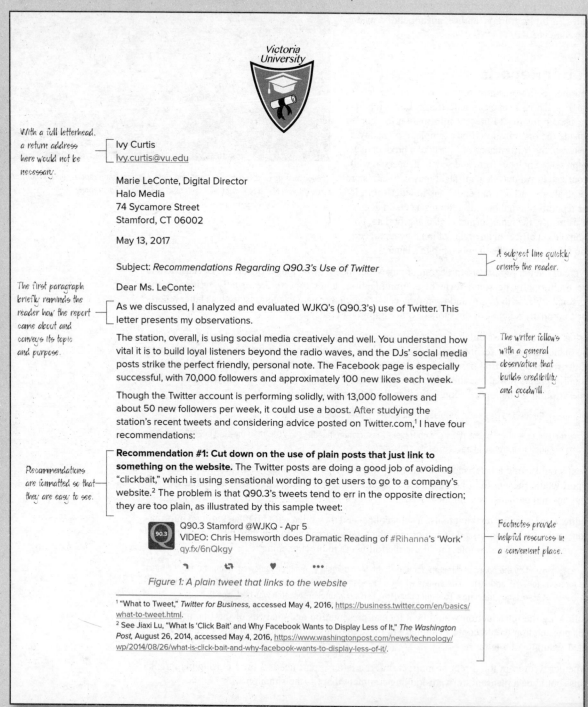

With a full letterhead, a return address here would not be necessary.

A subject line quickly orients the reader.

The first paragraph briefly reminds the reader how the report came about and conveys its topic and purpose.

The writer follows with a general observation that builds credibility and goodwill.

Recommendations are formatted so that they are easy to see.

Footnotes provide helpful resources in a convenient place.

Victoria University

Ivy Curtis
Ivy.curtis@vu.edu

Marie LeConte, Digital Director
Halo Media
74 Sycamore Street
Stamford, CT 06002

May 13, 2017

Subject: *Recommendations Regarding Q90.3's Use of Twitter*

Dear Ms. LeConte:

As we discussed, I analyzed and evaluated WJKQ's (Q90.3's) use of Twitter. This letter presents my observations.

The station, overall, is using social media creatively and well. You understand how vital it is to build loyal listeners beyond the radio waves, and the DJs' social media posts strike the perfect friendly, personal note. The Facebook page is especially successful, with 70,000 followers and approximately 100 new likes each week.

Though the Twitter account is performing solidly, with 13,000 followers and about 50 new followers per week, it could use a boost. After studying the station's recent tweets and considering advice posted on Twitter.com,[1] I have four recommendations:

Recommendation #1: Cut down on the use of plain posts that just link to something on the website. The Twitter posts are doing a good job of avoiding "clickbait," which is using sensational wording to get users to go to a company's website.[2] The problem is that Q90.3's tweets tend to err in the opposite direction; they are too plain, as illustrated by this sample tweet:

> Q90.3 Stamford @WJKQ - Apr 5
> VIDEO: Chris Hemsworth does Dramatic Reading of #Rihanna's 'Work'
> qy.fx/6nQkgy

Figure 1: A plain tweet that links to the website

---

[1] "What to Tweet," *Twitter for Business,* accessed May 4, 2016, https://business.twitter.com/en/basics/what-to-tweet.html.
[2] See Jiaxi Lu, "What Is 'Click Bait' and Why Facebook Wants to Display Less of It," *The Washington Post,* August 26, 2014, accessed May 4, 2016, https://www.washingtonpost.com/news/technology/wp/2014/08/26/what-is-click-bait-and-why-facebook-wants-to-display-less-of-it/.

Annotated Example (continued)

Ms. Marie LeConte   **May 13, 2017**   2

Subsequent pages of a letter need this kind of header.

When there are too many such tweets, readers begin to feel that the station is mechanically sending out notices about its website material without enough regard for what the viewers might really be interested in. If viewers click on the links and are uninterested in what they find on the website, they develop an even more negative impression and are likely to start ignoring such tweets altogether. They may even start regarding the tweets as essentially Twitter spam.[3]

Negative points are clearly but tactfully worded.

To prevent such reactions, the station should not overuse this type of link, and the text in these links should be as reader-focused and appealing as possible while still avoiding sensationalism.

Recommendation #2: Avoid unduly repetitive tweets. Multiple tweets to promote an event or promotion are a great idea—as long as those tweets are different enough to be interesting. The following three tweets about a recent promotion at Q90.3 are too similar:

 Q90.3 Stamford @WJKQ - Apr 19
#PickYourPurse is back at 7:40AM! Print your cheat sheet ----> qy.fx/3EQxgy

↰   ⇄   ♥ 1   •••

Q90.3 Stamford @WJKQ - Apr 18
We have PURSES!!! #PickYourPurse is comming up 7:40! Get your cheat sheet ----> qy.fx/5eQ33k

↰   ⇄   ♥   •••

Q90.3 Stamford @WJKQ - Apr 17
#PickYourPurse is back TMW at 7:40AM!!!

↰   ⇄   ♥ 1   •••

Figure 2: Tweets that are too repetitive

Instead of simply repeating the announcement about the promotion, the posts could feature various fun aspects of it—for example, reminding people to listen for the winners at certain times of day or piquing their curiosity with questions like "Will your purse be worth $50 or $500?!" Posting photos of sample purses would also likely increase viewer participation—which brings us to the next recommendation.

Recommendation #3: Post interesting media in the tweets and take advantage of Twitter cards. The station is on target with its posts about new music and videos, but readers currently have to click a link in the tweet to access those, as in the following example:

Brief but explicit captions capture the point of each visual.

 Q90.3 Stamford @WJKQ - Apr 15
Check out @Pink's new song "Just like Fire" qy.fx/8fmXnB

↰   ⇄ 5   ♥ 7   •••

Figure 3: A tweet that could have displayed the video instead of making viewers go to the website to see it

This post would have been more interesting had it included this clickable video visual from the station's website:

---

[3] "Reporting Spam on Twitter," *Twitter.com*, accessed May 4, 2016, https://support.twitter.com/articles/64986.

Ms. Marie LeConte   **May 13, 2017**   **3**

Figure 4: Video visual that could have been added to the post in Figure 3

© Shutterstock/Blue Planet Studio

When tweeting material from its own or others' websites, the station can also take advantage of Twitter cards, which are different types of enhanced displays for tweets. Twitter cards create better-looking posts and also enable the poster to defeat the 140-character limit for tweets by linking to a longer summary of the material being tweeted about. For example, if viewers click on the "View Summary" link, they can read a 200-word summary of the material, as shown in this example:

Colin Docherty @colin_docherty   15h
I've just learnt how to mark my webpages up for Twitter Summary Cards colindocherty.co.uk/twitter/summar... #twittercard
🗋 Hide summary   ← Reply   🗑 Delete   ★ Favourite   ••• More

🔹 Colin Docherty

Learn how to mark your webpages up for Twitter Card Summary Tweets
By Colin Docherty @colin_docherty

This tweet was created using Twitter's Summary Card HTML markup. Visit my tutorial page to learn how to apply this to your webpages to create richer & more engaging tweets.

learn twitter summary cards

View on www.colindocherty.co.uk/twitter

3:41 PM - 15 Nov 13 · Details   Flag media

Figure 5: A tweet that uses Twitter's summary card

Source: twitter.com; image © Westend61/Getty Images RF

There are also Twitter cards for linking to visual and audio material on websites, promoting products, displaying a gallery of photos, offering coupons, and more. These are enabled simply by adding some lines of code at the top of the code for the website that the tweet links to.[4]

Recommendation #4: Ask more questions and conduct more polls. Q90.3 has generated considerable activity with tweets like this one (which received 267 comments):

---

[4] Courtney Seiter, "The Everything Guide to Twitter Cards: How to Choose, Set Up, Measure Them, and More," *BufferSocial.com*, September 2, 2014, accessed May 4, 2016, https://blog.bufferapp.com/twitter-cards-guide.

The writer offers sufficient information—along with an example—to help the reader implement the suggestion.

Specific data like this show that the writer did careful, thorough research.

The writer saves the reader some work by sharing a helpful resource.

Ms. Marie LeConte   May 13, 2017   4

Figure 6: A Twitter poll conducted by the station

top-bottom: © UpperCut Images/SuperStock RF; © Ingram Publishing/Fotosearch RF; © PhotoAlto/SuperStock RF; © Jack Hollingsworth/Blend Images LLC RF

Tweeting more posts that ask questions—for example, which songs viewers prefer or whether they will be attending a certain event—will create more viewer engagement.

Q90.3 has done an excellent job of creating a social media presence with Facebook. By implementing these suggestions, the station can achieve similar success with Twitter:

- Cutting down on the use of posts that simply point to something on the website.
- Avoiding unduly repetitive tweets.
- Posting interesting media in the tweets and taking advantage of Twitter cards.
- Asking more questions and conducting more polls.

A summary in an easy-to-read format helps ensure the reader's comprehension.

The ending closes on a personal, goodwill-building note.

Thank you again for giving me the opportunity to do this project. It was a pleasure to learn more about one of the region's favorite radio stations, and I hope that you will find my suggestions helpful. Please email me if I can be of further assistance.

Sincerely,

Ivey Curtis

Ivey Curtis
Business Communication Student
Victoria University

Communication Matters

When Is a Report Not a Report?

One answer: When it is a **white paper**.

White papers are often categorized as reports because they share many characteristics with reports. They're based on research (many have footnotes or a references page); they present numerical data in tables and graphs; they have a title page and often have a table of contents and/or an executive summary (see the title page and executive summary of the sample white paper shown here); and they use levels of headings to indicate the document's structure. In other words, they look like reports.

They differ from reports, though, in one crucial way: They are almost always intended to be persuasive rather than objective.

White papers look like problem-solving reports, and in a way they are. They start by identifying a problem that their intended readers—usually other businesses—are likely to have. For example, a white paper may discuss the need for effective waste management or for an effective checkout system. To establish the existence and extent of the problem, the author will present data gathered from creditable sources. But then the solution the paper proposes will be the authoring company's own products or services (see page 18 of the example, which promotes Newsweaver software). In this part, little effort is made to objectively or thoroughly compare all possible solutions.

It's important to understand the difference between a report and a white paper. Readers bring different expectations to these documents. Failing to make clear which type you're writing is unethical, and it can sway readers to make a decision on insufficient or misinterpreted data.

You can learn more about white papers and their uses by visiting whitepaperguy.com, whitepapersource.com, and many other Web resources.

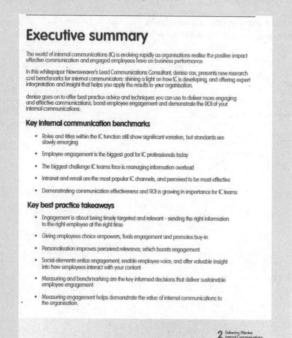

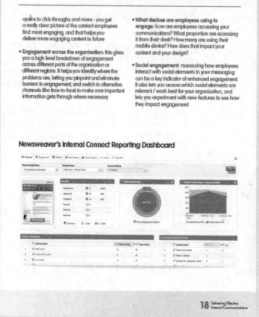

Email and Memo Reports

As we noted in Chapter 2, email is heavily used in business. It has largely eclipsed memos, but memos are still written, especially in cases where computers aren't easily accessible or the writer prefers to deliver a print message. Both email and memos can be used for internal reports—that is, for reports written by and to people in an organization.

Because email and memos are primarily communications between people who know each other, they are usually informal, though those directed to high-ranking administrators can be quite formal. Like the longer forms, they may use headings to display content and visuals to support the text. For the longer email reports, writers will often choose to make the report itself an attached document and use the email message as a transmittal message.

Because they are largely internal, email reports tend to be problem-solving reports. They are intended to help improve operations, lay the groundwork for an innovation, solve a problem, or otherwise assist decision makers in the organization.

Written Reports in Other Forms

While most written reports in business will take the form of short reports, letter reports, or email or memo reports, they can take a variety of other forms as well. The report featured in Exhibit 12-6 appeared on MailChimp's website. Companies often prepare and share studies like these as a service to their readers and as a form of content marketing (discussed in Chapter 10). Research can also be reported in pamphlets, white papers (see the preceding Communication Matters feature), and other publications; and many reports are uploaded to the Web as stand-alone documents in PDF format. You can apply your report-writing knowledge to all these forms and more. Just be sure to choose the appropriate form for your readers and purpose.

Sometimes it is courteous to deliver a report in both hard copy (to keep your reader from having to print it) and electronic form (so your reader can easily distribute it).
© Image Source/Stockbyte/Getty Images

Exhibit 12-6

A Report from an Email-Marketing Firm's Website

We work in an increasingly mobile-oriented world. The Pew Research Center found that the use of phones to read email doubled between 2009 and 2013, and the November 2014 Ericsson Mobility Report estimates that smartphone subscriptions and traffic per phone will have respective annual growth rates of 15% and 25% until 2020. These trends raise many questions, especially for email marketers. Here are two we wanted to answer: "What will mobile's impact be on email engagement? And can email campaign design counteract changing engagement rates?"

Methodology

We analyzed a random subset of email addresses that MailChimp sends to and determined their corresponding devices from their user agent strings. For each address in our sample, we considered the device that registered the most clicks to be that user's preferred device. To focus on recipients that actually engage with email, only addresses that had clicked on an email campaign since the beginning of 2013 were considered.

We aggregated sends and clicks to these addresses from MailChimp users within a 6 month period to see how preferred device impacts engagement. We looked to see if use of our Inbox Preview feature and responsive templates help engage mobile subscribers, and we looked at how different links within a campaign are impacted.

Readers click less on mobile

What did we find out? For starters, PCs, tablets, and mobile devices accounted for 64%, 9%, and 27% of email addresses, and 72%, 9%, and 18% of clicks, respectively. Right off the bat, we could tell that PC users click more.

Next, we calculated click rates at the address/campaign level. Unique click rates measure what percentage of sends received at least one click, and total click rates allow for multiple clicks for a single recipient/campaign. We found that PC and tablet users have unique click rates of 3.8%, a 40% increase over the 2.7% mobile click rate.

Unique click rates for PC and tablet users are similar, but PC users who click tend to click more links per email than tablet users, resulting in a 6.7% total click rate for PC users and a 5.6% rate for tablet users.

Recipients who use mobile phones had unique and total click rates of 2.7% and 3.9%, worse than all other device categories. Of the three platforms, PC users are more likely to click on an email, and those that do tend to click on a larger number of links within that email.

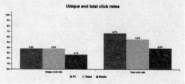

Common Types of Short Reports

Because organizations depend heavily on short reports, there are many varieties, written for many different purposes. We cover some of the most common types here, categorized on the basis of their main purpose, but the form they take will vary from company to company. Also, most companies will have developed unique types of reports to accomplish particular goals. Always consider your company's typical ways of reporting when deciding what to report and how.

Routine Operational Reports

The majority of the reports written within companies are **routine operational reports** that keep supervisors, managers, and team members informed about the company's operations. These can be daily, weekly, monthly, or quarterly reports on the work of each department or even each employee. They can relate production data, information on visits to customers, issues that have arisen, or any kind of information that others in the organization need on a routine basis.

The form and contents of these reports will vary from company to company and manager to manager. Many will be submitted on predesigned forms. Others may not use forms but will follow a prescribed format. Still others will be shaped by the writer's own judgment about what to include and how to present it.

The nature and culture of the organization heavily influence the forms taken by these reports. For example, one innovative format for weekly reporting is the 5-15 report.[1] The name comes from the fact that it is intended to be read in 5 minutes and written in 15 minutes. Its typical three-part contents are a description of what the employee did that week, a statement about the employee's morale and that of others he or she worked with, and one idea for how to improve operations. Clearly, this format would work best in an organization where employees have nonroutinized jobs and the management values the employees' opinions.

Whatever the form, the routine operational report should convey clearly and quickly what readers most need and want to know about the time period in question. It is also an opportunity for you, the writer, to showcase your ability to provide needed information on deadline.

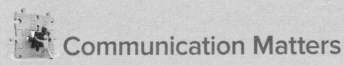

Communication Matters

The Monetary Value of a Good Report

A research-based report can save a business thousands of dollars or generate thousands of dollars in income. That's why companies are willing to pay well for industry reports like those prepared by such information brokers as ReportLinker. The 32-page sample report shown here carries a price tag of $1,020—but the cost is minimal for a company that can really benefit from the information.

Source: ReportLinker.com

Progress Reports

You can think of an internal **progress report** as a routine operational report except that it tends to be submitted on an as-needed basis, and, as its name implies, it focuses on progress toward a specific goal. If you are working on a project for an external client, you may also need to submit progress reports to show that your work is on track. For example, a fundraising organization might prepare weekly summaries of its efforts to achieve its goal. Or a building contractor might prepare a report on progress toward completing a building for a customer. Though these reports focus on the progress that has been made, they also may include such related topics as problems encountered and projections of future progress.

Progress reports can be quite formal, as when a contractor building a large manufacturing plant reports to the company for whom the plant is being built. Or they can be very informal, as in the case of a worker reporting by email to his or her supervisor on the progress of a task being performed. Some progress reports are quite routine and structured, sometimes involving filling in blanks on forms devised for the purpose. Most, however, are relatively informal narrative reports like the featured Annotated Examples. As these examples show, you should organize and format the "story" of your progress for easy comprehension.

As with most reports, you have some choice about the tone to use when presenting your information. With progress reports, you want to emphasize the positive if possible. The overall message should be "I (or we) have made progress." The best way to convey this message confidently, of course, is to be sure that you or your team has in fact made progress on the task at hand.

Annotated Example
A Progress Report in Email Form

This email report summarizes a sales manager's progress in opening a new district. It begins with the highlights—all a busy reader may need to know.

The factual information follows, grouped into three categories. The writer–reader relationship justifies a personal style.

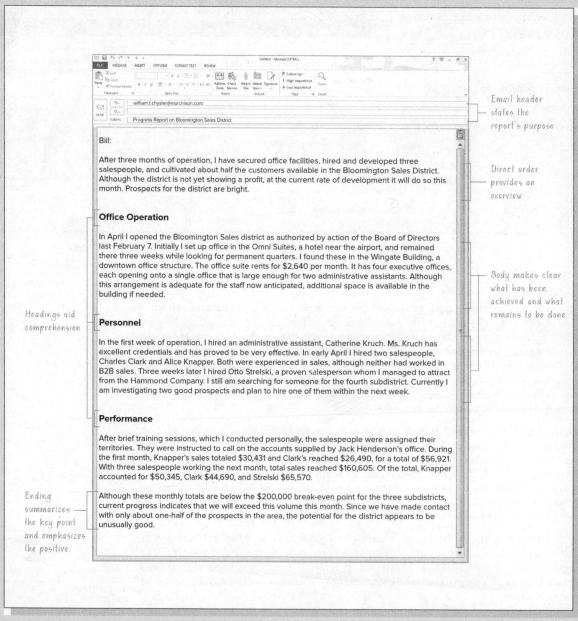

Email header states the report's purpose

To... william.t.chysler@murchison.com

Subject: Progress Report on Bloomington Sales District

Bill:

After three months of operation, I have secured office facilities, hired and developed three salespeople, and cultivated about half the customers available in the Bloomington Sales District. Although the district is not yet showing a profit, at the current rate of development it will do so this month. Prospects for the district are bright.

Direct order provides an overview

Office Operation

In April I opened the Bloomington Sales district as authorized by action of the Board of Directors last February 7. Initially I set up office in the Omni Suites, a hotel near the airport, and remained there three weeks while looking for permanent quarters. I found these in the Wingate Building, a downtown office structure. The office suite rents for $2,640 per month. It has four executive offices, each opening onto a single office that is large enough for two administrative assistants. Although this arrangement is adequate for the staff now anticipated, additional space is available in the building if needed.

Body makes clear what has been achieved and what remains to be done

Headings aid comprehension

Personnel

In the first week of operation, I hired an administrative assistant, Catherine Kruch. Ms. Kruch has excellent credentials and has proved to be very effective. In early April I hired two salespeople, Charles Clark and Alice Knapper. Both were experienced in sales, although neither had worked in B2B sales. Three weeks later I hired Otto Strelski, a proven salesperson whom I managed to attract from the Hammond Company. I still am searching for someone for the fourth subdistrict. Currently I am investigating two good prospects and plan to hire one of them within the next week.

Performance

After brief training sessions, which I conducted personally, the salespeople were assigned their territories. They were instructed to call on the accounts supplied by Jack Henderson's office. During the first month, Knapper's sales totaled $30,431 and Clark's reached $26,490, for a total of $56,921. With three salespeople working the next month, total sales reached $160,605. Of the total, Knapper accounted for $50,345, Clark $44,690, and Strelski $65,570.

Ending summarizes the key point and emphasizes the positive.

Although these monthly totals are below the $200,000 break-even point for the three subdistricts, current progress indicates that we will exceed this volume this month. Since we have made contact with only about one-half of the prospects in the area, the potential for the district appears to be unusually good.

Source: Kathryn Rentz.

Annotated Example
A Memo Progress Report on a Class Project

As a student, you will sometimes need to submit a progress report on a complex assignment, such as a group project. In such cases, the same goals apply here as to workplace progress reports—to show that you understand the project's purpose, that you have made good progress, that you have a good sense of what remains to be done, and that you're headed toward a successful conclusion.

Memo Report

Date: May 12, 2017

To: Professor Rodriguez

From: Sam Ellis *SE*

Subject: Group Four's Progress on the Report for Ms. Herbert

Our group consists of Bo Riddle, Ina Ward, Tiffany Paine, and me. We have made good progress on gathering information to help Ms. Herbert decide whether to include personality testing in her hiring process for Fashion Sense.

> *Direct opening orients the reader and announces good progress on the project*

Research Topics and Methods

In our first group meeting, on May 3, we decided to investigate the following topics, assigned as shown:

> *List shows that the group is well organized*

- Types of personality testing available (Tiffany)
- Use of personality testing in the retail industry (Ina)
- Cost of personality testing (Bo)
- Possible legal risks of personality testing (me)

To research the types of testing available, we conducted mostly Internet research. We did both Internet and library research to investigate the remaining topics. We also interviewed Amy Loehmann, a professor in the law school, about possible legal issues.

> *Discussion of research methods builds credibility*

Findings So Far

In the first week of work, we have gathered these main findings:

> *Informative headings and bulleted lists make the contents easy to digest*

- Companies use many different kinds of personality tests, such as the Big Five personality test (see queendom.com) and tests based on four personality types (see MaximumAdvantage.com). But the most popular is the Myers-Briggs Type Indicator. Given its proven track record, Ms. Herbert is likely to want to use some version of this test if she adopts personality testing.
- Large retail stores such as Macy's do use personality testing, but we have not yet found much use of such testing for smaller businesses like Ms. Herbert's.
- Personality testing can be extremely expensive if the company hires a trained consultant to conduct the testing. However, there are many small testing outfits that provide relatively simple, yet valid, tests. For example, for about $500, Proven Results will test a company's high-performing employees and develop a personality test based on those employees' traits (ProvenResults.com). This test can then be given to job applicants to determine their suitability for the work.
- Personality testing poses some legal risks. Mainly, one must be sure not to ask questions that discriminate against the test takers on the basis of religion, race, or gender. If a company hires a consultant or firm like ProvenResults to do the testing, that person or firm will be the responsible legal party. If one doesn't hire a third party, it is advisable to have an attorney review the testing procedure before it is used.

> *Convincing details and brief citations of sources attest to the group's hard work*

Next Steps

> *A good plan for completing the work builds the instructor's confidence in the group*

We will continue to explore the kinds of tests that might be suitable for Ms. Herbert. Specifically, we will try to find out what kinds of personality tests the smaller retail companies use and which of these might be appropriate for Fashion Sense. We will also try to determine the most cost-effective method for Ms. Herbert to adopt and acquire contact information for any testing services that look promising.

We are on track to have a complete draft of our report prepared by the May 22 deadline. This is an interesting project, and we believe we will be able to help Ms. Herbert make a well-informed decision.

> *Conclusion shows good awareness of the next major deadline and of the end goal*

Problem-Solving Reports

Like many long reports, many short reports are **problem-solving reports**. These reports help decision makers figure out what to do any time a problem arises within an organization—which is often. For example, a piece of equipment may have broken down, causing mayhem on the production line. Or employees may have gotten hurt on the job. Or, less dramatically, a company procedure may have become outdated, or a client company may want to know why it's losing money. If we define *problem* as an issue facing the company, we could include many other scenarios as well—for example, whether or not a company should adopt flextime scheduling or what location it should choose for a new store. Whatever the context, the writer of a problem-solving report needs to gather facts about the problem or issue, define it clearly, research solutions, and recommend a course of action.

Like progress reports, problem-solving reports can be internal or external. Internal problem-solving reports are usually assigned, but sometimes employees may need to write unsolicited problem-solving reports—for example, if they must recommend that a subordinate be fired or if they feel that a change in procedure is necessary. External problem-solving reports are most often written by consulting companies for their clients. In these cases, the report is the main product that the client is paying for.

A type of problem-solving report that deserves special attention is a **feasibility study**. For these reports, writers study several courses of action and then propose the most feasible, desirable one. For instance, you might be asked to compare Internet service providers and recommend the one that suits the company's needs and budget best. Or you might investigate what type of onsite child care center, if any, is feasible for your organization. Sometimes feasibility studies are not full-blown problem-solving reports. They may offer detailed analysis but stop short of making a recommendation. The analysis they provide nevertheless helps decision makers decide what to do.

In fact, many short reports that help solve company problems may not be complete problem-solving reports. As explained in the previous chapter, some decision makers who assign research reports will not want recommendations; they'll want only good data and careful analysis so that they can formulate a course of action themselves. Whether you are preparing an internal or external report, it is important to understand how far your readers want you to go toward proposing solutions.

You have some latitude when deciding how direct to make your opening in a problem-solving report. If you believe that your readers will be open to any reasonable findings or recommendations, you should state those up front. If you think your conclusions will be unexpected or your readers will be skeptical, you should still state your report's purpose and topic clearly at the beginning but save the conclusions and recommendations until the end, after leading your readers through the details. Exhibit 12-7, a pattern for a problem-solving report used by the U.S. military, follows this indirect plan. As always, try to find out which method of organization your readers prefer.

While they usually propose action, problem-solving reports are not true persuasive messages. Because they either have been assigned or fall within an employee's assigned duties, the writer already has a willing reader. Furthermore, the writer has no obvious personal stake in the outcome the way he or she does with a persuasive message. However, when writing a problem-solving report, especially one that makes recommendations, you do need to show that your study was thorough and your reasoning sound. The decision makers may not choose to follow your advice, but

Exhibit 12-7

Military Form for Problem-Solving Report

DEPARTMENT OF THE AIR FORCE
HEADQUARTERS UNITED STATES AIR FORCE
WASHINGTON, DC 20330

REPLY TO
ATTN OF

SUBJECT

TO:

AFODC/Colonel Jones

Staff Study Report

PROBLEM

1. --
--.

FACTORS BEARING ON THE PROBLEM

2. Facts.

a.--
--.

b.--.

3. Assumptions.

4. Criteria.

5. Definitions.

DISCUSSION

6. --.

7. --.

8. --.

CONCLUSION

9. --.

ACTION RECOMMENDED

10. --.

11. --.

JOHN J. JONES, Colonel, USAF   2 Atch
Deputy Chief of Staff, Operations   1. ----------------------
                                    2. ----------------------

your work, if it is carefully performed, still helps them decide what to do and reflects positively on you.

Meeting Minutes

Many short reports in business, especially internal ones, do not recommend or even analyze. Instead, they describe. Trip reports, incident reports, and other such reports are meant to provide a written record of something that happened. Whatever their type and specific purpose, they all share the need to be well organized, easy to read, and factual. Perhaps the most common of these reports is **minutes** for meetings.

Minutes provide a written record of a group's activities, which can include announcements, reports, significant discussions, and decisions. They include important details, but they are primarily a summary that reports the gist of what happened, not a verbatim transcript. Minutes include only objective data; their writer carefully avoids using such judgmental words as *excellent* or *impractical* or such descriptive words as *angrily* or *calmly*. However, if the group passes a resolution that specific wording be officially recorded, a writer should include it. Accurate minutes are important because they can sometimes have legal significance, such as when shareholders or boards vote to approve certain corporate activities.

The expected format varies across organizations, but any format you use should enable the reader to easily review what happened and retrieve particular information. Headings in bold or italics are usually appropriate, and some writers find that numbering items in the minutes to agree with the numbering of a meeting's agenda is helpful. Additional advice on writing minutes can be found in Chapter 14.

It takes both skill and judgment to prepare accurate, neutral minutes for an important meeting.
© Image Source/Getty Images RF

The Annotated Example that follows illustrates typical minutes. Note that these preliminary, body, and closing items may be included:

Preliminary Items

- Name of the group
- Name of the document
- Type of meeting (monthly, emergency, special)
- Place, date, and time called to order
- Names of those attending including guests (used to determine if a quorum is present)
- Names of those absent and the reasons for absence

Body Items

- Approval of the minutes of previous meeting
- Meeting announcements
- Old business—Reports on matters previously presented
- New business—Reports on matters presented to the group

Closing Items

- Place and time of the next meeting
- Notation of the meeting's ending time
- Name and signature of the person responsible for preparing the minutes

Annotated Example
Illustration of Meeting Minutes

Minutes of the Policy Committee
Semiannual Meeting
November 21, 2017, 9:30–11:30 A.M., Conference Room A

Present: Elaine Horn (chair), D'Marie Simon, DeAnne Overholt, Michelle Lum, Joel Zwanziger, Rebecca Shuster, Jeff Merrill, Donna Wingler, Chris Woods, Tim Lebold (corporate attorney, guest).

Absent: Joan Marian, Jeff Horen (excused), Leonna Plummer (excused)

> *Complete preliminary information provides a good record*

Approval of Minutes

Minutes from the May 5, 2017, meeting were read and approved.

Announcements

Chris Woods invited the committee to a reception for Milton Chen, director in our Asia region. It will be held in the executive dining room at 3:00 P.M. tomorrow. Chris reminded us that Asia is ahead of the United States in its use of wireless technology. He suggested that perhaps we can get an idea of good policies to implement now.

> *Headings help readers retrieve information*

Old Business—Email Policy

Joel Zwanziger reported the results of his survey on the proposed email policy. While 16 percent of the employees were against the policy, 84 percent favored it. A January 1, 2018, implementation is planned, subject to its distribution to all employees before the Christmas break.

Web-Surfing Policy

D'Marie Simon reported on her study of similar companies' Web-surfing policies. Most have informal guides but no official policies. The guidelines generally are that all surfing must be related to the job and that personal surfing should be done on breaks. The committee discussed the issue at length. It approved a policy that reflects the current general guidelines.

> *Discussions are summarized and actions taken are included*

Temp Policy

Tim Lebold presented the legal steps we need to take to get our old and new temporary employees to sign a nondisclosure agreement prior to working here, as we've been discussing in relation to a new temp policy. The committee directed Tim to begin the process so that the policy could be put in force as soon as possible.

New Business—Resolution

Michelle Lum proposed that a resolution of thanks be added to the record recognizing Megan for her terrific attention to detail as well her clear focus on keeping the committee abreast of policy issues. It was unanimously approved.

> *Resolutions often include descriptive language*

Next Meeting

The next meeting of the committee will be May 3, 2018, from 9:30–11:30 A.M. in Conference Room A.

> *Closing gives reader complete needed facts*

Adjournment

The meeting was adjourned at 11:25 A.M.

Respectfully submitted,

Elaine Horn
Elaine Horn

> *Signing signifies the minutes are an official record*

When you are responsible for preparing the minutes of a meeting, you can take several steps to make the task easier. First, get an agenda in advance. Use it to complete as much of the preliminary information as possible, including the names of those expected to attend. If someone is not present, you can easily move that person's name to the absentee list. You might even set up a table in advance with the following column headings to facilitate your note taking:

Topic	Summary of Discussion	Action/Resolution

Bear in mind that meeting minutes, while they look objective, almost always have political implications. Because minutes are the only tangible record of what happened, meeting participants will want their contributions included and cast in a positive light. Since you will not be able to record every comment made, you will need to decide which ones to include, whether or not to credit a particular speaker, how to capture the group's reaction, and so forth. Use your good judgment when translating a rich oral event into a written summary.

Long, Formal Reports

The preceding sections have already discussed the prefatory pages that accompany long reports and several traits that distinguish long reports from short reports. In this section, we elaborate further on the special features and components of long reports and then provide an annotated example of a long report.

LO12-5 Write longer reports that include the appropriate components, meet the readers' needs, and are easy to follow.

Additional Components of Long, Formal Reports

Because of their length and the scope and complexity of their contents, long reports have several other features besides prefatory pages that aid the readers' comprehension, help the report meet their information needs, and build credibility.

The Introduction   The introduction is the first section of the report itself, coming after all the prefatory pages, and in long reports, it can be quite elaborate. Its purpose is to prepare the readers to receive the report. Whatever will help achieve this goal is appropriate content. Giving your readers what they need makes a good first impression and displays good you-viewpoint.

To determine what content is appropriate, consider all the likely readers of your report. As noted earlier, the readers of many shorter reports are likely to know the problem well and have little or no need for an introduction. But such is not often the case for longer reports.

Many of these reports are prepared for a large number of readers, some of whom know little about the problem. These reports often have long lives and are kept on file to be read in future years. Your introductory material will need to prepare both immediate and later readers.

Ask yourself what you would need or want to know about the problem if you were in your readers' shoes. As the report's author, you know more about the report than anyone else, so you will need to work hard not to assume that readers have the same knowledge of the problem that you do. The following list of common components can help you decide what to include in your introduction. Remember, though, that you should adapt the introduction's contents to your situation. Only on rare occasions, such as for the longest, most complex reports, would you include all the items.

A long report can be daunting to readers. Be sure to provide prefatory material that invites them in and makes the key information easy to find.
© Dean Drobot/123RF

Origin of the Report The first part of your introduction might be a review of the **facts of authorization**. If you decide to include this part, you should present such facts as when, how, and by whom the report was authorized. Information of this kind is particularly useful in reports that have no transmittal message.

Problem and Purpose As Chapter 11 explains, a vital part of almost every report's introduction is a statement of its problem and purpose.

The problem statement is a description of the problem or situation that prompted the investigation. The complexity of the problem and the readers' familiarity with it will determine how much description you need to provide. In many cases, one or two statements will suffice. In cases where the problem is very complex, you may need to provide a short description of the problem here and then go into further detail in a later section of your report (for example, the background section).

The purpose statement conveys the goal of your investigation. In essense, it says, "given the problem or situation that needed addressing, this is what I tried to find out." For example, if your company needs an Internet-use policy, your purpose statement might say that you analyzed other companies' policies to determine guidelines for your company's policy. See the last two paragraphs of the sample long report in this chapter for an illustration.

Scope If the **scope** of your report is not clearly indicated in any of the other introductory parts, you may need to include it in its own subsection. By *scope* we mean the boundaries of your investigation. In this part of the introduction—in plain, clear language—you should describe what parts of the problem you studied and what parts you didn't.

Limitations In some reports, you will need to explain **limitations**. By *limitations* we mean anything that keeps your report from being an ideal treatment of the problem. No real-world problem can be completely explored, and because different writers will approach the same problem differently, what seems complete to one person may not seem complete to another. But in certain cases, you will want to state explicitly what forms of research were not employed so your readers will know how to evaluate your information.

For example, if time constraints permitted only a quick email survey rather than in-depth interviews of your sources, you would say so. Or if a major source of information was unavailable (perhaps a key expert had left the company or relevant industry reports were too expensive), you would note this limitation in your report. You might also indicate the extent to which your findings can be applied to similar situations.

Be frank in this section but not too negative. State clearly what was not done and why, but do so without apology or such negative wording as "impair" or "compromised the validity of our findings." If you have done a good job with the resources at your disposal, this section of the report can use a directness that shows confidence in the report's usefulness despite its limitations.

Background Knowledge of the history of the problem is sometimes essential to understanding the report, so you may need to cover that history in your introduction. Your general aim in this part is to acquaint the readers with how the problem developed and what has been done about it thus far. You should bring out the main issues and then focus on the part of the problem that your report will address.

Sources and Methods of Collecting Information You usually need to tell the readers how you collected the information in the report. You should specify whether you used published research, surveys, experiments, qualitative research, or a combination of methods and describe the steps you followed. Include enough detail about your research to allow your readers to assess it and to convince them that your work was done competently.

In reports based on published research, this section can be short. If most of your findings came from a few sources, you can name the sources. If you used a large number of sources, you can just describe the types of sources you used and then cite the sources with footnotes as you use them. If you include a bibliography, you may refer to that as well.

Using a Table of Contents Generator for Speed and Accuracy

Word's table of contents generator frees you from having to format the table of contents and make sure its entries and their page numbers match those in the report. Just a few clicks produce and format the table of contents, along with leaders and page numbers. Additionally, this tool enables you to add links so that those reading the report on the screen rather than on paper can easily navigate to a particular section or page by simply clicking it in the table of contents.

The table of contents generator works with Word's built-in styles, which you use as tags to mark the different levels of headings that will be included in the table of contents. If you are using a standard report template, styles are already incorporated in it. If you are creating your own report from a blank document, you could use predefined styles or define your own styles to create titles, headings, and subheads. Styles provide consistency so that headings at certain levels always appear the same, helping the reader see the relationship between the parts of your report.

Furthermore, if you decide to change the material in your report after you have generated the table of contents, you can simply regenerate it to update the headings and page numbers.

Shown here is a sample table of contents automatically created in Word 2016.

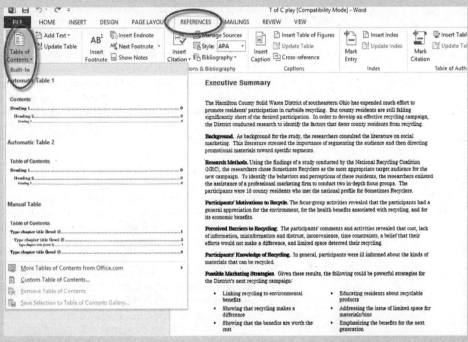

Source: Microsoft Word 2016.

Contents

Source: Kathryn Rentz.

More complex research requires a more detailed description. If you conducted a survey, for example, you probably would need to explain how you chose your sample, how you developed the survey, and how and when you administered it. If you conducted an experiment, you would need to describe its design carefully. Whatever your method, you should include enough detail so that readers can judge the reliability and validity of your findings.

Definitions of Special Terms and Acronyms If you use terms or acronyms that are likely to be unfamiliar to readers of the report, you'll need to define these. For extremely long technical reports, you may need to provide a separate terminology page after the table of contents or at the end of the report. But for most reports, you can define each term in the text or in a footnote when it is first used, or you can define all unfamiliar terms in a separate part of the introduction. If you use the latter method, begin this part with an introductory statement and then list the terms with their definitions.

Report Preview In very long reports, the final part of the introduction should preview the report structure. In this part you tell the readers how the body of the report is organized—what topics will be taken up first, second, third, and so on. Such forecasting statements aid your readers' comprehension by giving them an orderly framework for what they're about to read.

The Report Body
After the introductory material comes the body of the report. Here is where the information that has been collected is presented and related to the problem. In a sense, the report body *is* the report. With the exception of the conclusion or recommendation sections, the other parts of the report are attached parts.

You can use the advice presented in Chapter 11 to organize your content. As that chapter also advises, you may choose the personal or impersonal style, but whichever you choose should be interesting and clear. Using guidelines discussed in Chapter 3, you should format this part of the report for easy comprehension, and any visuals you include should follow the guidelines discussed in Chapter 4. If you've used outside sources, these should be noted and documented as illustrated in this chapter's sample long report and in Reference Chapter B. In short, writing this major section of the long, formal report will require virtually all your organizing, writing, and formatting skills.

The Ending of the Report
You can end your report in any number of ways: with a **summary**, a **conclusions section**, a **recommendations section**, or a combination. Your choice depends on the purpose of your report. But whatever your choice, be sure to use helpful formatting to make the key points stand out. This section is where the main payoffs of the report are stated. Do not make your reader struggle through dense paragraphs of text to find them.

Ending Summary When the purpose of the report is to present information, the ending is logically a summary of the major findings. Long informational reports often have minor summaries at the ends of the major sections. These can be collected and restated to form your report's overall summary.

You should not confuse the ending summary with the executive summary. The executive summary is a prefatory part of the report; the ending summary is part of the report text. Also, the executive summary is more complete than the ending summary. The executive summary reviews the entire report, from the problem and purpose statements to the research methods to the findings and conclusions and/or recommendations, whereas the ending summary reviews only the major findings of the report.

Conclusions Reports must often do more than just present information; they usually need to analyze that information in light of the problem and, from this analysis, reach a conclusion or conclusions.

The makeup of the conclusions section varies from case to case. In investigations for which a single answer is needed (e.g., "Has our new schedule reduced our utility costs?"), this section normally reviews the preceding information and analyses and, from this review, arrives at the answer. For more complex investigations (e.g., "How do employees feel about the new schedule?"), the report may treat each topic in a separate section and draw conclusions in each section. The conclusions section of such a report would then collect and summarize these previous conclusions.

On the other hand, you should avoid mechanically repeating the findings you've already stated in earlier sections. Some interpretation is appropriate here. Put the findings back into the context of the overall problem and help the reader see what they mean in terms of the problem (e.g., why employees may have responded as they did).

Recommendations When the goal of the report is not only to draw conclusions but also to present a course of action, recommendations are in order. You may provide them in a separate section following the conclusions section, or you may include them in the conclusions section. Whether you include recommendations should be determined by whether the readers want or expect them.

Appended Parts Sometimes you will need to include a **bibliography**, an **appendix**, or both at the end of the report, depending on the report's contents and purpose.

Bibliography When your investigation makes heavy use of published sources, you will normally need to include either footnotes, a bibliography, or both. The construction of these is described in Reference Chapter B.

Appendix An appendix, as its name implies, is something appended (attached) to the main report and, for that reason, is always put last. You use appendices for supplementary information that supports the body of the report, such as questionnaires, summary tables, and relevant documents.

As a rule, an appendix should not include the charts, graphs, and tables that directly support the report's findings. These should be placed in the body of the report because it is not convenient for readers to have to flip to the appendix to find the data they need. Put in the appendix only those visuals that are too large or complex to insert into the body of the report.

The Formal Report Illustrated

Falling at the top level of formality and length in Exhibit 12-1, the Annotated Example that follows includes all the prefatory parts listed in the exhibit. Because it contains numerous graphs, it also includes a list of figures, and because it reports survey findings, it presents a copy of the survey as an appendix.

The president of a successful company that is anticipating significant growth wanted to know the extent to which the company might already have begun to outgrow its informal internal communication methods. He assigned the human resources director the task of finding out. After receiving further direction from the president, she designed, tested, and conducted an employee survey. This report presents her findings. Realizing that the report will be shared with the whole executive team, if not all the managers, and that it may be used as a reference for some time to come, she prepared the report in full formal style.

Identifying the Communication Gaps

at WorkWare:

Results of a 2017 Employee Survey

Title fly—for the most formal reports

WorkWare, Inc.

Identifying the Communication Gaps at WorkWare:

Results of a 2017 Employee Survey

Title page repeats the title . . .

Prepared for
Joseph Bryson, President

Prepared by
Sarah Lockwood, Human Resources Director

. . . and adds additional information

February 16, 2017

WorkWare, Inc.
Berkshire Office Park, Suite 700
Atlanta, GA 30327
(404) 233-3197
www.workware.com

February 16, 2017

Joseph Bryson, President
WorkWare, Inc.

Dear Joe,

First paragraph contains orienting information

This report contains the results of the communication study that we discussed on January 23. As you requested, I conducted a company-wide online survey to identify the areas in which employees feel well informed as well as any areas in which their communication needs are not being met.

Body conveys the gist of the report

The report revealed several topics on which employees would like to receive and send more information. I believe we can interpret this desire, in large part, as a result of the great team spirit that has been cultivated at WorkWare. Employees want to be an even more integral part of the company's success while also achieving personal success here.

In light of these findings, the report recommends several strategies that can be implemented to strengthen internal communication at WorkWare as the company continues to grow.

Ending is positive and forward looking

Thank you for helping me conduct this informative study. I look forward to discussing the findings and recommendations with you and the rest of the executive team.

Sincerely,

Sarah

Sarah Lockwood
Human Resources Director

Letter of transmittal "hands over" the report

Table of Contents

Entries match the report's headings

Table of contents previews the report's structure

[iv]

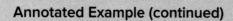

List of Figures

Separate figures list makes it easy to go directly to a figure

[v]

Executive Summary

Over the course of a mere 12 years, WorkWare has become an employer of almost 100 people and the leading developer of software for independent construction contractors. A strong element of this success has been the company's tight-knit culture. With growth, however, have come "stress fractures," to use President Bryson's words, and these will only intensify as WorkWare expands. To determine how well the company's internal communication is currently meeting employees' needs and to plan for their future information needs, President Bryson asked me to conduct an employee survey.

Identifies the problem and the research purpose

Survey Method

Working with President Bryson, I developed a brief SurveyMonkey survey that asked employees about the sufficiency of the information they receive and send on various work-related topics. I then pilot-tested the survey with five employees. The survey was sent to all employees on January 30, 2017, and they were given two weeks to participate. They received one reminder before the survey closed on February 13. Of the 98 recipients, 49 responded to at least part of the survey, for a response rate of 50%.

Provides considerable detail to build credibility

Findings

Presents the report in brief and matches its indirect pattern

In terms of information they receive, the participants indicated that they feel relatively well informed about *benefits and pay, what to do each day, how hard to work,* and *the company's successes, goals, and business environment.* They indicated a particular need for additional information on these topics:

- *Promotion and advancement paths, how they're being evaluated,* and *how to succeed at WorkWare.*

- *How well WorkWare is performing, organizational decisions that will affect them,* and *what's going on with other employees and in other departments.*

They also would like to have *more timely communication.* The managers registered greater communication needs than the non-managerial employees on several topics related to being kept in the loop on company operations.

In terms of information they send, employees are relatively satisfied with the information they share about *their daily work* and *their peers' performance.*

The employees overall would like to contribute more to *decisions regarding their workgroup and the company* and to give more *feedback on their managers' performance.*

The managers would especially like to give *more performance feedback to their direct reports as well as to their superiors,* to have a greater amount of *communication with those in other departments,* and to have more input into *decisions affecting the company and their workgroups.* They also feel that they should be *communicating more with their workgroups.*

Captures the key findings

Recommendations

The executive team is on target with its efforts to create more room for advancement in the company. A more systematic performance-feedback system, an enhanced internal communication network, the designation of a part-time internal-communications director, and more managerial training can all help the company maintain its team-like culture during the next period of growth.

Previews the recommendations but minimizes them to prevent a resistant reaction

[vi]

Identifying the Communication Gaps at WorkWare:
Results of a 2017 Employee Survey

Introduction

WorkWare has experienced much success since its beginnings 12 years ago. It has grown from a one-office operation into the industry leader in its software niche. It also leads in terms of employee engagement and satisfaction, as evidenced by the fact that its employees have voted the company onto the region's "Best Places to Work" list for the last five years.

Provides the context and puts readers in a receptive mood

Having reached a size of nearly 100 employees, the company is now poised to move into its next developmental stage. It is of great importance to the executive team that the company maintain its close-knit culture as much as possible during the anticipated expansion.

Identifies the report problem

President Bryson thus requested that I conduct a survey to determine how well the company's internal communication is currently meeting employees' needs. As he said in a pre-survey interview, the company is already showing "stress fractures" because it is starting to outgrow its small-business model. He wanted to identify any communication gaps the employees are experiencing and to begin collecting ideas for ways to meet their information needs as the organization grows.

Identifies the report's purpose and main contents

To achieve these purposes, I conducted a brief company-wide survey. This report discusses the communication gaps revealed by the study and proposes several actions that WorkWare might take in order to strengthen and maintain its cohesive culture.

Survey Method

I met with President Bryson on January 23, 2017, to learn what he wanted the survey to achieve. During this hour-long interview, we discussed what kinds of questions to ask on the survey and how to conduct it.

Based on my conversation with President Bryson, I drafted a SurveyMonkey survey to send to all non-executive employees. I then met with two employees in the Tech Department (one employee, one manager) and three in Customer Services (one employee, two managers) to have them walk through the survey and indicate ways it could be improved. Their input led to the final version of the survey.

I sent a link to the online survey to all employees via an email message on January 30. I assured the employees that their responses would be kept anonymous. President Bryson also sent out an employee-wide email encouraging the employees to participate and to provide their honest feedback. The recipients were given two weeks to participate. Toward the end of that time period, I sent out one more request for participation. The survey was closed on February 13.

Research specifics build confidence in the study

The recipients were asked to indicate the following:

Previewing the survey questions aids readers' comprehension

- The amount of information they currently receive on 18 topics versus the amount they would like to receive. To do so, they used a scale from 1 to 5, with 1 meaning "very little or no information" and 5 meaning "a lot of information."
- How satisfied they are with the timeliness of the information they receive, with 1 meaning "very dissatisfied" and 5 meaning "very satisfied."
- The amount of information they currently send on nine topics versus the amount they would like to send. To do so, they used a scale from 1 to 5, with 1 meaning "very little or no information" and 5 meaning "a lot of information."

A demographic question at the beginning of the survey enabled me to compare the responses of the managerial and non-managerial employees. A copy of the survey is provided in the appendix to this report.

Of the 98 recipients, 49 responded to at least part of the survey, for a response rate of 50%. The response rate for managers was 16 out of 18, for an 89% response rate; for non-managerial employees, it was 33 out of 80, for a response rate of 41%.

Findings: Information Received

This section presents the respondents' answers to the question asking them to rate how much information they receive and how much they would like to receive. For ease of reading, I have divided their ratings on 18 topics into two categories: *information received about their jobs* and *information received about WorkWare*.

Previews the section's contents

This section also presents the respondents' answers to the question *"How satisfied are you with the timeliness of the information you receive?"*

Finally, it compares the managers' information needs to those of the non-managerial employees.

Levels of headings are formatted to convey a clear hierarchy

Total Responses

In all, there were 49 respondents for this question—16 managers and 33 non-managerial employees.

About Their Jobs

Figure 1 shows how the respondents as a whole assessed the amount of information they receive regarding their jobs.

Provides a lead-in to the visual

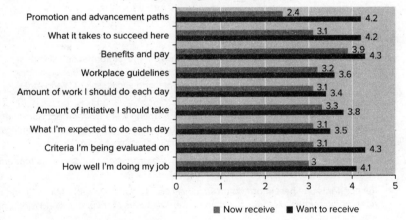

Figure 1:

Total Responses on Information Received about Their Jobs

(n=49 [16 managers, 33 employees])

All visuals are numbered and clearly labeled

In this figure, two main patterns stand out:

- Respondents registered the biggest information gaps on the top two and bottom two topics: *promotion and advancement paths* (a 1.8 gap), *what it takes to succeed here* (1.1), *criteria I'm being evaluated on* (1.2), and *how well I'm doing my job* (1.1).

- Respondents feel a greater need for information about the top three and the bottom two topics (each with a "want to receive" level of 4.1 or higher) than for the four topics in between (with a "want to receive" level between 3.4 and 3.8).

Analysis notes the most important information in the visual

These findings indicate that WorkWare managers and employees feel relatively well informed about their daily work and about employee benefits and policies, but they do not feel well informed about their longer-term prospects of succeeding and advancing at WorkWare.

Provides a helpful interpretation and summary

[2]

Annotated Example (continued)

About the Company

Figure 2 shows how the respondents feel about the information they receive regarding the company as a whole.

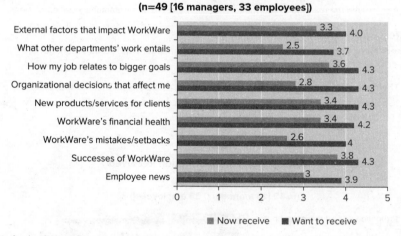

Figure 2:
Total Responses on Information Received
about WorkWare
(n=49 [16 managers, 33 employees])

As the figure shows,

- The four topics on which the respondents want the most information (all with a 4.3 rating) are *how my job relates to bigger goals, organizational decisions that affect me, new products and services for clients,* and *successes of WorkWare.* A fifth topic, *WorkWare's financial health,* followed closely (4.2).

- The two topics that got the lowest "importance" rating were *what other departments' work entails* (3.7) and *employee news* (3.9)—but respondents registered a significant information gap on both these topics (1.2 and .9 points, respectively).

- The topics with the largest information gaps were *organizational decisions that affect me* (1.5) and *WorkWare's mistakes/setbacks* (1.4).

- Respondents feel best informed on *successes of WorkWare* (a gap of only .5) and on *how my job relates to bigger goals* and *external factors that impact WorkWare* (both with a gap of .7)

Notes the highlights and interprets them

Internal communications about WorkWare's successes, goals, and business environment seem to have been quite effective, as one would expect given our company's team-like culture. But employees crave more of this information, as well as additional company information (e.g., WorkWare's setbacks; employee news) and more communication about organizational decisions.

Timeliness of Information

Using boldface type makes the key findings stand out.

Respondents were also asked to rate their degree of satisfaction with the *timeliness* of the information they receive, with 1 meaning "very dissatisfied" and 5 meaning "very satisfied." The **average rating on this question was 3.4** (n=48). The **most common answer was 3** (the answer for 20 out of the 48 responses).

[3]

Respondents added these comments in the comment box that accompanied the question:

Provides all the comments because the readers will want them (could be put into an appendix instead, depending on the number of comments and the readers' likely preference)

- "Usually we will get the information after the incident. However, it would be much better if we get the information in advance."
- "It happens usually via email or face to face contact."
- "Usually get everything in a timely manner."
- "On some things I get the information right away but others I don't. Like when someone leaves the company a company notice should go out. It has at certain times but not others."
- "We always have an open forum throughout the company, and I feel very comfortable speaking to my direct managers, my VP, as well as other executives about anything. They're always open to discuss anything freely with us that they feel is pertinent to our performance. The executive team is a unique, honor driven group that actually looks out for the best not only for the company, but their employees as well. This is a unique culture we have, and we are all truly a 'Family'!"
- "There are times when we are provided information it is timely (email from the CEO, for example). There are other times when information is not provided at all."
- "Extremely important news comes quickly almost too soon and when it does, it ruins a holiday for people. Then the smaller items are non-existent or the information comes too late."
- "I often feel out of the loop."
- "An internal newsletter or feed from an intranet would be helpful on new announcements from each department."
- "Could use more updates on company news, financial goals, career paths, etc."
- "Most communications come out within a timely manner."
- "I am confident that any important information has been and will be shared with me quickly as needed."
- "The only thing I'd like is more feedback on my performance, but I've spoken with my manager about this before and I understand that this point is a struggle for them too. If I worry about something and want immediate feedback, I just go ask for it."

Section Summary

Several executives have mentioned that finding ways to promote employees in a company with so little room at the top is a problem, so the employees' strong desire to learn more about advancement paths (the topic with the biggest information gap) is not surprising.

But these other points also seem to warrant executive attention:

Provides a summary that distills the information presented thus far before providing more data

- The information gaps on *what it takes to succeed here* (1.1), *criteria I'm being evaluated on* (1.2), and *how well I'm doing my job* (1.1) suggest that WorkWare needs more robust performance-feedback methods.

- While employees feel relatively well informed about WorkWare's successes, the notable information gaps on *organizational decisions that affect me* (1.5) and *WorkWare's mistakes/setbacks* (1.4) indicates a strong desire to be better informed about the company as a whole.

- Employees are a bit less interested in *what other departments' work entails* and *employee news,* probably because these factors affect them less directly than the others. But they still reported significant information gaps on these topics (1.2 and .9).

The latter two points, as well as respondents' relatively low rating for the timeliness of the information they receive, indicate that WorkWare needs a better system for communicating news about the company as a whole, as well as about departments and individuals.

[4]

Annotated Example (continued)

Managers' vs. Non-managerial Employees' Responses

The following sections compare the managers' and non-managerial employees' information needs as indicated by their responses to the "information received" question.

About Their Jobs

Figures 3 and 4 show how the managerial and non-managerial employees feel about the information they receive about their jobs.

Appropriately discusses these two graphs together since their data are being compared.

Uses lead-ins to avoid stacked headings and abruptness

Figure 3:
Managers' Responses on Information Received about Their Jobs
(n=16)

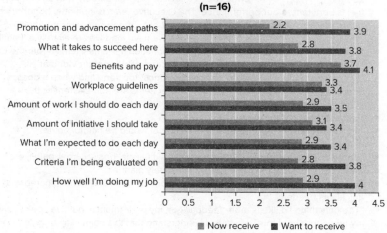

Figure 4:
Non-managerial Employees' Responses on Information Received about Their Jobs
(n=33)

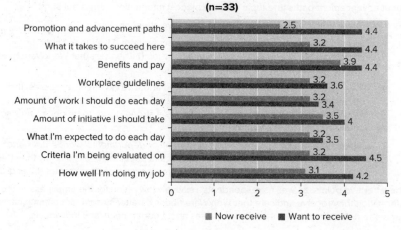

[5]

Annotated Example (continued)

The two most noteworthy findings were these:

- As the "want to receive" ratings in the two graphs show, employees tend to want/ need more information than the managers. Their indicated desire for information often reached into the 4 range, whereas the managerial employees' responses tended to be in the 3 range.

- The two groups registered the largest information gaps on the same four topics (*promotion and advancement paths, what it takes to succeed here, criteria I'm being evaluated on,* and *how well I'm doing my job*). The gaps they registered on these topics are very similar.

It makes sense that the managers feel somewhat more satisfied with the information they receive about their jobs than the non-managerial employees. They have more face time with the company leaders and tend to have been at the company longer.

Uses knowledge of the context to interpret the data

Like the non-managerial employees, though, the managerial employees crave performance feedback and a better sense of how to shape a successful career with WorkWare.

About the Company

Figures 5 and 6 show how managers and employees feel about information they receive about the company as a whole.

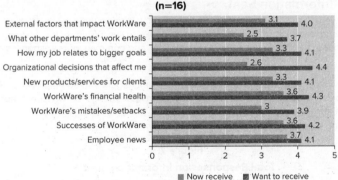

Figure 5:

Managers' Responses on Information Received about WorkWare

(n=16)

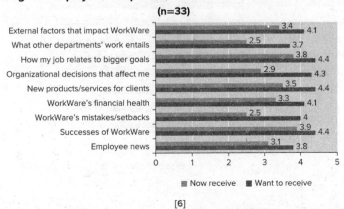

Figure 6:

Non-managerial Employees' Responses on Information Received about WorkWare

(n=33)

[6]

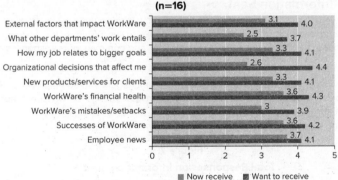

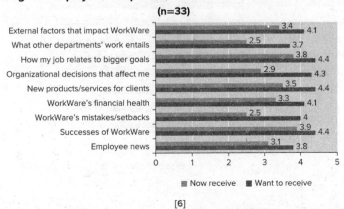

As you can see,

- Here, too, the employees registered larger information needs overall than the managers.

- But the reported information gaps were a bit larger for the managers on four topics:

    ○ *External factors that impact WorkWare* (.9 versus .7 for the employees)

    ○ *How my job relates to bigger goals* (.8 versus .6)

    ○ *Organizational decisions that affect me* (1.8 versus 1.4)

    ○ *Successes of WorkWare* (.6 versus .5).

- Both groups registered a large (and the same) information gap—1.2—on *what other departments' work entails.*

Section Summary

Both employees and managers experience a shortage of information on *promotion and advancement paths, what it takes to succeed here, criteria I'm being evaluated on, how well I'm doing my job,* and *what other departments' work entails.* Becoming a manager, then, does not seem to reduce employees' desire for more performance feedback and for information on how their department's work relates to that of the other departments.

The managers reported noticeably larger information gaps than the non-managerial employees on *external factors that affect WorkWare, how my job relates to bigger goals, organizational decisions that affect me,* and *successes of WorkWare.* In other words, they feel that they need a better view of the bigger managerial picture to be able to manage as effectively as possible.

Provides another section summary to help readers retain what they just read

Findings: Information Sent

Participants were then asked to indicate for 9 work-related topics *how much information they're expected to send* and *how much they would like to send.* This section first presents the total responses and then compares the managers' and non-managers' responses.

Total Responses

In all, there were 47 respondents for this question—17 managers and 30 employees. (Note: Since most of the employees do not have direct reports, the ratings for "My direct reports' performance" include only 7 employees' responses.)

Explains a seeming quirk in the data

Figure 7 shows the overall responses.

Figure 7:

Total Responses on Information Sent

(n=47 [17 managers, 30 employees])

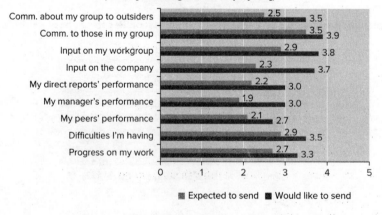

[7]

The respondents indicated a desire to send more information on all nine topics, particularly on the following (listed in descending order):

- *Input on the company* (a 1.4 gap)
- *My manager's performance* (a 1.2 gap)
- *Communication about my group to outsiders* (a 1.0 gap)
- *Input on my workgroup* (a .9 gap)
- *My direct reports' performance* (a .8 gap)

As in previous analyses, does the math for the readers

They are the most satisfied with *communication to those in my group* (only a .4 shortfall) and seem to be relatively satisfied with the amount of communication they're sending about *my peers' performance, difficulties I'm having,* and *progress on my work.*

Overall, they seem to feel well connected to their workgroups and to their managers, but they want greater input on decisions and processes at both the workgroup and the company level. They also want more opportunity to evaluate their managers and share with other departments what their group does.

The respondents made these additional comments:

Provides the comments to aid the readers' interpretation

- "No mistake, not looking for daily or weekly micro reporting. Would like productive exchange of ideas monthly or quarterly."
- "I'd like to tell somebody what a good job my boss is doing, but they know that already."
- "Information I am expected to send? There are currently no set expectations—we've got an open door policy, so much of this is accomplished without providing specific information."
- "I don't understand how or what information I am supposed to send about my managers performance."
- "Again—we have a very unique culture where there is no 'Competition' to 'Get Ahead' for promotional aspects. We all work together as a cohesive unit."
- "For the majority of these items, no expectations were set with me. The impression I get is that my input and suggestions are not valuable enough for me to submit them. Or, management has already made up their mind and asking for input is just procedural."
- "Inter-department communication is an issue but there has not been enough definition around what is desired by whom."

Managers' vs. Non-managerial Employees' Responses

Figures 8 and 9 show the managers' and non-managerial employees' desire to communicate, as indicated by their responses to this question. (Note: The employees' responses on *my direct reports' performance* represent only 7 people.)

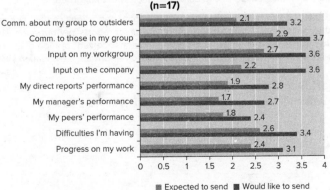

Figure 8:

Managers' Responses on Information Sent

(n=17)

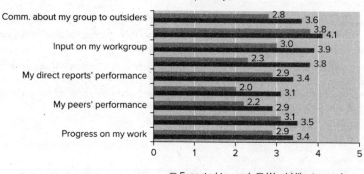

**Figure 9:
Non-managerial Employees' Responses
on Information Sent
(n=30)**

Comm. about my group to outsiders: 2.8, 3.6
3.8, 4.1
Input on my workgroup: 3.0, 3.9
2.3, 3.8
My direct reports' performance: 2.9, 3.4
2.0, 3.1
My peers' performance: 2.2, 2.9
3.1, 3.5
Progress on my work: 2.9, 3.4

■ Expected to send ■ Would like to send

Both groups reported relatively large communication gaps on these topics:

- *Input on the company* (a gap of 1.4 for the managers, 1.5 for the employees)
- *My manager's performance* (a gap of 1.0 for the managers, 1.1 for the employees)
- *Input on my workgroup* (a gap of .9 for both groups)

The managers reported a notably larger gap on *communication to outsiders* (a 1.1 gap versus .8 for the employees), *communication to those in my group* (a .9 gap versus only a .3 for employees), and *my direct reports' performance* (a .9 versus .6 for the employees). They are also somewhat less satisfied than the employees on information sent about *difficulties I'm having* and *progress on my work.*

Overall, the managers are experiencing more of a communication gap in terms of information sent than the non-managerial employees are. One likely reason is that, as managers, they would naturally want to contribute more to company decisions and represent their workgroups to other groups more than non-managerial employees would.

What is less clear is why they feel they send too little communication to those in their workgroups and provide too little input into how their own groups operate. Perhaps they simply wish they had more time to manage their groups. But they may also need more guidance on management of and communication with their groups.

It also seems noteworthy that the managers want to send significantly more information than they're currently expected to send on *my direct reports' performance.* This finding, together with several findings from the "information received" portion of this report, suggests that they would like a better-developed performance-evaluation system.

Summary and interpretation of the preceding data help prepare readers for the writer's recommendations

Now puts all the findings together for easy review/ reference

Report Summary

This section provides a synopsis of the key findings from the survey.

[9]

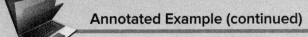
About Information Received

WorkWare has dedicated employees who have been encouraged to think of themselves as team or "family" members. Not surprisingly, then, the respondents registered a desire for more information on all 18 work- and company-related topics they were asked about. But they need more information on some topics than on others:

- Overall, the team feels quite knowledgeable about *benefits and pay* and fairly secure about *what to do each day* and *how hard to work*. But they want much more information about *promotion and advancement paths* (something the executive team already knows), as well as about *how they're being evaluated* and *how to succeed at WorkWare*.

- They feel relatively well informed about *the successes, goals, and business environment in which WorkWare operates,* but they want to be in the know more about *how well WorkWare is performing, organizational decisions that will affect them,* and *what's going on with other employees and in other departments.*

- The company's communications were not rated highly on *timeliness* (an average score of only 3.4 on a 5-point scale). The informal communications that worked well when WorkWare was a smaller company now seem to be falling short of the employees' needs. The employees still indicate a strong team spirit, but the company has grown to the point where intermittent executive emails, employee meetings, and face-to-face encounters are not sufficient to keep people informed.

- The managers indicated greater communication needs than the non-managerial employees on *external factors affecting WorkWare, how their jobs fit into WorkWare's goals, organizational decisions,* and *WorkWare's successes.* In other words, they want more information about and involvement in the big picture.

Readable formatting helps the key findings stand out: negative findings are clearly but tactfully reported

About Information Sent

Incorporates positive language when possible

The respondents registered a need to send more information on all nine topics they were asked about. Here, too, this can be viewed as a good sign: People who work at WorkWare want to be an active part of the team because that is the culture that WorkWare has cultivated. But as with "information received," several reported gaps warrant attention.

- The employees overall are relatively satisfied with the *information they share about their daily work* and *their peers' performance,* but they indicated a noticeable desire to contribute more to *decisions regarding their workgroup and the company* and to give *feedback on their managers' performance.*

- The managers registered an especially noteworthy desire to give *more performance feedback to their direct reports as well as to their superiors.* More so than the non-managerial employees, they would also like to have a greater amount of *communication with those in other departments* and have more input into *decisions affecting the company and their workgroups.* They also feel that they should *communicate with their workgroups* more.

Recommendations

"The good and bad thing is that WorkWare is a family." That comment, made by President Bryson during my interview with him, goes a long way toward summing up what is working well at WorkWare and what practices are becoming problematic as WorkWare continues to grow.

Captures the gist of the report

[10]

The survey findings indicate that these areas need to be addressed:

- **The need for greater opportunity for advancement.** The executive team is well aware that there is little vertical room at WorkWare. In fact, this factor has played a role in their decision to expand the company. The survey responses indicate that employees' desire for promotion room is indeed very real.

  ➢ Recommendation: When the time seems right, communicate with employees about the executive team's efforts to address this problem so that loyal employees who are getting frustrated with the lack of upward mobility will know that the team is working on it.

- **The need for clearer performance evaluation criteria and a more systematic evaluation process.** A subset of the "information received" data—findings regarding *what it takes to succeed here, criteria I'm being evaluated on,* and *how well I'm doing my job*—indicates a strong desire for more explicit performance criteria and clearer evaluative feedback. The respondents also indicated a relatively strong desire to be able to evaluate their managers' and peers' performance.

  ➢ Recommendation: Assess the ways we currently give performance feedback and explore options for adopting a more systematic method, one that would enable upward, lateral, and downward feedback.

- **The need for better support for internal communication.** The findings indicate strongly that the time has come for more a more robust internal communication system at WorkWare.

  ➢ Recommendation: Set up a cross-functional, intergenerational team to explore various platforms (electronic newsletter? intranet with social-networking capabilities? virtual town-hall meetings?) for keeping the "family" in the loop—not only in terms of company news but also in terms of what's going on in the different departments. This team will need to take into account the critical role that face-to-face communication has played in WorkWare's success and find creative ways to sustain and/or mimic this important medium.

  ➢ Recommendation: When the time seems right, designate an internal-communication director. Overseeing this area of operations has become too big a job to tack onto a busy executive's list of responsibilities. Perhaps the company could assign a current or new employee this responsibility as well as a role in another area of the company, such as marketing or HR. A full-time position for a director of communications could be created later, if warranted by the company's growth.

- **The need for more systematic managerial training.** Most of WorkWare's managers worked their way up from entry-level jobs or are friends or family of people who already worked here, so their company loyalty is very strong. The knowledge that they have absorbed about WorkWare's culture is one of their best assets. But they would like to understand better how they fit into the company's strategic goals and overall operations, and they could use more coaching on communicating with, and giving feedback to, their groups.

  ➢ Recommendation: Create a more formal version of the mentoring that is currently taking place; and hold managerial events, such as retreats and regular meetings, to enable the managers to learn from each other and be more involved in the executive team's thinking.

Recommendations show an understanding of the company and are worded to keep the focus on the ideas, not the writer

Formatting aids comprehension

Looking Ahead

WorkWare has a close-knit culture in which employees feel known, valued, and engaged in a meaningful team effort. Sustaining this culture will be one of the company's main challenges as it grows. But as the relatively high level of participation in this study and the apparent honesty of the respondents attest, WorkWare's "no fear" climate has encouraged a strong sense of ownership on the part of the employees. The evidence is strong that, with their creative input, WorkWare will find ways to grow while maintaining the qualities that have made it the undisputed leader in its market and a workplace where dedicated employees pull together to achieve success.

Provides a forward-looking but realistic ending

[11]

Annotated Example (continued)

Appendix: The Employee Survey

Shows readers exactly what was asked and how

Page 1:

Which group of employees do you fall within?
- o People manager (with direct reports)
- o Professional/technical/other salaried employee

Page 2:

For each topic below, indicate . . .
—the amount of **information you now receive** (1 = very little or no information; 5 = a lot of information) and
—the amount of **information you would like to receive** (1 = very little or no information; 5 = a lot of information)

	Amount of information I now receive	Amount I'd like to receive
How well I'm doing my job		
The criteria I'm being evaluated on		
What I'm expected to work on each day		
The amount of initiative I'm expected to take		
The amount of work I'm expected to do each day		
Workplace guidelines (e.g., attendance, conduct)		
Company-wide employee news (e.g., new hires, promotions)		
Employee benefits and pay		
What it takes to succeed here		
Promotion and advancement paths here		
Successes of WorkWare		
WorkWare's mistakes and setbacks		
WorkWare's financial health		
New applications and services for our clients		
Organizational decisions that affect me		
How my job relates to company goals		
What other departments' work entails		
External factors that impact WorkWare (e.g., our clients, our industry)		

You can add explanations or comments here [a text field was provided].

Page 3:

How satisfied are you with the **timeliness** of the information you receive? (1 = very dissatisfied; 5 = very satisfied) _____
Explain briefly [a text field was provided].

[12]

Page 4:

For each topic below, indicate . . .
—the amount of **information you're expected to send** (1 = very little or no information; 5 = a lot of information) and
—the amount of **information you would like to send** (1 = very little or no information; 5 = a lot of information).

	Amount I'm expected to send	Amount I'd like to send
Progress on the projects I'm working on		
Difficulties I'm having on the job		
My peers' performance		
My manager's performance		
My direct reports' performance (if applicable)		
Input on company-wide decisions that affect me		
Input on my workgroup's decisions and processes		
Communication to members of my workgroup		
Communication to those in other workgroups about the work my group does		

You can add explanations or comments here [a text field was provided].

[13]

Power Charge Your Professionalism: Use Apostrophes Correctly

Many writers throw up their hands in defeat when it comes to apostrophes, feeling that they can't possibly remember the rules. You don't have to! You can use Reference Chapter A or a grammar handbook (in print or online) to help you. But, in truth, the rules are not that hard to learn. You could probably master them in 30 minutes or less.

Using your memory or a guide, choose the correct answer in the following sentences. Then explain why you made the choice you did for each one.

1. This report has eight entries in (its/it's/its') list of illustrations.
2. All the (figure's/figures/figures') titles in this report are missing the figure number.
3. The report did not identify (whose/who's) error caused the problem.
4. All of the upper-level (manager's/managers/managers') requested a copy of the report.
5. The reports produced by this research firm are regarded as the (industries/industries'/industry's) best.
6. In some (people's/peoples') opinion, an executive summary should always be in the direct order.
7. The report described (men's/mens') shopping habits.
8. The report represented two (week's/weeks/weeks') worth of work.

Using apostrophes correctly is important because . . .

- Sometimes a misused apostrophe can cause your reader to take a misstep (until he or she figures out that there's an apostrophe error).
- Incorrectly used apostrophes are distracting and convey a negative impression of you as a writer.

For further instruction and practice, do the "Apostrophes" activities under "Punctuation and Mechanics" in LearnSmart Achieve.

Key Terms

Critical-Thinking Questions

1. Which of the prefatory pages of reports appear to be related primarily to the length of the report? Which to the need for formality? **LO1**

2. Describe the role and content of a transmittal message. **LO1**

3. Why is the personal style typically used in the transmittal message? **LO1**

4. Explain how to write the executive summary of a report. **LO1**

5. Why does the executive summary include key facts and figures in addition to the analyses and conclusions drawn from them? **LO1**

6. Explain why some routine report problems require little or no introduction. LO2

7. Why is the direct order generally used in the shorter reports? When is the indirect order desirable for such reports? LO2

8. Describe a situation in which you would use short-report format rather than email format for an internal report. Why would you choose the short-report format? LO3

9. Describe a situation in which you would prepare a memo report rather than an email report for an internal report. Why would you choose the memo format? LO3

10. What kinds of information might go into routine operational reports for different kinds of organizations? Why would these organizations need this information regularly? LO4

11. Given what you've learned about progress reports, suggest a general structure for these reports. What might go into the beginning? What might the middle parts be? What would the conclusion do? LO4

12. How might an internal problem-solving report that has been assigned differ from one on the same subject that an employee generated on his or her own? LO4

13. Discuss the pros and cons of including a list of absentees in meeting minutes. LO4

14. Give examples of long-report problems whose introduction could require historical background or a discussion of the report's limitations. LO5

15. Give examples of report problems that would require, respectively, (a) an ending summary, (b) a conclusion or conclusions section, and (c) a recommendation or recommendations section. LO5

16. Find a long report or white paper and identify the devices it uses to help guide the reader through the report and keep the report's purpose clearly in mind. LO5

Skills-Building Exercises

1. Review the following report situations and determine for each the makeup of the report you would recommend for it. LO1, LO3
   a. A professional research organization has completed a survey of consumer attitudes toward BankOne. The survey results will be presented to the bank president in a 28-page report, including seven charts and three tables.
   b. Joan Marion was asked by her department head to inspect the work area and report on safety conditions. Her report is two pages long and written in personal style.
   c. Bill Wingler has an idea for improving a work procedure in his department at McLaughlin Body Company. His department head suggested that Bill present his idea in a report to the production superintendent. The report is five pages long, including a full-page diagram. It is written in the personal style.
   d. Karen Canady, a worker in the corporate library of Accenture, was asked by Doug Edmunds, its president, for current inventory information on a number of subscriptions. Her report is less than a full page and consists mostly of a list of items and numbers.
   e. Bryan Toups, a sales manager for Johnson and Johnson, was asked by the vice president of marketing to prepare an analysis of the results of a promotional campaign conducted in Toups's district. The report is six pages long (including one chart).

2. Making any assumptions needed, construct complete yet concise titles for the reports described here. LO1
   a. A report writer reviewed records of exit interviews of employees at Marvel-Floyd Manufacturing Company who left their jobs voluntarily. The objective of the investigation was to determine the reasons for their leaving.
   b. A researcher studied data from employee personnel records at Magna-Tech, Inc. to determine whether permanent long-term employees differ from short-term employees. Some of the differences found would be used in hiring employees in the future. The data studied included age, education, experience, and scores on pre-employment tests.

c. A report writer compared historical financial records (2006 to the present) of Super Saver Foods to determine whether this grocery chain should own or rent store buildings. In the past it has done both.

3. Critique the following beginning sentences of transmittal messages. LO1, LO5
    a. "In your hands is the report you requested January 7 concerning. . . ."
    b. "As you will recall, last January 7 you requested a report on. . . ."
    c. "I recommend that we open a new outlet in Bragg City, based on the research you asked me to conduct."
    d. "Thank you for giving me this interesting report assignment."

4. Following is a report that was written for the manager of a large furniture retail store by the manager's assistant. The manager was concerned about customer complaints of late deliveries of their furniture and wanted to know the cause of the delays. Critique this report. LO2, LO4

> 11-17-16
>
> TO: Martina Kalavoda
>
> FROM: Anthony Dudrow
>
> SUBJECT: Investigation requested 11-17-16
>
> This morning at the staff meeting it was requested that an investigation be made of the status of home deliveries and of the causes of the delays that have occurred. The investigation has been made with findings as follows.
>
> Now that a new driver's helper, Morris Tunney, has been hired, there should be no more delays. This was the cause of the problem.
>
> Over the past two weeks (10 working days), a total of 143 deliveries were made; and of these, 107 were made on or before the date promised. But some of the deliveries were late because of the departure two weeks ago of the driver's helper, Sean Toulouse, who had to be fired because of dishonesty and could not be replaced quickly with a permanent, qualified helper. Now that a permanent, qualified helper has been hired, there should be no more delays in delivery as this was the cause of the problem.
>
> The driver was able to find a temporary helper, a man by the name of Rusty Sellers, for some help in the unloading work, but he got behind and couldn't seem to catch up. He could have caught up by working overtime, in the opinion of the writer, but he refused to do so. Of the 36 deliveries that were late, all were completed within two days. The problem is over now that the driver has a helper, so there should be no additional delays.

Problem-Solving Cases

Short to Mid-Length Reports

1. **Researching the Risks of Going More Social:** Your company (you decide what kind) is deciding whether to up its social media game. Right now, it has a blog and a Facebook page, but these sites don't get a lot of action or attract much attention. So your boss, one of the marketing staff, has asked you, an intern, to gather data on the potential risks involved in becoming active on Twitter. What kinds of problems have other companies encountered in the Twitterverse? How have their marketing efforts gone awry? What have been the consequences? How can such problems be prevented—and can they all be prevented?

    Your task will be to gather lessons and information that will help your boss, her boss, and the company president decide whether/how to jump into Twitter. You will not be doing thorough enough research to be able to recommend a course of action, but you can help your bosses decide what to do by relating the facts you find to the situations that are likely to come up for your company if it decides to move forward. Send your report to your boss as an email attachment.

2. **Recommending Ways for Employees to Stay Informed with LinkedIn:** You're a new hire in the _____ department of _____ company (you fill in the blanks). Your boss drops by your

desk and tells you about a webinar he recently attended that extolled the benefits of using social media to stay abreast of trends in one's field. He was particularly surprised at how useful LinkedIn can be for this purpose. He thinks the others in your department would be surprised, too, because most people think of LinkedIn as an employment-networking tool. But it's also a great way to see what people are talking about in various professional areas. "Organizations, groups, and individuals share a lot of useful information there," he says, "so we should be following what's going on." He plans to send the department a persuasive message along these lines—but first he wants you to further scope out LinkedIn's educational potential. Who are the thought leaders in the field? What kinds of things do they write about? How easy is it to contact a specific individual to ask questions? What groups are available, and how easy is it to join them? Can you see what your competition is up to? In what other ways might LinkedIn be a valuable resource for those in your department?

You'll do this research for your boss and send him your findings in an email report. Try to tell him everything he needs to be able to prepare a persuasive and knowledgeable message to the team.

3. **Researching the Career Outlook in Your Field:** Take advantage of the many career resources to research the current and likely future status of a career you're interested in. Research the employment prospects, typical jobs, advancement opportunity, salary range, career advantages/disadvantages, typical responsibilities—whatever you can find. You might start with the U.S. Government Occupational Outlook Handbook (http://www.bls.gov/ooh/). Professional societies also sometimes have excellent statistics on salaries and working conditions in their fields. And don't neglect such job-search sites as Monster.com. If your instructor directs, interview someone in your field who can give you an insider's view. Write up your findings as a well-organized short report, and be sure to interpret your findings in terms of their likely significance to you.

4. **Helping Your Boss Create an Internet-Use Policy:** The online retail company where you work as an assistant to the information technology (IT) manager is doing well. It began as a tools and equipment company 30 years ago, but it is now a popular seller of whimsical and hard-to-find items for home, garden, and fun—such as patio furniture, bug zappers, recreational accessories, remote-control toys, and novelty gadgets. Counting the three recent hires, the company now has 24 full-time employees, with the largest departments being product procurement, sales, order fulfillment, and customer service. With this growth have come IT headaches. Employees are visiting sites that lock up their computers, downloading large and/or malicious files, and even including proprietary information in some of their Internet-based correspondence. While it's important to the business for the employees to have free access to the Internet, it's also important that they use it safely and for the benefit of the company.

It's time for an Internet-use policy, and your boss thinks you're just the person to help write it. Your assignment is to study the current wisdom on workplace Internet policies and send your findings to him in an email report. He will use the report as the basis for a meeting with the chief operations officer on the subject next week.

5. **Recommending Where a Company Should Spend Its Radio-Advertising Dollars:** This is the third summer you've worked for SunLand, an outdoor-furniture and swimming-pool supplies company in Terre Haute, Indiana. It's early in the season, so the store isn't that busy, but the owners are working overtime to get the store fully stocked and shipshape. "Hey," one of them says to you today. "You're a college kid! I wonder if you'd help me out with something. I've read that businesses can really increase local traffic to their stores with strategically placed radio ads. I want to try this out, but I'm not sure which of the different stations in our area we should start with. Will you take a look on the Internet and tell me what you come up with? What stations are available, what do they charge, and—most importantly—who are their listeners? Obviously we want to reach people who would buy what we sell."

You don't know anything about this topic, but you're glad to give it a try. You enjoy working for this company—and you'll probably want a letter of recommendation (or perhaps even a full-time job) from the owner someday! Plus, you may well learn something that will help you in a business venture of your own. The boss didn't specify what written format to use, so you'll use the one that you think is best for the situation. (If your instructor permits, you can choose a different city and/or type of business, or different advertising media.)

6. **Finding Out How to Generate Positive Customer Reviews:** As with every other facet of online sales, good customer reviews don't just happen; they can be cultivated as well. Research the Internet and social media posts to find out how companies (1) encourage customers to post reviews on their websites and (2) try to ensure that those reviews are positive. Find out, also, what tactics one should *not* use and why. You'll write up your findings as a letter report to Mindy Swales, a small-business owner whom your instructor recruited as a client for this assignment. Mindy runs a coffee and wine shop in an upper-middle-class neighborhood in your city—and she has some stiff competition. She can really use your help.

7. **Exploring Online Meeting Options:** You were recently hired as an intern at Mayim's, a distributor of high-end cosmetics and skin care products. Kori Roberts, sales manager and your supervisor, drops by your office to chat one day and brings up a subject she's been wondering about. "Our sales staff have been communicating with each other and our retailers fairly effectively via phone and email, but I think it's time to look into an online meeting application to supplement these methods. Do you know what kind of tool I'm talking about?" she asks. You nod, having just covered online meeting tools in your Technology for Business Communication class. "I heard some of these options were totally free and really easy to use," she continues, "so I looked into a few. Skype, Google Hangouts, WebEx, and OpenMeetings seem to be pretty popular for businesses. I'm thinking about recommending that all the sales staff subscribe to one of these. Then maybe they could talk to each other and the retailers more easily. I wonder which of these tools is better for us. And is there any downside to online meetings? What works best for small companies? Are there security issues?" You take the hint and offer to look into the matter for her.

   Do the necessary research—and, if you haven't yet done so, try one or more of these services yourself—and then write Kori a report giving her the information she needs in order to decide whether or not to pursue this idea further. She may want to share your report with other managers in the company, so this is a good opportunity to make an impression and someday advance your career.

8. **Researching a Social Media Platform for Your Organization:** Think of a company or non-profit organization that you know well or want to learn more about and assume that you're an employee there. The organization has a nice website and Facebook page, but now it's considering doing more. You've been given the task of exploring whether the organization should promote itself through one of the following channels (you choose which one, based on the nature of your organization and its audiences):

   • YouTube

   • Pinterest

   • Tumblr

   • Instagram

   • Slideshare

   Research and prepare a report of approximately four pages in which you inform your boss, one of the managers, about the potential value of this platform to the organization. Do not assume that your boss, or anyone else who may read your report, knows much about the tool you chose. You'll need to educate him/her about the tool before you assess its appropriateness for the organization. (And to be able to assess its appropriateness, you will need to research the organization first.) Be sure you answer the reader's likely questions (e.g., about cost and potential drawbacks). Also, be careful that your recommendation is supported by the data you present. If you're not sure whether the organization should adopt this platform, you might recommend that the matter be explored further.

9. **Reporting on Students' Attitudes toward a Smoke-Free Campus:** A few U.S. states have passed legislation preventing smoking on the campuses of all their state-supported universities. While your school, a private liberal arts college, is not a state school and is not in a state that has passed such legislation, the administration is considering banning smoking on its campus for the same reasons that state-supported schools have done so. Currently, smokers on campus cannot smoke indoors anywhere on campus or within 15 feet of any building. The student affairs office, headed by Dean James Kirkland, has asked the student government organization to find out how students would feel about having a smoke-free policy instead. As a member of the student senate, you volunteered to be on a three-person team that would find out.

Your team conducted a student survey in two ways: online and in person. You got permission to send the online survey to the whole student body of 2,300 students. You also positioned four volunteers around campus on one day to conduct the survey in person, with each surveyor asking 25 passers-by what they thought.

Here are the data you gathered:

Overall results:

Strongly favor	Favor	Neutral	Dislike	Strongly Dislike
205	137	147	122	118

Results broken down by survey method:

Online:

Strongly favor	Favor	Neutral	Dislike	Strongly Dislike
191	120	114	102	102

In person:

Strongly favor	Favor	Neutral	Dislike	Strongly Dislike
14	17	33	20	16

Results broken down by year in school:

	Strongly favor	Favor	Neutral	Dislike	Strongly Dislike
First-year (N=149)	49	32	35	21	12
Sophomore (N=184)	51	36	46	28	23
Junior (N=202)	58	37	35	37	35
Senior (N=194)	47	32	31	36	48

Here are sample comments that the students made online and in person:

"Great idea. I hate walking through smoke on my way into the building."

"We're a progressive school. We should have a progressive smoking policy [in favor of a smoke-free campus]."

"This is a ridiculous idea. It makes us look like we can't think for ourselves."

"I think it's people's right to smoke as long as they're outside and being considerate. We should limit people's rights as little as possible."

"Isn't the purpose of a college education to teach people to make their own decisions? A smoke-free policy would completely contradict that."

"I pay this school a lot of money, so I think it should stay out of my business when it comes to smoking."

"We're paying a lot to go here, so the campus should be as pleasant as possible for everyone" (supports a smoke-free campus).

"I really don't care."

"Did someone complain? Why are we even discussing this?"

"A lot of kids start smoking on campus because they see others doing it. I think that would happen less if we had a smoke-free campus."

"It gives a bad impression to visitors when students are smoking. We look like we don't care about medical research or health."

"If this school had had a smoke-free policy when I was applying to schools, I wouldn't have come here."

"I think you're going to run a lot of people out of campus housing if you adopt a smoke-free policy."

"We already have to smoke at least 15 feet away from the buildings. I'm starting to feel discriminated against."

"C'mon—other cultures aren't so smoking phobic. This policy would make us look backwards and puritannical."

"Definitely should have the policy. People have plenty of other places to smoke if they want to."

"Doesn't the administration have something more important to think about? How about working on lowering our tuition?!"

"It seems like the right thing to do [to have the policy]."

"Let's face it—smoking is dumb. When we tolerate it as a school, we look dumb."

Now it's time to prepare the report for Dean Kirkland. The report will also be made available, in pdf format, on the student government webpage. Create a title page and a combined letter of transmittal and executive summary for this mid-length report. Include a copy of the survey at the end as an appendix.

10. **Recommending a Charity for Your Company to Support:** You're part-time assistant to the business manager of a successful veterinary clinic with four locations in the greater _____ area (you pick the city). The practice's three owners have been building the clinic's image as a strong supporter of the community. They have created a thriving employee-volunteer program, they sponsor community events, and they convey their genuine interest in animal welfare in their advertising.

Now they want to add another piece to their social-responsibility portfolio: adopting a charity to support.

They've asked your boss to come up with three charities who would make worthy recipients of donations from the company. From these, they will choose one. Since you're a college student with good writing and research skills and free access to your university's extensive online resources, she asks you to tackle this task. You decide you'll start your research by consulting your library's resources on corporate philanthropy and on veterinary philanthropy in particular. You'll also look at the websites for various relevant charities. Once you believe you've found everything useful, you'll digest it, interpret it, and present the results in a well-organized, well-written report that your boss can hand over to the owners during her meeting with them next month. Keep your report to about three pages, but be sure to include your sources so your readers can consult them if they want.

11. **Researching the Viability of QR codes:** It wasn't very long ago that including QR codes in print promotional material was at the cutting edge of marketing. Now your boss, marketing manager for a local chain of restaurants, isn't so sure. So he turns to you, the restaurant's trusty hospitality co-op. "We've been including our QR code in print ads in the city's business newspaper, free local papers, coupon books, and magazine. But now I'm wondering if it's worth the trouble. Even more so, I'm wondering if they make us look behind the times. Is anybody using QR codes anymore? If not, why not, and what has replaced them? If so, how does a business use them effectively?"

You're happy to take on this challenge. It'll teach you something about marketing resources in your field as well as give you attractive details to include when describing your co-op experience on your resume. Prepare an email report of about two pages for your boss that'll answer all of his likely questions. Be sure to include your sources.

12. **Helping Employees Interact with New Colleagues outside the United States:** You work in the human resources department of a clinical research organization with about 2,000 employees. Like other companies in this industry, your company arranges, runs, and reports on clinical trials of new drugs, biomedical devices, and promising medical treatments. Your company recently expanded beyond U.S. borders for the first time by opening a new research facility in Montreal, Canada (or some other country that you or your instructor chooses).

Your boss wants to be sure that all U.S. employees who'll be interacting with the Canadian employees understand that Canada, and Montreal in particular, has its own culture. Toward that end, she has asked you to prepare a short report on what people should keep in mind when conversing with those who manage and work at the Montreal branch. For example, how formal are the Canadians in their correspondence? Do they value directness or indirectness, or does it depend on the circumstances? What's their attitude toward hierarchy? What might be topics or wording to be careful about? And when visiting the Canadian site, what should U.S. employees know about the business and social protocol that is likely to be used there?

Write her a report in which you convey a helpful, accurate picture of the culture in Montreal and offer well-researched advice for U.S. employees that she can share with them as she sees fit. Cite your sources—and be careful to use reliable ones.

13. **Substituting One Benefit for Another:** You work in human resources for Wiley, Renn, and Long, a large law firm. The firm offers both single-person and family health insurance coverage to its 150 employees.

Last week you hired Rebecca Chang. You sent her the standard paperwork all new hires complete. When Rebecca stopped by today to submit her paperwork, she said that she had turned down the health insurance, as she has health insurance coverage through her spouse. In telling you this, she mentions that her spouse's company offers an annuity the equivalent of a single-person premium as an alternative benefit for employees who decline the health insurance, and she wants to know if Wiley, Renn, and Long will do the same for her. The cost of a single-person premium per month is $510.

You present the idea to your boss, who initially says "absolutely not" but then decides that you should research the issue first. What are the advantages and disadvantages for the employee and for the company? How much will this potentially cost if other employees choose an annuity over health insurance? What if the cost of a single-person premium increases? Can you go back? That is, can you decide to discontinue this benefit at any time? Present your research in a report so your boss can make an informed decision.

14. **Helping Your Boss Promote Mindfulness:** You're a management major on co-op with a large customer-data company. Your company sells technology that collects detailed records of what customers buy, at what price, and when, and then crunches those data to help companies improve their revenue. The employees include computer engineers, salespeople, client consultants, customer support staff, technicians, and professionals in other business areas. You've been assigned to various areas of the company to "learn your chops," so to speak, and you're currently reporting to Jennifer Sachs, the director of communications. One of Jennifer's duties is to work with the president to write the script for his monthly video to the employees. Jennifer has been coming across more and more articles about the detrimental effects of multitasking and the benefits of focused, "mindful" work, so she thinks she'll recommend that the president's next talk be on this subject. That's where you come in. "See what you can find out about mindfulness on the job," she asks you. "Find out what it means, how to have it, what its benefits are, who's practicing it."

Do the research and then write Jennifer an email report answering her (and the president's) likely questions and helping them see what approach to take to this topic in the video.

15. **Dealing with Tardy Employees:** You are quite comfortable in your position as supervisor at a commercial printing office in your hometown, but you find some employees a bit more challenging than others. Alex, your receptionist, is one of those challenges.

Alex is a terrific receptionist—in fact, he is the best you have ever had. He is a whiz on every computer program you use. His organizational skills are exceptional. Losing him would have a detrimental impact on your customers and on the office in general. Besides, he's a really nice person. Unfortunately, he is frequently late for his shift, causing you to answer the phones or leave your office to greet customers. You have reminded Alex of his hours, and he always indicates he will change his behavior, but he continues to be late. To make things worse, you've noticed recently that others in the office are arriving late for work because, you believe, Alex has not suffered any consequences for his actions. Quite honestly, you're not sure what the consequences should be. You don't want a negative work environment, but lately, it seems as though a practice that has always been taken for granted (employees being on time for work) is now one that you need a policy to enforce.

You ask your boss for some guidance with this matter. She asks you to do some research and to present some options. She agrees that a policy is needed, but she does not want it to seem parental or patronizing, and she does not want to harm morale by making employees feel that they are being disciplined or punished. She just wants a policy that gives offenders the opportunity to improve their behavior while also giving her the flexibility to impose harsher sanctions if employees continue to be late. Write a report to your supervisor investigating the many options available to managers when dealing with tardy employees. Address in a general sense any legal challenges you may encounter. You may consider interviewing a human resource specialist regarding your options and for tips on having difficult conversations with employees when issues such as this arise.

16. **Deciding Which Pizza to Put on the Main Menu:** You're an assistant manager in the home office of Dandy's Pizza, a local business with several locations in your city. To find out which of three popular seasonal pizzas to add to the regular menu, you conducted a poll that allowed viewers to vote for the one they thought should win. The choices were the Mi Amigo, a Mexican-style pizza; the Ballpark, a pizza with a spicy mustard sauce, sauerkraut, and slices of mettwurst sausage; and Autumn Harvest, a veggie pizza with goat cheese, butternut squash, roast pumpkin seeds, and kale. Customers could vote either on Facebook or in person at the restaurants (by checking their choice on a card). In an effort to get unbaised results, the company conducted the poll during two weeks in March, when none of these pizzas were on the menu.

Here are the results:

Facebook votes: 603 for Mi Amigo; 249 for Ballpark; 323 for Autumn Harvest.

Votes in-store: 1,023 for Mi Amigo; 320 for Ballpark; 563 for Autumn Harvest.

You also gathered sales data for the three pizzas for the past year. Each pizza was featured as the specialty pizza for two months. Here's how they compared on sales revenue over the course of that period:

Mi Amigo: weeks 1–2, $14k; weeks 3–4, $13.3k; weeks 5–6, $13.9k; weeks 7–8, $12.9k.

Ballpark: weeks 1–2, $8.4k; weeks 3–4, $9.1k; weeks 5–6, $7.8k; weeks 7–8, $6.3k.

Autumn Harvest: weeks 1–2, $6.5k; weeks 3–4, $7.9k; weeks 5–6, $6.9k; weeks 7–8, $6.2k.

Now it's time to interpret these data, share them with your boss, and make your recommendation. Send him your report as an email attachment.

17. **Analyzing the Results of a Schedule Change:** You work as an operations assistant at Mayer Tool and Die, a large manufacturer of machine tools. Three months ago, your company switched from a typical five-day work week to a four-day work week. Under the new arrangement, employees at Mayer work 10-hour days, Monday through Thursday. The change was made to save money on utility expenses, specifically electricity. Under the new arrangement, the plant is completely closed on Friday, Saturday, and Sunday.

Your supervisor, the operations manager, wants to know two things about the schedule change. First, have utility expenses actually decreased, and second, what do employees think about the schedule change? You make a visit to the accounting department, where you ask for the gas and electric bills for the previous six months. The total cost for utilities is displayed in Table 1:

▼ **Table 1** Mayer's Gas and Electric Expenses for the Last 6 Months

Month	Total Expense
March 2016	$21,364
April 2016	$24,567
May 2016	$28,526
June 2016	$33,426
July 2016	$39,217
August 2016 (current month)	$42,357

The accounting clerk, Beth Li, suggests that you also look at the gas and electric bills for the same three months (June, July, and August) of last year. Total gas and electric expenses for those three months are displayed in Table 2:

▼ **Table 2** June–August 2011 Gas and Electric Expenses for Mayer

Month	Total Expense
June 2015	$37,917
July 2015	$44,785
August 2015	$47,612

After collecting this information, you begin to analyze the data from a survey that your boss recently sent to all 1,500 employees at Mayer, which asked their opinions on the scheduling change. A total of 871 employees responded to the survey.

The survey asked a series of questions, but three in particular are of most interest to your boss. The first question is, "Do you like the new four-day work week?" The breakdown in responses was as follows: 375 "Strongly Agree," 141 "Agree," 147 "Neutral," 128 "Disagree," and 90 "Strongly Disagree." The second question is, "Do you think that the new four-day work week has made you more productive?" The breakdown in responses to the second question was as follows: 143 "Strongly Agree," 165 "Agree," 201 "Neutral," 189 "Disagree," and 173 "Strongly Disagree." The third question is "Do you recommend that we continue with the four-day work week?" The breakdown in responses to the third question was as follows: 237 "Strongly Agree," 192 "Agree," 226 "Neutral," 153 "Disagree," and 63 "Strongly Disagree."

Finally, there was an open-ended question that asked employees for any other thoughts they had on the four-day work week. Responses included "I like the three-day weekend," "This is another example of why I like working for this company," "I am very tired at the end of the 10-hour day," and "The lunch break is not long enough."

Using these data, write a report to your boss about the impact the schedule change has had on the plant's overall gas and electric costs, as well as the employees' perceptions of the schedule.

18. **Helping the Blood Bank at Your School Increase Student Blood Donations:** Your business communication instructor has put the class in groups and asked each group to do research that will help solve a campus problem. Your group has decided to help the Galway Center, the blood bank located on the medical-school campus, to increase blood donations by students.

You first met with Angela Locke, marketing director for the center, to find out what she would like to know. You also got some really interesting statistics from her about the importance of blood donations. You had no idea, for example, that blood can be stored for only so long; that's why blood centers are always running donation campaigns.

Angela wants your help with figuring out what motivates students to donate, what keeps them from donating, and what might increase donations. On the basis of your interview with her, you designed a quick survey for students to complete. You had to use a convenience sample to conduct your survey because you were not permitted to use the all-campus student email list. But you tried to get a somewhat representative sample by handing out surveys in your classes. These were junior- and senior-level classes in business and a few sophomore- and junior-level classes in other majors (English, political science, Spanish, journalism, and psychology).

You've now gathered and tabulated your data. Here's what you found out:

Have you donated blood while you've been a student here?

Yes, 30; No, 272.

*If yes, what is the **main** reason you donated?*

I wanted to help others, 15; My club or organization did it as a group, 7; I wanted the giveaway item, 5; Other, 3 (written in: "my friend dared me," "wanted to try it," "not sure")

If no, why haven't you donated? (Check all that apply.)

- Inconvenience: 132
- Fear: 144
- Health issues: 16
- Lack of information: 17
- Low level of importance: 12

How appealing would you find each of the following incentives for donating blood? Rate each on a scale from 1 (not appealing) to 5 (very appealing).

- Discounts to businesses on campus (e.g., eateries, bookstore): 4.2
- Credit toward required service hours: 3.4
- Tickets to a varsity basketball or football game: 3.0
- Tickets to concerts at University Music Hall: 2.4
- Tickets to movies on campus: 4.0

(Note: Only 243 answered this question.)

Analyze your findings and prepare a helpful report for Ms. Locke. You will need to fill in more details regarding your survey method, and you may use additional information about your school and the students to help you interpret the findings and create your recommendations.

Longer Reports

19. **Helping Your Company Choose an Email-Marketing Service:** Jake and Jeff Anderson started their tree and lawn service, Anderson's, 15 years ago, and they've decided they're ready to compete with the bigger players in town by bumping up their marketing efforts. They've been reading about the payoffs of email marketing, but they don't have anyone on staff who would be qualified to do it. Jake is an arborist, and Jeff is the accountant, business manager, and IT troubleshooter. They also have a couple of office staff who field customer calls, schedule appointments, and manage the billing, as well as several work crews. They contract out their human resources and website-maintenance services. Jeff has been the makeshift marketer for the company, but he'd be in over his head with email marketing. So they've decided that they'll depend on an outside firm to get them into this new territory. If it works out well, they might hire someone to handle all the sales and marketing for the company.

    You'be been working for them ever since you were a teenager, and you've continued on part time for them while pursuing your college degree. They know you're pretty sharp with technology, so they ask if you'll do the preliminary research toward finding the right email marketing service to work with. You'll be glad to—because you want to see the business grow, and you want to be that full-time marketer!

    This will take a good bit of research, though. As a student, you've got free access to e-Marketer's database, so you'll spend about an hour reading various email-marketing statistics and articles there. Then you'll get into the Internet research—scoping out what's available, reading reviews of various email-marketing service providers, finding out what types of services are offered, and exploring the potential cost. You know that Jake and Jeff are interested in a pretty minimalist approach at this point, so you won't spend much time looking at companies that want to sell more than Anderson's needs.

    You're planning to include the resulting report in your employment e-portfolio, so you will write up your findings for Jeff and Jake as a formal report, from title page to recommendations. You'll cite your sources by using footnotes and a list of works cited. (Or, if your instructor permits, do this report as a team project, with Anderson's as your client.)

20. **Reporting Marketing Data to Your Boss:** You're an event coordinator for The Phoenix, an event facility in the heart of downtown in your midsize city. The space used to be a museum for contemporary art, so it has a clean, contemporary look with wood floors, neutral-colored walls, natural light from large windows, and modern ceiling fixtures. There's an elegant foyer and staircase when you enter, and up the stairs is the main ballroom, with several small rooms adjoining. Your boss, the main owner, has been renting out the space as a corporate event and wedding center for about three years now. Your job is to field inquiries, arrange tours, encourage visitors to rent the space, and serve as the facility's main contact during the clients' event planning.

    Recently, three couples who toured the center declined to book their wedding receptions there, and sales in general are not what your boss hoped they would be. To find out why, you offered each of these couples a $50 gift card for a local restaurant if they would participate in an informal focus group at a coffeeshop near the center. They all agreed to participate.

    All three couples are in their mid to late twenties. They all learned about the venue from The Knot, the most popular wedding-planning site on the Internet, and from the Phoenix's own website. They plan to have 200–300 guests. Here are their bios:

Sean and Betsy live in a suburb north of downtown. They thought it might be nice to hold their wedding and reception in a downtown location for the convenience and entertainment of their many out-of-town guests. They expect to spend $4–5k on the venue and up to $25k on their wedding overall.

Andre and Kelly live downtown and enjoy the downtown atmosphere. They expect to spend up to $6k on the venue and up to $30k on their wedding overall.

Mark and Haley live on the west side of town, which is a bit rural. They're wondering whether to hold their reception in their neighborhood or treat their guests to something special by booking a downtown venue. They expect to spend $4k on the venue and $18–22k on their wedding overall.

You asked these questions, and got these replies:

1. *What positive things had you read or heard about the Phoenix before your visit?*

   - All had read about the beautiful space and viewed the photos on the Internet.

   - All had discovered, by looking at different venues' availability calendars online, that the center had more availability on Saturdays throughout the year than most of the other wedding venues in the city. (This is because the facility is relatively new, and the corporate events it hosts happen mostly on weekdays.)

   - Two couples (Sean and Betsy, Mark and Haley) had read in an online review that the alcohol cost would likely be lower at the Phoenix than at comparable venues. (This is true because the Phoenix has a license to buy liquor from distributors and then mark it up themselves, which enables them to keep the cost low.)

   - Sean and Betsy mentioned that they thought it would be cool to hold their event in a space that had been an art museum and that still had an artsy look. (Andre and Kelly agreed.)

   - All the couples thought it was neat that the venue was so close to the city's Central Square, and two couples (Sean and Betsy, Andre and Kelly) thought it was awesome that the venue was linked by skywalk to nearby hotels.

2. *What did you think when you first saw the space?* Here are the key comments from the conversation that ensued:

   "The foyer is gorgeous" (nods all around). "Very elegant venue." "Lovely space" (about the ballroom; nods all around). "Yes—but really plain! We were expecting more than just empty rooms" (Haley and Mark). "I loved that—I could imagine all kinds of ways to use this space!" (Kelly). "It'd be a really special, unique spot for a wedding" (Andre, with nods from Kelly and Betsy). "We liked that you could rent only as many rooms as you needed—whether just the foyer and ballroom or all four siderooms as well" (Haley and Mark, with nods from the other couples).

3. *After the tour, did you still consider booking here?*

   All three couples said no, giving these reasons:

   "It seemed like it would be a lot of work. I mean, all you'd supply is the space, valet parking, the tables and chairs, and setup and breakdown. You don't even have a preferred-vendors list. We'd have to find and line up all the vendors, arrange all the decorations, plan the layout, and so forth" (Sean and Betsy, with nods from Mark and Haley). "Sounds like you'd basically have to hire a wedding or reception planner" (Haley, with nods from Betsy and Kelly).

   "Yeah, and the price ($5k) seems pretty high considering that" (Mark, with nods from the other two guys). "Yes, the place is pretty and unique, but it seemed expensive for what you got" (Haley). "It also felt like we'd be nickled and dimed to death. I mean, in a way it's good that you charge separately for each space, and that you charge for extra time (beyond four hours) by the hour, but it kind of conveys a greedy message" (Sean, with nods from Mark and Haley). "And $500 for each extra hour seems like a lot" (Kelly, with nods from Haley and Betsy).

   "Also, I didn't understand that alcohol policy. So, you buy the alcohol wholesale from a list that changes each month and the client picks from that? But the client can also special-order certain beverages? Does that cost extra?" (Sean). "And I didn't understand the buy-back policy. So you'll buy back all unopened products except for special orders? But not any liquor, even if it was picked from the inventory list?" (Mark, with nods from almost everyone). "Yeah, it's very confusing. It seemed like I got a different description of the alcohol policy from each person at the Phoenix I spoke with" (Betsy).

Now it's time to interpret these findings, write them up, and offer suggestions for improving sales. You'll enhance the reasoning behind your suggestions by making a few comparisons to comparable wedding venues downtown. (Hint: Choose a midsize city and use the Internet to look at downtown wedding venues there.) Your boss has three business partners, and probably others, with whom she'll share and discuss your report.

21. **Recommending a Sports Trip for International Guests:** You recently got your dream job: You were hired by Ben and Dan Bender, two young entrepreneurs, to help them operate Get the Gear, a business that sells authentic U.S. professional sportswear to fans around the world. Most of its sales are online, but the brick-and-mortar store in Columbus, Ohio, has become a popular shopping destination. Business there has been so good, in fact, that Ben and Dan are considering opening a store in Japan. They've been discussing the possibility with a company in Tokyo, and two of the Japanese executives are planning to come to Columbus to see the store and meet with Ben and Dan this summer. Ben and Dan also want to treat their Japanese guests to a major-league baseball game while they're in the United States.

This is where you come in. Your boss, the business manager, asks you to research the cost and relative advantages of trips to four ballparks: one in Cincinnati, one in Pittsburgh, one in Cleveland, and one in Detroit. He wants you to research the prices for good regular seats (not guest boxes or party rooms) at the various stadiums (you can assume that all four baseball teams will be playing at home when your guests are here). In addition, he suggests that you research transportation to the cities, parking, concessions, possible hotels for a two-night stay (hotels that should be within walking distance of the stadiums), and anything else that might be relevant.

Make your recommendation for a city in the form of a report addressed to your boss. The report should include an estimate of the total trip cost to each of the four cities, as well as your recommendation for which city to visit. (If your instructor permits, you can choose a different city, sport, or nationality for your international visitors.)

22. **Researching e-Portfolio Platforms for Your Boss:** The University Career Center is a great place to begin your career in information systems, so you were thrilled to land a full-time position there as manager of the student workers and assistant to the center's director. Your boss, the director, selected you because she wants you to help ensure that the center is digitally current.

On your first day of work you were surprised to learn that little emphasis is placed on helping students create e-portfolios. The center's website mentions e-portfolios but does not say why students should create them or how to do so. You share these thoughts with your boss, and she agrees that the center is behind in this area. She asks you to gather information that can be posted on the website and shared with students in other ways (e.g., through the center's advisors) to encourage them to create this important job-search tool.

Prepare a report for your boss in which you discuss, first, the benefits of having an e-portfolio (this material might wind up as persuasive text on the center's website). Then examine and evaluate three options for creating Web-based e-portfolios. Compare the platforms based on their cost, how easy they are to learn and use, their design features, the kinds of files they can display, and any other factors you believe to be important. This report will be shared with numerous people at the center, so it will need a certain amount of formality (as your instructor directs).

23. **Researching Delivery Vans for a Start-Up:** You've been invited by a married couple in your town to help them launch a business venture: a service that delivers organic and local produce to households and small businesses in town. You were recommended to them by your former entrepreneurship professor, for whom you'd written a great business plan when you took her class.

The couple is now preparing a business plan to attract investors. They have done the research to prove that there is sufficient demand for the business and that they will have sufficient and reliable suppliers. But they haven't yet figured out all the likely costs. One big cost yet to be determined is that of the vehicles they'll be using to deliver the produce.

They turn to you for help. They figure they'll need four large vans to start with, adding more as needed. Should they rent or buy? And if they buy, which makes and models might be best for their purposes?

Do the necessary research to find out what their options are and make a recommendation. Carefully consider all the criteria that would make one option better than another, and invent any additional realistic details that you need in order to do so (perhaps information on the website of

Green Bean Delivery, on which the company in this case was based, can help). Write a polished report so that these entrepreneurs can use appropriate parts of it in their business plan.

24. **Getting Employees' Opinions about Online Training and Education:** Every employee at Malcolm Industries needs to be current in his or her field. As a developer of medical practice management software for hospitals, clinics, and private practices, Malcolm requires everyone from the programmers to the sales staff to the communications specialists be up to date on current practices, trends, and client needs so that the company can survive in an extremely competitive industry.

To ensure that its employees have the most current knowledge, Malcolm invests a lot of money in employees' continuing education, which includes workshops, seminars, and continuing education courses at two-year colleges and four-year colleges and universities; the company has even paid for some employees' courses toward an MBA. Wherever the education is, Malcolm sends its employees.

This practice for continuing education has become too costly. As a result, the company has decided that nearly all employees might be able to remain current in their fields by taking advantage of more cost-effective online opportunities.

Your boss sees two issues. The first is that he needs to know if online opportunities provide the same quality of training or education as face-to-face opportunities. The second is that in talking with a few department heads and employees informally, your boss senses some resistance to online learning. Your boss wants to learn whether there really is widespread resistance to online learning and, if so, where the points of resistance are. Your boss also wants to know some best practices for promoting online training opportunities as valid options for continuing education. You have been assigned the task of gathering the information your boss requires and presenting both the information and recommendations for ensuring that employees see online education opportunities as useful.

Write a report that answers your boss's questions and provides direction to him for how to best proceed with the plan to use online continuing education in your workplace.

You will need to do secondary research to answer your boss's questions regarding issues surrounding the quality of online learning and how to promote it to employees, especially those who are resistant. Cite your sources in the style required by your instructor.

Your primary research, however, is complete. You surveyed your 2,100 employees and received 735 responses. The survey results are provided below. The numbers represent frequency data (the number of respondents, not percentages).

Survey Questions and Responses:

Q1: In what department do you work?

82 Research and Development

300 Sales

27 Communications

59 Accounting

68 Training and Education

28 Marketing

30 Human Resources

54 Hardware and Software Support

51 Information Technology

36 Legal

Q2: What is the nature of your position?

130 Manager

137 Supervisor

383 Subject matter expert (accountants, technical writers, programmers, salespeople)

85 Clerical/support

Q3: Have you ever participated in any of the following online education opportunities? Check all that apply.

23 Online workshop

102 Webinar (online seminar)

65 Online course

54 Other (please specify): 24 bachelor's degree from an online university or a face-to-face university with an online program; 30 technical/vocational degree through an online program

Q4: Do you participate in any of the following? Check all that apply.

311 Professionally related blog

602 Professionally related online social networking site (e.g., Twitter, LinkedIn, Facebook)

Q5: What is your perception of the workload in online seminars/workshops/courses?

187 More work than face-to-face opportunities

144 About the same work as face-to-face opportunities

404 Less work than face-to-face opportunities

Q6: What is your perception of the quality of online seminars/workshops/courses?

117 Better quality than of face-to-face opportunities

201 About the same quality as face-to-face opportunities

417 Less quality than face-to-face opportunities

Q7: Indicate your level of agreement with this statement: People can learn as much in an online environment as they can in a face-to-face environment.

82 Strongly agree

138 Agree

65 Neither agree nor disagree

358 Disagree

92 Strongly disagree

Q8: Indicate your level of agreement with this statement: If the following online continuing education opportunity presented itself, I would willingly take it.

An online seminar (1–2 hours)

105 Strongly agree

468 Agree

29 Neither agree nor disagree

82 Disagree

51 Strongly disagree

An online workshop (1–2 days)

52 Strongly agree

164 Agree

312 Neither agree nor disagree

163 Disagree

44 Strongly disagree

An online course (1–3 weeks)

92 Strongly agree

222 Agree

151 Neither agree nor disagree

202 Disagree

68 Strongly disagree

An online course (4–8 weeks)

75 Strongly agree

120 Agree

81 Neither agree nor disagree

279 Disagree

180 Strongly disagree

An online course (9–16 weeks)

54 Strongly agree

92 Agree

192 Neither agree nor disagree

197 Disagree

198 Strongly disagree

Q9: My general attitude toward online learning in any form is

99 Strongly positive

185 Positive

137 Neutral

213 Negative

101 Strongly negative

Cross tabulations for "Q 9: My general attitude toward online learning in any form is"

99 Strongly Positive (25 managers, 26 supervisors, 42 subject matter experts, 6 clerical/support staff)

185 Positive (45 managers, 50 supervisors, 70 subject matter experts, 20 clerical/support staff)

137 Neutral (14 managers, 21 supervisors, 88 subject matter experts, 14 clerical/support staff)

213 Negative (31 managers, 30 supervisors, 138 subject matter experts, 14 clerical support staff)

101 Strongly negative (15 managers, 10 supervisors, 45 subject matter experts, 31 clerical support staff)

Employee comments on the survey:

"How will I network in an online class like I would in a face-to-face seminar?"

"Getting away from the company for a few days of training is a nice break from the routine."

"I worry that I won't be motivated to stick with an online class. If I go face-to-face, I feel more accountable to the teachers and the students I can see and get to know."

"This is just one more way for the company to cut costs and quality. You get what you pay for, and I think we will find that our training and continuing education will suffer."

"I think I am the kind of learner who needs to be in a regular classroom. It won't feel like a class if I'm sitting at work or home on my computer—too many distractions."

"I got my entire bachelor's degree online. It was so convenient! I didn't have to leave my family or my office for classes. Plus, if I ever had questions, I could discuss them any time with the class or the instructor."

"Online seminars are great! With video conferencing, you can see other participants. It's like being in the same place—and at the end of the training, I can go to my own home without having to travel or stay in hotels."

"I just finished a webinar and loved it! That said, I've also attended webinars that are a total waste of time. Online training is a good idea as long as we have quality options."

25. **Assessing Customer Service at a Health Clinic:** You are the assistant to the clinic manager for the West Union branch of Tri-City Healthcare Systems, which operates about 25 health facilities in the area. Tri-City recently announced that it would be reducing the number of staff by 120, primarily by not replacing vacant positions but also by eliminating and combining positions. This will require that your boss reduce the staff at her clinic by seven people; the rest of the positions will be eliminated at other clinics in the system and at company headquarters.

Tri-City's news release to local media outlets cited rising health care costs, a poor economy, and fewer patients seeking care due to high insurance deductibles as reasons for the layoffs. You boss is sure that the reasons cited in the press release have a lot do to with the downsizing, but she has also gathered from comments on the newspapers' websites and the company's Facebook page that there might be other reasons. Only a few of these 40 or so comments are complimentary; the rest cite billing errors, poor customer service, excess or unfair charges on their bills, long waits for appointments, and long waits to see a physician as reasons they have sought health care at a competitor's clinics. Even if Tri-City's reasons for the layoffs are accurate, she wants to find out how satisfied her clinic's patients are and address any problems.

Together, she and you developed a survey to find out from current and recent patients what the clinic is doing well and what it can do better. You surveyed these two groups over the past three weeks by using print questionnaires in the waiting room and a mailing to those who had no appointment during those three weeks or who had left the clinic. The questions asked respondents to evaluate not only the clinic's staff but also the performance of the billing staff, who work at corporate and do the billing for all the clinics.

Now your boss wants you to interpret the data. Write her a report on what the clinic's employees and the billing staff are doing well and what they need to improve on. She'll then use these findings as the basis of a comprehensive report and a PowerPoint presentation that she can share with the clinic's management team and/or Tri-City's corporate office. N=718 (601 of 740 possible respondents filled out surveys in the office; 117 of 400 randomly chosen patients who did not visit the office during the survey period returned mailed surveys.)

Demographic Information

Q1. How many times have you visited the clinic in the past six months?

0: 68

1–5: 572

6–10: 61

11–15: 10

16 or more: 7

Customer Service

Q2. How would you rate the ease of getting through to one of the clinic staff on the phone?

Very good: 167

Good: 349

Fair: 122

Poor: 75

Very poor: 5

Comments: Generally very quick; I once waited seven minutes to talk to someone; if the wait is longer than three minutes, you should have some way to let the caller know; if you say someone is going to call back, give a time frame and follow through; physicians/nurses/staff are terrible at returning calls (mentioned by several respondents).

Q4. How would you rate the ease of scheduling an appointment?

Very good: 60

Good: 174

Fair: 188

Poor: 208

Very poor: 88

Comments: I read that you're laying off people because of lower patient demand. Really? If you have so few patients, how come I had to wait five months to see a dermatologist? | I've been asked to reschedule several times because the doctor will be out of the office—can't you plan any better than that? | I know a same-day appointment is not often possible, but it seems like the wait time for any appointment is at least three weeks. | No complaints—I can usually get in right away. | This clinic is not for sick people—you have to hope that what you have can wait for a couple of days, a week, or even a month until you can get an appointment.

Q5. How would you rate the courtesy of the staff in the registration area?

Very good: 231

Good: 222

Fair: 155

Poor: 75

Very poor: 35

Comments: Very helpful and friendly; the courtesy seems to depend on the time of day—in the morning, they are very nice; but in the afternoon, they are sometimes really crabby; overall, friendly and helpful; they get curt when they get busy.

Q6. Once you are in the waiting room, the amount of time you wait before seeing your provider is

Never longer than 25 minutes: 65

Occasionally longer than 25 minutes: 218

Regularly longer than 25 minutes: 295

Always longer than 25 minutes: 140

Comments: The wait time is absolutely ridiculous—if I didn't like my provider so much, I would go elsewhere [this comment was made by several people]. I I have complained about this to anyone who will listen; if I don't see changes, I'll find another clinic. I My last three visits? 35-, 50-, and 65-minute waits; this has been a problem for some time now—there must be a way to do better [this comment was echoed by several people].

Q7. Are the bills sent from Tri-City's billing office (not those you may receive from your insurer) accurate?

Always: 157

Usually: 312

Sometimes: 159

Almost never: 70

Never: 20

Comments: To be honest, I just pay the amount on the bill—I don't question it. I Your bills are really hard to understand. I Usually, the bills are accurate—it's my insurer who disputes them [mentioned by several respondents]. I How hard is it to calculate a bill? It seems like every bill is calculated wrong and requires six phone calls to get it fixed. I The billing errors are ridiculous; I get a lot of refund checks for overcharges—wouldn't it be easier to just get the bill right in the first place? I I'm really tired of calling billing to get my bills straightened out.

Q8. Think about the times when you have had to contact Tri-City's billing office (not your insurer) regarding questions about your bill. How would you rate the courtesy and helpfulness of the staff?

Always courteous: 40

Usually courteous: 208

Sometimes courteous: 242

Almost never courteous: 210

Never courteous: 10

I've never had to contact the billing office: 8

Comments: It's really hit and miss—you just have to hope you don't get any of them on a bad day. I Very impersonal. I They get really defensive when you ask a question [mentioned by several respondents]. I Bad attitude [mentioned by several respondents]. I I have to say my bill always gets corrected, though I don't get why they make so many mistakes in the first place [mentioned by several respondents]. I They are helpful, just not friendly [mentioned by several respondents]. I They are almost always helpful.

26. **Finding the Right Price and Marketing Methods for an Entrepreneur's Product:** Like many retired businesspeople, Craig Stevens has decided to try running a small business of his own. He traveled a good bit when he was an executive, and he learned that the Bohemian area of the Czech Republic is renowned for its gorgeous cut crystal. Once he retired, he returned to that area and arranged to have one of the glass cutters design a unique vase, about 12 inches tall, and make 100 of them for Stevens to sell in the United States. The vases have arrived in perfect condition—and now Stevens has come to one of your classes to ask for the students' help with determining the price and marketing strategy for his merchandise. He paid the artist roughly $1,000 for the vases and about $1,000 in shipping costs.

With a couple of team members, do the research that will enable you to advise Mr. Stevens. Where and how should he sell his product? What additional costs might be involved? What price point would enable him to cover his costs and make a decent profit? Toward what groups of consumers should he direct his marketing efforts? How can he best differentiate his product from competing products? Try to anticipate any additional questions he would have and answer them. You do not have to create any actual marketing or sales materials, but you should give Mr. Stevens a clear idea of the marketing strategy you have in mind. (With your instructor's permission, you may choose a different product.)

27. **Advising an Organization on How to Become an Official Nonprofit:** You've been working for Sarah Gallagher, who started an organization called Metro Eats a couple of years ago. She rented a small space, outfitted it with a kitchen, and got volunteers to help her collect leftover perishable food from a few local grocery stores. She then turned the foods into delicious meals (mostly soups and vegetarian dishes) and distributed them to the city's poor and homeless, usually through an established food pantry or church. The idea attracted a lot of positive attention, donations, and volunteers—to the point where Metro Eats now gathers donated food from over 15 grocery stores and restaurants and turns out about 300 meals a week. It has its own website and social media promotions, two paid employees (you and Sarah), and about two dozen full- and part-time volunteers.

Sarah thinks the time has come to seriously consider acquiring official nonprofit status for the organization. She knows that a 501(3)(c) organization enjoys such benefits as enabling donors' contributions to be tax-deductible (which would thus encourage more donations). But she suspects there may be downsides, too. The thing is, she's too busy to find out. So she turns to you: "Will you find out what we'd need to do to acquire nonprofit status? And which category of nonprofit we should apply to be? What's involved in setting up and running a nonprofit? How hard or complicated would it be?"

Do the research that will help Sarah figure out what to do, and prepare your findings in the form of a report that Sarah and others can consult when setting up and managing the nonprofit. Seeing what comparable organizations have done would probably aid her in her decision making.

28. **Helping Your Bosses Find a Good Investment:** You're a finance co-op working in the executive office of a successful public relations firm. The three partners who own the firm rely on an investment advisor to advise them on managing their assets, but sometimes they decide on their own to add or remove companies from their investment portfolio. They're interested in catching one of the current technology waves. Should they buy some shares in Yelp? Groupon? WebMB? Uber? Something else? A combo?

One of the partners turns this research task over to you. You decide to start with the Internet since it provides a lot of investor news and advice, as well as some companies' annual reports (on their investor relations page) and financial reports (at www.sec.gov, the U.S. Securities and Exchange Commission's site). You'll also go to Hoover's Online (or some other company-information database), a great research tool you learned about in your classes. You'll compare the three companies on all factors that you think would be of interest to your employers.

Using your resourcefulness and great research skills, scout out the opportunities and write a clear, well-organized report on three of them that will help your readers decide what ideas to pursue with their investment advisor.

29. **Helping to Launch an Employee-Volunteer Program:** Last month your boss, HR director for the building supplies company where you work, got the executives' approval to launch an employee-volunteer program. As assistant HR director, you were tasked with conducting phase one of the plan: surveying the 420 employees to find out what kind of program they would be most likely to support. You designed an online survey to gather this information, and you got 300 complete replies. Here are the results:

Q1: Have you volunteered for a cause in the past year? Yes: 190; No: 110

Q2: If yes, about how many hours per week do you volunteer? 0.8

Q3: With what type of organization have you volunteered? Choose all that apply.

School: 32	National nonprofit organization: 14
Church: 77	Local nonprofit or health organization: 22
Neighborhood/community: 55	Other: 10

Q4: What type(s) of activity did you do? Choose all that apply.

Tutoring/teaching: 35	Community governance/development: 23
Construction/maintenance: 62	Promoting a social cause: 20
Help at food pantry/homeless shelter: 20	Coaching: 31
Beautification work: 39	Other: 4 (e.g., hospital)

Q5: Why do you volunteer? Rate each reason on a scale from 1 (not important) to 7 (very important).

It's important to help others: 5.5

I'm needed: 6.5

It broadens my world: 2

It makes me feel good to share what I'm good at: 5

I learn new things: 3.5

It feels good to work with others for a good cause: 4.5

I meet others and make friends: 2.5

Other reasons (write-ins): I needed something outside of work. | It helps promote our company. | A friend recruited me (three comments like this).

Q6: If you don't volunteer, why not? Rate each reason on a scale from 1 (strongly disagree) to 7 (strongly agree).

I'm too busy: 6

I feel I give enough to others already: 3

It's too hard for me to find the right volunteer opportunity: 4.5

It just sounds like more work: 5

Other reasons (write-ins): I want a life. | I need to have my family time (two comments like this). | It should be enough that I do my job.

Q7. If the company were to create a volunteer program, how would you feel about each of the following types? Rate each on a scale from 1 (not very positive) to 7 (very positive).

Individuals report their volunteer hours (honor system) and receive recognition at an annual company celebration: 3.5

Individuals receive up to two hours of unpaid time off per month, depending on the amount of service (must be documented): 5.0

Individuals receive up to two hours of paid time off per month, depending on the amount of service (must be documented): 5.5

The company holds a special volunteer event (e.g., community fix-up day): 5.5

The company chooses one special organization to support based on an employee vote, and becomes known as the benefactor of that organization: 4.3

The company creates a list of volunteer options based on an employee survey, and teams can choose which one they want to support: 4.8

Other options (write-ins): I like the idea of doing something as a team or company. | It would be a pain to have to document my community service (two comments like this). | What if I couldn't participate in the volunteer event? Would I be penalized? | I think we should be like other leading companies and have a "signature" cause that we support—and that would keep things simple.

Q4: My general attitude toward a company volunteer program in any form is

Strongly positive: 52

Positive: 90

Neutral: 76

Negative: 56

Strongly negative: 26

Comments: I don't want it counting against me on my performance review that I didn't volunteer—I work hard enough already (two comments like this). | I don't want the company telling me what do to with my personal time or where to give my service (two comments like this). | We are a great company with a big heart—we should show it more! | I love the idea of our company getting behind community service; a lot of us volunteer, and our contributions should be recognized. | I like the idea of the company helping us figure out where and how to volunteer.

Write your boss a report that helps him/her interpret these data and decide what kinds of parameters the new program should have. Remember that your recommendations can go only so far since your boss has additional data on such programs that you have not studied. Also keep in mind that your boss may want to share your report with the company executives.

30. **Recommending a City for a Business Getaway:** When the employees at Strategic Advantage, a communications firm, exceed their performance goals for the year by a wide margin, they're invited to "President's Club," which means that they and their families get to go on an all-expenses-paid trip to a cool U.S. city. As the president's administrative assistant, you research the places the president has in mind each year to help him choose the destination.

For this year, the president wants you to research two cities in the Southwest: Sedona and Santa Fe. Both are popular, highly rated vacation cities, and both are somewhat out of the way; it's unlikely that many of the company's employees have ever been to either. He's asked you to research and compare the relative advantages of the two cities. Is there golf? Other recreational opportunities? Shopping? Great food? Natural beauty? How hard is it to get there? Are interesting side trips possible? And how much money would we be talking for a nice hotel or resort there? (Forty-plus people will be going.) Is there sufficient opportunity for socializing? (This is supposed to be a team-building experience, too). Do sufficient Internet research to answer all of your boss's likely questions. Then write up your findings in an attractive document that he can share with the other executives.

31. **Helping to Ensure Visitors' Safety at the U.S. National Parks:** Lucky you! You just got a summer job with the _____ Regional Office of the US National Parks Service (you can visit https://www.nps.gov/aboutus/contactinformation.htm to pick your region). Your boss, the assistant director of communications, just gave you your first assignment. The office recently received a directive from national headquarters requiring the regions to ensure that visitors to their parks can acquire sufficient safety information from the parks' websites. To begin to address this directive, your boss wants you to study and assess the safety information on the websites of three parks in the region. For example, is the information provided for each park accessible and sufficient? Is it clear and useful? Does it make the danger clear without scaring people off? Is there information on one or more of the sites that the others should have as well? Can visitors easily access the information once they're at the park?

Choose three parks based on some kind of reasoning and then gather the information she is requesting. Evaluate the websites' safety information on logical, consistent criteria; and, in the last section of your report, suggest guidelines that the parks' websites could follow to ensure the completeness and helpfulness of this kind of information.

Topics for Projects with Real Clients

Following are several topics that would work especially well when clients can give students access to company or organizational information beyond what is available publicly. These topics can be developed into reports of varying length and difficulty.

1. Whether/how the company or department should use personality testing to improve its teamwork or operations

2. How effectively an organization's website is meeting the needs of the users

3. What kind of collaborative-writing or virtual-meeting platform would work best for this organization

4. How a local business can attract more student customers

5. How a local nonprofit can attract more student volunteers

6. How to raise money for a certain cause or event

7. Whether there is sufficient demand for the college to offer a new major or certificate program; whether a current major should be revised

8. What skills alumni are using in the workplace and areas in which they wish they had been better prepared

9. How to attract more students to a major or program at your university

10. How to solve a problem at your school or workplace

11. What kind of ad campaign would resonate with a new segment of customers that a company wants to attract

12. Whether a company should develop its own downloadable app and, if yes, how to do it and what it should do

13. How well a company's internal communication methods are meeting the company's and employees' needs

14. How to increase employee retention at a company

15. How to improve the accessibility (by those with disabilities) of an organization's website; how to boost accessibility awareness in an organization

16. How to improve employee performance reviews

17. The public's perception of a company or organization and how to correct or enhance that perception

18. Whether an organization should use email marketing

19. How an organization can generate more social media fans/followers

20. How an organization can increase email subscriptions to its blog

21. What application and/or service an organization should use for its webinars

22. The effectiveness of the communication in a company or department

23. Whether a company should consider developing an employee wellness program

24. The best practices for communication when using a company intranet to manage projects

25. The usability of a company's software, online ordering system, website, forms, or training materials

Delivering Business Presentations and Speeches

© hxdbzxy/123RF

Thirteen

Researchers consistently note the growing importance of oral communication skills even as technologies such as email, blogs, and social networking tools demand more of our writing skills. One heavily used form of oral communication in business is the presentation. A recent survey of 1,610 business-school alumni who had been in the workplace from 2 to 12 years found that 37.1% of them present monthly and 27.9% present weekly.[1] People who have been out of school longer and risen higher in their organizations are likely to present even more.

Why so much presenting? Because, depending on the nature of their work, business people need to give **oral reports** upwards and downwards in their organizations as well as outwards to clients, regulatory groups, citizens, and other external audiences. They may also need to deliver speeches, proposals and sales pitches, training talks, conference presentations, and many other kinds of talks to many other kinds of listeners.

This chapter will help prepare you for the various presentation challenges that await you in the professional world.

Learning Objectives

LO13-1 Prepare the right kind of presentation for your purpose and audience.

LO13-2 Determine the appropriate topic, purpose, structure, delivery method, and means of audience interaction for a presentation or speech.

LO13-3 Plan visual aids and handouts to support your presentation.

LO13-4 Describe the personal, physical, and vocal traits that contribute to an effective presentation.

LO13-5 Use visual aids effectively when speaking.

LO13-6 Manage audience interactions skillfully during your presentation.

LO13-7 Plan and deliver effective Web-based presentations.

LO13-8 Work effectively with a group to prepare and deliver a team presentation.

Problem-Solving Challenge

Meeting the Challenge of Formal Speaking

You joined the Corporate Affairs team at Sunfield Cereals only a few months ago, but you can already see that your work will involve several kinds of oral presentations.

For example, at its monthly meeting last week Sunfield's executive committee assigned your department the task of preparing a special oral report. The report will present the results of a survey that your department conducted to find out how a shipment of flawed products had affected the company's public image. Because you designed and conducted the survey, your boss has asked

you to give this report. The audience will be not only the company executives but also the managers at all 10 Sunfield locations across the United States. You must find a way to deliver your report to all these audiences simultaneously.

Then today, your boss asked you to do something very special for the company. It seems that each year Sunfield Chemicals awards a $5,000 scholarship to a deserving business student at State University. The award is presented at the business school's annual Honors Day Convocation, usually by your boss. To show

the business school's appreciation for the award, its administration requested that your boss be the speaker at this year's convocation. But she has a conflicting engagement, so you got the assignment. You are excited but nervous about this challenge.

Presentations are beginning to factor into your work more than you anticipated, and it's clear that such assignments will only become more frequent as you move up the ladder. Time to start developing your public-speaking skills. . . .

Preparing the Right Kind of Talk

LO13-1 Prepare the right kind of presentation for your purpose and audience.

When you're preparing a business presentation, a decision you'll need to make wisely, and early, is what kind of presentation you should make. In the words of Bob Adams, publisher of a series of business guides, "defining your presentation is half the battle."[2] That's because the kind of presentation you're creating will influence a lot of your other decisions.

Citing Daria Price Bowman's *Presentations: Proven Techniques for Creating Presentations That Get Results,* Adams describes 10 types of presentations (see the Communication Matters feature "10 Types of Business Presentations"). In this section, we'll focus on the three most common types, categorized by main purpose, and explain the special considerations and likely features for each one.

Informative Presentations

In this category fall the talks that are primarily informative in nature, such as oral reports and educational talks. These can be internal (e.g., presenting the results of a committee's work to an association's members, facts about a department's operations to executives, or training information to employees) or external (e.g., public-information talks on community issues or talks to particular groups to share your or your company's expertise in a certain area).

Special Considerations The key fact to keep in mind with an **informative presentation** is that *your audience's information needs are primary*. In developing this kind of presentation, you should learn all you can about amount and type of knowledge the audience already has and the amount and type they want to gain from you. You need to anticipate their likely questions and plan your answers. You also need to provide definitions, examples, and explanations to help your readers understand you. But perhaps most importantly, you need to understand *why* they want this information from you. As with written reports, informational presentations need to have a purpose that matches the audience's "problem" or need.

This doesn't mean that your own goals aren't important. Whatever informative talk you're giving, you will have a stake in it—whether it's wanting to convey a creditable image, wanting to be sure you represent your company appropriately, wanting to allay the listener's possible fears, or some other goal. But by definition, effectively conveying the information will be the main goal of this kind of talk.

Communication Matters

10 Types of Business Presentations

According to *Presentations: Proven Techniques for Creating Presentations That Get Results*, by Daria Price Bowman, business presentations can be divided into the following 10 types. While they're not completely distinct from one another, they convey a good sense of the variety of presentations you might be expected to give.

1. **Informative presentations.** This category includes oral reports, informational reports on one's area of expertise, and explanations of procedures.

2. **Persuasive presentations.** Besides persuading people to buy something, the goal of this kind of presentation is to gain support for an idea, motivate, or change people's minds.

3. **Goodwill presentations.** These are talks that are intended to celebrate noteworthy accomplishments and build camaraderie. They are upbeat and sometimes funny (e.g., "roasts" of honorees).

4. **Sales.** This category refers to the type of presentation you give when invited to compete for a company's business—say, for example, a full-blown multimedia sales presentation with the top brass. With this type of presentation, you have already made prior contact with the company and have begun to build rapport. Your presentation is thus your final, most elaborate effort to win the business.

5. **Training.** Employees need training on dozens of new and ongoing topics. Because you are often talking to a captive audience—people who may not want to be participating—you'll need to make special efforts to build rapport and maintain interest during your talk.

6. **Entertainment.** This is the category of the after-dinner speech and other speeches intended to amuse and enlighten.

7. **Image building.** Businesspeople often give speeches to external parties, such as community groups, parents and school officials, and professional associations. Often, such speeches have the purpose of enhancing the image of the organization for whom the speaker works.

8. **Motivational presentations.** This is the type of speech intended to inspire. It often uses high-energy tactics and is carefully tailored to the needs and desires of the audience.

9. **Interviews.** In your role as a professional and a representative of your organization, you may be interviewed by a radio or talk show host or a writer for a magazine or newspaper. You can approach the task as if it were a presentation, especially since the interviewers will often share the questions with you in advance. The job interview might also be considered a type of presentation—an interactive one that you need to be well prepared for.

10. **Multipurpose presentations.** A presentation intended to sell might be largely informational. Or an interview might be motivational. All the types listed above can be mixed and matched, depending on the particular requirements of the situation.

Source: Bob Adams, "Defining Your Type of Presentation Is Half the Battle," *BusinessTown*, accessed August 27, 2016, https://businesstown.com.

Likely Structure and Features With this kind of talk, you can get down to business quickly because the topic and purpose of the talk will probably already be known. After just a few opening words, you can get right into what you'll be discussing.

In general, oral reports are more likely to be delivered indirectly than are written reports. Perhaps this is because listeners expect an oral report to be more or less like a story, with the beginning and middle leading up to the main point. Whatever the reason, oral reports usually begin with the purpose, provide any helpful background information, present the facts and analysis, and then give the conclusions or recommendations. On the other hand, the direct structure may be more appropriate for some oral reports. For example, if you've been asked to report on the impact of a new federal regulation on the company's operations, your listeners may grow impatient if you do not reveal the main findings up front and then fill in the details.

Besides choosing between an indirect or direct structure, you'll need to choose a logical pattern for the contents of your talk. The structural patterns for written reports that are discussed in Chapter 11 ("Organizing the Report Information") are just as handy for oral presentations. Choose a pattern that matches the type of information you want to present—whether time based, factors based, cause/effect based, or some other logical pattern. Then, following the advice in that chapter, create an outline that divides your material into digestible chunks and puts them in an appropriate order.

Oral reports to managers, executives, boards of directors, and other company stakeholders tend to be relatively unemotional and focused on the data.

© PeopleImages/Media Bakery RF

Keep in mind that your listeners are forced to comprehend the information at the pace you're delivering it; they can't read more slowly or review earlier material the way they can with written reports. For this reason, planning the pacing of your talk is a special consideration, as is the preparation of helpful visual aids. Slides with bullet points have gotten a bad reputation from poor presenters and books like *Death by Power-Point* and *slide:ology*,[3] but when the information is relatively dense and complicated, well-designed text-based slides (with a bit of visual interest) can be your best presentation aid.

Like written reports, informative presentations may end with a summary, a conclusion, a recommendation, or a combination of the three. But the oral report is likely to have a more extensive closing statement. In a sense, your ending will serve the purpose of an executive summary by bringing together all the important information, analyses, conclusions, and recommendations.

Persuasive Presentations

Proposals and sales pitches are the main types of presentations in this category. These can be internal (e.g., persuading employees that an organizational change is needed or persuading your bosses to hire another staff member) or external (e.g., selling your products or services to potential customers).

Special Considerations
Like written persuasive messages and proposals, *persuasive oral presentations are primarily intended to sell.* When preparing this kind of talk, you will need to be especially analytical and creative when figuring out what will best move your listeners from lack of interest, skepticism, or even resistance to "yes."

Sales presentations usually involve more creativity and emotion than informative presentations.

© Monkey Business Images/Shutterstock

A **persuasive talk** doesn't just require logical organization, then; it requires a strategy. What kind of opening will bring your audience on board right away? How will you methodically build the need for your product or plan? What features of what you're selling will you highlight? What evidence will you provide that your idea or product will meet the listeners' needs? How will you use ethos, logos, and/or pathos to build desire and belief? What will you ask the audience to do, and how will you encourage them to do it? As you can see, all the questions you must answer when planning written persuasive messages, as discussed in Chapter 10, will need to be answered for oral ones, too.

Likely Structure and Features
In some situations, such as when the topic is serious and/or the main content is data, the listeners may expect a persuasive approach that is low key and even somewhat dry. For example, if you're proposing that a company choose your financial services firm to create and manage its investment portfolio, you'll want to convey an appropriate level of seriousness and focus on numbers that convey your expertise.

But more often, audiences will expect presentations in the persuasive category to be somewhat flashier than informative presentations. They'll expect an interesting, or even unorthodox, opening, verbal and visual material that keeps them engaged, and a higher level of involvement or enthusiasm on the part of the speaker. A deck of PowerPoint slides consisting of bullet points won't do the job here; you'll need engaging graphics and perhaps even animation, sound, and video. Audiences for this kind of talk also expect to be kept engaged through interaction. You can ask questions, tell stories, and use a conversational tone. As much as possible, keep your eyes on your audience, not on your notes or slides.

Entertaining or Ceremonial Presentations

Lots of business presentations can be better described as **speeches**. They're talks that may teach and may persuade, but *their main function is to engage the audience and reward their attention.* Inside the organization, the executives make most of the speeches, but there are times when employees give speeches, too—for example, when giving an inspirational talk at a company retreat or accepting an award at a recognition ceremony. You may be asked to give a speech to an audience outside your organization either because of your professional expertise or because you are an appropriate spokesperson for your organization.

Special Considerations

Of the three main types of talks discussed here, this is the type that is likely to involve an uninterrupted presentation by the speaker, especially if the speech is being delivered on a formal occasion and/or you are the featured speaker. With this trait comes special challenges. One is that of maintaining interest throughout. As with sales presentations, listeners expect entertaining speeches to surprise, amuse, challenge, or otherwise affect them emotionally while they're learning from the speaker's content. They also typically expect the speaker to achieve this feat without overt interactions with them besides eye contact (until the question-and-answer period, if there is one). Most listeners for such speeches don't expect or want to work very hard to comprehend or evaluate the contents; instead, they sit back and wait for what they hope will be a pleasant experience, one from which they'll carry away an interesting insight, a bit of humor, or a new attitude toward something.

Likely Structure and Features

Of the three types, this is the type that will be most likely to require that you choose your subject. For informative presentations, the speaker's educational goals and the audience's information needs help determine the topic, and for sales presentations, the product you're selling and the needs of the potential customers help determine the topic. For entertaining presentations, the range of choices will be greater, so determining your topic and purpose, discussed in the next section, will take more thought.

You will also have great latitude in deciding how to open your speech. The best openings will put the audience at ease, begin to develop rapport with them, and indicate that you are likely to have something interesting to say. See the Communication Matters box, "Getting Your Speech Off on the Right Note," for strategies that can help you achieve these goals. (These strategies can work well for many sales presentations, too.)

To plan the rest of your speech, think about the contents you want to include and what kind of structure would best match those contents. It is well documented that people respond well to articles or speeches that have an introduction, three middle parts, and a conclusion (despite the overuse and abuse of the five-paragraph essay in composition classes).[4] More points than four or five—unless you're going with a "Top Ten" theme—is probably too many. For each of the main points, try to plan an interesting story, example, or statistic to share.

When considering using visual support for your speech, you'll need to find out first if visuals can be shown in the context where you'll be presenting (some venues and occasions won't accommodate the display of electronic contents). If they can, create visuals that capture the gist of what you're saying or show interesting data; lists of bullet points may or may not be appropriate, depending on the topic and purpose of your talk.

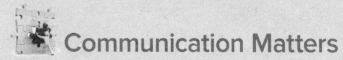

Communication Matters

Getting Your Speech Off on the Right Note

The introduction of a speech has much the same goal as the introduction of a written or oral report: to prepare the listeners (or readers) to receive the message. But the opening of a speech usually needs some kind of attention-gaining material as well.

Here are some possibilities:

- **A human-interest story.** People love stories, so consider opening with one. For example, a speaker presenting a message about the opportunities available to people with original ideas might open this way: "Nearly 150 years ago, an immigrant boy of 17 walked the streets of our town. He had no food, no money, no belongings except the shabby clothes he wore. He had only a strong will to work—and an idea."

- **Humor.** If you know a joke that's relevant to your topic, you might open with it—though, as one expert advises, you have to be a good joke teller to pull off this kind of opening without making the humor seem forced.* A strategy that many speakers seem to use is to say something humorous that is apropos of the situation. If someone gives you a glowing introduction, for example, you might say, "Wow, after that introduction, I can hardly wait to hear what I'm going to say!"

- **Quotations.** By quoting a person the audience would view as creditable, especially a comment with catchy wording, you can both spark their attention and introduce your key theme. A speech about building employee engagement might open with this quote from Mary Kay Ash, founder of Mary Kay Cosmetics: "A company is only as good as the people it keeps" (found on BrainyQuote.com, one of many sources of quotable remarks).

- **Questions.** Asking a question can generate immediate engagement. One kind of question that could open your talk is the rhetorical question, a question meant to establish commonality with the audience, such as "Who wants to be free of burdensome financial responsibilities?" Or, you can ask a genuine question, such as "How many of you have Roth IRAs?" Besides gaining attention, this kind of question can help you gauge the audience's knowledge so that you'll know how long to spend on each of your topics.

- **Startling statements.** If you can identify a relevant fact that will surprise the audience, that can be a good opener. A speech to an audience of merchants on a plan to reduce shoplifting could begin this way: "Last year, right here in our city, in your stores, shoplifters stole over $3.5 million of your merchandise."

*Bill Lampton, "5 Reasons You Shouldn't Start Your Speech with a Joke," *Business Know-How*, accessed May 9, 2016, http://www.businessknowhow.com/growth/speechjokes.htm.

The audience will expect you to end your speech with something catchy, inspirational, and/or forward looking. Give it some stylistic flair to make it memorable and an ending that is fit for a great talk.

Hybrid Presentations

While traits of all three types of presentations can be heard in every talk, some presentations are a more overt mixture than others. A **hybrid presentation** is fine as long as having more than one purpose is warranted by the situation.

A good example is the keynote speech that was given at a recent Association for Business Communication meeting. The speaker, who represented Corporate Media Relations for the agrochemical-biotechnology company Monsanto, described the media-relations makeover that Monsanto had recently undergone to connect better with the public, many of whom are suspicious of genetically modified organisms (GMOs). The speech was, on its surface, informational, consisting of many bullet-point-based slides that described Monsanto's customer research and the strategies that resulted. But the talk was equally an image-building presentation intended to humanize the company and emphasize its social awareness. Considering the context and content, having a two-purpose speech was appropriate.[5]

As with the other genres of communication discussed in this book, this discussion of common presentation types is intended to aid, not replace, your communication problem solving. To figure out what kind of talk to give, learn all you can about the situation and the audience, think about your own areas of expertise, and go with your best judgment.

You Make the Call

Can you think of other situations, like the one described here, in which a talk might have two equally important purposes? Or one that might seem like one kind of speech on the surface but is actually also serving another purpose?

Planning the Content and Delivery

Identifying the type of presentation you need will get you thinking about your talk in the right way. But to plan its specific contents and delivery, you'll need to consider the topics in this section and the next one more carefully.

LO13-2 Determine the appropriate topic, purpose, structure, delivery method, and means of audience interaction for a presentation or speech.

The Topic and Purpose

Whatever type of presentation you've chosen, your first step is to determine its topic and purpose. Sometimes, the topic and purpose will be assigned to you. Perhaps you've been asked to share with the rest of the marketing team how well the current mix of email, social media, and direct mail is working. Perhaps you've been asked to describe your company's community-enhancement efforts to the city's chamber of commerce. Or perhaps your job is to introduce a featured speaker at a gathering.

In other cases, you'll be asked to speak on a topic of your choice. In your search for a suitable topic, you should be guided by these three basic factors:

- *Your background and knowledge.* Any topic you select should be one with which you are comfortable. As much as possible, pick a topic that you feel quite knowledgeable about and that also affords you some opportunity to share your personal experiences.

- *The interests of your audience.* As with all the other types of communication discussed in this book, selecting a topic that your audience can appreciate and understand is vital to the success of your speech.

- *The occasion of the speech.* Is the occasion a meeting commemorating a historic event? A monthly meeting of an executives' club? The keynote address at a professional conference? Whatever topic you select should match the occasion in terms of formality and contents.

Also, whatever type of talk you'll be giving, find out, and stay within, the expected time limit. Nothing exasperates an audience more than a speaker who rambles on beyond the allotted time or, worse, takes up some of the time allotted to others who may be speaking. So plan the **scope** and **duration** of your speech accordingly. It is better to err on the side of saying too little than saying too much.

The Structure

After you have decided what to talk about, why, and for how long, it's time to start roughing out your **structure**. As discussed in Chapter 11 and the preceding section in this chapter, the topic and purpose will often suggest a structure. Just be sure that it is logical and that your choice of directness or indirectness matches the audience's expectations.

To flesh out your planned contents, you will need to gather additional information, whether by recalling relevant experiences or generating ideas, conducting research in a library, searching through company data, gathering information online, or consulting people in your own company or other companies. Chapter 11 can help you choose the right research methods and resources.

When you have your information, you are ready to begin planning a detailed outline. To do so, you can follow basically the same guidelines as those discussed in Chapter 11 or, if you're preparing an oral proposal, Chapter 10. If you prefer a more visual process, you can do some form of storyboarding, as discussed in the next section.

To avoid exasperating your audience, don't try to cover too much, and be sure to stay within the allotted time limit.
© Image Source/Getty Images RF

Plans for oral presentations need to differ somewhat from those for written reports or proposals, however, as discussed in this section.

Introduction The beginning of a presentation, like that of a written report or proposal, should convey the central topic of the talk and provide enough context for the audience to care about what you're about to say.

With oral presentations, though, you cannot simply jump into your content. The audience will expect you to make a **personal connection** with them first, whether by thanking them for inviting you, introducing yourself, or simply saying "Good morning." The opening of your talk also needs to begin to build your credibility, even if someone has introduced you or your audience already knows you.

When preparing your talk, then, you must put careful thought into your **opening remarks**. If you're an inexperienced speaker, you may want to write these out word for word and even plan the body language that will go with them.

Body Because of its oral delivery, the body of a presentation also needs to be planned somewhat differently from that of a written report or proposal.

- *A presentation needs to be simpler and shorter.* As mentioned earlier, readers can study written material at their own pace and reread sections as needed; they can even take a break and finish reading later. They also have such visible structural cues as levels of headings and formatting devices. By contrast, an audience must build a mental model of what you're saying as you speak. To help them follow you, keep the structure of your talk as simple as possible. In most cases, you should use only two levels of hierarchy, especially if you will not be using presentation software to aid your listeners' comprehension. Look for other ways to respect their limited energy, too, such as cutting out extraneous material and avoiding unnecessarily difficult content. Put detailed definitions, data, references, and other such information in a handout.

- *Presentations need more coherence helpers.* Because they're not reading, audiences need more, and more elaborate, **transitions**. When creating your presentation, figure out how you will move the audience from one section to the next, and include these transitions in your outline.

- *Presentations are less formal.* While a formal written report can be delivered in an impersonal style, that is not possible for a presentation, even a formal one, because the speaker is standing right there. For this reason, audiences expect some degree of **informality** in both delivery and content. Look for places in your presentation plan where you can add stories, examples, and even humor.

Conclusion An oral report is likely to have a more extensive ending than a written report. Here again, your listeners cannot flip back through the report the way they could with a written report, so you need a close that will help them pull all the parts of your report together and remember the key points. You can then invite questions, if that is part of your plan.

For other types of presentations, you can follow the summary with a creative and memorable flourish, such as an appropriate quote, call for action, or clever final remark.

The Delivery Method

In addition to determining the speech's content and structure, you'll need to decide whether you'll deliver your talk from notes, deliver it from memory, or read it.

Presenting Extemporaneously **Extemporaneous presentation** is by far the most popular and effective method. With this method, you first thoroughly outline your talk. Then you prepare notes to refer to when giving your presentation. Next, you rehearse your talk, using your notes as prompts, until you feel comfortable doing so. Resist the temptation to plan every word of your talk, even though the impromptu element in extemporaneous presentations requires a bit of bravery. The reason such presentations are preferred is they have a conversational feel. Practice your talk enough so that you can deliver it smoothly and efficiently while also sounding natural.

Memorizing The most difficult method is to present your speech from memory. If you are like most people, you find it hard to memorize a long succession of words. Also, if you memorize, you can get flustered if you miss a word or two during your talk.

For this reason, few speakers who use this method memorize the entire speech. Instead, they memorize key passages and use notes to help them through the speech. A delivery of this kind is a cross between an extemporaneous presentation and a **memorized presentation**.

Reading The third presentation method is reading. Most of us tend to read aloud in a monotone, with our eyes glued to the page. For this reason, it is considered inappropriate to read in most business situations, since your audience will want more personal interaction than that. However, when you're acting as the official spokesperson for a company or organization—for example, when responding to a crisis or giving an important announcement—reading from a carefully prepared speech is appropriate and even expected. Many top executives today use teleprompters when delivering **read speeches**, and many of these speeches are well done.

Extemporaneous presentations are the result of thorough preparation, even though they incorporate informal elements.
© Digital Vision/Getty Images RF

You can learn to read a speech in an interesting, smooth way, too. The key is to practice it enough so that it sounds almost as though you're talking. You should print your speech in a large enough font so that it is easy for you to look up at the audience at various points and then find your place when you look back down. You can also mark up your speech to remind yourself when to pause, look up, and vary the pace.

The Means of Audience Interaction

In the past, presentations were largely one-way communication, with the presenter delivering a well-prepared talk and restricting audience participation to applause or questions at the end. This kind of talk is still appropriate in many circumstances, but today's speakers often invite two-way communication while they're speaking. You will need to plan what kind of **interaction** to include.

With webinars, or live presentations conducted via the Web, participants expect to be kept involved through polls, questions, and even live chat with the speaker. In real settings, audiences can be invited to contribute by raising their hands, asking questions, voting with a clicker,[6] or tweeting their answers or comments.[7]

You may also want to incorporate other kinds of audience participation. In training talks, for example, presenters often give the attendees a chance to practice something on their own. In speeches designed to raise the audience's awareness about something, speakers sometimes ask the audience to do an activity in groups.

Whether or not you invite audience feedback during your talk, consider inviting the audience to email you afterward with their questions and comments. Many webinar presenters follow up their online sessions with evaluation forms that they email to the participants. This kind of post-presentation interaction can help you improve your presentations, acquire positive statistics to show to your boss, and build productive relationships with those who heard you speak.

Planning the Visuals to Support Your Talk

LO13-3 Plan visual aids and handouts to support your presentation.

Audiences have become much more visually oriented than they used to be. They expect most presentations to include a visual component to help them follow along and stay interested.

Plus, as professional trainers know, visuals also aid immensely in retention of the presented information. In *e-Learnng and the Science of Instruction,* Ruth Colvin Clark and Richard E. Mayer cite numerous studies to support the point that "people learn more deeply from words and graphics than from words alone."[8]

Planning the visual support for your oral report or speech should thus be integral to planning the talk overall.

Using Presentation Software Effectively

When most people think of designing visuals to go with a report or speech, they automatically think of PowerPoint—the first widely used, and still the most popular, presentation software. But cloud applications and apps for mobile devices have broadened your options.

For example, you may have tried Prezi, a cloud application that enables you to zoom in and out as you move around an online canvas. And of course there's Google Drive's Presentation, which has almost as many features as PowerPoint, along with the added benefit of enabling easy online collaboration.

Whichever tool you use, you can apply many of the visual-design principles discussed in Chapters 3 and 4 to make your slides clear and appealing. Use **grids** to create a balanced layout, and use **contrast**, **repetition**, **alignment**, and **proximity** to enable quick comprehension of how the elements on each slide go together.

You should also try to steer clear of these common slide-design pitfalls:

- *Putting too much on a slide.* As Garr Reynolds, author of *Presentation Zen,* points out, "One of the biggest mistakes that typical business people make with presentation slides . . . is going out of their way to seemingly use every centimeter of space on a page, filling it up with text, boxes, clip art, charts, footers, and the ubiquitous company logo."[9] Remember that your talk, not your slides, should convey most of your detailed information. Making a slide or Prezi object too crowded is a surefire way to make your audience stop looking at it. For text-based slides, we recommend no more than eight brief bullet points per slide and no more than two levels of bullet points (Exhibit 13-1).

- *Making the contents on the slide too small.* This is probably the second most common error. When you're designing your slides, you're looking at them on your computer, so small type and visuals are legible. But your audience for an in-person speech will be trying to read your slides from many feet away from the screen, and even those viewing webinar slides on their computers won't like tiny content. For text, we recommend 30-point type or larger for headings and 24-point type or larger for the text. Graphic elements also need to be large enough to be legible from a distance.

- *Overlooking chances to represent your content visually.* Reynolds is a big advocate of using most of your slides' real estate for visuals because "images are powerful, efficient, and direct."[10] So look for ways to use visuals to enhance the meaning of your slides. If you're showing how something is organized, for example, you might embed your text in one of the relationship or hierarchy graphics in PowerPoint's SmartArt. You can also look for information that can be illustrated or replaced with a photo or line art. The two slides in Exhibit 13-2 show one way to give your slides more visual appeal.

- *Using an inappropriate theme or unreadable color combinations.* Novices tend to want to choose elaborate and flashy designs for their slides. But many templates included with the software are too busy for most presentation purposes, and certain text and background color

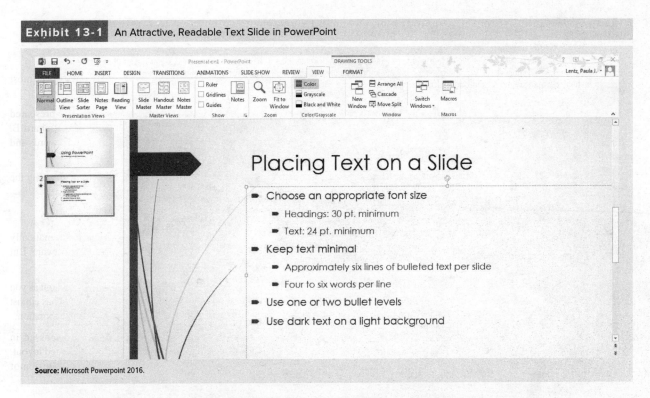

Source: Microsoft Powerpoint 2016.

combinations, such as red text on a blue background, make the slides difficult to look at, let alone read. Err on the side of conservatism. For text-based slides, dark text on a pale background that has a bit of visual interest (e.g., a gradient or a simple decorative graphic) can make for easily readable slides as well as a clean, professional look.

- *Using too much animation.* Another tendency amateurs have is to go wild with the options for transitions between slides and with other dynamic features. Prezi is particularly susceptible to this problem; all of the zooming in and out can actually make viewers dizzy. Again, err on the side of conservatism. Remember that the goal is not to dazzle the audience with visual activity but to achieve your communication purpose.

- *Being inconsistent across slides.* Your whole presentation should have a consistent look. This means that similar slides should be formatted similarly. For text-based slides, use the same font throughout for the slide titles, as well as the same body font. Your use of SmartArt, photos, and other visuals needs to be consistent as well; you shouldn't have clip art on some slides, photos others, and SmartArt on yet others. No slide should look as though it belongs in a different presentation.

Another issue to think about is how to cite visuals (or wording) that you've borrowed from other sources. We recommend using an abbreviated form like the one used in Exhibit 13-2, which provides just enough information to credit the source. For books, you can use just the author's name and book title (e.g., "Source: Chip Heath and Dan Heath, *Made to Stick*"), and for some online resources, you can provide just the title (e.g., "Source: *eMarketer.com*"). On the other hand, if you'll be providing your listeners with an electronic copy of your slides, you might want to include a references slide that lists the full publication information for your sources.

When your talk will not be electronically supported—and such talks still take place frequently— you should consider incorporating visuals (except animation and multimedia, of course) into a print handout for your listeners. Many of these types of visuals can also be adapted to a flip chart or whiteboard.

The first slide here isn't bad. It avoids being too crowded, the bullet points are clear, and the photo adds visual interest. But compare it to the next one, which conveys the same information but in a more visually pleasing form. Watch for opportunities to make your meaning stand out by minimizing the text and maximizing the visuals.

Female Employees in Japan

- Make 40% less than men
- Hold only 10% of the management roles.

Source: Christina Cauterucci, "What the U.S. Can Learn from Japan's Working Women," *Slate*, October 8, 2015.

© Indeed/Getty Images RF

Female employees in Japan make 40% less than men and hold only 10% of the management roles.

Source: Christina Cauterucci, "What the U.S. Can Learn from Japan's Working Women," *Slate*, October 8, 2015.

© Brock Jones

Creating a Storyboard

One way to plan the visuals that will go with your presentation is simply to make rough notes as you outline your talk. Another way is to jump into your presentation software and just rough out the text and the visuals as you're drafting your show. But for a fairly long, complex talk, especially one you're preparing with a team, you should consider creating a **storyboard**.

Storyboards originated in the film industry as a way to plan what would be happening on screen when the different sounds, such as dialog and music, were playing. They're now used for creating PowerPoint shows, videos, online tutorials, websites, and other genres that require the coordination of visuals, sound, and action.

Exhibits 13-3 and 13-4 show the first slides of a sample storyboard. The table format makes it easy to see at a glance what will be happening as each screen or slide appears. Like an outline, the storyboard can start out as just a way to plan the sequence of screens and indicate with placeholders what kind of content will be added, as shown in Exhibit 13-3. As you develop your talk, you can replace the placeholders with sketches and more information. If you're working alone, you can decide when the storyboard is complete enough for you to start building your show. If you're working with a group or someone wants to review your talk before you give it, you can fill in all the visuals, oral commentary, and animation (if there is any), as shown in Exhibit 13-4.

When making and reviewing your plan, use the checklist in Exhibit 13-5 to guide you.

Preparing Handouts

Should you supplement your presentation with **handouts**? If so, what kind? And at what point in the talk? These are good questions. You know from experience that some speakers provide no handouts, while others provide complete copies of their slides. If they have handouts, some speakers distribute them at the beginning of the talk, while others wait until the end.

Make your decisions given the purpose and occasion of your talk. If you're presenting information that your listeners will want to be able to review later, give them complete copies of your slides or even a complete copy of your report or proposal. If you think your listeners will want to take notes as you go, give a handout at the start of the talk that has room for notes; otherwise, save the handout until the end so that your speech can benefit from the element of surprise. If the

You Make the Call

Can you think of situations in which you might want to deliver both a written and an oral report to your audience members? Why would this be appropriate in some circumstances?

Exhibit 13-3	First Slides of a Rough Storyboard for a Training Talk	
Slide Number	**Content**	**Oral Comments/Actions**
1	Title: Something like "How to Use SmartArt" Visual: Some different examples of SmartArt	Motivational beginning—why to use SmartArt, how easy it is.
2	Text: What is SmartArt? Visuals: Two different examples	Definition of SmartArt. Have a couple of good examples appear on click. "Let's get started!"
3	Text: Step 1—select the slide where you want SmartArt Visual: Show a sample slide w/bullet points for a talk on China	Set up the sample scenario—giving a talk about China. Now want to make the bulleted list more appealing.
4	Text: Step 2—show how to access/apply SmartArt Visual: Show right-clicking and choosing Vertical Picture Accent List. Use arrows to show where to click.	How to access SmartArt from your list. Note default and additional choices. Select the graphic. Click to show arrows/shapes as needed during demo.
5	Text: Step 3—show how to enhance the chosen SmartArt graphic with visuals Visual: Slide showing list in SmartArt format. Arrow points to visual placeholder.	Note how much nicer the slide looks. Point out that you can add visuals to this particular SmartArt graphic. Example: Insert small graphic of Chinese flag for first topic.

Exhibit 13-4

First Slides of a Storyboard with the Content Filled in (Angle Brackets Indicate Where to Trigger the Animation)

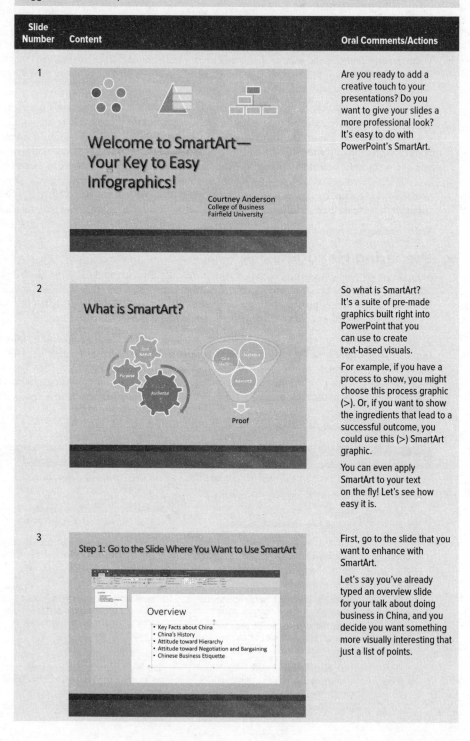

Slide Number	Content	Oral Comments/Actions
1	**Welcome to SmartArt— Your Key to Easy Infographics!** Courtney Anderson College of Business Fairfield University	Are you ready to add a creative touch to your presentations? Do you want to give your slides a more professional look? It's easy to do with PowerPoint's SmartArt.
2	**What is SmartArt?** Proof	So what is SmartArt? It's a suite of pre-made graphics built right into PowerPoint that you can use to create text-based visuals. For example, if you have a process to show, you might choose this process graphic (>). Or, if you want to show the ingredients that lead to a successful outcome, you could use this (>) SmartArt graphic. You can even apply SmartArt to your text on the fly! Let's see how easy it is.
3	**Step 1: Go to the Slide Where You Want to Use SmartArt** Overview • Key Facts about China • China's History • Attitude toward Hierarchy • Attitude toward Negotiation and Bargaining • Chinese Business Etiquette	First, go to the slide that you want to enhance with SmartArt. Let's say you've already typed an overview slide for your talk about doing business in China, and you decide you want something more visually interesting that just a list of points.

Exhibit 13-4 *Continued*

4

Step 2: Right-Click on the Text That You Want to Format with SmartArt

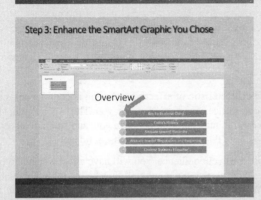

All you have to do is right click in the list, and a menu will pop up. Hover over "Convert to SmartArt" (>), and that will open the SmartArt choices.

If you don't like the ones SmartArt thinks you might want, you can click "More SmartArt Graphics" (>).

But let's say we like this one (>)—so we'll click it.

5

Step 3: Enhance the SmartArt Graphic You Chose

Voilà! Your list now has visual appeal! And with this particular SmartArt graphic, you can add an icon or photo at the beginning of each bullet point (>) to add even more interest.

For example, you could use a graphic of China's flag for the first topic. Let's see how.

Exhibit 13-5 Tips for Effective Presentation Visuals

Checklist for Preparing/Editing Presentation Slides

Questions about the presentation as a whole:

- Is there an attractive, clearly worded, readable title slide?
- Does the writer make good use of an outline slide? Is it titled effectively, and are the items in the list of topics grammatically parallel?
- Do the slides seem to cover all the important information?
- Do the slides seem to be in the most logical order?
- Is there a final slide that sums things up or leaves people with a significant thought or finding?
- Does the whole presentation have a consistent look?

Questions about every slide:

- Is there enough contrast between the background and the textual and/or visual components?
- Is there any type that is too small to be read? (Remember, no typeface should be smaller than 24 points.) Conversely, is any type too big (yelling)? Is any typeface hard to read (as with italics or too fancy a font)?
- Is there too much or too little information on any slide? Should any slides be combined or divided up?
- Are slide titles accurate, informative, and parallel?
- Has the writer managed the hierarchy of the information well on text-based slides (not using more than two levels of information and making clear which is on the top level and which is on the secondary level)? Are items in all lists grammatically parallel?
- Is the wording on each slide clear and grammatically correct?
- Is each slide visually clean and attractive? Should/could the writer add visuals anywhere or replace text with visuals? Do any of your visuals need captions and/or citation of the source?
- Are the dynamic elements (e.g., slide transitions) appropriate for the topic and audience? Should you use more or less animation at any point?

information you're covering can be distilled into a useful quick-reference sheet or a list of resources, handing that out at the end of your talk is sufficient. As you can see, there is no over-arching rule; what's best will depend on the situation.

If possible, always bring one complete print copy of your slides or a detailed outline of your talk to the presentation venue. Computers crash; projector bulbs go out; Internet connectivity sputters. If technological disaster strikes, it's likely that the venue will still have a copier, enabling you to deliver your talk with print support.

Delivering Your Talk

Whatever type of oral report, speech, or presentation you will be giving, you'll need to prepare yourself to deliver it. The following points will help ensure that your audience will respond positively.

Projecting Appealing Personal Traits

LO13-4 Describe the personal, physical, and vocal traits that contribute to an effective presentation.

In oral presentations you, the speaker, are a very real part of the message. How the audience perceives you can significantly affect how they will respond to your content. Every speaker has a unique personality, of course, but everyone can also choose to project certain traits instead of others. As part of getting yourself into the right mindset to present, focus on the qualities described in this section.

Confidence A primary characteristic of effective speaking is confidence—both your confidence in yourself and the confidence of your audience in you. The two are complementary: Your confidence in yourself gives your audience confidence in you, and your audience's confidence in you gives you a sense of security that increases your self-confidence.

When you know the members of your audience, you will have already begun to earn their confidence through your earlier contact with them and will thus be likely to feel relatively confident when speaking to them. When you must speak to a room full of strangers, you'll need to work harder to generate confidence. Preparing your presentation diligently and practicing it thoroughly is the best way to prepare for such situations. Also helpful is having an appropriate physical appearance. Looking like those your audience respects will give you credibility and help you get into your role as presenter. Yet another confidence-building strategy is simply to talk in a strong, clear tone. Speaking as though you are relaxed and self-assured will actually help you feel this way. See the Communication Matters feature "Controlling Nervousness During Your Talk" for more ways to feel confident and relaxed while speaking.

Good presenters project confidence, competence, sincerity, and friendliness.
© Photodisc/Getty Images

Competence Audiences expect speakers to be knowledgeable on the topic they're discussing. Do your homework so that you'll have the knowledge your audience will require of you. Anticipate the listeners' likely questions so that you'll be prepared to answer them. And spare no effort in making the presentation itself well designed and well written. Grammatical errors or poorly designed slides can sabotage an otherwise great speech.

Sincerity Because your **ethos**—your character as a speaker—is front and center in a presentation, it is a key element of your talk. As soon as your listeners see you and begin to hear you, they will be assessing who you are and whether you can be trusted. They will be quick to detect insincerity, and if they detect it, they are likely to give little weight to what you say. The way to project an image of sincerity is simple: *Be* sincere. Be yourself, and avoid hype or pretense. Show that your topic is of genuine interest to you and that it is more important than your ego.

Communication Matters

Controlling Nervousness During Your Talk

It's well known that some people have a strong fear of public speaking. But most can control that fear and give excellent talks by using certain calming strategies.

Here are some of the best ones we've learned about (and used):

- *Prepare well for your talk.* This is one of the most successful strategies. Good preparation prevents feelings of worry and uncertainty during your talk and helps you feel optimistic about how it will go.
- *Realize that nobody can control everything that will happen during a talk.* For this reason, allow yourself to relax a bit before you speak. Part of the excitement and appeal of a live talk is that unexpected things will happen—to every speaker. People realize this and allow some room for mishaps (e.g., announcing an award winner only to find that he/she hasn't attended the event; having the technology misfire; following a speaker who has used up almost half

of your speech time; having to field negative comments from an unreasonable audience member). To some extent, you must simply roll with these things and not feel too embarrassed about them because they're par for the course.

- *Get to the gathering early and meet some of the participants before giving your speech.* When you've chatted with people who will be in the audience, it is much easier to approach your talk as a conversation, not a performance, and the audience seems much less daunting.
- *Realize that the audience hasn't come there to see you fail.* In fact, they want you to do well and want to have a pleasant experience themselves. They're behind you, not against you.
- *Care about what you're talking about.* You know how you feel when you're explaining something to someone or sharing something you care about? Bring some of that feeling into your talk. It will help you focus on your content, not yourself.

- *Calm yourself physically.* Before your talk, take a few deep breaths; let your shoulders relax; let your mind rest. This will help calm irrational fears and let you focus on your talk.
- *If you're easily distracted, don't stare people right in the eyes as you speak.* Instead, let your eyes rest a bit on people's faces as you look at the audience. That way, you still look as though you're making eye contact, but you won't be distracted by personal contact while you're trying to focus on your speech.
- *Realize that a bit of anxiety is normal—and good.* Read your jitters as a sign that you're pumped for your speech and ready to do a good job.
- *Plan the beginning of your talk especially carefully.* When your speech gets off to a good start, you'll have more confidence about delivering the rest of it, and you'll feel the audience's goodwill. Plan the opening word for word and gesture by gesture if you have to. Then practice giving it in a natural, conversational way.

Friendliness A speaker who projects an image of friendliness has a significant advantage. Audiences simply like friendly people, and they are generally receptive to what such people say. To project friendliness, smile, make eye contact, and learn and use audience members' names. You can also watch yourself in a mirror as you practice speaking to improve your projection of friendliness.

Managing the Physical Elements
In face-to-face presentations and many videos and online presentations, your listeners will be looking at you and your surroundings. What they will see is a part of the message and can affect the success of your speech. Do your best to make these visual elements contribute to, not detract from, your talk.

The Communication Environment Whenever you'll be visible, a background will be visible as well. For actual presentations, try to visit the room ahead of time to see what adjustments to the setting you might want to request. For example, you might want the podium moved or the lighting managed in a certain way. For virtual presentations, be sure to test how you'll actually look on camera so you can check the backdrop, the lighting, and how much of you will show. In both environments, ensure that your voice will be appropriately amplified and that extraneous noise will be kept to a minimum.

You Make the Call
Audience members can help or hinder the speaker with their reactions during the talk. What behaviors are polite and encouraging? What behaviors have you seen that could be discouraging for a speaker?

Effective presenters wear appropriate, nondistracting clothing, use friendly facial expressions, and look directly at the members of their audience.

© Eric Audras/PhotoAlto/Getty Images

Personal Appearance Your personal appearance is a part of the message your audience receives. Dress in a manner appropriate for the audience and the occasion. You should also be sure that nothing about your appearance (e.g., hairstyle or jewelry) is distracting.

Posture Your posture is also part of the visual message you project. Keep your body erect without appearing stiff, and comfortable without appearing limp. Try to appear naturally poised and alert.

Walking Your audience will form an impression of you from the way you walk, so walk confidently to the place where you will speak. During the presentation, you can step forward and to the side to emphasize points and keep the audience's attention. But don't walk so much or so far that you detract from your message, and be sure not to walk away from the microphone.

Facial Expression Probably the most communicative physical movements are facial expressions. Using an appropriate expression, such as a smile, a look of concern, or a puzzled frown, can enhance your content.

You should also look at your audience often to show that you are speaking directly to them and have a genuine interest in them. Try to look at different parts of the audience as you talk to indicate that you are including everyone. If it will help you speak more naturally and confidently, make **eye contact** with some of the audience members. If you find actual eye contact too distracting, you can "fake it" by simply looking at people's faces during your talk and then make eye contact during the question-and-answer period.

Gestures Like facial expressions, gestures are strong, natural aids to speaking. You might emphasize a plea with palms up, for example, or show disagreement by shaking your head. You can raise first one hand and then the other to indicate alternatives or to emphasize contrasting points, or use a shrug to mean "who knows?"

The gestures you use will also depend on your personality. the size and nature of the audience, and the occasion. A speaker appearing before a formal group will tend to use somewhat conservative gestures (e.g., slight head and hand movements). As with the other elements of your talk, you'll need to adapt your physical movements to the situation.

Using a Pleasant Voice and Speaking Style

An interesting, pleasant voice is an important element of good speaking. To be sure your voice enhances your message, practice speaking in a way that avoids these common problems: (1) lack of pitch variation, (2) lack of variation in speed, (3) lack of vocal emphasis, and (4) unpleasant voice quality.

Lack of Pitch Variation Speakers who talk in a monotone won't hold the interest of their listeners for long. Listening to your voice and making a conscious effort to vary your **pitch** can help you develop a more interesting style.

Lack of Variation in Speaking Speed Delivering your whole talk at the same speaking speed can be boring as well. To vary the **pace** of your presentation, you can deliver the easy

Look Like a Pro with PowerPoint Keyboard Shortcuts

If you've ever attended a presentation during which the speaker had trouble finding the right view, going back to an earlier slide, or using other features of the software, you know how distracting that can be. Familiarizing yourself with keyboard shortcuts can help you move around quickly and skillfully in your presentation. Here are some commonly used shortcuts for managing your slides like a pro in PowerPoint 2013 and 2016.

To Do This	Press
Start your presentation in Slide Show view.	Alt + S, B
Perform the next animation or advance to the next slide.	N, Enter, Page Down, Right Arrow, Down Arrow, or Spacebar
Perform the previous animation or advance to the next slide.	P, Page Up, Left Arrow, Up Arrow, or Backspace
Go to a slide number.	number + Enter
Display a blank black slide, or return to the last-viewed slide from a blank black slide.	B or Period
Display a blank white slide, or return to the last-viewed slide from a blank white slide.	W or Comma
End a presentation	Esc
Erase on-screen annotations	E
Return to the first slide.	Press and hold Right and Left Mouse buttons for 2 seconds
Change the pointer to a pen (to draw on your slides while presenting).	Ctrl + P
Change the pen back to an arrow.	Ctrl + A
Change the pointer to an eraser.	Ctrl + E
Show or hide the ink markup.	CTRL + M

To see all the PowerPoint shortcuts, press Shift + F10.

Source: "Use Keyboard Shortcuts to Deliver Your Presentation," Microsoft.com, accessed May 14, 2016, https://support.office.com.

parts of your message at a fairly fast rate and the more difficult parts and the parts you want to emphasize at a slower rate. You can also use pauses at appropriate points to let what you've said sink in. When you pause, be sure to avoid such **fillers** as *uh, like, you know,* and *OK.*

Lack of Vocal Emphasis Delivering all parts of your talk as if they were equally important will hinder your audience's comprehension and lose their attention. To give words their proper emphasis, you can vary the pitch of your voice, the pace of your presentation, and the **volume** of your voice. When varying your volume, keep in mind that decreasing your volume can sometimes be more dramatic and effective than increasing it.

Unpleasant Voice Quality It is a hard fact that some voices are more pleasant than others. But whatever the quality of your **speaking voice**, you can improve it, in much the same way as you can learn to speak a foreign language with appropriate accents, vowels, and consonants.

First, capture your voice on audio or video and assess how you sound. Then practice changing your pitch, speed of delivery, and volume to make your voice more pleasant and engaging. You might want to watch videos of speakers you admire and mimic their style to some extent.

Referring to Your Visuals as You Speak

Visuals have become an expected part of most presentations, and for good reason: They add interest and aid comprehension. But you need to strike a good balance between helping the

LO13-5 Use visual aids effectively when speaking.

audience read what's on the screen and keeping the focus on you and what you have to say. Here are some basic dos and don'ts:

- Talk to the audience—not to the visuals. Look at the visuals only when the audience should look at them.

- Don't read the points on your slides verbatim. The audience can read these as long as you've made them big enough. Instead, allude to the key points as you deliver your oral commentary.

- Be sure that your commentary matches and elaborates on what's on your slides. The audience should be able to connect your comments to the slides' contents easily, and they will expect your comments to flesh out what's on the slides.

- When discussing a visual, refer to it with physical action and words. Use a laser pointer or point to the slide with your hand or eyes. You can also have each point appear or fly in as you're discussing it.

- If necessary, explain the visual. Remember that the visual is there to help you communicate content, not just to add visual interest.

From the Tech Desk

Presentation Delivery Tools Help You Convey Your Message Effectively

Have you ever used PowerPoint's Presenter View? It can really enhance the smoothness of a presentation. You can see its major tools in the screenshot here. While your slides are being displayed to the audience in Slide Show view, Presenter View lets you view not only the slides but also your notes. Additionally, you see the title to the upcoming slide as well as the elapsed time since the beginning of the presentation. Furthermore, a menu under the current slide allows you to start or end the show on one click, black out that screen to bring the attention back to you, and perform other actions. As the presenter, you have the flexibility to skip slides or change the ordering on the fly.

In PowerPoint 2016 you can enable presenter view by going to the Slide Show tab > Monitors box and being sure "Use presenter view" is checked. *Note:* You need to have your computer connected to two monitors—usually a laptop and a projector—to be able to set up and use Presenter View. For setup instructions, search "presenter view" in PowerPoint's Help feature.

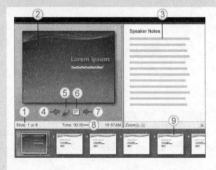

1 The slide number (for example, slide 1 of an 8-slide presentation)

2 The slide you are currently showing to the audience

3 The speaker's notes, which you can use as a script for your presentation

4 Click to go to the previous slide

5 The pen or higlighter

6 Click to display a menu that enables you to end the show, darken or lighten the audience screen, or go to a specific slide number

7 Click to go to the next slide

8 The elapsed time of your presentation, in hours and minutes

9 Slide thumbnails that you can click to skip a slide or to return to a slide that you already presented

Source: Microsoft, "What Is Presenter View?" Microsoft.com, accessed May 14, 2016, https://support.office.com/en-us/article/What-is-Presenter-view-98f31265-9630-41a7-a3f1-9b4736928ee3.

Managing the Interactions with Your Audience

For many presentations, interacting with your audience will be appropriate and expected. As mentioned in the section on planning your talk, you should decide up front what kind of interaction you'll be inviting and during what part of your talk. If it's okay for people to ask questions as you're speaking, tell them. Otherwise, most people will assume that they must wait until the end to do so.

LO13-6   Manage audience interactions skillfully during your presentation.

During the audience-interaction parts of the speech, unexpected and sometimes bothersome things can happen. Here are some issues that might arise and how to deal with them:

- *You're asked something you don't know.* Don't try to fake an answer. Instead, acknowledge that you don't know the answer and invite others to share their ideas. Then graciously compliment their contributions and add what you do know. If the question really needs an answer from you, you can offer to find the information and share it with the audience later (e.g., by email).

- *Someone wants to talk about a pet topic and steer everyone away from the topics of your talk.* Let the person share his/her point, but after about 30 seconds, indicate with your body language (nodding, turning your head, beginning to walk away) that it's time to move on. Call on someone else who had a hand up; but if no one else did, ask the group a question that's related to what you talked about.

- *Someone wants to show off his/her expertise.* It's fine to let this go on for a while; in fact, the person might actually be adding something valuable. But here, too, after about 30 seconds, nod and make a remark like "Thank you, that's certainly worth thinking about" or "I'd like to talk with you further about this after we're finished," and move on to a new question.

- *Someone disagrees with you.* The most important advice here is not to get hooked emotionally by this challenger. Stay calm and objective, and when you get a chance to speak, acknowledge why the person might think that way, reiterate why you think the way you do, and then move on.

- *Some audience members are carrying on a distracting side conversation.* If you're getting annoyed by audience members who are talking with each other while you talk, you can bet that the rest of the audience is annoyed, too. Pause for a moment until the offenders' chatter is the only sound in the room. That will usually give them the message, as will walking over to them as you're speaking. If they persist, you may have to hold up a hand toward them as you're speaking or even stop to say, "I'm sorry—could I ask you to hold your comments until the end of the talk? Thank you."

- *Nobody says anything when you ask a question.* This rarely happens because people usually like to talk when they've come together to hear a presentation. But if people are slow to participate, be ready to rephrase your question in a more provocative way. For example, if "What kind of people make the best salespeople?" doesn't draw much response, ask "Which do you think would make a better salesperson—an introvert or an extrovert? Or does it depend?"

Reviewing Presentation Basics

There's a lot to think about when planning a presentation. When you get caught up in the preparations, use Exhibit 13-6 to help you focus on the basics.

Exhibit 13-6   Summary of Guidelines for Oral Reports and Public Presentations

Oral Presentation Basics

- Be sure your report or speech has a clear, audience-adapted objective.
- Organize the talk so that it leads the listeners logically to your conclusion. The situation may call for either the direct or indirect order.
- Plan an engaging beginning.
- Plan for appropriate audience participation.
- Plan the visuals, if any, that will support your talk.
- Choose your speaking method (extemporaneous, memorization, reading, or a hybrid).
- Choose your presentation tools (if any), and be sure the venue is optimized for your talk. Manage any other visual elements of your talk (e.g., your appearance, the background) to your advantage.
- Project confidence, competence, sincerity, and friendliness.
- Employ body language to your advantage. Be relaxed and natural, and use appropriate gestures and facial expressions.
- Articulate clearly, pleasantly, and with proper emphasis. Avoid mumbling and the use of such fillers as *ah*, *er*, *like*, and *OK*.
- Punctuate the presentation with references to well-designed, nondistracting visuals.
- Field audience questions and comments with honesty, interest, and professionalism.
- End your presentation with a striking quote, statistic, or other comment that will reinforce your communication purpose.
- Provide handouts as needed to enable the audience to follow and use the information.

Delivering Web-Based Presentations

LO13-7   Plan and deliver effective web-based presentations.

Live Web presentations—commonly called *webinars* or *Web events*—have become a popular genre of business communication. They eliminate the speakers' and participants' travel expenses, and they can reach huge audiences. Plus, many powerful, easy-to-use applications for conducting such events are available. WebEx, once the undisputed leader in this area, now has competitors with such products as Citrix's GoToMeeting, Onstream Webinars, Adobe Connect, and more. The affordable costs make this technology attractive to both large and small businesses for presentations to both large and small audiences.

Varieties of Web Presentations

While the terms *webcast, Web meeting,* and *webinar* are sometimes used interchangeably, and one Web-based application might support all three types of communication, the consensus of those in the industry seems to be that the terms have—or should have—different meanings.

A **webcast** typically consists of live video being "broadcast" to the audience. Like a television or radio show, it provides no means of audience participation. A **Web meeting** is a Web-based get-together, usually for a small group of people who have chosen to conduct their interactions online rather than in a conference room. Of the three terms, **webinar** is the most synonymous with *presentation*. Here, a main speaker or speakers present on their topic of expertise, but the audience almost always has an opportunity to participate.

Special Guidelines for Web Presentations

To deliver a live virtual presentation effectively, you'll need to prepare for certain preliminary, delivery, and closing activities. Your first step is to choose a user-friendly technology that supports the type of webinar you want to give. Then you'll prepare and send out announcements of the presentation along with a note encouraging the audience to pretest their systems before the designated start time for the presentation. A day or two before and the day of the presentation, most presenters send email reminders of the event.

It is a good idea to line up a technical person to troubleshoot during the presentation since some participants will have trouble connecting, others will fall behind, and software or Internet glitches can occur. Also, you'll need to arrange ahead of time for an assistant if you need one. An assistant can help you keep track of time, take over if necessary, and provide other help to keep the presentation going smoothly.

You may want to create something for early arrivers to view in the first 5 to 10 minutes before you start. This could be an announcement, news of an upcoming presentation, or information about your products and services. At the end of the talk, you will want to tell participants where to access additional information, including your slides, a video recording of the presentation, and/or other materials.

Delivering your virtual presentation will be like delivering other presentations except that you'll be doing it from your desktop using a microphone and perhaps a Web camera (if the talk will include video). You may want to use the highlighter, drawing tools, or animation features of PowerPoint or the webinar application to help you emphasize key points that you would otherwise physically point to in a face-to-face presentation. You will want to plan breaks during which you will poll or quiz the audience or handle questions that have come in through the chat tool.

In the closing, you will want to allow time to make any final points and answer any remaining questions. Watching your time is critical because some systems will drop you if you exceed your requested time.

Overall, presenting virtually requires the same keys to success as other presentations—careful planning, attentive delivery, and practice.

Virtual Presentations: The Next Best Thing to Being There

Web-based presentation tools offer many options for participant interaction. Featured here is the control panel of Citrix's GoToWebinar. You can see who is attending, call them by name, show their desktops, give them the mic, show them on live video (if they have webcams), conduct polls, chat, and more.

Source: *GoToWebinar User Guide*, Citrix, 2015, accessed May 16, 2016, http://support.citrixonline.com/servlet/file Field?retURL=%2Fapex%2FCPDownloadStarter%3Farticle LinkId%3DG2WD00001%26l%3Den_US%26product %3Dwebinar&entityId=ka350000000TrytAAC&field= Content__Body__s.

Giving Team (Collaborative) Presentations

LO13-8   Work effectively with a group to prepare and deliver a team presentation.

Team presentations are a common school assignment, and they're common in business as well. To give this type of presentation, you can apply all the preceding advice about giving individual presentations and speeches. You can also use much of the advice from Chapter 11 on preparing written reports collaboratively. But you will need to adapt the ideas to an oral presentation setting.

First, you will need to take special care to plan the presentation—to determine the sequence of the presentation as well as the content of each team member's part. You also will need to select supporting examples and design any visual components carefully to build continuity from one part of the presentation to the next. A storyboard, as discussed earlier, can be a great tool for planning the verbal and visual components of a group presentation.

Groups should plan for the physical aspects of the presentation, too. You should coordinate the type of delivery, use of notes, and attire to present an impression of competence and professionalism. You should also plan the transitions from one presenter to the next so that the team will appear coordinated.

Another presentation aspect—**physical staging**—is important as well. For face-to-face presentations, team members should decide where they will sit or stand, how visuals will be presented, how to change or adjust microphones, and how to enter and leave the speaking area. For videotaped and virtual presentations that will show the speakers and their settings, you will need to determine what kind of background to have and what distance the presenter will sit from the camera.

Attention to the close of the presentation is especially important because you'll need to ensure that all the pieces delivered by the team members are brought together into a coherent, complete conclusion. Teams need to decide who will present the close and what will be said. If a summary will conclude the talk, the member who presents it should attribute key points to appropriate team members. If there is to be a question-and-answer session, the team should plan how to conduct it. For example, will one member take the questions and direct them to a specific team member? Or will the audience be permitted to direct questions to specific members? Some type

Besides planning their talk's contents, a team needs to plan its choreography—who will do what, when, and how.
© Purestock/Superstock RF

of final note of appreciation or thanks needs to be planned, with all the team nodding in agreement or acknowledging the final comment in some way.

Teams should also allow for plenty of rehearsal time. They should practice the presentation in its entirety several times as a group before the actual presentation. During these rehearsals, individual members should critique each other's contributions, offering specific ways to improve. After first rehearsal sessions, outsiders (nonteam members) might be asked to view the team's presentation and critique the group. Moreover, the team might consider videotaping a rehearsal of the presentation so that all members can evaluate it.

As you can see, effective presentations, whatever their form, take knowledge, preparation, and skill. But the rewards justify the effort. By following this chapter's advice and using good judgment, you can communicate orally in any medium or situation. This ability will make you a valued asset to your employer and further your professional success.

Power Charge Your Professionalism: Use Adjectives and Adverbs Correctly

Remember that adjectives modify nouns and pronouns—that is, adjectives say *which one*, *what kind*, and *how many*. Adverbs modify verbs, adjectives, and other adverbs—that is, they say *how*, *when*, *where*, *to what extent*, and *why*.

Find the sentences below that use adjectives or adverbs incorrectly and correct them. Use Reference Chapter A to explain your decisions.

1. Using well-designed slides will help your audience get your point quicker.
2. If you do poorly on a talk, just learn from your mistakes and do good on the next one.
3. When you're well prepared, you'll feel good about giving your presentation.
4. Projecting the right ethos will help your audience take your presentation seriously.
5. If your listeners look confused, you might want to go more slow.
6. She felt well about promoting her favorite nonprofit organization in her speech.
7. All the presenters delivered their parts perfect.
8. Getting in an argument with an audience member made Janice look badly.

Using adjectives and adverbs correctly is important because . . .

- Adjective and adverb errors will distract your readers/listeners.
- This type of error makes you sound uneducated. It can be a credibility killer in a written message or presentation.

For further instruction and practice, do the "Adjectives and Adverbs" activities under "Grammar and Common Sentence Problems" in LearnSmart Achieve.

Key Terms

Critical-Thinking Questions

1. As you consider your future career, think of three scenarios in which you might need to make a presentation. What would be the purpose of these talks, and who would be their audiences? In light of these factors, what kinds of content would you include? LO1

2. Explain the principal differences between oral and written reports. What do these differences mean in terms of how you'd need to adapt a written report for presentation to an audience? LO1, LO2

3. Give an example of a scenario in which you'd be wise to organize a presentation indirectly. Then give one in which the direct order would be preferable. Explain the rationale behind your choices. LO1, LO2

4. Assume that your boss, the director of marketing, has asked you to prepare an oral report for the marketing team on the status of the current sales campaign. The sales messages have been designed for viewing on three different technologies: PCs, tablets, and smartphones. List, in order of presentation, the content you might include, along with any visuals that would go with it. LO2, LO3

5. Assume that you must prepare a speech on the importance of community service for an audience of business majors. Develop two attention-gaining openings for this speech. LO1, LO2

6. Assume that as a successful young _____ [fill in an appropriate job title], you've been asked to give a speech to a college honorary society or club in your area of professional expertise. Generate two good topics for your speech, and be ready to explain the reasoning behind your choices. LO2

7. Assume that in the scenario described in question #6 you invite questions at the end of your talk, and an arrogant-seeming student in the audience contradicts something you said. How would you handle this situation? LO6

8. Recall an effective speech you heard or viewed in which the speaker read his or her remarks. What made the speech effective even though it was read? LO2

9. View a TED talk (TED.com) and evaluate the projected personal qualities, use of body language, and speaking style/voice of the presenter. What techniques might you emulate? Which, if any, would be ones you'd want to avoid? LO4

10. Go to YouTube.com and examine a video in which a business professional is giving advice about making oral presentations. Evaluate the advice, and also evaluate the speaker's own presentation skills. LO1–LO5

11. View a TED talk (TED.com) and evaluate both the visuals the speaker uses and how he or she integrates them into the talk. What techniques might you emulate? Which, if any, would be ones you'd want to avoid? LO3, LO5

12. For the same TED talk or a different one, identify the strategies the speaker uses to build rapport with the audience. LO2, LO4

13. Find an online video or tutorial about designing effective presentation slides. Evaluate the advice being given. LO4

14. Recall a presentation you attended that effectively used supporting visual material. Then recall one that didn't. What were the differences? LO4, LO5

15. If you were giving a presentation and you saw that your audience's eyes were glazing over, what might you do to regain their attention? LO2, LO6

16. Find a videotaped webinar (e.g., those available at www.webex.com/webinars), and evaluate it. What were its strengths? How might it have been improved? LO7

17. If you've taken any online courses, make a list of the presentation features (e.g., use of media, types of audience participation) that you liked about them. Then list the drawbacks that these courses had. LO7

18. Assume that you and some classmates have been asked to prepare a team presentation that will be videotaped. What logistics do you need to work out before you tape the presentation? LO8

19. Recall the team presentations that you've seen in your classes. What qualities made some team presentations better than others? LO8

Skills-Building Exercises

The topics here can be used for various activities, including analyzing the audience and situation, planning the right kind of talk, gathering appropriate and sufficient information, organizing the talk, planning and designing visual aids, and delivering presentations. Many of the Problem-Solving Cases at the end of Chapter 12 can also serve as oral presentation topics.

1. Survey the major business publications for information about the outlook for the national (or world) economy for the coming year. Then present a summary report to your entrepreneurship class.

2. Select a current technological innovation for business use and prepare an oral report on it for a company's top administrators (you select the company). You will describe the innovation and point out how it will benefit the company. If appropriate, you may recommend its purchase.

3. Report to a meeting of a wildlife-protection organization on the status of an endangered species. You will need to gather the facts through research, probably in wildlife publications.

4. A national chain of _____ (your choice) is opening an outlet in your city. You have been assigned the task of reviewing site possibilities. Gather the pertinent information and make an oral recommendation to the board of directors.

5. The Future Business Leaders Club at your old high school has asked you to give a talk on what it takes to succeed in business school. You will cover all the factors that you think high school students need to know. Include visuals in your presentation.

6. You're one of a group of students who have been selected to go to Germany (or pick another country) to represent your school at a conference. Prepare a report to give to the group that will prepare them to behave appropriately in this culture.

7. As a member of an investment club, report to the membership on whether the club should purchase shares of a certain high-tech company. Your report will cover past performance, current status, and future prospects for the short and long run.

8. Use your library's resources and the Web to find the best available information on the job outlook for this year's college graduates. You will want to look at each major field separately. You also may want to show variations by geographic area, degree, and schools. Present your findings in a well-organized and illustrated oral report.

9. Present a plan for improving some phase of operations on your campus (e.g., registration, housing, grade appeals, library, cafeteria, traffic, curricula, athletics, computer labs).

10. Prepare a report for your classmates on some legislation of importance to business (e.g., right-to-work laws, ethics, environmental controls, taxes). Take care to present evidence and reasoning from all the major viewpoints. Support your presentation with appropriate visuals.

11. Assume that you are being considered by a company of your choice for a job of your choice. Your prospective employer has asked you to make a ____-minute report (your instructor will specify) on your qualifications. You may project your education to the date you will be on the job market, making assumptions that are consistent with your record to date.

12. Prepare and present a report on how individuals may reduce their federal or state income tax payments. You will want to emphasize the most likely sources of tax savings, such as tax sheltering and avoiding common errors.

13. Make a presentation to a hypothetical group of investors that will get you the investment money you need for a purpose of your choice. Your purpose could be to begin a new business, to construct a building, to develop land—whatever interests you. Make your presentation as real (or realistic) as you can. And support your appeal with visuals.

14. As chairperson of the site-selection committee of the National Federation of Business Executives, present a report on your committee's recommendation. The committee has selected a city and a convention hotel (you may choose each). Your report will give your recommendation and the reasons that support it. For class purposes, you may make up whatever facts you need about the organization and its convention requirements and about the hotel. But use real facts about the city.

15. Prepare a presentation about a nonprofit organization or a cause that you support. Your primary purpose will be to inform your audience, but your secondary purpose will be to gain their support for the organization or cause. You choose the audience/occasion.

16. The top administrators of your company have asked you to look into the matter of whether the company should own its own vans, lease them, or pay mileage costs on employee-owned vans. Gather the best available information on this topic and report it to the top administrators. You may make up any company facts you need, but make them realistic.

17. You work for a professional speakers bureau (a company that hires out speakers). Your boss has asked you to prepare a report on incorporating Twitter into presentations. Your report will be videotaped and distributed to the bureau's speakers to advise them on the potential uses of this tool.

18. Assume again the role described in topic #17, but this time your topic is the comparative advantages of Prezi and PowerPoint. Prepare a report that will help the bureau's speakers choose the better tool for a given situation and type of speech.

19. Prepare a speech on a school-related topic of your choice for a meeting of your school's alumni association. You'll be playing the role of yourself—a current student at the school. Make the audience feel good about the state of their alma mater.

20. The career services center at your school is conducting a series of brief presentations on companies both local and national/international that students might want to learn about as potential employees. Your business communication teacher has gotten wind of this initiative and has offered to have her class prepare and deliver some of these as their report assignments. The director of the center has enthusiastically agreed! In this pretend scenario, you'll be preparing an oral report about a company of your choice for students at your school who are entering the job market. Your instructor and the director of your career services center are your secondary audiences.

    Carefully plan your report to be between 8 and 10 minutes long. Support your talk with PowerPoint slides that have the following:

    - An introductory slide to identify your company
    - An overview slide, listing the topics your talk is going to cover
    - A slide for each main section of your talk
    - A closing slide with the main point you want to leave with people

The following kinds of information might be appropriate to include in your talk:

- Company's outputs (products/services); the industry to which it belongs
- Company's size (dollars in sales/revenue; number of employees), ownership, financial health
- Company's plants/facilities/location
- Company's history (how founded? when? by whom? main achievements and/or crises in the company's history?)
- Company's structure (if possible, include an organizational chart at the end of the report and refer to it in your report)
- Company's employees (labor force, unionized or not, kinds of expertise, values)
- Company's position in its industry or main competitors; company's market/customers
- Company's culture/missions/policies/management style/work environment
- Current problems/challenges facing this company
- Any unique traits of this company or industry that are important to mention to the prospective employee

Include at least two Web and two non-Web references in your report (that is, material in a publication or database).

Putting Interpersonal Communication Skills to Work in Conversations and Meetings

Chapter Fourteen

M uch of the oral communication that goes on in business is **interpersonal communication**, the informal, person-to-person interaction that occurs whenever people get together in meetings, over the phone, or in casual conversations. Your ability to engage in interpersonal communication will be key to getting a job and succeeding in your work. In fact, researchers have found that companies most value their new employees' use of standard grammar, team communication, conversational abilities, ability to participate in meetings, and phone skills—all of which are qualities or skills that fall in the category of interpersonal communication.[1]

Learning Objectives

LO14-1 Understand how to learn the features of an organization's culture and to explain how these features affect communication.

LO14-2 Explain the types of nonverbal communication.

LO14-3 Explain the challenges of listening and how to overcome them.

LO14-4 Describe the strategies for engaging in conversation and small talk.

LO14-5 Explain how to handle difficult conversations.

LO14-6 Explain how to give and receive constructive feedback.

LO14-7 Describe the strategies for resolving a conflict.

LO14-8 Explain the steps for successful negotiation.

LO14-9 Describe the strategies for leading successful meetings and teams.

LO14-10 Describe good phone and voice mail techniques.

Problem-Solving Challenge

Getting Along in the Workplace

You are in the third week of your first post-college job as an accountant at Timon, David, and McGee, a public accounting firm. You expected that you would have to interact with other staff and clients, but you are amazed at the amount of interpersonal communication you engage in each day.

Take today, for example. This morning you had a question about the implications of a newly passed U.S. tax law. You thought your question was simple, but the senior partner you asked seemed impatient with you. It was almost as though she thought you were wasting her time or should have found the answer on your own. When you had another question for someone else, you decided to ask it via email

rather than risk his impatience, but then your supervisor told you the senior partners prefer you to ask questions in person rather than over email. How were you supposed to know? All you do know is that you feel as though you cannot win.

Then, you returned from lunch to find seven voice mails. You needed to return five of the seven calls because the caller left incomplete or vague messages. Not having to return those phone calls would have saved you 45 minutes. You feel pretty comfortable communicating over the phone, but you do wish your co-workers and customers had better phone skills or that they would just send you an email, but people in this company would much

rather talk to each other than send emails, and you know the senior partners prefer that you speak directly with clients whenever possible.

You are fast realizing interpersonal communication is much more difficult than you thought. It's more than just communicating with people wherever, whenever, and however you like. In fact, you've discovered it's a lot like writing—you have to tailor your communication to your audience, context, and purpose.

This chapter will show you how to read an organization's culture and how to develop interpersonal skills that enable you to be a successful business professional.

LO14-1 Understand how to learn the features of an organization's culture and to explain how these features affect communication.

Communication and Organizational Cultures

Your success in developing effective interpersonal communication skills begins before you have that first conversation, meeting, or phone call. To have truly effective interpersonal communication skills, you have to understand your culture and your audience. You can also refer to Chapter 1 to learn more about the role of organizational culture in workplace communication.

Learning Your Organization's Culture

An **organizational culture** comprises the beliefs, values, practices, and norms that govern all aspects of organizational life, including what you can and cannot say, write, or do in the workplace.

Written and oral communications play a critical role in creating and reinforcing an organization's culture and also in changing an organization's culture. Your own interpersonal communication skills, then, are critical in helping you become an integral part of the life of your organization.

Navigating Your Organization's Culture

Many times, employers use the job interview as an opportunity to assess your potential to be a good fit for their culture. If they hire you, though, it does not mean this fit is automatic. Once you are hired, your success depends on your ability to analyze

The effectiveness of a person's interpersonal skills depends on the person's ability to read and respond to his or her organization's culture.
© nyul/123RF

Communication Matters

Can You Be Fired for Using Profanity at Work?

Profanity is seemingly everywhere—on television, in the movies, on the Internet, and in our daily conversations. In fact, profanity has become so common that in many cases people are no longer shocked when they hear it and likely face no consequences for using it. But can someone be fired or disciplined for swearing at work?

Law professor Christine Neylon O'Brian of Boston College says whether profanity is acceptable in the workplace depends on a company's culture. Furthermore, she says profanity may be protected by law if an employee is merely discussing his or her job or working

conditions. However, employees may be fired if their language is so "'egregious, dishonest, threatening, violent or insubordinate' that it exceeds the protection of labor law." That is, employees may be fired if their language is threatening or discriminatory.

Lorman, a continuing education company specializing in compliance in the fields of medicine, business, law, and finance, advises companies to have profanity policies in their employee handbooks defining language that is unacceptable (e.g., sexist, racist) and the consequences for employees who use it.

Of course, as an employee you want to observe whether profanity is acceptable in your workplace and know what the consequences are for using it. Even if it is acceptable, however, you have to ask yourself about the effect such language has on the respect your co-workers and customers have for you. The consequences of using profanity may not be as severe as losing your job, but the damage to your professional image is something to consider.

Source: Phyllis Korkki, "Fired for Cursing on the Job, Testing the Limits of Labor Law," *The New York Times*, February 13, 2016, accessed March 10, 2016, http://www.nytimes.com; "Take Steps to Clean up Workplace Profanity," *Lorman*, January 9, 2014, accessed March 10, 2016, http://www.lorman.com.

and appropriately respond to the culture—and each organization's culture is different. One culture might be highly formal; another, highly informal. One culture might see the work day as fluid, allowing employees to arrive or leave as they wish; another might adhere to a rigid schedule and see a late arrival as a sign of laziness or disrespect.

Much of what we discussed in Chapter 2 regarding audience analysis applies to learning and adapting to an organization's culture. That is, you must examine your relationships with your various audiences, discover the norms that govern communication in your workplace, and use communication channels and language that are appropriate for your audience and message. You can learn what is appropriate in your workplace by being observant and asking questions regarding some of these important markers of an organization's culture:

- What is the power structure in the organization? Does management exert a high level of control, or is power more decentralized and democratically dispersed?

- Who are the top employees? What sets them apart? Can you emulate some of these behaviors?

- Do people of lower rank approach or talk to those of the highest rank? Are people of a higher rank addressed by their first names, or are they addressed with courtesy titles (e.g., Mr., Ms., Dr.) and their last names? Is there a chain of communication that flows upward or downward? Or do employees of all rank communicate comfortably with one another?

- When does the work day start and end? If the day starts at 8 a.m., does this mean that you arrive at 8:00 or begin your work at 8:00? What happens when people arrive late or leave early? Are these people viewed as lazy or uncommitted to the company?

- What is the dress code for your job and rank?

- How much do employees socialize during the work day? What types of interactions do they have?

- When people have questions, do they send emails, call, or talk face to face?

- What language is appropriate? Do people speak formally? Informally? Is profanity acceptable?

As you can see, adapting your communication to the culture of your organization requires a lot of work. The work is well worth it when people respect you for your professionalism and your

You Make the Call
Should you put in your ear buds and listen to music while you work?

competence as a communicator. Furthermore, your ability to fit in with the organization's culture is critical to your success in making conversation with co-workers or clients in person or on the phone, managing conflict, engaging in negotiations, or leading teams and meetings.

Nonverbal Communication

LO14-2 Explain the types of nonverbal communication.

In your role of either speaker or listener in oral communication, you will need to be aware of your **nonverbal communication**—communication that does not involve the use of written or spoken words. In face-to-face communication, nonverbal communication can account for a larger part of the total message than do the words you send or receive. Usually, we use nonverbal communication to supplement and reinforce our words. Sometimes, nonverbal communication such as a smile or a frown communicates by itself.

In a world dominated by text messaging, social media, and other technology-enabled communication, we may neglect the nonverbal skills that are critical to interpersonal communication. Savvy businesspeople know, though, that nonverbal skills create a powerful impression and that a bad first impression is difficult to overcome. You can ensure you always make a good impression by paying as much attention to your nonverbal communication as you do to the words you use in your interactions.

The Nature of Nonverbal Communication

The vocabulary for nonverbal language is broad and imprecise. For instance, a frown on someone's forehead is sometimes interpreted to mean worry. Or could it be that the person has a headache? Or is the person in deep thought? Consider this example: Younger employees were using computers or other technology during meetings. Senior employees took the use of technology to mean that employees were not paying attention or were engaged in activities unrelated to the meeting. The employees, however, thought they were making a positive contribution as they used their technology to research topics related to the meeting and provide input.[2]

The number of possible meanings is multiplied even more when we consider the cross-cultural side of communication. As noted in Chapter 7, culture teaches us about body positions, movements, and various factors that affect human relationships (e.g., intimacy, space, time). Thus, the meanings we give to nonverbal communication will vary depending on how our culture has conditioned us.

Because of these numerous meanings, you need to be sensitive to what others intend with nonverbal communication, and you need to make some allowance for error in the meanings you receive from nonverbal cues. As a listener, you need to go beyond the obvious to determine what nonverbal communication means.

Types of Nonverbal Communication

Although nonverbal communication can be classified in many ways, we examine four common types: **body language, use of space, use of time**, and **paralanguage**.

Body Language   Much of what we say to others without using words is sent through the physical movements of our body. When we wave our arms and fingers, wrinkle our forehead, stand straight, smile, gaze at someone or something, or wear a coat and tie, we convey certain meanings; and others convey meanings to us in return.

Nonverbal communication can be as essential to the meaning of your message as the words you use.
© Périg Morisse/123RF

The face and eyes are by far the most important means of body language. For example, happiness, surprise, fear, anger, and sadness usually are accompanied by definite facial expressions and eye patterns. Eye contact is also an important nonverbal behavior. In some cultures, making eye contact shows concern, truthfulness, and trustworthiness; a lack of eye contact is a sign that someone may be lying to you. In other cultures, eye contact is considered too forward or disrespectful.

Gestures are another way we send nonverbal messages. Through body movements, we can accent and reinforce our spoken messages, and we can observe how others punctuate their oral communication with gestures. For example, if you observe the hand movements of another person while he or she is talking, you will get a good picture of the person's emotional state. Moreover, speaking and gestures appear to be linked. That is, the louder someone speaks, the more emphatic the gestures become and vice versa.

Another type of body language is physical appearance—our clothing, hair, and accessories. Consider, for example, how people would perceive you if you came to a professional interview in shorts and flip flops. You always want to make sure your clothes, style, and general appearance are consistent with the role you occupy.

Use of Space

Our use of space is another type of nonverbal communication that tells much about us and our culture.

We create four different types of space: intimate (physical contact to 18 inches), personal (18 inches to 4 feet), social (4 to 12 feet), and public (12 feet to the outer range of seeing and hearing). In each of these spaces, our communication behaviors differ and convey different meanings. For example, consider the volume of your voice when someone is 18 inches from you. Do you shout? Whisper? Now contrast the tone of your voice when someone is 12 feet away. Unquestionably, there is a difference just because of the distance involved.

You should think, also, about how the physical arrangement of a room sends a message. What type of environment do you create if you seat people in a row and talk in front of them instead of around a table where you sit with them as you talk? What message do you send if you have a conversation where you are on one side of a desk and the person you are speaking to is on the other? Use of space is another type of nonverbal communication heavily influenced by culture. As noted in Chapter 7, when people's attitudes toward space are different, the odds of miscommunication increase.

Use of Time

A third type of nonverbal communication involves time. That is, how we use time sends a message. To illustrate, think about how you manage your daily schedule. Do you arrive early for most appointments? Do you prioritize phone calls? Do you prepare agendas for meetings? Your response to time in these ways communicates to others, and, of course, others' use of time communicates to you. As we mentioned earlier in this chapter, your ability to understand the value and use of time in your organization is key to reading your organization's culture.

In Chapter 7, we discussed how various cultures approach time differently. For Americans, Canadians, and many others from English-speaking countries, time values are monochronic. Monochronic people tend to view time as linear and always moving ahead. They expect events to happen at scheduled times. Polychronic people—such as those from Asian, Arabic, and Spanish-speaking countries—have a more indefinite view of time. Unlike the monochronic person who expects a meeting to start precisely at 9:00 a.m., the polychronic person sees a 9:00 a.m. meeting as an objective to be accomplished if possible. Such time orientations are part of the messages we send to and receive from one another.

Paralanguage

Paralanguage, meaning "along with language," is a fourth type of nonverbal communication. Of all the types, it is the most closely tied to communication with words. It has to do with the sound of a speaker's voice—those hints and signals in the way words are delivered,

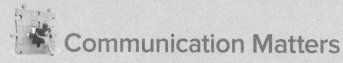
Communication Matters

Introverts and Extraverts: Personality Types and Interpersonal Communication

Much has been made in the media lately of the difference between introverts and extraverts. A common misconception is that these terms refer to people who are shy (introverts) or outgoing (extraverts).

In truth, these terms refer to the location of a person's energy or motivation. Introverts, according to the Myers & Briggs Foundation, derive their energy internally from ideas, pictures, memories, or reactions. They like to work alone and are likely to have a small circle of friends. While they may be described as "shy," they are more likely just reserved.

Extraverts, on the other hand, derive their energy by engaging others and activities in the world around them. They like a lot of activity and to be part of a large circle of friends. They are frequently described as "outgoing" or as "people persons."

It is unlikely that anyone is a pure introvert or extravert, and both personality types are valuable in the workplace depending on the task or interaction required. Extraverts prefer oral communication and will frequently talk or volunteer their thoughts as a means of thinking through an issue. Introverts prefer to think through the issue first and then voice their thoughts; they are not likely to contribute without first thinking through what they will say and feeling as though their contribution is substantive. Extraverts prefer working in groups and will initiate social activities, while introverts prefer individual tasks and business-related interaction.

Extraverts' and introverts' preferences for interaction and communication are highly nuanced, but a basic knowledge of each type can help you understand you and your colleagues' needs in one-on-one conversations, meetings, conflicts and negotiations, or other contexts.

To learn more about your own introvert or extravert tendencies, you may want to take a personality test such as the Jung Typology Test.

Sources: The Myers & Briggs Foundation, *Extraversion or Introversion,* accessed November 18, 2016, http://www.myers-briggs.org/my-mbti-personality-type/mbti-basics/extraversion-or-introversion.htm; "Introverted Versus Extroverted Personalities & Interest Inventory Career Infographic," *Career Assessment Site*, accessed November 18, 2016, http://careerassessmentsite.com/tests/mbti-test/strong-interest-inventory/personality-types/careers-infographic.

such as emphasis, pitch, volume speed, and connectivity—that also give meaning to a speaker's message. Are words spoken quickly or slowly? Are they high pitched or deep? Are they loud and forceful or barely audible? Are they smooth or disjointed? These questions are examples of the types you would ask to analyze the nonverbal cues of paralanguage. The cues become a part of the meaning that is conveyed by a spoken message.

To illustrate, read the following series of statements, emphasizing the underlined word in each.

I am a good communicator.

I am a good communicator.

I am a good communicator.

I am a good communicator.

I am a good communicator.

By emphasizing the underscored word in each statement, you change the meaning of that statement from the others even though you use the same words. As another example, try counting from 1 to 10 a number of times, each time expressing a different emotional state—say anxiety, anger, or happiness. The way you state each sequence of numbers will show what you intend quite accurately.

Paralanguage meanings also are conveyed by consistencies and inconsistencies in what is said and how it is said. Depending on the circumstance, a person's voice may or may not be consistent with the intended word meanings. Consistency between the words you choose and how you deliver them to create clear meaning should be your goal. For example, if you are happy or angry, your voice will be loud; if you are sad or delivering bad news, you will likely speak quietly.

Keep in mind that all communicators have certain assumptions about how a message should sound. Whether real or imagined, people infer background factors (e.g., race, education); physical appearance (e.g., age, height, gender); and personality (e.g., introversion, social orientation) when they hear and interpret paralanguage. When you speak, you should do whatever you can to influence these assumptions positively. Many of the suggestions in this chapter and in Chapter 13 should help you deliver a consistent and effective message. Active listeners will also want to listen between the lines of a spoken message to determine the true meaning a speaker is sending.

Other Types of Nonverbal Communication   The preceding four types are the primary forms of nonverbal communication, but others exist. For example, artists, interior decorators, and image consultants believe that different colors project different meanings. What meanings do you get from red, yellow, black, or blue? The colors in visual aids (see Chapters 3 and 4), wardrobe, and office decor all send nonverbal messages that you will want to attend to when you communicate.

Listening

Up to this point, our review of interpersonal communication has been about outward communication—communicating appropriately in your organizational culture and using appropriate nonverbal communication. However, having excellent interpersonal communication skills also requires that you know how to receive information as well, and this means that you must develop your listening skills.

LO14-3   Explain the challenges of listening and how to overcome them.

The Nature of Listening

From a communication standpoint, the listening process involves not only the **sensing** of sound but also the addition of **filtering** and **remembering** what you have heard.

Sensing   How well we sense the words around us is determined by two factors. One factor is our ability to sense sounds—that is, how well our ears can hear them.

The other factor is our attentiveness or concentration. Our concentration on the communication varies from moment to moment. From your own experience, you can recall moments when you were oblivious to the words spoken around you and moments when you listened intently. Most of the time, your listening falls somewhere between these extremes.

Filtering   From your study of the communication process in Chapter 1, you know that interpretation enables you to give meanings to the sounds you hear. In this process, your personal context affects how you filter these sounds and give meaning to incoming messages. This filter is formed by the unique contents of your mind: your knowledge, emotions, beliefs, biases, experiences, and expectations. In addition, larger social or workplace cultures affect how you filter sounds. As a result, you sometimes give messages meanings that are different from the meanings that others give them.

Remembering   Remembering what we hear is the third activity involved in listening. Unfortunately, we retain little of what we hear. We remember many of the comments we hear in casual conversation for only a few minutes or hours. In addition, we live in a world where multitasking (focusing on several activities simultaneously) is a common practice. Unfortunately, research indicates that multitasking not only makes people less productive, but it also impacts our ability to retain what we hear—even for students who multitask on their phones or computers during a classroom lecture.[3]

Improving Your Listening Ability

Improving your listening is largely a matter of concentrating on the activity of sensing. If you are like most people, you are often tempted not to listen, find it easier not to listen, or even think that you can listen well while attending to other tasks or people. Listening may seem like a passive activity, but it can be hard work.

Communication Matters

The Ten Commandments of Listening

1. Stop talking. Unfortunately, most of us prefer talking to listening. Even when we are not talking, we are inclined to concentrate on what to say next rather than on listening to others. So you must stop talking before you can listen.

2. Put the talker at ease. If you make the talker feel at ease, he or she will do a better job of talking. Then you will have better input to work with.

3. Show the talker you want to listen. If you can convince the talker to understand rather than to oppose, you will help create a climate for information exchange. You should look and act interested. Reading, looking at the clock, sneaking a look at phone messages, and looking away distract the talker.

4. Remove distractions. The things you do also can distract the talker. So don't doodle, tap with your pencil, send text messages or type at your computer, or shuffle papers.

5. Empathize with the talker. If you place yourself in the talker's position and look at things from the talker's point of view, you will help create a climate of understanding that can result in a true exchange of information.

6. Be patient. You will need to allow the talker plenty of time. Remember that not everyone can get to the point as quickly and clearly as you. And do not interrupt. Interruptions are barriers to the exchange of information.

7. Hold your temper. Anger impedes communication. Angry people build walls between each other; they harden their positions and block their minds to the words of others.

8. Go easy on argument and criticism. These tend to put the talker on the defensive, creating anger or avoidance issues. Thus, even if you win the argument, you lose. Rarely does either party benefit from argument and criticism.

9. Ask questions. By frequently asking questions, you display an open mind and show that you are listening. And you assist the talker in developing his or her message and in improving the correctness of meaning.

10. Stop talking! The last commandment is to stop talking. It was also the first. All the other commandments depend on it.

Source: Anonymous.

Successful businesspeople will have excellent speaking skills as well as excellent listening skills.

© Monkey Business Images/123RF

Active listening is one technique individuals can use successfully. It involves focusing on what is being said and reserving judgment until the message is complete. Other components include sitting forward and acknowledging with "um-hm," nodding, making eye contact, and leaning forward.

Back-channeling (repeating what you think you heard) is an effective way to focus your attention, as is asking questions. You might even think about using technologies such as chat and Twitter to comment on and enhance online communication in real time to keep people focused on what is being said.

Improving your listening also requires that you develop your ability to accurately interpret what you hear. To do this, you will need to think in terms of what words mean to the speakers who use them rather than what the dictionary says they mean or what they mean to you. You must try to think as the speaker thinks—judging the speaker's words by considering the speaker's knowledge, experiences, culture, and viewpoints. Improving your ability to hear what is intended requires conscious effort—asking questions, taking notes, and removing distractions.

Conversation and Small Talk

The ability to initiate and hold a conversation is a fundamental business skill. Most of us do a reasonably good job of informal talking. In fact, we do such a good job that we often take talking for granted and overlook the need to improve our conversational abilities. We also may not think about how a conversation in business might be different from the conversations we have with friends or family.

LO14-4 Describe the strategies for engaging in conversation and small talk.

As a first step in improving your conversational skills, think for a moment about the people you enjoy talking with in an ordinary conversation. Then think about the opposite—the worst conversationalist you can imagine. With these two images in mind, you can form a good picture of the characteristics of good conversation. The following section covers the most important of these.

Starting a Conversation

Conversations in business range from formal to informal with new clients, people in your professional network, or colleagues in the office. Your ability to read the context and be purposeful in your communication will define your professional image.

Timing The key to any conversation, formal or informal, is timing. You may have an important topic to talk about, but as we've discussed, your audience must find your message important as well. If people are busy, distracted, tired, or even in the middle of a meal, they are not likely to attend to what you say if they have something more pressing in the moment. Likewise, unless you have a true emergency, your conversation is never so important that you interrupt another conversation. Good manners require that you wait.

Thus, even though you think your conversation is critical and in need of immediate attention, if you delay it until your audience is likely to be most receptive, you may find that you get better results or leave the audience with a better impression of you.

Approaching Someone for Conversation Of course, if you know the person you are speaking with, introductions are not necessary, and you can simply start your conversation. If you have to introduce yourself in a general gathering, simply approach the person, smile, make eye contact, extend your hand for a handshake, and say, "Hello, I am _____."

If you are entering someone's office or other private space, you should first knock and then ask, "May I come in?" Only in the most informal conversations with close colleagues or clients should you enter without first being invited. Even then, if the person's body language suggests that he or she is busy, it is polite to ask, "Is this a good time?" before assuming you should enter.

If your relationship with your audience is informal, such as with a close client or colleague, you can enter the room and be seated. Otherwise, once you are invited to enter, you should wait to sit until you are invited to do so. If you are not invited, you may ask, "May I sit?" Yes, it is likely all right for you to sit without asking first, but you show good manners and project a professional image if you ask or wait until you are invited.

Selecting Appropriate Topics for Discussion Conversations in the workplace frequently are with people you know well or at least have a professional relationship with. Usually, these conversations take place in the course of a work day and serve the purpose of accomplishing your work or carrying out the duties of your job. For these conversations, many of the tips in Chapters 8 and 9 about the direct and indirect approaches apply.

Sometimes, though, business situations require you to make **small talk**, a conversation on neutral topics with people you may have just met or may not know all that well. Business etiquette expert Patricia Napier-Fitzpatrick provides these tips for making small talk:

1. Smile, make eye contact, and use other body language that suggests you're approachable.

2. Be the first to say "hello."

Communication Matters

What's in a Handshake?

A handshake is a common part of the greeting in U.S. business culture, especially in formal situations, in situations where individuals have not seen each other in a long time, or when people are meeting for the first time.

In fact, your handshake may be among the most critical nonverbal behaviors in the initial stage of any business relationship, such as the job interview or a meeting with a potential client. The professional handshake requires more than extending your hand. It requires that you practice so you are prepared for any situation. Here are the rules according to Innovative Training and Communication Solutions:

• Know when to shake hands. Shake hands when (1) you are introduced to someone, (2) someone introduces himself or herself, (3) you introduce yourself to someone, or (4) the conversation is over.

• Shake for no more than three "pumps." Another rule is to shake for about three seconds. Any longer than that and you make the situation awkward for everyone.

• Shake from the elbow, not your shoulder. This allows you to have a smooth handshake that is not rough or too forceful for the other person.

• Don't be a "dead fish" or "wet fish." Just as you do not want to shake too roughly, you do not want a limp handshake either. If your hands are sweaty, have some way to wipe them off (on your slacks or in the bathroom) before meeting people.

• Don't be a "bone crusher." Don't grip the other person's hand too hard. Not only do you not want to inflict pain, you don't want to appear too aggressive. Use the same force you would use to turn a door handle.

• Don't give the "little lady" handshake. Extend your whole hand, not just your fingertips. Extending just your fingertips signals that you are weak (especially if you are a woman).

• Shake with one hand, not two. Using both hands is too personal for a business setting. It also makes you look like you're trying too hard.

Source: Amy Castro, "7 Handshake Rules You Shouldn't Break," *Innovative Communication and Training Solutions*, January 15, 2015, accessed March 10, 2016, http://www.amy-castro.com/7-handshake-rules-you-shouldnt-break/.

3. Start with a compliment, neutral statement, or question about the event, weather, or how the person came to be there.

4. Prepare for small talk by being up to date on current events. Doing so ensures you will have a variety of interesting topics to choose from.

5. Focus your topics and questions on the other person rather than on yourself.

6. Listen.

7. Don't engage in too serious a conversation until you find something that interests both you and the other person.

8. Stick to topics that are of interest to most people such as movies, theater, sports, books, movies, food, travel, and hobbies.

9. Think before you speak so that you don't say something you regret.

10. Leave a conversation with a polite comment such as "It's been great talking with you. I really enjoyed hearing about _____."

Napier-Fitzpatrick also advises people to avoid topics of ". . . health or diet habits; the cost of things; personal questions; mean gossip; off-color jokes; and controversial issues, such as politics or religion, when you don't know the others in the group." The goal is to ensure the other person is comfortable.[4]

Approaching Difficult Conversations

LO14-5   Explain how to handle difficult conversations.

Whether you are giving a negative performance review, telling a customer that you cannot meet his or her needs, or giving negative feedback to a co-worker about his or her work on a project, you will have to engage in difficult conversations in the workplace.

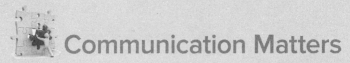

Communication Matters

Thinking before You Speak

We have all had those moments where we have gotten emotional and said something we later regret. Many times, all we can do is apologize and then be more careful the next time.

CEO Peter Bregman offers tips for responding in emotional or high-pressure situations.

1. Think about the outcome you want. Do you want people to get angry with you? Do you want them to disconnect? Or do you want people to feel respected or supported? It's likely you want the latter, which means your communication style has to be consistent with that outcome.

2. Think about what to communicate to achieve that outcome. For example, saying, "I am hurt" brings you closer to people than "I am angry" or "I can't believe you didn't . . . ," which introduces issues of power. Good leaders, he says, will have the "emotional courage" to be vulnerable in these angry situations.

3. Think about how you communicate to achieve that outcome. You should listen first to ensure you understand the other person's perspective; then you can share yours by first asking, "Can I share my perspective?"

4. Think about your timing. As we've mentioned, timing is key in effective communication. Bregman advises that you "ask yourself when you are most likely to approach the communication with curiosity, compassion, and clarity and when the other person is likely to be generous and calm."

Source: Peter Bregman, "Outsmart Your Next Angry Outburst," *Harvard Business Review*, May 6, 2016, accessed May 7, 2016, https://hbr.org/2016/05/outsmart-your-next-angry-outburst.

While it is tempting to try to avoid these conversations by sending an email or even a text message, doing so when your motive is to avoid someone is not professional. Fortunately, much of what we discussed in Chapter 6 and Chapter 9 can help you frame your message. That is, you want to think about buffering any bad news, remaining objective, using facts and logic to deliver your message, incorporating any positive news, and avoiding an accusatory or hostile tone. Delivering these messages requires preparation so that you deliver a polished and thoughtful message.

Communication experts suggest that the success of a difficult conversation may lie in how you think of it. They say that if you approach these conversations as negative or difficult, you will be nervous and tense and likely to make the conversation even more uncomfortable. For example, if you are delivering a difficult performance review, you will be less tense and have a better outcome if you see this as an opportunity for the employee to grow rather than as time for you to criticize.

In addition, these experts note that difficult conversations can go more smoothly if you take time for the conversation rather than rush it just to get it done, listen to the other person, and show empathy for his or her viewpoint. Lastly, they say you want to remember that this conversation is not about you, so if you say "I feel bad about saying this . . ." or "This is hard for me . . ." you are asking the other person to have sympathy for you when, really, you should be the one showing compassion.[5]

Giving and Receiving Feedback

Two common types of conversations that may be either easy or difficult involve giving and receiving feedback. Because of this, you need to carefully analyze your audience, keeping in mind the audience may feel differently about the feedback than you do; conversely, you need to be able to respond appropriately to feedback you receive, either good or bad.

LO14-6   Explain how to give and receive constructive feedback.

Giving Feedback   Whether your message is positive or negative, you want to make sure you give **constructive feedback**—objective, helpful comments that improve others' work, build goodwill, and help both parties achieve their communication and business goals. Giving constructive feedback requires careful consideration of your audience and your tone. You may think your suggestion to reword a sentence or your observation of a calculation error is fairly neutral feedback. The person you are speaking to, however, may perceive your feedback as a personal comment on his or her competence and become offended.

When delivering negative feedback, you can use many of the strategies discussed in Chapter 9 for delivering bad news or discussed in this chapter in the section on having difficult

Giving and receiving feedback requires careful planning, audience analysis, and attention to nonverbal communication.

© nakophotography/123RF

conversations. Whether the feedback is positive or negative, you can use the following strategies to ensure your feedback is heard:

- *Stick to the facts.* Your feedback should be based on facts, logic, and other evidence that both you and the other person would likely agree on. For example, instead of saying, "You never meet your deadlines . . ." or even "Most of the visuals in this presentation are really good, but some of the others . . . ," you can say, "The workplace climate survey was submitted at three days after its deadline . . ." or "The bar charts are especially effective in highlighting the sales in each territory; the pie chart on page 5 would be more effective if. . . ."

- *Watch your pronoun use.* Careful use of pronouns will help you depersonalize your feedback. In some cases, you can use the you-view (see Chapter 6) to help others identify benefits of heeding your feedback. In other cases, you can avoid blaming or accusatory language by saying, "I noticed . . ." or "The document could be stronger if the visuals . . ." rather than "I think you should . . . ," "You didn't . . . ," or "Why didn't you . . . ," which may cause your audience to see your feedback as a personal attack.

- *Ask for clarification.* Saying to someone, "Could you please help me understand . . ." or "Can you tell me why . . . ," or "What do you think we can do to . . ." gives the other person an opportunity to explain. Allowing the other person to be part of the conversation can minimize resistance to the criticism and encourage compliance with steps moving forward.

- *Watch your tone.* Even if your feedback is well intended, a disapproving, condescending, patronizing, or angry tone will make your audience defensive and unwilling to accept your feedback.

Receiving Feedback

Receiving feedback is difficult because it feels highly personal, even when it is supposed to be objectively focused on your work. You cannot control how well the feedback is delivered to you, which can make it hard not to react emotionally in situations where the other person is insensitive or rude. And even when the feedback is positive and you feel good about receiving it, you may become nervous at the very thought of being critiqued. Regardless of how the feedback is delivered and how you feel about it, you should still receive it professionally:

- *Separate the feedback from the person who is giving it.* Whether the person delivers the feedback well or poorly, be sure to listen to the substance of the feedback. Even when the feedback is full of praise, you cannot get so lost in how wonderful you are that you miss opportunities for improvement. If the feedback is negative, be honest with yourself. Is it true? If so, this feedback is an opportunity to become better at your job, even if the message is painful to hear.

- *Express your thanks.* Whatever the feedback, thank the deliverer for the input. Giving feedback takes time, effort, and thought, so an expression of gratitude is generally appropriate.

- *Take the opportunity to respond.* Sometimes the feedback is positive or neutral or involves a minor issue where your only response needs to be "Thank you for the feedback. I am happy you like my work." Other times, you may have questions about what to do or you may feel the feedback is inaccurate or unfair. In these cases, if you have the opportunity to respond to the feedback, it is appropriate to share your thoughts. Without being defensive or angry, you can propose a plan of action, offer explanations (but not excuses) that correct inaccurate information or incorrect perceptions, or ask questions that will help you improve.

You Make the Call

What is the difference between an explanation and an excuse?

- *Think carefully before you apologize.* The rules for apologies that we discuss in Chapter 9 apply here, too. If you have done something wrong or offended someone, you can offer a sincere apology and then move on. If not, do not apologize, as you may convey the impression that you have done something wrong when you have not. Remember that the apology is only sincere if your actions demonstrate a change in your behavior or attitude.

  Be sure you avoid the fake apology that begins with the "*I* am sorry . . . *you* . . ." pattern: "I am sorry if you were offended by what I said," or "I am sorry that you felt my work didn't meet your expectations," or "I am sorry the report was late, but you were not clear about the deadline." These apologies suggest the other person is unreasonable and that you are not really sorry for anything you have done.

  Instead, use the "*I* am sorry . . . *I/my* . . ." pattern: "I am sorry that my words were offensive," "I am sorry my work was not up to our company standard," or "I am sorry; I misunderstood the deadline and should have asked for clarification." In other words, if you truly did something wrong, your apology should show your ownership of the issue and indicate a willingness to improve.

- *Be aware of the power dynamics.* Your opportunity to respond to feedback and the nature of the response will depend on your relationship to the person delivering the feedback. The greater the power distance, the less likely you may be able to respond. If you do respond, you can offer a simple "Thank you for the feedback. I appreciate the opportunity to develop as a professional and grow as an employee." If you do not respect the power dynamics, you risk being seen as unprofessional or inappropriate.

As you can see, having a conversation in a business setting requires a lot more thought and planning than many of the conversations you have in your daily life. Being aware of the differences between your personal and professional communication will help you develop conversational habits that serve you well in the workplace.

Conflict and Negotiation

Conflict and negotiation frequently go hand in hand—you disagree with others and have to work with them to negotiate a solution. Of course, much of what we have discussed to this point about being courteous, using an appropriate tone and style, and adapting your nonverbal communication are all part of being able to successfully work through conflict or engage in successful negotiation.

LO14-7 Describe the strategies for resolving a conflict.

Defining the Conflict The key to managing a conflict is first defining the conflict. Defining the conflict may seem simple. Maybe team members disagree about the best way to deliver a presentation, or perhaps you and others disagree about how to best manage a staffing shortage, or maybe the conflict is about something as seemingly small as who gets a vacant corner office.

Regardless of the circumstances, many people make the mistake of thinking that the conflict is about the circumstances themselves when, really, the conflict stems from how people feel about the circumstances. One popular definition of **conflict** used in studies of organizational and business communication is that conflict is "the interaction of interdependent people who perceive opposition of goals, aims, and values, and who see the other party as potentially interfering with the realization of these goals."[6]

Notice that the focus is on feelings and goals related to the conflict rather than the nature of the conflict. In other words, the conflict may not be about about differing opinions on how to give a presentation; it is about people who do not feel their input is valued. The conflict is

Conflict may be inevitable, but it can be an opportunity to consider new ideas or explore possibilities.
© Katarzyna BiaÅ,asiewicz/123RF

not about how to fill positions in a staffing shortage but about the fear people have that their departments will be understaffed or marginalized. Or maybe the conflict is not about the location of a vacant office; it is about the status associated with those who occupy that office. Being able to define the conflict in terms of its practical and emotional natures and then acknowledge the feelings of those involved are the first steps in identifying the true conflict and working toward a resolution.

Managing Conflict

Susan Raines identifies five primary ways people generally manage conflict in the workplace.[7] She notes that any of these strategies could be appropriate depending on the conflict but that many people prefer one or two styles consistent with their cultural or family experiences. It is important, therefore, that people be aware of these preferences and be willing to adjust their approaches based on the situation and people involved. The five strategies Raines identifies are as follows:

Conflict Avoidance Strategy   As the name indicates, this strategy is used by people who avoid conflict. Raines says people who prefer this style see conflict as a win–lose proposition in which they are likely to lose. This style is preferred by those with little power, those who privilege harmony, and those with low verbal and social skills. This strategy is useful, though, when the conflict is small and walking away from it allows the conflict to resolve itself.

Accommodative Strategy   People who use this strategy prioritize relationships and others' feelings over their own wishes. The key to success with this approach is balance. You want to be flexible enough to accommodate others' ideas but not so flexible that your ideas are not heard or valued. This strategy is effective when you are not in a position of power and are not likely to get what you want or when someone else has a strong preference and you do not. It presents a good opportunity to build goodwill that perhaps will be returned to you when another situation arises.

Collaboration Strategy   This strategy is useful when two people work toward a common goal. It is frequently referred to as the "win–win" strategy because it requires that people work for a resolution that meets everyone's needs. Collaboration is essential in teamwork and in building trust, but it is not always the best strategy. For example, it is frequently difficult to achieve consensus in large groups. Furthermore, some decisions need to be made quickly; taking the time for collaboration may not be feasible. Plus, people who trust their leaders may not want that much input and instead prefer to rely on their leaders to make decisions.

Compromising Strategy   The compromising strategy requires both sides of the conflict to make concessions so that each party believes the resolution is fair. This style works well if a decision needs to be made quickly and if the decision is not terribly complex. The drawback to this style is that in making concessions, people may leave behind opportunities for a collaborative solution that incorporates the best of all possible solutions. Further, people may make too many concessions or feel pressured into making unwanted concessions and later be unhappy.

Competitive Strategy   This strategy requires you to get your way as much as you can, regardless of the relationships involved. Sometimes, competition is inherent in a conflict (e.g., in an election), but Raines says unless competition is used to achieve positive ends or build teams, it will most likely result in hard feelings.

As we've mentioned, the strategy you choose will depend on the situation. Once again, as a good business communicator, you will analyze your audience, context, and purpose to ensure that your communication goals and business goals lead to effective business solutions.

You Make the Call
Do you recognize any of these strategies as your preferred way to address conflict?

Negotiating

One common type of interpersonal communication you'll engage in as a professional is that of **negotiation**, the process of discussion that leads to an agreement. Many times people engage in negotiation to resolve a conflict. Other times, you might negotiate a raise, a contract with a client, or even a deal with co-workers about sharing office equipment.

LO14-8 Explain the steps for successful negotiation.

As with any conversation, you want to do as we discussed earlier in this chapter regarding the timing, planning, and approach to a conversation. You will also present your best professional image, achieve your communication goals, and preserve your listener's goodwill by heeding the following advice from author and entrepreneur Kevin O'Leary:[8]

1. *Know What You Want.* Be sure you know, exactly, the goals of the negotiation and how to make your point in a way that makes sense to your audience. Also anticipate your audience's questions and have answers ready to show you've thought through your points. You will find many strategies in Chapter 10 that can help you be persuasive in a negotiation.

2. *Know That Your Audience Is Judging You.* Your audiences are judging you on everything from how you're dressed to your body language to how well you're using their time. If you do not look the part, are not confident, or don't get to your point immediately, you lose your credibility.

3. *Help Others Help You.* Focus on benefits to your audience. Your audiences are not likely to negotiate if they cannot see any outcomes that benefit them.

4. *Know Your Facts.* Know everything you can about the audiences you're negotiating with (and about the issue you're negotiating). If you look like you haven't done your homework, you lose your advantage or give your audience little reason to continue negotiating.

5. *Know When to Walk Away.* The goal of negotiation should be that everyone leaves with some type of satisfaction. When this doesn't happen (or looks like it's not going to happen), it's all right to walk away.

6. *Remember the Bottom Line.* In business, the success of a negotiation may be the extent to which you show the audience how your idea helps the bottom line (making money). Depending on what you're negotiating, if the negotiation does not look financially advantageous, your audience may lose interest.

7. *Don't Get Greedy.* Once you've gotten what you want, be done. If you press the issue, you may quickly lose what you've just received.

Managing conflict and negotiating solutions are skills that are developed through practice and experience. Each audience is different, but over time if you are sensitive to your audience and your context, you will learn what is most effective for the people you work with.

Meetings and Teams

Meetings and teamwork are a common occurrence in business. In fact, one estimate is that businesspeople attend an average of 60 meetings per month.[9] Whether these meetings are formal or informal, they will obviously involve communication, and the quality of the communication will determine their success.

LO14-9 Describe the strategies for leading successful meetings and teams.

Conducting Meetings

How you conduct a meeting depends on the formality of the occasion. Meetings of such groups as formal committees, boards of directors, and professional organizations usually follow generally accepted rules of conduct called **parliamentary procedure**. These very specific rules are too numerous and detailed for review here, but when you are involved in a formal meeting, you can study one of the many books and websites covering parliamentary procedure before the meeting so that you know, for example, what it means to make a motion, second a motion, open the floor for discussion, or call for a vote. For less formal meetings, you probably won't follow parliamentary procedure, but keep in mind that every meeting has goals, and every meeting needs some structure to help participants meet your goals. The following practices will help you conduct a successful meeting.

Plan the Meeting

A key to conducting a successful meeting is to plan it thoroughly. For informal meetings, just knowing your plan may be sufficient, but before conducting formal or complex meetings, you may want to prepare an **agenda** (a list of topics to be covered). To prepare an agenda, select the items that need to be covered to achieve the goals of the meeting. Then arrange these items in the most logical order. Items that explain or lead to other items should come before the items that they explain or lead to. After preparing the agenda, make it available to those who will attend. Exhibit 14-1 shows an agenda created for a student organization meeting, but you can tailor an agenda to whatever will help you accomplish your goals. Word processing programs also have templates that may be helpful.

Follow the Plan

You should follow the plan for the meeting item by item. In most meetings the discussion tends to stray, and new items tend to come up. As the leader, you should keep the discussion on track. If new items come up during the meeting, you can take them up at the end or perhaps postpone them for a future meeting.

Whether meetings are formal or informal, good planning and communication will ensure their success.
© Joshua Hodge Photography/Getty Images RF

Move the Discussion Along

Another job you have as the leader is to control the agenda. After one item has been covered, bring up the next item. When the discussion moves off subject, move it back on topic. In general, you want to do what is needed to proceed through the items efficiently, but you do not want to cut off discussion before all the important points have been made. You will have to use your good judgment to permit complete discussion on the one hand and to avoid repetition, excessive details, and off-topic comments on the other.

Control Those Who Talk Too Much

Keeping certain people from talking too much is likely to be one of your harder tasks. A few people usually tend to dominate the discussion, and one of your tasks as the leader is to control them. Of course, you want the meeting to be democratic, so you will need to let these people talk as long as they are contributing to the goals of the meeting. However, when they begin to stray, duplicate what's already been said, or bring in irrelevant topics, you should step in. You can do this tactfully by asking for other viewpoints or by summarizing the discussion and moving on to the next topic.

Encourage Participation from Those Who Talk Too Little

Just as some people talk too much, some talk too little. People may not speak for many reasons. They may be in a lower position of power relative to other members in the group, or they may not feel they have anything relevant to contribute. Others are quiet or more introverted by nature. You should encourage these people to participate by asking them for their viewpoints and by showing respect for the comments they make.

Control Time

When your meeting time is limited, you need to determine in advance how much time will be needed to cover each item. Then, at the appropriate times, you should end discussion of the items. You may find it helpful to announce the time goals at the beginning of the meeting and to help the group members keep track of the time during the meeting. You might also consider including the time limits next to each item on the agenda so that readers know the time constraints before they attend the meeting and can plan their contributions accordingly.

Summarize at Appropriate Places

After a key item has been discussed, you should summarize what the group has covered and concluded. If a group decision is needed, the group's vote will be the conclusion. In any event, you should formally conclude each point and then move on to the next one. At the end of the meeting, you can summarize the progress the group has made.

Exhibit 14-1 Illustration of a Meeting Agenda

Agenda

International Association of Business Communicators (IABC)
Executive Board Meeting
February 23, 2019
Clearwater Room, 7 p.m.

I. **Officer Reports**
  A. President
  B. Vice president
  C. Secretary
  D. Treasurer

II. **Committee Reports**
  A. Public Relations Committee
  B. Web Development Committee
  C. Social Committee

III. **Old Business**
  A. Bake sale fundraisers
  B. Community service project

IV. **New Business**
  A. Election of new officers
  B. Attendance at exec board meetings
  C. Hot chocolate promo

V. **Adjournment**

You also should summarize whenever a review will help the group members understand what they agreed upon.

Take Minutes People at meetings may hear or interpret what is said differently. In addition, you may need to refer to the discussions or to the decisions made at a meeting long after the meeting when people's memories are even less reliable. To ensure you have an accurate, objective account of the topics covered and decisions made at a meeting, assign the task of recording **meeting minutes** (a record of the decisions and discussions at a meeting) to someone. In particularly contentious or detailed discussions, it is important that everyone have a shared understanding of what has transpired.

The format of meeting minutes will depend on the nature of the meeting, group preferences, and company requirements. Some minutes are highly formal, with headings and complete sentences, while others might simply resemble casually written notes. The minutes of a meeting usually list the date, time, and location along with those persons who attended and those who were supposed to attend but were absent; some minutes may also note excused or unexcused absences.

If there is an agenda, the minutes will usually summarize the discussion of each agenda topic. Exhibit 14-2 provides an example of minutes based on the meeting agenda presented in Exhibit 14-1. Generally, the person who takes minutes sends them to those who attended the meeting and requests corrections, or he or she presents the minutes at the next meeting and asks for changes or corrections at that time. Group members may also vote on whether to accept the minutes as they were recorded.

Minutes

International Association of Business Communicators (IABC)
Executive Board Meeting
February 23, 2019
Clearwater Room, 7 p.m.

Attended: Jim Solberg, Aaron Ross, Linda Yang, Tyler Baines, Sara Ryan
Absent: Jenna Kircher (excused), Rebecca Anderson (unexcused)

I. Officer Reports

A. *President:* Jim Solberg. Jim received a message from the director of university programs reminding him to view IABC's officer roster. He reviewed it on February 16 and signed the required forms.

B. *Vice president:* Linda Yang. Linda compiled job descriptions for all officer positions. Jenna put them on the IABC website. The link to the description of the secretary's position was not working. She is contacting Jenna to fix the link.

C. *Secretary:* Aaron Ross. Minutes of the last meeting were read and approved. He sent a thank-you note to Village Pizza for letting us have our last social there. Our average general meeting attendance is 15 even though we have 27 people who have paid dues. At the next exec board meeting, we should discuss ways to improve attendance.

D. *Treasurer:* Rebecca Anderson. No report.

II. Committee Reports

A. *Public Relations Committee:* Tyler Baines. The committee wants to have a public relations campaign in place for next fall. He will be asking for volunteers at the next general meeting.

B. *Web Development Committee:* Jenna Kircher. No report.

C. *Social Committee:* Sara Ryan. The next social will be at the campus bowling alley on March 12 at 7 p.m.

III. Old Business

A. *Bake sale fundraisers:* The $76 we earned this time is less than the $102 we earned at the last one. We will discuss creative fundraising ideas at the next general meeting.

B. *Community service project:* Linda has the forms for participating in IABC's Relay for Life team on April 26–27. She will present them at the next general meeting and ask for volunteers.

IV. New Business

A. *Election of new officers:* Linda. Officers will be elected at the April meeting. We need to encourage people to run.

B. *Attendance at exec board meetings:* Jim. Rebecca has missed every exec board meeting this semester without an excuse. The bylaws state that anyone with more than three unexcused absences in an academic year can be removed from the exec board and office. Jim sent Rebecca an email reminding her of the bylaws, but she did not respond. The Executive Board voted unanimously to remove Rebecca from the board and office. Jim will send her a letter thanking her for her service and telling her she is off the board and no longer treasurer.

C. *Hot chocolate promo:* Sara. Sara requested $20 to buy supplies to serve hot chocolate on the quad from 7:30–9:30 a.m. on Monday, March 9, to promote IABC. Linda moved to spend the $20. Jim seconded the motion. Motion carried unanimously.

V. Adjournment

The meeting adjourned at 8:30 p.m. The next general meeting will be Monday, March 2, at 7 p.m. in the Alumni Room. The next exec board meeting will be Monday, March 9, at 7 p.m. in the Clearwater Room.

Respectfully submitted,

Aaron Ross

Collaborative Tools Support Virtual Meetings

It used to be that long-distance meetings or other types of collaboration required sophisticated tele-conferencing or videoconferencing equipment. Today, however, anyone with Internet access can use virtual meeting software to collaborate with anyone anywhere in the world. Businesses routinely take advantage of this technology to save time and money while enhancing productivity.

In fact, you may have already used some of these online meeting tools, such as Skype, to communicate with your friends, family, and classmates or other tools such as WebEx or GoToMeeting to communicate in an internship or other job. If not, becoming familiar with these tools is a good idea if you plan to enter the business world.

What can you do with a virtual meeting tool? Depending on the tool, you can meet with individuals or with hundreds of people; and you can share files, videos, or even your computer's desktop so that you collaborate directly using spreadsheets, slide shows, or docu-

© Blend Images/Ariel Skelley/Getty Images RF

ments. Because most also have mobile apps, you can meet using your phone. All tools for virtual meetings have features that ensure you and your colleagues use your time efficiently. The key is to do your research and find the right one for you.

Participating in a Meeting

Participating in meetings also requires business professionals to engage appropriately with their group members. You will see that many of the strategies below for participating in a meeting mirror the expectations for leading a meeting. When all parties (the leader and the team members) participate appropriately, teams can be productive and effective in accomplishing tasks and business goals.

Follow the Agenda When an agenda exists, you should follow it. Specifically, you should not bring up items not on the agenda or comment on such items if others bring them up. When there is no agenda, you should stay within the general limits of the goals for the meeting.

Participate The purpose of meetings is to get the input of everybody concerned. Your participation, however, should be meaningful. That is, you should participate when your input helps move the meeting toward its goals.

Do Not Talk Too Much As you participate in the meeting, you should speak up whenever you have something to say, but as in all matters of etiquette, always respect the rights of others to have the opportunity to speak, too. As you speak, ask yourself whether what you are saying really contributes to the discussion. Not only is the meeting costing you time, but it is costing other people's time and salaries as well as the opportunity costs of other work they might be doing.

Cooperate Respect the leader and her or his efforts to make progress. Respect the other participants, and work with them in every practical way. You can demonstrate your willingness to cooperate by attending all meetings, completing your assigned tasks, or volunteering to lead or serve on a committee—anything that outwardly shows your desire to help your group achieve its objectives.

Working in Teams

As with meetings, teamwork is an integral part of life in the workplace. Many times teams are more effective than individuals at generating ideas, developing solutions, and executing plans. Teams are only effective in their work, though, to the extent that the team itself has the structure and communication that enables the individuals in the team to work well together. Chapter 11 and Chapter 13 address collaborative writing and team presentations, and much of what is discussed there applies to teams in general.

In addition, leadership and training expert Elaine Biech says that functional teams demonstrate a multilayered set of foundational, secondary, and tertiary characteristics.[10]

Foundational Characteristics Foundational characteristics—those on which all other team functions depend—must be in place from the very beginning of the team's work. These characteristics include clear goals, clearly defined roles related to both the task and interpersonal functions of the team, open and clear communication, and a system for effective decision making (e.g., consensus vs. majority rule). Having these characteristics established unites team members around the goals, motivates action, and ensures efficient interactions among members.

Secondary Characteristics Secondary characteristics build from the foundational characteristics and must also be in place early in the team's work. These include balanced participation, valued diversity, and managed conflict. Effective teams allow everyone to participate and respect and value the variety of ideas that arise. It is inevitable that conflicts arise, but group members see conflict as an opportunity to challenge assumptions, consider many points of view, and build consensus.

Tertiary Characteristics Characteristics at this level are a positive atmosphere and cooperative relationships. Beich notes that while these characteristics are not necessary to do the work of the team, they are certainly essential for making the teamwork enjoyable and rewarding. Much of what we have discussed regarding conversations, interpersonal skills, and giving constructive feedback will help you build these relational skills that help teamwork be a pleasant experience.

Biech says a final characteristic, participative leadership, may not be present or necessary or may evolve as the team does its work. This characteristic is reflected through teams where leadership qualities are seen or delegated among team members. Leaders share credit and become good role models for other team members.

As you can see, teamwork is much more than getting through the work. Teamwork is a system of people, values, behaviors, and tasks and as such requires excellent communication skills among its members to be accomplished successfully.

Telephone Skills

Most of us use our phones every day for phone calls, texting, emails, and Internet use. In fact, research suggests 99% of Americans have cell phones, and while they spend 26 minutes a day texting, they spend only 6 minutes talking on their phones.[11] Whether you use the phone to text or talk, you will find that doing so for business purposes is likely to differ from how you text and talk for professional purposes. This chapter focuses on using the phone for talking; Chapter 2 can show you best practices for text messaging.

Professional Voice Quality

Keep in mind that a phone conversation is a unique form of oral communication because the speakers cannot see each other unless they have phones that allow face-to-face conversation. As a result, impressions are formed only from the words and the quality of the voice. Thus, when speaking by phone, you must work to make your voice sound pleasant and friendly.

One often-suggested way of improving your phone voice is to talk as if you were face-to-face with the other person—even smiling and gesturing as you talk if this helps you be more natural. In addition, you want to be aware of your voice quality, pitch, and speed, just as you would in a face-to-face setting.

You Make the Call

When you work in a team and a conflict arises, what do you do?

LO14-10 Describe good phone and voice mail techniques.

You may even want to record a phone conversation and then judge for yourself how you come across and determine what you need to do to improve.

Courtesy

As in written communication, your goal in oral communication is to build goodwill. One way to do this over the phone is to always be courteous to your listener.

When you initiate the call, introduce yourself immediately and then ask for the person with whom you want to talk:

> This is Anthony Todd of Robie Realty. May I speak with Kate Sorensen?

If you are not certain with whom you should talk, explain the purpose of your call:

> This is Anthony Todd of Robie Realty. I have a question about next week's photo shoot of your property. May I speak with someone who can help me?

If a call is coming directly to you, identify yourself.

> Brule Industries. Kate Sorensen speaking. May I help you?

If you are screening calls for others, first identify the company or office and yourself and then offer assistance:

> Brule Industries. This is Audrey Peters. How may I help you?

> This is Ms. Sorensen's office. I am Audrey Peters. May I help you?

Whether in or out of the office, be sure to project your best professional image when talking on the phone.
© wavebreakmedia/Shutterstock RF

If the person whose calls you're screening is not available, be helpful by saying, "Ms. Sorensen is not in right now. May I ask her to return your call?" You could also ask "May I tell her who called?" "Can someone else help you?" or "May I connect you with Rick Cruz? Mr. Cruz is Ms. Sorensen's associate and may be able to help you."

Assistants to busy businesspeople often screen incoming calls. If you are screening calls, you should courteously ask the purpose of the calls. The response might prompt you to refer the caller to a more appropriate person in the company. If the businessperson is busy at the moment, you should explain this and either suggest a more appropriate time for a call or promise a callback by the executive. However, promise a call back only if one will be made.

If the person being called is on another line or involved in some other activity, you can place the caller on hold or ask if the caller would like to leave a message. Good business etiquette requires that the choice should be the caller's. However, if you have to put a caller on hold, be sure the hold time is reasonable. You don't want to put the caller on hold for a long time just waiting for the person whom he or she called to have a chance to talk.

Effective Phone Procedures

At the beginning of a phone conversation you have initiated, state the purpose of the call and then use your listener's time efficiently by sticking to your point. To stay on point, you may want to outline an agenda for your call beforehand. You also want to eliminate distractions so that you can listen attentively when the other person is talking, and as in a face-to-face conversation, you want to refrain from interrupting or dominating the conversation.

Effective Voice Mail Techniques

Sometimes when the person you are calling is not available, you will be able to leave a voice message in an electronic voice mailbox. Not only does this save you the time involved in calling back the person you are trying to reach, but it also allows you to leave a more detailed message than you might leave with an assistant.

Telephobia: It's a Thing

In a world where many people like to text, it is no wonder that talking on the phone can cause stress and anxiety. When the stress and anxiety become so great that they keep someone from working or cause serious physical symptoms, the fear may be considered a phobia.

Treatment can include cognitive-behavioral therapies that help individuals positively visualize phone conversations or make phone calls that gradually move them from easy phone calls (e.g., calling a recorded customer service number where no interaction is expected) to more difficult ones (e.g., talking on the phone when others in the room can hear them).

You may not have a full-blown phobia, but if you are uncomfortable talking on the phone, you may want to do the following:

• Smile to relax yourself.
• Reward yourself after a phone call.
• Visualize your call being a success.
• Ask if you can call at a more convenient time if you sense the other person is busy.

• Don't take a "no" answer personally; think of reasons for the "no" that have nothing to do with you.
• Plan your message and prepare key points.
• Let some incoming calls go to voicemail.
• Make sure that the phone is the best communication channel for your message.

Source: Arlin Cuncic, "Phone Anxiety? How to Know if You Have a Phone Phobia; How to Overcome Your Fear of Making Phone Calls" *Very Well*, April 27, 2016, accessed May 10, 2016, https://www.verywell.com/afraid-making-phone-calls-tips-3024317.

You begin the message nearly the same way you would a phone call. Be as courteous as you would on the phone and speak as clearly and distinctly as you can. Tell the listener your name and affiliation. Begin with an overview of the message and continue with details. If you want the listener to take action, call for it at the end. If you want the listener to return your call, state that precisely, including when you can be reached. Slowly give the number where your call can be returned and then repeat it. Close with a brief goodwill statement. Using the example above, here is how Anthony Todd might leave a message for Kate Sorensen:

> Hello, Ms. Sorensen. This is Anthony Todd from Robie Realty. I'm calling to remind you about the photo shoot of your offices on May 2 at 8 a.m. I also have a few questions about the shoot and the timing of the final walkthrough on April 30. Please call me at 323-304-5902. I will be here until 5 p.m. I look forward to working with you and meeting your staff.

Courteous Use of Cell Phones

Cell phones have greatly expanded our ability to communicate. To ensure that you project your best professional image, you'll want to keep in mind these tips for using your cell phone—whether you're calling, texting, or using any of your phone's other features.

1. Turn off the ringer and sound in meetings and other places where it would be disruptive.

2. Do not use the cell phone at social gatherings.

3. Do not place the phone on the table while eating.

4. Avoid talking whenever it will annoy others. Usually this means when others are close enough to hear you.

5. Avoid discussing personal or confidential matters when others can hear you.

6. Do not talk in an excessively loud voice.

7. Preferably call from a quiet place, away from other people.

8. If you must talk while around people, be conscious of them and try to be discreet.

9. Don't hold up lines. If talking on your phone delays your ability to place an order or check out of a line, put the caller on hold or step out of the line and let others go ahead of you.

10. Avoid using the phone while driving (the law in some states).

Power Charge Your Professionalism: Put Your Editing Skills to Work

The following operational message informs employees of a new time-saving routing process for creating a bill of materials (BOM) for manufacturing your company's circuit boards. The BOM includes all resources for making the circuit boards, from purchasing raw materials and parts to assembling and selling the boards, so creating the BOM requires the approval of several divisions within the company.

This message is indirect and unclear. In addition, the message contains several sentence errors (sentence fragments, run-on sentences, and comma splices), punctuation errors, pronoun errors, subject-verb and pronoun-antecedent agreement errors, hidden verbs, cluttering phrases, and homophone errors.

As your instructor directs, revise the message as follows:

1. Correct the sentence errors and fix the hidden verbs, cluttering phrases, and homophone errors. Reference Chapter A: Correctness of Communication and Chapters 5 and 6 can help you identify and correct these issues.
2. Applying what you learned in Chapter 8, indicate how you would revise the message to make it more direct and clear. You can assume the audience requires all of the information in the message, so be sure your edits preserve all of the ideas even as you revise the wording.
3. Retype the message to reflect the revisions you indicated in steps 1 and 2.

To: <MGMT@forwardcircuits.com>; <supstaff@forwardcircuits.com>

From: Ross Gilman <rgilman@forwardcircuits.com>

Subject: Circuit Boards

I initiated and lead a process review for the reduction of the routing time our BOM's, two parts of the process were slowing it down. First, Purchasing's function are in the middle of the process. Which means the purchase order cannot be issued until the three departments before we in the process take up to three days to finish there assigned tasks. Also, once the Purchasing Department places the order, we have to wait five days for the supplier to ship the ISO 9001:2000/AS9100-compliant parts.

As you know, at the present time, the BOM's are routed as follows: Accounting, Sales, Scheduling, Purchasing, Accounting, Scheduling, Master Scheduling

In the new process we are able get the consolidation of the number of steps from seven to five. Non-value added processes were removed steps were eliminated. So that no department will be effected by long wait times. We have had two jobs that have went through the new process to test its effectiveness, average time from issuance of the purchase order is in the neighborhood of one day. The average total time for creating the BOM are 21 days, down from 28 days.

The new process routes the BOMs in the following order: Purchasing, Accounting, Scheduling, Sales, Master Scheduling

Please follow the new process outlined above to route any BOM's contact me with any questions or concerns.

Ross

_____

Ross Gilman, CPM & Senior Buyer
Purchasing Department
Forward Circuits, Incorporated
Office: 715-555-5550 | Cell: 715-555-5551

Good editing skills are important because . . .

- Grammar, punctuation, and mechanics impact the clarity and readability of a message.
- Editing and revising are critical steps to ensuring that you project a professional image.

If you need additional practice, be sure to visit the grammar, mechanics, and punctuation exercises in LearnSmart Achieve.

Key Terms

interpersonal
    communication 531
organizational culture 532
nonverbal
    communication 534
body language 534
use of space 534

use of time 534
paralanguage 534
sensing 537
filtering 537
remembering 537
active listening 538
back-channeling 538

small talk 539
constructive feedback 541
conflict 543
negotiation 545
parliamentary procedure 545
agenda 546
meeting minutes 547

Critical-Thinking Questions

1. What types of questions can you ask to ensure you understand your organization's culture? LO1

2. What might these nonverbal communication behaviors communicate? Think of at least two possibilities for each. LO2
   a. A nod of the head
   b. Avoidance of eye contact
   c. Being asked to sit on the other side of the desk from your boss
   d. Shouting "WHAT!"
   e. Showing up late for a meeting
   f. Using your computer while someone else is talking

3. Discuss why we have difficulty listening well. LO3

4. What can you do to improve your listening? LO3

5. Talking is something we do every day, so we can be confident that these everyday skills are ready for use in the workplace. Discuss. LO4

6. Being able to start a conversation is especially important when meeting clients in social settings. Discuss the types of topics that would and would not be appropriate. LO4

7. Why is timing an important consideration in starting a conversation? LO4

8. What should you do upon approaching someone to start a conversation? LO4

9. What are three techniques for approaching difficult conversations? LO5

10. What strategies should you use to deliver feedback? Receive feedback? LO6

11. Identify which conflict resolution strategy would work best in the following situations. LO7
    a. Your team members disagree about whether to conduct a survey or hold focus groups. It's one of your first big group decisions, so it is important that everyone feels that he or she wins.
    b. Two co-workers are involved in a minor conflict about who gets to leave early and who should stay to answer the phones. They ask you for your opinion, but you don't want to make either of them unhappy with you.
    c. You (a staff accountant) and a senior partner both need to use the same conference room at the same time. You really want the room, but clearly you lack seniority.
    d. You and your team of five are not going to finish your presentation by the deadline, so you have to work on the weekend. Your team members are not happy, but there is no alternative. Maybe you can offer them something in exchange for getting them to work on a Saturday.

12. What can you do to ensure a successful negotiation? LO8

13. The people attending a meeting—not the leader—should determine the agenda. Discuss. LO9

14. As meetings should be democratic, everyone present should be permitted to talk as much as they want without interference from the leader. Discuss. LO9

15. Describe an annoying phone practice that you have experienced or know about (other than the ones discussed in the chapter). Explain and/or demonstrate how it should be corrected. LO10

Skills-Building Exercises

Organizational Cultures LO1

1. **Examining Your Workplace Culture:** Using a current or former workplace as your example, answer the questions in the section of this chapter called "Communication and Organizational Cultures" about how to understand a workplace culture. What conclusions can you draw about your workplace culture regarding the "rules" for communicating in this workplace? As your instructor directs, you can present your answers in a written document or oral presentation.

2. **Exploring a Company Culture:** Choose a company that you think you might want to work for someday or that hires people in your field. Interview someone at this company about the organizational culture. Is this a culture you would like to work in? Why or why not? As your instructor directs, you can summarize the culture and present your thoughts in a written document or oral presentation.

Nonverbal Communication LO2

1. **Identifying the Meanings behind Nonverbal Behaviors:** Find three to five pictures of people with different facial expressions (happiness, sadness, anger, etc.) or gestures. Ask those native to your area to identify the emotions or the meanings of the gestures the pictures convey. Then ask at least three others from different countries to identify the emotions. Report your results to the class.

2. **Observing Others' Interactions:** Go to a public place (e.g., your school's cafeteria, the library, a park, or a mall). Observe the interaction between two people whom you can see but not hear. In a short memo to your instructor, describe the setting, the participants, the interaction, and the nonverbal behaviors. Analyze their nonverbal communication and present two possible interpretations of these behaviors. Be sure to justify your interpretations with evidence from your observation.

3. **Evaluating Your Oral Communication:** Record yourself in some type of oral communication setting (e.g., the meetings described in this chapter's exercises, a mock job interview with your school's career services office, a conversation with a customer or co-worker). Watch the recording without the sound, and pay attention to your nonverbal behaviors. In a short memo to your instructor, describe what you saw and evaluate what you do well and what you will work to improve.

Listening LO3

1. **Playing the Classic Game of "Telephone":** After the class has been divided into two or more teams, the instructor reads some factual information (newspaper article, short story, etc.) to only one member of each team. Each of these team members tells what he or she has heard to a second team member, who in turn tells it to a third team member, and so on until the last member of each team has heard the information. The last person receiving the information reports what she or he has heard to the instructor, who checks it against the original message. The team able to report the information with the greatest accuracy wins.

2. **Evaluating Your Listening Skills:** This exercise is similar to Exercise #1 under Conversations, but in this exercise, you will analyze your listening skills. Reflect on a recent conversation with a friend, oral instructions you received from your boss, or a class lecture where you demonstrated what you believe is representative of your listening skills in general. Use a SWOT analysis to evaluate your listening skills. What are your *strengths* as a listener? What are your *weaknesses*? Identify some *opportunities* for improving your skills. Identify possible *threats* (e.g., physical limitations, lack of interest) that may hinder your ability to improve your skills. What can you do to address these threats? Present your analysis in a memo report to your instructor.

Conversations LO4

1. **Evaluating Your Conversational Skills:** Record yourself in conversation with three different audiences (e.g., a friend, your parents, a customer or client at work, an instructor). Conduct a SWOT (strengths, weaknesses, opportunities, threats) analysis of your talking using the four elements of good talking discussed in this chapter. What are your *strengths*? What are your *weaknesses*? Identify *opportunities* for improving your talking. Discuss *threats* to improving

your talking (e.g., nervousness, lack of interest). What will you do to address the threats? Present your analysis in a memo report to your instructor. Be sure to explain to your audiences why you're recording your conversation and seek permission as appropriate.

2. **Making Small Talk:** Approach someone you don't know (e.g., at a social gathering, in the elevator, or in a checkout line) and make small talk. Reflect on how well you did and what you could do better. Be sure you approach people in a way that is appropriate for the context, and do not approach people if their nonverbal communication suggests that you should leave them alone.

3. **Observing Others' Conversations:** Observe conversations in your workplace. Are they productive? What do people do well? What could they improve?

Conflict and Negotiation LO5–8

1. **Playing "Divide the Loot":** Develop your conflict and negotiation skills by playing Divide the Loot.[12] Instructors, before this activity, you will have to give each student a different amount of play money.
   - Within a group, divide into two teams: managers and employees.
   - Put the money your instructor gave you into the group's employee pot or manager pot, depending on your role, but be careful not to let your team members know how much money you contributed. (You may want to put the money in an envelope.)
   - Your instructor will collect both pots, combine them, and add his or her own money. The instructor will count the money and let the group know how much is in the combined pot. You will still only know how much you contributed; you won't know how much anyone else contributed.
   - Take 10 minutes to decide how to divide the pot among your group members.
   - As your instructor directs, write or present an individual or team reflection on the strategies you used to resolve conflicts and negotiate the division of the money. Were they effective? Why or why not? What would you have done differently?

Meetings LO9

1. **Solving a Campus Problem:** For one of the following topics, develop a specific problem that would warrant a group meeting. (*Example:* For student government, the problem might be: "To determine the weaknesses of student government on this campus and what should be done to correct them.") Then lead the class (or participate) in a meeting on the topic. Class discussion following the meeting should reinforce the text material and bring out the effective and ineffective parts of the meeting.
   a. Scholastic dishonesty
   b. Housing regulations
   c. Student–faculty relations
   d. Student government
   e. Library
   f. Grading standards
   g. Attendance policies
   h. Varsity athletics
   i. Intramural athletics
   j. Degree requirements
   k. Parking on campus
   l. University calendar
   m. Homework requirements
   n. Tuition and fees
   o. Student evaluation of faculty
   p. Community–college relations
   q. Inclusivity and diversity issues on campus
   r. A policy for phone and computer use in the classroom

2. **Resolving a Problem of Your Choice:** Using one of the topics in the above exercise (or another topic as your instructor directs), work in groups of four to present a solution to the problem you decide to address. You should meet at least four times. One person should be designated to establish an agenda for and lead each meeting and another to take minutes

at each meeting. Each person in the group should take a turn leading a meeting and taking minutes. After each meeting, group members should evaluate the group leader's abilities. Let your leader know of at least one strength and one area needing improvement. Submit your agendas, minutes, and leader evaluations to your instructor as directed. Present your group's solution to your class as a short presentation or to your instructor in a memo.

2. **Debating a Current Topic:** Working in groups of four or five, debate the following statement. *As long as the information they provide is truthful, employers should be able to give a negative reference without fear of lawsuits or other negative effects for a former employee seeking employment with another company.* Examine arguments that might lead you to agree with the statement or disagree with it, and come to a consensus. Tape the meeting and analyze the group members' performances. You may analyze the recording as a group or individually as your instructor directs. Who emerged as the leader of the discussion? How could you tell this person was the leader? Did anyone dominate the discussion? Did anyone not participate or participate very little? Why do you think this person did not participate as much as he or she could have? What could people in the group do to improve their skills? What did they do well?

Talking on the Phone LO10

1. **Reflecting on Bad Phone Practices:** Make a list of bad phone practices that you have experienced or heard about. With a classmate, first demonstrate the bad practice and then demonstrate how you would handle it. Some possibilities: rudely putting a caller on hold, using an unfriendly tone, unintentionally insulting the caller, sounding uninterested.

2. **Making Sure Your Outgoing Message Is Professional:** Think about your outgoing message on your phone. For whom is your message appropriate? Are the voice quality, style, and word choice appropriate? Is it courteous? Is there anyone you would not want to hear this message (e.g., a potential employer)? Does the message contain sufficient detail? Is it too detailed or too long? In a memo to your instructor, include the text of your current outgoing message. If your message needs revision, include the text of your revised message. Explain why you are revising the message and describe the audience for which you are making the message more appropriate. If you do not believe your message needs revision, explain how your message meets the needs of your current audiences.

Communicating in
the Job Search

© George Doyle/Stockbyte/
Getty Images

Chapter Fifteen

D id you know that 93% of recruiters say they are likely to search for information about you on your social networking sites, regardless of whether you tell them what those sites are? Or that recruiters spend approximately 20% of the time in a face-to-face interview assessing your skills and 80% assessing your fit for the organization's culture?[1] These numbers can be intimidating, but they also show how important it is for you to be prepared, polished, and professional at every stage in the job search process.

Whether it involves an internship, your first job, or a job further down your career path, job seeking is directly related to your success and your happiness. This chapter will help you conduct your search and prepare the documents essential for your success.

Learning Objectives

LO15-1 Develop and use a network of contacts in your job search.

LO15-2 Assemble and evaluate information that will help you identify appropriate jobs.

LO15-3 Identify the sources that can lead you to an employer.

LO15-4 Compile résumés for print and electronic environments that are strong, complete, and organized.

LO15-5 Write targeted cover messages that skillfully sell your abilities.

LO15-6 Explain how you can participate effectively in an interview.

LO15-7 Write application follow-up messages that are appropriate, friendly, and positive.

LO15-8 Maintain your job-search activities.

Problem-Solving Challenge

Finding Your First Post-College Job

Introduce yourself to this chapter by assuming the role of either a college student seeking an internship or a graduating student seeking your first professional position in your field.

You believe that it is time to begin seeking the internship or job for which your studies have

been preparing you. But how do you do this? Where do you look? What does the search involve? How should you present yourself for the best results? Once you get an interview, how should you prepare for it? After the interview, what should you say in a thank-you note to the

employer? And what about other correspondence you might have to write to accept a position, decline a position, or perhaps resign from your current job?

The answers to these and related questions are reviewed in the following pages.

Conducting the Job Search

LO15-1 Develop and use a network of contacts in your job search.

Of all the things you do in life, one of the most important is getting a job. Being methodical, thorough, careful, and even a little creative in how you conduct the search will ensure you find a position that is not only a fit for your skills and talents but also a fit for your personality and preferences as an employee.

Building a Network of Contacts

You can begin the job search long before you are ready to find employment. In fact, you can do it now by building a **network of contacts**. More specifically, you can build relationships with people who can help you find work when you need it such as classmates, professors, and businesspeople.

Right now, your classmates are not likely to be holding positions in which they make or influence hiring decisions, but some of them may know people who can help you. Furthermore, in the future, when you want to make a career change, they may hold positions that allow them to help you. The wider your circle of friends and acquaintances, the more likely you are to make employment contacts.

Knowing your professors, and making sure that they know you, can also lead to employment contacts. Because professors often consult for businesses, they may know key executives and be able to help you contact them. Professors sometimes hear of position openings and can refer you to the hiring executives. Demonstrating your work ethic and your ability in the classroom is a great way to get your professors to know you and help you. Take advantage of opportunities to meet your professors outside the classroom, especially the professors in your major field.

Obviously, meeting business professionals can also lead to employment contacts. You may already know some through family and friends. But broadening your relationships among businesspeople is helpful. You can do this in various ways, especially through college professional groups such as the Association for Information Technology Professionals, Student Accounting Society, American Marketing Association, Collegiate DECA, International Association of Business Communicators, and the Society for the Advancement of Management. By taking an active role in the organizations in your field of study, especially by working on program committees and by becoming an officer, you can get to know the executives who serve as guest speakers.

You also might meet businesspeople online. If you share a particular interest on a blog or are known as one who contributes valuable comments to others' blogs, you may get some good job leads there. Likewise, you can network on social media sites such as LinkedIn by starting a group or actively contributing to one.

In addition to these more common ways of making contacts, you can use some less common ones. By working in community organizations (charities, community improvement groups, fundraising

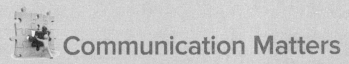
groups), you can meet community leaders. Even making small talk with the person working out next to you at the gym or with your favorite customer at the restaurant where you work could potentially lead to a professional contact. In fact, participation in virtually any activity that provides contacts with businesspeople can be mutually beneficial, both now and in the future.

Obtaining an Internship

Internships and **cooperative learning experiences** are short-term, educational employment experiences that are an effective way to network with people in your field, gain professional knowledge and experience, or simply learn whether your current field is where you want to build a career.

One source estimates that as many as 75% of employers prefer some type of relevant work experience, and 60% say they prefer work experience from internships or co-op experience.[2] While many students may find paid internships more desirable, unpaid internships can also be valuable. Usually the law requires that for-profit businesses compensate interns; nonprofit organizations are not required to provide a salary or stipend.

The key is to make sure that an unpaid internship provides the opportunity to gain marketable skills and to make sure the employer does not unfairly take advantage of an intern's unpaid time, expertise, and labor. Regardless of whether the internship is paid, you may also receive academic credit for your work.

Though a quick Web search for internships will net several links to internship types, the first step in finding an internship may be to contact your school's career services office. You may also want to use many of the networking strategies discussed earlier in this chapter.

Identifying Appropriate Jobs

To find the right job, internship, or co-op experience, you need to investigate both internal and external factors. The best fit occurs when you have carefully looked at internal factors: your education, personal qualities, experience, and any special qualifications. However, to be realistic, these internal qualities need to be analyzed in light of the external factors. Some of these factors may include the current and projected job market, economic needs, location preferences, and family needs.

LO15-2 Assemble and evaluate information that will help you identify appropriate jobs.

The website of a university's career center, such as the one shown here, can be a great place for students to start their job search.

Courtesy University of Wisconsin-Eau Claire Career Services

Analyzing Yourself   When you are ready to search for a job, you should begin the effort by analyzing yourself. In a sense, you should look at yourself much as you would look at a product or service that is for sale. After all, when you seek employment, you are really selling your ability to work—to do things for an employer.

A job is more than something that brings you money. It is something that benefits both you and your employer. Thus, you should think about the personal qualities you have that enable you to be an accountable and productive worker that an employer needs. This self-analysis should cover the following categories.

Education   Perhaps you have already selected your career area such as accounting, communication, economics, finance, information systems, international business, management, marketing, health care, or education. If you have, your task is simplified because your specialized curriculum has prepared you for your goal.

Even so, you may be able to note special points that have given you additional skills or that show something special about you that would be applicable to a particular field (e.g., psychology courses that have improved your human relations skills, communication courses that have improved your writing and speaking skills, or foreign language courses that have prepared you for international assignments).

If you have pursued a more general curriculum, such as one in general business or liberal arts, you will need to examine what skills and knowledge will transfer to the workplace. Perhaps you will find an emphasis on computers, written communication, human relations, or foreign languages—all of which are highly valued by businesses. Or perhaps you will conclude that your training has given you a strong general base from which to learn specific business skills.

In analyzing your education, you should look at the quality of your record—grades, projects, honors, and any special recognitions you can highlight in an application.

Personal Qualities   Your self-analysis also should cover your personal qualities and preferences for interacting with others and with your environment. Employers often use **personality tests** such as the Myers-Briggs to screen new hires for these qualities and preferences; you can take them online as well as at most campus career centers. Qualities that relate to working with people are especially important as are those that indicate an aptitude for leadership or teamwork ability.

Of course, you may want to check with friends to see whether they agree with your assessments. You also may need to check your record for concrete evidence supporting your assessments. For example, organization membership and participation in community

You Make the Call

What types of qualities do you have that a personality test might not reveal about you?

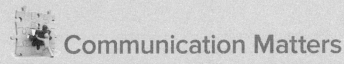

Communication Matters

Are You Sure You're Qualified? Employers May Not Agree

The American Association of Colleges and Universities surveyed 613 students at two- and four-year colleges and 400 employers regarding students' preparedness and readiness for the workplace. While students and employers were closest in agreement regarding students' aptitude with technology, they were farthest in agreement regarding skills associated with effective communication.

While it is true that such qualities as proficient creative or analytical skills can look different among individuals and that proficiency can be hard to define, it is also true that employers are seeking these skills as they apply to their situation. As we have said throughout the book, your perception matters much less than your audience's perception.

The survey underscores the importance of internships, cooperative learning, or other school-to-work opportunities that allow you to see what these traits look like in the workplace. You will gain experience, polish your skills, and be more confident that you meet the needs of your audience (employer) and project a professional image.

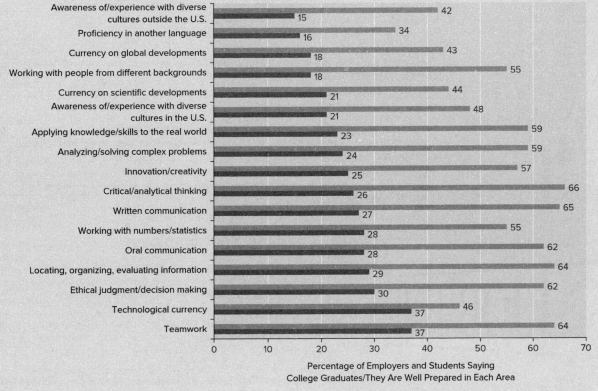

Percentage of Employers and Students Saying College Graduates/They Are Well Prepared in Each Area

■ Students ■ Employers

Source: Scott Jaschik, "Well-Prepared in Their Own Eyes," *Inside Higher Ed*, January 20, 2015, accessed May 7, 2016, https://www.insidehighered.com/news/2015/01/20/study-finds-big-gaps-between-student-and-employer-perceptions.

activities are evidence of people and teamwork skills. Holding an office in an organization is evidence of leadership ability. Participation on a debate team or collegiate business sales team is evidence of communication skills.

Work Experience Work experience in your major field deserves the most emphasis, but work experience not related to the job you seek also can tell something important about you.

Your part-time server job or summer construction job may not seem like a big deal to you, but these jobs provide you with assets that any employer in any company can use, such as attention to detail, initiative, team skills, communication skills, and the ability to work well under pressure. You don't want to undersell this experience.

Special Interests As we've mentioned, your self-analysis should include special qualifications that might be valuable to an employer. Your analysis can also include personal interests that may be relevant to types of positions you are seeking. To illustrate, athletic experience might be helpful for work with a sporting goods distributor, a hobby of automobile mechanics might be helpful for work with an automotive service company, and an interest in music might be helpful for work in arts administration.

You also might take an **interest inventory** such as the Strong Campbell Interest Inventory or the Minnesota Vocational Interest Inventory. These tests help match your interests to those of others successful in their careers. Most college counseling and career centers make these tests available to their students, and some are available online. Getting good help in interpreting the results is critical to providing you with valuable information.

Analyzing Outside Factors

After you have analyzed yourself, you need to combine this information with the work needs of business and other external influences to give realistic direction to your search for employment. Is there a demand for the work you want to do? Are jobs readily available? Can you make a living at doing what you want to do? Where is the kind of work you are seeking available? Are you willing to move? Is such a move compatible with others in your life—your partner, your children, your parents? Does the location meet your lifestyle needs?

Although the job market may drive the answer to some of these questions (e.g., Are you willing to relocate in order to get the job you want?), you should answer them on the basis of what you know now and then conduct your job search accordingly. Finding just the right job should be one of your most important goals. Reading about various careers in the *Occupational Outlook Handbook* at www.bls.gov/ooh/ is one way to learn about the nature of the jobs you seek as well as salary range and demand.

LO15-3 Identify the sources that can lead you to an employer.

Career fairs and job boards are good places to look for announcements of job openings.
Shutterstock / Gustavo Frazao

Finding Your Employer

You can use a number of sources in your search for an employer with whom you will begin or continue your career. Your choice of sources will probably be influenced by the stage of your career.

Career Centers

If you are seeking an internship or just beginning your career, one good possibility is the career center at your school. Most schools have career centers, and these attract employers who are looking for suitable applicants. Many centers offer excellent job-search counseling and maintain databases on registrants' school records, résumés, and recommendations that prospective employers can review. Most have directories listing major companies with contact names and addresses. Most also provide interviewing opportunities.

Campus career centers often hold **career fairs**, which are an excellent place to find employers who are looking for new graduates or interns as well as to gather information about the kinds of jobs different companies offer. By attending them early, you often find out about internships and summer jobs or gather ideas for selecting courses that might give you an advantage when you do begin your career search.

Network of Personal Contacts As we have noted, the personal contacts you make can be the leading means of finding employees. Business acquaintances may provide job leads outside those known to your friends.

Classified Advertisements Help-wanted advertisements in newspapers and professional journals, whether online or in print, provide good sources of employment opportunities for many kinds of work. Keep in mind that they provide only a partial list of jobs available. Many positions are filled before they reach the classifieds, so be sure you are part of the professional networks in your field.

Online Sources In addition to finding opportunities in classifieds, you also will find them in online databases. Monster.com, for example, lists jobs available throughout the United States and beyond, with new opportunities posted regularly. Many companies post job openings on the Web, some with areas dedicated to new college graduates. If you are working now, you may want to check your company's intranet for positions. And professional associations often maintain job databases. Furthermore, you could use social media such as blogs, Facebook, LinkedIn, and Twitter to search for jobs or post queries about job openings that readers might know of.

From the Tech Desk

Make Your LinkedIn Profile Work for You

According to a study by the Society of Human Resource Management, 43% of organizations say they use social media to screen candidates. The most popular site they use is LinkedIn (90%), but Facebook (66%) and Twitter (53%) are also popular. Over a third of the respondents (36%) say they have disqualified a job candidate as a result of their search. Most organizations (82%) say they use social media to recruit passive job seekers (those with an online presence who are not submitting application materials).

Although you want to review all of the social media sites you use, search engine optimization expert Brian Shumway provides these tips for ensuring you impress employers who visit your LinkedIn profile:

1. Fill out the profile completely. The more fields you complete, the greater the odds that people will find you in a search.

2. Customize your URL for your profile at www.linkedin.com/YourName and then use the URL on your résumé and website.

3. Use descriptive key words for your job titles.

4. Expand your network. When you expand the number of your connections, you can then see those connections' level-two and level-three connections and perhaps further expand your network.

5. Join and participate in groups. The groups give you an opportunity to network more closely with professionals in your field, and your contributions will help you get noticed.

6. Upload a photo. Include in your profile a professional photo, not a glamour shot or an informal picture of you at a party.

7. Optimize your job descriptions. Describe your jobs using common terminology and present the description in short paragraphs or lists.

8. Get and give endorsements. Get people to endorse your skills so that an employer can see what others think you are good at. Giving endorsements is one good way to get people to return the favor to you.

9. Update your summary. Keeping your summary updated is a good way to show that you are active. Remember, too, that you can add links or upload files within your summary. This is a great way to show your work.

10. Proofread. Because this is a professional site, any typos convey that you are not detail oriented or that you are not careful in your work.

Sources: Thomas Ahearn, "SHRM Survey Finds Employers Use Social Media to Both Hire and Disqualify Job Candidates," *Employment Screening Resources*, January 21, 2016, accessed May 10, 2016, http://www.esrcheck.com; Brian Shumway, "LinkedIn SEO–30 Tips to Increase Your Visibility," *LinkedIn*, July 8, 2015, accessed May 10, 2016, https://www.linkedin.com.

Employment Agencies Companies that specialize in finding jobs for employees can be useful. Of course, these companies charge for their services, but the employer sometimes pays the charges, especially if qualified applicants are scarce. **Executive search consultants** (headhunters) are commonly used to place experienced people in executive positions.

Employment agencies are another way job seekers gain employment, though it is usually temporary; however, temporary employment can lead to permanent employment. It allows the worker to get a feel for the company and the company to observe the worker before making a job commitment. You can also gain valuable on-the-job training in a temporary assignment.

Prospecting Some job seekers approach prospective employers directly, by either personal visit, mail, or email. Personal visits are effective if the company has an employment office or if a personal contact of yours can arrange a visit. Mail contacts typically include a résumé and a cover message. An email contact can include a variety of documents and be sent in various forms. The construction of these messages is covered later in the chapter.

Preparing the Application Documents

Once you have done your research, you are ready to apply for a job. If the distance is not great or if the employer has invited a personal contact, you can visit the company to apply for a position. When a personal visit is not convenient and appropriate, you may have to apply online or by mail or email.

Whether or not you apply in person, you are likely to need some written material about yourself. If you apply in person, you probably will take a résumé and cover message with you to leave as a record of your qualifications. If you do not apply in person, of course, the application is conducted completely in writing. Typically, it consists of a résumé and a cover message.

Approach preparing a résumé and cover message as you would when preparing a sales campaign (see Chapter 10). Use the self-analysis discussed earlier in the chapter to take a personal inventory, listing all the information about you that you believe an employer would want to know.

Then learn as much as you can about the company—its plans, its policies, and its operations. You can study the company's website, read its annual report and other publications, find any recent news articles about the company, and consult a variety of business databases. You should also learn as much as you can about the requirements of the work the company wants done.

With this preliminary information assembled, you are ready to plan the application. First, you need to know what the employer is requesting from applicants. Is it only a cover message? Only a résumé? A cover message and a résumé (also called a *vita, curriculum vita, qualifications brief,* or *data sheet*)? A cover message, résumé, and reference sheet? Many employers require the combination of a cover message and résumé, but some prefer to see a detailed cover message alone, while others require all three documents.

The Occupational Outlook Handbook is one of the best resources for finding out about a wide variety of jobs, including their education requirements, expected earnings, job duties and conditions, and more.

US Department of Labor, Bureau of Labor Statistics. http://www.bls.gov/ooh/; image: © Monkey Business Images/Shutterstock RF

Constructing the Résumé

LO15-4 Compile résumés for print and electronic environments that are strong, complete, and organized.

Writing a résumé requires you to use many of the same strategies we've discussed in previous chapters for writing business documents. To plan your résumé, you'll analyze your goals, purpose, and audience. Then you will draft your résumé and revise and edit it until it represents your best professional work.

As with any other business document, you also need to consider your communication channel—whether your audience will read your résumé as a printed (hard copy) document or an electronic document. Constructing the content for each type is similar, but because you are likely to need both printed and electronic copies of your résumé, you will need to be familiar with the special considerations for each type.

Résumé Content

Your **résumé** presents qualifications and experiences that show you are a good candidate for a position. Designed for quick reading, the information is arranged for easy scannability. It should also be tailored to the position for which you are applying.

The arrangements of résumés differ widely, but the following process represents how you generally approach them.

Selecting the Content
Your first step in preparing the résumé is to review the information you have assembled about yourself and then select the information that will help your reader evaluate you. You want to make sure that the information you select is tailored and relevant to the position for which you are applying. This means that each time you apply for a position, you may have to update the information you include in your résumé.

Arranging the Content into Groups
Many arrangements are possible, but the most conventional is the grouping of *Objective, Education, Internships, Work Experience,* and *Skills* or *Interests.* Another possibility is grouping by job functions or skills, such as *Selling, Communicating,* and *Managing.*

You might have a group of *Achievements* taken from your experience and education. Another possibility is to have a group consisting of information highlighting your major *Qualifications.* Here you would include information drawn from the areas of experience, education, and skills or personal qualities. Illustrations of and instructions for constructing groups such as these appear later in the chapter.

Constructing the Headings
With your information organized, a logical next step is to construct the headings for the résumé. Common headings include *Objective, Education, Experience,* and *Internship.* Exhibit 15-1 provides a list of category headings to consider.

The next level of headings might be *Objective, Education, Experience,* and *Skills.* These headings can be placed to the left or centered above the text that follows.

Consider using more descriptive headings that tell the nature of what follows. For example, instead of using the head *Education* and listing under that heading the software skills you acquired while a student, you might use *Computer Skills* and list your skills there. These headings better indicate the information covered, and they help the reader interpret the facts that follow.

As you can see from Exhibits 15-3, 15-5, 15-6, and 15-7, the headings are distinguished from the other information in the résumé by the use of different sizes and styles of type. The main heading (your name) should appear to be the most important of all. Your goal is to choose forms that properly show the relative importance of the information and are pleasing to the eye.

Exhibit 15-1   Résumé Headings and Titles

Academic Achievements	Credentials	Professional Affiliations
Academic History	Degree(s)	Professional Affiliations & Awards
Academic Honors	Designations	Professional Employment
Academic Training	Dissertation	Professional Experience
Accomplishments	Education	Professional Leadership
Activities	Education Highlights	Professional Memberships
Additional Experience	Education & Training	Professional Organizations
Additional Professional Training	Educational Background	Professional Objective
Additional Training	Employment	Professional Qualifications
Affiliations	Employment History	Professional Seminars
Appointments	Employment Objective	Professional Summary
Areas of Expertise	Exhibitions & Awards	Publications
Associations	Experience(s)	Published Works
Athletic Involvement	Experience Highlights	Qualifications
Awards	Extracurricular Involvement	References
Awards & Distinctions	Field Placement	Related Course Work
Background and Interests	Foreign Language	Related Experience
Business Experience	Graduate School	Relevant Course Work
Career Goal	Graduate School Activities	Research Experience
Career Highlights	Graduate School Employment	Seminars
Career History	Hardware/Software	Skill(s) Summary
Career Objective	Highlights of Qualifications	Skills & Attributes
Career Profile	Honors	Skills & Qualifications
Career-Related Experience	Honors, Activities, & Organizations	Special Abilities
Career-Related Fieldwork	Honors and Awards	Special Awards & Recognitions
Career-Related Training	International Experience	Special Courses
Career-Related Workshops	International Travel	Special Interests
Career Skills & Experience	Internship Experience	Special Licenses & Awards
Career Summary	Internship(s)	Special Projects or Studies
Certificate(s)	Job History	Special Skills
Certifications	Languages	Special Training
Classroom Experience	Leadership Roles	Strengths
Coaching Experience	License(s)	Student Teaching
Coaching Skills	Major Accomplishments	Student Teaching Experience
College Activities	Management Experience	Study Abroad
Communication Experience	Memberships	Summary
Community Involvement	Memberships & Activities	Summary of Experience
Computer Background	Military Experience	Summary of Qualifications
Computer Experience	Military Service	Teaching Experience
Computer Knowledge	Military Training	Teaching & Coaching Experience
Computer Languages	Objective	Teaching & Related Experience
Computer Proficiencies	Occupational History	Thesis
Computer Skills	Other Experience	Travel
Computer Systems	Other Skills	Travel Experience
Consulting Experience	Overseas Employment	Volunteer Experience
Cooperative Education	Overseas Experience	Work Experience
Cooperative Education Experience	Planning & Problem Solving	Work History
Course Highlights	Portfolio	Workshops & Seminars
Course Work Included	Position Objective	
Courses of Interest	Practicum Experience	

Source: Career Services, "Sample Résumé Headings & Titles," UW-Eau Claire, http://www.uweccareerservices.org.

Creating the Header

Place your name and contact information at the top of the résumé. Your address, phone number, and email address are the most likely means of contacting you. When it is likely that your contact information will change before the job search ends, you may want to include current and permanent contact information. Most authorities recommend that you display them prominently somewhere in the résumé. You also may want to display your website address or addresses for your social networking sites. The most common location for displaying contact information is at the top under your name.

The logic of making the contact information prominent and inclusive is to make it easy for the employer to reach you. However, in the interest of privacy, for résumés shared through the Internet, you may want to include only an email address created specifically for job searches and a phone number. For business use, a professional email address such as meganromero@yahoo.com is always preferable to an informal one, such as surferchick@yahoo.com or hunkman@gmail.com.

Writing a résumé requires careful planning, data gathering, and organization.
© momentimages/Getty Images RF

Because your name should be considered the main heading, it should be presented in type that is larger and bolder than the rest of the document so that it stands out. If an employer remembers only one fact from your résumé, that fact should be your name.

Including Your Objective

Although not a category of background information, a **statement of your objective** is appropriate in the résumé. Headings such as *Career Objective, Job Objective,* or just *Objective* usually appear at the beginning after your name.

Not all authorities agree on the value of including the objective, however. Some argue that the objective includes obvious information that is clearly found in the remainder of the résumé. Moreover, they point out that an objective can be unhelpful either because it is too general for the employer to know what type of work the applicant is seeking or so specific that it limits the applicant to a single position and eliminates consideration for other jobs that may be available.

Those who favor stating the objective say that it helps the recruiter see quickly where the applicant might fit in the company. For example, in large companies where the human resources office sees applications for many types of positions, a clear objective can be helpful in routing the résumé to the appropriate hiring personnel.

Primarily, your objective should describe the work you seek:

> Objective: To obtain a marketing research internship in the arts and entertainment industry for the summer of 2019

Another technique includes using words that convey a long-term interest in the targeted company, as in the following example.

> Objective: To secure a full-time sales representative position for McGraw-Hill leading to sales management

Also, wording the objective to point out your major strengths can be effective. It also can help set up the organization of the résumé.

> Objective: To apply three years of successful e-commerce accounting experience in a transaction management and analysis position with a large company

Presenting the Information

After crafting your job objective, you need to determine what information to present under the rest of your headings. Though the order of the headings will largely depend on your organizational strategy, the information under each heading generally appears as follows.

Work Experience The description of your work experience should contain your job title, position, company name, location, and dates of employment. You should also include your job duties and the skills you acquired, especially those that relate to the position for which you are applying.

Marketing and Public Relations Intern

Alliant Health Plans, Incorporated, Boston, MA

Jan. 2019–May 2019

- Created a Web page, brochure, and press release for a community wellness program
- Interviewed and wrote about physicians, customers, and community leaders for newsletter articles
- Worked with a team of interns in other departments to analyze and update the company's website

Note in the above example that in addition to the basic information regarding the job, the writer lists duties that anyone in a marketing or public relations field would likely use in a related position. The duties are represented with **action-oriented, past tense verbs** (e.g., *interviewed, wrote*) because the position has ended. If the intern were still in the position, he or she would have used **simple present tense verbs** for duties he or she currently performs (e.g., *interview, write*).

The use of these action verbs strengthens a job description because verbs are the strongest of all words. If you choose them well, you will do much to sell your ability to do the jobs you are targeting. A list of the more widely used action verbs appears in Exhibit 15-2.

Note also that the writer uses both months and dates. This is especially important when you consider that simply saying "2019" doesn't let the reader know how long the internship was. In another example, if a reader sees dates of employment as 2018–2019, he or she does not know if that included a full year of employment or if the writer started on December 31, 2018, and quit on January 1, 2019. Including the months along with the dates is the clearest and most ethical way to represent your employment timeline.

Education Because your education is likely to be your strongest selling point for your first job after college, you will cover it in some detail. Unless it adds something unique, you usually do not include your high school education once you have enrolled in college. Similarly, you also minimize the emphasis on all your education as you gain experience. At a minimum, your coverage of education should include institutions, dates, degrees, and areas of study.

For some jobs, you may want to list and even describe specific courses, especially if you have little other information to present or if your course work has uniquely prepared you for those jobs. In particular, if you are applying for an internship, you may want to list your course work as an indication of your current level of academic preparation as it relates to the requirements of the position.

If your grade-point average (GPA) is good, you may want to include it. Remember, for your résumé, you can compute your GPA in a way that works best for you as long as you label it accurately. For example, you may want to select just those courses in your major, labeling them "Major GPA." Or if your last few years in college were your best ones, you may want to present your GPA for just that period. In any case, include a GPA when it works favorably for you and be clear what grades or time period you are using to calculate it.

Personal Information Personal information regarding race, religion, gender, age, and marital status is not indicated on a résumé because current laws prohibit hiring based on it.

Personal information that is generally appropriate includes information on your organization memberships, civic involvement, and social activities. This information provides evidence of experience and interest in working with people. Such information can be quite useful to some employers, especially when personal qualities are important to the work involved. Exhibit 15-3 presents a résumé that emphasizes education and experience.

You Make the Call
Which action verbs in Exhibit 15-2 best describe your experience?

Exhibit 15-2 Action Verbs That Add Strength to Your Résumé

Communication Skills
Address
Arbitrate
Arrange
Author
Correspond
Develop
Direct
Draft
Edit
Enlist
Formulate
Influence
Interpret
Lecture
Mediate
Moderate
Motivate
Negotiate
Persuade
Promote
Publicize
Recruit
Spoke
Translate

Management Skills
Administer
Analyze
Assign
Attain
Chair
Contract
Consolidate
Coordinate
Delegate
Develop
Directed
Evaluate
Execute
Improve
Increase
Organize
Plan
Prioritize
Produce
Recommend
Review

Schedule
Strengthen
Supervise
Wrote

Teaching Skills
Adapt
Advised
Clarify
Coach
Communicate
Coordinate
Develop
Enable
Encourage
Evaluate
Explain
Facilitate
Guide
Inform
Initiate
Instruct
Persuade
Setting goals
Stimulate

Creative Skills
Act
Conceptualize
Create
Design
Develop
Direct
Establish
Fashion
Found
Illustrate
Institute
Integrate
Introduce
Invent
Originate
Perform
Plan
Publish
Revitalize
Shape

Helping Skills
Assist

Assess
Clarify
Coach
Counsel
Demonstrate
Diagnose
Educate
Expedite
Facilitate
Familiarize
Guide
Refer
Rehabilitate
Represent
Service
Support
Tend

Research Skills
Clarify
Collect
Critique
Diagnose
Evaluate
Examine
Extract
Identify
Inspect
Interpret
Interview
Invented
Investigate
Organize
Review
Summarize
Survey
Systematize

Financial Skills
Administer
Allocate
Analyze
Appraise
Audit
Balance
Budget
Calculate
Compute
Develop

Forecast
Manage
Market
Plan
Project
Research

Administrative Skills
Approve
Arrange
Catalog
Classify
Collect
Compile
Dispatch
Execute
Generate
Implement
Inspect
Monitor
Operate
Organize
Prepare
Process
Purchase
Record
Retrieve
Screen
Specify
Systematize
Tabulate
Validate

Information Skills
Catalog
Clarify
Classify
Compile
Compose
Convey
Copy
Correct
Define
Document
Gather
Inform
Kept records
Memorize
Proofread

Question
Review
Specify
Study
Survey
Tabulate
Test
Verify

Leadership Skills
Appoint
Approve
Arrange
Assess
Assign
Authorize
Carry out
Chair
Coach
Complete
Consult
Delegate
Demonstrate
Determine
Devise
Direct
Enlist
Facilitate
Head
Initiate
Launch
Motivate
Negotiate
Nominate
Preside
Set goals
Start

Problem-Solving Skills
Analyze
Apply
Calculate
Compile
Consult
Correct
Create
Critique
Design
Develop

Diagnose
Discover
Dissect
Examine
Explore
Problem solve
Propose
Research
Resolve
Revise
Search
Study
Track
Troubleshoot
Uncover

Technical Skills
Assemble
Built
Calculate
Compute
Design
Devise
Engineer
Fabricate
Maintain
Operate
Overhaul
Program
Remodel
Repair
Solve
Train
Upgrade

Teamwork Skills
Accomplish
Assist
Collaborate
Coordinate
Corroborate
Dispatch
Encourage
Explain
Follow
Help
Share
Team built
Volunteer

Source: Career Services, "Sample Résumé Headings & Titles," UW-Eau Claire, http://www.uweccareerservices.org.

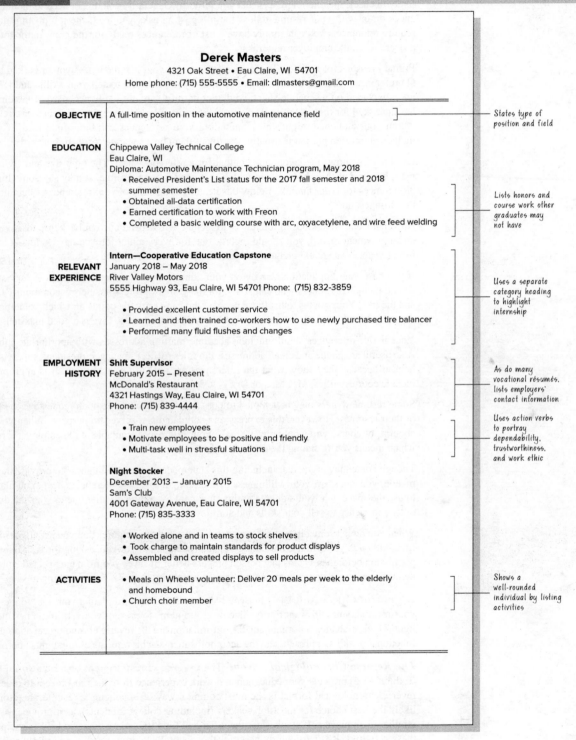

Derek Masters
4321 Oak Street • Eau Claire, WI 54701
Home phone: (715) 555-5555 • Email: dlmasters@gmail.com

| OBJECTIVE | A full-time position in the automotive maintenance field | States type of position and field |

EDUCATION
Chippewa Valley Technical College
Eau Claire, WI
Diploma: Automotive Maintenance Technician program, May 2018
- Received President's List status for the 2017 fall semester and 2018 summer semester
- Obtained all-data certification
- Earned certification to work with Freon
- Completed a basic welding course with arc, oxyacetylene, and wire feed welding

Lists honors and course work other graduates may not have

RELEVANT EXPERIENCE
Intern—Cooperative Education Capstone
January 2018 – May 2018
River Valley Motors
5555 Highway 93, Eau Claire, WI 54701 Phone: (715) 832-3859

- Provided excellent customer service
- Learned and then trained co-workers how to use newly purchased tire balancer
- Performed many fluid flushes and changes

Uses a separate category heading to highlight internship

EMPLOYMENT HISTORY
Shift Supervisor
February 2015 – Present
McDonald's Restaurant
4321 Hastings Way, Eau Claire, WI 54701
Phone: (715) 839-4444

As do many vocational résumés, lists employers' contact information

- Train new employees
- Motivate employees to be positive and friendly
- Multi-task well in stressful situations

Uses action verbs to portray dependability, trustworthiness, and work ethic

Night Stocker
December 2013 – January 2015
Sam's Club
4001 Gateway Avenue, Eau Claire, WI 54701
Phone: (715) 835-3333

- Worked alone and in teams to stock shelves
- Took charge to maintain standards for product displays
- Assembled and created displays to sell products

ACTIVITIES
- Meals on Wheels volunteer: Deliver 20 meals per week to the elderly and homebound
- Church choir member

Shows a well-rounded individual by listing activities

References Even though employers can (and do) check your social media sites, they are also likely to check specific references that you provide. Generally, you do not need to include references on or with your résumé unless the job posting asks you to. If the job posting does not require references, you can simply have a list of references ready for the point in the interview process when the employer requires it.

Primary reasons for not including your references on your résumé unless you are asked are that (1) references added to a résumé take up space you could use to sell your skills, and (2) references included on a separate sheet, while not harmful, are not likely necessary if the employer has not asked for them. However, if you have a particularly impressive reference or a reference whom your audience might know, including your references can be a good idea. If you do include your references, it is usually best to put them on a separate **reference sheet**.

Exhibit 15-4 shows the layout and content for a reference sheet. The type size and style of the main heading of this sheet should match that used in your résumé. It may say something like "References for [*your name*]." Below this heading is a listing of your references, beginning with the strongest one.

How many and what kinds of references to include will depend on your background. If you have an employment record, you should include one for every major job you have held—at least for recent years. You should include references related to the work you seek.

If you base your application heavily on your education or your personal qualities, or both, you should include references who can vouch for these areas: professors, clergy, community leaders, and the like. Your goal is to list those people who can verify the points on which your appeal for the job is based. At a minimum, you should list three references. Five is a good maximum.

Your list of references should include accurate mailing addresses with appropriate job titles. Also useful are phone and email addresses. Job titles (officer, manager, president, supervisor) are helpful because they show what the references are able to tell about you. It is appropriate to include courtesy titles: Mr., Ms., or Dr.

Some résumé writers may be tempted to put "References available upon request" at the bottom of their résumés. However, this expression is outdated and serves no purpose. When you think about it, of course you would always make your references available at the employer's request, which means you're stating the obvious.

Though some may argue that including this statement shows a willingness to provide the information, you can show your willingness by including a separate references sheet. You may want to use the space you would devote to this statement by adding another line to your job duties or other experience to sell your skills and abilities.

When you do list someone as a reference, business etiquette requires that you ask for permission first. Although you will use only those who can speak highly of you, asking for your reference's permission beforehand helps that person prepare better. It saves you from unexpected embarrassment if a reference does not remember you, is caught by surprise, or has nothing to say.

Organizing for Strength
After you have identified the information you want to include on your résumé, you will want to organize or group items to present yourself in the best possible light. Three strategies for organizing this information are the reverse chronological approach, the functional or skills approach, and the accomplishments/achievements or highlights approach.

The Reverse Chronological Layout
The **reverse chronological organizational layout** (Exhibit 15-5) presents your education and work experience from the most recent to oldest. The reverse chronological format is the most common way of organizing a résumé; therefore, it is likely the best choice for most job seekers (including college students), as it provides a format familiar to employers. It emphasizes the order and time frame in which you have participated in these activities. It is particularly good for those who have progressed in an orderly and timely fashion through school and work.

Exhibit 15-4 Illustration of a References List

References for Julia M. Alvarez

3177 North Hawthorne Boulevard
St. Louis, MO 63139
314.967.3117
jmalvarez358@hotmail.com

Format matches résumé

Mr. John Gibbs
Human Resources Director
Upton Industries
7114 East 71st Street
St. Louis, MO 63139
Phone: 314.342.1171
Email: John.Gibbs@upton.com

Mr. Todd E. Frankle, Store Manager
The Gap, Inc.
Four Points Mall
St. Louis, MO 63139
Phone: 314.466.9101
Email: tfrankle@gap.com

Professor Helen K. Robbins
Department of Management
Wilmont University
St. Louis, MO 63139
Phone: 314.392.6673
Email: Helen.Robbins@wilmont.edu

Professor Carol A. Cueno
Department of Psychology
Wilmont University
St. Louis, MO 63139
Phone: 314.392.0723
Email: Carol.Cueno@wilmont.edu

Complete information allows for easy contact

Exhibit 15-5 Illustration of a Résumé in Reverse Chronological Format

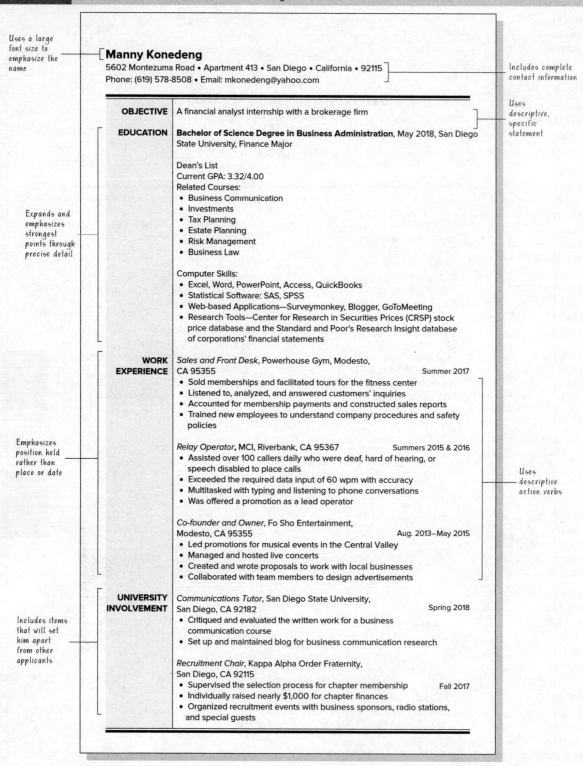

Uses a large font size to emphasize the name

Manny Konedeng
5602 Montezuma Road • Apartment 413 • San Diego • California • 92115
Phone: (619) 578-8508 • Email: mkonedeng@yahoo.com

Includes complete contact information

Uses descriptive, specific statement

OBJECTIVE	A financial analyst internship with a brokerage firm
EDUCATION	**Bachelor of Science Degree in Business Administration**, May 2018, San Diego State University, Finance Major

Dean's List
Current GPA: 3.32/4.00
Related Courses:
- Business Communication
- Investments
- Tax Planning
- Estate Planning
- Risk Management
- Business Law

Computer Skills:
- Excel, Word, PowerPoint, Access, QuickBooks
- Statistical Software: SAS, SPSS
- Web-based Applications—Surveymonkey, Blogger, GoToMeeting
- Research Tools—Center for Research in Securities Prices (CRSP) stock price database and the Standard and Poor's Research Insight database of corporations' financial statements

Expands and emphasizes strongest points through precise detail

WORK EXPERIENCE

Sales and Front Desk, Powerhouse Gym, Modesto, CA 95355   Summer 2017
- Sold memberships and facilitated tours for the fitness center
- Listened to, analyzed, and answered customers' inquiries
- Accounted for membership payments and constructed sales reports
- Trained new employees to understand company procedures and safety policies

Relay Operator, MCI, Riverbank, CA 95367   Summers 2015 & 2016
- Assisted over 100 callers daily who were deaf, hard of hearing, or speech disabled to place calls
- Exceeded the required data input of 60 wpm with accuracy
- Multitasked with typing and listening to phone conversations
- Was offered a promotion as a lead operator

Co-founder and Owner, Fo Sho Entertainment, Modesto, CA 95355   Aug. 2013–May 2015
- Led promotions for musical events in the Central Valley
- Managed and hosted live concerts
- Created and wrote proposals to work with local businesses
- Collaborated with team members to design advertisements

Emphasizes position held rather than place or date

Uses descriptive action verbs

UNIVERSITY INVOLVEMENT

Communications Tutor, San Diego State University, San Diego, CA 92182   Spring 2018
- Critiqued and evaluated the written work for a business communication course
- Set up and maintained blog for business communication research

Recruitment Chair, Kappa Alpha Order Fraternity, San Diego, CA 92115
- Supervised the selection process for chapter membership   Fall 2017
- Individually raised nearly $1,000 for chapter finances
- Organized recruitment events with business sponsors, radio stations, and special guests

Includes items that will set him apart from other applicants

You may wonder whether a college student or new graduate should use this format given many do not have a lot of work experience. Keep in mind that employers realize college students and new graduates do not have a lot of professional work experience; they are looking instead for transferable skills you could use in the internships or postcollege jobs you apply for. The important point is that this format is one you should likely choose because employers expect and readily recognize it, regardless of your level of experience.

The Functional or Skills Layout A **functional or skills layout** (Exhibit 15-6) organizes the résumé's contents around three to five areas particularly important to the job you want. Rather than showing that you developed one skill on one job and another skill on another job, this organizational plan groups related skills. It is particularly good for those who have had many jobs, have taken nontraditional career paths, or are changing fields.

Creating this kind of résumé takes much work and careful analysis of both jobs and skills to show the reader that you are a good match for the position. If you use a functional résumé, be sure that readers can see from the other sections—such as employment and education—where you likely developed the skills that you are emphasizing. Enabling your readers to make these connections quickly lends credibility to your claims to have such skills. If the reader has to guess where you might have learned the skills or cannot readily see where you learned them, he or she may disregard the résumé. This format is not as common as the reverse chronological order, so be sure you use it only for the reasons suggested here. Generally, college students and new college graduates should use the reverse chronological format.

The Accomplishments/Achievements Layout An **accomplishments/achievements layout** (Exhibit 15-7) foregrounds the most impressive factors about you.

It features a *Highlights* or *Summary* section that includes key points from the three conventional information groups: education, experience, and personal qualities. This information comes near the beginning of the résumé, usually following the objective. Typically, this layout emphasizes the applicant's most impressive background facts that pertain to the work sought, as in this example:

Summary

- Experienced: Three years of full-time work as programmer/analyst in designing and developing financial databases for the banking industry.

- Highly trained: BS degree with honors in management information systems.

- Self-motivated: Proven record of successful completion of an online degree while working full time.

Keep in mind that this section (and the accomplishments/achievements format) is usually for job seekers who have substantial experience. Therefore, its purpose is not to repeat sections of the résumé; its purpose is to highlight strengths for someone who may have a long list of jobs and experiences. If your résumé is short and your summary is just a repeat of other content, you will not want to include this section.

After the *Summary* or *Highlights* section, accomplishments should appear in a separate section rather than individually under an *Education* or *Employment* heading. Also keep in mind that like the functional or skills résumé, this format is not as common as the reverse chronological format, so be sure to use it only if you have a compelling reason to do so. Again, most college students and recent college graduates should use a reverse chronological résumé because it is the format employers expect to see.

Writing Impersonally and Consistently Because the résumé is a listing of information, you should write without personal pronouns (no *I, we, you*). You should also write all equal-level headings and the parts under each heading in the same parallel grammatical structure. For example, if one major heading in the résumé is a noun phrase, all the other major headings should be noun phrases. Chapter 5 can help you learn to use parallel structure.

Emphasizes tight organization through use of horizontal ruled lines

Charles Workman
12271 69th Terrace North
Seminole, FL 33772
727.399.2569 (Voice/Message)
cworkman@msn.com

Objective

An entry-level tax accounting position with a CPA firm

Education

Emphasizes degree and GPA

Bachelor of Science: University of South Florida, December 2018
Major: Business Administration
Emphasis: Accounting
GPA: 3.42 with Honors

Uses internal bullets to increase readability

Accounting-Related Course Work:
Financial Accounting ❖ Cost Accounting and Control ❖ Accounting Information Systems ❖ Auditing ❖ Concepts of Federal Income Taxation ❖ Financial Policy ❖ Communications for Business and Professions

Activities:
Vice-President of Finance, Beta Alpha Psi
Editor, Student Newsletter for Beta Alpha Psi
Member, Golden Key National Honors Society

Emphasizes key skills relevant to objective

Skills
Computer

- Assisted in installation of small business computerized accounting system using QuickBooks Pro.
- Prepared tax returns for individuals in the VITA program using specialty tax software.
- Mastered Excel, designing data input forms, analyzing and interpreting results of most functions, generating graphs, and creating and using macros.

Accounting

- Reconciled accounts for center serving over 1,300 clients.
- Prepared income, gift, and estate tax returns.
- Processed expense reports for twenty professional staff.
- Generated financial statements and processed tax returns using Great Plains and Solomon IV.

Varies use of action verbs

Business
Communication

- Conducted client interviews and researched tax issues.
- Communicated both in written and verbal form with clients.
- Delivered several individual and team presentations on business cases, projects, and reports to business students.

Work History
Administrative
Assistant

Office of Student Disability Services, University of South Florida
Tampa, FL. Spring 2018.

Tax Assistant

Rosemary Lenaghan, Certified Public Accountant. Seminole, FL Jan. 2015–May 2018.

Kimberly M. VanLerBerghe

2411 27th Street
Moline, IL 61265
309.764.0017 (Mobile)
kmv@yahoo.com

JOB TARGET   Trainer/translator for a large, worldwide company with operations in Spanish-speaking markets

HIGHLIGHTS OF QUALIFICATIONS

Emphasizes those qualifications most relevant to position sought

- Experienced in creating and delivering multimedia PowerPoint presentations.
- Enthusiastic team member/leader whose participation brings out the best in others.
- Proficient in analytical ability.
- Skilled in gathering and interpreting data.
- Bilingual—English/Spanish.

EDUCATION

Presents the most important items here

DEGREE	B.A. English, June 2018, Western Illinois University	
EMPHASIS	Education and Spanish	MAJOR GPA: 3.87/4.00
HONORS	Dean's List, four semesters	Chevron Scholarship, Fall 2016
MEMBER	Mortar Board, Women's Golf Team	

EMPLOYMENT

Identifies most significant places of work and de-emphasizes less important work

DEERE & COMPANY, INC.   **SENATOR KERRY ROSS**
Student Intern, Summer 2017   Volunteer in Computer Services, Fall 2017

Several years' experience in the restaurant business including supervisory positions.

ACCOMPLISHMENTS

Presents only selected accomplishments from various work and volunteer experience that relate to position sought

- ▶ Trained executives to create effective cross-cultural presentations.
- ▶ Developed online training program for executive use of GoToMeeting.
- ▶ Designed and developed a database to keep track of financial donations.
- ▶ Coded new screens and reports; debugged and revised screen forms for easier data entry.
- ▶ Provided computer support to virtual volunteers on election committee.
- ▶ Provided translation services for Hispanic employees.

The following four job duties illustrate the point. All but the third are verb phrases. The error can be corrected by making the third a verb phrase, as in the examples to the right:

Not Parallel	Parallel
Greeted customers	Greeted customers
Processed transactions	Processed transactions
Data entry in Excel spreadsheets	Entered data in Excel spreadsheets
Balanced a cash drawer	Balanced a cash drawer

The following items illustrate grammatical inconsistency in the parts of a group:

- Have fluency in Spanish
- Active in sports
- Ambitious

The understood word for the first item is *I* and for the second and third, the understood words are *I am*. Any changes that make all three items parallel would correct the error (e.g., fluent in Spanish, active in sports, ambitious).

Printed (Hard Copy) Résumés

As we've mentioned, one aspect of résumé writing you must consider is the environment in which your audience will read your document. Knowing whether your reader will read a printed or an electronic document helps you create résumés that are easily accessible to readers and ensures that you present a professional image.

A printed résumé is meant to be sent in hard copy format through the mail and used in face-to-face interviews. Generally, a printed résumé is one or two pages. Whether a résumé is one or two pages is determined by the skills and other information that best demonstrate your qualifications for a position. A two-page résumé is not more impressive than a one-page résumé if the information on the second page is irrelevant. On the other hand, you should not feel pressured to have a one-page résumé and then cram two pages of content onto one page; doing so will crowd the page and make important information less obvious to your reader.

However, knowing that some audiences prefer one-page résumés and may only read the first page, you want to make sure all of your most important information and qualifications appear on that first page.

Printed résumés should be formatted so that they are visually appealing and easily read. If you have a two-page résumé, be sure that your name, the word *résumé*, and the page number appear on page two as a page header.

The attractiveness of your résumé will determine the reader's initial impression. Thus, an attractive physical arrangement is a must. A sloppy, poorly designed presentation may ruin your chances of getting the job. While using a template is one solution, you will look like many other applicants. A layout designed with your reader and your unique data in mind will probably do a better job for you. Not only will your résumé have a distinctive appearance, but the design should sell your professional image.

You have many design possibilities. Your objective is to design an arrangement of type and space that appeals to the eye. Chapter 3 may provide design tips to get you started and help you with some general formatting principles.

White space is important in a résumé, so a good guide is to use one-inch margins on all sides. As you set up your categories and lists, you want to create additional white space by making sure your lists are short (three to six items) and that your items within each list are short as well. Be sure to check, too, that you have consistent spacing before and after headings and within your categories.

As you set up columns and bulleted lists, you will want to use tables and ruler guides rather than your space bar or tab key to align information. This allows you more control over your formatting and ensures that the alignment of the information in your columns is consistent and perfect.

While layout is important in showing your ability to organize and good spacing increases readability, other design considerations such as font and paper selection affect attractiveness almost as much. Type size for headings should be at least 12 to 14 points and for body text, 10 to 12 points. The size of your name at the top of your résumé, however, may be as large as 16 or 18 points (or more), depending on the font and the size of your other headings.

As we note in Chapter 3, you don't want to use more than two fonts in the document. Further, you can choose a serif font, sans serif font, or one of each. Whatever you choose, be sure it presents a professional business image. Script fonts such as Monotype Corsiva and informal fonts such as Comic Sans would not be good choices. Calibri, Helvetica, Arial, Times New Roman, or Cambria would work, depending on the audience and the image you want to project.

Another factor affecting the appearance of your application documents is the paper you select. The paper should be appropriate for the job you seek. In business, erring on the conservative side is usually better. The most traditional choice is white, 100% cotton, 20- to 28-lb. paper. When you mail your printed résumé, do not fold it; mail it in a 9 × 12 envelope and be sure to type (not handwrite) the mailing labels.

Comparing Examples of Résumés

The following two résumés show ineffective and effective layouts. The first one, scant in coverage and poorly arranged, does little to help the applicant or persuade an employer that the applicant is qualified. The second one is more complete and better arranged.

An Incomplete and Poorly Arranged Résumé
The format of this résumé is not pleasing to the eye. The weight of the type is heavy on the left side of the page. The failure to indent wrapped lines makes reading difficult. Overall, it does not effectively present Julia Alvarez's qualifications.

This résumé also contains numerous errors in wording. The headings are not parallel in grammatical form. All are in topic form except the first one. The items listed under *Personal* are not parallel either and contain irrelevant and inappropriate personal information.

Throughout, the résumé coverage is scant, leaving out many of the details needed to present the best impression of the applicant. Under *Experience,* little is said about specific tasks and skills in each job; and under *Education,* high school work is listed. The references are incomplete, omitting street addresses and job titles.

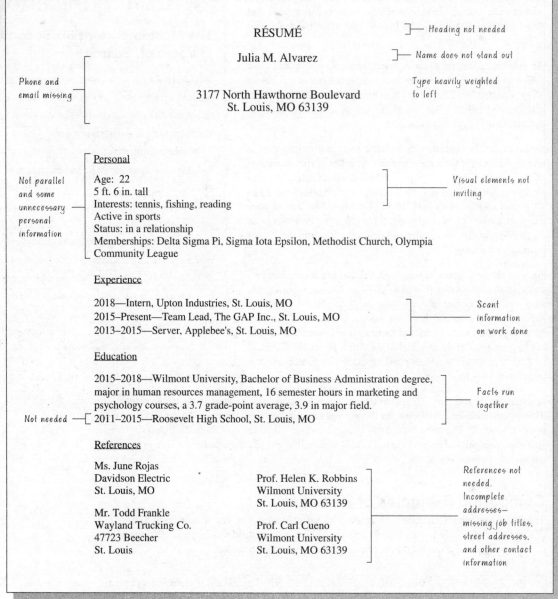

RÉSUMÉ ⟩— Heading not needed

Julia M. Alvarez ⟩— Name does not stand out

Type heavily weighted
to left

Phone and
email missing

3177 North Hawthorne Boulevard
St. Louis, MO 63139

Personal

Not parallel
and some
unnecessary
personal
information

Age: 22
5 ft. 6 in. tall
Interests: tennis, fishing, reading
Active in sports
Status: in a relationship
Memberships: Delta Sigma Pi, Sigma Iota Epsilon, Methodist Church, Olympia
Community League

Visual elements not
inviting

Experience

2018—Intern, Upton Industries, St. Louis, MO
2015–Present—Team Lead, The GAP Inc., St. Louis, MO
2013–2015—Server, Applebee's, St. Louis, MO

Scant
information
on work done

Education

2015–2018—Wilmont University, Bachelor of Business Administration degree,
major in human resources management, 16 semester hours in marketing and
psychology courses, a 3.7 grade-point average, 3.9 in major field.

Not needed — 2011–2015—Roosevelt High School, St. Louis, MO

Facts run
together

References

Ms. June Rojas
Davidson Electric
St. Louis, MO

Prof. Helen K. Robbins
Wilmont University
St. Louis, MO 63139

Mr. Todd Frankle
Wayland Trucking Co.
47723 Beecher
St. Louis

Prof. Carl Cueno
Wilmont University
St. Louis, MO 63139

References not
needed.
Incomplete
addresses—
missing job titles,
street addresses,
and other contact
information

A Thorough Résumé with Good Visual Appeal The revised résumé for Julia Alvarez appears better even at first glance. Its content is also superior to that of the other example. Additional words show the quality of Ms. Alvarez's work experience and education, and they emphasize points that make her suited for the work she seeks.

This résumé excludes inappropriate personal information and has only the facts that tell something about Ms. Alvarez's personal qualities. A bulleted list of duties under each job describes the skills and qualities Ms. Alvarez brings to a human resources position. The references have been moved to a separate references sheet (see Exhibit 15-4), and information about Ms. Alvarez's qualifications fills the space instead.

Julia M. Alvarez

3177 North Hawthorne Boulevard
St. Louis, MO 63139
314.967.3117 (Voice/Message)
jmalvarez358@gmail.com

Presents contact data clearly

Objective

To obtain a full-time position in human resources management specializing in safety and OSHA compliance.

Education

Bachelor of Business Administration
Wilmont University, St. Louis,
MO University—May 2018
GPA: 3.7/4.0

Major: Management:
           Human Resources Emphasis
Minor: Psychology
Certificate: Advanced Business
              Communication

Emphasizes key educational facts

Highlights most relevant courses and subjects

Related Coursework:
- Compensation Theory and Administration
- Organizational Change and Development
- Industrial Relations
- Advanced Human Resource Management

- Managerial Accounting
- Training and Human Resource Development

SHRM Certification

- Passed the Society for Human Resource Management (SHRM) Certification Examination

Internship

Human Resource Intern, Upton Industries, St. Louis, MO, June 2018–August 2018
- Consulted with management to ensure compliance with OSHA and state safety regulations
- Analyzed data from Upton's human resource database and created reports to guide management decisions
- Researched industry trends and reported them to management
- Participated in personnel-related tasks such as recruiting, reviewing candidates' résumés, conducting interviews, completing new hires' paperwork, training both new and current employees, determining compensation and benefits, and facilitating exit interviews
- Prepared timesheets for payroll

Special Project: Created and maintained an "HR News and Updates" page for the company intranet

Uses action verbs to portray an image of a hard worker with good interpersonal skills

Employment

Team Lead, The Gap, Inc., St. Louis, MO, October 2015–Present
- Was promoted to team lead after two months of employment
- Was named top store sales associate four of eight quarters
- Create merchandise displays
- Train new sales associates
- Participate in interviews and hiring
- Set the weekly schedule

Host and Server, Applebee's, St. Louis, MO, September 2013 – September 2015
- Provided exceptional customer service
- Worked well as part of a team to seat and serve customers quickly and efficiently

Activities

Includes only most relevant information

Delta Sigma Pi (professional); Sigma Iota Epsilon (honorary), served as treasurer and president; Board of Stewards for church; Society for Human Resources Management (SHRM), served as chapter vice president

You Make the Call

If an employer told you that he or she would be checking your LinkedIn profile or other social media sites, would you be ready?

Electronic Résumés

While some employers require printed résumés, others will require that you submit your résumé electronically via email or perhaps through an online application form or database. You might even create your own website to showcase your résumé or post a profile using sites such as LinkedIn.

Using a Social Networking Site or a Webpage Social networking sites such as LinkedIn provide a convenient way to present your professional qualifications. Exhibit 15-8 presents an example of a well-designed LinkedIn page. This Web-based profile presents not only the candidate's qualifications as they might appear on a printed résumé but also a personal summary and a recommendation. Links allow readers to access additional information regarding a candidate's education, employment, and skills.

Also, several free sites such as Weebly and Yola provide professional templates for creating personal webpages. All you need to do is input the content using the guidelines presented earlier in this chapter. Whether you are creating your own webpage or using a template, you have a variety of options for creating a visually appealing, easily navigable Web résumé. The tips for Web writing presented in Chapter 2 can guide your design and presentation decisions; guidelines presented earlier in this chapter will help you develop the content.

Creating an Unformatted Résumé As you will learn in upcoming paragraphs, you'll want to have an **unformatted (plain-text) version** of your résumé to use when sending your résumé in an email, applying via an online application, or sending your résumé to a company that uses an applicant tracking system. A plain-text résumé contains no formatting such as italics, tables, lists, bullets, and centered text. It also does not contain visuals or visual elements such as lines or shading. Exhibit 15-9 illustrates a plain-text résumé.

To create a plain-text résumé, just open your formatted résumé in Microsoft Word, select File > Save As > Save as Type dropdown list > "Plain text." You'll see that the file now has a .txt file extension. If you close the file and reopen it by clicking the file itself, the document will likely open in Notepad or WordPad. If you want to open the .txt file in Word, open Word first and then go to File > Open.

From there, you can adjust reordered text or odd formatting that happened in the conversion. As we have mentioned, you want to avoid italics, tables, lists, bullets, and centered text. Instead, as you format your plain-text résumé, you can format text using boldface and capital letters, and you can use asterisks (*) or hyphens (-) in place of bullets. You will also want to use a common sans serif font such as Arial.

Once your file is reformatted and saved as a .txt file, you can copy and paste the text into online databases or use it in other electronic environments without worrying about unexpected formatting issues. As you read the following discussion about sending your résumé via email or uploading it to be read by an applicant tracking system, you will learn why this formatting is important.

Sending Your Résumé via Email If an employer requests that you send your résumé by email, he or she may specify how to submit it. Always follow those directions. In the absence of directions, you can place the résumé text in the body of the email, attach your formatted résumé to the email, or do both.

One reason to copy the text of your résumé into an email is that you will know your reader received the information. Another is that the reader may find it helpful to have the text in the body of the email—especially if he or she is using scanning software to screen candidates. If you're copying the text of your résumé into the body of the email, always copy from an unformatted (plain-text) résumé referenced above. You cannot be sure that your reader is able to read HTML or formatted messages; he or she may be only able to read plain-text messages, so, for example, any information in tables in your formatted résumé may appear scattered throughout the email

(text continues on page 591)

Exhibit 15-8 Illustration of a LinkedIn Profile

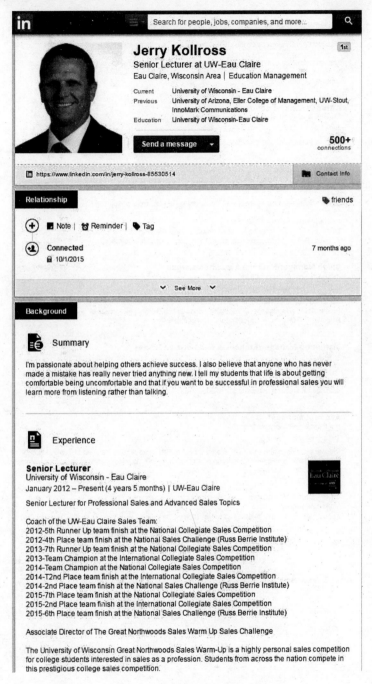

Continued

Exhibit 15-8 *Continued*

Assistant Director of the UW-Eau Claire College of Business Center for Sales and Sales Management

Board of Director member for the L.E. Phillips Career Development Center

The mission of the CDC is to be a viable business enterprise as a means to provide meaningful and appropriate vocational services and employment opportunities for individuals with disabilities or disadvantages.

Adjunct Senior Lecturer
University of Arizona, Eller College of Management
June 2015 – July 2015 (2 months) | Tucson, Arizona

Teaching Marketing 308 (Personal Selling) during session 1 of the Eller Marketing Minor Program

Senior Lecturer
UW-Stout
January 2006 – January 2012 (6 years 1 month)

Teaching 300 level Marketing and Professional Selling Courses both on campus and on-line

Coach of the UW-Stout Sales Team:
2010-Team Champion at the Great Northwoods Sales Warm Up
2011-9th Runner Up team finish at the National Collegiate Sales Competition

Sales Manager/National Account Manager
InnoMark Communications
May 1998 – June 2006 (8 years 2 months)

Managed 5 national consumer product and retail accounts in the Midwest territory
Promoted to sales manager in 2005 and managed four regional sales people
Billed $2,500,000 in new promotional business in 2004

Marketing Manager/Franchise Relations and Sales
Golf USA
1995 – 1998 (3 years) | Edmond, OK

Developed marketing programs for products (Acumark) sold in franchise stores. Started a promotional products corporate golf division (Golf Products USA).

Account Manager
Printing Service Company
1992 – 1995 (3 years)

Prospected, closed and serviced national accounts. First sales person assigned to display sales for PSC. First sales employee of display spin off company of PSC (Display Graphics) which later became Innomark Communications.

Other Sales Positions
Other Companies
August 1984 – January 1992 (7 years 6 months)

I have also worked in sales for the following companies: American Printing Company (Madison, WI)
Agfa Corporation (Dayton, OH)

Source: Jerry Kollross. Used by permission. https://www.linkedin.com/in/jerry-kollross-85530514

Continued

Exhibit 15-8 *Continued*

Skills

Top Skills

75 Marketing
74 Sales
56 Public Speaking
44 Teaching
39 Leadership
36 Higher Education
30 Selling
17 Customer Service
17 Coaching
15 Sales Management

Jerry also knows about...

13 Social Networking   13 Time Management   12 Sales Operations
9 PowerPoint   8 Social Media   4 Retail   4 Research
3 Event Planning   3 Strategic Planning   3 Market Research
2 Data Analysis   1 Social Media Marketing

Education

University of Wisconsin-Eau Claire
MBA, Business Administration
2004 – 2006

Activities and Societies: UW-Eau Claire Graduate Studies Outstanding Student Award

▾ 1 recommendation

Professional Clothier

Jerry was my professor for the entry level and advanced sales class at the University of Wisconsin- Eau Claire. He is an outstanding individual who goes above and beyond the call of duty to help his students. The style of both classes not only... View ↓

University of Wisconsin-La Crosse
BS, Marketing
1980 – 1984

Activities and Societies: American Marketing Association Member UW-LaCrosse Marketing Consultants, Alumnus Member UW-LaCrosse Athletic Wall of Fame Member (Swimming)

Continued

Exhibit 15-8 *Continued*

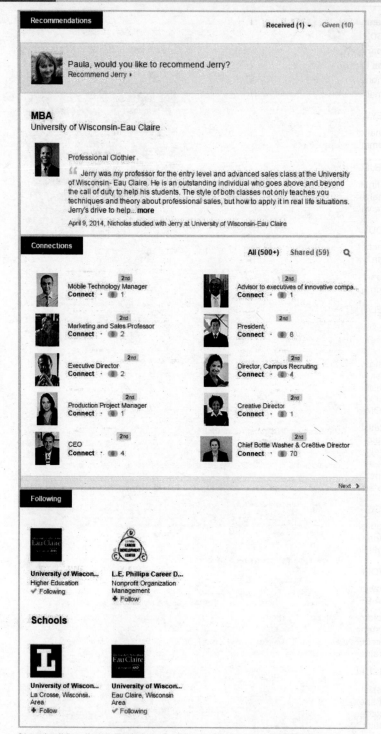

Recommendations

Received (1) ▾   Given (10)

Paula, would you like to recommend Jerry?
Recommend Jerry ▸

MBA
University of Wisconsin-Eau Claire

Professional Clothier

" Jerry was my professor for the entry level and advanced sales class at the University of Wisconsin- Eau Claire. He is an outstanding individual who goes above and beyond the call of duty to help his students. The style of both classes not only teaches you techniques and theory about professional sales, but how to apply it in real life situations. Jerry's drive to help... **more**

April 9, 2014, Nicholas studied with Jerry at University of Wisconsin-Eau Claire

Connections

All (500+)   Shared (59)   🔍

2nd Mobile Technology Manager **Connect** · 🔘 1	2nd Advisor to executives of innovative compa... **Connect** · 🔘 1
2nd Marketing and Sales Professor **Connect** · 🔘 2	2nd President, **Connect** · 🔘 8
2nd Executive Director **Connect** · 🔘 2	2nd Director, Campus Recruiting **Connect** · 🔘 4
2nd Production Project Manager **Connect** · 🔘 1	2nd Creative Director **Connect** · 🔘 1
2nd CEO **Connect** · 🔘 4	2nd Chief Bottle Washer & Cre8tive Director **Connect** · 🔘 70

Next ▸

Following

University of Wiscon...
Higher Education
✓ Following

L.E. Phillips Career D...
Nonprofit Organization Management
✚ Follow

Schools

University of Wiscon...
La Crosse, Wisconsii.
Area
✚ Follow

University of Wiscon...
Eau Claire, Wisconsin
Area
✓ Following

Manny Konedeng
5602 Montezuma Road
Apartment 413
San Diego, California 92115
Phone: (619) 578-8058
Email: mkonedeng@yahoo.com

Avoids italics and underlines yet is arranged for both scanner and human readability

KEYWORDS

Finance major, bachelor's degree, leadership skills, ethics, communication, teamwork

Includes a keywords section of terms a tracking system may scan for

OBJECTIVE

A financial analyst internship with a broker-dealer where both analytical and interpersonal communication skills and knowledge are valued

Uses all caps and white space for enhanced human readability

EDUCATION

Bachelor of Science Degree in Business Administration, May 2018
San Diego State University, Finance Major

Dean's List
Current GPA: 3.32/4.00

RELATED COURSES

Business Communication
Investments
Tax planning
Estate Planning
Risk Management
Business Law

Places each item on its own line and avoids tabs

COMPUTER SKILLS

Statistical Software: SAS, SPSS Excel, Word, PowerPoint, Access, QuickBooks
Web-based Applications: Surveymonkey, Blogger, GoToMeeting
Research Tools: Center for Research in Securities Prices (CRSP) stock price database and the Standard and Poor's Research Insight database of corporations' financial statements

ACCOMPLISHMENTS

Published in Fast Company Magazine and the San Diego Union Tribune
Won Greek scholarship
Finished in top five mathematics competition

WORK EXPERIENCE

Powerhouse Gym, Sales and Front Desk, Summer 2017, Modesto, CA 95355

Integrates precise nouns and industry-specific jargon as keywords

Sold memberships and facilitated tours for the fitness center
Listened to, analyzed, and answered customers' inquiries
Accounted for membership payments and constructed sales reports
Trained new employees to understand company procedures and safety policies

MCI, Relay Operator, Summer 2015 & 2016, Riverbank, CA 95367

Assisted over 100 callers daily who were deaf, hard of hearing, or speech disabled to place calls
Exceeded the required data input of 60 wpm with accuracy
Multitasked with typing and listening to phone conversations
Was offered a promotion as a Lead Operator

Continued

Exhibit 15-9 *Continued*

Fo Sho Entertainment, Co-founder and Owner, Aug. 2013–May 2015
Modesto, CA 95355

Led promotions for musical events in the Central Valley
Managed and hosted live concerts
Created and wrote proposals to work with local businesses
Collaborated with team members to design advertisements

ACTIVITIES AND SERVICE

Information Decision Systems, Communications Tutor, Spring 2018,
San Diego, CA 92182
Critiqued and evaluated the written work for a business
communication course

Set up and maintained blog for business communication research
Kappa Alpha Order Fraternity, Recruitment Chairman, Fall 2017,
San Diego, CA 92115
Supervised the selection process for chapter membership
Individually raised nearly $1,000 for chapter finances
Organized recruitment events with business sponsors, radio stations,
and special guests

Recruitment Chair, Kappa Alpha Order Fraternity
Supervised all new member recruitment
Coordinated fundraisers for chapter finances
Organized recruitment events with business sponsors, radio stations,
and special guests
Advocated Greek Freshmen Summer Orientation and Greek life

Correspondent for External Chapter Affairs, Kappa Alpha Order
Fraternity
Communicated with chapter alumni and national office to fulfill
chapter obligations

Upsilon Class Treasurer, Kappa Alpha Order Fraternity
Managed chapter budgets and expenditures
Held several Interfraternity Council Roles

Member, Fraternity Men against Negative Environments and Rape
Situations

Cochairman, Greek Week Fundraiser

Candidate, IFC Treasurer

Professional and Community Service

Member, Finance & Investment Society
Presenter, Peer Health Education
Marshal, SDSU New Student & Family Convocation
Volunteer, Muscular Dystrophy national philanthropy
Volunteer, Service for Sight philanthropy
Volunteer, Victims of Domestic Violence philanthropy
Volunteer, Camp Able philanthropy
Associated Students' Good Neighbor Program volunteer
Volunteer, Designated Driver Association
Volunteer, Beach Recovery Project

Avoids graphics and extra lines

Adds other relevant information since there is no physical page limit

Uses black on white contrast for improved scanning accuracy

rather than organized in columns and rows. Copying from the unformatted résumé ensures that your text appears in order and readable in plain format. It also saves you time from having to "unformat" anything as you copy from your formatted résumé to a plain-text message.

While copying the text of a résumé into the body of an email is functional, it does not leave you with a résumé as nice as the one you've formatted. For this reason, many job candidates will attach a copy of the formatted résumé to the email. It is especially important in formatted résumés sent as attachments that you do not format your résumé using the space bar or tab key. Many times when you use tabs or the space bar, the résumé format will look fine when you are working at your computer, but occasionally the reader will open a résumé formatted this way only to see text scattered across the page, as the tabs and the spacing were not preserved.

To ensure that your text and lists stay aligned, use the ruler or a table (just make sure you turn off "View Gridlines" before emailing the document). Also be sure to use a standard font so that the font you use is the font the reader sees. For example, if you use Calibri but your reader is using an older version of Word that does not have Calibri, Word will substitute a new font. If you use Arial, a font all versions of Word have, you know your reader will see your document as you created it.

As a courtesy to your reader, use a common file format for attached documents. Because many people use Word, a .docx file or .doc file will work for most readers. In addition, include your name in the file name. Instead of a generic "résumé.docx," use "karen_jones_résumé.docx" so the reader can easily identify your résumé.

Lastly, before sending your résumé to an employer, always test it by sending it and any attachments to yourself and a few others to ensure that the formatting is preserved. Another option for ensuring that the résumé you create in Microsoft Word or other program looks the same to both you and your reader is to save the résumé as a pdf and attach it to your email. Word's "Save As" feature will let you save files in this manner. If you are not using Word, free pdf converters are available online.

Submitting an Online Job Application If you're applying online, you may be asked to attach a résumé in the same way you would attach a file to an email. If this is the case, the same guidelines discussed above apply. However, applying online may require that you enter information into text boxes or fields. Because these fields are not likely to allow text formatting, you will want to copy the information from your unformatted (plain-text) résumé into the fields. Many times if you copy from a formatted résumé, you have to delete tabs or extra spaces, so copying from an unformatted résumé will save time. If you want to use any kind of formatting, you can always capitalize headings or use an asterisk or hyphen in place of a bullet.

Preparing a Résumé for an Applicant Tracking System As résumé expert Lisa Rangel explains, an **applicant tracking system (ATS)** is a database of résumé information. Employers advertise for positions online (e.g., on the company's website or on a job board); when people apply to these online postings, the tracking system uses key words to search for applicants who may be qualified for a position. Your goal is to make sure that your résumé is easily searchable within these systems. Because you cannot know how the system scans your data, it is hard to know if you are formatting your information correctly. However, Rangel offers these tips that can help your chances for success.[3]

First, you need to make sure you answer all of the questions on the online application. Skipping even one question may disqualify you. Second, you need to format your résumé so that the ATS can read it:

- Give your résumé a title with your name and desired job title.
- Use common headings such as *Work Experience* and *Education.*
- Don't use images, columns, tables, fields, text boxes, graphics, special characters, or colors. An ATS may not be able to read them or recognize data in them.

- Use a standard font such as Arial, Georgia, or Trebuchet; don't use color or underlining.

- Spell check. An ATS won't be able to determine what was meant by a misspelled word.

- Include contact information in the main area of the document, not in the header or footer.

- Save the résumé as a .doc/.docx or .txt file.

- Present your employment history information in a chronological and consistent order (e.g., company, title, city, state date).

Lastly, Rangel says that to increase your odds of the ATS picking out your résumé, you want to pay attention to the résumé content:

- Include industry-specific terminology using both the abbreviation and the full term.

- Use words from the job description frequently.

Manny Konedeng's résumé in Exhibit 15-9 is an example of a text-only résumé that would be read by an applicant tracking system. While it is true that the résumé is not as attractive as a standard formatted résumé, it is more important that the résumé be functional. You can always submit an attractive, formatted résumé if you are asked to send one or if you are invited for an interview.

Today, companies accept résumés by mail, email, and the Internet. You will use whatever channel the employer wants, but when given the choice, choose the one that serves you best. Obviously, when speed gives you an advantage, you'll choose the email or Internet options.

Writing the Cover Message

LO15-5   Write targeted cover messages that skillfully sell your abilities.

The **cover message** is a direct message that matches your qualifications to the position requirements. Even though you are writing about yourself, you want to write an audience-centered message that focuses on what you will bring to the employer rather than what the employer can do for you.

Cover Messages

Cover messages come in two types: **solicited (invited)** and **unsolicited (prospecting)**. As their names suggest, a solicited messsage is written in response to an actual job opening, and an unsolicited message is written when you don't know whether a job exists but would like to investigate the possibility of employment. Generally, a cover message is organized according to the following plan:

- An introduction that gets the reader's attention and provides just a brief summary of why you are interested or qualified or previews the information in the body of the message. If you are writing a solicited message, you will also mention where you learned of the position.

- A body that matches your qualifications to the reader's needs. You should also use a good sales strategy (see Chapter 10) and the you-viewpoint and positive language (see Chapter 6).

- A conclusion that requests action such as an interview and provides contact information that makes a response easy.

Gaining Attention in the Opening
As in sales writing, the opening of the cover message has two requirements: It must gain attention, and it must set up the information that follows.

Gaining attention is especially important in prospecting messages. Such messages are likely to reach busy executives. Unless the résumé gains favorable attention right away, the potential employer probably will not read it. Even solicited messages must gain attention because they will compete with other applicants' messages.

In choosing the best opening, you should consider whether you are writing a prospecting or a solicited message. If the message has been solicited, your opening words should refer to the job posting and begin qualifying you for the advertised work, as in these examples:

> As an honors graduate in accounting with experience in tax accounting, I believe I qualify for the position you listed in today's *Times*.

> Your advertisement in the *Journal* for a tax accountant particularly interests me because my education and accounting internship have provided me with the qualifications you are looking for.

You can gain attention in the opening of an unsolicited message in many ways. One way is to use a topic that shows understanding of the company or the type of employees it might need. Employers are likely to be impressed by applicants who have made the effort to learn something about the company, as in this example:

> Now that Taggart, Inc. has expanded operations to Central America, can you use a broadly trained international business major who knows the language and culture of the region?

Another way is to make a statement or ask a question that focuses attention on a need of the reader that the writer seeks to fill. The following opening illustrates this approach:

> Are you interested in hiring a University of Cincinnati business major to fill in for your vacationing summer employees?

Sometimes you will learn of a job possibility through a company employee. Mentioning the employee's name can gain attention, as in this opening sentence:

> At the suggestion of Mr. Michael McLaughlin, supervisor at your Hamilton Road office, I am sending the attached résumé as my application for the open loan supervisor position.

Whatever you use, you want to make sure it is relevant and tailored to your audience. If you use the outdated, trite. or clichéd "This is to apply for . . ." or writer-centered beginnings such as "I am writing to apply for . . ." or the tentative "I would like to apply for . . ." you will not be as effective in getting your reader's attention.

Selecting Content Following the opening, you should present the information about your qualifications as they relate to the position you're applying for.

If your application has been solicited, you may learn about the job requirements from the source of the invitation. If you are answering an advertisement, study it for the employer's requirements. If you are following up on an interview, review the interview for information about job requirements. If you are prospecting, your research and your logical analysis should guide you.

In any event, you are likely to present facts from three background areas: education, experience, and skills and/or personal details.

How much you include from each of these areas and how much you emphasize each area will depend on the job and on your background. Most of the jobs you seek as a new college graduate will have strong educational requirements, and your education is likely to be your strongest selling point at this stage of your career. Thus, you should stress your education. When you apply for work after you have accumulated experience, you will probably need to stress experience.

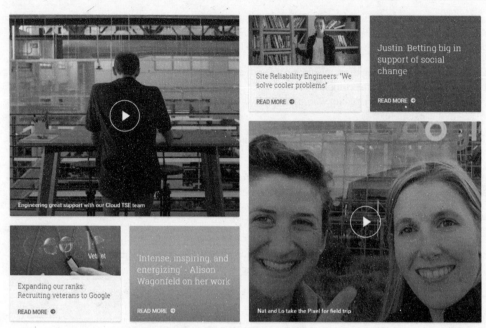

Bring questions. Build answers.

Site Reliability Engineers: "We solve cooler problems"
READ MORE

Justin: Betting big in support of social change
READ MORE

Engineering great support with our Cloud TSE team

Vet Vet

Expanding our ranks: Recruiting veterans to Google
READ MORE

'Intense, inspiring, and energizing' - Alison Wagonfeld on her work
READ MORE

Nat and Lo take the Pixel for field trip

Many companies have search features on their websites that help applicants find open positions.
Source: https://www.google.com/about/careers. Google and the Google logo are registered trademarks of Google Inc.

The message should contain the major points around which you build your case, and the résumé should include these points plus supporting details. As the two are parts of a team effort, somewhere in the message you should refer the reader to the résumé.

Organizing for Persuasion

In general, the plan you select is likely to follow one of three general orders. The most common order is a logical grouping of the information, such as education, experience, and skills and/or personal details. A second possibility is a time order. For example, you could present the information to show a year-by-year preparation for the work. A third possibility is an order based on the job requirements. For example, selling, communicating, and managing might be the requirements listed in an advertised job, and you would use those to group the content in your letter.

As you present your qualifications, you want to use language that shows what you can do rather than simply tells the reader what you can do. You could tell the reader, for example, that you "held a position" as sales manager, but it is much more convincing to show your competence by saying that you "supervised a sales force of 14."

Likewise, you do more for yourself by writing that you "earned a degree in business administration" than by writing that you "spent four years in college." And it is more effective to say that you "assisted 200 clients through the Volunteer Income Tax Assistance program" than it is to say that you "helped low-income people with their taxes."

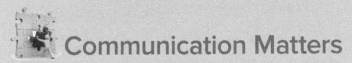

Communication Matters

Developing a Professional Portfolio

Imagine yourself in an interview. The interviewer says, "This position requires you to use Power-Point extensively. How are your presentation and PowerPoint skills?" What do you say? Of course you say your skills are excellent. And so does everyone else who interviews.

One way you can set yourself apart from other applicants and supplement your online presence on LinkedIn is to take a professional portfolio to an interview to demonstrate your qualifications. A portfolio may contain a title page, your résumé, references list, cover message, a transcript, a program description, copies of licenses and certifications, work samples, letters of recommendation—whatever creates your best professional image.

All you need to do is put your documents in sheet protectors in a professional-looking three-ring binder for easy editing and updating and create tab dividers for the sections of the portfolio, and you're on your way.

One note of advice, though: Protect your information by including a confidentiality statement; removing any student ID numbers, social security number, or other private information from your documents; and using copies rather than originals of any licenses or certificates.

You also can help your case by presenting your facts in the you-viewpoint discussed in Chapter 6. For example, you could present a writer-focused statement:

> I have an interest in mechanical operations and processes. Last summer I worked in the production department of a container plant.

Or you could show how your experience meets the reader's needs:

> Last summer's experience working 10- and 12-hour days in the production department of Miller Container Company is evidence of my interest in mechanics and shows that I can and will work hard.

Since you will be writing about yourself, you may find it difficult to avoid overusing *I* references, but an overuse of *I* sounds egotistical and creates the impression that you are more focused on yourself than on the reader's needs. Some *I* use, however, is acceptable. After all, the message sells your skills and abilities.

Overall, you are presenting your professional image, not only as a prospective employee but also as a person. Carefully shaping the professional you are projecting is arguably just as important to the success of your cover message as using convincing logic.

Driving for Action in the Close The presentation of your qualifications should lead logically to the action that the close proposes. You should drive for whatever action is appropriate in your case. It could be a request for an interview or an invitation to engage in further communication (perhaps to answer the reader's questions). You are concerned mainly with opening the door to further negotiations.

Your action words should be clear and direct. As in the sales message discussed in Chapter 10, the request for action may be made more effective if it is followed by words recalling a benefit that the reader will get from taking the action. The following closes illustrate this technique:

> The highlights of my education and experience show that I have been preparing for a career in human resources. May I now discuss how I might put my skills to work for you? You can reach me at 727-921-4113 or by email at owensmith@att.com.

> I welcome the opportunity to meet for an interview to discuss with you how my skills can contribute to your company's mission.

Exhibits 15-10, 15-11, 15-12, and 15-13 provide examples of effective cover messages.

Exhibit 15-10 Illustration of a Prospecting Email

From: Molly Everson <mheverson@creighton.edu>
To: Marlene O'Daniel <modaniel@cic.org>

SUBJECT: Application—Communications Specialist Position

Dear Ms. O'Daniel:

One of your employees, Victor Krause, suggested that I apply for the communications specialist position you have open. My résumé is attached for your review.

Gains attention with an associate's name

Shows the writer knows the skills needed for the job

Presently, I am a communications intern for Atlas Insurance. My work consists primarily of writing a wide variety of documents for Atlas policyholders. This work has made me an advocate for well-crafted business communication, and it has sharpened my writing skills. More importantly, it has taught me how to get and keep customers for my company through writing well.

Employs a conservative style and tone

Additional experience working with businesspeople has given me insight into the communication needs of business. This experience includes planning and presenting a communication improvement course for Atlas employees.

Uses subtle you-viewpoint-implied by the writer's understanding of the work

My college training provided a solid foundation for work in business communication. Advertising and public relations were my areas of concentration for my BS degree from Creighton University. As you will see on the enclosed résumé, I took all available writing courses in my degree plan. I also studied writing through English and journalism courses.
You can view samples of my work and learn more about my qualifications by visiting my LinkedIn profile: linkedin.com/mollyheverson.

References the résumé

Summarizes her qualifications

My education and experience have prepared me for work as your communication specialist, as the attached writing samples show. I know business writing, and I know how it can be used to your company's advantage. May we discuss my qualifications in an interview? You can reach me at 402-786-2575 to arrange a convenient time and place to meet.

Appropriately requests an interview

Sincerely,

Molly H. Everson

Exhibit 15-11 | Illustration of a Solicited Cover Letter

4407 Sunland Avenue
Phoenix, AZ 85040-9321

July 8, 2018

Ms. Anita O. Alderson, Manager
Tompkins-Oderson Agency, Inc.
3901 Tampico Avenue
Los Angeles, CA 90032-1614

Dear Ms. Alderson:

Gains attention by using the reader's words

Marketing student ... interest in advertising ... team skills....

Uses a writing style that demonstrates his ability to write advertising copy.

These keywords in your July 6 advertisement on State University's Career Finder student website describe the intern you want, and I believe I am that person.

Shows clearly what the writer can do on the job

I have gained experience in every area of retail advertising while working for the *Lancer*, our college newspaper, selling advertising, planning layouts, and writing copy. During the last two summers, I obtained firsthand experience working in the advertising department of Wunder & Company. My main responsibility was to write copy, some of which is enclosed for your inspection; you will find numerous other examples on my blog at http://janekbits.blogspot.com.

Shows practical experience, initiative, and leadership

In my major, I am studying marketing with a specialization in advertising and integrated marketing communications. My course work has provided several opportunities to participate in real-world projects, including one where my teammates and I used a variety of media to raise money for schools in Louisiana, Texas, and Mississippi's hurricane damaged areas. Understanding the importance of being able to get along well with people, I actively participated in Sigma Chi (social fraternity), the Race for the Cure (breast cancer fundraising event), and Pi Tau Pi (honorary business fraternity).

Provides good evidence of social skills

Leads smoothly to action

I ask that you review my qualifications and contact me for an interview. You can email me at janek@hotmail.com or call and text message me at 602-713-2199 to arrange a convenient time to talk about my joining your team.

Sincerely,

Michael S. Janek

Michael S. Janek

enclosures

12712 Sanchez Drive
San Bernadino, CA 92405
http://www.LinkedIn.com/jimmygoetz

April 9, 2018

Mr. Conrad W. Butler
Office Manager
Darden, Inc.
14326 Butterfield Road
San Francisco, CA 94129

Dear Mr. Butler:

Gains attention with a question

Can Darden, Inc., use a hardworking Grossmont College business administration major seeking an internship in management or office administration? My experience, education, and personal qualities have prepared me to contribute to your operations.

Sets up the rest of the letter

As the attached résumé indicates, I have worked as a receptionist for the past three summers. My duties have included managing a multi-line telephone system, using Excel and Access to monitor office traffic, and greeting visitors. I am excited about the possibility of developing more skills through an internship with Darden.

Highlights relevant experience and transferable skills

Complementing my work experience are my studies at Grossmont College. In addition to studying the prescribed courses in my major field of business office technology, I have completed electives in Dreamweaver, QuickBooks, and professional speaking to help me in my career objective. In addition, I am proud that while working full time during most of my college career, I was able to earn an Associate of Arts degree with a 3.3/4.0 GPA. But most important, I am learning from my studies how office work can be done efficiently.

Ties his education to his skills

In addition, I have the personal qualities that would enable me to fit smoothly into your organization. I like people, and through work and academic experiences, I have learned how to work with them as both a team player and a leader.

May I meet with you to talk about interning for Darden? Please call me at 714-399-2569 or email me at jgoetz@gmail.com to arrange an interview.

Requests action clearly and appropriately

Sincerely,

Jimmy I. Goetz

Jimmy I. Goetz

Enc.

Exhibit 15-13 Illustration of a Prospecting Letter

MARY O. MAHONEY

May 17, 2018

Mr. Nevil S. Shannon
Director of Personnel
Snowdon Industries, Inc.
1103 Boswell Circle
Baltimore, MD 21202

Dear Mr. Shannon:

Gains attention with an effective question

Will you please review my qualifications for work in your management trainee program? My education, work attitude, and personal skills qualify me for this program.

Sets up the paragraphs that follow

Ties her education to the position

My management education consists primarily of four years of business administration study at State University. The Bachelor of Business Administration degree I will receive in June has given me a broad foundation of business knowledge. As a general business major, I studied all the functional fields (management, marketing, information systems, finance, accounting) as well as the other core business subjects (communications, statistics, law, economics, production, and human resources). I have the knowledge base that will enable me to be productive now, and I can build upon this base through practical experience.

In addition, I completed an internship last summer in the claims department of Advantage Insurance. My duties included accurately processing a high volume of claims and documenting interactions with both our customers and other claimants. At the end of the internship, my supervisors commented on my ability to diffuse tense situations and work with people of all types and backgrounds. In addition, they noted the creative thinking and team skills I demonstrated as we all worked to make the claims process more efficient.

Emphasizes skills transferable to the position applied for

Demonstrates leadership and diverse interests

Throughout college, I developed my personal skills. As an active member of the student chapter of the Society for the Advancement of Management, I served as treasurer and program chairperson. I participated in intramural golf and volleyball, and I was an active worker in the Two to Tango dance club, serving as publicity chairperson for three years. All this experience has helped me to acquire the balance you seek in your administrative trainees.

These highlights and the additional evidence presented in the enclosed résumé present my case for a career in management. May I have an interview to continue my presentation? You can reach me at 301.594.6942 or marymahoney@yahoo.com. Thank you for your consideration.

Presents a request for action that flows logically from the preceding paragraphs

Sincerely,

Mary O Mahoney

Mary O. Mahoney

Enclosure

1718 CRANFORD AVENUE • ROCKWELL, MD • 20854
VOICE/MESSAGE/FAX: 301.594.6942 • EMAIL: MARYMAHONEY@YAHOO.COM

Comparing Examples of Cover Messages

These two examples present the qualifications of Julia M. Alvarez, the job seeker described in the Problem-Solving Challenge at the beginning of the chapter. The first message follows a few of the suggestions given in the preceding pages, whereas the second message is persuasive and well organized and clearly asks for action in the closing.

A Poorly Written Cover Message The cover messsage in this bad example contains many of the writer's qualifications. However, it simply tells the reader of the writer's qualifications instead of showing what the writer is capable of. It also uses the *I* pronoun frequently. As a result, this prospecting message is dull and lacks the you-viewpoint.

Dear Mr. Stark:

This is to apply for a position in marketing with your company.

At present, I am completing my studies in marketing at Wilmont University and will graduate with a Bachelor of Business Administration degree with an emphasis in human resource management this May. I have taken all the courses in marketing available to me as well as other helpful courses such as statistics, organizational psychology, and ecommerce.

I have had good working experience as a host and food server, a sales associate, and an HR intern. Please see the details on the enclosed résumé. I believe that I am well qualified for a position in human resource management and am considering working for a company of your size and description.

Because I must make a decision on my career soon, I request that you write me soon. For your information, I will be available for an interview on March 17 and 18.

Sincerely,

Julia M. Alvarez

A Well-Written Cover Message The better message begins with an interesting question that sets the stage for the rest of the contents. Notice the writer shows she knows the position requirements. Notice, too, that the you-viewpoint is stressed throughout, but the moderate use of *I* gives the message a personal quality. The details show the writer to be thoughtful and engaged. The closing request for action is a clear, direct, and courteous question. Julia also links to her LinkedIn profile, which allows the reader to learn more about her quickly and easily.

Dear Mr. Stark:

Is there a place in your Human Resources Department for someone who is well trained in the field and can communicate easily and competently with employees? As a June graduate with a degree in human resource management and internship experience, I am well qualified to meet your needs.

My studies at Wilmont University were specially planned to prepare me for a career in human resource management. I have taken courses in compensation theory and administration, organizational change/development, and training and development. I have also passed the Society for Human Resource Management (SHRM) Certification Examination.

As my résumé shows, I have completed an HR internship, where I performed tasks ranging from researching and reporting data on company and industry trends to participating in the hiring process.

My work experiences have also prepared me for a career in human resource management. While in college I worked as a server at Applebee's and as a team lead for The Gap, where I was the top seller for four of eight quarters. From these experiences, I have learned to understand human resource management, work with diverse groups of people, and communicate professionally.

These brief facts and the information in my résumé describe my diligent efforts to prepare for a position in human resource management. You can also learn more about me via LinkedIn (www.linkedin/juliamalvarez). May I talk with you about my qualifications for a position with Sunrise Enterprises? You can reach me at 917.938.4449 to arrange an interview.

Sincerely,

Julia M. Alvarez

Email Cover Messages

Like other email messages, an email cover message needs a clear subject line; like print cover messages, it needs a formal salutation and closing. It can be identical to one you might create for print, or you may opt to introduce yourself and your purpose in a short email message and attach your full cover message. The primary job of the email cover message is to identify the job, highlight the applicant's strengths, and invite the reader to review the résumé.

Notice how the following solicited email cover message quickly gains the reader's attention in the opening, highlights the skills in the body, and calls for action in the closing. The writer also takes advantage of the online environment by including a link to her personal webpage so that the reader can view her online portfolio.

To: Kate Troy <kate_troy@thankyoutoo.com>

From: Jessica Franklin <jessica_franklin@yahoo.com>

Subject: Web Design Intern Position

Dear Ms. Troy:

Yesterday my advisor here at Brown University, Dr. Payton Kubicek, suggested that I contact you about the summer intern position in design you recently announced on your website.

As my résumé shows, I have experience in HTML/CSS and Java as well as course work in graphic design and typography. I know how to listen to clients, help them meet their business goals, and design sites for the best search engine optimization.

I would enjoy applying some of these skills to help build a successful site targeted toward Thankyoutoo.com's high-end customers. You will see from my webpage profile at www.jessicafranklin.com/ that my design preferences and styles complement those of your company's website. I can be available for an interview at any time.

Sincerely,

Jessica Franklin
Phone: 934.122.3923

LO15-6   Explain how you can participate effectively in an interview.

Handling the Interview

Your initial contact with a prospective employer can be by mail, email, phone, or a personal (face-to-face) visit. If all goes well, your application will eventually involve a personal visit—an interview. Sometimes, before inviting candidates to a formal interview session, recruiters use phone interviews for preliminary screening.

In a sense, the interview is the key to the success of the application—the "final examination." You should carefully prepare for the interview, as the job may be lost or won in it. The following review of employment interview highlights should help you do your best in your interviews.

Investigating the Company

Before arriving for an interview, you should learn what you can about the company: its products or services, its personnel, its business practices, its current activities, its management, its mission statement, and its philosophy. This knowledge will inform your answers during the interview, and perhaps more important, the interviewer is likely to be impressed that you took the time to investigate the company. That effort can give you an advantage.

Making a Good Impression

How you look to the interviewer is a part of your message. Interviewers differ to some extent on what that image is, but a conservative appearance is usually the standard. This means avoiding trendy styles and preferring conservative business

Some employers use phone interviews for initial screening of job candidates. Being both well rested and well prepared for those initial contacts will help ensure that one gets an opportunity for a face-to-face interview later.

© Purestock/SuperStock RF

Websites Offer Valuable Interview Advice

The Web is a rich resource for help with interviewing. Sites such as Monster.com and many of the other online job database sites offer tips on all aspects of interviewing. You can get ideas for questions to ask interviewers, techniques for staying calm, and methods for handling a phone interview. They even include practice interactive virtual interviews with immediate feedback on your answers as well as suggestions and strategies for handling difficult questions.

The Monster site includes a planner listing commonsense tips such as polishing your shoes and keeping an interview folder to store all written and oral communication. Using these sites when preparing for interviews will help you not only feel more confident and interview more effectively but also be ready to evaluate the company.

colors such as black, brown, navy, and gray. It may also mean covering tattoos or removing piercings. Remember that the interviewer wants to know whether you fit into the role you are seeking. You should look like you are right for the job.

Some may argue that conformity in dress and grooming infringes on one's personal freedom. Perhaps it does, but if the people who can determine your future have fixed views on matters of dress and grooming, it is good business sense to respect those views. You may also wonder whether you want to work for this type of company if these expectations for dress represent expectations in the company's culture (see Chapter 14). If you do not think you can work in a company with certain expectations for dress and grooming, you will want to seek employment with companies that are more diverse in their standards.

Anticipating Questions and Preparing Answers

You should be able to anticipate some of the questions the interviewer will ask. Questions about your education (courses, grades, honors) are usually asked. So are questions about work experience, interests, career goals, location preferences, and activities in organizations. You should prepare answers to these questions in advance. During the interview your answers will then be thorough and correct, and your words will display poise and confidence. Your preparation will also reflect your interest.

In addition to general questions, interviewers often ask more complicated ones. Some of these are designed to test you—to learn your views, your interests, and your ability to deal with difficult problems. Others seek more specific information about your ability to handle the job in question. Although such questions are difficult to anticipate, you should be aware that they are likely to be asked. You want to be prepared, though, to address the following:

> Tell me about yourself.
>
> What can you do for us?
>
> Would you be willing to relocate? To travel?
>
> Do you prefer to work with people or alone?
>
> What are your strengths and weaknesses?
>
> How well has your performance in the classroom prepared you for this job?
>
> What do you expect to be doing in 10 years? In 20 years?
>
> Why should I rank you above the others I am interviewing?
>
> Why did you choose _____ for your career?
>
> How do you feel about working overtime? Nights? Weekends?
>
> Did you do the best work you are capable of in college?
>
> Is your college record a good measure of how you will perform on the job?
>
> What are the qualities of the ideal boss?
>
> What have you done that shows leadership potential? Teamwork potential?
>
> What are your beginning salary expectations?

You can also search reputable websites such as Monster.com or your school's career services office for common questions and answers.

Some questions, though, may not be legal regardless of the interviewer's intent, whether the interviewer is making small talk, is unaware the questions are illegal, plans to discriminate against you, or just wants to test whether you respond. How you respond is up to you; before you respond, you may want to ask how the question is relevant to the position, or you may politely decline to answer. The following are examples of illegal interview questions.

> What religion do you practice?
>
> How old are you?
>
> Are you married?
>
> Do you plan to have children?

Recently, the **behavioral interview style** has become popular with recruiters. Rather than just determining your qualifications for the job, interviewers are attempting to verify whether you can do the work. They ask questions about what you would do in certain situations because how you behave now is likely to transfer to similar situations in another job. Here are a few examples of behavioral questions:

> What major problem have you faced in group projects and how have you handled it?
>
> Can you tell us about a time when you had to choose between following the rules or stretching them?
>
> Describe a conflict you had with someone and how you resolved it.

Keep your answers concise. Briefly state the situation, describe the steps you took, and summarize the results. You can also share what you learned from the experience that you would carry into similar situations that might arise.

You Make the Call
How would you respond to an illegal interview question?

Communication Matters

Answers to the 10 Toughest Interview Questions

Forbes published the following advice regarding common interview questions and their answers.

1. **Why should I hire you?** Know the job description and then tie your skills and knowledge to the employer's specific needs.

2. **Why is there a gap in your work history?** Explain the reason. Employers understand that there are good reasons for being unemployed, especially for college students (e.g., heavy course load, study abroad), but dwell on what you did during the gap, such as taking classes, taking care of family members, or volunteering.

3. **Tell me one thing you would change about your last job.** Be careful not to criticize your previous employer and be prepared to tell why you didn't change what you didn't like. Pick a safe topic such as updating the technology to make a process more efficient.

4. **Tell me about yourself.** Because this is a "warm-up" question for the rest of the interview, give yourself only a minute or two. Summarize your early experience, your education, your work history, and your current experience (with emphasis on the current experience). Do not talk about your social life or your personal life.

5. **Explain a complicated database (or any other concept or procedure) to your eight-year-old nephew.** Your answer should show you know your industry so well that you could explain it even to an eight-year-old. Do your research and be able to talk about your field.

6. **What would the person who likes you least say about you?** Pick a true fault that could be leveraged as a strength (e.g., impatience).

7. **Tell me about a time when old solutions didn't work.** The employer is testing your creativity and problem-solving ability. A good topic might be a time when you had to learn a new technology to accomplish a task.

Explain the issue, what you did to resolve it, and the results.

8. **What's the biggest risk you've ever taken?** The employer is assessing your resiliency and your ability to make good decisions. Be sure you have examples of risks that paid off.

9. **Have you ever had a supervisor challenge a decision?** Your answer to this indicates your ability to take direction and remain humble. Focus on what you learned from the situation rather than the situation itself.

10. **Describe a time when your team did not agree.** The employer sees your answer as an indicator of how you will behave in the workplace. Make sure your answer focuses on the process—what happened, what you did, and what you learned. Concisely describe how your group came to consensus.

Sources: Meghan Casserly, "Why Are Manholes Round? The 10 Toughest Interview Questions," *Forbes*, July 27, 2011, accessed May 10, 2016, http://www.forbes.com/sites/meghancasserly/2011/07/27/the-10-toughest-interview-questions/#3f434b0a62b2.

The job interview is the final stage of the job application. Appearing professional, calm, and enthusiastic will help you succeed.

© Brand X Pictures/Getty Images RF

Putting Yourself at Ease

Perhaps it is easier to say than to do, but you should be calm throughout the interview. Remember that you are being inspected and that the interviewer should see a calm and collected person. Appearing calm involves talking in a clear and strong voice. It also involves controlling your facial expressions and body movements.

Developing such controls requires self-discipline and reassuring self-talk. You may find it helpful to convince yourself that the stress experienced during an interview is normal. Or you may find it helpful to look at the situation realistically—as merely a conversation between two people who have the same goal in mind: hiring the right person for the position.

Practicing your answers to common interview questions out loud may be helpful. You may even want to record one of these practice sessions and analyze your performance. Your school's career services office may be able to help with this. The more prepared you are, the calmer you will be.

Helping to Control the Dialog

Just answering the interviewers' questions is often not enough. The questions you ask and the comments you make should bring up what you want the interviewer to know about you. Your self-analysis revealed the strong points in your background. Now you should make certain that those points come out in the interview.

You have several options for bringing up points about you that the interviewer does not ask for. For example, a student seeking a job in advertising believed that her teamwork skills should be brought to the interviewer's attention. So at an appropriate time in the interview, she asked, "How important is the ability to collaborate in this company?" The anticipated answer—"very important"—allowed her to discuss her skills. To take another example, a student who wanted to bring out his knowledge of the prospective employer's operations did so with this question: "Will your company's expansion in the Madison area create new job opportunities there?" How many questions of this sort you should ask will depend on your need to supplement your interviewer's questioning.

Although you want to ask questions that highlight your skills, you should also ask questions to determine if the company is a good fit for you, such as "How would you describe the culture here?" Your goal should be to make certain that both the interviewer and you get all the information you consider important.

Leading an Interview

At some point in your career, you will likely be in the position of the interviewer. As an interviewer, you need to understand that an interview is more than just asking the questions. An interview is a business meeting that helps you accomplish a business goal—hiring qualified, talented staff. As such, you need to approach this meeting much like you approach other types of business communication by analyzing your audience, context, and purpose and then developing your materials accordingly.

Because your ultimate goal in an interview is to hire a qualified candidate, you need to consider the qualities the candidates must possess, the types of questions that will help you determine the best candidate, and the structure of the interview itself.

Determining Position Requirements To determine the position requirements, you need to ask yourself what characteristics the best candidate would possess. You can look at job descriptions or at the performance of others in your company, especially of those in similar positions. Generally, you can divide these characteristics into educational requirements (which can also include licenses or certifications); technical requirements or skills; and soft skills such as communication, team skills, and leadership abilities.

Once you have developed your lists, you can further refine them by dividing the position requirements into lists of those that are required and those that are preferred. For example, you can list a bachelor's degree as a requirement for the position and an MBA as a preferred requirement. This means that all candidates you interview will have at least a bachelor's degree but that you will look more favorably on those who have a master's degree in business.

Developing and Asking the Interview Questions Once you have determined the position requirements, you can determine the interview questions you will ask. The questions you ask should be ones you can ask consistently to all candidates and should be tied specifically to the employment requirements.

Illegal Interview Questions As we've mentioned already, there are some questions you cannot ask. The United States Equal Opportunity Commission (EEOC) says that it is against the law to base employment decisions on "race, color, religion, sex (including gender identity, sexual orientation, and pregnancy), national origin, age (40 or older), disability, or genetic information."[4] This means you cannot ask questions related to these topics unless you can support that these questions are relevant to employment.

Even then, the way you ask the question is important. For example, if you are hiring for a position where the duties require someone to be at least 18, instead of asking "How old are you?," you can ask, "Are you older than 18?" Or if you are hiring for a sales position and want to know if the person is willing to travel, instead of asking "Are you married? Do you have children?" (which are factors in applicants' personal lives that may make them unwilling to travel), you can say, "This job requires at least 10 days of travel per month. Are you able to do this?" Likewise, instead of asking "Do you have a disability?," you can ask, "Are you able to stand for at least 30 minutes?" As you can see, these questions address job qualifications; they do not address private or potentially discriminatory issues.

Common Questions You have many options for interview questions. Because you can see an individual's educational or technical qualifications in a résumé, you will not want to spend time with questions such as "What is your degree?" Instead, you want to see how well an individual is prepared to transfer what he or she knows to the workplace.

You can, of course, ask common interview questions such as those presented earlier in the chapter if you feel those questions will help you meet your hiring goals. And while it is important that applicants prepare for interviews, management professor John Sullivan notes that readily available answers to common interview questions are available on the Internet, thus increasing the odds that you will get canned answers to these questions.

Sullivan encourages interviewers to ask more challenging questions to get to the heart of an individual's readiness and qualifications for a position. Specifically, he advocates for questions that assess the following:[5]

- *Problem-solving ability:* Requiring candidates to solve a problem they might encounter on their first day of work or identify the flaws in a current process is a good way to assess problem-solving skills via work the employee would have to do for the company.

- *The ability to be forward-looking:* Good employees look ahead, so you may want to ask candidates what their goals would be for the first three to six months and how they might accomplish them; you can also ask them about changes they anticipate in the job or industry.

- *The ability to learn, adapt, and innovate:* These questions might require candidates to explain how they would remain current in their field, adapt to changes in technology or customer expectations, or become more innovative to remain competitive.

- *How sold the candidates are on the position:* Asking candidates the factors they consider when accepting a job offer is a good way to get them excited about the job and company.

Whatever you ask, keep in mind that the more targeted you can be, the more likely you are to get a match between your candidate and your company.

Structuring the Interview
While the questions are surely an important part of the interview, so, too, is the way you structure the conversation. Will you have a committee conduct the interview? Will everyone ask questions or just one person? How long will the interview be? How much time will you spend on each question? Will you use a rating sheet to assess the candidates' answers? On what type of scale will you assess the candidates' answers? What does a "good" answer look like? How will you determine the best candidate?

Your answers to these questions will ensure not only a smooth interview but also a logical process for evaluating a candidate and arriving objectively at a good decision. Especially once the interviews are finished, you and your hiring committee will appreciate a uniform process for quickly selecting the best candidate and proceeding with a job offer.

Following Up and Ending the Application

The résumé, cover message, and interview are not the only types of employment communication. You also need to be able to thank the interviewer, follow up on an application, accept a position, turn down an offer, or even resign from a position after you have been in it for a while.

LO15-7 Write application follow-up messages that are appropriate, friendly, and positive.

Writing a Thank-You Message

Sending a brief **thank-you message** is essential both to be courteous and to gain an advantage over your competitors who may not send one. Keep in mind, though, that the thank-you message helps your case only if it is delivered well—tailored to the employer and interview, spell checked and proofread, and sent immediately after the interview.

Thank-you messages are usually short. They begin with an expression of gratitude; say something about the interview, the job, or the company; and take care of any additional business (such as submitting information requested). Then they end on a goodwill note—perhaps a hopeful look to the next step in the negotiations. While you can send your message by mail, an email will quickly convey your thanks as the following message illustrates:

Sending a thank-you note shows professionalism and good manners.
© Antonio Guillem/123RF

> Dear Mr. Woods:
>
> Thank you for talking with me yesterday about the finance internship. I enjoyed learning more about Sony Corporation of America and the financial analyst position.
>
> As you requested, I have attached samples of the financial analysis I developed as a class project. If you need anything more, please let me know.
>
> I look forward to the possibility of discussing employment with you soon.
>
> Sincerely,

Constructing a Follow-Up to an Application

When a prospective employer is late in responding or you receive another offer with a time deadline, you may need to call the company or write a **follow-up message**. Employers are often just slow, but sometimes they lose the application. Whatever the explanation, a follow-up message may help to produce action.

Follow-up messages are routine inquiries (see Chapter 8). The following messages are examples. The first is what you might say in a phone call; the second, in an email.

> Hello, my name is Dawna Firth. Last week, I interviewed for the staff accountant position, and I am calling to check on the status of my application.

> Dear Ms. Yang:
>
> Because the time is approaching when I must make a job decision, could you please tell me the status of my application with you?
>
> You may recall that you interviewed me in your office November 7. You wrote me November 12 indicating that I was among those you had selected for further consideration.
>
> SAIC remains one of the organizations I would like to consider in making my career decision. I would very much appreciate hearing from you by December 3.
>
> Sincerely,

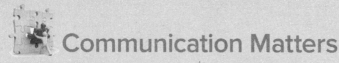
Communication Matters

What's the Number One Interviewing Mistake?

As manager of the business news site *Business Insider*, Jessica Liebman says she does a lot of hiring. She also says the number one interview mistake isn't wearing the wrong clothes, showing up with a cup of coffee, being late, having a limp handshake, or opening the interview by asking if you'll get a free iPad.

It's an action (or nonaction) that takes place after the interview: failing to send a thank-you message.

As Liebman says, even a brief email of thanks helps seal a positive impression, whereas no message indicates that "you don't want the job" or "you're disorganized and forgot about following up."

So the next time you have an interview, be sure you get everyone's name. As soon as possible after the interview (preferably the same day), send your interviewers a thank-you email. It could

mean the difference between getting your job and continuing your search.

Source: Jessica Liebman, "The Number One Mistake People I Interview Are Making These Days," *Business Insider*, February 24, 2013, accessed May 15, 2016, http://www.businessinsider.com/the-number-one-mistake-people-i-interview-are-making-these-days-2012-2.

Planning the Job Acceptance

Job acceptances are favorable response messages with an extra amount of goodwill. Chapter 8 can help you review routine responses. Because the message should begin directly, a "yes" answer in the beginning is appropriate. The remainder of the message should contain a confirmation of the starting date and place and comments about the work, the company, the interview—whatever you would say if you were face to face with the reader. The message need not be long. This one does the job well:

> Dear Ms. Garcia:
>
> Yes, I accept your offer of employment as a junior analyst. After my first interview with you, I was convinced that Allison-Caldwell was the organization for me. I am delighted that you think I am right for Allison-Caldwell as well.
>
> Following your instructions, I will be in your Toronto headquarters on May 28 at 8:30 a.m. ready to work for you. Thank you for this opportunity.
>
> Sincerely,

Writing a Message Refusing a Job

Messages refusing a job offer follow the indirect refusal pattern (see Chapter 9). One good technique is to begin with a friendly comment—perhaps about something that happened during the interview process. Next, explain and present the refusal in clear yet positive words. Then end with a friendly comment. This example illustrates the plan:

> Dear Mr. Chen:
>
> Meeting you and the other people at Northern was a genuine pleasure. Thank you for sharing so much information with me and for the generous job offer.
>
> As we discussed, a special interest of mine is to work abroad. After considerable thought, I have decided to accept an offer with a firm that has extensive opportunities along these lines.
>
> I appreciate the time and the courteous treatment you gave me.
>
> Sincerely,

Writing a Resignation

At some point in your career you are likely to resign from one job to take another. When this happens, you will probably inform your employer of your resignation orally. Other times, you will find it more practical or comfortable to resign in writing. In some cases, you may do it both ways. As a matter of policy, some companies require a written resignation even after an oral resignation has been delivered.

Your **resignation message** should be as positive as the circumstances permit. Even if your work experiences have not been pleasant, you want to depart without a final display of anger. As an anonymous philosopher once explained, "When you write a resignation in anger, you write the best letter you will ever regret."

The indirect order is usually the best strategy for negative messages such as a resignation (see Chapter 9), but some are written in the direct order (see Chapter 8). They present the resignation right away, following it with expressions of gratitude or favorable comments about past working experiences. Either approach is acceptable. Even so, using the indirect order may help you to build the goodwill you want to leave behind you.

The following example illustrates the indirect order. It begins with a positive point—one that sets up the negative message. The negative message follows, clearly yet positively stated. The ending returns to positive words chosen to build goodwill and fit the situation.

> Dear Ms. Shuster:
>
> Working as your assistant for the past five years has been a genuinely rewarding experience. Under your direction I have grown as an administrator, and I have learned a great deal from you about retailing.
>
> As you may recall from our past discussions, I have been pursuing the same career goals that you held early in your career. To achieve these goals, I am now resigning to accept a store management position with Lawson's in Belle River. I would like my employment to end on the 31st, but I could stay a week or two longer if needed to help train my replacement.
>
> I leave with only good memories of you and the other people with whom I worked. Thanks to all of you for a valuable contribution to my career.
>
> Sincerely,

Continuing Job-Search Activities

Continuously keeping your finger on the pulse of the job market is a good idea. Not only will it provide you with information about changes occurring in your field, but it will also keep you alert to better job opportunities as soon as they are announced.

Maintaining Your Résumé
While many people intend to keep their résumés updated, they just do not make it a priority. Updating your résumé as you gain new accomplishments and skills is important. Otherwise, you will be surprised to find how easily you can lose track of important details.

Reading Job Ads and Professional Publications
Nearly as important as keeping your résumé updated is keeping up on your professional reading. Most trade or professional journals have job notices or bulletin boards you should check regularly. These ads give you insight into what skills are in demand, perhaps helping you choose assignments where you get the opportunity to develop new skills.

Staying up to date in your field can be stimulating; it can provide both challenges and opportunities. As you progress through your career, you will write a variety of messages as you encounter these challenges and opportunities. Your ability to tailor your messages to the audience and purpose will serve you well.

LO15-8   Maintain your job-search activities.

You Make the Call
What professional publications should people in your field be reading?

Power Charge Your Professionalism: Put Your Editing Skills to Work

During a recent storm, several trees fell on Elizabeth Sampson's porch, damaging the porch and its roof. Ms. Sampson claimed the trees belonged to Nelson Insurance's client, so the claims field representative, Carl Anderson, inspected the damage.

Mr. Anderson discovered that the trees were on Ms. Sampson's side of the lot line. Ms. Sampson contested Mr. Anderson's investigation and took her claim to the field claims manager, Ryan Bayes. He reviewed Ms. Sampson's claim and responded with the message below.

The message he has written to Ms. Sampson, however, is too direct and poorly punctuated and contains unnecessarily negative and hostile language. It also includes subject-verb agreement errors, pronoun errors, and several other errors discussed throughout the chapters in this book.

As your instructor directs,

1. Punctuate the message correctly using commas, colons, and semicolons. Cite the correctness standard from Reference Chapter A that you applied.
2. Applying what you learned in Chapter 9, indicate how you would revise the message to improve the tone. While you may need to delete some words or sentences or add content, be sure your edits preserve the writer's ideas and relevant content.
3. Retype the message to reflect the revisions you indicated in Steps 1 and 2.

> July 1, 2019
>
> Ms. Elizabeth Sampson
> 10586 California Avenue
> Hayward, WI 54843
>
> Dear Ms. Sampson:
>
> This letter is to inform you that as per your request I have completed a review of you're claim.
>
> You claimed that you believe our ensured, Mr. Conrad Dodge, is responsible for the cost of replacing the porch roof the dented siding and the screens that were tore because the trees that fell were his. Following the inspection by Carl Anderson, our field claims representative, it showed that the trees are yours. Nelson Insurance have secured a copy of the most recent survey of the properties I have enclosed a copy of those documents.
>
> My review of this matter has came to the same conclusion as Carl. Unfortunately, we simply cannot honor your claim the current survey of your property and Mr. Dodges property clearly shows that the trees are your's. While I can understand your disappointment you can obviously see these are your trees if you look at the survey, therefore, Nelson Insurance has determined the following your claim lacks legal standing and our insured are not liable to you in any way.
>
> If you have any further evidence that you wish for me to consider please provide it to Carl or I and we will review that information quick. If you have any questions or concerns I can be contacted at 715-432-4321, ext. 4. I apologize for any inconvenience.
>
> Sincerely,
>
> Ryan Bayes, CPCU, AIC, AIS
> Nelson Insurance: Field Claims Manager
> Phone: 715-432-4321, ext. 4
> Email: rbayes@nelsoninsurance.com

Good editing skills are important because . . .

- Grammar, punctuation, and mechanics impact the clarity and readability of a message.
- Editing and revising are critical steps to ensuring that you project a professional image.

If you need additional practice, be sure to visit the grammar, mechanics, and punctuation exercises in LearnSmart Achieve.

Key Terms

Critical-Thinking Questions

1. "Building a network of contacts to find jobs seems selfish. It involves acquiring friendships just to use them for one's personal benefit." Discuss this view. LO1

2. Do employers who offer unpaid internships take unfair advantage of students' knowledge and skills? Under what circumstances might it be a good idea to take an unpaid internship? When might it not be a good idea? LO1

3. Maryann Brennan followed a broad program of study in college and received a degree in general management.

    She did her best work in English, especially in the writing courses. She also did well in history, managerial leadership, organizational behavior, and psychology. As much as she could, she avoided math and computer courses.

    Her overall grade point average of 3.7 (4.0 basis) placed her in the top 10 percent of her class. What advice would you give her as she begins her search for a career job? LO1–3

4. Discuss the value of each of the sources presented in the chapter for finding jobs (a) before an internship, (b) right after graduation, and (c) after 20 years of work in a specialty. LO1–3

5. Assume that, in an interview for the job you want, you are asked the questions listed in the text under the heading "Anticipating Questions and Preparing Answers." Answer these questions. Compare your answers with your classmates' answers. LO6

6. The most popular arrangement of résumé information is the reverse chronological order with a three-part grouping: education, experience, and personal details. Describe two other arrangements. When would each be used? LO4

7. Distinguish between the print résumé and the electronic résumé. When would each be most appropriate? LO4

8. What is meant by parallelism of headings? LO4

9. Describe the cover message and résumé you would write (a) immediately after graduation, (b) 10 years later, and (c) 25 years later. Point out similarities and differences, and defend your decisions. LO2, 4, 5

10. What differences would you suggest in writing cover messages for jobs in (a) accounting, (b) banking, (c) advertising copy writing, (d) management, (e) sales, (f) consulting, (g) information systems, and (h) healthcare? LO5

11. Discuss the appropriateness of beginning a cover message with these words: "This is to apply for . . ." and "I would like to. . . . " LO5

12. How should you end a cover message? LO5

13. Discuss some of the advantages that writing a thank-you note to the interviewer gives the writer. LO7

14. Identify some of the benefits one gains from continuing to read professional journals for job information after one is employed. LO8

Skills-Building Exercises

1. Criticize the following excerpts from résumés. (They are not from the same résumé.) LO4
    a. Work Experience

        2016–2019 Employed as sales rep for Lloyd-Shanks

        Tool Company

        2015–2016 Office manager, Drago Plumbing Supply, Toronto

        2014–2015 Matson's Super Stores. I worked part time as sales clerk while attending college.

b. References

Mr. Carl T. Whitesides
Sunrise Insurance, Inc.
317 Forrest Lane
Dover, DE 19901-6452

Patricia Cullen
Cullen and Cullen Realtors
2001 Bowman Dr.
Wilmington, DE 19804

Rev. Troy A. Graham
Asbury Methodist Church
Hyattsville, MD 20783

D. W. Boozer
Boozer Industries
Baltimore, MD 21202

c. Qualifications

- Know how to motivate a sales force. I have done it.
- Experienced in screening applicants and selecting salespeople.
- Know the pharmaceutical business from 11 years of experience.
- Knowledgeable about realistic quota setting and incentives.
- Proven leadership ability.

d. Education

2018 Graduated from Tippen H.S. (I was in top 10 percent of class.)

2020 BS from Bradley University with major in marketing

2016 to present Enrolled part time in MBA program at present the University of Phoenix

2. Criticize these sentences from cover messages. LO5

Beginning Sentences
   a. Please consider this my application for any position for which my training and experience qualify me.
   b. Mr. Jerry Bono of your staff has told me about a vacancy in your loan department for which I would like to apply.
   c. I am that accountant you described in your advertisement in today's Times-Record.
   d. I want to work for you!

Sentences Presenting Selling Points
   a. From 2014–2018 I attended Bradley University where I took courses leading to a BS degree with a major in finance.
   b. I am highly skilled in trading corporate bonds as a result of three years spent in the New York office of Collins, Bragg, and Weaver.
   c. For three years (2015–2018) I was in the loan department at Bank One.
   d. My two strongest qualifications for this job are my personality and gift of conversation.

Sentences from Action Endings
   a. I will call you on the 12th to arrange an interview.
   b. If my qualifications meet your requirements, it would be greatly appreciated if you would schedule an interview for me.
   c. Please call to set up an interview. I anticipate several interviews and offers but would prefer to be with your company.

Problem-Solving Cases

1. You have successfully prepared yourself for the career of your choice, but the recruiters visiting your school have not yet offered you a job. Now you must look on your own. So by searching newspapers, online job databases, and company website announcements, find the best job for which you believe you are qualified. Write two cover messages that you might use to present your qualifications for this job: one for print presentation and one for email. Attach a copy of the job description to the messages. Write the résumé and reference sheet to accompany the message.

2. Project yourself three years past your graduation date. If you already have three years of professional experience, use that as your starting point. During these years, you have had a good experience working for the company. Unfortunately, your progress hasn't been what you had expected. You think that you must look around for a better opportunity. You search through the classified advertisements in your area newspapers, online, and in *The Wall Street Journal,* and you turn up one promising possibility. Write a cover message that skillfully presents your qualifications for this job. (You may make logical assumptions about your experience over the three-year period.) For class purposes, attach the advertisement to your message. Write the résumé and reference sheet to accompany the message.

3. Assume you are in your last term of school, and graduation is just around the corner. Your greatest interest is in finding work that you like and that would enable you to support yourself now and to support a family as you win promotions.

   You have not been able to find a job you want to apply for in the want ads of newspapers, your school's career services office, online job sites, or trade magazines. So you decide to do what any good salesperson does: survey the product (yourself) and the market (companies that could use a person who can do what you are prepared to do) and then advertise (send each of these companies a résumé with a cover message). Write a prospecting cover message. Write the résumé and reference sheet to accompany the message.

4. Graduation is fast approaching, and you are now ready to sell your working ability in the job market. Besides canvassing likely firms with the help of prospecting messages and diligently following up with family contacts, you have decided to look into anything that appears especially good in the ads of newspapers, online sources, and magazines. The latest available issues of large city publications and online services yield the jobs listed below.

   Concentrate on the ad describing the job you would like most or could do best and then write a cover message that will get you that job. Your message will first have to survive the filtering that eliminates dozens (sometimes hundreds) of applicants who lack the expected qualifications. Toward the end you will be getting into strong competition in which small details give you the superiority that will get you an interview.

   Study your chosen ad for what it says and even more for what it implies. You may imagine far enough ahead to assume completion of all the courses that are planned for your degree. You may build up your case a bit beyond what you actually have. Sort the qualifications for the job, organize them strategically, and then present them in a cover message. Write a résumé and reference sheet to accompany your message.

   a. *Office manager.* Currently seeking an office manager with initiative and flexibility for work in a fast-paced environment. Must have an outgoing personality and excellent communication skills and be a team player. Must be a "power user" of Word and Excel and have excellent Internet search skills. Knowledge of PowerPoint is a plus. Some overtime expected during crunch periods. Send application materials to Chris Eveland at ceveland@qconline.com.

   b. *Assistant webmaster.* Outstanding information technology, organizational, and interpersonal skills are needed for work on a company portal. Mastery of HTML and CSS, experience with website design including graphic design, and knowledge of client/server technology are vital. Candidates should be able to communicate with international audiences. Candidates also must possess excellent writing skills and the ability to effectively manage multiple projects while interfacing with company employees. A bachelor's degree with a background in information systems, marketing, or communications is required. Please send résumé to Megan Adami in Human Resources, 7165 North Main Street, (your city and state), or fax it to 1-888-444-5047, or email it to megan_adami@cnet.com.

   c. *Management trainee.* Named by *Fortune* magazine as one of the best places to work, this constantly expanding international company uses shared decision making and clear career paths so that employees can be productive and well rewarded. The challenging management training program requires candidates with good communications skills and high energy levels to be successful. Applicants must be computer literate and possess good interpersonal skills. Fax résumé to Don Zatyko at 1-888-399-2569.

   d. *Staff accountant—payroll specialist.* We are looking for an accountant who desires to grow and move up the ladder. One should be motivated and willing to work in a fast-paced, multitasking environment. An associate's degree in accounting or finance is required. Additionally, the ideal candidate will be detail-oriented and able to meet deadlines. The job involves coordinating transfers of time worked data from time collection systems to payroll systems. Must have extended knowledge of Excel to compute withholdings and deductions, and must stay up-to-date on multiple state laws regarding payroll. Excellent compensation package and benefits. Apply to Carolynn Workman, accounting director, at carolynn_workman@adelphia.net.

e. *Staff accountant.* Successful candidate should have a BS in accounting and be proficient in QuickBooks and/or Excel. Would be responsible for performing account analysis for corporate accounts, assisting in consolidation of subsidiaries, and assisting in the preparation of annual and quarterly financial statements and financial reports for certain subsidiaries. Experience in the local environment of small business is desirable. If you are concerned with order, quality, and accuracy, please contact us by mail at Administrative Partner, Winship and Acord, P.C., 3013 Stonybrook Drive, (your city and state), or by email at CWA@msn.com, or by fax at 1-217-399-2569.

f. *Network specialist.* We seek someone who can help deliver reliable, secure, and integrated networks. Must be able to bring together data and voice, WAN and LAN, fiber optics and wireless. Opportunity to learn newest technologies. Must have network certification such as MCP, MCSE, CNA, or CNE as well as a college degree or the equivalent experience. Requires excellent interpersonal and problem-solving skills. Experience with multiplatform computing is preferred. Will be expected to develop technical documentation and help establish network policies, procedures, and standards to ensure conformance with information systems and client objectives and strategy. Qualified applicants should send application documents to Robert Edwards at redwards@tyt.com.

g. *Technology analyst/consultant.* A fast-growing, highly regarded information technology assessment/consulting firm has a position for someone with expertise in client/server technology and Access. Must have excellent written communication and interpersonal skills. Vendor or user organization experience is highly desirable. Position is in the Bay Area. Send or fax your résumé to director of human resources at 500 Airport Road, Suite 100, (your city and state), or 415-579-1022.

h. *Financial analyst.* An eastern-based investment firm is seeking an analyst to help with the evaluation of potential private equity investments and marketing of an existing and a new leveraged buyout fund. Should have a bachelor's degree from a good school and some experience in banking. Ideal candidates will have strong analytical capabilities and excellent computer skills, particularly spreadsheet, statistics, and database. Please email your résumé to andrew-winston@fidelity.com.

i. *Trade show exhibits coordinator.* Position reports to the national sales manager and requires an individual who can work independently as well as part of a team. Professional telephone and computer skills are essential. Coordinator will maintain exhibitor contact databases, serve as an internal liaison to accounting and as an external liaison to vendors, and assist the on-site floor managers with various exhibitor-related responsibilities. Also must create exhibitor and attendee pre- and post-show surveys, collect data, and compile results. Trade show, association, or convention services experience is a plus. Some limited travel is expected. Send your résumé to lmiller@gmail.com.

j. *Sales representative.* Major pharmaceutical company is expanding and looking for a sales representative in your area. Ideal candidate will have a successful record of sales experience, preferably in a business-to-business environment. Candidate must be well versed in science and willing to continually learn about new products. Good knowledge of your area is highly desirable. Send your résumé to Jane_Adami@pfizer.com.

k. *Human resources generalist.* Seeking a professional individual to work in our human resources department. Familiarity with OSHA laws, EEOC requirements, and state employment laws is required. Experience in talent recruitment and development is preferred. Send your résumé and cover message to rickyoung@sampsonindustries.com.

l. *Marketing professional.* An international, rapidly growing consumer and trade publisher is seeking a self-motivated individual to help us reach our goal of doubling revenues by the year 2021. Ideal candidate will be an innovative, results-oriented professional willing to take the challenge of developing new markets in Central and South America. Should be good at packaging and repackaging information products for a large and expanding customer base. We are looking for those with some experience, creative writing talent, leadership skills, good communication skills, and strong interpersonal skills. Sell yourself through your cover message and résumé. Send a rich media text to Thomas McLaughlin, corporate vice president, Blackhawk Publishing at tjmclaughlin@blackhawk.com.

m. *Executive administrative assistant.* Vice president of a Fortune 500 manufacturing company seeks a highly competent, personable, organized, and dependable executive assistant. College degree desired. Must have excellent communication skills and thorough command of Internet navigation as well as word processing and presentation programs. In addition to basic business knowledge in accounting, economics, computer systems, finance, marketing, and management, an understanding of manufacturing in a global market would be desirable. Apply to Director of Human Resources, P.O. Box 3733, (your city and state).

n. *Graphic artist.* An employee-owned systems integration firm has an immediate need for a graphic artist. A bachelor's degree or an associate's degree with some experience desired. Must be proficient in PhotoShop and Illustrator, preferably in a Windows environment. Will prepare presentation and curriculum support graphics for government customer. Knowledge of project management software is a plus. Must have a work portfolio. Send résumé to the attention of KML, P.O. Box 900, (your city and state).

o. *IT specialist.* A local medical clinic is seeking an individual to manage a multisite, multiplatform computer system. Will be responsible for troubleshooting and coordinating problems in a Windows Vista environment and writing reports for management. A background in the health care/medical field combined with a good knowledge of computing is highly desirable. Send résumé to (your city's name) Community Clinic, 1113 Henderson, (your city and state), or fax to 888-316-1026.

p. *Financial manager.* Multispecialty medical group (60 doctors) needs dedicated professional to work in providing financial planning and control in a growing organization. Join a team of financial specialists who bear responsibility for budgeting, general accounting, reimbursement, billing processes, and external reporting. Also responsible for development of long- and short-range financial goals and evaluation of their impact on strategic objectives and service mission. Degree in accounting/finance. Technical and team skills needed. Competitive salary and benefits package. Send letter and résumé to Mount Renault Medical Group, Box 14871, New York, NY 00146.

q. *Accountant.* A major real estate developer and property management company seeks an accountant. Must have a bachelor's degree in accounting. Will assist in financial reporting, tax preparation, cash flow projections, and year-end audit work and paper preparation. Mastery of Excel is required as are good communication skills. Some work experience in accounting is desirable; internship experience in an accounting or real estate environment is also desirable. Send your résumé and cover letter to TPL, P.O. Box 613, (your city and state) or email it to tpl@yahoo.com.

r. *Accounting majors.* Multinational consumer electronics firm seeks entry-level accountant for work in its controller's division. This person must be knowledgeable in financial and managerial accounting, internal auditing, budgeting, and capital investments. A multinational orientation, degree in accounting, and progress toward completion of CPA or CMA are a plus. Good communication skills (written and oral) and computer applications are required. Interested applicants should send message and résumé to hrdirector@circuitcity.com.

s. *Bank examiner.* Federal Reserve Bank (nearest to your location) seeks career-oriented individuals. Persons hired will conduct onsite examinations of foreign banks operating in the United States in their lending activities, derivative products, bank operations, and financial information. Applicants must possess a bachelor's degree in accounting, finance, or economics. Evidence of cross-cultural sensitivity and foreign language proficiency is preferred. Travel 30–50% of the time. Excellent oral/written skills and U.S. citizenship required. Apply with a cover letter, résumé, and reference sheet to Federal Reserve Board, Human Resources Department, (your city and state).

t. *Proposal writer.* Global leader in high-technology asset management needs individual to prepare proposals for clients. Person selected must be a team player, thrive on high-tech challenges in fast-paced environment, and possess a state-of-the-art solution orientation. Excellent writing skills essential, along with BBA degree and experience with various hardware/software technologies. Job includes coordinating appropriate persons to define solutions and preparing program plans with cost estimation for clients. Send a cover letter, résumé, and writing sample to Department SAS, (your city and state).

u. *Assistant to operations manager.* Proven leader in the insurance industry seeks a highly motivated assistant to the operations manager of regional service center. Technical skills include proficiency in Internet use and Microsoft Word, Excel, PowerPoint, Access, and other database applications. College training preferred with good people skills. Person selected must be able to develop and maintain effective working relationships with internal and external customers. Apply to HR Department, Box 7438, (your city and state) or email to hrdirector@statefarm.com.

v. *Environmental safety and health assistant.* World leader in battery manufacturing is looking for an individual to work in safety and health area of production plant and distribution center. The successful candidate will need to have a business or environmental engineering degree and possess excellent organizational and people skills. Job duties involve administering health/safety programs, conducting training, and working with governmental agencies and regulatory personnel. Excellent opportunity for results-oriented individual seeking to work for a safe, attractive, and sanitary environment. Send cover message and résumé to Box SH, (your city and state).

w. *Account executive for display advertising.* State business journal invites applications for career-oriented individuals. Qualified candidates must be college graduates (business preferred) and have work background to demonstrate reliability and commitment. Job scope involves selling display advertising in creative ways for specialized business print and online publications. Applicants should be of high energy, aggressive, and creative. Send applications to Drawer HBD, (your city and state), or salesmgr@busjrnl.com.

x. *Financial consultant.* Large communications services company needs qualified person to provide communication-based utility automation consulting to electric utilities. Must have comprehensive financial management knowledge. Perform economic analyses on current and proposed projects; assist in development of budgets; evaluate budget to actual performance; prepare monthly reports. Demonstrated knowledge of strategic planning, valuation techniques, accounting principles, and economic forecasts. Must communicate well orally and in writing. Email a cover message, résumé, and references to applications@alc.com.

y. *SEO blogger.* New website is seeking a writer/intern for its search engine optimization (SEO) blog. This new site, which has free SEO tools, is attracting a growing worldwide interest. We are seeking two writers for three to five posts per week. Must have a background in SEO and be abreast of the field in order to write on current topics. Telecommuting is OK. Please send samples of your work or links to it along with your SEO credentials to jobs@nonbot.com.

z. *Corporate trainer.* Exciting opportunity is available for a professional with strong presentation skills, good organizational skills, and excellent written and oral communication skills. Successful trainer will be able to effectively communicate technical information to both technical and nontechnical users. Should be able to design classroom training modules and measure their effectiveness. Good time management and use of Outlook are required. Some travel to clients' sites may be required. Application documents including a sample PowerPoint presentation should be sent to Sharon Garbett, President, Sedona Training, P.O. Box 1308, Moline, Illinois 61266.

5. You are looking ahead to your graduation soon. You've decided to begin to look for jobs online. Tap into a system that you know posts jobs in your major or a corporate website that posts job openings. Browse through the jobs until you see one that appeals to you and for which you will be qualified when you graduate. Print (or save) a copy of the ad so you will have it handy when you write your résumé and cover messages. Address the points covered in the ad and explain that you learned about the position from a particular online system. Plan to send your résumé electronically via email. Plan to send both a formatted and a .txt version of your résumé.

6. Create a LinkedIn profile complete with links that provide supporting details. Take care that your online portfolio is easy to navigate as well as pleasing to view.

7. You are seeking an internship in your field. Using your school's career services office, online internship sites, personal contacts, or other sources, find an internship in your field that you are currently qualified to hold. Write a résumé, references list, and cover message for the position. Print a copy of the position description for your instructor. If you find the information through a personal contact or have no official job posting to print, write a brief paragraph describing the position. Be sure the description includes your personal contact's name, job title, company name, and contact information as well as a list of job duties and qualifications.

8. You are seeking an internship but have not yet found a job posting that fits your interests and abilities. However, you know of a company that you've always wanted to work for, and even though the company has no positions advertised, you decide to send an unsolicited/prospecting cover message, résumé, and references to this company. Before you write the cover message and résumé, though, you will want to analyze your purpose and goals; your audience; and the skills, experience, and qualifications you could bring to an internship with this company. Submit this analysis in a short memo to your instructor. Then prepare a résumé and cover letter targeted to the internship.

Correctness of Communication

The correctness of your communication will be important to both you and your company. It will be important to you because people will judge you by it, and how they judge you will in part determine your professional success. It will also be important to your company because correctness in communication will help convey the image of competence that companies require. People judge a company by how its employees act, think, talk, and write, so you want to be sure your speaking and writing reflect a high degree of professionalism.

To read more and get free access to full chapter, visit and register at **www.mheducation.co.in** or scan the given QR Code*

*For more details, see the inside back cover

Documentation of Sources

When writing reports and other business documents, you will frequently use information from other sources. If this information can't be considered common knowledge, you'll need to give credit to the authors by citing the source. Providing source information is also an aid to your readers, who might want to access the resources you used.

This chapter explains how to reference such borrowed material. As you'll see, we recommend using the Chicago style in situations where you need to use a formal citation system. If your instructor prefers APA or MLA style, you can still use this chapter to see how to employ those styles.

To read more and get free access to full chapter, visit and register at **www.mheducation.co.in** or scan the given QR Code*

Reference Chapter B

Documentation of Sources

When writing reports and other business documents, you will frequently use information from other sources. If this information can't be considered common knowledge, you'll need to give credit to the authors by citing the source. Providing source information is also an aid to your readers, who might want to access the resources you used.

This chapter explains how to reference such borrowed material. As you'll see, we recommend using the Chicago style in situations where you need to use a formal citation system. If your instructor prefers APA or MLA style, you can still use this chapter to see how to employ those styles.

When to Acknowledge

Your decision to acknowledge or not acknowledge a source should be determined mainly on the basis of giving credit where credit is due. If you are quoting verbatim (using the original author's exact words), you must give credit. If you are paraphrasing (expressing someone else's ideas in your own words), you should still give credit unless the material covered is general knowledge.

Most colleges and universities have academic honesty or academic integrity policies. Many businesses, too, have ethics policies and codes. Following the policies not only ensures that you get full credit for your own work but also helps you build a reputation as an ethical person. This reputation will lead others to trust you, serving you well both professionally and personally.

Plagiarism and falsifying data are two unethical practices plaguing schools and businesses alike. These practices range from carefully planned, intentional acts to careless, unintentional ones. Whether intentional or not, such misrepresentations can have damaging results. Plagiarism, or presenting others' work as your own, steals from the real authors, depriving them of credit for their work and sometimes of the financial rewards they have earned. Additionally, being caught for or even accused of plagiarism affects your reputation as well as the reputation of your company or your school. Falsifying data is equally harmful, especially when others rely on the information you present to make decisions. Worse yet, if you are successful in passing off falsified or plagiarized work as your own, it tempts you to behave unethically in the future. Being sloppy or deceitful is a slippery slope toward potential disgrace and loss of your job.

The following advice will help you avoid such problems.

Documentation of Sources B-1

*For more details, see the inside back cover

Appendix A

The Power of Attention and Mindfulness

Why Being Attentive is Essential?

Good listening skills and being attentive to what we do help us develop and improve our personal relationships. Steven Covey in his book *The Seven Habits of Highly Effective People* shares how the CEO of a multinational with 35,000 employees came to acknowledge the importance of listening[1]: 'He said, "My wife had told me I didn't listen to our daughter." After he honed his listening skills, he and his daughter grew closer. He realized the value of listening and applied his experience to business.

Being mindful and attentive allows us to demonstrate that we are paying attention to whatever is happening around us. This, in turn, enables us to be well informed of the situations. Similarly, effective listening allows us to be attentive to the thoughts, feelings and behaviors of the other person. Unfortunately, while speaking, reading, and writing are formally or informally taught to most of us, we are rarely taught how to be attentive and, as a result, develop poor listening skills. Although the importance of effective listening skills is largely ignored, research on human communication indicates that it helps maintain productive relationships[2]. In fact, being attentive to others is sometimes the only way to establish communication, and the only way to entertain some people is to listen to them.

How does Mindfulness help us do Meaningful Business?

It is especially important to be attentive to people we interact with, processes that enable us to complete tasks, and places in which we function. For example, when we are mindful of our actions and are attentive to people who matter the most at that point, we are likely to make sound decisions. When we make sound decisions, we are more likely to reach to agreements with our stakeholders, which, in turn, shall enable us to influence them and sell our products, services and ideas. Furthermore, managers who have developed good listening skills and are able to pay attention to details are able to recruit and train people more effectively than those who do not have these traits. For instance, a unique response from a service representative of a large toy company to a kid who had lost his favorite toy had once gone viral. It was an international toy production company – best known for the manufacture of interlocking plastic bricks. The following story shows how an attentive person can dig deeper into a matter and respond beyond the routine act of communication.

The Lego-Evo Das Case – Story of a Seven Year Old Girl

Those who deal with kids would know how painful it could be for a kid to lose her/his favorite toys. In their imaginary world, they interact with their toys and thus they assign their favorite toys beautiful names. Long-time Lego fan Evo Das spent all of her birthday money to buy a Ninjago (Lego ninja) named Jay XZ. Against her dad's advice, Evo brought her Ninjago on a shopping trip and lost it. Being devastated, Evo wrote a letter to Lego explaining her loss and assuring the Lego staff that she would take extra-special care of her action figure if they sent her another one.

Evo Das wrote:

> Hello
>
> My name is Evo Das and I am seven years old. With all my money I received on my sixth birthday I bought the Ninjago kit of the Ultrasonic Raider. The number is 9XXX. It is really good. My Dad just took me to a supermarket and told me to leave the people at home but I took them and I lost Jay ZX at the shop as it fell out of my jacket. I am really upset I have lost him. Dad said to send you an email to see if you will send me another one. I promise I won't take him to the shop again if you can.
>
> – Evo

The response she received from a Lego customer support representative Rubai was not only atypical but also drew the attention of many. Rubai wrote to Evo stating that he had talked to Sensei Wu (a Ninjago character):

> He told me to tell you, – Evo, your father seems like a very wise man. You must always protect your Ninjago minifigures like the dragons protect the Weapons of Spinjitzu!
>
> Sensei Wu told me it was okay if I sent you a new Jay and also told me it would be okay if I included something extra for you because anyone that saves her birthday money to buy the Ultrasonic Raider must be a really big Ninjago fan.
>
> So, I hope you enjoy your Jay minifigure with all his weapons. You will actually have the only Jay minifigure that combines 3 different Jays into one! I am also going to send you a bad guy for him to fight!
>
> Just remember, what Sensei Wu said: keep your minifigures protected like the Weapons of Spinjitzu! And of course, always listen to your Dad.

....

It is indeed rare to see such a thoughtful, creative response to a distraught customer. That is why this story went viral. The question is, what did Rubai write that made it viral? Rubai seemingly went beyond the surface information that Evo's letter carried. He understood Evo did not just lose a toy but lost someone who was an integral part of her imaginary world. In his response, Rubai wrote to Evo that her father seemed to be a wise man and she should listen to her dad always. These statements are likely to appeal to the parents in general. Since parents are the one who ultimately decide on what toys to buy for their kids and when, such statements are likely to evoke positive sentiments among the potential buyers. Additionally, by sending her an extra toy (a bad guy for Sensei Wu to fight) the service representative Rubai not only won Evo's heart but also offered parents (in general) subtle parenting tips, i.e., kids must be taught to fight against evil and protect the ones who save good people. Rubai's ability to go beyond the surface level of Evo's message was possible not only because he was analytical and creative but also attentive to what was hidden in the message.

Being attentive is essential to our effectiveness not only as a manager but also as a speaker. To be an effective speaker, we need to take feedback from the audience (i.e., paying attention to how our audience react to our speech) and adjust our presentations according to what works most effectively for them[3].

When the benefits of being attentive to people who matters and what we do are so huge, why a large number of people, including managers, fail to be attentive? Why most people have poor listening skills and have little or no patience to be mindful of what they are supposed to attend to? It is perhaps because of the amazing nature of the human brain. On the one hand, it got us to the moon, built the Taj Mahal, cured smallpox and, on the other, it also can't seem to go beyond six minutes without checking social media.

The Barriers to Mindfulness

In their book *The Distracted Mind: Ancient Brains in a High-Tech World*, Adam Gazzaley and Larry Rosen wrote[4] – Students, regardless of their age, are unable to stay focused more than three to five minutes. Most students self-interrupt their studies to switch to another task.

Incidentally, the above findings came out after observing the students under lab conditions when they were specifically instructed to focus as long as they could on something they were told was important. The fact is that our attention spans are going down drastically. Focus appears to be a lost art. Research indicates we check our phones up to 150 times a day—about every six to seven minutes that we are awake.

First of all, we need to stop blaming technology. Technology is neither good nor bad. The valuation of technology depends largely on how and for what purpose we use them. Often, we put the blame on our phones for our addiction to them, when it is actually our brain's fault. Our brains are designed to seek new information. In fact, it is the same system that keeps us on the lookout for food and water and rewards us for discovering novel information.

Now, the more pertinent question is, when our brain is so good at seeking out new information, why is it so bad at following through? The answer is simple. It is because the information-seeking part is much stronger than the "cognitive control" part that allows us to complete our tasks. In fact, focusing is not the only activity that taxes our grey matter. FMRI studies of the brain show ignoring irrelevant stimuli is not a passive process[5]. Just like noise-canceling headphones need batteries, our brain, too, has to expend precious resources in order to filter distractions around us. So, doing the same task is harder in environment with more tempting or annoying stimuli. It gets worse for those of us who have hectic work schedule and very little scope for work-life balance. The final question, then, is, what is the way out?

Research indicates that there are multiple ways in which we can help improve our attention span and enhance our mindfulness that enables us to remain focused on our tasks. Five such ways are:

1. Stop Multitasking
2. Get Regular Exercise
3. Meditate daily
4. Call Mother Nature
5. Reduce Interference

Juggling multiple activities certainly divides our attention among the tasks. Furthermore, we also pay a cognitive "penalty" on top of that to manage the switching. Consequently, we are more prone to errors when we multitask. Additionally, multitasking makes things take longer than they would have if you had done them each separately. However, just avoiding multitasking is not enough to increase our attention span. We need to stay healthy to strengthen our body and mind. In fact, scientists have measured that our cognitive control is better even after a single exercise session. However, while just one exercise session boosts our cognitive control, just one bad night's sleep reduces it. Therefore, if we are sleep-deprived, our ability to focus on the important tasks is greatly reduced. However, the most direct way to improve our attention span is perhaps to meditate.

Meditation, as prescribed by many practitioners, is a process through which we can enhance our cognitive control. However, many of us avoid doing it since we find it difficult to spare time in our already full schedule of working and caring for our family. However, Dr Jan Chozen Bays in her handy popular book *"Mindfulness on the go – simple meditation practices you can do anywhere*[6]*"* offers a few excellent methods of mindfulness. These methods can easily be integrated in our daily schedule and do not require any special arrangements. Dr Bays defines mindfulness as a process that enables us to pay full attention to what is happening around us and within us, i.e., in our body, heart, and mind. She further states that mindfulness is awareness without criticism.

Ways to Improve Our Attention Span

There are several different ways to meditate. One very common way that is often suggested and followed by many is to chant a mantra (it can be anything that we believe in) repeatedly in our mind as we take slow deep breaths. Since some of us may find it difficult to follow for whatever reasons, Dr Bays suggests we take a few minutes to practice mindfulness through our daily routines. She lists down a few ways that enable us to pay attention to what we see, hear, taste, touch, and smell. In other words, we need to be able to fully awaken our five sensory organs to consciously interact with our surroundings. A partial list of which would be as follows:

1. Use your nondominant hand to perform regular tasks This method informs us how impatient we are. Further, it reveals that how strong and unconscious our habits are and how challenging they are to change without awareness and determination. By using our nondominant hand, we can become more flexible and learn new tricks which, in turn, shall enable us to develop new skills.

2. Identify filler words in your conversations with others and try reducing them There are only a few people who have the ability to speak fluently without hesitation. For the rest of us, however, words like "um," "er," and "I mean," (filler words) are a common part of our communication. Linguists do not think that the use of filler words makes us less smart. They observe that we are more conscious of who we are talking to and what we are saying. However, when we use the filler words less and pause less frequently while conversing, we are likely to become more eloquent. Incidentally, this unconscious habit will slowly go away only when we bring the light of awareness to a pattern of filler word usage and we begin to work on this aspect of our conversation and modify it.

3. Pay genuine compliments to people around you Once a day, think of someone we know and give them a genuine compliment on their behaviors, achievements, traits, etc. Since many of us are connected to several others through social media, it is even easier for us to pay compliments to their status updates or photos on Facebook, WhatsApp, Instagram and other social media platforms. In fact, instead of hitting the 'like' button, if we pay a genuine compliment on someone's photo or status updates, we are likely to initiate a pleasant conversation, even if it is a brief one. When we pay compliments to others, we are likely to receive compliments from others. We need to be aware of any compliments others give us. Furthermore, we need to understand the purpose of compliments and the effect on us of being given a compliment. We need to remember that compliments are magic words and they make us feel happy.

4. Actively listen to sounds, music, and stories It is important that we stop a few times a day and listen to sounds around us actively. Listening practice is an important way to quieten the mind. To listen actively, we need to calm down and be quiet for a while. Active listening helps us disengage from the endless ruminations of the anxious mind. Thus, once in a while on a day, listen to either a new music or story intently. For stories, we can resort to audio books.

5. *Say Thank You* Scientists have for long acknowledged the powers of gratitude. In fact, gratitude decreases the stress hormone cortisol in us. Furthermore, a study out of the University of California San Diego's School of Medicine found that grateful people were happier, slept better, had more energy, and had lower levels of inflammatory biomarkers—some of which correlated with heart health.

6. *Stop the Snowball Effect* Time and again, researchers have convincingly proved that dwelling or ruminating over things that have happened or things that may happen is very dangerous. A research article published in the *Journal PLOS One* finds that brooding over negative events is the biggest predictor of issues like depression and anxiety. Additionally, it plays a huge role in how much stress we experience. Keeping ourselves away from past events and future fears are rubrics that are likely to make us cool and serene.

7. *Be Positive in Attitude* We must focus on the positives in life and things for which we are grateful than the things that bother us or the things we do not have. It is beneficial for us to try to be a glass half full instead of a glass half empty. We could try writing down 3 things that went well, or for which we are grateful, at the end of every day. Attitude counts! Many of our problems diminish and are easily solved if we have positive attitude. Thus, we can conserve energy and focus in a better way on things that matter to us.

8. *Enjoy Aromatherapy* Aromatherapy has benefits for stress relief as it can help us feel energized, more relaxed, or more present in the moment. Emerging research indicates certain scents can alter brain wave activity and/or decrease stress hormones in the body. So we need to enjoy candles, diffusers, or body products to incorporate some aromatherapy into our daily lives.

9. *Create Artwork* We all are born creative; but we lose our creativity as we grow up aiming to be successful in our professional life. However, as we grow older, we tend to realize the importance of creativity both in our personal and professional lives. Thus, it is important that we get in touch with our creative side time to time. If we are not into drawing or painting, we could consider coloring in a coloring book. Research suggests that coloring can have a meditative effect. One study found that anxiety levels decline in people who were coloring complex geometric patterns, making it a suitable outlet for stress reduction.

10. *Develop a Positive Self-Talk Habit* The way we talk to ourselves matters because harsh self-criticism, self-doubt, and catastrophic predictions enhance anxiety level and make us stressful. If we constantly think things like, "I don't have time for this," and "I can't stand this," we are very likely to be stressed out. It is important that we learn to talk to ourselves in a more realistic, compassionate, and positive manner. When we doubt our ability to succeed, we need to be able to reply with a kinder inner dialogue. Positive self-talk helps us develop a healthier outlook, and an optimistic and compassionate conversation with ourselves can help us manage our emotions and take positive action.

The above mentioned acts are certainly not an exhaustive list of how we can be more attentive. There are several other ways in which we can practice mindfulness. For that we need to get in touch with expert practitioners. However, if we follow either all or a few of the ten acts suggested above, we are very likely to overcome many of the barriers to listening, such as different types of noises. In communication, noises are those that either hamper or interrupt our attention and, consequently, our communication.

Scholars of communication studies have identified three types of noises that stand as barriers to listening – **physical**, **physiological**, and **psychological**[7]. Physical noises mean any unwanted sound. They are great impediments to carry on communication – especially face-to-face and telephonic conversations. It is difficult to listen in a noisy environment – it becomes a frustrating experience for both the speaker and the listener. In such cases methods of mediation listed above may or may not help us pay attention to the other person's speech much. Therefore, we need to avoid conversations in noisy surroundings and, if possible, eliminate the source of such physical noises whenever possible. Physiological noises relate to our health issues, such as headache, fever, and body pain. Due to these unusual physiological issues, we are often unable to pay attention to what require our attention. For removing these physiological barriers, we need to consult a doctor rather than focusing on mindfulness strategies. However, when we practice mindfulness, we are likely to eliminate many of the psychological barriers, such as prejudice, fear, and ideological misalignment and be able to listen to people who have different opinions and offer different perspectives from what we believe to be true.

Appendix B

Internet-Mediated Organizational Communication

Internet-Mediated Communication in Organizations and its Future

Like many changes experienced in other areas of business either before or after the most recent pandemic, the integration of Internet-Mediated Communication (also known as Computer-Mediated Communication or CMC) brought about unprecedented changes in the way organizations manage their communication processes[1]. From their use in product development to surveys of after sales customer satisfaction, the Internet has been playing crucial roles in the flow of information, not only within individual organizations but also between organizations[2]. Although face-to-face communication is the richest medium of communication, it is very difficult to arrange frequent face-to-face communication for various reasons, such as non-availability of the people at the same time and place for a face-to-face meeting. Therefore, Internet-Mediated Communication (IMC) has replaced many of the traditional forms of business communications[3]. IMC offers interactive processes that facilitate two-way interpersonal communication among individuals or groups. IMC provides instant access to employees working at different places, with the advantage of accessibility to all the relevant information. With the advantages of communication technologies over more traditional modes of communication, the emphasis has increasingly turned to understanding how IMC has affected organizational effectiveness, which in turn would guide us how and how not to incorporate IMC in organizations. Moving forward, we will know more about the relationship between IMC and organizational effectiveness.

What is Organizational Communication?

Organizational communication is a multi-dimensional process through which a group of people attempt to achieve organizational goals. Organizational communication, in plain terms, is a process by which information is exchanged and understood by two or more people, typically with the intent to motivate or influence behavior. In this process, the sender intends to influence the receiver to do what the sender wants[4]. For example, if a team leader wants the team members to work hard for a certain task, he/she may promise to pay some incentives if they successfully accomplish the task within the time limit. Here the team leader motivates the team to work harder in order to gain some incentives. The sender is influencing the receiver to buy into what the sender wants to happen in a specific situation.

Internet-Mediated Organizational Communication **App-B.1**

What Purpose does IMC serve in Organizations?

Although voice communication such as Skype, Zoom and other forms of Voice-over-Internet Protocol (VoIP) transmission have become popular in recent years, text-based IMC is still predominantly used in workplace communications[5]. In fact, email is the most commonly used form of IMC in organizations, and is a powerful communications tool[6]. It plays an important role in organizations as often email is used instead of a written memorandum. Typically, a memorandum, in short memo, is a brief message or record used for internal communication in a business. Once the primary form of internal written communication, memorandums have declined in use since the introduction of email and other forms of electronic messaging. One research that compares email with memo found that organizational emails differed markedly from the memoranda in containing more structural reductions, expressive features, greeting and leave-taking formulas, and instances of linguistic innovation. The popularity of emails over memorandum is argued to be for the following few reasons: 1) linguistic economy in email is tempered by the need to maintain social (phatic) contact between users; 2) email style tends to be less formal than other varieties of written workplace communication; and 3) email contains features traditionally considered 'oral.'[7]

Selection of an Appropriate Medium

The integration of new network technologies and the expansion of the Internet have improved organizations' internal and external communication capabilities. However, the decision to use a telephone, text-based IMC, or VoIP can often be complex because of the many factors involved. The mode of communication chosen by managers is essentially based on how communicative they are. In fact, Richard L. Daft and Robert H. Lengel's **Media richness theory**[8], sometimes referred to as information richness theory or MRT, describes that a communication medium's ability is dependent on how it reproduces the information sent over it. It ranks and evaluates the richness of certain communication media, such as phone calls, VoIP, and text-based IMC. For example, a phone call cannot reproduce visual non-verbal cues such as gestures and emotive expressions which make it a less rich communication channel than VoIP, which affords the transmission of gestures, emotive expressions, and body language. MRT explains that the richer a personal communication media is, the more effective it is for communicating equivocal issues. However, often, other factors, such as the resources available to the communicator, become a deciding factor for an organization as well as an individual to opt one over others. Daft and Lengel assume that managers mostly focus on achieving the communicative goal as efficiently as possible and do not usually take into consideration other factors, such as relationship development and rapport management. However, subsequent researchers have argued that media usage is not always voluntary and one's attitudes towards a medium may not accurately predict a person's likelihood of using that medium over others. In reality, managers are often obliged to abide by the organization's norms and resources that support one medium. Therefore, it may be difficult for a manager to choose a medium of her/his choice to communicate her or his message.

Managers in any communication can feel either attached or removed from each other based on their social presence in the communicative event. **Social presence**[9] refers to the degree to which a medium permits communicators to experience others as being psychologically present. Alternatively, it also indicates the degree to which a medium is perceived to convey the actual presence of the communicating participants. Tasks that require managers to have good interpersonal skills, such as resolving disagreements or negotiation, demand high social presence. In contrast, tasks such as exchanging routine information require less social presence. Therefore, face-to-face group meetings are more appropriate for performing tasks that require high social presence.

Likewise, media such as email and written letters are more appropriate for tasks that require low social presence.

In addition to the Media Richness Theory, in selecting an appropriate medium, managers need to consider the **social influence model**[10]. How to decide where a medium falls on the richness scale, also depends on users' perceptions of media characteristics that are socially created. These characteristics reflect social forces and social norms at play in a given environment and the context that determines the needed use. Each organization is unique in its goal and culture. Thus, with different organizational cultures and environments, the way each organization perceives a medium is different. Consequently, the way each organization uses media and deems media as more or less rich will vary.

Furthermore, communicators need to consider how personal or impersonal a message should be when determining the appropriate media for communication. In general, richer media are more useful in exchanging personal messages as they include various nonverbal and verbal cues, such as body language, inflection, and gestures. These cues, in turn, signal a person's reaction to a message. Thus, rich media is likely to promote a closer relationship between a manager and a subordinate if all other influencing factors remain constant. Additionally, the sentiment of the message may also have an influence on the medium chosen. Typically, managers are advised to communicate negative messages in person or via a richer media, even if the equivocality of the message is not high. This process of sharing negative messages is more likely to facilitate better relationships with subordinates than sharing it through any leaner medium. Generally, it is observed that sending a negative message over a leaner medium would weaken the immediate blame on the message sender and prevent him from observing the reaction of the receiver.

As current business models continue to evolve, allowing more employees to work outside the office, organizations need to rethink about the reliance on face-to-face communication. Furthermore, the fear of more lean channels' ineffectiveness must be rid of. In this current pandemic context, managers have no option but to decide through trial and error which medium is best suited for a situation. For example, an employee who works from the office vs. an employee who works outside the office. Business is being conducted on a global scale. The world has finally realized that they are better off being interdependent on each other rather than just looking inwards. In order to save various types of energy including money and cut back on travel time, organizations must adopt new media pragmatically in order to stay up-to-date with business functions in the modern times.

Internet-Supported Collaborative Learning

What is Collaborative Learning?

There are several approaches to effective learning and one of them is collaborative learning. Collaborative learning is a fundamental educational approach to teaching and learning. It involves groups of learners working together to solve a problem, complete a task, or create a product. J M Gerlach, a reputed scholar in the field of education, explains that collaborative learning has a social component[11]. It is based on the idea that learning is a naturally social act in which the learners talk among themselves. It is through the talk that learning occurs.

Computer-Supported Collaborative Learning (CSCL)

As the business models continue to evolve, face-to-face meetings in a shared physical space are increasingly becoming a difficult proposition for organizations. Therefore, organizations are bound to find alternative ways to hold meetings including brainstorming sessions that promote learning for participants. One such effective means is computer-supported collaborative learning (CSCL)[12]. It is a pedagogical approach wherein learning takes place via social interaction among managers using their inter-connected computers through the Internet or other means. Although CSCL is typically used in classroom learning environments either synchronously or asynchronously, it can also be used for intra or inter organizational training and learning purposes. Synchronous Internet-supported communication requires immediate responses which limit the use of outside resources while asynchronous communication supports delayed interactions. Depending on the time sensitivity of the task as well as depth of knowledge required to complete the task, organizations need to decide whether to go for synchronous or asynchronous Internet-supported collaborative learning.

In the recent past, this approach of learning was adopted in teaching an online Managerial Communication course to 119 business executives at the Indian Institute of Management Kozhikode by one of the authors. The executives were located at different cities in India owing to their jobs. They were placed in 12 different groups and each group had ten members. The composition of the group was guided by the diversity factors. It is a well-known fact that learners benefit when exposed to diverse viewpoints from people with varied backgrounds. Thus, the groups were formed based on executives' educational background, nature and duration of work experience, sex, and personality traits. While information related to education, work experience, and sex was readily available, the executives' personality traits were assessed through the responses to a set of behavioral questions. Subsequently, they were categorized into one of the following four dominant personality types:

Driver — a fact-based extrovert person

Analytical — a fact-based introvert person

Amiable — an introvert person who focuses on relational issues

Expressive — an extrovert person who focuses on relational issues

Drivers are very strong personalities. Typically, they are high on energy and achievement-oriented. However, what is negative about them is that they can sometimes come across as stubborn or arrogant. **Analytical types** are constantly assessing, determining pros and cons, and making lists of to-do items. They are the ones who constantly ask questions, almost to the point of getting too much information. Others see them as people with brilliant ideas. However, they can suffer from analysis paralysis, i.e., analyzing situations too much. As for the **amiable personality types**, they are very calm. They are usually laid back and are hard to excite. Moreover, they seem relaxed all the time and desire a peaceful environment over anything else. They will go out of their way not to upset people. Amiable types will often wait until the last minute to make decisions and will often go with what everyone else is doing. **Expressive personality types** are seen as people persons. They thrive on socializing and talking. They are great story tellers. Furthermore, they are good at communicating vision, getting others excited about ideas and issues. However, they often overcommit themselves in an attempt to please people. Thus, they, sometimes, cannot be relied upon to get things done.

As much as possible, these four different types were evenly distributed to each group. Subsequently, each group was asked to form a WhatsApp group and study and analyze a business case among the group members on their respective WhatsApp group. They were given a week's time to do so and the members were instructed to analyze the case only through text-chat and nothing else. Afterward, each group submitted a typed case analysis report to the instructor for evaluation.

A few screenshots of the actual WhatsApp discussion from a group are displayed below to illustrate how the team has achieved what they were meant to achieve through this collaborative learning experience.

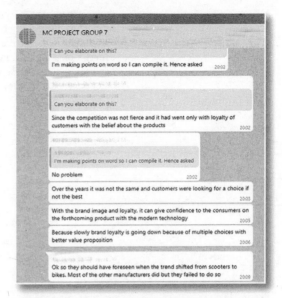

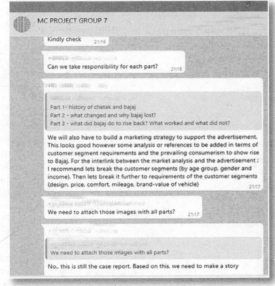

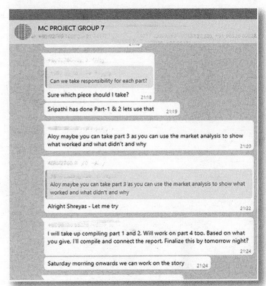

After closely analyzing the collaborative case discussions of all the 12 groups, a few important points related to computer-supported collaborative Case Study emerged.

It is very much possible to have an effective collaborative problem solving session involving spatially distributed people through computer-supported learning environment. Since learning requires challenges that open the door for the learners to actively engage her/his peers, it is important to create groups in such a way that promotes diversity of knowledge, thoughts, and perspectives. This process of learning helps learners to process and synthesize information rather than simply memorize and regurgitate it. Furthermore, it was observed that learning flourishes in a social environment such as WhatsApp chat where text-based conversations between learners take place. During this intellectual gymnastics, the learners created a framework and meaning to the discourse.

In this experimental exercise, the learners were challenged both socially and emotionally as they listened to different perspectives, and were required to articulate and defend their ideas. In so doing, they began to create their own unique conceptual frameworks and not rely solely on an expert's or a text's framework. Thus, in this collaborative learning setting, learners had the opportunity to converse with peers, present and defend ideas, exchange diverse beliefs, question other conceptual frameworks, and remain actively engaged for a week.

Computer-Supported Collaborative Case Study Exercise

A Note for the Instructors

For replicating the method of computer-supported collaborative learning, the learners can be placed in multiple groups based on their level of knowledge, experience, socio-economic background, sex/gender, and if feasible, assessment of their personality types. After this, a case of the instructor's choice that is appropriate for the learners' age can be shared with each group. The group will be advised to create a WhatsApp group including all the group members and the instructor. While the group members need to study and analyze the case on the respective WhatsApp group textually, the instructor needs to remain a silent spectator. The timeframe for solving the problem and presenting their ideas either in writing or through an oral presentation shall be fixed after due diligence.

Below is a marketing communication case that can be utilized for this collaborative experiment. The learners can be asked to prepare a marketing communication report based on this case.

Buland Bharat Ki Buland Tasveer – The Case of Bajaj Chetak

(A hypothetical case based on information collected from various newspaper articles)

The Bajaj Chetak was a popular Indian-made motor scooter produced by Bajaj Auto Limited. The scooter is named after Chetak, the legendary horse of Indian warrior Rana Pratap Singh. Originally based on Italian Vespa Sprint, Chetak was an affordable means of transportation for millions of Indian families for decades and is lovingly called Hamara Bajaj (Our Bajaj). 'Hamara Bajaj'—a campaign that fuelled pride in the brand that aspired to be a global player. However, in the face of rising competition from bikes and cars, Chetak lost ground in India, and production was discontinued in 2009. Lately, Bajaj Auto is believed to be re-entering the scooter segment. The report states that the Bajaj Auto is redesigning its iconic 'Chetak' in a modern avatar to capture the lost market. The big question is, whether it will be able to regain its lost glory.

Overview of the Company

Founded in 1926, at the height of India's movement for independence from the British, the group has an illustrious history. Kamalnayan Bajaj, then 27, took over the reins of business in 1942. The present Chairman of the group, Rahul Bajaj, took charge of the business in 1965. Under his leadership, the turnover of the Bajaj Auto, the flagship company, has gone up from INR 72 million to INR 120 billion, its product portfolio has expanded and the brand has found a global market.

Bajaj Auto came into existence on 29 November 1945 as M/s Bachraj Trading Corporation Private Limited. It started off by selling imported two- and three-wheelers in India. In 1959, it obtained a license from the Government of India to manufacture two-wheelers and three-wheelers and it became a public limited company in 1960. In 1970, it rolled out its 100,000[th] vehicle. In 1977, it sold 100,000 vehicles in a financial year. In 1985, it started producing at Waluj near Aurangabad. In 1986, it sold 500,000 vehicles in a financial year. In 1995, it rolled out its ten millionth vehicle and produced and sold one million vehicles in a year.

With the launch of motorcycles in 1986, the company has changed its image from a scooter manufacturer to a two-wheeler manufacturer.

Once the country's undisputable scooter czars, the Bajaj's saw the ground move away from under their feet in the late 90s when customers shifted dramatically from buying scooters to buying motorcycles. Before this, Bajaj was used to customers queuing up for its products, not saying no to it. Change had to be brought in to survive. On taking over the operational control of the company from Rahul Bajaj, his sons, Rajiv and Sanjiv, made a major overhaul in the way the company operated and also on how it developed a market orientation by understanding customer needs through proper research. This resulted in the conceptualization of the Pulsar and Discover which addressed the needs of the customers to have a bike with rugged styling and more power. The products took the markets by storm and started eating away at other competitors' products and achieved a market share of 28% by 2004–05.

But by his own admission, Rajiv Bajaj was in all kinds of trouble in 2008—three years after he took over as Managing Director and CEO of Bajaj Auto. The company had a string of failures with the XCD, Caliber and Wind. It hurt even more because the company had always prided itself on being a market leader. In 2008, the situation at Bajaj Auto was uncertain and Rajiv Bajaj had to take a decisive call about Bajaj Chetak.

The Recent Past

Rahul Bajaj, President of Bajaj Auto, said during an interview that he was 'hurt' by his son's decision to stop production of scooters. However, son Rajiv opined that solutions should come more from logic than emotions.

Rajiv Bajaj, who took over the reins of the Rs. 8,500-crore group as Managing Director in 2005, had said that scooter production would be stopped to pave way for augmenting growth in the motorcycle segment as part of the company's aim to become the world's biggest bike maker in future.

Differentiate or Die

Sometime in 2008, when Bajaj Auto was on a sticky wicket, CEO Rajiv Bajaj, addressed his top generals, with a copy of Jack Trout's *Differentiate or Die* in his hands. The young Bajaj read out passages for a good 90 minutes, expounding the key messages gleaned, why Bajaj Auto was floundering, and how some of Trout's theories could come in handy. Finally, as Bajaj wrapped up the last chapter, Tom Ishikawa, a Japanese executive who had joined Bajaj Auto from Yamaha, said to Rajiv Bajaj that all he had said was ok, but that was just a book. But Bajaj was quickly disillusioned with modern management science as the failure rate of new products still exceeded 90%. At that point of time, he had also been grappling with a question: the Japanese (Sony), or Korean (LG) or Taiwanese companies, which had mastered technology, quality, efficiency and productivity, weren't making money. Why? He turned to unlikely places – yoga, homeopathy and even philosophers, like Seneca and Confucius – to glean management lessons. Rajiv finally learned a lesson when he was reading Trout's and Steve Rivkin's *Differentiate or*

Die. He understood that people don't actually buy products, they buy brands. Further, he stated that if we take the brand out of the equation, we reduce everything to the product level . Rajiv realized that brands that are more sharply positioned are the ones that are more profitable. It (scooter) is not a really profitable market and thus he decided to discontinue it. He, however, hinted the company might one day come back into the scooter segment, stating that Bajaj Auto has some good ideas on how to bring back the magic of a new kind of scooter. He wished to come back on the strength of a new category and with it he optimistically stated that they will not only have a scooter business but also a very profitable scooter business.

By focusing entirely on the motorcycle segment and thus ignoring scooter altogether, Bajaj has lost a big opportunity. During all the slowdown, it is the scooter segment, especially variants from Honda Motorcycle & Scooter India Pvt. Ltd. (HMSI), the unit of Japanese Honda Motor Co Ltd. which had kept its volumes soaring. In fact, even today, there is a certain waiting period (varies from location to location and dealer to dealer, but about one month) for Honda Activa, which is now into its third generation mode. Not only that, scooters made by Hero MotoCorp (erstwhile Hero Honda), TVS Motor Co Ltd., Suzuki Motorcycle India Pvt. Ltd., Mahindra Two Wheelers Ltd. and Vespa are also selling like hot cakes. In fact, it was the delay in delivery by Honda that seems to have helped others, especially Suzuki, TVS Motors and Mahindra to capture a significant market share. Unfortunately, Bajaj, once the 'king of scooters', was nowhere in the picture. According to the Society of Indian Automobile Manufacturers (SIAM), in February 2015 scooter volumes jumped 18.8% to 3.70 lakh units from 3.12 lakh units, same month last year. At the same time, motorcycle volumes declined 8.22% to 7.77 lakh units. Even the cumulative figures between April 2014 and February 2015 are in favor of scooters. Data from SIAM shows during the 11 months of Fiscal Year 2015, scooter volumes grew 26.6% to 41.1 lakh units, while motorcycle sales increased marginally 3.2% to 98.84 lakh units. Another interesting take-out from the SIAM report is that except Bajaj, all other two-wheeler makers are present across categories, be it Honda, Hero MotoCorp, TVS Motors, Suzuki or Mahindra. In short, by balancing their offerings in both scooters and motorcycles, these manufacturers are making sure to survive unexpected setbacks from each category. Since Bajaj exited from scooters, it did not have the same benefit and had to depend solely on motorcycle sales. Therefore, the company is making a comeback with its iconic 'Chetak' in a new, modern avatar. The new Chetak is being redesigned with a four-stroke, single-cylinder and air-cooled engine, displacing somewhere in the region of 125-150cc. Additionally, it is expected to offer gearless ease, unlike old Chetak scooters. The big question is, will Rahul Bajaj's 'magic of logic' comeback into its once 'famed' scooter segment make his father Rahul Bajaj smile again?

Nostalgia

Some brands become part of national consciousness. As Bajaj scooter rode into history, the country saw a kind of emotional outpouring as if a family member is no more. Spin-doctors are calling it a generational shift linking it to the change of guard in the Bajaj family, but for the man on the street it is the demise of his trusted Chetak. Almost everybody has a Bajaj moment to share. Rajesh Khanna reminisces how he took his newly- wed all the way from Aligarh to Hissar on his Chetak with the luggage. "I had a kind of belief that it will not ditch me. After all, my father rode his Bajaj Cub till he died at the age of 75." Medical student Ranbir Malik relates how his faith in his father's scooter multiplied the day he travelled from Mathura to Delhi to appear in CBSE Medical entrance. "There was a bus strike but my father was confident that the scooter will see us through. The stepney (spare wheel) used to add to the confidence."

Adman Prahlad Kakkar puts things in perspective. When asked about the scooter, he stated that the scooter was originally designed for the young, but in India Bajaj and the advertising agencies hyped it as a family vehicle. It worked because women loved it for the space it offered on the pillion seat and the variety of things one can carry on scooter. As it began to lose out to relatively sturdy and racy bikes, the company did try to reinvent it with four stroke and gearless scooters. They did manage to attract girls from the pillion to the front seat but lost the young male customer. Suddenly, young males had plenty of options and nobody can beat a Bajaj no longer remains a fact.

As for emotional connect, R. Balki, Chairman of Lowe India, the agency which created the legendary *Hamara Bajaj* campaign stated that the '*Humara Bajaj*' commercial would have worked for any other vehicle as well. Bajaj didn't mean scooters; it meant it made vehicles which the nation drove. At that time it was scooters, now it is motorcycles. Kakkar holds that the swagger and the connect came from the fact that it was the first 'thet' (desi) brand that gave us enhanced mobility after Hero cycles. Though initially the technology came from Italian Vespa, there was no Vespa or Suzuki attached to the brand.

Over the years, the generation which believed in *Buland Bharat ki buland tasveer* has lost out to a fill it, shut it, forget it generation. Kakkar says the company could reinvent the brand as an antique vehicle for export market like Bullet and Harley Davidson.

Anupam Batra, technical in-charge at a Bajaj service station, says, "It worked for a generation when the service station culture had not set in and the vehicles were easily maintained by the neighborhood mechanic. The low maintenance cost and long life contributed to its popularity. It used to be a great option to gift to the groom." Anupam indicates towards the changing decision makers in Indian families. "Earlier, it was the head of the family who used to decide what's good for the family. Today, it's the youngsters who prefer fashionable vehicles with speed. Also, technically speaking, mileage, placement of engine and wheel base tilted the balance in bikes' favor."

Rakesh Mohan, manager of a Bajaj showroom, says, "Though practically the scooter is not in the showrooms in the National Capital Region (i.e, Delhi and adjacent satellite citieslike Gurugram and Noida) for years, we still get queries about Chetak. Mostly it is from the middle-aged people. They get shocked when I say we no longer sell Chetak."

However, the Internet, the medium of expression for the young, is full of sentimental messages. Neha Dhupia, a young college student, writes, "My dad had a Bajaj Priya for 13 years, followed by a Chetak for 16 full years before we kind of blackmailed him to switch to a Honda Activa. This news makes me so sad! Brings in a gushing load of memories." Perhaps the youth connect comes from the fact that for many of us it was the first motor vehicle in life and the one on which we polished our driving skills. "My uncle booked it for himself. After patiently waiting for days when he got it, he realized Chetak was too high for his comfort. My father bought it from him. I used to clean it for Abbu every morning and loved standing in the spacious front. Then one day he decided to teach me. I carried on the tradition when my brother started feeling the rush of hormones," says Shahid Ali, another college student, showcasing the 1988-model. "Its strength has been an inspirational factor. I can still exert all my weight on its chassis. You can't do it with new versions. Now we use it for carrying load for our pharmaceuticals business." At the Ghazipur crossing in Delhi you can see meat vendors carrying loads of chicken, and Pizza delivery boys rely on scooters for keeping pace with the quick delivery time their companies promise.

Bajaj Chetak does not seem to be lacking masculine appeal. Shah Rukh Khan drove it when he played a docile government babu, Suriji in *Rab Ne Bana De Jodi* and Ranvir Kapoor in *Rocket Singh* carried his crusade against corruption on a scooter gifted by his grandfather. Model Milind Soman, who loves to drive a gearless scooter, says it's a marketing gimmick to present bikes as a masculine option.

Hamara Bajaj Campaign

When the new version of '*Hamara Bajaj*.' was launched in 2001, the younger generation had a sort of *déjà vu* because they faintly remembered the music and the words. However, they quickly fell in love with the new fast paced music and feel of the film. The older generation had a nostalgic moment because they were transported back to the times when '*Hamara Bajaj*' presented a mirror to their old middle class aspirations. One can watch the old *'Hamara Bajaj'* promotional campaign on YouTube.

R. Balki, chairman and CEO of Lowe (which has worked on the iconic campaign *'Hamara Bajaj'* and continues to handle the account till today), feels that Bajaj captures the spirit of India every time. He seems to think that right in the beginning, Bajaj was the vehicle that India rode on. Old *'Hamara Bajaj'* captured the mood and aspirations of the country then. While tracing the evolution of the campaign, one could notice that in 2001, the same theme *'Hamara Bajaj'* was re-launched and this time it was a perfect combination of India being a global player and still preserving its roots. The campaign was for the Bajaj bikes. In 2007, *'Hamara Bajaj'* for Pulsar 220 was when India was exploring biking. This campaign was about competing with oneself and once again, it captured the spirit of India. It was further observed that the first part was about patriotism. The second was to show that India was a global player and it assimilates from the west while maintaining its roots. The third part is about that the fact that 'We are good. Now let's be better than ourselves.' Thus, India's evolution has been tied up with Bajaj's evolution.

Re-Branding through Visual Narratives

In order to address the big question, an idea needs to be generated that will help Chetak differentiate itself from its competitors. It is argued that for re-branding Chetak, a television commercial needs to be conceptualized that would appeal to potential consumers. To make an advertisement popular, advertisers must construct narratives that are recognizable to viewers; moreover, they must produce narratives that are sufficiently compelling that viewers are motivated to decipher them. Both advertisers and the viewers apply a social grammar – a shared set of propositions about how commercials are structured and how the narrative of a commercial will unfold.

Fam and Waller (2006) reported that Indians favor funny, humorous, lively, and entertaining television advertisements that have a storyline. In addition, they noted that settings with a touch of warmth, happiness, refreshing atmosphere, and adherence to tradition draw viewers' attention. Consequently, a story writing exercise is planned to elicit the most compelling narrative for re-branding Chetak. You are required to come up with a compelling story that would help Chetak regain its lost glory. The following guidelines are for the participants.

Guidelines

First, each group needs to produce an analytical case report of the case that will be the foundation of your story. The report must be written in a word document and it shall not exceed 1000 words. Next, based on your case analysis report, each group needs to conceptualize a story interpreting the set of images that are appended below. A group of artists and creative writers believed these images, if interpreted from different perspectives and then arranged in a meaningful order, could potentially help one write a story for Chetak. No additional images are required and all the images in the set must be used at least once; however, if required one or more images may be used multiple times.

The images are marked (as Image A, Image B and so on) for you to identify them easily. However, the marking of the images **does not** indicate any particular sequence. You are required to re-arrange them to create a logical coherence between scenes/events of the story. There are a few common techniques that are used to structure a relevant plot. A plot is the sequence of events that make up a narrative. The common techniques include backstory, flashback, flash-forward, and foreshadowing. Common techniques relevant to narrative perspective, or who is telling the story, include first person, second person, third person, and third-person omniscient.

Your story needs to have three components.

1. **The title**
2. **The fictional narrative**
3. **The tagline**

Your story will be evaluated based on the following two criteria.

(A) Analysis of the case and

(B) Narrative style and structure

An effective narrative draws and retains readers' attention. Consequently, it shall have recall value.

The following two figures illustrate the fundamental framework of a story. While conceptualizing a plot and subsequently the story/narrative, please follow either of the two frameworks.

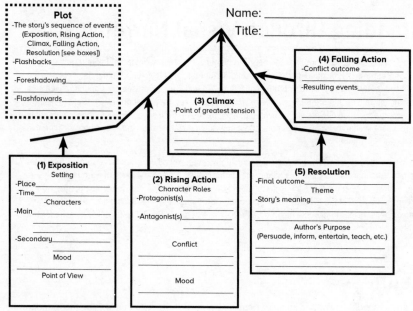

Plot
-The story's sequence of events (Exposition, Rising Action, Climax, Falling Action, Resolution [see boxes])
-Flashbacks_____
-Foreshadowing_____
-Flashforwards_____
_____

Name: _____
Title: _____

(3) Climax
-Point of greatest tension
_____
_____
_____
_____

(4) Falling Action
-Conflict outcome _____
_____
-Resulting events_____
_____
_____
_____

(1) Exposition
Setting
-Place_____
-Time_____
-Characters
-Main_____
_____
_____
-Secondary_____
_____
Mood
_____
Point of View

(2) Rising Action
Character Roles
-Protagonist(s)_____
_____
-Antagonist(s)_____
_____
Conflict
_____
_____
_____
Mood
_____

(5) Resolution
-Final outcome_____
Theme
-Story's meaning_____
_____
_____
Author's Purpose
(Persuade, inform, entertain, teach, etc.)
_____
_____
_____

Figure 1 *Mono-Act Narrative Structure*

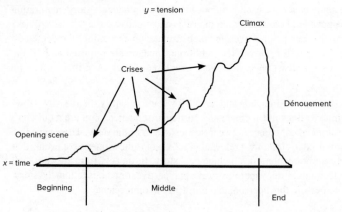

Figure 2 *Three-Act Narrative Structure*

Image A

Image B

Image C

Image D

Image E

Image F

Image G

Image H

Critical Crisis Communication

What is a Crisis?

Crisis is typically understood as either an event or activity that is expected to lead to an unstable and unfavorable situation affecting an individual, group, or whole organization[1]. The word 'crisis' is believed to be linked to two Chinese words – Danger and Opportunity. Thus, with each danger comes an opportunity to resolve it. On the one hand, a crisis can help an organization grow stronger than before if it is addressed appropriately on time while, on the other, a crisis can be the reason for the destruction of an organization or a group if it is not managed properly. Crisis Management is a well thought-out process by which an organization deals with a major event that threatens to harm the organization, its stakeholders, or the general public[2]. There are three elements that are common to most crisis situations. First of all, it threatens the organization in many ways. Further, there would always be elements of surprises that routine events and activities do not have. Finally, there is usually a short window to address it adequately[3]. The first step to manage a crisis is to be able to identify and accept that there is one. A crisis can typically be classified as one among the following six types[4].

Natural crisis It is a crisis that occurs due to natural disasters, e.g., four people died, over five were left injured after a major fire broke out in the storm water drainage in the Uran plant of Oil and Natural Gas Corporation (ONGC).

Organizational Misdeed crisis These types of crises occur when management takes actions that harm stakeholders without suitable precautions, e.g., Yes Bank has experienced serious governance issues and practices in the recent years which have led to steady decline of the bank.

Deception crisis A crisis of this nature occurs due to lack of transparency from the management about certain information, e.g., Enron and Satyam Computer Services hid financial losses from the stakeholders and went bankrupt.

Workplace violence crisis A crisis of this nature occurs when a member or a group of members commits violence to other members, e.g., Maruti Suzuki's General Manager, Human Resources, was burned to death in the violence in its car plant in Manesar (near Gurgaon, Haryana) allegedly triggered by the workers for which 91 workers were arrested. A worker allegedly beat him up following which the worker was suspended and that triggered the large-scale violence.

Skewed values crisis Such types of crises occur when short term economic gains are sought by neglecting social values, stakeholders and investors. Typically, it arises when the business pays more attention to revenue over its functioning and its commitment to customers or employees or to the world.

Rumors crisis A crisis may occur when false information about an organization and its product hurts the organization's reputation.

Despite having such objective classification of crisis, there may be situations that may not be strictly categorized into one or the other. In some cases there may be elements of more than one type of crisis. In a complex situation where more than one type of crisis is present, one needs to do further due diligence to prepare for the crisis.

In preparing for the crisis, one needs to focus on two primary areas – **Vulnerability Assessment** and **Crisis Planning**[5]. In assessing the potential damage that might have been caused by the crisis, one needs to determine current and potential areas of operational and communications weakness. Subsequently, one needs to plan how to control the damage. There are crucial steps that need to be followed. The first step of planning involves **operational issues**, i.e., **what we do, who does it, and when it is done**. Furthermore, one needs to appropriately communicate the message to the aggrieved stakeholders to lead the crisis situation to an acceptable outcome. In doing so, organizations need to deliberate on what to communicate, who to communicate the message, and finally how they get the messages out. However, getting the appropriate messages out will require due diligence. Thus, an effective crisis response needs to include a set of response modules, preset activation protocols and clear communication channels.

Crisis Communication on Social Media

With the popularity of web 2.0, especially social media, the focus of organizational crises management has somewhat shifted from the way crisis communication was handled traditionally. Social media crises are largely on reputational concerns[6]. An organization mishandles a social media crisis often when it fails to assess the nature of the crisis and thus it uses inappropriate communication strategies. Consider the following hypothetical case. One of the oldest and widely known name in fine dining restraunts, Mugambo causes outrage for refusing to serve customer and her not-so-elite driver. On a Saturday, Jhanvi decided to have dinner in the restaurant with her driver Ishaan, but was shocked when she was told that he wouldn't be allowed inside. She wrote about the incident on Facebook, which has been shared over 15,800 times since.

A Business Executive, Jhanvi wrote:

"How hollow and inhuman have we become?

Last night being my last day in Mumbai, I decided to try out this popular restaurant called Mugambo. I went with my driver – Ishaan bhaiya there. Ishaan bhaiya's great service and care throughout my stay in Mumbai for a week was superb. (Also through this act I wanted to lessen my burden of guilt. In one of the afternoons during my stay in Mumbai, Ishaan bhaiya missed his lunch because I forgot to tell him to go for lunch – uncertain about the time it would take me to finish the meeting – and he missed his lunch.)

As soon as I reached Mugambo at around 8:25 PM, I asked the staff to give me a table for 2.

Staff: There is a waiting of 10 to 15 minutes.

Me: *As I was excited to try out this popular restaurant* happily agreed.

Staff: *By this time they observed I was with Ishaan bhaiya* walked up to me and said it would take 45 minutes to an hour for the table to get ready.

Me: *Little confused by time communicated earlier* now eagerly asked, but you said 10 to 15 minutes?

Staff: Yes, the table was going to get empty, but they ordered more food.

Me: *Peeping through the transparent windows* but I can see some empty tables inside.

Staff: They are four seaters. Today is Friday so we cannot give that table.

Me: Ok.

After waiting for 10-15 minutes, when I see people coming after me getting the table.

Me: Why are you not giving me the table?

Staff: Maam, we can't give you a table.

Me: But why?

Staff: Who are you with?

Me: Subtly pointing towards Ishaan bhaiya.

Staff: Aahhh....Maam he is not suitably dressed .

*Me: *He was cleanly dressed in a blue trousers and a white shirts tucked out ... And floaters**

I asked what Mugambo's dress code was.

Staff: We don't have a dress code.

Me: Then?

Staff: I'm sorry, Mam. He is not appropriately dressed for a fine dine restaurant.

*Me: *Agitated by now* What's wrong with his dressing? Do you have a written dress code that he is not following?*

By this time Ishaan bhaiya understood parts of the conversation in English and by the daunting looks of the staff -walks up to me and says – 'Didi, hum nahi khaenge aap khana kha lijiyega na .'(Meaning, Mam, I will not eat, you please go ahead and have your food.)

*Me: *Touched by his innocence, and hurt by the inhuman inconsiderate behavior of the staff at Mugambo **

Me: Call your manager. I need a valid reason why he cannot come in.

Staff: Goes and calls another person.

Me: Sir, why can't he come in?

Staff: Well, he is drunk.

*Me: *Furious and baffled by the audacity of the staff* How do you know he is drunk?*

Staff: Because I could make out from his appearance.

*Me: On what basis do you make such assumptions? Did he drink in front of you or did you even go near him *they were standing 2-3 meters apart* He is driving me around since 9 o clock in the morning. Leave apart being drunk, he is not even had food.*

Staff: But I know he is drunk.

Me: Prove it then.

Me: What's your name?

Staff: I can't tell you my name.

Me: Why?

Staff: I'm sorry. I just can't let you in with him.

Me: I don't want to get into your obnoxious restaurant.

I walked away with Ishaan bhaiya with deep grief in my heart on how inhuman and hollow the world has become.

Ishaan bhaiya is one of the finest human beings I have met in a long time. He took good care of me and did his duty with all his heart. He is a simple man, makes Rs375 a day for 12 hours of driving, and sends more than half of the money back home. He has a difficult life, still he laughs a lot, shares a lot of stories, and is more human and empathetic than many I know.

To Mugambo staff and restaurant that doesn't consider humans as humans and differentiates, discriminates and stratifies them into classes just because they do not fit into your description of a perfect customer (doesn't own an iPhone, maybe doesn't talk in English), I'm sorry you don't deserve a fine human like Ishaan bhaiya sitting and eating in your obnoxious restaurant.

In their defence, Mugambo issued the following public statement.

"The driver was very indecently dressed. He was wearing one pant and shirt. Moreover, he was not in proper state. He was having roadside food and just standing, not in proper state of mind. We couldn't allow him in our fine dining restaurant. We told her (Ms Jhanvi) we cannot give her driver a table, but we can give her one. We've such high standard guests coming here, it's a fine dining restaurant, we cannot have such a roadsider coming and sitting here."

"We do not have a dress code. But at least a person should be neat and clean. He was having roadside food while walking around and grazing people. We don't entertain such types of people in to our restaurant, This is not a dhaba."

After further inquiry it appeared that neither the driver's clothes and behaviour nor the fact that he was eating *road-side food* were the real offences. The only reason, which the management at Mugambo repeatedly stated was that the driver wasn't given a table because he was a "roadsider" which made him a less privileged social class.

In a situation like this, the stakeholders, in this case a portion of actual and potential customers, appeared to have perceived that *Mugambo's* behaviors and/or policies are inappropriate, irresponsible and discriminatory. This negative perception generated out of the social media narrative of one of the customers and subsequently Mugambo's attempt to refute the claim made by the customer did harm the reputation of Mugambo, even if it was temporary in nature.

Certainly, in organizational crisis the notion of challenge is multidimensional. Scholars of crisis management, such as Coombs, have identified three types of challenges: (1) **organic**, (2) **expose**, and (3) **villain**. Having stated that, a crisis may have all three of these challenges either present at the same time or may appear one after the other. Implications for crisis communication may vary depending on the nature of the challenges as they impact how the reputation is affected and how best to respond to the challenges. An organic challenge occurs when an organization is either unable to identify or fails to meet the stakeholders' expectations appropriately. For example, when a hospital, in order to manage the initial screening of the patients, introduced a mandatory automated screening process through an AI induced robot instead of human intervention, many elderly patients felt uncomfortable and intimidated. Gradually, the hospital started losing many of their loyal customers.

An expose challenge arises when the stakeholders argue that an organization's claims are inconsistent with its actions. For example, while most malls in India claim to be modern and are designed to cater to the needs of their stakeholders of all kinds, a recent incident in a popular mall revealed that many of the malls in India do not have even the secluded space for breastfeeding. On a Sunday, when a young mother Tua Das needed to breastfeed her child in a Central City Mall, she was denied a private space by storekeepers and security staff despite repeated pleas before an apparel storekeeper offered her a private space. The Facebook posts— the young mom's plaint and the response from one of the India's biggest malls—had gone viral. This incident brought into focus one of the most urgent needs that often go ignored at public spaces in India. The posts also triggered a public outcry that forced the mall officials on the defensive. An attempt to issue an "unconditional apology" was met with such anger that the mall management had to remove the feedback option from its page.

The villain challenge typically leads to a series of arguments between an organization and a specific group of stakeholders. Usually the stakeholders are professional activists who have a long-standing dispute with an organization. The stakeholders' goal is to inform and convince the larger community of the organization's misdeeds and thus project it as a villain that needs to reform its evil ways. For instance, Kodaikanal mercury poisoning[7] is a case of mercury contamination at the hill station of Kodaikanal by Hindustan Unilever in the process of making mercury thermometers. Although Hindustan Unilever claims to be an environment friendly company, they failed to adhere to protocols when disposing off mercury waste in their unit in Kodaikanal. The factory imported mercury from the United States, and exported finished thermometers to markets in the United States and Europe. Around 2001, a number of workers at the factory started having kidney and related ailments[8]. Public interest groups such as Tamil Nadu Alliance Against Mercury (TNAAC) suspected some foul play on the part of Hindustan Unilever. Subsequently, in early 2001, public interest groups unearthed a pile of broken glass thermometers with remains of Mercury from an interior part of the shola forest, which,they alleged, could have come from the company. In March 2001, a public protest led by local workers' union and international environmental organization Greenpeace forced the company to shut down the factory[9]. This revelation of the environmental abuse led to the closure of the factory in 2001 and opened up a series of issues in India such as corporate liability, corporate accountability and corporate negligence.

Crisis Communication Strategies

Managers resort to one or more of the following four communication strategies to respond to these types of challenges: (1) **refutation**, (2) **repression**, (3) **reform**, and (4) **repentance**. The refutation strategy attempts to invalidate the challenge. For example, in the Mugambo case, the management evidently made an attempt to refute the claims of the aggrieved customer. The repression strategy seeks to prevent stakeholders from making others aware of their challenge. This form of crisis communication attempts to silence challengers either by lawsuits or other form of intimidation. Scholars of crisis communication argue that this form of communication is potentially dangerous since it precludes the free exchange of ideas and creates the impression of censorship. Typically other stakeholders tend to react negatively to the repression strategy, leaving a scope for backlash against the organization. The reform strategy admits that there is a violation of expectations and explains how the organization is trying to meet those expectations. For instance, when the top management of the Central City Mall realized that the initial rude reaction to the aggrieved Tua Das's Facebook compliant in the Central City Mall went viral and the Mall's reputation was in question, the management quickly made an unconditional apology to all the stakeholders on their Facebook page. This is what they had written in their apology post on their Facebook page:

> Dear Patrons,
>
> Please accept our unconditional apology for the remark/comment made by one of our agents in accordance to the feedback/comment written by our very valuable visitor in relation to her inconvenience for feeding the baby.
>
> Please find attached the response made by the Central City Management yesterday night at around 10:30 pm upon noticing the remark made by our Agent handling the Facebook page. We have provision for Baby changing/feeding room, Kids toilet, etc. on every floor. Unfortunately, as the Mall is partly operational and partly under renovation, all services are not active. However, one Baby Changing room on the 1st level along with Kids Toilet is available.
>
> We clarify that Central City tries to take care of the smallest requirement a Patron would need at the Mall at any time and we would continue to strive to look after our patrons. It is our agent who, without knowing the facts, made such a comment in response to the feedback of our Patron. Please be informed that we have taken the duly required action against the same yesterday itself.
>
> Once again we apologize for the inconvenience caused to the patron concerned despite all the amenities available at the Mall. We never intend to hurt anyone's sentiment and/or disrespect.
>
> #CentralCityMall #anamivapal #TrinaGuhaMallik

The repentance strategy is most useful with the exposed challenges. Normally in an exposed challenge, management admits its claims were exaggerated and is working to meet the expectations the organization had claimed to be meeting. However, in a situation like this the management must sincerely put effort to rectify the mistake and meet the expectations of the stakeholders. For example, Nestle India Limited (NIL) in May 2015 witnessed a nation-wide food scare. One of their most popular food products Maggi became the bone of contention. Maggi claims to have 'No Monosodium Glutamate', commonly known as MSG, in it[10]. However, in March, 2014, a Maggi sample was sent for test in Gorakhpur, Uttar Pradesh and the lab analyst found samples of lead and MSG. Next, NIL took the samples for further tests to a central food laboratory in Kolkata where illegal levels of lead were found[11]. Consequently, NIL was advised to recall Maggi products in Uttar Pradesh in June 2015. However, soon after this Nestle held a press conference after testing 125 million packets and claimed that the noodles are safe to eat. Food Safety and Standards Authority of India (FSSAI) four days later had ordered NIL to withdraw all nine variants of Maggi instant noodles from the market, terming them "unsafe and hazardous" for human consumption. Subsequently, NIL destroyed Rs.3 billion worth of Maggi noodles products without going for any further tests. The Maggi fiasco had repercussions on the company as a whole and NIL sustained its first quarterly loss in 17 years. Furthermore, in an attempt to control the damage, NIL appointed Suresh Narayanan as its MD, replacing India head Etienne Benet[12]. In late August 2015, NIL had come up with short video ads leveraging on nostalgia and emotional quotient attached with Maggi instant noodles. Meanwhile, NIL invested time and effort to genuinely fix the problem. In October 2015, Nestlé claimed that it had cleared three lab tests mandated by a court in Maharashtra, and would relaunch Maggi by November 2015. Finally, Maggi geared for its relaunch.

Exercise

The curious case of Rukmini Devi and the Bank

Given below is a hypothetical letter that was sent to a private bank by a 76-year-old woman Rukmini Devi. She is a retired high school principal and a widow. Furthermore, she currently has no other family support system. She is well educated and survives entirely on her pension. Rukmini Devi lives in a traditional close-knit suburban residential complex all by herself. She is an independent person and takes pride in being so. One fine day, Rukmini Devi needed to get a crucial plumbing issue fixed for which she called a plumber who regularly serves the residential complex in which she lives. After the issue was fixed, Rukmini Devi wrote the plumber a check. Since the plumber was a busy person and had other clients to attend, he asked his young daughter to deposit the check to his bank after which she could withdraw Rs. 25000/- for her college admission fee. Soon after depositing the check written by Rukmini Devi, the daughter of the plumber learned that the check bounced back and her father did not have enough balance in his account that would enable her to pay the college admission fees. It was the last day of the admission and she panicked thinking that she would probably miss her admission. The daughter then informed her father about the incident and being fearful of losing her chance to get an admission to a college, she tweeted describing the entire incident and linked the tweet to her Facebook account. The daughter's friends started commenting on the post and also retweeted.

Meanwhile, the plumber, after knowing the incident, borrowed the required amount money from his current client to manage the deficit and asked his daughter to pay the admission fee at the last moment. Furthermore, before borrowing the money from his current client, the plumber, too, narrated the incident to his current client. In the meantime, Rukmini Devi's bank (different from the Plumber's bank) notified her through an automated SMS that due to insufficient balance in her account her check bounced back for which she would have to pay a heavy penalty. However, Rukmini Devi, being not so tech-savvy, did not notice the SMS her bank had sent her. Finally, when the plumber called her to draw her attention to the matter, she became very emotional and upset with the bank. Meanwhile, a former student of Rukmini Devi whose daughter was a friend of the Plumber's daughter learned about the incident through her daughter's Facebook wall and called Rukmini Devi to find out what happened actually. At this point, Rukmini Devi realized the matter has gone public and she felt insulted. She then asked her former student help her submit a letter of complaint on her behalf to the bank to which she agreed. The former student, with Rukmini Devi's permission, also posted the letter to Rukmini Devi's Facebook wall and soon after many of her former students started commenting on the post asking the bank to be more considerate to senior citizens.

One of her former students responded to the original post on Rukmini Devi's Facebook stating that she is not sure how bank will deal with her. Her doubts comes as a result of her perception of Rukmini Devi's character. The former student depicted Rukmini Devi as –

Mam is a peace-loving lady and she is very passionate. However, she can be very stubborn, and her emotions can be very confusing for others. She can be gentle, affectionate, and agitated at the same time.

Her moods wax and wane like the lunar cycle. But the difficult thing for others is that there is no particular pattern in which her moods swing so one can never accurately anticipate what will come next. She is prone to pessimism and negative attitude.

Mam is known for building a fortress around her emotions, and she takes a lot of time to trust someone and open her heart. As far as I know, she dislikes criticism and rejection and will do everything in her capacity to avoid them.

In a situation like this, she feels extremely hurt, she can withdraw into a silent spell; go deep into her shell where she is unreachable. However, she will not plan revenge against the person who has hurt her. She may become extremely irritable but will rarely do anything to hurt others on purpose, because she is very sensitive to the feelings of others.

Mam is cautious, and she will not take impulsive decisions. She will carefully consider all the pros and cons and then make a move.

Mam is creative and has an artistic leaning. Poetry, music, paintings and the serenity of nature help her relax and unwind.

Although she is very much capable of looking after herself and not emotionally weak, she needs the reaffirmation that she is loved and needed. It is this assurance that keeps her going and gives her strength to take up difficult tasks.

Please read the letter below and based on your understanding of the process followed in the crisis situation, suggest the bank how to resolve the issue that will help it create a long lasting positive impression. For a business organization, impression management and customer care go hand in hand.

Dear Sir:

I am writing to thank you for bouncing my check with which I endeavored to pay my plumber last month. By my calculations, three nanoseconds must have elapsed between his presenting the check and the arrival in my account of the funds needed to honor it. I refer, of course, to the automatic monthly deposit of my entire pension, an arrangement which, I admit, has been in place for only eight years. You are to be commended for seizing that brief window of opportunity, and also for debiting a hefty amount by way of penalty for the inconvenience caused to your bank.

My thankfulness springs from the manner in which this incident has caused me to rethink my errant financial ways. I noticed that whereas I personally answer your telephone calls and letters,—when I try to contact you, I am confronted by the impersonal, overcharging, pre-recorded, faceless entity which your bank has become.

From now on, I, like you, choose only to deal with a flesh-and-blood person.

My mortgage and loan repayments will therefore and hereafter no longer be automatic, but will arrive at your bank, by check, addressed personally and confidentially to an employee at your bank whom you must nominate. Be aware that it is an OFFENSE under the Postal Act for any other person to open such an envelope. Please find attached an Application Contact which I require your chosen employee to complete. I am sorry it runs to eight pages, but in order that I know as much about him or her as your bank knows about me, there is no alternative.

Please note that all copies of his or her medical history must be countersigned by a Notary Public, and the mandatory details of his/her financial situation (income, debts, assets and liabilities) must be accompanied by documented proof. In due course, at MY convenience, I will issue your employee with a PIN number which he/she must quote in dealings with me. I regret that it cannot be shorter than 28 digits but, again, I have modeled it on the number of button presses required of me to access my account balance on your phone bank service.

As they say, imitation is the sincerest form of flattery. Let me level the playing field even further. When you call me, press buttons as follows:

IMMEDIATELY AFTER DIALING, PRESS THE STAR (*) BUTTON FOR ENGLISH

#1. To make an appointment to see me.

#2. To query a missing payment.

#3. To transfer the call to my living room in case I am there.

#4 To transfer the call to my bedroom in case I am sleeping.

#5. To transfer the call to my toilet in case I am attending to nature.

#6. To transfer the call to my mobile phone if I am not at home.

#7. To leave a message on my computer, a password to access my computer is required.

Password will be communicated to you at a later date to that Authorized Contact mentioned earlier.

#8. To return to the main menu and to listen to options 1 through.

#9. To make a general complaint or inquiry.

The contact will then be put on hold, pending the attention of my automated answering service.

#10. This is a second reminder to press* for English.

While this may, on occasion, involve a lengthy wait, uplifting music will play for the duration of the call.

Regrettably, but again following your example, I must also levy an establishment fee to cover the setting up of this new arrangement.

May I wish you a happy, if ever so slightly less prosperous New Year? Your Humble Client And remember: Don't make old people mad. We don't like being old in the first place, so it doesn't take much to p**s us off.

Best regards,
Rukmini Devi

A Note for the Instructors

The students can be asked to complete this assignment either individually or in a group. If it is group assignment the instructor can decide whether to have the students do it in face-to-face context or online through text chat following the method of Computer-Supported Collaborative Learning (CSCL). The process of CSCL is described in the Appendix B. The instructor can decide on the time to be given to the student to complete the assignment and submit either a written case analysis report or make a time-bound class presentation.

On Making an Impactful Speech

Public speaking is neither easy nor difficult. The first and foremost factor that determines our success in public speaking is our motivation[1]. Our desire to be an impactful public speaker is either self-driven or controlled by external factors. Intrinsic motivation involves doing something because it is personally rewarding to us. Extrinsic motivation, on the contrary, involves doing something because we want to earn a reward or avoid punishment. On the surface level, it might seem like it is better to be intrinsically motivated than extrinsically motivated. After all, is it not ideal if we do not need anyone, or anything, motivating us to accomplish tasks? However, we do not live in such an ideal world, do we? Being extrinsically motivated does not mean anything bad; extrinsic motivation is just the nature of being a human being sometimes. While a few have the inherent ability to motivate themselves intrinsically, others may need extrinsic motivations to push themselves to accomplish a task. For example, if you have a job, and you have to complete a project and make a presentation to the clients, you will probably need extrinsic motivation to do so, if you detest public speaking or have public speaking anxiety. However, your boss may help if he/she knows how to motivate you further to energize you and boost your confidence. Soon after you get motivated, you will probably find out ways to make an impactful presentation.

It is seemingly not possible for us to make an impactful speech on the stage without any preparation. The question is, what helps us do so. The answers to this fundamental question are hidden in the quotes of some of the great personalities. For example, Mark Twain – an American writer, humorist, entrepreneur, publisher, and lecturer – once stated, "It usually takes me more than three weeks to prepare a good impromptu speech." With this quote what essentially Twain perhaps conveyed is that there is no alternative to preparation for public speaking.

The next question then is, what it takes to prepare well for a public speech. Alexander Gregg, an American Episcopal clergyman, explained, "There are three things to aim at in public speaking: first, to get into your subject, then to get your subject into yourself, and lastly, to get your subject into the heart of your audience." Ultimately the content of our speech must be well accepted by our audience. Harvey Diamond, the author of *Fit for Life*, stated, "If you don't know what you want to achieve in your presentation your audience never will." Subsequently, we need to focus on how to gather knowledge for our speech, how to assimilate them, and how to deliver them to our audience.

Create Content for the Speech

Let us assume that we are part of a guided tour to an exciting tourist destination, like Rome, and our guide, without briefing us about the places/things to see, started off the journey. Most of us are very likely to feel tired after sometime and be disinterested in travelling further if the first few places/things we visited did not excite us. On the contrary, if our guide briefs us about the places to be seen and shares stories of how exciting they are at the beginning of the tour, we are very likely to complete the tour with excitement even if we are physically tired. Likewise, when we deliver a speech, our audiences expect two things from us – **a destination and a path**. Without knowing where we are going and why, we might not be very comfortable taking this journey, especially if the speaker is lesser known to the audience. Thus, it is important to set the expectation at the opening of our speech on what we will be covering. Subsequently, we need to write and revise, focus on structuring and simplifying. Thereafter, get rid of anything that is extraneous, contradictory, or confusing. We need to keep in mind if our points do not help us get our core message across, drop it.

Let us closely examine and understand how effective speeches are written point by point.

1. The title Creating Content for Effective Speeches

2. Introducing self Hello! I am Anupam Das, Associate Professor of Humanities & Liberal Arts in Management at the Indian Institute of Management Kozhikode – commonly addressed as IIM Kohikode. I regularly teach Managerial Communication, Communication as Impression Management, and Public Speaking to Postgraduate MBA students and Business executives. I am honored to join Professor Kathryn Rentz of University of Cincinnati and Professor Paula Lentz of University of Wisconsin – Eau Claire to help you out in your Public Speaking lesson! Let's get started! This will be so much F-U-N!

3. Clearly offer the outline of your speech at the onset Writing an effective speech is very similar to making a beautiful collage. Typically you can make a photo collage in a few steps. First, you need to select photos that would help you create a bigger picture. Thus, you need to choose photos with a theme to make use of the collage's storytelling power. Thereafter, arrange those photos on a select layout to bring your story to life. For better effect, you need to customize borders, add color, texture, and patterns to enhance the theme of your collage. Finally, you may consider adding texts to create a tagline. Since one-size-fit-all approach does not work, you need to first identify the purpose of your speech by identifying the types of audience you will be delivering it to. Typically, a speech aims at achieving one or more of the following four purposes – drawing attention of the audience to explain something, generating interest among the audience to follow something or to take up cause, creating positive impression by sharing stories of one's achievements, and giving directions to some who might need it to complete a task.

4. Crafting an appropriate speech begins with identifying the audience type The speaker's task to creating content further depends on the type of audiences involved, which include the following five types: PEDESTRAIN Audience, SELECTE Audience, ORGANIZED Audience, CAPTIVE Audience, and CONCERTED Audience. As you already know that one size does not fit all, you need to have an appropriate approach for each of these audience types.

5. Identifying the right approach So, what approach is to be adopted for Pedestrian Audience? People who belong to this type display lowest degree of orientation. How could you reach out to these people to deliver the intended messages through your speech? Certainly, it would be ATTENTION since they lack them. Selected audience usually assemble for a pre-defined purpose, like a seminar or convention. As a speaker you need to keep in mind that they are well informed people and thus you need to focus on creating positive IMPRESSION to retain their attention. As for the captive audience, they are partially oriented and are generally found in classrooms and social organizations. You, as a speaker, need to create content of your speech with CONVICTION. The organized audience are those where the orientation between the speaker and the audience is the most structured. There is a division of labor and authority, supported with a common interest and purpose. The task left to be done here is – DIRECTION. With concerted audience, there is an active purpose, and they share on common interest. What is to be done in this audience is creating positive IMPRESSION.

6. Selecting your message topic   After you have correctly identified your audience type, you need to select your message topic. There are only four major rules of thumb for you to remember in selecting your speech topic – **the 4Ks to speech selection:** I. Keep it simple. II. Know your audience. III. Know the occasion. IV. Know the message purpose.

7. Main purpose of a speech   There are three main purposes of a speech: INFORMING, PERSUADING, and RITUALIZING. For example, when doing an informative speech presentation, you can use four ways to achieve this purpose. One of them is trying to clarify information. A doctor explains to a group of paramedical and nursing staff during a symposium how to identify potentially infected COVID-19 patients and treat them. The other purpose is to narrate factual information. For instance, as a sales manager you need to share the features of the latest version of a smart phone to the sales trainees so that they can recall this factual information when required to sale. The remaining two are – establishing boundaries or limits concerning the amount of information required to inform the audience and how to use information, rather than on what it is. For example, as I have finished drafting this speech, I had to go back and forth to edit it further not only for grammatical errors but also for the amount of information to be provided so that my audience can assimilate them. As for how to use information, a sales person in an electronic gadget store must be able to assess a potential customer's requirement by asking a few basic questions related to dominant purpose of the phone he/she intends to buy. Thereafter, the sales person can present the available items in the store and help him/her make an informed decision by providing necessary (but not all) factual information.

For a persuasive speech, you need to remember that persuasion is often a process, and not an event. For some, persuasion is inducing others to change or winning by some power or force. For some others, persuasion is creating satisfaction or reinforcing assurance in the mind of the listener. When you want to persuade, there are three basic assumptions at work. First of all, you need to assume that the audience is already informed about the speech subject. Your second assumption should be that the speech is a debatable issue. Finally, make an assumption that there is a good chance that the audience may hold a different view, concerning the subject, from that of the speaker.

As for a ritualizing speech, you will find that the occasion dictates what kind of speech should be used. Ritual speeches are often done to entertain audiences. They may be any of the following: I. After-dinner speech II. Goodwill speech III. Speech of Nomination IV. Dedication Speech V. Commemorative Speech VI. Anniversary Address VII. Eulogy VIII. Ceremonial Speech IX. Courtesy Speeches – a. Speech of Introduction b. Speech of Presentation c. Speech of Acceptance d. Speech of Welcome e. Speech of Response to a Welcome f. Speech of Farewell.

8. Giving your thoughts a shape   This part is as challenging as preparing yourself to speak in front of a large gathering – preparing the speech itself. You now get ready in front of your computer, and put all your thoughts and researches down into the right words. You are now ready to plan your speech message into an organized, outlined structure – introduction, body, and conclusion.

9. Introducing the speech   In introducing the speech the speaker attempts to serve three special purposes: I. Gaining attention. II. Establishing rapport. III. Previewing signalling – a. Briefing b. Introducing your subject and purpose. Please do not work on your introduction mechanically. For an impactful introduction, you need to be creative. You can incorporate numerous creative techniques in introducing your speech. What are these techniques?

I. Quotations II. Storytelling /Narration III. Rhetorical Question IV. Props / Visuals V. Situational Approach VI. Audience – Participation. For instance, Steve Jobs in the introduction of his commencement speech in Stanford in 2005 made use of narrative approach[2]. In his introduction he stated, "I am honored to be with you today at your commencement from one of the finest universities in the world. I never graduated from college. Truth be told, this is the closest I've ever gotten to a college graduation. Today I want to tell you three stories from my life. That's it. No big deal. Just three stories."

10. Developing the body of the speech You need to structure your message so that the ideas follow a sequence. Organizational structures help you sequence your ideas in an easy, logical, and coherent manner. Let's have an overview of them as we move forward.

11. Organizational structures Priority There are three primary elements to structure the main body of your speech – **Chronological Classification, Historical Problem, and Logical Solution**. This classification is arranged from the most important to the least important or vice versa. Chronology signifies it follows a time sequence, based on a piece of information that happened first, second, so on. Thereafter, you view your subject as the problem. As you narrate the problem, your audience will automatically seek solutions to it. Thus, you present each main idea of the speech as the cause and you go on demonstrating the effects. This pattern is effective for speeches to inform through explaining and demonstrating. Some communication experts suggest dividing a message into three parts or stories is a simple, memorable, and effective technique to structure it.

For example, Steve Jobs in his commencement speech in Stanford in 2005 wrapped three lessons in just three stories. Jobs' first story was about connecting the dots. He talked to the graduates about dropping out of his College so he could "drop in" to the courses he wanted to take, like calligraphy, a course that had no practical application to his life. Ten years later, he incorporated what he had learned into the design of the Macintosh. "It was the first computer with beautiful typography…You can't connect the dots looking forward; you can only connect them looking backwards. You have to trust the dots will somehow connect in your future." Jobs' second story was about love and loss. He recalled falling in love with computers at an early age, meeting Steve "Woz" Wozniak, building Apple, and losing Apple after a falling out with the Board of Directors. "Getting fired was the best thing that could have ever happened to me…I'm convinced that the only thing that kept me going was that I loved what I did. You've got to find what you love." Jobs' third and final story was about death. "Remembering that you are going to die is the best way I know to avoid the trap thinking you have something to lose. You are already naked. There is no reason not to follow your heart."

12. Concluding the speech There are valuable purposes of conclusion in a speech. This is where you get a chance to review by pulling it all up before you thank your audience. It is advisable that you divide your conclusion into two parts: Part 1 – a brief summary of the main ideas you presented in the body of speech. Part 2 – Audience impact: the final moment of spoken words makes the greatest impact on us once presentation is over. Thus, a good conclusion is extremely important. In concluding his speech, Jobs emphasized triumph over adversity. Each of the three vignettes from Jobs' life involves struggle or sacrifice. Stories of triumph over struggle resonate with audiences because humans, by default, can empathize with one another. When he shared his life experiences through stories, they became the vehicles through which he could connect with his audience. Once they're connected to a speaker, an audience is likely to follow the speaker's advice or buy into her/his idea. Steve Jobs saves his call to attention for the end of the speech: "Stay Hungry. Stay Foolish. I have always wished that for myself. And now, as you graduate to begin anew, I wish that for you. Stay Hungry. Stay Foolish."

It is time to write your own speech. I hope my speech helps you get started! **Don't forget to follow the steps presented here** – I. What is your desired speech topic? II. What made you choose this topic? III. What is your message purpose? IV. How do you plan to start your speech? (Write an ideal introduction that suits your chosen topic, 3–5 sentences will do. You can always add/improve it later.) V. Now you are getting the ball rolling! What organizational structure are you planning to use in presenting your ideas in the body of your speech? VI. Why are you planning to use this structure? VII. How will it help strengthen your topic?. Thank you for your attention.

I hope you gather courage to give it a try and write your next speech following the framework presented here. Jobs' speech has been inspiring people for a decade and will continue to do so. You too could inspire people with your speech only if you "Stay hungry. Stay foolish."

Assimilating Your Speech

In "*Becoming Steve Jobs*[3]", Laurene, wife of Jobs, confessed that Steve Jobs wasn't always the confident showman he seemed to be on stage during his famous keynotes. On the morning of June 12, 2005, hours before Jobs was scheduled to deliver the commencement speech in Stanford University, "He woke up with butterflies in his stomach," says his wife. She went on stating that "I'd almost never seen him more nervous." Evidently, the speech meant a lot to Steve Jobs and thus he had practiced the speech endlessly, often talking out loud as he walked around the house. It was further learned that he gave the speech several times during family dinners, taking advantage of the captive audience. In fact, the best speeches and presentations are those that connect deeply with one's audience. As of March 2020, Jobs's commencement speech had 34 million views on YouTube. Steve Jobs' speech did connect deeply with millions of souls around the world. The reason for such impactful speech is that it is a finely crafted speech. It was emotional, inspiring, and simply structured. Furthermore, before it was delivered, it was well assimilated in the speaker through practice.

Several rounds of practices help speakers assimilate a well-crafted speech and thus words come out from the depth of truth. Through this process, a speaker gradually reaches towards perfection.

For a better outcome, speakers are advised to practice their speech, and not rehearse. With rounds of practices a speaker can constantly try to improve the skills for any specific aim. On the contrary, with rehearsal speakers tend to invite more trouble for themselves as it is likely to increase the level of anxiety in the speaker. This is because in practice sessions one can have flaws whereas in a rehearsal the speaker is not supposed to have any imperfections associated with the speech. Furthermore, in a practice session, a person is free to express any emotion or make changes while in a rehearsal, one is restricted to a perfect coordinated and unconcealed mind. Moreover, as practice may be done in bits and pieces, a speaker may want to practice only the opening part of the speech leaving the rest of the matter for a later time whereas a rehearsal is made as a complete act. Therefore, in the process of rehearsing the speech the speaker is usually very tensed and anxious.

While in public speaking anxiety is very common and, to a certain extent, is considered natural, it is important that speakers try to get rid of anxiety as soon as and as much as possible. We need to be able to identify the factors causing public speaking anxiety and how to address them[4]. First of all, it is novel. We do not do it regularly and lack necessary skills as a result. Furthermore, it is done in formal settings. Consequently, our behaviors, when giving a speech, are more prescribed and rigid. Moreover, often the audience acts as a critic and the speaker stands apart from the audience. Additionally, a speech is often delivered in front of an audience that is unfamiliar, which is the cause for additional anxiety. A formal presentation is also a unique situation in which the degree of attention paid to the speaker is quite noticeable.

As the saying goes, where there is a will there is a way. For overcoming public speaking anxiety, there are several ways. **The most commonly suggested methods of overcoming the fear and anxiety are**: I. Start planning and preparing your speech early. II. Choose a topic you care about if you have that freedom. III. Become an expert on your topic by digging deeper into the subject matter. IV. Research your audience to orient your speech according to their needs. V. Practice your speech as much as possible, and VI. Know your introduction and conclusion well.

How to Deliver an Effective Presentation or Speech

Often, you would hear speakers saying "I had written an impressive speech; but my hands started shaking and legs continued to tremble when I stood in front of the audience." Effective, confident public speaking should look effortless. In reality most people, including TED[5] speakers, need considerable time and practice before they can talk confidently in front of an audience. You can use a number of techniques to overcome stage fright, present yourself confidently and keep your audience engaged.

How to Avoid Signs of Nerves During Your Speech?

A few generic techniques that may help many of you gradually overcome your stage fright are presented below. However, for a few, these techniques may not work and they may need special assistance in overcoming their public speaking anxiety. In fact, public speaking anxiety can come from various sources and even for those coming from a privileged background. For example, if you know the story of a famous film 'The King's Speech[6]' you would know even a prince is no exception when it comes to public speaking.

As and when you stand on the stage to deliver a talk or make a presentation, assume yourself as someone who is sharing valuable information with willing listeners. Try not to get so worked up about how you will come across in your nervous state. As long as you appear calm, it does not really matter that you are feeling nervous. The question is how to appear calm on the stage before a speech. Here are a few tips that you may master to appear calm.

> **Fidgeting** Avoid touching your face or playing with jewellery and/or phone. Keep your hands in front of you.
>
> **Pacing** Move strategically so that you do not appear to your audiences that you are panick- stricken. Move a few steps and then stop. This can help keep an audience engaged, and you can use it to emphasize the message you are communicating.
>
> **Hands shaking** Use a neatly arranged stack of cards rather than sheets of paper for your notes. This will make your shakiness much less apparent. However, there is no need to hide it from your audiences. Hold them smartly to indicate that you are comfortable.

Develop Good Body Language

For our body language, the most important part of our body is our face and the most important facial expression is arguably the **smile**. Our friendly smile is likely to create an instant rapport and will make your audience warm to us. Use facial expressions to help convey key points -this will help to make your speech seem more convincing. In doing so, you need to pay attention to the emotive words in your speech and try to map your facial expressions accordingly. **Posture**, too, is crucial as it indicates your level of confidence. Stand up straight with your feet slightly apart and your arms loose. Recall the scene from the popular Bollywood film 'Lagaan' where the lead character Bhuvan addressed his peers and neighbors to persuade them to speak to the king so that the tax is exempted for them. Bhuvan stood firm with his feet slightly apart and his arms were loose and his confidence was reflecting through his facial expressions and posture. It is important that you look rooted which will make you appear more confident and believable. Avoid placing your hands on your hips and avoid swaying while you talk. Furthermore, avoid closed gestures such as crossing your arms or legs and standing with your arms behind your back. These gestures are inappropriate for a formal presentation since they create a mental barrier between you and your audience. Additionally, during your speech, look at your audience from time to time. Engaging your audience visually makes you appear secure and confident.

Gesticulate for Success

Gesticulation is an effective method of human communication as it helps emphasize one's words. Use your hands and arms to help your audience follow your speech. Often, effective and confident gestures command attention from listeners. When your body language and words work together, they create a powerful message. However, you need to vary gestures so that you do not look like a robot.

It is important that you adjust your body language to fit the size of the space you are working with to emphasize points effectively. When delivering a speech, use bold gestures! Tentative, half-hearted actions can make you appear unsure and unconvincing, especially in some cultures.

Exercise

You are required to craft an impactful speech using the images given below. After interpreting the images, first in isolation and then in connection to other images, you are required to identify a macro and a micro problem and then offer solutions to these problems. In presenting your arguments and ideas you need to build a powerful narrative either in 1st person or in 3rd person. You must use all the images in crafting your speech. However, you are allowed to rearrange the images to create a compelling narrative.

Our behavior is dictated by a desire for external rewards

"I am not a machine, Chanda. I can't just turn my greed on and off."

The Lost Generation

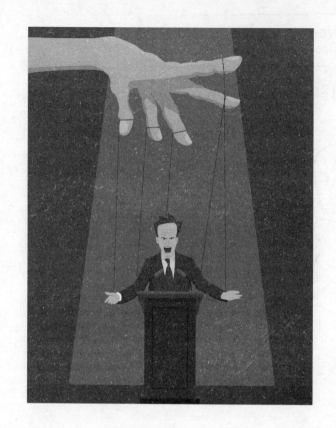

Chapter 1

1. "Job Outlook 2016: Attributes Employers Want to See on New College Graduates' Résumés," *NACE*, November 18, 2015, accessed February 20, 2016, http://www.naceweb.org/s11182015/employers-look-for-in-new-hires.aspx.

2. The Conference Board, Corporate Voices for Working Families, the Partnership for 21st Century Skills, and the Society for Human Resource Management, "Are They Ready to Work? Employers' Perspectives on the Basic Knowledge and Applied Skills of New Entrants into the 21st Century Workforce," October 2, 2006, p. 21, accessed February 20, 2016, http://www.p21.org/storage/documents/FINAL_REPORT_PDF09-29-06.pdf.

3. Shirley Taylor, "Why Are Communication Skills Important?," July 22, 2011, accessed February 20, 2016, http://www.shirleytaylor.com.

4. Jonathan Farrington, "The MOST Important Leadership Trait?—It's a 'No-Brainer,'" *Blogit*, September 26, 2008, http://www.socialmediatoday.com.

5. Rich Maggiani, "The Costs of Poor Communication," 2014, accessed February 20, 2016, http://www.solari.net/documents/position-papers/Solari-Costs-of-Poor-Communication.pdf.

6. SIS International Research, "SMB Communications Pain Study White Paper: Uncovering the Hidden Cost of Communications Barriers and Latency," February 1, 2015, accessed February 21, 2016, https://www.sisinternational.com/smb-communications-pain-study-white-paper-uncovering-the-hidden-cost-of-communications-barriers-and-latency/.

7. "PMI 2013 Pulse of the Professions: The High Cost of Low Performance: The Essential Role of Communications," May 2013, accessed February 21, 2016, http://www.pmi.org/~/media/PDF/Business-Solutions/The-High-Cost-Low-Performance-The-Essential-Role-of-Communications.ashx.

8. For discussions of problem solving, see the following print resources (in chronological order): John R. Hayes, *The Complete Problem Solver*, 2nd ed. (Hillsdale, NJ: Lawrence Erlbaum, 1989); Morgan D. Jones, *The Thinker's Toolkit* (New York: Three Rivers Press, 1998); Janet E. Davidson and Robert J. Sternberg, eds., *The Psychology of Problem Solving* (Cambridge, UK: Cambridge University Press, 2003); Dan Roam, *The Back of the Napkin* (London: Portfolio, 2008); John Adair, *Decision Making and Problem Solving Strategies*, 2nd ed. (London: Kogan Page, 2010); Jonathan G. Koomey, *Turning Numbers into Knowledge*, 2nd ed. (Oakland, CA: Analytics Press, 2010); Daniel Kahneman, *Thinking, Fast and Slow* (New York: Farrar, Straus and Giroux, 2011); Michael Kallet, *Think Smarter: Critical Thinking to Improve Problem-Solving and Decision-Making Skills* (Hoboken, NJ: Wiley, 2014).

9. Thomas Politzer, "Vision Is Our Dominant Sense," *BrainLine.org*, June 3, 2015, accessed February 21, 2016, http://www.brainline.org/content/2008/11/vision-our-dominant-sense_pageall.html; Ruth Colvin Clark and Richard E. Mayer, *e-Learning and the Science of Instruction*, 2nd ed. (San Francisco, CA: John Wiley & Sons, 2008).

10. "Job Outlook 2016."

11. "Job Outlook 2016."

12. Institute for the Future for the University of Phoenix Research Institute, *Future Work Skills 2020* (2011), 10, accessed February 22, 2016, http://www.iftf.org/uploads/media/SR-1382A_UPRI_future_work_skills_sm.pdf.

13. Institute for the Future for the University of Phoenix Research Institute, 10.

14. Institute for the Future for the University of Phoenix Research Institute, 8.

15. David Bollier, "The Future of Work: What It Means for Individuals, Businesses, Markets, and Governments," *Aspen Institute*, 2011, p. 8, http://www.aspeninstitute.org.

16. Bollier, 15.

17. Bollier, 19.

18. Bollier, 19.

19. Institute for the Future for University of Phoenix Research Institute, *Future of Work Report: Summary Map* (2011), accessed February 22, 2016, http://www.iftf.org/uploads/media/IFTF_FutureWorkSkillsSummary_01.gif.

20. Institute for the Future for University of Phoenix Research Institute, *Future Work Skills 2020,* 9.

21. Nielsen, *Millennials: Breaking the Myths* (February 2014), 6, accessed February 19, 2016, http://www.nielsen.com/content/dam/corporate/us/en/reports-downloads/2014%20Reports/nielsen-millennial-report-feb-2014.pdf.

22. Jacqueline Whitmore, "Good Manners Are a Career and Business Necessity," *Entrepreneur,* February 9, 2016, accessed February 23, 2016, https://www.entrepreneur.com/article/270214.

23. Kristie Lorette, "Essentials of Business Communication," *Chron,* accessed February 26, 2016, http://smallbusiness.chron.com/essentials-business-communication-116.html.

24. B. Lynn Ware, "Career Development for Millennials," Association for Talent Development, March 17, 2014, webinar.

25. "PMI 2013 Pulse of the Professions," 4–5.

26. Diana Laurillard, "Styles and Approaches in Problem-Solving," in *The Experience of Learning: Implications for Teaching and Studying in Higher Education*, eds. F. Martin and N. Entwistle, 3rd ed. (Edinburgh: University of Edinburgh, Centre for Teaching, Learning, and Assessment, 2005), 106–125, accessed February 23, 2016, http://www.ed.ac.uk/institute-academic-development/learning-teaching/staff/advice/researching/publications/experience-of-learning.

27. Chip Spinoza, Mick Ukleja, and Craig Rusch, *Managing the Millennials: Discover the Core Competencies for Managing Today's Workforce* (Hoboken, NJ: Wiley, 2010), 33–36, 119–123.

28. Kay Sargent, "Google Didn't 'Get It Wrong': A Deeper Look into That Recent Wapo [Washington Post] Piece about Open Offices," *Workspace Design Magazine*, January 7, 2015, accessed February 23, 2016, http://workdesign.com/2015/01/google-didnt-get-wrong-deeper-look-recent-wapo-piece-open-offices/.

29. See Edgar H. Schein, *Organizational Culture and Leadership*, 4th ed. (San Francisco: Jossey-Bass, 2010), which reviews the literature on this important concept.

30. See research by Dorothy A. Winsor, especially *Writing Power: Communication in an Engineering Center* (Albany: SUNY Press, 2003).

Chapter 2

1. NACE, "Job Outlook 2016: The Candidate Skills/Qualities Employers Want, the Influence of Attributes," *NACE*, November 18, 2015, accessed March 11, 2016, http://www.naceweb.org/s11182015/employers-look-for-in-new-hires.aspx.

2. JoAnne Yates, *Control through Communication: The Rise of System in American Management* (Baltimore: The Johns Hopkins UP, 1989), 95.

3. Kristin Naragon, "Subject: Email, We Just Can't Get Enough," *Adobe News*, August 26, 2015, accessed March 11, 2016, http://blogs.adobe.com/conversations/2015/08/email.html.

4. David Grossman, "Unproductive Time on Email Quickly Becoming a Corporate Productivity Concern," *Leader Communicator Blog*, June 11, 2015, accessed March 11, 2016, http://www.yourthoughtpartner.com/blog/unproductive-time-on-email-quickly-becoming-a-corporate-productivity-concern.

5. Heidi Schultz, *The Elements of Electronic Communication* (Boston: Allyn and Bacon, 2000), 43–47.

6. Career Builder, "More Employers Checking out Candidates on Social Media," *The Hiring Site Blog*, May 14, 2015, accessed March 11, 2016, http://thehiringsite.careerbuilder.com/2015/05/14/employers-checking-candidates-social-media/.

Chapter 3

1. National Eye Institute, "Facts about Color Blindness," February 2015, accessed March 22, 2015, https://nei.nih.gov/health/color_blindness/facts_about.

2. Janice Redish, *Letting Go of the Words: Writing Web Content That Works*, 2nd ed. (San Francisco: Elsevier, 2012), 20.

3. Jakob Nielsen, "Writing Style for Print vs. Web," *Alert Box*, June 7, 2008, accessed March 22, 2016, https://www.nngroup.com/articles/f-shaped-pattern-reading-web-content/.

4. Redish, 102.

5. Emil Towner and Heidi Everett, e-mail message to author, March 16, 2016.

6. Towner and Everett.

7. Lance Hiley, "Do Glossy Brochures Still Work or Has Digital Marketing Killed the Power of Print?," accessed March 22, 2016, http://www.themarketingcentre.com/do-glossy-brochures-still-work-or-has-digital-marketing-killed-the-power-of-print/.

Chapter 4

1. Anne Trafton, "In the Blink of an Eye: MIT Neuroscientists Find the Brain Can Identify Images Seen for as Little as 13 Milliseconds,'" *MIT News*, January 16, 2014, accessed October 18, 2016, http://news.mit.edu/2014/in-the-blink-of-an-eye-0116.

2. Thomas Frank, "The Science Behind How Fast Humans Can Read," *College Info Geek*, August 26, 2015, accessed April 10, 2016, http://collegeinfogeek.com/speed-reading-science/.

3. Xerox Corporation, "20 Ways to Share the Color Knowledge: Color Captures Attention, Enhances Productivity, Improves Communications and Helps Boost Sales," *Xerox*, 2014, accessed April 10, 2016, http://www.office.xerox.com/latest/COLFS-02UA.PDF.

Chapter 5

1. "What Is Plain Language?," *PlainLanguage.gov/*, accessed March 4, 2016, http://www.plainlanguage.gov.

2. Helen Sword, "Yes, Even Professors Can Write Stylishly," *The Wall Street Journal*, April 6, 2012, accessed March 5, 2016, http://www.wsj.com.

Chapter 6

1. U.S. Census Bureau, "Nearly 1 in 5 People Have a Disability in the U.S., Census Bureau Reports," July 25, 2012, accessed March 12, 2016, https://www.census.gov/newsroom/releases/archives/miscellaneous/cb12-134.html.

2. Brian Tracy, "Top 7 Qualities Employers Are Looking for in Candidates," *Undercover Recruiter,* December 17, 2014, accessed March 10, 2016, http://theundercoverrecruiter.com.

3. "How to Help Graduates Develop a Professional Mindset," *Undercover Recruiter*, March 11, 2016, accessed March 12, 2016, http://theundercoverrecruiter.com/graduates-professional-mindset/.

4. Tracy.

5. For fuller discussions of these approaches, see Paul Dombrowski, *Ethics in Technical Communication* (Needham Heights, MA: Allyn & Bacon, 2000).

Chapter 7

1. Laurel Delaney, "The World Is Your Market: Small Businesses Gear up for Globalization," *Scribd*, 2004, accessed June 7, 2016, http://www.scribd.com.

2. Abraham T. Mosisa, "Spotlight on Statistics: Foreign-Born Workers in the U.S. Labor Force," United States Department of Labor, Bureau of Labor Statistics, July 2013, accessed November 2016, http://www.bls.gov/spotlight/2013/foreign-born/.

3. Jena McGregor, "The Average Work Week Is Now 47 Hours," *Washington Post*, September 2, 2014, accessed March 19, 2016, https://www.washingtonpost.com/news/on-leadership/wp/2014/09/02/the-average-work-week-is-now-47-hours/.

4. Geert Hofstede, "National Cultures and Corporate Cultures," in *Communication Between Cultures*, eds. Larry A. Samovar and Richard E. Porter (Belmont, CA: Wadsworth, 1984), 51.

5. Fons Trompenaars and Peter Woolliams, *Business across Cultures* (London: Capstone, 2003), 53.

6. Thomas L. Friedman, *The World Is Flat: A Brief History of the Twenty-First Century* (New York: Farrar, Straus, and Giroux, 2005).

7. John Mattock, ed., *Cross-Cultural Communication: The Essential Guide to International Business*, rev. 2nd ed. (London: Kogan Page, 2003), 15–23.

8. Roger E. Axtell, *Gestures: The Do's and Taboos of Body Language around the World* (New York: John Wiley & Sons, 1998), 43.

9. Wang De-hua and Li Hui, "Nonverbal Language in Crosscultural Communication," *Sino-US English Teaching* 4, no. 10 (2007): 67, accessed March 19, 2016, www.linguist.org.cn.

10. Allan Pease and Barabara Pease, *The Definitive Book of Body Language* (New York: Bantam, 2006), 111.

11. Iris Varner and Linda Beamer, *Intercultural Communication in the Global Workplace*, 5th ed. (New York: McGraw-Hill/Irwin, 2011), 101–102.

12. "Power Distance Index," *ClearlyCultural,* accessed March 19, 2016, http://www.clearlycultural.com/geert-hofstede-cultural-dimensions/power-distance-index/.

13. Sejung Mariana Choi, Shu-Chuan Chu, and Yoojung Kim, "Culture-Laden Social Engagement: A Comparative Study of Social

Relationships in Social Networking Sites among American, Chinese and Korean Users," in *Cross-Cultural Interaction: Concepts, Methodologies, Tools and Applications* (Hershey, PA: IGI Global, 2014), 63–79, accessed March 19, 2016, *Safari Books Online*.

14. Kirk St. Amant, "Culture, Context, and Cyberspace: Rethinking Identity and Authority in the Age of the Global Internet," paper presented at the Association for Business Communication Southeast Regional Conference, St. Petersburg, FL, March 2013.

15. "Doing Business in Spain," *WorldBusinessCulture*, accessed March 19, 2016, http://www.worldbusinessculture.com/Business-in-Spain.html.

16. Jensen J. Zhao, "The Chinese Approach to International Business Negotiation," *Journal of Business Communication* 37 (2000): 225.

17. Zhao.

18. Naoki Kameda, *Business Communication toward Transnationalism: The Significance of Cross-Cultural Business English and Its Role* (Tokyo: Kindaibungeisha Co., 1996), 34.

19. Mattock, 14–15.

20. Danielle Medina Walker, Thomas Walker, and Joerg Schmitz, *Doing Business Internationally: The Guide to Cross-Cultural Success,* 2nd ed. (New York: McGraw-Hill/Irwin, 2003), 211.

21. Jean-Claude Usunier, "Ethical Aspects of International Business Negotiations," in *International Business Negotiations,* eds. Pervez N. Ghauri and Jean-Claude Usunier, 2nd ed. (Amsterdam: Pergamon, 2003), 437–438.

Chapter 9

1. Valerie Creelman, "The Case for 'Living' Models," *Business Communication Quarterly* 75 (2012): 176–191.

2. Jennifer R. Veltsos, "An Analysis of Data Breach Notifications as Negative News," *Business Communication Quarterly* 75 (2012): 192–203; Creelman.

3. Veltsos.

Chapter 10

1. Danile H. Pink, *To Sell Is Human* (New York: Riverhead Books, 2012), 21, 24.

2. See Helen Rothschild Ewald and Roberta Vann, "'You're a Guaranteed Winner': Composing 'You' in a Consumer Culture," *Journal of Business Communication* 40 (2003): 98–117.

3. Charles A. Hill, "The Psychology of Rhetorical Images," *Defining Visual Rhetorics*, eds. Charles A. Hill and Marguerite Helmers (Mahwah, NJ: Lawrence Erlbaum, 2004), 30–38.

4. Pink, 45–56.

5. Internet Society, *Global Internet Report 2015*, accessed March 22, 2016, http://www.internetsociety.org/globalinternetreport/?gclid=CJz_u9731MsCFYMehgodDCgBJQ.

6. "Internet Users by Country (2016)," *InternetLiveStats,* March 22, 2016, accessed March 22, 2016, http://www.internetlivestats.com/internet-users-by-country/.

7. "Percentage of U.S. Population with a Social Network Profile from 2008 to 2016," *Statista*, accessed March 22, 2016, http://www.statista.com/statistics/273476/percentage-of-us-population-with-a-social-network-profile/.

8. Internet Society.

9. Maria Pergolina, "10 Best Practices for Using Links in Emails," *Marketo*, December 4, 2009, accessed March 22, 2016, http://blog.marketo.com/2009/12/10-best-practices-for-using-links-in-emails.html.

10. Niti Shah, "8 Little Tricks to Make Your Emails More Clickable," *Hubspot*, November 22, 2013, accessed March 22, 2016, http://blog.hubspot.com/marketing/make-emails-more-clickable-list.

11. Movable Ink, *Email and Social Media Marketing: How to Leverage Engagement to Drive ROI* (March 3, 2015), accessed March 22, 2016, https://www.digitaldoughnut.com/knowledge/movable-ink/email-and-social-media-marketing.

12. Niti Shah, "Plain Text vs. HTML Emails: Which Is Better?," *Hubspot*, July 27, 2015, accessed March 22, 2016, http://blog.hubspot.com/marketing/plain-text-vs-html-emails-data.

13. Nora Ganim Barnes, Ava M. Lescault, and Kevin D. Augusto, "LinkedIn Dominates, Twitter Trends and Facebook Falls: The 2014 Inc. 500 and Social Media," UMass Dartmouth, 2014, accessed March 23, 2016, http://www.umassd.edu/cmr/socialmediaresearch/2014inc500/.

14. Douglas Karr, "2014 Statistics and Trends for Businesses on Social Media," *Marketing Tech Blog*, October 1, 2014, accessed March 23, 2016, https://www.marketingtechblog.com/2014-statistics-trends-businesses-social-media/.

15. "What Is Content Marketing?," *Content Marketing Institute*, accessed March 23, 2016, http://contentmarketinginstitute.com.

16. Corey Wainwright, "Why Blog? The Benefits of Blogging for Business and Marketing," *Hubspot*, September 30, 2015, accessed March 23, 2016, http://blog.hubspot.com.

17. Brittney Helmrich, "Social Media for Business: 2016 Marketer's Guide," *Business News Daily*, January 29, 2016, accessed March 23, 2016, http://www.businessnewsdaily.com/7832-social-media-for-business.html.

18. Marissa Burdett, "How to Optimize Your Twitter Chat Strategy," *UpContent*, accessed March 23, 2016, https://upcontent.com/post/twitter-chat-strategy/.

19. Molly Buccini, "How Many Times Should Brands Tweet per Day?" Brafton, accessed March 23, 2016, http://www.brafton.com/news/social-media-news/many-times-brands-tweet-per-day/.

20. Evan LePage, "A Long List of Instagram Statistics and Facts (That Prove Its Importance)," Hootsuite, September 17, 2015, accessed March 23, 2016, https://blog.hootsuite.com/instagram-statistics-for-business/.

21. "Fashion Brands Strike a Pose for Instagram," *eMarketer*, July 2, 2015, accessed March 23, 2016, http://www.emarketer.com/Article.aspx?R=1012684.

22. Sue Zimmerman, "Should You Go with Pinterest or Instagram for Your Business? 7 Factors to Consider," *Agorapulse,* April 1, 2015, accessed March 24, 2016, http://www.agorapulse.com/blog/pinterest-or-instagram-for-business.

23. "What It Takes to Win," *CapturePlannning*, accessed March 24, 2016, http://www.captureplanning.com/articles/what-it-takes-to-win.cfm.

24. Carl Dickson, "What a Private Sector Company Can Learn from Government Proposals," *CapturePlanning*, accessed March 24, 2016, http://www.captureplanning.com/articles/12548.cfm.

Chapter 11

1. Caroline Molina-Ray, email message to author, June 1, 2012. Dr. Molina-Ray is a content marketer for the global HR company Aquent and former Executive Director of Research and Publications, University of Phoenix, Apollo Education Group.

2. "Top 15 Most Popular Search Engines, April 2016," *eBizMBA*, accessed April 10, 2016, http://www.ebizmba.com/articles/search-engines.

3. Guy McDowell, "Is RSS Dead? A Look at the Numbers," *makeuseof.com*, March 25, 2015, accessed April 11, 2016, http://www.makeuseof.com/tag/rss-dead-look-numbers/.

4. Craig Smith, "By the Numbers: 90 Amazing Facebook Stats," *DMR*, January 27, 2016, accessed April 11, 2016, http://expandedramblings.com/index.php/facebook-page-statistics/.

5. Shea Bennett, "67% of Americans Use Social Media (with One in Six Active on Twitter)," *Adweek.com*, April 2, 2014, accessed April 11, 2016, http://www.adweek.com/socialtimes/social-media-america/497615.

6. Tom Webster, "Twitter Use in America: 2010," *Edison Research*, April 29, 2010, accessed April 11, 2016, http://www.edisonresearch.com/twitter_usage_in_america_2010_1/.

7. "Usability Evaluation Basics," U.S. Department of Health & Human Services, n.d., accessed April 11, 2016, http://www.usability.gov/what-and-why/usability-evaluation.html.

8. Daniel B. Felker et al., *Guidelines for Document Designers* (Washington, DC: American Institutes for Research, 1981).

Chapter 12

1. For a fuller description and history, see Leigh Buchanan, "How Patagonia's Roving CEO Stays in the Loop," *Inc.*, March 18, 2013, accessed June 12, 2016, http://www.inc.com/leigh-buchanan/patagonia-founder-yvon-chouinard-15five.html.

Chapter 13

1. Mary Marcel, "What's the Best Course? Evidence from Alumni on the Value of Business Presentation Preparation," *Journal of Education for Business* 90, no. 1 (2015): 10–17.

2. Bob Adams, "Defining Your Type of Presentation Is Half the Battle," *BusinessTown*, accessed August 27, 2016, https://businesstown.com.

3. Cherie Kerr, *Death by PowerPoint: How to Avoid Killing Your Presentation and Sucking the Life out of Your Audience* (Santa Ana, CA: ExecuProv, 2002); Nancy Duarte, *slide:ology: The Art and Science of Creating Great Presentations* (Sebastopol, CA: O'Reilly Media, 2008).

4. Brian Clark, "How to Use the 'Rule of Three' to Create Engaging Content," *Copyblogger*, September, 10, 2015, accessed May 9, 2016, http://www.copyblogger.com/rule-of-three/; "Presentation Skills 3: The Rule of Three," *Presentation Magazine*, April 20, 2009, accessed May 9, 2016, http://www.presentationmagazine.com/presentation-skills-3-the-rule-of-three-7283.htm.

5. Christi Dixon, "Let's Dig In: Engaging with Audiences Beyond Your Customers," PowerPoint presentation at the Midwest/Southeast Regional Meeting, Association for Business Communication, St. Louis, MO, April 22, 2016.

6. Jan Hoffman, "Speak Up? Raise Your Hand? That May No Longer Be Necessary," *The New York Times*, March 30, 2012, accessed May 15, 2016, http://www.nytimes.com/2012/03/31/us/clickers-offer-instant-interactions-in-more-venues.html?_r=0.

7. Lisa B. Marshall, "How to Use Twitter to Supercharge Presentations," *QuickAndDirtyTips.com*, March 20, 2012, accessed May 15, 2016, http://www.quickanddirtytips.com/business-career/public-speaking/how-to-use-twitter-to-supercharge-presentations.

8. Ruth Colvin Clark and Richard E. Mayer, *e-Learning and the Science of Instruction: Proven Guidelines for Consumers and Designers of Multimedia Learning*, 3rd ed. (San Francisco, CA: Pfeiffer, 2011).

9. Garr Reynolds, *Presentation Zen: Simple Ideas on Presentation Design and Delivery* (Berkeley, CA: New Riders, 2008), 145.

10. Reynolds.

Chapter 14

1. Lorelei A. Ortiz, Michelle Region, and Catherine MacDermott, "Employer Perceptions of Oral Communication Competencies Most Valued in New Hires as a Factor in Company Success," *Business and Professional Communication Quarterly* 79, no. 3 (September 2016): 317–330.

2. Eric Savitz, "Generation Gap: How Technology Has Changed How We Talk about Work," *Forbes*, May 16, 2012, accessed May 4, 2016, http://www.forbes.com/sites/ciocentral/2012/05/16/generation-gap-how-technology-has-changed-how-we-talk-about-work/#4ebf07c271e3.

3. Yvonne Ellis, Bobbie Daniels, and Andres Jauregui, "The Effect of Multitasking on the Grade Performance of Business Students," *Research in Higher Education Journal* 8 (2010): 1–10; James M. Kraushaar and David C. Novak, "Examining the Effects of Student Multitasking with Laptops during Lecture," *Journal of Information Systems Education* 21, no. 2 (2010): 241–251; Lizy Mathew, "The Effect of Multitasking and Grade Performance of Undergraduate Nursing Students," *Open Access Library Journal* 2 (2015): e2059, accessed November 19, 2016, doi: 10.4236/oalib.1102059.

4. Patricia Napier-Fitzpatrick, "10 Tips to Master Small Talk in Business," *The Etiquette School of New York*, 2012, accessed May 1, 2016, http://etiquette-ny.com/10-tips-to-master-the-art-of-small-talk-in-business/.

5. Rebecca Knight, "How to Handle Difficult Conversations at Work," *Harvard Business Review*, January 9, 2015, accessed May 1, 2016, https://hbr.org/2015/01/how-to-handle-difficult-conversations-at-work.

6. Linda L. Putnam and Marshall Scott Poole, "Conflict and Negotiation," in *Handbook of Organizational Communication*, eds. Frederic M. Jablin, Linda L. Putnam, Karlene H. Roberts, and Lyman W. Porter (Newbury Park, CA: Sage, 1987), 552.

7. Susan S. Raines, *Conflict Management for Managers: Resolving Workplace, Client, and Policy Disputes* (San Francisco: Jossey-Bass, 2013), 5–32.

8. Kevin O'Leary, "How to Win in Business Negotiations: Never Forget, It's All About the Money," *Huffington Post–Business: Canada*, July 26, 2012, accessed May 1, 2016, http://www.huffingtonpost.ca.

9. Infocom, "Meetings in America: A Verizon Conferencing White Paper," *Verizon*, accessed May 6, 2016, https://e-meetings.verizon-business.com/global/en/meetingsinamerica/uswhitepaper.php.

10. Elaine Biech, *The Pfeiffer Book of Successful Team-Building Tools: Best of the Annuals*, 2nd ed. (San Francisco, CA: John Wiley and Sons, 2007), 13–26.

11. "We Just Don't Speak Anymore. But We're 'Talking' More Than Ever," accessed May 7, 2016, http://attentiv.com/we-dont-speak/.

12. Management Training Specialists, "Conflict Management," accessed May 7, 2016, http://www.mtdtraining.com/blog/a-conflict-management-exercise.htm.

Chapter 15

1. Amanda Augustine, "The Numbers That Matter Most in Your Job Search," *Ladders*, August 28, 2015, accessed May 10, 2016, info.theladders.com/career-advice/job-search-by-the-numbers.

2. "Percentage of Students with Internship Experience Climbs," October 7, 2015, accessed May 10, 2016, *National Association of Colleges and Employers*, www.naceweb.org/s10072015/internship-co-op-student-survey.aspx.

3. Lisa Rangel, "The Easy How-To Guide to Formatting Resumes for Applicant Tracking Systems," accessed May 12, 2016, https://premium.linkedin.com/jobsearch/articles/the-easy-how-to-guide-for-formatting-resumes-for-applicant-tracking-systems.

4. U.S. Government Equal Opportunities Commission, "Prohibited Employment Practices/Policies," accessed November 20, 2016, https://www1.eeoc.gov//laws/practices/index.cfm?renderforprint=1.

5. John Sullivan, "7 Rules for Job Interview Questions That Result in Great Hires," *Harvard Business Review*, February 10, 2016, accessed May 15, 2016, https://hbr.org/2016/02/7-rules-for-job-interview-questions-that-result-in-great-hires.

Reference Chapter B

1. Based on *The Chicago Manual of Style Online*, 16th ed., http://www.chicagomanualofstyle.org/home.html; Kate L. Turabian: *A Manual for Writers of Research Papers, Theses, and Dissertations*, 8th ed. (Chicago: The University of Chicago Press, 2013).

2. "14.2 Chicago's Two Systems of Source Citation," *The Online Chicago Manual of Style*, accessed May 24, 2016, http://www.chicagomanualofstyle.org.proxy.libraries.uc.edu/16/ch14/ch14_sec002.html.

3. Timothy McAdoo, "The Frankenreference," *APA Style Blog*, February 11, 2010, accessed May 3, 2016, http://blog.apastyle.org/apastyle/2010/02/the-frankenreference.html.

4. The Chicago style also allows you to use the short form for all your footnotes and then provide the complete source information in your bibliography. But because this method forces the reader to flip to the bibliography to see all the citation information for a given source, we recommend using complete footnotes and subsequent footnotes instead.

5. Here again, Chicago gives a choice: You can cite the author and page only, or you can cite the author, a short form of the title, and the page. Make your choice based on what you think your readers will prefer.

Appendix A

1. Covey, S. R. (1989). *The seven habits of highly effective people: Restoring the character ethic*. New York: Simon and Schuster.

2. West, R., & Turner, H. L. (2009). *Understanding Interpersonal communication: Making choices in changing times*. Belmont, CA: Thomson/Wadsworth.

3. Bentley, S. C. (2000). Listening in the 21st century. *International Journal of Listening*, 14, 129-142.

4. Gazzaley, A., & Rosen, L. D. (2016). *The distracted mind: Ancient brains in a high-tech world*. Cambridge, MA: MIT Press.

5. Lenartowicz, A., Simpson, G. V., Haber, C. M., & Cohen, M. S. (2014). Neurophysiological signals of ignoring and attending are separable and related to performance during sustained intersensory attention. *J. Cogn. Neurosci.* 26, 2055–2069. doi: 10.1162/jocn_a_00613.

6. Bays, J. C. (2018). *Mindfulness on the go: Simple meditation practices you can do anywhere*. Boulder, CO: Shambhala.

7. Vangelisti, A. L., Knapp, M., & Daly, J. (1990). Conversational narcissism. *Communication Monographs*, 57, 251-274.

Appendix B

1. Boczkowski, P., & Orlikowski, W. (2004). Organizational discourse and new media: A practice perspective. In D. Grant, C. Hardy, C. Oswick, & L. Putnam (Eds.), *The Sage handbook of organizational discourse* (pp. 359-377). London: Sage.

2. Adam, K., & Galanes, G. (2009). *Communicating in groups: Application and skills*. New York, NY: McGraw-Hill.

3. Heracleous, L., & Barrett, M. (2001). Organizational change as discourse: Communicative actions and deep structures in the context of information technology implementation. *Academy of Management Journal*, 44, 755-778.

4. Murphy, H. A., & Peck, C. E. (1980). *Effective business communication*. New York, NY: McGraw-Hill.

5. Skovholt, K., & Svennevig, J. (2006). Email Copies in Workplace Interaction. *Journal of Computer-Mediated Communication*, 12(1):42–65, https://doi.org/10.1111/j.1083-6101.2006.00314.x.

6. Derks, D., & Bakker, A. B. (2010). The Impact of E-mail Communication on Organizational Life. *Cyberpsychology: Journal of Psychosocial Research on Cyberspace*, 4(1), Article 4. Retrieved from https://cyberpsychology.eu/article/view/4233/3277.

7. Cho, T. (2007). Linguistic features of electronic mail in the workplace: A comparison with memoranda. *language@internet*, 7.

8. Daft, R.L., & Lengel, R.H. (1986). Organizational information requirements, media richness and structural design. *Management Science*. 32 (5): 554–571. doi:10.1287/mnsc.32.5.554.

9. King, R. C. Y Weidong, X. (1997). Media appropriateness: Effects of experience on communication media choice. *Decision Sciences*. 28 (4): 877–910. doi:10.1111/j.1540-5915.1997.tb01335.

10. Turner, J. (2007). The Business Communicator as Presence Allocator. *International Journal of Business and Communication*. 44: 36–58. doi:10.1177/0021943606295779.

11. Gerlach, J. M. (1994). Is this collaboration? In Bosworth, K. & Hamilton, S. J. (Eds.), *Collaborative Learning: Underlying Processes and Effective Techniques, New Directions for Teaching and Learning No. 59*.

12. Stahl, G., Koschmann, T., & Suthers, D. (2006). Computer-supported collaborative learning: An historical perspective. In R. K. Sawyer (Ed.), *Cambridge handbook of the learning sciences* (pp. 409-426). Cambridge, UK: Cambridge University Press.

Appendix C

1. Bajaj hurt by son's decision to scrap scooter production (2009, December 16). *The Hindu*. Retrieved from http://www.thehindu.com/news/bajaj-hurt-by-sons-decision-to-scrap-scooter-production/article66028.ece?ref=relatedNews

2. Fam, K.S., & Waller, D.S. (2006). Identifying likeable attributes: A qualitative study of television advertisements in Asia. *Qualitative Market Research*, 9(1), 38 – 50. doi:10.1108/13522750610640549

3. Hamara Bajaj' making comeback in Scooters! (2015, March 12). *Moneylife*. Retrieved from http://www.moneylife.in/article/bajaj-scooters/40797.html

4. How do you visualize a story-flow (n.d.). *Story Arcs & Storyline Visualisation*. Retrieved from https://www.pinterest.com/timeldridge/story-arcs-storyline-visualisation/

5. Kumar, A. (2014, November 29). Driven by Nationalism. *The Hindu*. Retrieved from http://www.thehindu.com/todays-paper/tp-features/tp-metroplus/driven-by-nationalism/article6644794.ece

6. Kumar, A. (2009, December 16). Bye bye Bajaj. *The Hindu*. Retrieved from http://www.thehindu.com/features/metroplus/society/article65961.ece

7. Sulivan, T. (2010, March 14). Bye bye Bajaj: Sun sets on India's beloved scooter. *The Seattle Times*. Retrieved from http://old.seattletimes.com/html/businesstechnology/2011344373_apasindiawealthandscooters.html

8. "The Company". (n.d.). Retrieved from http://www.bajajauto.com/bajaj_corporate.asp

9. The semiotics of advertising. (n.d.). *Representing Global Capital*. Retrieved from http://it.stlawu.edu/~global/pagessemiotics/menuframesem.html

Appendix D

1. Perry, R. W. (2007). What is a crisis? In H. Rodriguez, E. L. Quarantelli, & R. R. Dynes (Eds.). *Handbook of disaster research* (pp. 1-15). New York, NY: Springer.

2. Coombs, W. T. (2006). The protective powers of crisis response strategies: Managing reputational assets during a crisis. *Journal of Promotion Management*, 12, 241-259.

3. Coombs, W. T. (2018). *Ongoing crisis communication: Planning, managing, and responding.* Los Angeles, CA: Sage.

4. Quarantelli, E. L. (2005). A social science research agenda for the disasters of the 21st century. In R. W. Perry, & E. L. Quarantelli (Eds.). *What is a disaster? New answers to old questions* (pp. 325-296). Philadelphia, PA: Xlibris.

5. Miroff, I. I. (1994). Crisis management and environmentalism: A natural fit. *California Management Review*, 36(2), 101-113.

6. Conway, T., Ward, M., Lewis, G., & Bernhardt, A. (2007). Internet crisis potential: The importance of a strategic approach to marketing communications. *Journal of Marketing Communications*, 13, 213-228.

7. "Prevent mercury pollution". *The Hindu*. 29 September 2016 [August 23, 2007]. Retrieved 6 June 2019.

8. "Studies and Reports on environmental pollution and public health hazard caused by Hindustan Lever in Kodaikanal". *Struggle for Justice in Kodaikanal*. Retrieved 6 June2019.

9. "Greenpeace calls on Hindustan Lever to Address Liabilities in Kodaikanal" (Press release). Greenpeace. 8 December 2003. Retrieved 6 June 2019.

10. https://fortune.com/longform/nestle-maggi-noodle-crisis/

11. https://www.businesstoday.in/current/corporate/maggi-samples-fail-lab-test-nestle-distributers-fined-rs-62-lakh-fsda-fssai/story/264964.html

12. https://www.businesstoday.in/current/corporate/maggi-samples-fail-lab-test-nestle-distributers-fined-rs-62-lakh-fsda-fssai/story/264964.html

Appendix E

1. Pintrich, P. R. (2003). A Motivational Science Perspective on the Role of Student Motivation in Learning and Teaching Contexts. *Journal of Educational Psychology*. 9(4):, 667–686.

2. https://news.stanford.edu/2005/06/14/jobs-061505/

3. Schlender, B. & Tetzeli, R. (2015). *Becoming Steve Jobs*. New York, NY: Random House.

4. https://www.mayoclinic.org/diseases-conditions/specific-phobias/expert-answers/fear-of-public-speaking/faq-20058416

5. www.ted.com

6. http://www.kingsspeech.com/

Index